D0162914

The Musician's Guide to Theory and Analysis

THIRD EDITION

Jane Piper Clendinning
Florida State University College of Music

Elizabeth West Marvin
Eastman School of Music

W. W. NORTON & COMPANY
NEW YORK · LONDON

W. W. Norton & Company has been independent since its founding in 1923, when William Warder Norton and Mary D. Herter Norton first began publishing lectures delivered at the People's Institute, the adult education division of New York City's Cooper Union. The Nortons soon expanded their program beyond the Institute, publishing books by celebrated academics from America and abroad. By mid-century, the two major pillars of Norton's publishing program—trade books and college texts—were firmly established. In the 1950s, the Norton family transferred control of the company to its employees, and today—with a staff of four hundred and a comparable number of trade, college, and professional titles published each year—W. W. Norton & Company stands as the largest and oldest publishing house owned wholly by its employees.

Copyright © 2016, 2011, 2005 by W. W. Norton & Company, Inc.

All rights reserved
Printed in the United States of America

Third Edition

Editor: Justin Hoffman
Developmental editor: Susan Gaustad
Media editor: Steve Hoge
Managing editor, College: Marian Johnson
Managing editor, College Digital Media: Kim Yi
Production managers: Andy Ensor and Jane Searle
Editorial assistant: Grant Phelps
Media editorial assistant: Stephanie Eads
Marketing manager, Music: Mary Dudley
Design director: Rubina Yeh
Designers: Lissi Sigillo and Rubina Yeh
Composition, layout, and music setting: David Botwinik
Permissions manager: Megan Jackson
Permissions clearing: Kathleen Karcher
Indexer: Marilyn Bliss
Manufacturing: LSC Communications, Kendallville

Library of Congress Cataloging-in-Publication Data
Names: Clendinning, Jane Piper, author. | Marvin, Elizabeth West, 1955-
    author.
Title: The musician's guide to theory and analysis / Jane Piper Clendinning,
    Florida State University College of Music ; Elizabeth West Marvin, Eastman
    School of Music.
Description: Third edition. | New York ; London : W. W. Norton & Company,
    [2016] | ?2016 | Includes index.
Identifiers: LCCN 2015043308 | ISBN 9780393263053 (hardcover)
Subjects: LCSH: Music theory. | Musical analysis.
Classification: LCC MT6 .C57 2016 | DDC 781--dc23
LC record available at http://lccn.loc.gov/2015043308

W. W. Norton & Company, Inc., 500 Fifth Avenue, New York, NY 10110
www.wwnorton.com
W. W. Norton & Company, Ltd., 15 Carlisle Street, London W1D 3BS

7 8 9 0

To our teachers, colleagues, and students—
with whom we have shared the joy of music,
and from whom we continue to learn—
and, with thanks, to our families
for their patience and support

Kurt

Brief Contents

Part I   Elements of Music

1. Pitch and Pitch Class 2
2. Simple Meters 21
3. Pitch Collections, Scales, and Major Keys 45
4. Compound Meters 67
5. Minor Keys and the Diatonic Modes 85
6. Intervals 109
7. Triads 129
8. Seventh Chords 146
9. Connecting Intervals in Note-to-Note Counterpoint 165
10. Melodic and Rhythmic Embellishment in Two-Voice Composition 181

Part II   Diatonic Harmony and Tonicization

11. From Species to Chorale Style: Soprano and Bass Lines 208
12. The Basic Phrase in SATB Style 228
13. Dominant Sevenths, the Predominant Area, and Chorale Harmonization 254
14. Expanding the Basic Phrase 275
15. New Cadence Types and Diatonic Root Progressions 297
16. Embellishing Tones 321
17. Voice-Leading Chords: vii°6, vii°7, vii⌀7, and Others 345
18. Phrase Structure and Motivic Analysis 361
19. Diatonic Sequences 385
20. Secondary Dominant and Leading-Tone Chords to V 409
21. Tonicizing Scale Degrees Other Than V 427

Part III   Chromatic Harmony and Form

22. Modulation to Closely Related Keys 448
23. Binary and Ternary Forms 470
24. Invention, Fugue, and Baroque Counterpoint 490
25. Variation 514
26. Modal Mixture 530

27. The Neapolitan Sixth and Augmented-Sixth Chords 548
28. Vocal Forms 569
29. Popular Music 593
30. Chromatic Harmony and Voice-Leading 618
31. Chromatic Modulation 641
32. Sonata, Sonatina, and Concerto 663
33. Rondo, Sonata-Rondo, and Large Ternary 692

Part IV The Twentieth Century and Beyond

34. Modes, Scales, and Sets 708
35. Rhythm, Meter, and Form in Music after 1900 730
36. Music Analysis with Sets 749
37. Sets and Set Classes 772
38. Ordered Segments and Serialism 793
39. Rhythm, Meter, and Form after 1945 823
40. Recent Trends 849

Contents

Preface xxi

To Our Students: Why Study Music Theory? xxxi

Part I Elements of Music

Chapter 1 Pitch and Pitch Class 2

Introduction to Pitch: Letter Names 3 • Pitch Classes and Pitches 4

The Piano Keyboard 5 • White Keys 5 • Black Keys: Flats and Sharps 5 • Enharmonic Equivalents 6 • Intervals: Half Steps and Whole Steps 6 • Double Flats and Sharps 8

Reading Pitches from a Score 8 • Staff Notation 8 • Treble Clef 9 • Bass Clef 11 • C-Clefs 12 • Naming Registers 13 • Ledger Lines 13 • Writing Pitches on a Score 16

Dynamic Markings 17

Style Periods 18

Did You Know? 19

Terms You Should Know 19 • **Questions for Review 20**

Chapter 2 Simple Meters 21

Dividing Musical Time 22 • Beat, Beat Division, and Meter 22 • Conducting Patterns 23 • Tempo 24 • Rhythm and Meter 25

Rhythmic Notation for Simple Meters 25 • Rhythmic Values 25 • Meter Signatures 26

Counting Rhythms in Simple Meters 28 • Beat Subdivisions 30 • Stems, Flags, and Beaming 30 • Counting Rests and Dots 32 • Slurs and Ties 34 • Metrical Accents and Syncopation 35 • Hemiola 37 • Anacrusis Notation 38

Beat Units Other Than the Quarter Note 40

Implications for Performance: Metric Hierarchy 42

Did You Know? 43

Terms You Should Know 43 • Questions for Review 44

Chapter 3   Pitch Collections, Scales, and Major Keys 45

Chromatic and Diatonic Collections 46

Scales: Ordered Pitch-Class Collections 47 • Scale Degrees 49 • Spelling Major Scales 50 • Spelling Chromatic Scales 52

Major Keys 54 • Key Signatures 54 • The Circle of Fifths 56 • Identifying a Key from a Key Signature 57 • Writing Key Signatures 58 • Identifying the Key of a Piece 59 • Scale-Degree Names 62

The Major Pentatonic Scale 63

Implications for Performance 64

Did You Know? 65

Terms You Should Know 66 • Questions for Review 66

Chapter 4   Compound Meters 67

Hearing Compound Meters 68

Meter Signatures 68

Rhythmic Notation in Compound Meters 70 • The Dotted-Quarter Beat Unit 70 • Subdividing the Beat 72 • Beat Units Other Than the Dotted Quarter 74

Syncopation 76

Mixing Beat Divisions and Groupings 77 • Triplets 77 • Duplets, Quadruplets, and Polyrhythm 79 • Hemiola in Compound Meter 81

Metric Accent and Implications for Performance 82

Did You Know? 83

Terms You Should Know 83 • Questions for Review 83

Chapter 5   Minor Keys and the Diatonic Modes 85

Parallel Keys: Shared Tonic 86

Relative Keys 88 • Relative Minor: Shared Key Signatures 88 • Finding the Relative Minor and Major Keys 89

Variability in the Minor Scale 92 • The "Forms" of Minor 93 • Identifying the Key of a Musical Passage 95 • Hearing Minor Scale Types 96 • Writing Minor Scales 97

Scale Degrees in Minor 100

The Minor Pentatonic Scale 101

Modes of the Diatonic Collection 102 • The "Relative" Identification of Modes 104 • The "Parallel" Identification of Modes 105 • Spelling Modal Scales 105 • Twentieth-Century and Contemporary Modal Practice 106

Did You Know? 107

Terms You Should Know 108 • **Questions for Review 108**

Chapter 6   Intervals 109

Combining Pitches 110 • Interval Size 110 • Melodic and Harmonic Intervals 111 • Compound Intervals 112

Interval Quality 114 • Major, Minor, and Perfect Intervals 115 • Inverting Intervals 116

Spelling Intervals 117 • Smaller Intervals: 2, 3, and 4 117 • Larger Intervals: 5, 6, and 7 119 • Semitones and Interval Size 121 • Augmented and Diminished Intervals 121 • Enharmonically Equivalent Intervals 123

Consonant and Dissonant Intervals 124 • Analyzing Intervals in Music 125

Did You Know? 127

Terms You Should Know 127 • **Questions for Review 127**

Chapter 7   Triads 129

Chords and Triads 130 • Triad Qualities in Major Keys 131 • Triad Qualities in Minor Keys 133

Spelling Triads 135 • By Interval 135 • By the C-Major Method 136 • By Key Signature 136

Triad Inversion 137

Figured Bass 139

Triads in Popular-Music Notation 142

Did You Know? 144

Terms You Should Know 144 • **Questions for Review 144**

Chapter 8   Seventh Chords 146

Seventh Chords 147 • Diatonic Seventh Chords in Major Keys 148 • Seventh Chords in Inversion 150 • Diatonic Seventh Chords in Minor Keys 152 • Spelling Seventh Chords 153

Seventh Chords in Popular Styles 155 • Less Common Seventh Chords 156

Triads and Seventh Chords in Musical Textures 157 • Arpeggiated Triads and Seventh Chords 157 • Triads and Seventh Chords in Transposing Scores 159 • Seventh Chords and Musical Style 162

Did You Know? 162

Terms You Should Know 163 • **Questions for Review 163**

Chapter 9   Connecting Intervals in Note-to-Note Counterpoint 165

Species Counterpoint 166

Connecting Melodic Intervals 167

Connecting Harmonic Intervals 169 • Four Types of Contrapuntal Motion 170 • Consonant Harmonic Intervals 171

Writing Note-to-Note Counterpoint in Strict Style 175 • Beginning and Ending a First-Species Counterpoint 175 • Completing the Middle 175

Did You Know? 179

Terms You Should Know 179 • **Questions for Review 180**

Chapter 10   Melodic and Rhythmic Embellishment in Two-Voice Composition 181

Melodic Embellishment in Second-Species (2:1) Counterpoint 182 • Passing Tones 183 • Consonant Skips 184 • Neighbor Tones 184

Writing 2:1 Counterpoint 186 • Opening and Closing Patterns 186 • Melodic Considerations 187 • Harmonic Considerations 189

Further Melodic Embellishment in Third-Species (4:1) Counterpoint 191

Writing 4:1 Counterpoint 194

Rhythmic Displacement in Fourth-Species Counterpoint 197 • Types of Suspensions 198 • Rhythmic Character of Fourth Species 199 • Breaking Species and Tying Consonances 199 • Chains of Suspensions 200

Writing Fourth-Species Counterpoint 201

Fifth Species and Free Counterpoint 203

Did You Know? 205

Terms You Should Know 205 • **Questions for Review 205**

Part II Diatonic Harmony and Tonicization

Chapter 11 **From Species to Chorale Style: Soprano and Bass Lines 208**

Note-to-Note Counterpoint in Chorale Style 209 • Contrapuntal Motion 210 • Chordal Dissonance 211 • Characteristics of Bass and Melody Lines 214 • Writing Counterpoint with a Given Line 220

Melodic Embellishment in Chorale Textures 223 • Passing Tones, Neighbor Tones, and Consonant Skips 223 • Suspensions 225

Did You Know? 227

Terms You Should Know 227 • **Questions for Review 227**

Chapter 12 **The Basic Phrase in SATB Style 228**

The Basic Phrase 229 • Defining the Phrase Model: T-D-T 230 • Establishing the Tonic Area 230 • Cadential Area and Cadence Types 232

The Notation of Four-Part Harmony 235 • Writing for Voices: SATB 235

Connecting the Dominant and Tonic Areas 242 • Resolving the Leading Tone in V and V⁶ 242 • Perfect Consonances 243

Melody and Accompaniment 245 • Writing for Keyboard 245 • Harmonizing a Melody 247 • Creating an Accompaniment 248

Did You Know? 251

Terms You Should Know 252 • **Questions for Review 252**

Chapter 13 **Dominant Sevenths, the Predominant Area, and Chorale Harmonization 254**

Writing V⁷ and Its Inversions 255 • Resolving the Leading Tone and Chordal Seventh 255 • Approaching Perfect Intervals 257

Expanding the Basic Phrase: T-PD-D-T 261 • Predominant Function: Subdominant and Supertonic Chords 261 • Voice-Leading from Predominant to Dominant 262 • Predominant Seventh Chords 264 • Harmonic Function and Principles of Progression 265

Realizing Figured Bass 266

Harmonizing Chorale Melodies 268 • Soprano-Bass Counterpoint and Chord Choice 269 • Completing the Inner Voices 270

Did You Know? 273

Terms You Should Know 273 • **Questions for Review 273**

Chapter 14 Expanding the Basic Phrase 275

Expanding Harmonic Areas with ⁶₄ Chords 276 • The Cadential ⁶₄ 276 • The Pedal or Neighboring ⁶₄ 279 • The Arpeggiating ⁶₄ 282 • The Passing ⁶₄ 283 • The Four ⁶₄ Types 286

Other Expansions of the Tonic Area 287 • The Subdominant in Tonic Expansions 287 • The Dominant in Tonic Expansions 288 • Contexts for the Submediant 290 • Embedding PD-D-T Within the Tonic Area 292 • Extending the Final Tonic Area 293

Did You Know? 295

Terms You Should Know 295 • **Questions for Review 295**

Chapter 15 New Cadence Types and Diatonic Root Progressions 297

New Cadence Types 298 • The Deceptive Cadence and Resolution: V-vi (or V-VI) 298 • The Plagal Cadence and Extension: IV-I (or iv-i) 301 • The Phrygian Cadence: iv⁶-V 304

Basic Root Progressions 306 • Root Motion by Descending Fifth 306 • Root Motion by Descending Third 309 • Root Motion by Second 312

Other Diatonic Harmonies 314 • About Mediant Triads 314 • The Mediant and Minor Dominant in Minor Keys 316 • Parallel ⁶₃ Chords 318

Did You Know? 319

Terms You Should Know 319 • **Questions for Review 319**

Chapter 16 Embellishing Tones 321

Embellishing a Harmonic Framework 322 • Passing and Neighbor Tones in Chorale Textures 323

More on Suspensions 326 • Suspensions in Four Parts 326 • Suspensions with Change of Bass 327 • Combining Suspensions 328 • Embellishing Suspensions 329 • Retardations 331

More on Neighbor and Passing Tones 332 • Chromatic Neighbor and Passing Tones 332 • Incomplete Neighbors 333 • Double Neighbors 335 • Passing Tones, Chordal Skips, and Scales 336

Other Types of Embellishments 338 • Anticipations 338 • Pedal Points 339

Embellishing Tones in Popular Music 341

Did You Know? 343

Terms You Should Know 344 • **Questions for Review 344**

Chapter 17   Voice-Leading Chords: vii°6, vii°7, vii⌀7, and Others 345

Dominant Substitutes: Leading-Tone Chords 346 • Contexts for the vii°6, vii⌀7, and vii°7 Chords 346 • Writing and Resolving vii°6 350 • Writing and Resolving vii⌀7, vii°7, and Their Inversions 352

Voice-Leading ⁶₄ Chords 356

Did You Know? 359

Terms You Should Know 359 • **Questions for Review 359**

Chapter 18   Phrase Structure and Motivic Analysis 361

Phrase and Motive 362 • Motives and Motivic Analysis 363 • The Sentence 366

Phrases in Pairs: The Period 368 • Phrase Diagrams 369 • Parallel and Contrasting Periods 369 • Writing Parallel and Contrasting Periods 372 • Other Period Types 373

Phrase Rhythm 376 • Phrase Structure and Hypermeter 376 • Linking Phrases 378 • Phrase Expansion 379

Did You Know? 383

Terms You Should Know 384 • **Questions for Review 384**

Chapter 19   Diatonic Sequences 385

Sequences 386

Descending Sequences 389 • Descending-Fifth Sequence 389 • Pachelbel Sequences 398 • Descending Parallel ⁶₃ Chords 402

Ascending Sequences 404 • Ascending-Fifth Sequence 404 • Ascending Parallel ⁶₃ Chords 405

Did You Know? 407

Terms You Should Know 408 • **Questions for Review 408**

Chapter 20   Secondary Dominant and Leading-Tone Chords to V 409

Intensifying the Dominant 410

Secondary Dominants to V 411 • Spelling Secondary Dominants 411 • Tonicization and Modulation 414 • Secondary Dominants to V in the Basic Phrase 416 • Writing and Resolving 418 • Cross Relations 419

Secondary Leading-Tone Chords to V 420 • Writing and Resolving 421

Secondary-Function Chords in Dominant Expansions 423

Did You Know? 426

Terms You Should Know 426 • Questions for Review 426

Chapter 21   Tonicizing Scale Degrees Other Than V 427

Secondary-Function Chords Within the Basic Phrase 428 • Identifying Secondary Dominant and Leading-Tone Chords 429

Secondary-Function Chords in Musical Contexts 432 • Tonicizing Harmonies Within a Phrase 432 • Providing a Temporary Harmonic Diversion 434 • Creating Forward Momentum 434 • Evading an Expected Resolution 435 • Text Painting 436

Spelling Secondary Dominant and Leading-Tone Chords 438

Resolving Secondary Dominant and Leading-Tone Chords 440 • Irregular and Deceptive Resolutions 441

Secondary Dominants in Sequences 443

Did You Know? 444

Terms You Should Know 444 • Questions for Review 444

Part III   Chromatic Harmony and Form

Chapter 22   Modulation to Closely Related Keys 448

Common Pivot-Chord Modulations 449 • Modulation or Tonicization? 450 • Modulation from a Major Key to Its Dominant 451 • Modulation from a Minor Key to Its Relative Major 452 • Closely Related Keys 456

Other Pivot-Chord Modulations 458 • From a Minor Key to v 458 • From a Major Key to ii, iii, IV, and vi 459 • Writing a Pivot-Chord Modulation 461

Direct Modulations 461 • Modulations Introduced by Secondary Dominants 463

Locating Modulations 464

Modulations in Musical Contexts 464 • Harmonizing Modulating Melodies 466

Did You Know? 468

Terms You Should Know 468 • Questions for Review 469

Chapter 23   Binary and Ternary Forms 470

Binary Form 471 • Phrase Design 471 • Sections 475 • Tonal Structures 476 • Writing Binary-Form Pieces 480

Simple Ternary Form 484

Binary Forms as Part of a Larger Formal Scheme 486 • Composite Ternary 486 • Composite Binary 487

Did You Know? 488

Terms You Should Know 488 • **Questions for Review** 489

Chapter 24   Invention, Fugue, and Baroque Counterpoint 490

Baroque Melody 491 • *Fortspinnung* 491 • Compound Melody and Step Progressions 492

Invention and Fugue: The Exposition 493 • The Subject 494 • The Answer and Countersubject 495

Episodes and Later Expositions 500

Special Features 503 • Double and Triple Fugues 503 • Stretto 506 • Inversion, Augmentation, Diminution, and Other Subject Alterations 507 • Canon 509 • Vocal Fugues 510

Did You Know? 512

Terms You Should Know 513 • **Questions for Review** 513

Chapter 25   Variation 514

Continuous Variations 515 • Formal Organization 517

Sectional Variations 520 • Themes and Formal Organization 520 • Variation Procedures 521

Musical Topics 526

Performing Variations 528

Did You Know? 528

Terms You Should Know 529 • **Questions for Review** 529

Chapter 26   Modal Mixture 530

Harmonic Color and Text Setting 531

Mixture Chords 532 • The Spelling and Function of Mixture Chords 534 • Tonicizing Mixture Chords 538 • Embellishing Tones 540 • Mixture and the Cadential $^6_4$ Chord 540 • Intonation and Performance 542 • Mixture in Instrumental Music 543

Mixture and Modulation 544

Did You Know? 546

Terms You Should Know 546 • **Questions for Review** 547

Chapter 27   **The Neapolitan Sixth and Augmented-Sixth Chords 548**

Chromatic Predominant Chords 549

The Neapolitan Sixth 549 • Spelling and Voicing 550 • Voice-Leading and Resolution 551 • Intonation and Performance 556 • Tonicizing the Neapolitan 556

Augmented-Sixth Chords 558 • Voice-Leading, Spelling, and Resolution 561 • Italian, French, and German Augmented Sixths 562 • Approaches to Augmented-Sixth Chords 563 • Aural Identification and Performance 564 • Less Common Spellings and Voicings 564 • Secondary Augmented-Sixth Chords 566

Did You Know? 567

Terms You Should Know 567 • **Questions for Review 567**

Chapter 28   **Vocal Forms 569**

Three-Part Vocal Forms 570 • Aria da capo 570 • Other Ternary Arias 572 • Recitatives 574

Text and Song Structure 577 • Strophic Form 579 • Text Painting 581 • Analysis and Interpretation 583

Other Vocal Forms 584 • Modified Strophic Form 584 • Through-Composed Form 585 • French Mélodie 589

Did You Know? 591

Terms You Should Know 591 • **Questions for Review 591**

Chapter 29   **Popular Music 593**

Popular Song 594 • Quaternary and Verse-Refrain Forms 594 • Harmonic Practices 596 • Suspensions and Rhythmic Displacement 600 • Altered Fifths and Tritone Substitutions 600

The Twelve-Bar Blues 602 • Pentatonic and Blues "Scales" 602 • Blues Harmonic Progressions and Phrase Structure 604

Post-1950 Popular Song 606 • New Elements of Form 606 • Harmony and Melody 612

Did You Know? 616

Terms You Should Know 616 • **Questions for Review 616**

Chapter 30   **Chromatic Harmony and Voice-Leading 618**

Chromatic Elaboration of Diatonic Frameworks 619 • Chromatic Sequence Patterns 619 • Descending Chromatic Bass Lines 621 • Chromatic

Voice Exchanges and Wedge Progressions 625 • Common-Tone Diminished Seventh and Augmented-Sixth Chords 627 • The Raised Chordal Fifth 632

Chromatic Mediant Relations 633

Did You Know? 639

Terms You Should Know 639 • **Questions for Review 639**

Chapter 31   Chromatic Modulation 641

Chromatic Modulation Employing Common Tones 642 • By Common Tone 642 • By Common Dyad and Chromatic Inflection 644 • Through Mixture 645 • Enharmonic Modulation with Augmented-Sixth Chords 646 • Enharmonic Modulation with Diminished Seventh Chords 650

Chromatic Modulation with Sequences 653 • By Descending-Fifth Sequence 654 • Other Chromatic Sequences 655

Linear Chromaticism 656 • Chromaticism and Voice-Leading Chords 656 • Intentional Harmonic Ambiguity 658 • Analyzing and Performing Chromatic Passages 660

Did You Know? 661

Terms You Should Know 661 • **Questions for Review 661**

Chapter 32   Sonata, Sonatina, and Concerto 663

Sonatas and Sonata Form 664

Classical Sonata Form 664 • The First Large Section: Exposition 664 • The Second Large Section: Development and Recapitulation 669

Sonata Form in the Romantic Era 674 • Increasing Length and Complexity 674 • Key Areas and the Organization of the Exposition 674 • The Development Section 679 • The Recapitulation and Coda 681

Related Forms 684 • Sonatina 684 • Concerto Form 686

Performing and Listening to Sonata-Form Movements 688

Did You Know? 690

Terms You Should Know 690 • **Questions for Review 690**

Chapter 33   Rondo, Sonata-Rondo, and Large Ternary 692

Five-Part Rondo 693 • Refrain (**A** Section) 693 • Episode (Contrasting Section) 694 • Transition and Retransition 695 • Coda 697

Seven-Part Rondo and Sonata-Rondo 698

Large Ternary Form 699

Did You Know? 705

Terms You Should Know 706 • **Questions for Review 706**

Part IV The Twentieth Century and Beyond

Chapter 34   Modes, Scales, and Sets 708

Listening to Twentieth-Century Compositions 709

Pitch-Class Collections and Scales Revisited 709 • Analyzing Mode and Scale Types 712 • Composing with Diatonic Modes 713 • Sets and Subsets 719

Other Scale Types and Their Subsets 721 • Pentatonic Scales 721 • Whole-Tone Scales 723 • Octatonic Scales 725 • Hexatonic Scales 726

Did You Know? 728

Terms You Should Know 728 • **Questions for Review 728**

Chapter 35   Rhythm, Meter, and Form in Music after 1900 730

Rhythm and Meter 731 • Asymmetrical Meter 731 • Perceived and Notated Meter 733 • Changing Meter and Polymeter 734 • Ametric Music 736 • Additive Rhythm 738

Form after the Common-Practice Era 740 • Scale Analysis and Formal Design 740 • Form and Register 742 • Substitutes for Tonal Function 744 • Canon and Imitation 745 • The Fibonacci Series 746

Did You Know? 747

Terms You Should Know 747 • **Questions for Review 747**

Chapter 36   Music Analysis with Sets 749

Relationships Between Sets 750 • Listing the Elements of a Pitch-Class Set 751

Pitch and Pitch-Class Intervals 753 • Pcset Transposition and mod12 • Arithmetic 755 • Interval Classes and the Interval-Class Vector 759

The Inversion of Pitch Sets and Pitch-Class Sets 762 • The Inversion of Pitch Sets 763 • The Inversion of Pitch-Class Sets 764 • Identifying Transposition and Inversion 766

Did You Know? 770

Terms You Should Know 770 • **Questions for Review 770**

Chapter 37   Sets and Set Classes 772

Set Classes and Their Prime Forms 773 • Finding Prime Form 774 • Set-Class Labels 779

Characteristic Trichords of Familiar Scales and Modes 780 • Whole Tone 780 • Pentatonic 780 • Hexatonic 781 • Octatonic 782 • Chromatic 783

Reading Set-Class Tables 784 • Complementary Sets 784 • Using ic Vectors 786

Set Classes and Formal Design 789

Did You Know? 791

Terms You Should Know 792 • **Questions for Review** 792

Chapter 38   Ordered Segments and Serialism 793

Serial Composition 794 • Ordered Pitch Segments 794 • Labeling Pitch-Class Segments 797 • Operations on Pitch Classes 797

Twelve-Tone Rows 799 • Labeling Rows 801 • Choosing Row Forms 803 • Hearing Row Relationships 804

Realizing Twelve-Tone Rows 805 • The Row Matrix 807 • Heaxchordal Combinatoriality 809 • Finding Combinatorial Row Pairs 811

Serialism and Compositional Style 814

Serialized Durations 819

Did You Know? 821

Terms You Should Know 821 • **Questions for Review** 821

Chapter 39   Rhythm, Meter, and Form after 1945 823

New Approaches to Traditional Form 824 • Sectional Forms 824 • Canon and Imitation 825

Variants on Traditional Rhythmic Notation 830 • Ametric Music 830 • New Approaches to Meter and Polymeter 832 • Metric Modulation 834

New Developments in Musical Form and Notation 837 • Time-line, Graphic, and Text Notation 837 • Moment Form and Mobile Form 841 • Indeterminacy and Chance 843 • Minimalism and Form as Process 844

Analyzing Form in Recent Music 846

Did You Know? 847

Terms You Should Know 847 • **Questions for Review** 848

Chapter 40   Recent Trends 849

Contemporary Composers and Techniques of the Past 850 • Materials from the Pretonal Era 851 • Materials from the Baroque, Classical, and Romantic Periods 855 • Materials from the Twentieth Century 860

A Look Ahead 867

Did You Know? 868

Terms You Should Know 868 • **Questions for Review** 868

Appendixes

1. *Try it* Answers A1

2. Glossary A47

3. The Overtone Series A68

4. Guidelines for Part-Writing A70

5. Ranges of Orchestral Instruments A74

6. Set-Class Table A78

Credits A81

Index of Music Examples A83

Index of Terms and Concepts A87

Preface

We are pleased to bring to you the third edition of *The Musician's Guide to Theory and Analysis* and its accompanying Workbook, Anthology, and media. With each revision, we hear from many colleagues around the country about what works best for their students, and we are proud to retain these features while introducing something new to each edition. Among the key pedagogical approaches that characterize the *Musician's Guide* series are

- student-centered pedagogy that features clearly written prose, recorded musical examples throughout, and multiple opportunities for reinforcement both in the text and online;

- introduction to each new topic through musical repertoire, using a spiral-learning approach that revisits familiar works while adding new layers of understanding;

- consideration of how analysis might impact performance decisions;

- incorporation of counterpoint and form chapters so that students can study complete works;

- reliance on the basic phrase model to teach principles of harmonic progression; and

- comprehensive coverage that extends through music of the twentieth and twenty-first centuries.

The Musician's Guide series is the most comprehensive and flexible set of materials available for learning music theory. For theory classes, this textbook and its accompanying Workbook cover a wide range of topics—from fundamentals to harmony, form and analysis, popular music, and twentieth and twenty-first century works. An Anthology features core repertoire for study along with recordings for each work. In this edition, we have added a new **Know It? Show It!** pedagogy, which provides unprecedented opportunities for online learning. Meanwhile, the accompanying *Musician's Guide to Aural Skills* offers complete coordination between theory and aural skills courses, so that the two are mutually reinforcing. Instructors can mix and match the components that are ideal for their classroom.

Features

- Each chapter of the text begins with an **Outline** and an **Overview** paragraph, which serve as a chapter preview.

- The **Repertoire** list specifies which pieces are featured in the chapter. *The Musician's Guide* uses real music to explain every concept. Each time students encounter a piece from the Anthology, their understanding deepens, as does their knowledge of masterworks of music.

- **Boldface** type signals a new and important term. These terms are listed together at the end of the chapter and defined in the Glossary in Appendix 2. In the ebook, students can simply mouse over or tap on a term to retrieve its definition.

- **Key Concept** and **Summary** boxes in every chapter identify the most important ideas and summarize key information so that it is instantly available.

> **KEY CONCEPT** Classical-era sonata-form expositions are usually repeated, and generally consist of the following sections:
>
> | First theme group | Transition | Second theme group (optional codetta) |
> |---|---|---|
> | Major key: I | Modulates to V. | V (may include a closing theme, still in V). |
> | Minor key: i | Modulates to III (or v). | III (or v) (may include a closing theme in the same key). |

SUMMARY

> Intervals may be
> - melodic—measured between successive notes,
> - harmonic—measured between pitches sounding at the same time,
> - simple—spanning an octave or less, or
> - compound—spanning more than an octave.
>
> Intervals are labeled by their size and quality.
> - Size measures the number of letter names spanned: U, 2, 3, 4, 5, 6, 7, 8.
> - Intervals 2, 3, 6, and 7 may be major or minor, but not perfect (e.g., m2, M3, m6).
> - Intervals U, 4, 5, and 8 may be perfect, but not major or minor (PU, P4, P5, P8).

- *Try it* boxes, scattered through every chapter, provide immediate opportunities to practice every core concept. Many of these exercises preview upcoming Workbook assignments. Answers appear in Appendix 1 or can be revealed by clicking the "reveal answers" button in the ebook.

Try it #3

Fill in the space between the I and I⁶ (or i and i⁶) with a passing $\frac{6}{4}$, from the bass and figures provided. Include a voice exchange with the soprano, and write a Roman numeral analysis.

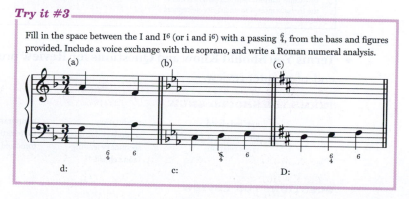

- **Listening icons** (🎧) identify opportunities for listening—either to the excerpt immediately at hand or to a complete work in the Anthology. These recordings are all accessible online; in the ebook, a click on the icon brings you immediately to a recording of the example shown.

- Since many theory concepts can be learned in more than one way, **Another Way** boxes offer alternative explanations.

> ### *Another Way*
>
> Another way to spell secondary dominants quickly is to imagine them as "altered" diatonic chords, following the chart below (in C major). Add whatever accidentals are necessary to create a Mm7 quality. Use this method as a shortcut for spelling only; in analysis, you should write V7/IV, not I7, to capture more accurately how the chord functions.
>
> | TO MAKE A . . . | | START WITH . . . | | ALTER QUALITY TO Mm7 |
> | --- | --- | --- | --- | --- |
> | V7/IV | → | I7 (C-E-G-B) | → | I7 (C-E-G-B♭) |
> | V7/V | → | ii7 (D-F-A-C) | → | II7 (D-F♯-A-C) |
> | V7/vi | → | iii7 (E-G-B-D) | → | III7 (E-G♯-B-D) |
> | V7/ii | → | vi7 (A-C-E-G) | → | VI7 (A-C♯-E-G) |
> | V7/iii | → | vii∅7 (B-D-F-A) | → | VII7 (B-D♯-F♯-A) |

- **Did You Know?** boxes at the end of each chapter explain certain historical developments, fill in background for composers and pieces featured in the chapter, or supply more advanced information. These are a source of enrichment and come from stories that we have told in class to our students.

> ### Did You Know?
>
> You will find a complete list of Messiaen's modes of limited transposition in his book *The Technique of My Musical Language*, translated by John Satterfield (Paris: Leduc, 1956). Messiaen wrote the *Quartet for the End of Time* while incarcerated in a prisoner-of-war camp during World War II. He chose his text from the Revelation of St. John. Messiaen says this about the instrumental ensemble, all fellow prisoners:
>
> > The unusual group for which I wrote this quartet—violin, clarinet, cello and piano—is due to the circumstances surrounding its conception.
>
> I was a prisoner-of-war (1941), in Silesia, and among my fellow prisoners were a violinist . . . a clarinetist . . . and a cellist . . . myself being the pianist. . . . Why this choice of text? Perhaps because, in these hours of total privation, the basic forces which control life reasserted themselves. (From the liner notes to Angel/EMI recording S-37587.)
>
> It is remarkable that an artwork of such power was composed in such dire circumstances—a testament to the human spirit.

- **Terms You Should Know** and **Questions for Review** provide essential end-of-chapter review.

TERMS YOU SHOULD KNOW

applied chord	modulation	temporary tonic
chromatic voice exchange	secondary dominant	tonicization
cross relation	secondary leading- tone chord	tonicized half cadence

QUESTIONS FOR REVIEW

1. Where are secondary dominants used? secondary leading-tone chords?
2. What do you need to remember when spelling secondary dominants? secondary leading-tone chords?
3. What are the special voice-leading guidelines for resolving secondary dominant chords? secondary leading-tone chords?
4. Under what circumstances are cross relations permitted in common-practice style?
5. In music for your own instrument, find two examples of secondary dominants (in two different pieces or keys). What guidelines can help you scan the score and find them quickly?

Workbook

Each **Workbook** chapter is organized so that ideas are reinforced in the same order they were presented in the chapter. Each assignment consists of a tear-out-and-turn-in worksheet. The Workbook includes the following:

- Short exercises such as chord spelling and two- or three-chord connections.

- Opportunities to write music—through melody harmonizations, figured bass realizations, or other short composition projects—most based on passages from music literature rather than contrived practice exercises. This edition features even more opportunities for composition.

- Analyses, from short passages to phrases, periods, and entire works. Longer analyses are often taken from works in the Anthology, allowing you to revisit the core repertoire and hear these works again.

We provide a **Teacher's Edition** that includes all answers, formatted to match the student pages, for easy grading. Contact your Norton representative to receive your copy.

Online Resources

An **ebook**, included with every new copy of the text, allows students to read on a wide variety of devices. Recordings of music examples are only a click or tap away.

Along with the ebook, there is a new **Know It? Show It!** online pedagogy, designed to enhance student learning.

- As they read each chapter, students watch short video tutorials, created by Brad Osborn (University of Kansas) and Anna Gawboy (Ohio State University), keyed to each topic discussed in the text. Tutorials show students how to work through the problems they will encounter in their Workbook assignments.

- Students take carefully graduated **adaptive online quizzes** to deepen their understanding and demonstrate mastery of the material. **InQuizitive**, a new formative assessment tool, with questions written by Philip Duker (University of Delaware) and Sarah Sarver (Oklahoma City University), asks students questions until they've demonstrated that they understand the chapter material. When students have trouble, tailored feedback points them back to specific spots in the book and video tutorials. And once students complete the activity, data about their performance can be reported to your campus learning-management system to help you assess which topics need more review and which are well understood.

- In addition to the print version, the **online Workbook** makes nearly all exercises available in Noteflight, an online notation program that allows students to complete their homework and send it to their instructor electronically. Instructors can grade work and return it to students paperlessly.

With **Total Access**, all students who purchase a new book—regardless of format—will receive access to all the media, including the ebook and **Know It? Show It!** pedagogy. Students can access the media in a variety of ways:

- The **ebook** includes links to all accompanying media.
- With Norton **Coursepacks**, instructors can bring the media into their campus learning-management systems.
- At digital.wwnorton.com/guidetotheory3, students and instructors can launch all the online resources included with this text.

Anthology

Study of the **Anthology** works is integral to the book's approach to learning music theory—we strongly believe that the concepts we teach must emerge from the music itself. We have chosen music that we like, that many of our students have performed, and that they (and we) have enjoyed exploring together (see the complete list at back of book). Some works should be familiar to students ("Greensleeves," "The Stars and Stripes Forever"), while others will probably be new (Edgard Varèse's *Density 21.5*, Clara Schumann's Romanze). There are classics of the repertoire (Mozart and Beethoven piano sonata movements, German Lieder selected from Schubert and Schumann song cycles, and groundbreaking compositions by Schoenberg and Webern); pieces for varied performing ensembles (solo flute, cello, and violin; chamber orchestra, string quartet, band, and choir, among others); and pieces in contrasting musical styles—from American popular songs to French mélodie, from piano ragtime to minimalist music, from marches for band to hymns and anthems for choirs. While the Anthology includes gems of familiar repertoire, we have also included wonderful but less familiar works by women and African American composers (Fanny Mendelssohn Hensel, Clara Schumann, Scott Joplin), as well as diverse works written within the last century.

Every chapter begins by discussing one or two examples from the Anthology. With the text's spiral-learning approach, students return to Anthology selections again and again. A single piece might be used to illustrate scales, triads, cadence types, secondary dominants, common-chord modulation, sequence, and binary form. Because the Anthology works hand-in-hand with the text, revisions to the chapters in the third edition have provided opportunities to explore new repertoire. For example, we have expanded coverage of early twentieth-century music before the advent of atonality; the Anthology now includes new songs by Ives and Debussy, Ravel's *Pavane pour une infant défunte*, and a movement from Stravinsky's piano transcription of *Petrouchka*.

Anthology recordings, performed by musicians at the Eastman School of Music, are included with each new copy of the text and are available online.

Aural Skills

The Musician's Guide to Theory and Analysis is the only theory book that is accompanied by a fully integrated companion text: *The Musician's Guide to Aural Skills*. This text consists of two volumes that can be used together with this text or on their own. Taken together, the two volumes provide all the materials needed for the aural skills sequence, from fundamentals to post-tonal ear training.

- The **Sight-Singing** volume features over 800 carefully selected melodies, rhythms, improvisation activities, and keyboard exercises.

- The **Ear-Training** volume includes hundreds of short, self-grading *Try it* dictations that help students identify common tonal gestures. Over 400 contextual-listening questions guide students through the process of taking dictation from performances of real music.

- New for this edition, both volumes of *The Musician's Guide to Aural Skills* have been organized in 40 chapters to match exactly the chapters of *The Musician's Guide to Theory and Analysis*, so that students can study the same concepts simultaneously in theory and aural skills. This coordination ensures that all terminology and pedagogical concepts match between the "written" and aural texts.

What's New?

We have worked to incorporate the ideas of many helpful reviewers, while retaining the key features of an effective pedagogical strategy.

- With new **Know It? Show It!** pedagogy, students get access to multiple short video tutorials for each chapter, adaptive written and aural quizzes, and an online Workbook free with every new copy of the text.

- Throughout the text, the prose has been streamlined, making important points even easier to grasp.

- Every chapter in the book has undergone revision, replacing repertoire from the second edition with fresh new pieces. We have revised and reorganized material in the chapter on sequences, introduced topic theory to our discussion of variation and sonata forms, and made countless small changes to improve clarity and better annotate musical examples so that you can see in a glance what they illustrate.

- Chapters on form and twentieth-century theory have been reorganized for a smoother pedagogical progression. We have placed the Variations chapter earlier, so that students can explore this form as soon as they have sufficient harmonic understanding to do so. We have expanded our discussion of the Concerto, and moved Rondo later, combined with Sonata-Rondo and Large Ternary. In Part IV, we have expanded our discussion of early twentieth-century works before atonality, and consolidated the discussion of serialism into a single chapter. We also reorganized our treatment of rhythm, meter, and form after 1900 so that it follows a roughly chronological sequence: an initial chapter early in Part IV explores innovations in the first half of the twentieth century, while a second chapter near the end of the book discusses innovations after 1945.

- The Anthology features 26 new works, including additional compositions by major composers such as Bach and Beethoven, as well as new twentieth-century works by Berg, Ives, Debussy, and Ravel. Other new additions complement the form chapters: a variation movement for band by Gustav Holst, a very early minuet by Mozart, a large Romantic ternary movement by Clara Schumann, a Broadway-style song from Jerome Kern, and so on.

Our Thanks to . . .

A work of this size and scope is helped along the way by many people. We are especially grateful for the support of our families—Elizabeth A. Clendinning, David Stifler, Rachel Armstrong Bowers, Rocky Bowers, and Glenn, Russell, and Caroline West. Our work together as co-authors has been incredibly rewarding, and we are thankful for that collaboration and friendship. We also thank Joel Phillips (Westminster Choir College) for his many important contributions—pedagogical, musical, and personal—to our project and especially for the coordinated aural skills component of this package, *The Musician's Guide to Aural Skills*, with Paul Murphy (Muhlenberg College), who has become a key member of our team. While working on the project, we have received encouragement and useful ideas from our students at Florida State University and the Eastman School of Music as well as from music theory teachers across the country. We thank these teachers for their willingness to share their years of experience with us.

For subvention of the recordings that accompany the text and Anthology, and for his continued support of strong music theory pedagogy, we thank Jamal Rossi (Dean of the Eastman School of Music). For performance of many of the short keyboard examples in the text, we thank Richard Masters, whose sight-reading abilities, flexibility, and good grace are all appreciated. We also thank Don Gibson (former Dean of Florida State University's College of Music) for his enthusiasm and unfailing support. For pedagogical discussions over the years, we are grateful to our colleagues and graduate students at Florida State University and the Eastman School of Music, and to the College Board's AP Music Theory Test Development Committee members and AP Readers. Special thanks to Mary Arlin for her thorough and meticulous checking and generous help with Workbook exercises.

We are indebted to the detailed work of our prepublication reviewers, whose careful reading of the manuscript inspired many improvements, large and small. For this edition, we thank Daniel Arthurs (University of Tulsa), Christopher Bartlette (Binghamton University), Jack Boss (University of Oregon), Lyn Burkett (University of North Carolina-Asheville), Gregory Decker (Bowling Green State University), Christopher Doll (Rutgers University), Ryan Jones, (University of Wisconsin-Eau Claire), Greg McCandless (Appalachian State University), Brad Osborn (University of Kansas), Matthew Santa (Texas Tech University), and Peter Silberman (Ithaca College). For previous editions, reviewers have included Douglas Bartholomew (Montana State University), Rhett Bender (Southern Oregon University), Vincent Benitez (Pennsylvania State University), Per Broman (Bowling Green State University), Poundie Burstein (Hunter College), Lora Dobos (Ohio State University), Nora Engebretson (Bowling Green State University), Benjamin Levy (University of California-Santa Barbara), Peter Martens (Texas Tech University), Paul Murphy (Muhlenberg College), Tim Pack (University of Oregon), Ruth Rendleman (Montclair State), Elaine Rendler (George Mason University), Stephen Rodgers (University of Oregon), Mark Spicer (Hunter College), Reynold Tharp (University of Illinois), Gene Trantham (Bowling Green State University), Heidi Von Gunden (University of Illinois), James Wiznerowicz (Virginia Commonwealth University), and Annie Yih (University of California at Santa Barbara). We also acknowledge that the foundation for this book rests on writings of the great music theorists of the past and present, from the sixteenth to twenty-first century, from whom we have learned the "tricks of our trade" and whose pedagogical works have inspired ours.

For production of all recordings, our thanks go to recording engineers Mike Farrington and John Ebert, who worked tirelessly with Elizabeth Marvin on recording and editing sessions, as well as to Helen Smith, who oversees Eastman's Office of Technology and Media Production. We also acknowledge the strong contributions of David Peter Coppen, archivist of the Eastman Audio Archive, for contacting faculty and alumni for permission to include their performances among our recordings. We finally thank the faculty and students of the Eastman School who gave so generously of their time to make these recordings. The joy of their music making contributed mightily to this project.

We are indebted to the W. W. Norton staff for their commitment to *The Musician's Guide* Series and their painstaking care in producing these volumes. Most notable among these are Justin Hoffman, who steered the entire effort with a steady hand and enthusiastic support; Susan Gaustad, whose knowledge of music and detailed, thoughtful questions made her a joy to work with; and Maribeth Payne, whose vision helped launch the series. We are grateful for Norton's forward-thinking technology editor Steve Hoge, who coordinated development of the ebook, video lessons, InQuizitive activities, online Workbook, and audio recordings with the assistance of Meg Wilhoite, Kate Maroney, William Paceley, and Stephanie Eads. Jodi Beder was invaluable in checking assignments, correcting errors, and copyediting the Workbook. Lissi Sigillo and Rubina Yeh created the book's design for all parts of the *Musician's Guide* package, Michael Fauver project-edited the Workbook and Anthology, Debra Nichols provided expert proofreading, Grant Phelps assisted in preparing the manuscript and arranging for reviews, Mary Dudley developed marketing strategies, and Megan Jackson pursued copyright permissions and helped us understand copyright law. David Botwinik set the text and Workbook, and Andy Ensor and Jane Searle oversaw the production of these multifaceted texts through to completion. Our gratitude to one and all.

Jane Piper Clendinning
Elizabeth West Marvin

To Our Students: Why Study Music Theory?

Have you ever tried to explain something without having the right words to capture exactly what you mean? It can be a frustrating experience. Part of the process of preparing for a professional career is learning the special language of your chosen field. To those outside the profession, the technical language may seem like a secret code intended to prevent the nonspecialist from understanding. For example, a medical doctor might speak of "cardiac infarction," "myocardia," or "angina" when referring to conditions that we might call (inaccurately) a heart attack. To those who know the technical terms, however, one or two words capture a wealth of associated knowledge—years of experience and books' worth of information.

Words and symbols not only let us name things, they also help us to communicate how separate elements work together and group into categories. Music theory provides useful terms and categories, but it does more than that: it also provides a framework for considering *how* music is put together, *what* musical elements are in play, *when* particular styles were prevalent, and *why* music sounds the way it does. Understanding the vocabulary for categorizing and explaining musical events will prepare you to develop your own theories about the music you are playing and studying.

The purpose of this book is to introduce you to the technical language of music. In the first part, you will learn (or review) basic terminology and notation. Mastery of terminology will allow you to communicate quickly and accurately with other musicians; mastery of notation will allow you to read and write music effortlessly. You will next learn about small- to medium-scale musical progressions and how they work. Knowledge of these progressions will help you compose music in particular styles, structure improvisations on your instrument, make interpretive decisions in performance, and improve your sight-reading skills.

Later parts of the book deal with larger musical contexts, such as how sections of music fit together to make musical form. You will learn how to write in standard musical forms in differing styles, how to divide the pieces you perform into sections, and how to convey your understanding of form in performance. In the final chapters, we explore ways that these concepts are transformed (or abandoned) in music of the twentieth and twenty-first centuries, and consider new theories that have arisen to explain music structure in this repertoire. We will apply this information in the same ways as in previous chapters—with direct links to performance, analysis, and writing.

We have written this text with you and your learning at the forefront. With the purchase of a new book, you receive **Total Access** to a wealth of media and learning aids—from an **ebook** version of the text to recordings, formative quizzes, an online Workbook, and even video lessons that you can watch and review as often as you wish. Each chapter begins with an overview of what you will learn and ends with a list of important terms and questions for review. In between, we provide clear prose dotted with many musical examples—nearly all of which you can hear with a click on the website or ebook. Our *Try it* exercises give you practice on concepts (with answers in an appendix, or with a click in the ebook) that will prepare you for **Workbook** assignments, and our **Another Way** and **Summary** boxes give you new ways to think about and consolidate the concepts you are studying. The **Anthology** that accompanies this text is full of pieces that we love, and that we hope you will come to love, too. We chose them for maximum variety of style, instrumentation, and genre; we also chose works that many college students will have performed in lessons and concerts themselves. Every piece in the Anthology comes with a recording so that you can listen easily. Feel free to compare and contrast these performances with others you find online and in the library; think about which ones you prefer and why. We encourage you to explore the ebook, online resources, and recordings even before class begins, and throughout each semester of your undergraduate training. We hope these tools will help make your learning more interactive and musical.

One of the most important things to remember about music theory is that it is all about *music*—how and why music sounds the way it does, and what elements of a piece or a performance move us. You will be listening to music in every chapter, so that you can associate terms and notation with sounding music. We want you to make connections every day between what you are learning in this book and the music you are playing, singing, hearing, and writing. Music theory is absolutely relevant to the music making we do—whether it's listening, performing, analyzing, or composing. You will see references in nearly every chapter to the way its content might inform your music making. Use this information! Take it to the practice room, the studio, and the rehearsal hall to make the connection between your coursework and your life as a practicing musician. We hope the concepts you learn here will impact the ways you think about music for many years to come.

PART

I

Elements of Music

Pitch and Pitch Class

Outline

**Introduction to Pitch:
Letter names**
- Pitch classes and pitches

The piano keyboard
- White keys
- Black keys: Flats and sharps
- Enharmonic equivalents
- Intervals: Half steps and
  whole steps
- Double flats and sharps

Reading pitches from a score
- Staff notation
- Treble clef
- Bass clef
- C-clefs
- Naming registers
- Ledger lines
- Writing pitches on a score

Dynamic markings

Style periods

Overview

When we read notated music, we translate its symbols into sound—sung, played on an instrument, or heard in our heads. We begin our study of music theory by learning to read and write the symbols that represent pitch, one of music's basic elements.

Repertoire

Scott Joplin, "Solace"

Wolfgang Amadeus Mozart, Piano Sonata in C Major, K. 545, mvt. 1

"Ubi caritas et amor" (Gregorian chant; "Where charity and love are")

Introduction to Pitch: Letter Names

Listen to an excerpt from a piano work by Wolfgang Amadeus Mozart as you follow Example 1.1, the musical notation (or **score**). Many of the score's elements will be introduced in this chapter, beginning with the notes you see here.

EXAMPLE 1.1: Mozart, Sonata in C Major, K. 545, mvt. 1, mm. 1–4

By the end of the chapter, you will be able to name each note in this example. The first piece of information you need is that musical notes are named with the first seven letters of the alphabet—A, B, C, D, E, F, G—repeated endlessly.

KEY CONCEPT Imagine these seven letters ascending like stairs or arranged around a circle like a clock, as in Figure 1.1. "Count" up or down in the series by reciting the letters forward (clockwise) or backward (counterclockwise). To count up beyond G, start over with A; to count down below A, start over with G.

FIGURE 1.1: Seven letter names

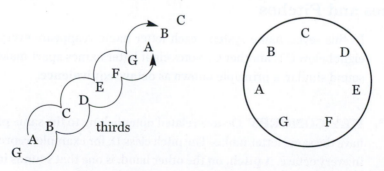

You will read music much more fluently if you also practice reading alternate letter names, as marked in the figure: G-B-D-F-A or A-C-E-G-B. This is called counting in thirds, because each pair of notes spans three letter names: A-C encompasses A, B, and C.

Learning to count in letter names is a fundamental musical skill. Practice counting backward and forward from A to A, C to C, G to G, and so on, until you feel as comfortable counting backward as forward. Think of the movement as "upward" when you count forward, and "downward" when you count backward. For example, five above C, counting forward, is G (C-D-E-F-G), and six below E, counting backward, is again G (E-D-C-B-A-G). Always include the first and last letters in the series, and count the first letter name as 1: three above F is A, not B (count F-G-A, not G-A-B).

Try it #1

Find each letter name requested.

A. Remember to count the given note as 1.

(1) 7 above G: __F__   (6) 5 below A: _____   (11) 2 above F: _____

(2) 6 above F: _____   (7) 3 above E: _____   (12) 4 above C: _____

(3) 2 above D: _____   (8) 2 below C: _____   (13) 6 below A: _____

(4) 4 below B: _____   (9) 3 above G: _____   (14) 7 below E: _____

(5) 3 below C: _____   (10) 2 above B: _____   (15) 5 above G: _____

B. Count in thirds above the pitch given. Write one letter name in each blank.

(1) G: __B__ - __D__ - _____ - _____   (2) D: _____ - _____ - _____ - _____

(3) A: _____ - _____ - _____ - _____   (4) B: _____ - _____ - _____ - _____

(5) C: _____ - _____ - _____ - _____

Pitch Classes and Pitches

In this seven-name system, each letter name reappears every eighth position: eight below C is another C. Notes eight letter names apart make an **octave**. They sound similar, a principle known as **octave equivalence**.

KEY CONCEPT Octave-related notes belong to the same **pitch class** and have the same letter name. The pitch class D, for example, represents every D in every octave. A **pitch**, on the other hand, is one that sounds in one particular octave.

Listen again to the first notes of the Mozart excerpt (Example 1.1) to hear pitch class C played in two octaves simultaneously: two different pitches that belong to the same pitch class.

The Piano Keyboard

White Keys

Throughout this text, we will reinforce concepts with the help of a keyboard. As a musician, you will find keyboard skills essential, whatever your primary instrument. Because of the piano's great range and ability to sound several pitches simultaneously, keyboard skills allow you to play simple accompaniments, demonstrate musical ideas, and harmonize melodies.

The white keys of the keyboard correspond to the seven letters of the musical alphabet, as shown in Figure 1.2. Immediately to the left of any group of two black keys is pitch class C; immediately to the left of any three black keys is pitch class F. **Middle C** is often used as a reference point; it is the C closest to the middle of the piano keyboard.

KEY CONCEPT No black key appears between white keys E and F or between B and C.

FIGURE 1.2: Piano keyboard with letter names

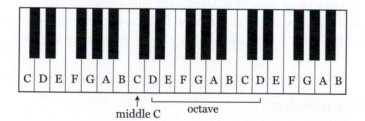

Black Keys: Flats and Sharps

The black-key pitches are named in relation to the white-key pitches. The black key immediately above (to the right of) any white key gets the white note's name plus a **sharp** (♯). As Figure 1.3 shows, each group of two black keys is called C♯ (C-sharp) and D♯, and each group of three black keys is F♯, G♯, and A♯. At the same time, the black key immediately below (to the left of) any white key gets the white note's name plus a **flat** (♭). That means the group of two black keys can also be called D♭ (D-flat) and E♭, and the three black keys G♭, A♭, and B♭. Every black key therefore has two possible names: one with a sharp and one with a flat. The two names are **enharmonic** spellings.

FIGURE 1.3: Keyboard with enharmonic pitches marked

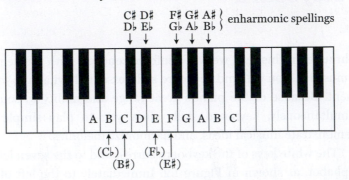

The sharp and flat symbols are called **accidentals** (although there is nothing "accidental" about them). A third common accidental, a **natural** (♮) cancels a sharp or flat. It returns the pitch to its "natural" state and white-key location on the keyboard.

Enharmonic Equivalents

Enharmonic pitches, with the same sound but different names (B♭ = A♯), belong to the same pitch class. Not all sharped or flatted pitches are black keys, however: if you raise an E or B to the closest possible note on the keyboard, you get a white key, not a black one. E♯ is a white key enharmonic with F, just as B♯ is white and enharmonic with C. On the flat side, C♭ is enharmonic with B, and F♭ is enharmonic with E. Find these pitches on a keyboard or in Figure 1.3.

Try it #2

Name the enharmonic equivalent.

(1) G♭: __F♯__   (5) B: _____   (9) D♯: _____

(2) B♯: _____   (6) A♭: _____   (10) E: _____

(3) A♯: _____   (7) E♯: _____   (11) F♯: _____

(4) D♭: _____   (8) B♭: _____   (12) F: _____

Intervals: Half Steps and Whole Steps

The distance between any two notes is called an **interval**. Two intervals that serve as basic building blocks of music are half steps and whole steps.

KEY CONCEPT A **half step** (or **semitone**) is the interval between any pitch and the next closest pitch on the keyboard. The combination of two half steps forms a **whole step** (or **whole tone**); a whole step always has one note in between its two notes.

On a keyboard, a half step spans a white note to a black note (or black to white)—except in the case of B to C and E to F, as shown in Figure 1.4. Whole steps span two keys the same color—again except in the case of B–C and E–F. A whole step above E is not F, but F♯; a whole step below C is not B, but B♭.

FIGURE 1.4: Examples of half and whole steps at the keyboard

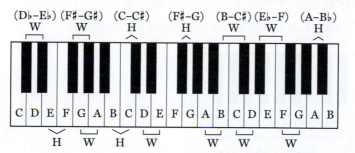

SUMMARY

1. The distance between any two notes is an interval. Two important intervals are half and whole steps.

2. Half steps span keys of different colors: white to black or black to white.
   - Exceptions are E-F and B-C, the white-key half steps.

3. Whole steps span keys the same color: white to white or black to black.
   - Exceptions are E♭-F, E-F♯, B♭-C, and B-C♯.

4. Double-check the spelling of any half or whole step that includes E, F, B, or C.

Try it #3

A. Name the pitch a half step above or below the given pitch, and give an enharmonic equivalent where possible.

(1) Above G: __G♯__ or __A♭__   (5) Above D: _____ or _____

(2) Below C♯: _____ or _____   (6) Below F: _____ or _____

(3) Above E: _____ or _____   (7) Below G♯: _____ or _____

(4) Below B♭: _____ or _____   (8) Below A♭: _____ or _____

B. Identify the distance between the two notes by writing W (whole step), H (half step), or N (neither).

(1) F♯ to E: __W__   (5) E to F: _____

(2) C♯ to D: _____   (6) F to G: _____

(3) B♭ to A♭: _____   (7) B♯ to C: _____

(4) C to B♭: _____   (8) D♭ to E♭: _____

Double Flats and Sharps

Two remaining accidentals appear less frequently in musical scores. A **double sharp** (×) raises a pitch two half steps (or one whole step) above its letter name; a **double flat** (♭♭) lowers a pitch two half steps below its letter name. For example, the pitches G♭♭ and F are enharmonic, as are A× and B (Figure 1.5).

FIGURE 1.5: Enharmonic pitches on the keyboard

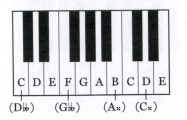

Reading Pitches from a Score

Staff Notation

The earliest forms of Western notation showed rising or falling melody lines, without identifying pitches by letter name. With the invention of the **staff** (the plural is "staves"), specific pitches could be notated by placing them on lines or spaces. Early staves had a variable number of lines (Figure 1.6a), but the modern staff consists of exactly five lines and four spaces (part b), which are generally read from bottom to top, with the bottom line called the first and the top line the fifth.

FIGURE 1.6: The staff 🎧

(a) Gregorian chant, "Ubi caritas et amor"

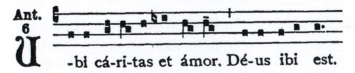

Translation: Where charity and love are, God is there.

(b) Modern staff

Treble Clef

To identify notes on the staff's lines and spaces, you need a **clef**, the symbol that appears to the far left of every staff. The clef tells which line or space represents which pitch (in which octave). The treble clef is used for higher notes (those played by a piano's right hand or higher instruments and voices). This clef is also called the G-clef: its shape resembles a cursive capital G, and the end of its central curving line rests on the staff line G. Example 1.2 shows how all the other pitches can be read from G, counting up and down in the musical alphabet, one pitch for each line and space.

EXAMPLE 1.2: Treble clef (G-clef)

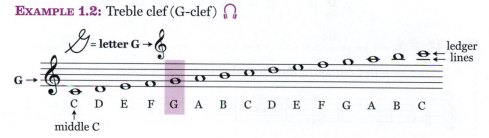

To write notes lower or higher than the staff, we add short lines called **ledger lines** below or above it, as in Example 1.2. Memorize the note names for each line and space. Learn the "line notes" together and the "space notes" together, as in Example 1.3 (these should be familiar from counting letter names in thirds).

EXAMPLE 1.3: Treble-clef lines and spaces

Another Way

To memorize the lines together or spaces together, you might make up sentences whose words begin with their letter names. The treble-clef lines (E–G–B–D–F), for example, might be "Every Good Bird Does Fly" or "Every Good Bond Drives Fast." The spaces of the treble clef make it easy for you: they simply spell F-A-C-E.

Example 1.4 shows whole and half steps on the treble staff, notated with accidentals. Listen to each one to hear the difference in sound between these intervals.

KEY CONCEPT When you write pitches on the staff, place the accidental before (to the left of) the **note head**, the main (oval) part of the note. When you say or write the letter names, however, the accidental goes after the letter name; for example, C♯ (C-sharp).

EXAMPLE 1.4: Half and whole steps on a staff

Try it #4

A. Write the letter names in the blanks below.

(1) **F♯**   (2) ___   (3) ___   (4) ___   (5) ___   (6) ___   (7) ___   (8) ___   (9) ___   (10) ___

B. Write the letter name in every blank below (including when the note is repeated).

John Lennon and Paul McCartney, "Eleanor Rigby," mm. 9–11

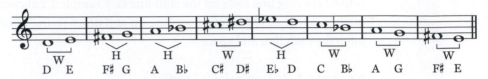

C. Identify whether each pair of pitches spans a whole step (W), half step (H), or neither (N).

(1) **H**   (2) ___   (3) ___   (4) ___   (5) ___   (6) ___   (7) ___

(8) ___   (9) ___   (10) ___   (11) ___   (12) ___   (13) ___   (14) ___

Bass Clef

Lower notes (for a pianist's left hand or lower instruments like the cello) are designated with a **bass clef**, or F-clef. This clef resembles a cursive capital F, and its two dots surround the line that represents F (Example 1.5). You can count other pitches from F or memorize them by their position on the staff.

EXAMPLE 1.5: Bass clef (F-clef)

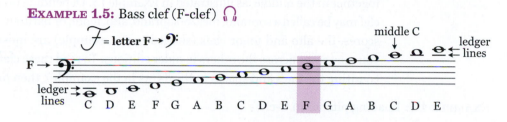

Example 1.6 shows the bass-clef lines and spaces. One way to remember the lines (G-B-D-F-A) might be "Great Big Doves Fly Away." The spaces (A-C-E-G) could be "All Cows Eat Grass" or "All Cars Eat Gas."

EXAMPLE 1.6: Bass-clef lines and spaces

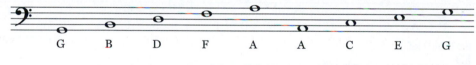

| G | B | D | F | A | A | C | E | G |

Try it #5

A. Write the letter names in the blanks below.

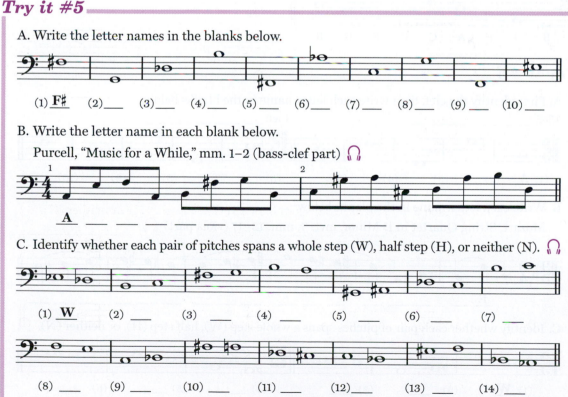

(1) **F♯**   (2)___   (3)___   (4)___   (5)___   (6)___   (7)___   (8)___   (9)___   (10)___

B. Write the letter name in each blank below.

Purcell, "Music for a While," mm. 1–2 (bass-clef part)

A ___ ___ ___ ___ ___ ___ ___ ___ ___ ___ ___ ___ ___

C. Identify whether each pair of pitches spans a whole step (W), half step (H), or neither (N).

(1) **W**   (2) ___   (3) ___   (4) ___   (5) ___   (6) ___   (7) ___

(8) ___   (9) ___   (10) ___   (11) ___   (12) ___   (13) ___   (14) ___

C-Clefs

Although music reading starts with knowledge of the treble and bass clefs, you should learn how to read the C-clefs as well, since they are standard in orchestral and chamber music scores. A **C-clef** is a "movable" clef: its distinctive shape—𝄡— identifies middle C by the point on the staff at which the two curved lines join together in the middle, as illustrated in Example 1.7. Depending on its position, the clef may be called a soprano, mezzo-soprano, alto, tenor, or baritone clef. In modern scores, the alto and tenor clefs (shaded in the example) are most common, but you may come across the others in older editions. To read these clefs well, practice counting the lines and spaces in thirds (as in the example), then memorize them.

EXAMPLE 1.7: Reading pitches in C-clefs

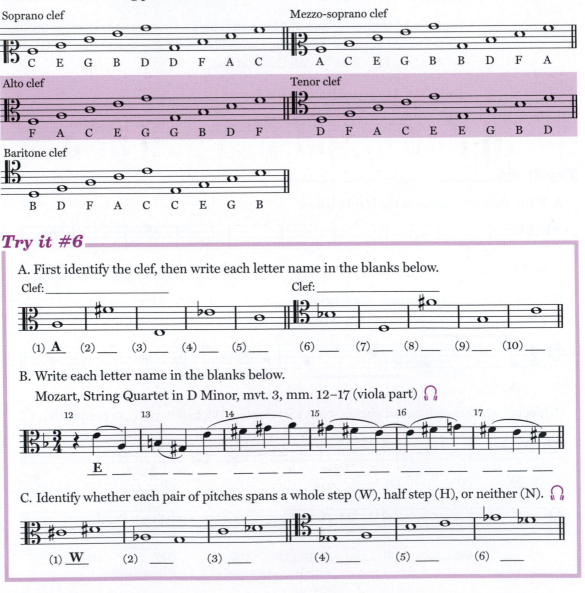

Try it #6

A. First identify the clef, then write each letter name in the blanks below.

Clef: _____   Clef: _____

(1) **A**   (2) ___   (3) ___   (4) ___   (5) ___   (6) ___   (7) ___   (8) ___   (9) ___   (10) ___

B. Write each letter name in the blanks below.

Mozart, String Quartet in D Minor, mvt. 3, mm. 12–17 (viola part) 🎧

E __ __ __ __ __ __ __ __ __ __ __ __ __ __ __

C. Identify whether each pair of pitches spans a whole step (W), half step (H), or neither (N). 🎧

(1) **W**   (2) ___   (3) ___   (4) ___   (5) ___   (6) ___

Musicians read different clefs because each one corresponds to the range of pitches needed for a particular instrument or voice type. The higher instruments, like the flute and violin, read treble clef. Lower instruments, like the cello and bass, generally read bass clef, while violas use the alto clef. Pianists read both bass and treble clefs, and bassoonists and cellists read both bass and tenor clefs. In choral scores, the tenor's voice part is often notated using a treble clef with a small "8" beneath it, known as the **choral tenor clef**. These pitches are read down an octave.

Naming Registers

When you name pitches, it helps to specify their precise octave placement. There are several systems for doing this: we will use the numeric system shown on the keyboard in Figure 1.7. The lowest C on the piano is C1 and the highest is C8; middle C is C4. The number for a particular octave includes all the pitches from C up to the following B, so the B above C4 is B4, and the B below C4 is B3. The three notes below the C1 on the piano are A0, B♭0, and B0.

FIGURE 1.7: Piano keyboard with octave designations

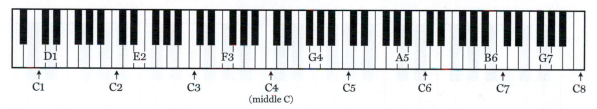

Ledger Lines

Listen to Example 1.8, the beginning of Joplin's rag "Solace." Like most piano music, this work is notated on a **grand staff**—two staves, one in treble clef and one in bass clef, connected by a curly brace. The shaded pitches are written with ledger lines, which may be written above, below, or between staves. Read ledger lines just like other staff lines, by counting forward or backward from pitches on the staff.

EXAMPLE 1.8: Joplin, "Solace," mm. 1-4

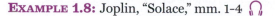

Pitches near middle C may be written between the two staves of the grand staff, as in the Joplin rag and Example 1.9 (arrows point to equivalent ledger-line pitches). In keyboard music, the choice of clef usually indicates which hand should play the note: bass clef for the left hand and treble clef for the right.

EXAMPLE 1.9: Ledger lines between staves on the grand staff

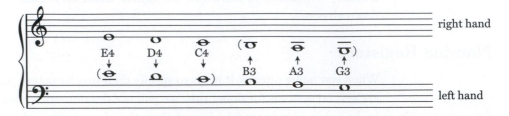

Example 1.10 shows pitches on a grand staff, extending over four octaves (some with ledger lines), and their positions on a keyboard.

EXAMPLE 1.10: Pitches on a grand staff and keyboard

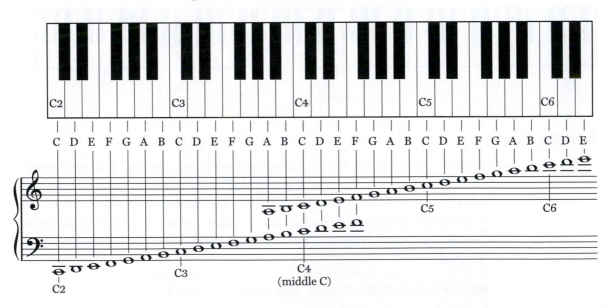

Notes higher than the staff have ledger lines drawn through them or below them, but never above them; notes below the staff have ledger lines through them or above them, but never below. Draw ledger lines the same distance apart as staff lines, as in Example 1.11.

EXAMPLE 1.11: Correct and incorrect ledger lines

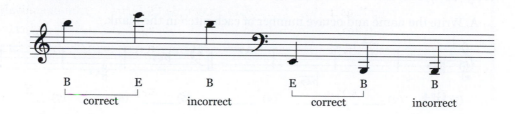

B		E	B		E		B		B

correct   incorrect   correct   incorrect

Memorize landmark pitches above and below the staves to help you read ledger lines quickly—as in Example 1.12, which gives the first three lines above and below each staff.

EXAMPLE 1.12: Landmark ledger-line pitches

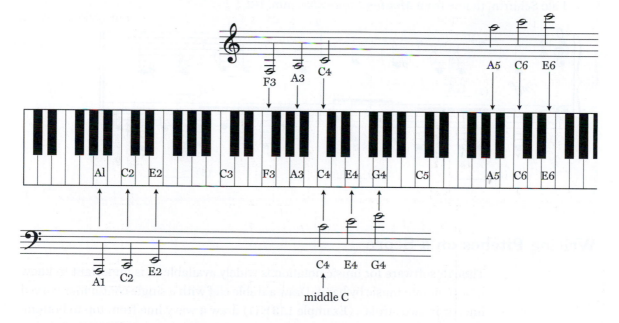

middle C

An alternative to ledger lines is the **ottava sign**. An "8va" above the staff means to play an octave higher (the "8v" stands for "octave," and the "a" stands for *alta*, Italian for "above"). An "8vb" beneath the staff means to play an octave lower (the "b" stands for *bassa*, or "below").

Try it #7

A. Write the name and octave number of each pitch in the blank.

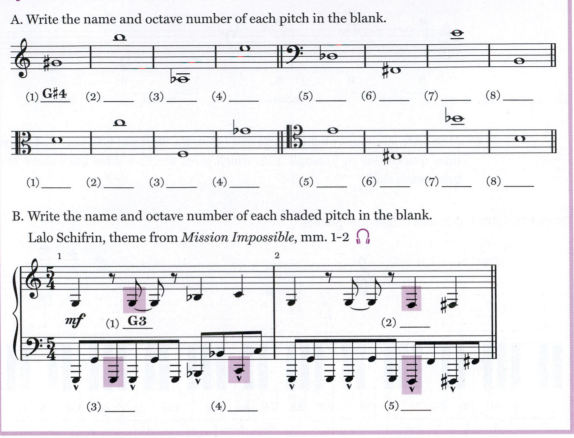

(1) <u>G♯4</u>   (2) _____   (3) _____   (4) _____   (5) _____   (6) _____   (7) _____   (8) _____

(1) _____   (2) _____   (3) _____   (4) _____   (5) _____   (6) _____   (7) _____   (8) _____

B. Write the name and octave number of each shaded pitch in the blank.

Lalo Schifrin, theme from *Mission Impossible*, mm. 1-2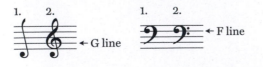

(1) <u>G3</u>   (2) _____

(3) _____   (4) _____   (5) _____

Writing Pitches on a Score

Though software for music notation is widely available, it is important to know how to notate music by hand. Draw a treble clef with a single continuous curved line, or in two strokes (Example 1.13): (1) draw a wavy line from top to bottom, like an elongated S; then (2) draw a second line that joins at the top and curves around it (ending on G4). To draw a bass clef, follow the diagram in the example, and make sure that the two dots straddle the F line.

EXAMPLE 1.13: Drawing treble and bass clefs

1.   2.   1.   2.

← G line   ← F line

When you draw note heads, make them oval-shaped rather than round, and not so large that it is hard to tell whether they sit on a line or space (Example 1.14a). Most notes are attached to thin vertical lines, called **stems**, that extend above or below the note head (♩ ♪). If a note lies below the middle line of the staff, its stem goes up, on the right side of the note head; if a note lies above the middle line, its stem goes down, on the left side (part b). A stem attached to a note *on* the middle line generally goes down (more about this in Chapter 2). The length of a stem from top to bottom spans about an octave.

EXAMPLE 1.14: Notation guidelines

(a)

(b)

too round   too big   too small   perfect ovals   correct   incorrect

Try it #8

Write each of the specified notes in the correct octave, using hollow note heads and correctly notated stems and ledger lines. Place accidentals before (to the left of) the note head.

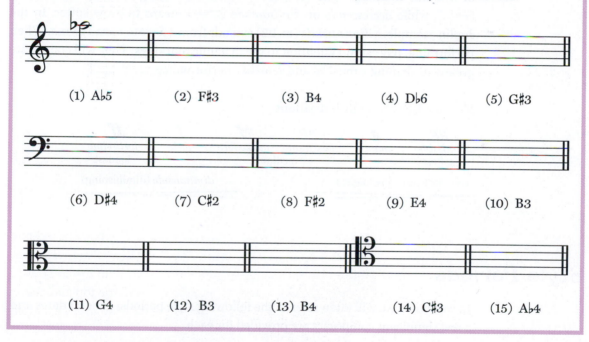

(1) A♭5   (2) F♯3   (3) B4   (4) D♭6   (5) G♯3

(6) D♯4   (7) C♯2   (8) F♯2   (9) E4   (10) B3

(11) G4   (12) B3   (13) B4   (14) C♯3   (15) A♭4

Dynamic Markings

Now listen to another excerpt from Joplin's "Solace," shown in Example 1.15. This passage begins with a full sound, marked with a large *f* in the score. This is a **dynamic** indication, which tells performers how soft or loud to play. Such markings also help musicians make decisions about the character or mood of a piece.

EXAMPLE 1.15: Joplin, "Solace," mm. 21–24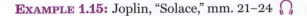

The **_f_** stands for _forte_, a loud dynamic marking; _piano_ (abbreviated **_p_**) is a soft one. Other frequently encountered markings are **_mp_** (for _mezzo piano_, "half as soft") and **_mf_** (for _mezzo forte_, "half as loud"). Figure 1.8 shows a typical range of dynamic markings. The indication that tells you to get louder is _crescendo_ (⟨⟩), while _decrescendo_ or _diminuendo_ (⟩⟨) means to grow softer. In the Joplin example, a _diminuendo_ (m. 22) extends from a _forte_ to _mezzo piano_. When performing, pay careful attention to the dynamic markings. They will contribute greatly to shaping a musical and sensitive performance.

FIGURE 1.8: Dynamic indications

_pp_	**_p_**	**_mp_**	**_mf_**	**_f_**	**_ff_**
pianissimo	_piano_	_mezzo piano_	_mezzo forte_	_forte_	_fortissimo_
softest		medium			loudest

crescendo (growing louder)   _diminuendo_ (diminishing)

Style Periods

In this book, we will often refer to the following style periods; general dates and a few significant composers are provided for each.

- **Early music**
  - **Medieval (c. 500–1400):** Gregorian chant, Hildegard von Bingen, Guido d'Arezzo
  - **Renaissance (c. 1400–1600):** Tomás Luis de Victoria, William Byrd, Giovanni Pierluigi da Palestrina

- **Common practice**
  - **Baroque (c. 1600–1750):** Elisabeth-Claude Jacquet de la Guerre, Arcangelo Corelli, Henry Purcell, Johann Sebastian Bach, George Frideric Handel
  - **Classical (c. 1730–1820):** Joseph Haydn, Wolfgang Amadeus Mozart, Ludwig van Beethoven
  - **Romantic (c. 1815–1910):** Franz Schubert, Robert and Clara Schumann, Frédéric Chopin, Fanny Mendelssohn Hensel, Richard Wagner, Johannes Brahms, Gabriel Fauré
- **Modern and contemporary**
  - **Early twentieth century and modernist (c. 1890–1945):** Scott Joplin, Claude Debussy, Maurice Ravel, Béla Bártok, Arnold Schoenberg, Anton Webern, Igor Stravinsky
  - **Post–World War II and late twentieth century (c. 1945–2000):** Pierre Boulez, Luciano Berio, György Ligeti, John Cage
  - **Twenty-first century:** Steve Reich, Arvo Pärt, John Corigliano, Ellen Taaffe Zwilich, Chen Yi

Did You Know?

Scott Joplin was born into a musical family: his father, a former slave, played violin, and his mother played the banjo. One of Joplin's most famous compositions, "Maple Leaf Rag" (published in 1899), earned him one penny for every sheet-music copy sold, an income that helped support him for the rest of his life. Although his opera *Treemonisha* (composed in 1911) won an award for being the "most American opera" ever written, Joplin never saw it fully staged. His music was played in bars, dance halls, and other popular gathering places from the 1890s to the 1910s—and became popular once again in the 1970s after it was featured in the movie *The Sting* (1973), with Paul Newman and Robert Redford. Joplin's rags have remained among the best-known American music of the early twentieth century.

TERMS YOU SHOULD KNOW

accidental	clef	counting in thirds	musical alphabet
• flat	• treble clef	dynamic marking	octave
• sharp	• bass clef	enharmonic pitch	octave equivalence
• natural	• C-clef	grand staff	pitch
• double flat	• alto clef	half step	pitch class
• double sharp	• tenor clef	interval	staff
		ledger line	whole step

QUESTIONS FOR REVIEW

1. How do a staff and clef work together to identify pitches?
2. How do pitches and pitch classes differ?
3. What is the function of (a) C-clefs, (b) accidentals, (c) ledger lines?
4. How do the piano's white and black keys help you determine whole and half steps?
5. Which white-key pairs of notes form half steps, without the addition of accidentals?
6. Give two guidelines each for notating ledger lines, note heads, and stems.
7. How are octave numbers assigned? What is the octave number for middle C?
8. Pick a melody from the anthology or music that you are playing that includes ledger lines. Identify all its pitches and octave numbers.

Know It? Show It!

Focus by working through the tutorials.

Learn with InQuizitive.

Apply what you've learned to complete the workbook assignments.

2

Simple Meters

Overview

We turn now to the organization of music in time. This chapter explains how beats are grouped and divided to create meter, then focuses on simple meters, whose beats divide into two parts.

Repertoire

Anonymous, Minuet in D Minor

Frédéric Chopin, Mazurka in F Minor, Op. 68, No. 4

"Greensleeves"

George Frideric Handel
  Chaconne in G Major
  "Rejoice greatly," from *Messiah*

Fanny Mendelssohn Hensel, "Neue Liebe, neues Leben"
  ("New Love, New Life")

Scott Joplin
  "Pine Apple Rag"
  "Solace"

John Newton, "Amazing Grace"

John Philip Sousa, "The Stars and Stripes Forever"

Tomás Luis de Victoria, "O magnum mysterium"
  ("O Great Mystery")

Antonio Vivaldi, "Domini Fili unigenite" ("Lord, the only-begotten Son"), from *Gloria*

Outline

Dividing musical time
- Beat, beat division, and meter
- Conducting patterns
- Tempo
- Rhythm and meter

Rhythmic notation for simple meters
- Rhythmic values
- Meter signatures

Counting rhythms in simple meters
- Beat subdivisions
- Stems, flags, and beaming
- Counting rests and dots
- Slurs and ties
- Metrical accents and syncopation
- Hemiola
- Anacrusis notation

Beat units other than the quarter note

Implications for performance: Metric hierarchy

Dividing Musical Time

Beat, Beat Division, and Meter

Listen to the opening of Joplin's "Pine Apple Rag" and Handel's "Rejoice greatly"—two lively works in contrasting styles. As you listen, tap your foot in time: this tap represents the work's primary pulse, or **beat**. You should also hear a secondary pulse, moving twice as fast. Tap the secondary pulse in one hand while your foot continues with the primary beat. This secondary pulse represents the **beat division**.

KEY CONCEPT Musical meters are defined by

(1) the way beats are divided, and

(2) the way beats are grouped into larger recurring units.

Beats typically divide into two or three parts. In the Joplin and Handel examples, the beat divides into twos. Now listen to the English folk tune "Greensleeves." Tap your foot along with the slow beat, as before. When you add the beat division in your hand, you'll notice that the beat divides not into twos, but into threes.

KEY CONCEPT There are two principal meter types: simple and compound. Works in **simple meters** have beats that divide into twos. Those in **compound meters** have beats that divide into threes.

There can be quite a difference in character between these two types: simple meters feel like walking or marching, while compound meters may sound lilting, like a waltz.

Try it #1

Listen to each piece below to determine the beat and its division. If the beat divides into twos, circle "simple"; if it divides into threes, circle "compound."

(a) Joplin, "Solace"	simple	compound
(b) Gilmore, "When Johnny Comes Marching Home"	simple	compound
(c) Mozart, *Variations on "Ah, vous dirai-je Maman"*	simple	compound
(d) Schumann, "Wilder Reiter" ("Wild Rider")	simple	compound

Listen now to the opening of Sousa's "Stars and Stripes Forever" and Chopin's Mazurka in F Minor. Tap the primary beat for each. In both works, the beat divides into twos: both are in simple meter. But besides dividing, primary beats also *group*—into twos, threes, or fours. As you listen to each piece, try counting "1-2, 1-2" (one number per beat); if the piece doesn't fit that pattern, try "1-2-3, 1-2-3" or "1-2-3-4, 1-2-3-4."

KEY CONCEPT When beats group into units of two, the meter type (either simple or compound) is **duple**. When they group into units of three, the meter type is **triple**; and when they group into units of four, it is **quadruple**.

As you may have heard, the meter type for the Sousa march is simple duple, and for the Chopin mazurka simple triple. In music notation, the beat groupings are indicated by **bar lines**, which separate the notes into **measures**, or **bars**. Measures are often numbered at the top, as in Example 2.1, to help you find your place in a score. Listen again to the mazurka while following the notation in the example and the counts written beneath.

EXAMPLE 2.1: Chopin, Mazurka in F Minor, mm. 1–4

Conducting Patterns

Conductors' motions outline specific patterns for each meter to keep an ensemble playing together and to convey interpretive ideas. The basic conducting patterns for duple, triple, and quadruple meters given in Figure 2.1 are the same whether the piece is in a simple or compound meter (although the conductor may distinguish between them by subdividing the basic pattern).

As you practice each pattern, you will feel a certain physical weight associated with the **downbeat**—the motion of the hand down on beat 1 of the pattern. You will probably feel anticipation with the **upbeat**—the upward lift of the hand for the final beat. Practice these patterns until you feel comfortable with them, and use them to help you recognize meter types by ear.

FIGURE 2.1: Conducting patterns

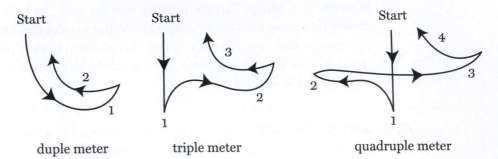

duple meter   triple meter   quadruple meter

Tempo

Conductors also use conducting patterns to establish a work's **tempo**, or speed (the plural is "tempi"), which in turn helps to convey the character or mood of a piece. The tempo is often indicated on a musical score with words in Italian or other languages. Following are the most common tempo indications in Italian.

- Slower tempi: *grave, largo, larghetto, adagio*

- Medium tempi: *andantino, andante, moderato, allegretto*

- Faster tempi: *allegro, vivace, presto, prestissimo*

- Increasing in tempo (gradually faster): *accelerando*

- Decreasing in tempo (gradually slower): *ritardando*

- Flexibility within tempo: *rubato*

Meter is considered *hierarchical* because you can perceive it simultaneously at different levels, depending on the tempo. You may have trouble hearing the difference between duple and quadruple meters by ear; you may hear one measure in quadruple meter as two bars of duple. It is also possible to hear two measures of simple triple meter as one measure of compound duple. Don't worry that you are "wrong"—you're simply identifying the meter at a different level of the metric hierarchy of beat divisions, beats, and measures. Tempo can provide an important clue. If you perceive a very fast beat in three, for example, chances are you are hearing the beat divisions in compound meter.

Try it #2

Listen to the beginning of each of these simple-meter compositions. Listen for the grouping and metrical accent, then circle either "duple or quadruple" or "triple."

(a) Bach, "O Haupt voll Blut und Wunden" 🎧   duple or quadruple   triple

(b) Mozart, Minuet in F Major 🎧   duple or quadruple   triple

(c) Mozart, Piano Sonata in C Major, mvt. 1 🎧   duple or quadruple   triple

(d) Bach, Passacaglia in C Minor for Organ 🎧   duple or quadruple   triple

Rhythm and Meter

Rhythm and meter are two different, but related, aspects of musical time. **Rhythm** refers to the durations of pitch and silence (notes and **rests**) used in a piece. Meter provides a framework of strong and weak beats against which the rhythms are heard.

SUMMARY

Music written in a meter has

- a recurring pattern of beats,
- perceivable divisions of beats (simple or compound),
- perceivable groupings of beats (duple, triple, or quadruple).

Rhythm consists of

- durations of pitch and silence, usually heard in the context of the underlying meter.

This summary applies generally to tonal music from the common-practice era, roughly 1600 through the early twentieth century. Some music is nonmetric—without meter—especially in early, non-Western, and post-1900 works.

Rhythmic Notation for Simple Meters

Rhythmic Values

The parts of a note are labeled in Figure 2.2. The wavy line attached to the stem of a single note is a **flag**, and the horizontal line connecting two or more notes is a **beam**.

FIGURE 2.2: Parts of a note

A chart of common note values and their equivalent rests (durations of silence) in simple meters is given in Figure 2.3: a **whole note** divides into two **half notes**, a half note divides into two **quarter notes**, and so on. You can create smaller note values by adding flags or beams to the stem: **eighth notes**, for example, have one beam, **sixteenth notes** two beams (a **thirty-second note** has three flags or beams, and a **sixty-fourth note** four). Flags and beams are notational choices; the rhythms they notate sound the same. In some meters, you will see longer note values, such as the **breve** (𝄺), which lasts twice as long as a whole note, sometimes written as a double whole note (∞).

FIGURE 2.3: Note values in simple meters

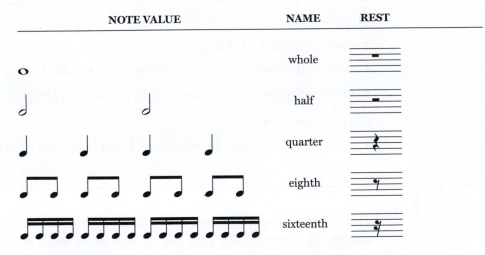

NOTE VALUE	NAME	REST
	whole	
	half	
	quarter	
	eighth	
	sixteenth	

Meter Signatures

A **meter signature** (or **time signature**) at the beginning of a score establishes the meter type and **beat unit** (the note value that gets one beat). In "Amazing Grace" (Example 2.2), the upper number (3) means that there are three beats in each full measure, while the lower number (4) indicates the beat unit: the quarter note gets one beat.

EXAMPLE 2.2: Newton, "Amazing Grace," mm. 1-4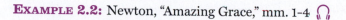

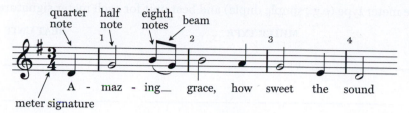

🔈 **KEY CONCEPT** Meter signatures are written with two numbers, one above the other, as in Figure 2.4. In simple meters:

- The upper number tells how many beats are in a measure; this number is **2**, **3**, or **4**, to represent simple duple, triple, or quadruple meter.

- The lower number indicates the beat unit (which note gets one beat): **2** (half note), **4** (quarter note), **8** (eighth note), or **16** (sixteenth note).

FIGURE 2.4: Meter signatures

(a) Quarter-note beat unit:

METER SIGNATURE	BEATS PER MEASURE	BEAT UNIT	METER TYPE
$\frac{2}{4}$	2	♩	simple duple
$\frac{3}{4}$	3	♩	simple triple
$\frac{4}{4}$	4	♩	simple quadruple

(b) Other beat units:

METER SIGNATURE	BEATS PER MEASURE	BEAT UNIT	METER TYPE
$\frac{2}{2}$	2	♩	simple duple
$\frac{3}{2}$	3	♩	simple triple
$\frac{3}{8}$	3	♪	simple triple
$\frac{4}{8}$	4	♪	simple quadruple
$\frac{4}{16}$	4	♪	simple quadruple

Try it #3

Name the meter type (e.g., simple duple) and beat unit for each meter signature given below.

	METER TYPE	BEAT UNIT
(a) $\frac{3}{16}$	_____	_____
(b) $\frac{4}{2}$	_____	_____

Besides numbers, you may see other symbols to represent meter signatures. For example, **c** (called "common time") represents $\frac{4}{4}$; and ¢ (called **alla breve** or "cut time"), represents $\frac{2}{2}$.

SUMMARY

Meter signatures you are likely to see in simple meters include:

- Simple duple $\frac{2}{2}$ ¢ $\frac{2}{4}$ $\frac{2}{8}$

- Simple triple $\frac{3}{2}$ $\frac{3}{4}$ $\frac{3}{8}$ $\frac{3}{16}$

- Simple quadruple $\frac{4}{2}$ $\frac{4}{4}$ c $\frac{4}{8}$ $\frac{4}{16}$

Counting Rhythms in Simple Meters

Look at Example 2.3 to see how to write counts into a score. In this simple-triple meter, each quarter note gets a count. If no new pitch sounds on a given beat (like the half note that extends into beat 2 of each measure), write the count in parentheses. The two eighth notes in measure 1—the **beat division**—are written "3 &" (or "3 +") and counted aloud as "three and"; the "and" is the **offbeat**. The quarter note D preceding the first full measure is an **anacrusis** (also called an **upbeat**, or **pickup**). Count it as the final beat (3) of an incomplete measure.

EXAMPLE 2.3: Newton, "Amazing Grace," mm. 1-4

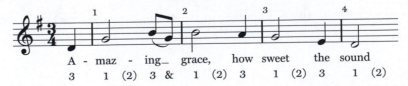

A - maz - ing_ grace, how sweet the sound
3   1 (2) 3 & 1 (2) 3   1 (2) 3   1 (2)

In Example 2.4, a composition with half-note beat unit, the counts for its soprano part are written above the staff.

EXAMPLE 2.4: Victoria, "O magnum mysterium," mm. 21–25

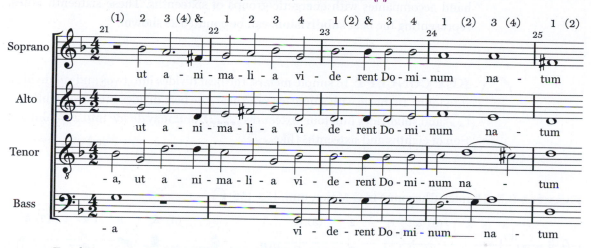

Translation: And animals saw the newborn Lord.

Try it #4

Write the counts beneath the following melodies. (The final measure of (c) is incomplete.)

(a) Bach, "Schafe können sicher weiden," mm. 24–26

(b) Anonymous, Minuet in D Minor, mm. 1–4

(c) Bono and U2, "Miracle Drug," mm. 29–32

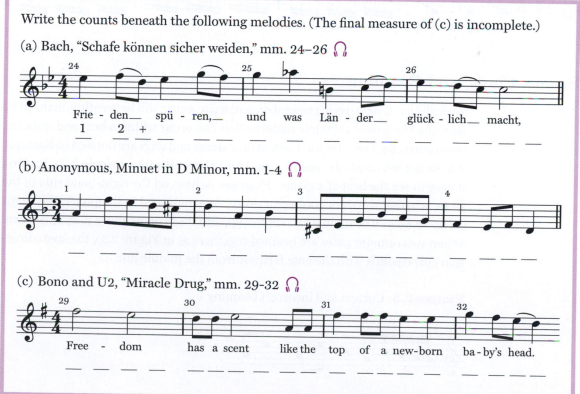

Beat Subdivisions

In Example 2.5, Variation 19 of Handel's Chaconne in G Major, the stately melody is played in quarter and eighth notes in the right hand, while the left hand accompanies with energetic groups of sixteenths. These sixteenth notes, representing the beat **subdivision**, can be counted as shown.

KEY CONCEPT In simple meters, the beat divides into twos and subdivides into fours. In music with a quarter-note beat, the beat divides into two eighths (♩) and subdivides into four sixteenths (♪♪♪), or it may divide into a combination of eighths and sixteenths (like ♪♪♪).

EXAMPLE 2.5: Handel, Chaconne in G Major, mm. 153–156 🎧

Stems, Flags, and Beaming

Your ability to sight-read, remember, and write music will be greatly enhanced by learning the typical rhythmic patterns that can occur within a beat and notating them correctly. Look, for instance, at how stems and flags are notated in Example 2.5. In the left hand, the beams group four sixteenths into a single beat, making it easy to see the beat at a glance. Flags are written on the right-hand side of the stem, whether the stem goes up or down. As mentioned in Chapter 1, the stems on notes below the middle line extend up, and those on or above it extend down. When two or more notes are beamed together (as in Figure 2.5), the stem direction corresponds with the note farthest from the middle line.

FIGURE 2.5: Correct and incorrect beaming

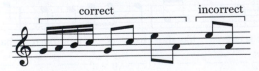

Try it #5

Renotate the pitches below onto the staff at the right. Correct all stems, flags, and beams.

🎵 **KEY CONCEPT** Rhythms should be beamed to reflect the beat unit. For example, groups of eighth and sixteenth notes that span a quarter-note beat unit, such as ♫♪, are beamed together. (Older vocal scores, though, sometimes beam to correspond with the sung syllables rather than the beat unit.)

Five rhythmic patterns for the quarter-note beat unit are given in Figure 2.6: learn each pattern with its correct beaming. Familiar patterns like these can be combined and recombined in different ways, just as words can be recombined in a sentence.

FIGURE 2.6: Five common simple-meter patterns

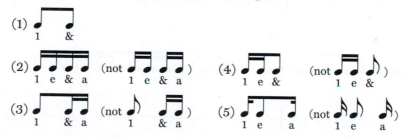

Another Way

Although this book uses the "1 e & a" syllables to count rhythms, teachers have developed other systems as well. Syllables for the five basic patterns in Edwin Gordon's system are shown on the left, and the "ta-ka-di-mi" system on the right.

Using a counting system can help you remember and identify rhythmic patterns; choose one and use it consistently.

The single-line rhythms that follow in *Try it #6* and elsewhere in the book are notated with **rhythm clefs**, which show only rhythm, not pitches. To draw a rhythm clef, write two vertical lines preceding the meter signature.

Try it #6

Circle beats that are beamed incorrectly, then renotate the entire rhythm on the second line with correct beaming. Write the beat-level counts beneath the given line, as in (a).

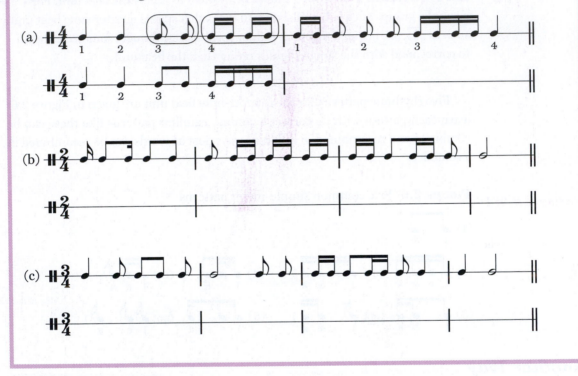

Counting Rests and Dots

Rests represent durations of silence. As you saw in Figure 2.3, each rest (e.g., eighth rest) lasts as long as the note that shares its name (eighth note). Be careful when you read and write whole and half rests, which resemble each other: the half rest sits on top of the third staff line, while the whole rest hangs from the fourth line. (You might think of the whole rest as "heavier," forced to hang from the line, while the "lighter" half rest can sit on top.)

A whole rest may be written to indicate silence that lasts a whole measure regardless of how many beats are in that measure. In music with a half-note beat unit, such as $\frac{4}{2}$, you may see a double whole rest or note (breve), which lasts four half-note beats (Figure 2.7a). Finally, some scores (particularly orchestra parts where players rest for many consecutive bars) include multiple-bar rests. The number above the rest tells the player how many bars to rest. The rest in part (b), for example, is counted **1**-2-3-4, **2**-2-3-4, **3**-2-3-4.

FIGURE 2.7:

(a) Breve: (b) Multibar rest:

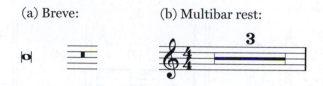

When a beat begins with a rest, write the appropriate beat number in parentheses, as in Example 2.6. This helps you count the durations of silence (or accompaniment) as accurately as the pitches.

EXAMPLE 2.6: Handel, "Rejoice greatly" (vocal part), mm. 8–11

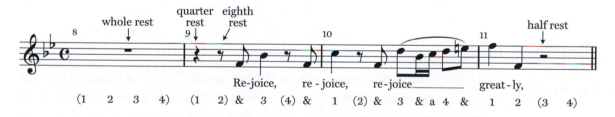

A **dot** adds to a note half its own value, as Figure 2.8a shows. That is, a dotted-quarter note equals a quarter plus an eighth, a dotted eighth equals an eighth plus a sixteenth, and so on. Dotted notes are generally paired with another note that completes a full beat or full measure. Some typical patterns are shown to the right, along with their counts in $\frac{4}{4}$. **Double dots** (relatively rare) add to a note half its value plus another quarter of its value (part b). The dot is always written on a space; if the relevant note falls on a line, the dot goes next to it on the space above, so that it can be clearly seen (part c).

FIGURE 2.8: Use of dots

(a) Single dots

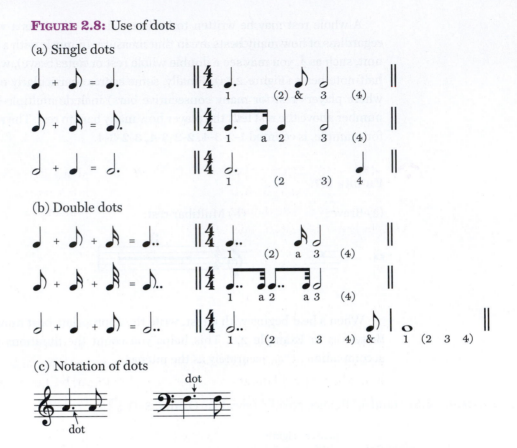

(b) Double dots

(c) Notation of dots

Slurs and Ties

Listen to the dotted passage from "Rejoice greatly" given in Example 2.7. The small arcs written above notes in measures 92-93 are **slurs**, which connect two or more different pitches. Slurs affect performance articulation—bowing or tonguing, for example—but not duration: the notes encompassed by a slur should be played smoothly, or **legato**, rather than detached. For singers, slurs identify groups of pitches sung to a single syllable.

EXAMPLE 2.7: Handel, "Rejoice greatly" (vocal part), mm. 92-96

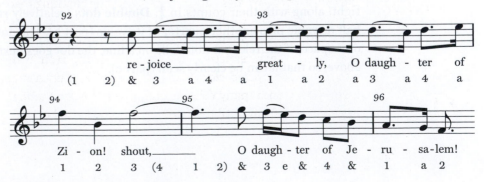

The small arc above the F in measures 94-95, on the other hand, is a **tie**, which connects two pitches that are the same. The F in measure 95 is not played again; rather the tie adds the duration of the two note values together, so "shout" lasts three and a half beats. Counts for the beats spanned by a tie are written in parentheses; and if an accidental is applied to the first note of a tie, it continues through the tie's duration.

KEY CONCEPT Ties and dots should be notated in a way that clarifies the meter rather than obscuring it. For example, an eighth tied to a quarter would be clearer than a dotted quarter in the rhythmic context below, because it makes the placement of beat 3 explicit.

instead of

1   (2) &   (3)   1   (2) &   (3?)

Dotted rhythms are made up of well-defined patterns that fit within a beat unit or half measure, and usually begin on the beat rather than on an offbeat. Write a tie when the held duration crosses over a bar line or beat unit, where writing a dot would obscure where the beat falls.

Metric Accents and Syncopation

One of the most important concepts to remember from this chapter is that meters are hierarchical: the beat division represents a low metric level, the beat unit a higher level, and the measure's downbeat an even higher level. Within each measure, the downbeat (beat 1) is the strongest. In duple meter, the beats alternate strong-weak; in triple meter, the accents are strong-weaker-weakest; and in quadruple meter, strongest-weak-strong-weak. Strong beats in a meter are heard as **metric accents**.

When an expected metric accent is displaced or moved to another beat or part of a beat—by ties, dots, rests, dynamic markings, accent marks, or the rhythm itself—the result is **syncopation** (marked by arrows in Example 2.8). Syncopations may occur at the level of the beat (accents on beat 2 or 4 rather than 1 or 3), the division (on "&"), or the subdivision (on "e" or "a"). Part (d) shows one of the syncopated *clave* patterns from Afro-Cuban music, which has been incorporated into many other popular styles. After the first note, all the notes begin on an offbeat until the last one, which falls on beat 2.

EXAMPLE 2.8: Syncopated rhythms 🎧

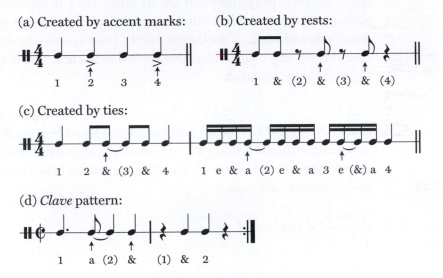

(a) Created by accent marks:

(b) Created by rests:

(c) Created by ties:

(d) *Clave* pattern:

Syncopations can be found in all styles, but they are especially prevalent in popular music, jazz, and ragtime. Within a quarter-note beat, the rhythms ♪♪♪ and ♪♩ are the most typical syncopation patterns, where the longest duration of the rhythm is on the "e" of "1 e & a" instead of the stronger "1" or "&."

Listen to the beginning of Joplin's "Pine Apple Rag" (Example 2.9) to hear the syncopations within the beat (mm. 1 and 3) and across the beat (mm. 2 and 4), marked by arrows. Syncopations across the beat are usually notated with ties, as here: the expected emphasis on beat 2 comes earlier, on the first of the tied notes.

EXAMPLE 2.9: Joplin, "Pine Apple Rag," mm. 1–4 🎧

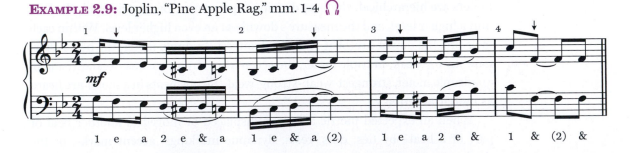

Joplin's "Solace" (Example 2.10) also includes many syncopations (see arrows above the counts). In fact, every measure of the excerpt shows a tie from the last sixteenth of beat 1 to the first sixteenth or eighth of beat 2, creating a syncopation mid-measure. In measures 10 and 12, syncopations are produced by ties from the last sixteenth of the previous measure. Such devices are highly effective because of the steady accompaniment pattern in the left hand: syncopations can only be perceived if there is a strong sense of the underlying beat for them to play against.

EXAMPLE 2.10: Joplin, "Solace," mm. 9-12

Hemiola

Another common metrical displacement pattern—the **hemiola**—is illustrated in Example 2.11. Read the rhythm aloud on "tah" or counting syllables while conducting—first level (a), then level (b). As you will discover, the beats in measures 3 and 4 group into twos, implying a temporary duple meter despite the overall triple meter. At level (c), you can hear a larger $\frac{3}{2}$ meter in those measures. You may hear a hemiola as a temporary change of meter, or as both meters (duple and triple) continuing at the same time, creating a type of syncopation.

EXAMPLE 2.11: Hemiola pattern in triple meter

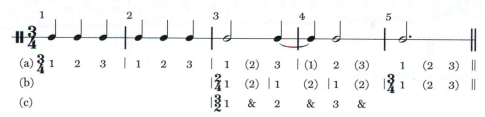

KEY CONCEPT A hemiola, often found in Baroque music to signal an important arrival point, is a temporary duple rhythmic grouping in the context of an underlying triple meter. Typically, two measures of meter $\frac{3}{4}$ are heard as three measures of $\frac{2}{4}$. A hemiola may be articulated by rhythmic durations, accents, or melodic patterns.

Example 2.12 shows a hemiola in context. At the beginning of the excerpt, the $\frac{3}{4}$ meter is strongly articulated in the lower three parts, while soprano pitches tied across the bar line add rhythmic and harmonic interest. In measures 88–90, the upper two voices move in half-note groupings against the underlying triple meter—making a hemiola, which might be conducted in $\frac{3}{2}$ as shown. (Note the double-dot notation in the tenor and bass parts in m. 85.)

EXAMPLE 2.12: Vivaldi, "Domine Fili unigenite," mm. 85–90

Translation: Lord, the only-begotten Son.

Anacrusis Notation

In music that begins with an anacrusis, the last measure is often notated as an incomplete bar to "balance" the opening incomplete measure. For example, in $\frac{4}{4}$ meter, a quarter-note anacrusis would be balanced by a final measure of only three beats. In Hensel's "Neue Liebe, neues Leben" (Example 2.13), the two-beat anacrusis at the beginning is balanced by a final bar of only two beats, shown in part (b).

EXAMPLE 2.13: Hensel, "Neue Liebe, neues Leben"

(a) Mm. 1-4

Herz mein Herz, was soll das_ ge - ben, was be - drän - get dich so_ sehr,___

3 & 4   1 & 2   3 & 4   1 & 2   3 & 4   1 & 2   3   4   1   2

Translation: Heart, my heart, what does this mean? What troubles you so much?

(b) Mm. 73-77 (piano postlude)

1 (2   3) 4   1   2

If you listen without a score, you might hear the beginning of this song as a downbeat. Why might Hensel have set this text with an upbeat? Perhaps her sensitivity to the accents and meaning of the text suggested that the second "Herz" ("heart"), on the downbeat of measure 1, was the more important word for a metric accent, as was "sehr" ("very") at the end of the phrase.

Try it #7

In the following melodies, identify what the duration of the last measure of the piece should be to balance the anacrusis.

(a) Meredith Willson, "Till There Was You," mm. 1-4 (melody only)

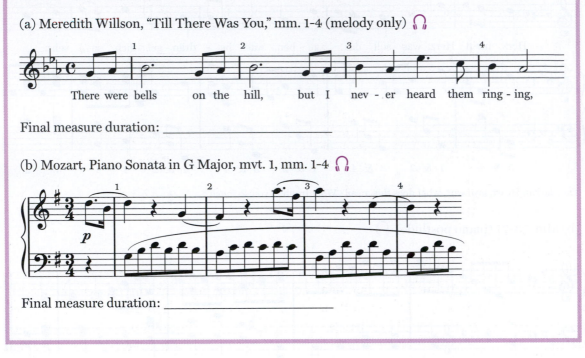

There were bells   on the   hill,   but I   nev - er   heard   them   ring - ing,

Final measure duration: _____

(b) Mozart, Piano Sonata in G Major, mvt. 1, mm. 1-4

Final measure duration: _____

Beat Units Other Than the Quarter Note

The way you count the rhythm in any passage of music depends on its meter. Even the idea that "a whole note gets four beats" is correct only in certain meters, such as $\frac{4}{4}$, where a ♩ gets one beat and a ♩ two beats; in $\frac{4}{2}$, a ♩ gets a half beat, a ♩ one beat, and a 𝅝 two beats. Listen to the opening of "The Stars and Stripes Forever" while following the piano score and counts above the staff in Example 2.14. The ¢ ($\frac{2}{2}$) meter instructs performers to think of these measures "in two" (two beats per measure). To develop good sight-reading skills, practice reading rhythms with half-note or eighth-note beat units, as well as the more familiar quarter-note unit.

EXAMPLE 2.14: Sousa, "The Stars and Stripes Forever," mm. 1-8 🎧

There are various reasons why you might see compositions written with a particular beat unit. Sometimes the meter is meant to remind the performer of a specific compositional type or character—such as *alla breve* for marches. Sometimes rhythms are notated with a longer beat unit for ease of reading, so that quick-moving or complex rhythms need not be notated in small note values. In the Sousa march, for example, the *alla breve* signature allows the quick-moving pitches to be notated as eighths rather than sixteenths. And sometimes the reason has historical roots: to eighteenth-century musicians, a signature of $\frac{3}{16}$ would indicate a sprightly jig, while $\frac{3}{4}$ would suggest the slower tempo of a minuet.

One way to gain facility with different beat units is to write equivalent rhythms in different meters, as in Example 2.15.

EXAMPLE 2.15: Equivalent rhythms notated in different meters 🎧

When you write in meters that are less familiar, make sure the beaming is correct for the new beat unit. For example, in $\frac{3}{8}$, write ♩♩♪ rather than ♪♪♪♪, in order to reflect the eighth-note beat unit. (Composers are not always consistent with this guideline, as Example 2.16 illustrates.)

Try it #8

Rewrite each rhythm in the meter specified. Check that your beaming correctly reflects the new beat unit. Write the counts (1, 2, 3, etc.) below the new rhythms.

Implications for Performance: Metric Hierarchy

Metric hierarchy is sometimes represented with rows of dots, as in Example 2.16, where a greater number of dots aligned vertically indicates a stronger metric position. The first beat of each measure, then, no matter the meter, receives the strongest metric accent.

EXAMPLE 2.16: Anonymous, Minuet in D Minor, mm. 1–4

At an even higher level of the hierarchy, measures themselves group together in what's called "hypermeter": measures 1 and 3 are heard as metrically stronger than measures 2 and 4. This hypermetric grouping of measures is also illustrated in Example 2.16 by the vertical columns of dots; in performance, think of strong and weak measures, just as you might think of strong and weak beats. Measure 4 of the hypermeter, then (which often coincides with the end of a phrase), will be a metrically weak resting point. Carefully studying a work's metric and harmonic organization can help you determine the relative importance of each beat and pitch, and thus shape an effective performance.

You may find it helpful sometimes to think "one to the bar" to create a large-scale hypermetric alternation between strong and weak measures. This can result in a performance with broader sweep, one that is not bogged down by rhythmic detail.

Did You Know?

Baroque musicians sometimes moved their hands down and up to conduct performances, but their patterns were somewhat different from those seen today. German composer and theorist Johann Mattheson (1681-1764), a contemporary of J. S. Bach, describes in one treatise the motions associated with duple and triple meters: both meters are based on a downward and upward motion, but in triple meters the up-stroke lasts twice as long as the down-stroke. Because the hand motion in triple meters was uneven, they were called "uneven" meters; duple meters were referred to as "even."

During this time, ensemble music was led by one of the players, usually the harpsichordist or organist, who signaled the first downbeat, then played with the ensemble. Sometimes opera or large-ensemble conductors indicated the downbeat by banging a large baton or staff on the floor. This proved hazardous in at least one case: Jean-Baptiste Lully, a ballet and opera composer at the French court of Louis XIV until 1687, died from an infection in his foot after energetically striking it with the conducting baton during a performance.

TERMS YOU SHOULD KNOW

alla breve	hemiola	metric accent	slur
anacrusis	hypermeter	note head	stem
bar line	measure	rest	syncopation
beam	meter	rhythm	tempo
beat	• simple	rhythmic value	tie
common time	• compound	• eighth note	time signature
cut time	• simple duple	• half note	upbeat
dot	• simple quadruple	• quarter note	
downbeat	• simple triple	• sixteenth note	
flag	meter signature	• whole note	

QUESTIONS FOR REVIEW

1. What is the difference between (a) simple and compound meters, (b) rhythm and meter, (c) beat division and subdivision, (d) a flag and a beam, (e) a tie and a slur, (f) a syncopation and a hemiola?

2. What do the two numbers in a simple meter signature represent?

3. Provide two appropriate meter signatures each for a simple duple, simple triple, and a simple quadruple piece. Write three measures of rhythm in each meter, using rhythm clefs.

4. What are the notation rules for (a) stem direction, (b) beaming beat divisions and subdivisions, (c) upbeats?

5. How are syncopations created? Write two syncopated rhythmic patterns.

6. Find a piece of music from the anthology in each of the following meters: simple duple, simple triple, simple quadruple. Choose at least one with an eighth- or half-note beat unit, and practice counting its rhythm while conducting the meter.

7. Choose a short passage from your repertoire. Try to perform it with equal stress on each beat. Then mark the strong and weak beats, and perform again.

Know It? Show It!

Focus by working through the tutorials.

Learn with InQuizitive.

Apply what you've learned to complete the workbook assignments.

3

Pitch Collections, Scales, and Major Keys

Overview

The concept of key is fundamental to Western music. In this chapter, we learn about keys by notating and playing major scales. The major key signatures and scale-degree names will serve as foundations for the study of harmony.

Repertoire

Johann Sebastian Bach
    Invention in D Minor
    Invention in F Major

Wolfgang Amadeus Mozart, Piano Sonata in C Major, K. 545, mvt. 1

"My Country, 'Tis of Thee"

John Newton, "Amazing Grace"

Dolly Parton, "I Will Always Love You"

Henry Purcell, "When I am laid in earth," from *Dido and Aeneas*

Robert Schumann, "Trällerliedchen" ("Humming Song"), from *Album for the Young*, Op. 68, No. 3

"Simple Gifts"

John Philip Sousa, "The Stars and Stripes Forever"

Outline

Chromatic and diatonic collections

Scales: Ordered pitch-class collections
- Scale degrees
- Spelling major scales
- Spelling chromatic scales

Major keys
- Key signatures
- The circle of fifths
- Identifying a key from a key signature
- Writing key signatures
- Identifying the key of a piece
- Scale-degree names

The major pentatonic scale

Implications for performance

Chromatic and Diatonic Collections

Listen to excerpts from two compositions written almost exactly 100 years apart: Purcell's *Dido and Aeneas* (1689, Example 3.1) and Mozart's Piano Sonata in C Major (1788, Example 3.2). Below the examples, write the letter names of the pitch classes in each excerpt, writing each letter name only once, in any order. When finished, you will have written a **pitch-class collection** for each excerpt—that is, the group of pitch classes found in the music, with no particular order and no duplications.

EXAMPLE 3.1: Purcell, "When I am laid in earth," mm. 10-17

Pitch-class collection: **G**

EXAMPLE 3.2: Mozart, Piano Sonata in C Major, mvt. 1, mm. 1-4

Pitch-class collection: **C**

The Purcell passage includes ten of the twelve possible pitch classes; two more and it would constitute a complete **chromatic** collection. (The word "chromatic" comes from the Greek *chroma*, meaning "color"; chromatic collections contain one of each possible pitch-class "color.") In contrast, the Mozart excerpt features only seven different pitch classes; these form a **diatonic** collection—seven different letter names in a particular arrangement. Because no ordering guidelines were given, you could have listed C D E F G A B, or C E G B D F A, or any other order. A diatonic collection is a subset of the chromatic collection.

Try it #1

Write the pitch-class collection for the passage shown below, and identify its collection type.

Bach, Invention in F Major, mm. 1–3

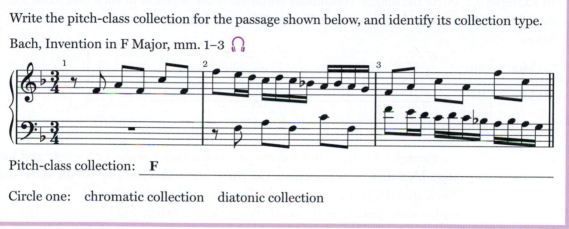

Pitch-class collection: **F** _____

Circle one: chromatic collection   diatonic collection

Scales: Ordered Pitch-Class Collections

Listen again to the opening of the Mozart sonata (Example 3.2), and sing the pitch that seems to be more stable than the rest. This pitch, C, provides the foundation for a special type of diatonic collection called a **major scale**.

Scales differ from collections in that they are ordered. When you play or sing a scale, there is a beginning pitch and an order to the notes that corresponds to the musical alphabet—in this case, C D E F G A B C, the pitches of a C major scale.

Similarly, when the chromatic collection is ordered, it becomes the **chromatic scale**, made up entirely of consecutive half steps. In musical works, composers may include only a segment of this scale. A descending chromatic segment often colors a slow, sad movement, like Purcell's aria (Example 3.1). Chromatic passages may also appear in showy music as a decorative or virtuosic element. For an example, listen to the Trio section of "The Stars and Stripes Forever" (Example 3.3).

EXAMPLE 3.3: Sousa, "The Stars and Stripes Forever," mm. 77-84

Try it #2

In Example 3.3, circle the longest continuous chromatic scale segment in each line. Look for numerous accidentals and consecutive half steps. Write the letter names of the scale segments below.

(a) Mm. 77-80: _____

(b) Mm. 81-84: _____

Example 3.4 illustrates a chromatic and a major scale, with whole and half steps identified for comparison. The chromatic scale's steps are all the same size: a half step (H, part a). In contrast, the pattern of whole (W) and half steps in the major scale (part b) is W–W–H–W–W–W–H. When you hear a half step in a major scale, you know it is in one of two specific locations, while in a chromatic scale the half step could be anywhere. The position of the half step thus helps us quickly locate the most stable pitches in a major scale.

KEY CONCEPT A major scale may begin on any pitch. It must include each of the seven letter names, as in Example 3.4b, and follow the W–W–H–W–W–W–H arrangement of whole and half steps from bottom to top.

EXAMPLE 3.4: Chromatic and major scale patterns

(a) Chromatic

(b) Major

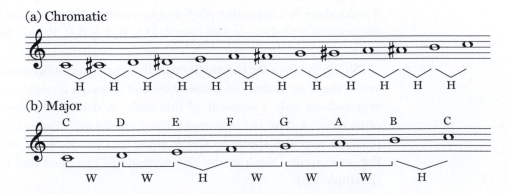

Another Way

One way to remember the W–W–H–W–W–W–H pattern is to think of the white-key notes on the piano: they match exactly the sequence of notes from C up to C.

Scale Degrees

The word "scale" comes from the Latin *scalae* (or the Italian *scala*), meaning "stairs" or "ladder." Each pitch of the scale is a **scale degree**—or **scale step**, in keeping with the stairs image. When you write or play a scale, its beginning note, called the **tonic**, is usually repeated one octave higher at the end. The tonic scale degree (C in the C major scale) is crucial to the sound and structure of scales and musical passages; it is the most stable scale degree and often serves as the final pitch of a melody. The other scale steps vary in structural weight, depending in part on the musical context.

Scale-degree numbers are written with a caret above: $\hat{1}$, $\hat{2}$, $\hat{3}$, $\hat{4}$, and so on. Some sight-singing methods encourage singing with these numbers. Another method, **movable-do solfège**, or **solfège** for short, assigns each scale degree a syllable—*do, re, mi, fa, sol, la, ti, do*—as in Example 3.5a. Part (b) gives scale-degree numbers and solfège syllables for the beginning of "Twinkle, Twinkle, Little Star."

EXAMPLE 3.5: Solfège syllables and scale-degree numbers

(a) Scale beginning on C

(b) "Twinkle, Twinkle, Little Star" (mm. 1–4)

Try it #3

For practice hearing scale-degree relationships in melodies:

(a) Sing up and down a major scale on scale-degree numbers or solfège syllables beginning on any C in a comfortable range. Then write the appropriate number or syllable below each pitch of the two melodies below (assuming C is $\hat{1}$, or *do*).

Mozart, Piano Sonata in C Major, mvt. 1, mm. 1–4

$\hat{1}$ *(do)* ___ ___ ___ ___ ___ ___ ___ ___ ___ ___ ___ ___ ___ ___

Mozart, "Alleluia," mm. 1–4

Al - le - lu - ia,   Al - le - lu - ia,   Al - le - lu - ia,   Al - le - lu - ia.

___ ___ ___ ___   ___ ___ ___ ___   ___ ___ ___ ___   ___ ___ ___ ___

(b) Sing the melodies above on scale-degree numbers or solfège in any comfortable octave. After giving yourself the starting pitch, use a piano or other instrument to check your pitch only if necessary. For now, don't worry about the rhythm; focus on singing the scale degrees in tune. After singing, listen to the sound file to check your accuracy.

(c) For more practice, sing some familiar tunes on numbers or solfège, such as "Frère Jacques" ("Are You Sleeping?"), which starts $\hat{1}$-$\hat{2}$-$\hat{3}$-$\hat{1}$ (*do-re-mi-do*); or "Happy Birthday," $\underline{\hat{5}}$-$\underline{\hat{5}}$-$\underline{\hat{6}}$-$\underline{\hat{5}}$-$\hat{1}$-$\underline{\hat{7}}$ (*sol-sol-la-sol-do-ti*). An underlined number or syllable indicates that it falls below the tonic.

Spelling Major Scales

Chances are, you are already familiar with the sound of major scales from playing and singing them as technical warm-ups. Here's how to write them.

KEY CONCEPT To write an ascending major scale from any given pitch:

(1) Write the given pitch (scale degree $\hat{1}$) on the staff.

(2) Write pitches with no accidentals on every line and space from that pitch, up to and including the same pitch class an octave higher (Example 3.6a).

(3) Label the space between each pair of consecutive pitches, from bottom to top, W–W–H–W–W–W–H (part b).

(4) Add an accidental (♯ or ♭) as needed to make the appropriate whole or half step (part c).

EXAMPLE 3.6: Steps in constructing a D major scale

(a) Write note heads on the staff.

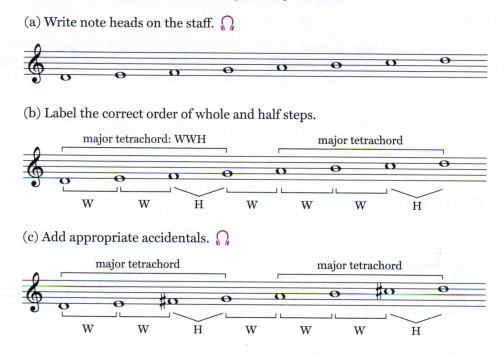

(b) Label the correct order of whole and half steps.

(c) Add appropriate accidentals.

Another way to remember the whole- and half-step pattern is to divide the scale into two four-note groups, or **major tetrachords** ("tetra-" means "four"): $\hat{1}$-$\hat{2}$-$\hat{3}$-$\hat{4}$ and $\hat{5}$-$\hat{6}$-$\hat{7}$-$\hat{8}$. Each major tetrachord consists of the pattern W–W–H, and the two tetrachords are a whole step apart, as marked in Example 3.6. Play major tetrachords, beginning on various pitches, on a keyboard or other instrument to become familiar with their sound.

KEY CONCEPT To "spell" a major scale with the correct letter name and accidental for each pitch:

- Write eight pitches—all seven letters of the alphabet plus the repeated tonic.
- Use accidentals that are either all sharps or all flats, not a mixture.

As Example 3.7a demonstrates, in B♭ major it would be incorrect to write D♯ instead of E♭: this spelling does not include all seven letter names (there is no E), and it mixes flats with sharps. Part (b) provides the correct spelling. When spelling scales, never change the given pitch. If your scale doesn't conform to these guidelines, go back and check your work.

EXAMPLE 3.7: Notation of the B♭ major scale

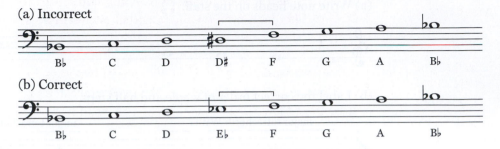

(a) Incorrect

B♭   C   D   D♯   F   G   A   B♭

(b) Correct

B♭   C   D   E♭   F   G   A   B♭

Try it #4

Follow the steps above to write a major scale from each given pitch.

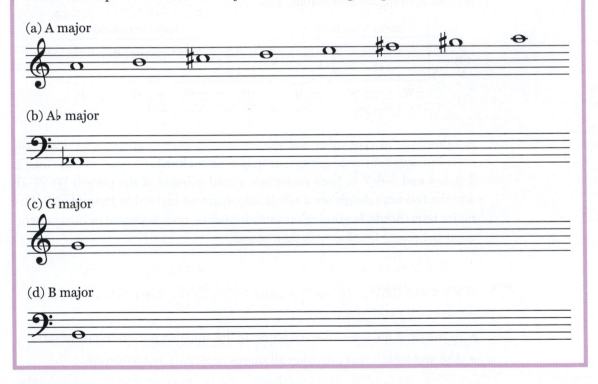

(a) A major

(b) A♭ major

(c) G major

(d) B major

Spelling Chromatic Scales

Unlike major scales, chromatic scales must include some letter names more than once.

🎵 **KEY CONCEPT** A half step spelled D-D♯ is a **chromatic half step**: the same letter name plus a chromatic alteration. A half step spelled D-E♭ is a **diatonic half step**: different letter names for adjacent pitches in a diatonic scale.

Chromatic scales may be notated in one of two ways, depending on the context. When no key is specified or the key is unclear, simply raise notes when ascending and lower them when descending, as in Example 3.8a.

EXAMPLE 3.8: Two ways to notate chromatic scales

(a) Sharps ascending, flats descending (when the key context is unclear)

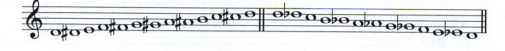

(b) In the context of a B♭ major scale (represented in whole notes)

Ascending

| 1̂ | ♯1̂ | 2̂ | ♯2̂ | 3̂ | 4̂ | ♯4̂ | 5̂ | ♯5̂ | 6̂ | ♯6̂ | 7̂ | 1̂ |

| do | di | re | ri | mi | fa | fi | sol | si | la | li | ti | do |

Descending

| 1̂ | 7̂ | ♭7̂ | 6̂ | ♭6̂ | 5̂ | ♭5̂ | 4̂ | 3̂ | ♭3̂ | 2̂ | ♭2̂ | 1̂ |

| do | ti | te | la | le | sol | se | fa | mi | me | re | ra | do |

Part (b) shows the chromatic scale spelled in the context of a B♭ major scale. If a key is specified, first write the underlying major scale in whole notes, then fill in each whole step with a chromatic half step: raise the scale degrees with ♯ or ♮ going up, and lower them with ♭ or ♮ going down. This results in a scale with mixed accidentals (and additional solfège syllables), but a clear underlying tonal context.

It is important to pay careful attention to how you spell scales and other musical elements. In practical terms, the correct spelling makes a score easier to sight-read. Once you are used to the look and feel of a particular key, unusual spellings can be distracting or confusing. Spelling anything incorrectly—even if the spelling "sounds" the same—changes its musical meaning.

Try it #5

Write a chromatic scale (ascending and descending) beginning with the pitches shown below. Base the spelling on the corresponding major scales you wrote for *Try it #4*. Label the diatonic scale degrees, and write these pitches with whole notes. Then fill in the half steps between them (with filled note heads) as appropriate.

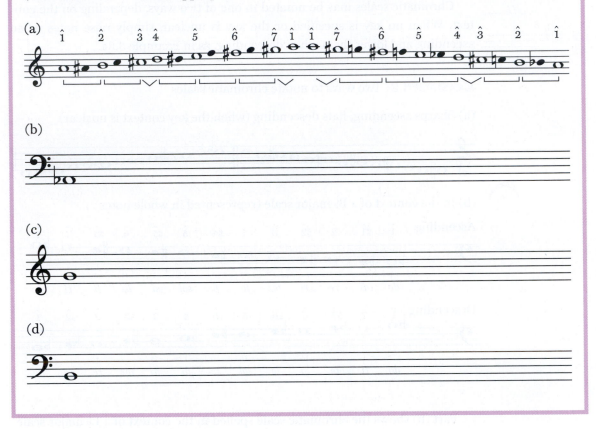

Major Keys

Key Signatures

In writing scales so far, we have added an accidental next to any note that needed it. In tonal music, however, this type of notation is not standard practice. Instead we use a shorthand notation, called a key signature, at the beginning of the score to specify consistent accidentals for the whole piece. Look at the beginning of Dolly Parton's "I Will Always Love You," given in Example 3.9.

EXAMPLE 3.9: Parton, "I Will Always Love You," mm. 1-5

This song is in A major, whose scale includes three sharps, yet not a single accidental is notated next to any pitch. Instead, the key signature at the beginning of each line instructs the singer to sharp every F, C, and G.

KEY CONCEPT A **key signature** shows which pitches are to be sharped or flatted consistently throughout a work. It appears at the beginning of each line of a score, immediately after the clef. (The meter signature, in contrast, is written only once at the beginning of the score, after the key signature, for most of the music we will study.) The key signature, together with the work's pitch collection and the relationships between its pitches, determine the key of the work.

To say that a piece of music is "in" a key (for example, A major) means that its pitches are drawn primarily from a single scale (A major), and that the pitches have predictable relationships of stability and instability. For example, the first note of the scale ($\hat{1}$) is the most stable (where a piece will usually end). Figure 3.1 presents all the major key signatures. Memorize them, together with their position on the staff, since many skills you will learn in later chapters build on this knowledge.

FIGURE 3.1: Major key signatures in four clefs

Try it #6

On the staves below, copy the major key signatures requested, taking Figure 3.1 as your model. Center each accidental on the appropriate line or space.

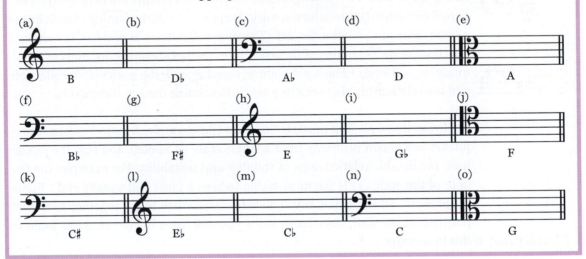

The Circle of Fifths

In key signatures, each time a new sharp is added, the new key is five steps higher than the last; and as a new flat is added, the new key is five steps lower than the last. This important relationship between keys, called the **circle of fifths**, is represented in the diagram in Figure 3.2. The sharp keys appear around the right side of the circle (each a fifth higher), while the flat keys appear around the left side (each a fifth lower). Keys at the bottom may be spelled with either flats or sharps; these are enharmonic keys (e.g., G♭ major and F♯ major). You may find the circle of fifths a helpful aid as you learn the key signatures. If so, you will be in good company: music students have relied on such a circle since the eighteenth century.

FIGURE 3.2: Circle of fifths

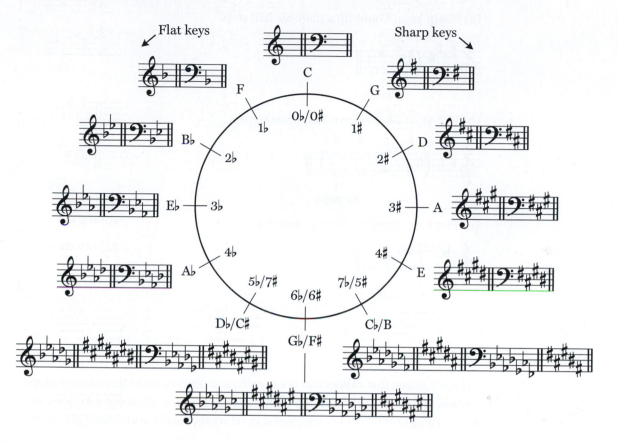

Identifying a Key from a Key Signature

Although you should memorize which key goes with each signature, you can also calculate the name of the key from the signature.

KEY CONCEPT To determine the major key from a key signature:

- For sharp keys, the last sharp of the signature is scale degree $\hat{7}$ (or *ti*). To find the tonic ($\hat{1}$, or *do*), go up a diatonic half step (Example 3.10a).

- For flat keys, the last flat is $\hat{4}$ (or *fa*); count down four diatonic steps to the tonic (part b).

  Shortcut: Since flats are spaced a fourth apart, the next-to-last flat (in a signature with two or more flats) represents the name of the key (part c).

EXAMPLE 3.10: Determining the major key

(a) Sharp keys: Count up a diatonic half step.

E major

(b) Flat keys: Count down four scale steps.

E♭ major

(c) Flat keys shortcut: Next-to-last flat.

E♭ major

Writing Key Signatures

To write music that others can read easily, you need to learn the standard order, octave, and spacing for each key signature, as shown in Example 3.11. Memorize these signatures with each accidental in its correct order and octave placement.

KEY CONCEPT The key signature goes between the clef and meter signature, which is easy to remember if you just think alphabetical order: clef, key, meter. The order of the sharps is F-C-G-D-A-E-B; the order of the flats is the same, only backward: B-E-A-D-G-C-F. The sharps are positioned on the staff alternating "down-up," while the flats alternate "up-down." (This pattern is occasionally broken to avoid writing an accidental on a ledger line.)

EXAMPLE 3.11: Order of the sharps and flats

Another Way

A helpful mnemonic (or memory device) for the first four flats is that they spell the word "bead." And a handy sentence to remember the order of both sharps and flats is "Father Charles Goes Down And Ends Battle." When you read it forward, the first letter of each word gives you the order of the sharps; when you read it backward ("Battle Ends And Down Goes Charles' Father"), it gives you the order of the flats.

SUMMARY

1. To write the key signature of a sharp key, think down a diatonic half step from the name of the key: this will be the last sharp of the signature.

   • In B major, the last sharp is A♯; the signature is F♯-C♯-G♯-D♯-A♯.

2. The name of a flat key is the next-to-last flat.

   • In A♭ major, the next-to-last flat is A♭; the signature is B♭-E♭-A♭-D♭.

Try it #7

Write key signatures for the major keys specified below from memory, in the treble and bass clefs.

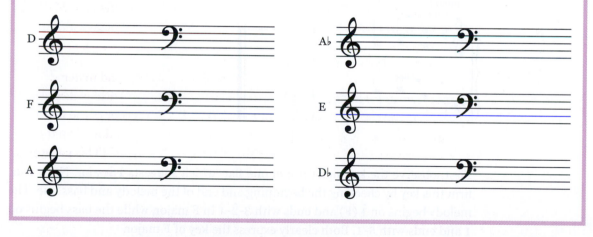

Identifying the Key of a Piece

If a piece begins with a key signature of one flat, you might assume that it is in F major, but the key signature alone is not enough to determine the key of a piece. As we will see in Chapter 5, it can indicate either a major or minor key.

KEY CONCEPT To find the key of a piece, first check the key signature, then check the beginning and end of the piece for characteristic scale degrees. The last note of the melody usually ends on $\hat{1}$ of the key. Typical patterns at the end are $\hat{2}$-$\hat{1}$ or $\hat{7}$-$\hat{1}$ in the melody and $\hat{5}$-$\hat{1}$ in the lowest-sounding voice (the bass). The most common scale degrees at the beginning of both melody and bass are $\hat{1}$, $\hat{3}$, and $\hat{5}$.

Listen to "My Country, 'Tis of Thee" (Example 3.12), and focus on the beginning and end to decide its key.

EXAMPLE 3.12: "My Country, 'Tis of Thee"

(a) Mm. 1-4

(b) Mm. 13-14

First, observe the key signature of one flat, which suggests F major. Next, confirm this key by checking the beginning and end of the melody and bass line. The melody begins on $\hat{1}$ (F) and ends with $\hat{3}$-$\hat{2}$-$\hat{1}$ in F major, while the bass begins on $\hat{1}$ and ends with $\hat{5}$-$\hat{1}$. Both clearly express the key of F major.

In contrast, look at the Bach invention excerpts given in Example 3.13. This piece also has a key signature of one flat, but the notes at the beginning and end emphasize D, not F. The melody begins in D in both voices (both lines), and it ends with $\hat{3}$-$\hat{2}$-$\hat{1}$ to D in the top voice and $\hat{5}$-$\hat{1}$ to D in the bottom voice. The piece is not in F major, but in D minor; minor keys will be discussed in Chapter 5.

EXAMPLE 3.13: Bach, Invention in D Minor

(a) Mm. 1-5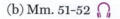

(b) Mm. 51-52

Try it #8

In what key is the excerpt below notated?

- Key signature suggests what key? _____
- First two scale degrees? _____
- Last scale degree? _____   Key of piece: _____

"Simple Gifts"

'Tis the gift to be sim-ple 'tis the gift to be free 'Tis the
gift to come down where you ought to be And when we find our-selves in the
place just right 'Twill be in the val-ley of love and de-light._____

Scale-Degree Names

In addition to numbers, scale degrees also have names, as specified in Example 3.14 and Figure 3.3. These names can indicate either the scale degree itself or the harmony built on it (which will be covered in Chapter 7).

EXAMPLE 3.14: Scale-degree names

(a) Arranged $\hat{1}$ to $\hat{1}$

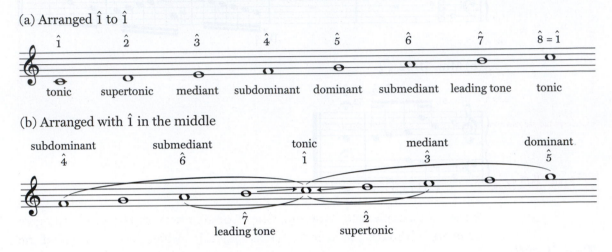

(b) Arranged with $\hat{1}$ in the middle

FIGURE 3.3: Scale-degree names and their meanings

SCALE DEGREE	NAME	MEANING
$\hat{1}$	**tonic**	The "tone" on which the scale is built.
$\hat{2}$	**supertonic**	"Super-" means "above"; its position is immediately above $\hat{1}$.
$\hat{3}$	**mediant**	Falls in the "medial" position midway between $\hat{1}$ and $\hat{5}$.
$\hat{4}$	**subdominant**	"Sub-" means "below"; the same distance below the tonic as dominant is above (part b).
$\hat{5}$	**dominant**	Its function "dominates" tonal music.
$\hat{6}$	**submediant**	Three scale steps below the tonic, just as the mediant is three scale steps above (part b).
$\hat{7}$	**leading tone**	Tends to lead upward toward the tonic; sometimes called a **tendency tone** because of this strong pull.

Try it #9

Fill in the letter name for the scale degree in each specified scale.

SCALE	SCALE DEGREE	LETTER NAME
F major	$\hat{4}$	_____
G major	leading tone	_____
A♭ major	$\hat{5}$	_____
E major	mediant	_____
B major	supertonic	_____
D♭ major	$\hat{6}$	_____

The Major Pentatonic Scale

Listen to Example 3.15, "Amazing Grace," or sing it on solfège or scale-degree numbers. Although the melody sounds major, it includes only a subset of the major scale: $\hat{1}$, $\hat{2}$, $\hat{3}$, $\hat{5}$, and $\hat{6}$ (*do, re, mi, sol, la*), missing $\hat{4}$ and $\hat{7}$ (*fa* and *ti*). Because this collection features only five of the seven diatonic pitches, it is called a **pentatonic** scale ("penta-" means "five"). Of the numerous pentatonic collections found in folk and popular music, world music, rock, and jazz, this one is called the **major pentatonic** because it begins with the first three degrees of the major scale.

EXAMPLE 3.15: Newton, "Amazing Grace," mm. 1-16

Try it #10

Write major pentatonic scales beginning on the following notes, and label the scale degrees $\hat{1}$-$\hat{2}$-$\hat{3}$-$\hat{5}$-$\hat{6}$ or *do-re-mi-sol-la*.

Implications for Performance

What are scales used for? For one thing, practicing scales on an instrument helps you gain finger facility in different keys, the better to meet the technical demands of works that include scalar passages. It also helps you to think in different keys, which in turn helps with memorization and improvisation. Melodies may not include all the notes of a scale; many are composed with only the first five, called the **major pentachord**, $\hat{1}$-$\hat{2}$-$\hat{3}$-$\hat{4}$-$\hat{5}$ (or *do-re-mi-fa-sol*; W-W-H-W).

EXAMPLE 3.16: The major pentachord: $\hat{1}$-$\hat{2}$-$\hat{3}$-$\hat{4}$-$\hat{5}$

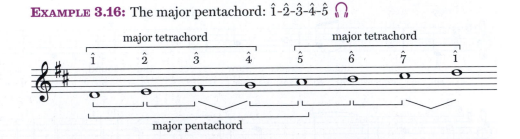

The melody of Schumann's "Trällerliedchen" (Example 3.17) does not venture beyond the major pentachord. If you practice playing ascending and descending major pentachords in every key, you will find your sight-reading much improved for melodies like this one.

EXAMPLE 3.17: Schumann, "Trällerliedchen," mm. 1-8

KEY CONCEPT The major pentachord is a scale segment of consecutive pitches: $\hat{1}$-$\hat{2}$-$\hat{3}$-$\hat{4}$-$\hat{5}$. Don't confuse it with the major pentatonic scale, which skips $\hat{4}$ and $\hat{7}$: $\hat{1}$-$\hat{2}$-$\hat{3}$-$\hat{5}$-$\hat{6}$.

Scales also make a helpful analytical tool: an abstraction from a piece that clarifies the function and relationship of pitches within it—especially the tendency tones and their expected resolutions (such as $\hat{7}$-$\hat{1}$). Eventually you may choose to bring out tendency tones and their resolutions in performance. In preparation for the analytical work in future chapters, you should be able to play all the major pentachords and major scales on a keyboard, as well as on your own instrument. Work with your performance teachers for the correct fingering and technique.

Did You Know?

The invention of solfège is usually attributed to Guido of Arezzo, an eleventh-century monk. Starting with a chant whose phrases began on C, D, E, F, G, and A, he represented each of those notes by the first syllable of the phrase's Latin text:

  C: Ut queant laxis,
  D: Resonare fibris,
  E: Mira gestorum,
  F: Famuli tuorum,
  G: Solve polluti,
  A: Labii reatum, Sancte Johannes

This six-syllable system worked well with the music of Guido's time, which could be sung using six-note segments called hexachords, starting on three different different notes: C, F, and G. In fact, the three hexachords (called the natural, soft, and hard hexachords) are also the source of our modern notation for natural, flat, and sharp signs. Singers back then sang on syllables by moving between the three hexachords, and they used a mnemonic device based on the knuckles of the hand to remember the syllable changes. Today we call this a "Guidonian hand." Since Guido's time, the system has been altered only a little—changing *ut* to *do*, and adding a seventh syllable, *ti*, for the leading tone.

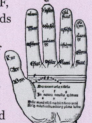

TERMS YOU SHOULD KNOW

chromatic	dominant	scale	subdominant
chromatic half step	key signature	• chromatic	submediant
circle of fifths	leading tone	• diatonic	supertonic
collection	major pentachord	• major	tendency tone
diatonic half step	median	• major pentatonic	tetrachord
	pentatonic	scale degree	tonic
		solfège syllables	

QUESTIONS FOR REVIEW

1. What are the whole- and half-step patterns in the major and chromatic scales?

2. What are two different systems for spelling chromatic scales? How do you decide which one to use?

3. What is the interval pattern for a major tetrachord? Spell the two major tetrachords in E major.

4. How can you identify the key of a flat-key work from its key signature? a sharp-key work?

5. What is the order of sharps in a key signature? of flats? What pattern do you follow to place them in the correct octave?

6. Name two systems for identifying scale degrees.

7. How is the circle of fifths constructed, and how can it help you learn key signatures?

8. In addition to the key signature, what other musical aspects should you check to identify the key of a work?

9. Which scale degrees form a major pentatonic scale? a major pentachord?

10. Find a passage of music for your instrument or voice that includes a portion of a chromatic scale. Find a complete major scale and major pentachord.

Know It? Show It!

Focus by working through the tutorials.

Learn with InQuizitive.

Apply what you've learned to complete the workbook assignments.

4

Compound Meters

Overview

In this chapter, we learn typical rhythmic patterns in compound meters, and how to notate and perform these patterns.

Repertoire

"Agincourt Song"

Johann Sebastian Bach, Fugue in E♭ Major for Organ (*St. Anne*)

Johannes Brahms, "Die Mainacht" ("The May Night")

Frédéric Chopin, Nocturne in E♭ Major, Op. 9, No. 2

"Down in the Valley"

"Greensleeves"

Gustav Holst, Second Suite for Military Band, mvt. 4 ("Fantasia on the 'Dargason'")

"Home on the Range"

Elisabeth-Claude Jacquet de la Guerre, Gigue, from Suite No. 3 in A Minor

Wolfgang Amadeus Mozart, Lacrymosa, from *Requiem*

Smokey Robinson, "You've Really Got a Hold on Me"

Franz Schubert, "Der Lindenbaum" ("The Linden Tree"), from *Winterreise* (*Winter Journey*)

Outline

Hearing compound meters

Meter signatures

Rhythmic notation in compound meters

- The dotted-quarter beat unit
- Subdividing the beat
- Beat units other than the dotted quarter

Syncopation

Mixing beat divisions and groupings

- Triplets
- Duplets, quadruplets, and polyrhythm
- Hemiola in compound meter

Metric accent and implications for performance

Hearing Compound Meters

🎧 Listen to the familiar folk song "Greensleeves." Tap the primary beat, then listen for a quick-paced secondary beat (the beat division) that helps establish the song's character. If you conduct along (using the same conducting patterns from Chapter 2) while tapping this beat division, you may recognize that the meter is compound duple. Because we associate a lilting quality with music in compound meter, composers often choose these meters for pastoral or folk-like music, lullabies, or dances.

Meter Signatures

Compound meter signatures differ from simple ones in several ways, the most important being that the lower number in compound meter signatures represents the beat *division* rather than the beat unit.

⌒ **KEY CONCEPT** In compound meters:

- The top number of the meter signature is 6, 9, or 12, representing duple, triple, or quadruple meter, respectively. Divide this by three to get the number of beats per measure (two, three, or four).

- The lower number is usually 8, but may also be 4 or 16 (rarely 2). This number shows the type of note that represents the division of the beat (usually ♪). Add three of these note values together to get the beat unit (♪♪♪ = ♩.), which will always be a dotted note.

The most common compound meters are summarized in Figure 4.1.

FIGURE 4.1: Compound meter signatures

(a) Dotted-quarter beat unit:

METER SIGNATURE	BEATS PER MEASURE	BEAT UNIT	METER TYPE
6/8	2	♩.	compound duple
9/8	3	♩.	compound triple
12/8	4	♩.	compound quadruple

(b) Other beat units:

METER SIGNATURE	BEATS PER MEASURE	BEAT UNIT	METER TYPE
$\frac{6}{4}$	2	𝅗𝅥.	compound duple
$\frac{9}{4}$	3	𝅗𝅥.	compound triple
$\frac{12}{4}$	4	𝅗𝅥.	compound quadruple
$\frac{6}{16}$	2	♪.	compound duple
$\frac{9}{16}$	3	♪.	compound triple
$\frac{12}{16}$	4	♪.	compound quadruple

Consider the $\frac{9}{8}$ meter signature for "Down in the Valley" (Example 4.1). To determine the number of beats per measure, divide the top number by three: three beats per measure. For the beat unit, add three eighth notes—from the bottom number, 8—to get a dotted quarter. The meter type is compound triple: three beats per measure with a ♩. beat unit. One possible counting system ("1 la li, 2 la li, 3 la li") is given beneath the words.

EXAMPLE 4.1: "Down in the Valley," mm. 1-4 🎧

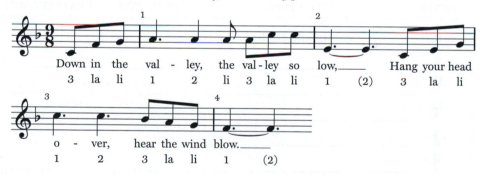

This tune begins with an anacrusis of three eighth notes, equaling one beat. As in simple meters, the final measure will be incomplete—with only two beats—to balance the anacrusis.

Look now at the meter signatures of Examples 4.2 and 4.3. The $\frac{12}{8}$ meter of Mozart's Lacrymosa has four beats per measure (12 ÷ 3 = 4) and a ♩. beat unit. The $\frac{6}{4}$ meter of the "Agincourt Song" has two beats per measure (6 ÷ 3 = 2) and a dotted-half beat unit (♩♩♩ = 𝅗𝅥.).

⌒ **KEY CONCEPT** At the beat level, metrical accents in compound meters are the same as in simple meters: compound duple ($\frac{6}{8}$) is strong-weak, compound triple ($\frac{9}{8}$) is strong-weaker-weakest, and compound quadruple ($\frac{12}{8}$) is strongest-weak-strong-weak. Conduct them in two, three, and four.

EXAMPLE 4.2: Mozart, Lacrymosa, from *Requiem* (soprano part), mm. 3-4 🎧

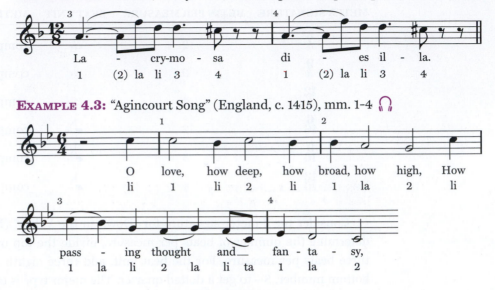

La - cry-mo - sa   di - es il - la.
1   (2) la li 3   4   1   (2) la li 3   4

EXAMPLE 4.3: "Agincourt Song" (England, c. 1415), mm. 1-4 🎧

O   love, how deep, how broad, how high, How
li   1   li   2   li   1   la   2   li

pass - ing thought and__ fan - ta - sy,
1 la li 2 la li ta 1 la   2

Try it #1

For each simple or compound meter in the chart below, provide the meter type (e.g., simple triple), beat unit, and number of beats per measure.

METER	METER TYPE	BEAT UNIT	BEATS PER MEASURE
$\frac{9}{8}$	compound triple	♩.	3
$\frac{2}{2}$	_____	____	____
$\frac{12}{8}$	_____	____	____
$\frac{12}{4}$	_____	____	____
$\frac{4}{8}$	_____	____	____
$\frac{3}{2}$	_____	____	____
$\frac{2}{4}$	_____	____	____
$\frac{6}{8}$	_____	____	____

Rhythmic Notation in Compound Meters

The Dotted-Quarter Beat Unit

Figure 4.2 provides note values and rests in compound meters, while Figure 4.3 shows common one-beat patterns in meters with a ♩. beat unit.

FIGURE 4.2: Note values and rests in compound meters with a ♩. beat unit

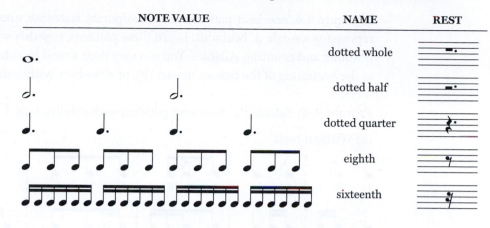

NOTE VALUE				NAME	REST
				dotted whole	
				dotted half	
				dotted quarter	
				eighth	
				sixteenth	

FIGURE 4.3: Five common one-beat patterns, with a ♩. beat unit

(1) 1

(2) 1 la li

(3) 1 li

(4) 1 la

(5) 1 ta li

Try it #2

Provide counting syllables for the melodies below, using Figure 4.3 as your model. Write the counts for rests in parentheses.

(a) "Greensleeves," mm. 1-4

li 1 li 2 ta li

(b) Hensel, "Nachtwanderer," mm. 3-6

Ich wand - re durch die stil - le Nacht, da schleicht der Mond so Heim-lich sacht

(c) Robinson, "You've Really Got a Hold on Me," mm. 6-9

I don't___ like you,___ but I___ love you;

Seems that I'm al - ways___ think - ing of you.___

Subdividing the Beat

In Figure 4.4, one-beat patterns that incorporate sixteenth notes, each pattern represents a single ♩. beat unit. Learn these patterns, together with their correct beaming and counting syllables. You can vary their sound by substituting rests—at the beginning of the beat as in part (b), or elsewhere within the beat.

FIGURE 4.4: Selected ♩. beat-unit patterns with subdivisions 🎧

(a) Without rests

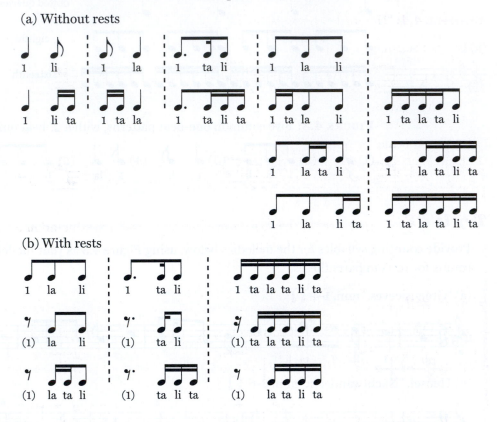

(b) With rests

Another Way

To read rhythms with the Gordon method, substitute "du da di" for "1 la li"; six sixteenths are read "du ta da ta di ta." In the "ta-ka-di-mi" system, each division and subdivision has its own syllable; ♫♩ is "ta ki da," and ♬♬ is "ta va ki di da ma." Sample rhythms are shown below. If you choose not to use any syllable system, you may still find it helpful to write the number counts on the score to mark where each beat begins.

KEY CONCEPT As in simple meters, rhythms in compound meters should be beamed to reflect the beat unit. For example, write ♩ ♪♫♫, not ♩ ♫♫♫ (which implies simple triple meter).

Example 4.4 shows an American folk tune notated correctly in part (a) and incorrectly in part (b). The incorrect beaming makes the beat unit unclear and, especially in measures 1 and 2, suggests a syncopated rhythm where none exists.

EXAMPLE 4.4: "Home on the Range," mm. 1-4 🎧

(a) Correct beaming

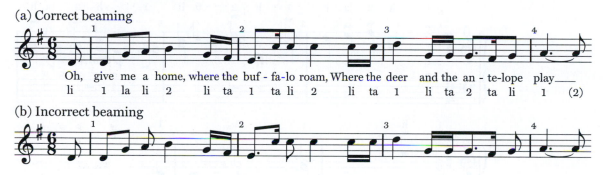

(b) Incorrect beaming

Likewise, when two rests appear together, choose a notation that makes the beat and its division clear: ♪· 𝄾, not ♩. Sometimes ♪· is notated ♩ 𝄾, and ♩ is notated 𝄾𝄾 —both reflect the beat division.

Try it #3

A. Decide which of the two rhythms below is beamed correctly, and write the counts below it.

B. For each rhythm, provide the missing bar lines that correspond with the meter signature, and write the counts below.

Beat Units Other Than the Dotted Quarter

Not all compound-meter music is notated with a dotted-quarter beat unit. Example 4.5 shows the opening of a keyboard piece with a 𝅗𝅥. beat unit and 𝅘𝅥 beat division. Counts for the melody (in the top voice) appear between the staves. (The symbols above and below some of the notes indicate ornaments, or embellishments, heard on the recording.)

EXAMPLE 4.5: Jacquet de la Guerre, Gigue, from Suite No. 3 in A Minor, mm. 1-6

One way to develop fluency with these less familiar meters is to transcribe music with a 𝅗𝅥. beat unit to meters with 𝅗𝅥. or 𝅘𝅥. units, as in Example 4.6. If performed with the same tempo for each beat unit, all three versions would sound the same, although they look quite different.

EXAMPLE 4.6: "Greensleeves," mm. 1-4

(a) Original notation (𝅘𝅥. beat unit)

(b) Transcribed to 6/4 (𝅗𝅥. beat unit)

(c) Transcribed to 6/16 (𝅘𝅥𝅮. beat unit)

Figure 4.5 illustrates the five main one-beat patterns for compound meters written with these three beat units.

FIGURE 4.5: One-beat rhythm patterns with different beat units 🎧

Counting compound meters with quarter-note beat divisions can prove challenging; since the quarter notes (♩♩♩♩♩♩) are not beamed together like eighths are in ⅜ meter (♪♪♪♪♪♪), that helpful visual cue is missing. Look, for example, at measures 78–80 of Example 4.7, from Bach's *St. Anne* Fugue. If we beamed the right hand's quarter notes in groups of three to show the dotted-half beat, that would turn them into eighths. In this example, only the beaming of the eighth notes into groups of six shows the beat unit clearly. It is left to the performer to group the rhythms mentally to reflect the proper metric accents. In this example, the strong-weak alternation occurs at the ♩. level (every half measure).

EXAMPLE 4.7: Bach, *St. Anne* Fugue, mm. 76–81 🎧

Try it #4

(a) For each rhythm below, provide the missing bar lines that correspond with the meter.

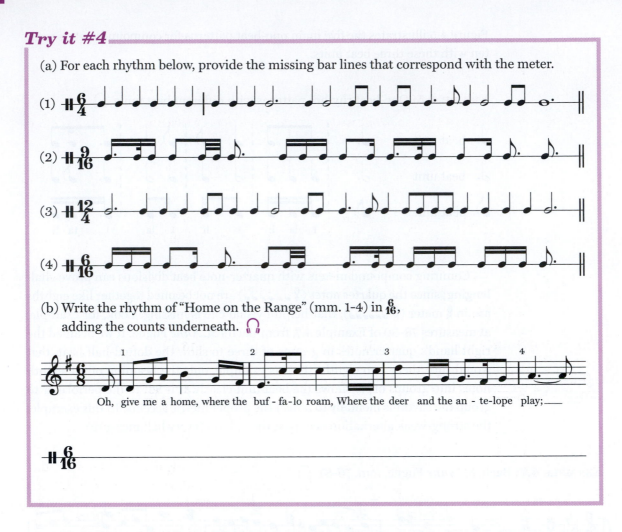

(b) Write the rhythm of "Home on the Range" (mm. 1-4) in $\frac{6}{16}$, adding the counts underneath.

Oh, give me a home, where the buf - fa - lo roam, Where the deer and the an - te - lope play;____

Syncopation

As in simple meters, ties and rests in compound meters can create offbeat accents, or syncopations.

 **KEY CONCEPT** Syncopations are created in compound meters by placing

(a) ties from a weak part of a beat across a stronger part;

1 la li (2) la   1 ta   ta   ta

(b) an accent mark on a weak beat or the weak part of a beat;

1 la li 2 la li

(c) a rest on the strong part of a beat that causes a weaker part to sound accented.

(1) la   (1) ta ta ta

Example 4.8 illustrates syncopations (marked with arrows) in the melody of "You've Really Got a Hold on Me." In measure 15, on "hold," the weaker third eighth note is tied across beat 2, delaying "on." This creates an offbeat emphasis on the second division (la) of beat 2. In measure 16, the singer enters (on "Baby") an eighth note ahead of the beat, creating an accented offbeat entrance—another syncopation.

EXAMPLE 4.8: Robinson, "You've Really Got a Hold on Me," mm. 14-16

You real - ly got   a hold_____ on me.   Ba - by__

(1) (2) li 3 li 4 li 1 la li (2) la 3 (4) (1) (2) li (3) 4 la

Typical syncopations within the beat are given in Figure 4.6, where the dotted-quarter note is the beat unit. As here, an eighth note often substitutes for two sixteenths tied together.

FIGURE 4.6: Typical syncopations within the beat (beat unit)

1 ta ta li   1 la ta ta   1 ta ta ta

Mixing Beat Divisions and Groupings

Triplets

Listen to the excerpt from Schubert's "Der Lindenbaum" given in Example 4.9. This simple-triple melody moves primarily in quarter and eighth notes, except for the last beat of measure 11, which is divided into three eighths instead of two (indicated with a small 3 above the group).

EXAMPLE 4.9: Schubert, "Der Lindenbaum," mm. 9–12

Translation: At the well in front of the gate, there stands a linden tree.

KEY CONCEPT In simple meters, the beat may occasionally be divided into three parts instead of the normal two. These beats, marked with a 3, are called triplets. Count triplets with syllables borrowed from compound meter (e.g., 1 la li).

Now compare this passage with Example 4.10, the second verse of the song. Here, Schubert develops the triplet idea by giving it to the piano accompaniment. In measures 29-30, the interplay of the piano's triplet division on beat 1 with the ♩. ♪ rhythms (beat 2 of the piano and beat 3 of the voice) propels the music forward and provides contrast with the more tranquil first verse.

EXAMPLE 4.10: Schubert, "Der Lindenbaum," mm. 29–32

Translation: I had to travel by it again today in dead of night.

Finally, listen to the beginning of the piano introduction to this song (Example 4.11). The triplets, here written as sixteenth notes—they divide the eighth note (rather than quarter note) into threes—create a wonderful effect, depicting the rustle of the linden tree's leaves.

EXAMPLE 4.11: Schubert, "Der Lindenbaum," mm. 1-2 🎧

> ⌢ **KEY CONCEPT** When notating triplets, use the same duration values for the triplet as the duple division it replaces (see Figure 4.7). That is, an eighth-note triplet replaces two eighth notes, and a sixteenth-note triplet replaces two sixteenths.

FIGURE 4.7: Notation of triplets

BEAT UNIT	DUPLE DIVISION	TRIPLET

Duplets, Quadruplets, and Polyrhythm

Just as triple divisions may appear in simple meters, so may duple or quadruple divisions appear in compound meters: these are called **duplets** (♫) or **quadruplets** (♩♩♩♩). Triplets, duplets, and quadruplets are sometimes collectively called "tuplets." In compound meter, composers might set a duple subdivision of the beat against the triple subdivision, as in Example 4.12. In measures 117–119, the melody in 6/8, played by the lower winds and brasses, is accompanied by duplet rhythms in the upper winds and brasses.

EXAMPLE 4.12: Holst, *Second Suite for Military Band*, mvt. 4, mm. 113–120 (condensed score) 🎧

polyrhythm: 2 against 3

As an example of a quadruplet, look at measure 18 from Chopin's Nocturne in E♭ (Example 4.13). Although the piece is in compound quadruple ($\frac{12}{8}$) meter, a group of four eighth notes appears in the right hand of measure 18, with a 4 beneath. To count the quadruplet, shift from compound-meter divisions (1 la li) to simple-meter divisions (1 e & a). This juxtaposition of two beat divisions—three (left hand) against four (right hand)—is called a **polyrhythm**.

EXAMPLE 4.13: Chopin, Nocturne in E♭ Major, mm. 17–18 🎧

polyrhythm:
3 against 4

Other types of tuplets include quintuplets (groups of five), sextuplets (groups of six), and septuplets (groups of seven). These appear most often in Romantic-era repertoire (around 1830 to 1910), including later in this Chopin nocturne, where they mimic the freedom of virtuoso improvisation.

Another polyrhythm, one you will encounter even more often, is two against three, shown in Example 4.14 (and Example 4.12 as well). In this song, Brahms introduces triplets in the right hand of the piano, while the singer continues with eighth-note divisions of the beat (beat 4 of mm. 33 and 34). To perform such polyrhythms, a good first step is to learn the composite pattern made by merging the two rhythms. For two against three, for example, tap one rhythm in each hand to the words "nice piece of cake": "nice" (both hands together) "piece" (hand 1) "of" (hand 2) "cake" (hand 1) "nice" (both hands), and so on; there should be equal time between "nice," "piece," "cake," and the next "nice." Hand 1 will be tapping threes and hand 2 twos. (When you have the hang of this, try tapping the rhythm of the vocal part in Example 4.14 with your right hand and the triplets of the piano's top line with your left.)

EXAMPLE 4.14: Brahms, "Die Mainacht," mm. 33-35

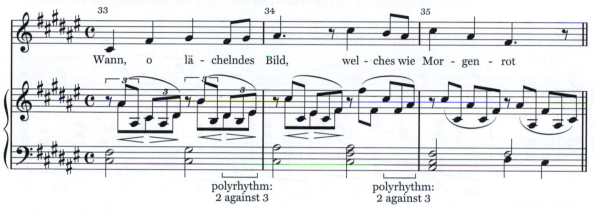

Translation: When, O smiling image, who [shines] like rosy dawn.

You can devise a similar strategy for performing three against four, taking a phrase like "pass the peanut butter": "pass," "pea,-" and "butt-" represent the triplet division of the beat, and "pass the" "-nut," and "-ter" represent the quadruple division (with equal time between those syllables).

Hemiola in Compound Meter

As in simple meters (Chapter 2), hemiolas in compound meters, though less common, propel the music forward toward the end of a piece or section. In Example 4.15, the normal three-part division of the beat is temporarily grouped in twos in the upper voice (m. 58). Here it is possible to hear both meters ($\frac{3}{2}$ for the three half notes in the highest voice and in $\frac{6}{4}$ the other voices) continuing simultaneously for a measure and then realigning into the notated meter at measure 59.

EXAMPLE 4.15: Bach, *St. Anne* Fugue, mm. 57-59

Metric Accent and Implications for Performance

Now listen to the opening of Chopin's Nocturne in E♭ (Example 4.16) to consider ways that knowledge of the metrical hierarchy might help to shape a performance. The left-hand part consists of a repetitive rhythm that sounds on every eighth note of the $\frac{12}{8}$ meter, but these eighths don't carry the same metrical weight, as the dots beneath the staff indicate. The pianist might want to bring out the lowest bass notes (E♭2, E♭2, D2, C2, etc.)—an eloquent melodic line whose pitches fall primarily on the beat—and minimize the chords on the offbeats.

EXAMPLE 4.16: Chopin, Nocturne in E♭ Major, mm. 1–4

Hypermeasure:
Measure:
Half-measure:
Dotted-quarter note:
Eighth note:

Similarly, the pianist might want to shape the right-hand melodic line in a pattern of strong and weak beats, with stronger beats on 1 and 3. Thinking in larger units sometimes raises interesting performance questions: for example, whether to aim measure 2 toward the highest pitch, C6, or beyond it to the metrically accented B♭ 5—while paying attention at the same time to the *crescendo* and *decrescendo* marks (⟨ ⟩) in the score. Such questions make the interaction of analysis and performance a fascinating topic for exploration. Compare some recordings of this nocturne to hear the choices great pianists have made.

At best, rhythmic notation only approximates a truly musical performance. The performer's interpretation will usually include tempo fluctuations that speed up or slow down slightly as the work approaches an important musical goal. This type of transitory tempo fluctuation is called **rubato**, and few Romantic-era pieces are performed without it.

Did You Know?

Composers and performers from earlier eras didn't think of meter in exactly the way we do now. For example, in the 1770s, German theorist and composer Johann Philipp Kirnberger (a student of J. S. Bach) wrote that simple meters can be divided into two *or* three parts: $\frac{2}{4}$ divides two beat units into two eighth notes per beat, and $\frac{6}{8}$ (also a simple meter) divides two beat units into three eighth notes per beat. What makes both these meters "simple" for Kirnberger is that they each require one main accent, on the downbeat of the measure.

Compound meters, for Kirnberger, are made of several measures of simple meter "put together," or "compounded": for example, $\frac{4}{4}$ is two $\frac{2}{4}$ measures combined, and $\frac{12}{8}$ is two measures of $\frac{6}{8}$. These meters take an accent on beats 1 and 3. Kirnberger even describes two types of $\frac{4}{4}$: one with a strong beat only on the downbeat of the measure ("simple" $\frac{4}{4}$) and the other with accents on beats 1 and 3 ("compound" $\frac{4}{4}$).

Clearly musicians of earlier eras understood beats within the measure to belong to an implicit hierarchy of strong and weak, which affected notation choices, performance practice, and conducting. Mozart's father, Leopold, commented in *Gründliche Violinschule* (a violin manual) that $\frac{12}{8}$ is more suitable for a quick melody than $\frac{3}{8}$ because the latter "cannot be beaten quickly without moving the spectators to laughter." From his remarks, Leopold presumably conducted $\frac{12}{8}$ in four.

TERMS YOU SHOULD KNOW

anacrusis	compound quadruple	metrical accent	rubato
compound duple	duplet	polyrhythm	triplet
compound triple	hemiola	quadruplet	tuplet

QUESTIONS FOR REVIEW

1. How are compound meters distinguished from simple meters?
2. When reading a compound meter signature, how do you determine (a) the number of beats per measure and (b) the beat unit?
3. Provide the number of beats per measure and the beat unit for each of the following meter signatures: $\frac{12}{4}$, $\frac{9}{16}$, $\frac{6}{4}$.
4. What guidelines should you follow in beaming rhythms together? What makes this difficult when the dotted-half note is the beat unit?
5. How do the guidelines for metrical accent compare in simple and compound meters?
6. If possible, find a piece of music in the anthology in each of the following meters: compound duple, compound triple, compound quadruple. Choose at least one with a beat unit other than ♩., and practice chanting its rhythm while conducting the meter.

Know It? Show It!

💻 **Focus** by working through the tutorials.

🐰 **Learn** with InQuizitive.

✍ **Apply** what you've learned to complete the workbook assignments.

5

Minor Keys and the Diatonic Modes

Overview

We continue our study of keys and scales by writing and playing in minor keys and diatonic modes. With this knowledge, along with that of major keys, we will be able to identify keys and modes in musical works.

Repertoire

Johann Sebastian Bach
 Violin Partita No. 2 in D Minor, Chaconne
 Invention in D Minor
Béla Bartók, "In Lydian Mode," from *Mikrokosmos* (No. 37)
Arcangelo Corelli
 Trio Sonata in A Minor, Op. 4, No. 5, Allemanda
 Sonata in D Minor, Op. 4, No. 8, Preludio
"Greensleeves"
John Lennon and Paul McCartney, "Eleanor Rigby," from *Revolver*
"Old Joe Clark"
Franz Schubert
 "Der Lindenbaum" ("The Linden Tree"), from *Winterreise* (*Winter Journey*)
 Waltz in B Minor, Op. 18, No. 6
"Wayfaring Stranger"

Outline

Parallel keys: Shared tonic

Relative keys
- Relative minor: Shared key signatures
- Finding the relative minor and major keys

Variability in the minor scale
- The "forms" of minor
- Identifying the key of a musical passage
- Hearing minor scale types
- Writing minor scales

Scale degrees in minor

The minor pentatonic scale

Modes of the diatonic collection
- The "relative" identification of modes
- The "parallel" identification of modes
- Spelling modal scales
- Twentieth-century and contemporary modal practice

Parallel Keys: Shared Tonic

If all music were composed in major keys, the palette of musical colors would be severely limited. Listen, for example, to the expressive qualities of the Schubert melody shown in Example 5.1. This melody begins on B and ends with the familiar $\hat{3}$-$\hat{2}$-$\hat{1}$ pattern leading to B; the key is B minor. Its sound is different from a major-key melody, in part because the whole- and half-step arrangement differs from major. The $\hat{3}$-$\hat{2}$-$\hat{1}$ ending of this minor melody, for example, descends by half then whole step, in contrast to two whole steps in major. We begin our study of minor keys by comparing a minor key with the major key that begins on the same note, a relationship called parallel minor and major.

EXAMPLE 5.1: Schubert, Waltz in B Minor, mm. 1-8 (melody only)

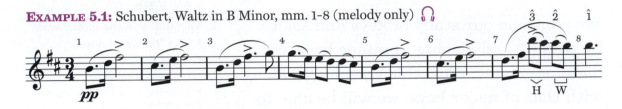

Listen to another work by Schubert, his now-familiar song "Der Lindenbaum," specifically the passages shown in Examples 5.2a and 5.3a. Part (b) in each example gives a portion of the scale—the pentachord from $\hat{1}$ to $\hat{5}$—that corresponds with the passage's melody pitches.

EXAMPLE 5.2: Schubert, "Der Lindenbaum," mm. 9-12

(a) Vocal line with piano accompaniment

Translation: At the well in front of the gate, there stands a linden tree.

(b) Major pentachord: Scale degrees $\hat{1}$ to $\hat{5}$ from the vocal line

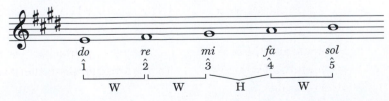

EXAMPLE 5.3: Schubert, "Der Lindenbaum," mm. 29-32

(a) Vocal line with piano accompaniment

Translation: I had to travel by it again today in dead of night

(b) Minor pentachord: Scale degrees $\hat{1}$ to $\hat{5}$ from the vocal line

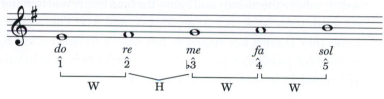

The two passages are written in **parallel keys**: E major and E minor. Parallel keys share the same tonic, but a different key signature and different arrangement of whole and half steps. The first five scale degrees of these keys differ by only one note: $\hat{3}$ (*mi*) in major is $\flat\hat{3}$ (*me*) in minor.

- The major pentachord is sung as *do-re-mi-fa-sol* and written $\hat{1}$-$\hat{2}$-$\hat{3}$-$\hat{4}$-$\hat{5}$.
- The minor pentachord is sung as *do-re-me-fa-sol* and written as $\hat{1}$-$\hat{2}$-$\flat\hat{3}$-$\hat{4}$-$\hat{5}$.

We write the third scale degree of the minor pentachord with a flat sign ($\flat\hat{3}$) even when (as in E minor) there is no flat in the key signature or next to the note; the $\flat$ symbol simply indicates that the third scale degree has been lowered. In some keys (as here), the correct spelling of $\flat\hat{3}$ will need no accidental at all.

KEY CONCEPT

- Parallel keys share the same tonic.
- Parallel-key pentachords share four scale degrees ($\hat{1}$, $\hat{2}$, $\hat{4}$, and $\hat{5}$).
- The third scale degree of the minor pentachord is a half step lower than in the major pentachord: $\flat\hat{3}$ (*me*) instead of $\hat{3}$ (*mi*).
- You could also think of the major and minor pentachords in terms of their whole and half steps: W-W-H-W for the major pentachord and W-H-W-W for the minor.

Parallel keys often appear within a single piece or movement, as in "Der Lindenbaum," to set a different mood. In this song, the minor-key passage reflects a change in the text from daytime to a foreboding "dead of night." Parallel keys might also be used for different variations in a theme-and-variations piece or for separate movements in a larger work.

Relative Keys

Relative Minor: Shared Key Signatures

Now listen to two brief passages from Corelli's Allemanda, while looking at the score excerpts in Example 5.4. Both passages share the same key signature (no flats or sharps)—yet part (a) is in A minor and part (b) in C major. Scale degrees written above the melody and below the bass line reveal familiar patterns that help establish these keys: $\hat{1}$-$\hat{2}$-$\hat{3}$ (or $\flat\hat{3}$), $\hat{7}$-$\hat{1}$, and $\hat{5}$-$\hat{1}$. These excerpts are in **relative keys**: they share a key signature but have different tonics. By moving between relative (or parallel) keys in a piece, a composer is able to vary the music's color and mood, heightening musical interest.

KEY CONCEPT Relative keys have different tonics, but share the same key signature and diatonic collection.

EXAMPLE 5.4: Corelli, Allemanda, from Trio Sonata in A Minor

(a) Mm. 1–3

(b) Mm. 13-15

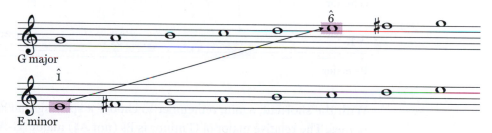

Finding the Relative Minor and Major Keys

Example 5.5 compares the scales for two relative keys: G major and E minor. As you can see, the relative minor scale is made from the same pitch-class collection as its relative major, but it begins on scale degree $\hat{6}$ of the major key.

EXAMPLE 5.5: Finding the relative minor key

KEY CONCEPT To find the relative minor of any major key, identify scale degree $\hat{6}$ of the major scale: that pitch is the tonic of the relative minor. (Shortcut: Count down three half steps from the major-key tonic.)

If you are counting half steps, be careful to choose the correct spelling: it should conform to the key signature of the major key *and* span three different letter names. The relative minor of A major, for example, is F♯ minor (A-G-F), not G♭ minor.

Try it #1

Given the major key below, supply the name of the relative minor.

KEY	RELATIVE MINOR	KEY	RELATIVE MINOR
E major	**C♯ minor**	A♭ major	
D major		E♭ major	
B major		F major	

KEY CONCEPT To find the relative major of any minor key, identify scale degree ♭$\hat{3}$ of the minor scale: that pitch is the tonic of the relative major (Example 5.6). (Shortcut: Count up three half steps from the minor-key tonic.)

EXAMPLE 5.6: Finding the relative major key

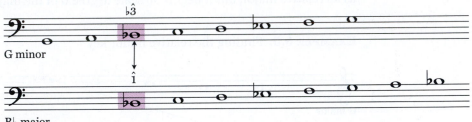

With the shortcut, again, remember to choose a spelling that spans three letter names. The relative major of G minor is B♭ (not A♯) major (G-A-B).

Try it #2

Given the minor key below, supply the name of the relative major.

KEY	RELATIVE MAJOR	KEY	RELATIVE MAJOR
A minor	**C major**	C♯ minor	
G♯ minor		F minor	
C minor		E minor	
D minor		B♭ minor	

For speed and facility in sight-reading and analysis, memorize the minor key signatures as well as the major. The circle of fifths in Figure 5.1, with the relative keys added, may help you. If you compare parallel keys in the figure, you will see that they differ by three accidentals: for example, B major (five sharps) and B minor (two sharps). You could think of this as three "steps" counterclockwise around the circle of fifths: D major (two sharps) is three steps away from D minor (one flat).

FIGURE 5.1: Circle of fifths with minor keys added

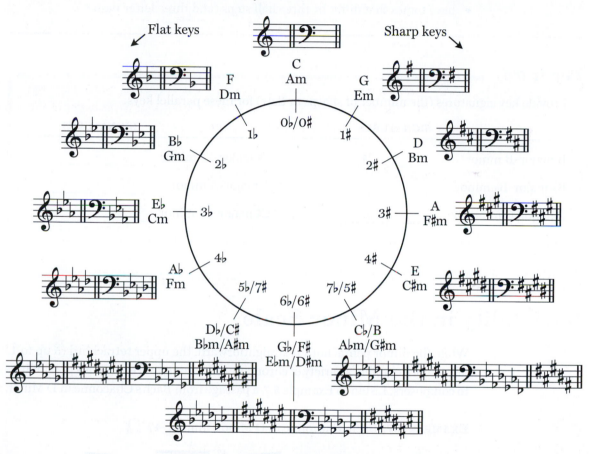

Try it #3

Given the key signature below, supply the name of the minor key.

KEY SIGNATURE	MINOR KEY	KEY SIGNATURE	MINOR KEY
(5 sharps)	G♯ minor	(2 sharps)	
(2 flats)		(3 flats)	
(4 flats)		(2 sharps)	

SUMMARY

Parallel keys
- share the same tonic, $\hat{1}$ (as well as $\hat{2}$, $\hat{4}$, and $\hat{5}$);
- have key signatures that differ by three accidentals.

Relative keys
- share the same key signature and diatonic collection;
- have tonics that differ by three half steps (and three letter names).

Try it #4

Provide key signatures (the number of sharps or flats) for these parallel keys:

	SIGNATURES				SIGNATURES	
B major-B minor	5♯	-	2♯	F♯ major-F♯ minor	____	- ____
B♭ major-B♭ minor	____	-	____	A major-A minor	____	- ____
C major-C minor	____	-	____	C♯ major-C♯ minor	____	- ____

Variability in the Minor Scale

While the minor pentachord is straightforward, the upper tetrachord ($\hat{5}$ up to $\hat{1}$) of a minor key offers a variety of chromatic inflections, and expressive possibilities to composers. Listen to Example 5.7, a passage from Bach's Chaconne in D Minor.

EXAMPLE 5.7: Bach, Chaconne in D Minor, mm. 41-47 🎧

Try it #5

On the staff below, write the scales bracketed in measures 41 and 45. Add all accidentals, including the B♭ of the key signature if needed. How do the pitch collections differ?

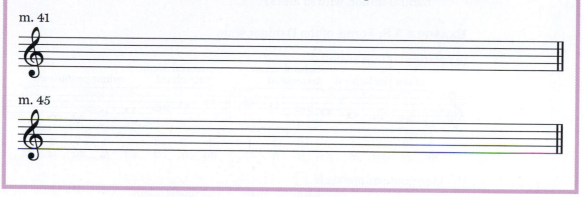

m. 41

m. 45

The bracketed scales are both D minor; they share the same minor pentachord (D-E-F-G-A). But the upper tetrachords differ. Sing or play the ascending A-B♮-C♯-D from measure 41 and the descending D-C♮-B♭-A from measure 45. This variability in scale degrees is typical in minor-key compositions: you may find ♭$\hat{6}$ or $\hat{6}$ (B♭ or B♮ in D minor), as well as ♭$\hat{7}$ or $\hat{7}$ (C♮ or C♯).

In musical contexts, as in Bach's Chaconne, rising lines are usually associated with the raised forms of $\hat{6}$ and $\hat{7}$: B♮-C♯ in measure 41. These pitches follow the tendency of the upward line toward the tonic. The A-B♮-C♯-D tetrachord is sung to the same syllables as in the parallel major, *sol-la-ti-do*, and written as scale degrees the same way as well: $\hat{5}$-$\hat{6}$-$\hat{7}$-$\hat{1}$.

Falling lines, on the other hand, are usually associated with ♭$\hat{6}$ and ♭$\hat{7}$: C♮-B♭ in measure 45. The lowered pitches here follow the tendency of the line to descend toward the tonic. The descending D-C♮-B♭-A tetrachord is sung with the syllables *do-te-le-sol* and written $\hat{1}$-♭$\hat{7}$-♭$\hat{6}$-$\hat{5}$ (even if the actual pitches are written without a flat). Think of "flat" as meaning "lowered" from the parallel major.

The "Forms" of Minor

Because of this variability in the upper tetrachord, musicians distinguish between different "forms" of the minor scale: natural, harmonic, and melodic minor. These are shown in Example 5.8.

- **Natural minor** (part a) is the scale whose accidentals exactly match the key signature of the relative major.

- **Harmonic minor** (part b) raises the seventh scale degree from ♭$\hat{7}$ to $\hat{7}$ to create a leading tone. This scale has a distinctive sound, because the distance between ♭$\hat{6}$ and $\hat{7}$—here, B♭ to C♯—is larger than a whole step: it is an **augmented second** (A2), equivalent to a step and a half.

- **Melodic minor** (part c) differs in its ascending and descending forms. Ascending, the sixth and seventh scale degrees are raised, corresponding exactly to the major scale. Descending, melodic minor is identical to natural minor, with ♭$\hat{6}$ and ♭$\hat{7}$.

EXAMPLE 5.8: Forms of the D minor scale

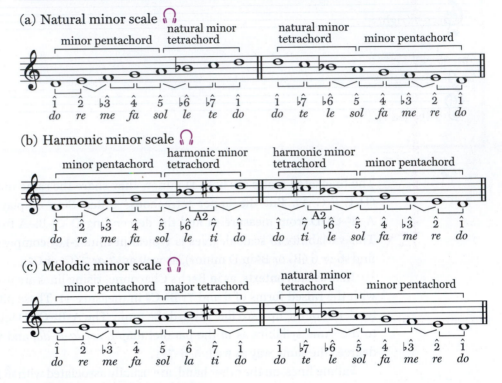

(a) Natural minor scale

(b) Harmonic minor scale

(c) Melodic minor scale

Another Way

You can form any of these scales by combining a minor pentachord with one of three different upper tetrachords, also marked in Example 5.8:

- the natural minor tetrachord, H–W–W (to make natural minor),
- the harmonic minor tetrachord, H–A2–H (to make harmonic minor), or
- the major tetrachord, W–W–H (to make ascending melodic minor).

One of the distinctive aural features of the natural minor scale is the absence of a leading tone, which leaves a whole step between ♭$\hat{7}$ and $\hat{1}$ (although composers will usually raise ♭$\hat{7}$ to $\hat{7}$ in a piece). In harmonic minor, the leading tone's presence poses a melodic problem: the distinctive sound of the A2 from ♭$\hat{6}$ to $\hat{7}$ stands out from the surrounding whole- and half-step motion. One way to solve this problem is to place the leading tone in the accompanying harmony—a reason for the harmonic minor scale's name. Another solution is shown in Bach's Invention in

D Minor (mm. 1-2 in Example 5.9a). When the entire harmonic minor scale appears in a melody, it often extends from $\hat{7}$ below the tonic to $\flat\hat{6}$ above (part b). This *embellished* minor pentachord features half-step motion at both extremes: above the dominant, $\hat{5}$–$\flat\hat{6}$–$\hat{5}$, and below the tonic, $\hat{1}$–$\hat{7}$–$\hat{1}$.

EXAMPLE 5.9: Bach, Invention in D Minor

(a) Mm. 1–7 (right hand)

(b) Embellished D minor pentachord

minor pentachord

KEY CONCEPT In harmonic minor scales, accidentals may be mixed (e.g., flats and sharps together, as in Example 5.10a), and double sharps may be necessary (part b).

EXAMPLE 5.10: Spelling harmonic minor scales

(a) Mixed accidentals in G harmonic minor

A2

(b) Double sharp in G♯ harmonic minor

A2

Identifying the Key of a Musical Passage

Because the upper tetrachord is variable, minor-key music often features accidentals—especially to raise $\flat\hat{7}$ to make the leading tone. Keep this in mind when identifying the key of a piece or passage.

KEY CONCEPT To identify a key:

1. Look at the key signature, and think of *both* the major and minor key associated with it.

2. Look at the beginning and end of the melody and bass line for motion to and from the major-key or minor-key tonic ($\hat{1}$).

3. Look for accidentals that might indicate the leading tone in minor.

In Example 5.11, the key signature of one flat suggests either F major or D minor. But when you see that the violins and bass line all begin on D, and the only accidental in the excerpt is C♯, the leading tone of D minor, you can safely assume the key is D minor. (The key itself is called D minor, not D harmonic minor.)

EXAMPLE 5.11: Corelli, Preludio, from Sonata in D Minor, mm. 1–7 🎧

Try it #6

Look at the anthology score for each of the following pieces to determine its major or minor key. Then listen to the beginning of each work to check your answer by ear.

	KEY
(a) Joplin, "Pine Apple Rag" 🎧	_____
(b) Mozart, Dies irae, from *Requiem* 🎧	_____
(c) "Chartres" (hymn) 🎧	_____
(d) C. Schumann, "Liebst du um Schönheit" 🎧	_____
(e) Schubert, "Du bist die Ruh" 🎧	_____

Hearing Minor Scale Types

Example 5.12 shows the C major scale and all three forms of the C minor scale. To distinguish between scale types by ear:

- Listen first for the quality of the third scale degree ($\hat{3}$ vs. ♭$\hat{3}$, *mi* vs. *me*).
- If minor, then listen for a leading tone: natural minor and descending melodic minor have no leading tone, but rather a whole step from ♭$\hat{7}$ to $\hat{1}$ (*te-do*). In harmonic minor, you hear the distinctive A2 approach to its leading tone (♭$\hat{6}$-$\hat{7}$, *le-ti*).

- If you hear $\hat{6}$-$\hat{7}$ (*la-ti*), the same as major, the scale is ascending melodic minor.

EXAMPLE 5.12: Scales beginning on C

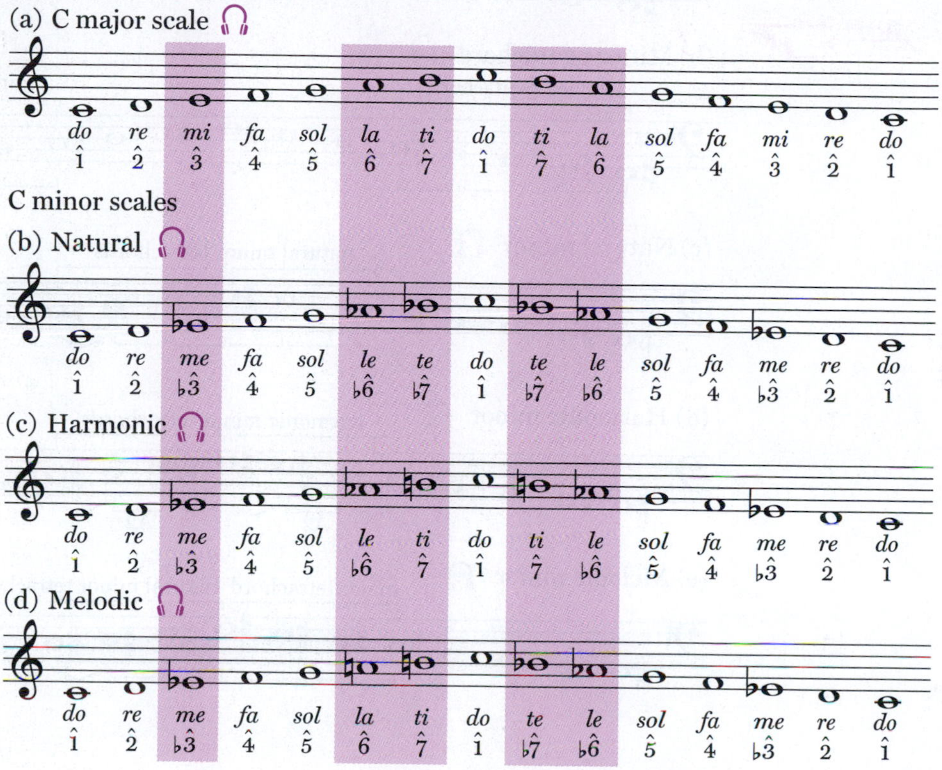

(a) C major scale

C minor scales

(b) Natural

(c) Harmonic

(d) Melodic

Writing Minor Scales

When writing minor scales, the relative-major key signature provides a good starting point; be sure you have memorized these.

(a) Begin your minor scale by writing note heads from tonic to tonic, as in Example 5.13a.

(b) Count up three half steps from the tonic, spanning three letter names, to get the relative major of F♯ minor: A major, three sharps. Add the appropriate accidentals from that key signature, and you have completed the natural minor scale (parts b and c).

(c) Add further accidentals as needed: raise ♭$\hat{7}$ to $\hat{7}$ for harmonic minor (part d).

(d) Raise ♭$\hat{6}$ and ♭$\hat{7}$ to $\hat{6}$ and $\hat{7}$ for ascending melodic minor. Descending melodic minor is the same as natural. Remember that ♭$\hat{6}$ and ♭$\hat{7}$ may be written with naturals (part e).

EXAMPLE 5.13: Writing F♯ minor scales

(a) Note heads F♯ to F♯ and back

(b) Minor pentachord

(c) Natural minor

(d) Harmonic minor

(e) Melodic minor

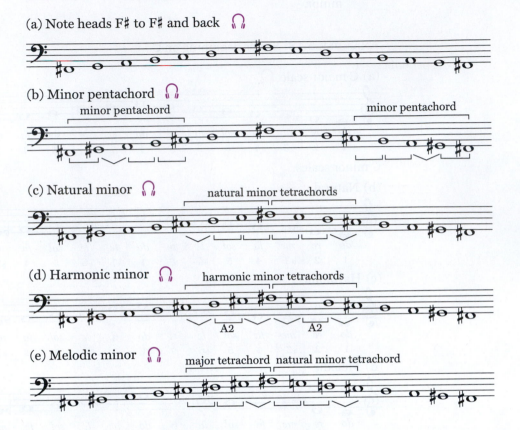

Another Way

You may prefer to write the minor scale beginning with the minor pentachord, then vary the type of tetrachord.

(a) Write pitches on the staff from tonic to tonic, ascending and descending.

(b) Add accidentals to make the minor pentachord, W–H–W–W (ascending and descending).

(c) For natural minor, add accidentals to create a natural minor tetrachord (H–W–W) on the upper part of the scale, both ascending and descending.

(d) For harmonic minor, add accidentals to create a harmonic minor tetrachord (H–A2–H), ascending and descending.

(e) For melodic minor, use the major tetrachord (W–W–H) ascending; descending is the same as natural minor.

Try it #7

Write, then play, the ascending forms of the minor scales below, paying special attention to the spelling of the upper tetrachord.

(a) C harmonic minor

(b) B♭ melodic minor

(c) F melodic minor

(d) G♯ melodic minor

(e) B harmonic minor

(f) C♯ melodic minor

(g) F♯ harmonic minor

(h) E harmonic minor

SUMMARY

Natural minor: Same key signature as the relative major, no additional accidentals.

Harmonic minor: Same key signature as the relative major, but raise ♭$\hat{7}$ a half step to $\hat{7}$.

Melodic minor, ascending: Same key signature as the relative major, but raise ♭$\hat{6}$ and ♭$\hat{7}$ a half step to $\hat{6}$ and $\hat{7}$.

Melodic minor, descending: Same as natural minor.

Scale Degrees in Minor

The scale-degree names in minor are identical to those in major with only a few exceptions (Example 5.14). The $\hat{7}$ in harmonic or melodic minor remains the leading tone, as in major. But in natural minor, $\flat\hat{7}$ is called the **subtonic**, a whole step below the tonic. When $\flat\hat{6}$ is raised to $\hat{6}$ in melodic minor, it is simply known as the **raised submediant**.

EXAMPLE 5.14: Scale-degree names in minor keys

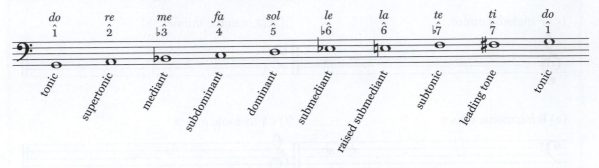

Musicians sometimes speak of a passage written in the "major mode" or "minor mode" (rather than "key"). Because scale degrees $\hat{3}$, $\hat{6}$, and $\hat{7}$ are crucial in the distinction between major and minor, they are often called the **modal scale degrees**—they create the distinctive sound of each mode. Example 5.15 highlights the modal scale degrees in the parallel keys E major and E minor.

EXAMPLE 5.15: Modal scale degrees in parallel keys 🎧

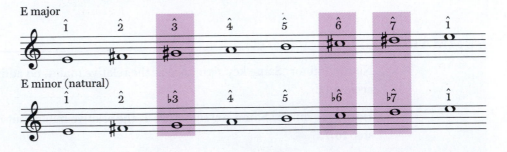

The Minor Pentatonic Scale

Embedded within the natural minor scale is a five-note scale often heard in folk melodies. For an example, listen to "Wayfaring Stranger" (Example 5.16), and identify which scale degrees of the natural minor scale are missing.

EXAMPLE 5.16: "Wayfaring Stranger," mm. 1–8 (melody)

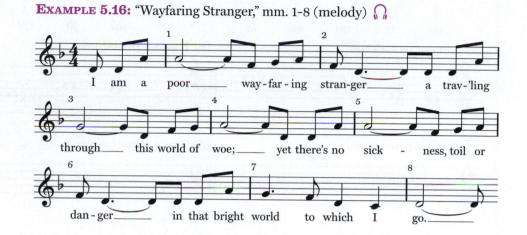

The melody includes $\hat{1}$, $\flat\hat{3}$, $\hat{4}$, $\hat{5}$, and $\flat\hat{7}$ (*do, me, fa, sol,* and *te*), but is missing $\hat{2}$ (*re*) and $\flat\hat{6}$ (*le*). These pitches make up a scale called the **minor pentatonic** (Example 5.17a), because it consists of only five diatonic pitches and gets its sound from $\hat{1}$, $\flat\hat{3}$, and $\hat{5}$ of the minor scale. Part (b) compares this collection with the major pentatonic (see Chapter 3), which gets *its* sound from $\hat{1}$, $\hat{3}$, and $\hat{5}$ of the major scale. The major and minor pentatonic scales are "rotations" of the same pitch-class collection, as are relative-major and natural-minor scales.

EXAMPLE 5.17: Pentatonic scales

(a) D minor pentatonic   (b) F major pentatonic

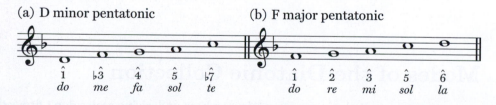

Try it #8

For each tonic pitch given, write the major pentatonic scale on the left and the minor pentatonic on the right. Think of the major and minor key signatures, and use the scale degrees below as a guide.

Modes of the Diatonic Collection

Perhaps you know pieces whose underlying scales don't fit neatly into the major or minor scale types discussed so far. Listen to the beginning of one such melody, "Greensleeves" (Example 5.18). The tune appears to be in A minor, since it begins and ends on A. Yet its key signature (F♯) yields the same pitch-class collection as G major (or E minor).

This type of scale is neither major nor minor, but **modal**—in this case, the mode known as **Dorian**. Dorian sounds like natural minor, but with a raised sixth scale degree. In some arrangements (as in your anthology version), the

Dorian melody is altered at the end (with an added G♯, the leading tone to A), but the version shown here is purely Dorian. Modal melodies are typically found in music of the Renaissance and early Baroque, folk and popular music, world musics, and some rock and jazz.

EXAMPLE 5.18: Dorian melody, "Greensleeves," mm. 1–8 🎧

Now listen to Example 5.19, "Old Joe Clark." This folk tune sounds somewhat major, with D as the tonic and starting on 5̂, but its key signature of only one sharp means that the seventh scale degree in D is lowered (C♮). This mode is called **Mixolydian**.

EXAMPLE 5.19: "Old Joe Clark" (melody) 🎧

Old Joe Clark, he had a house, fif-teen sto-ries high.

Ev-'ry sto-ry in that house was filled with chick-en pie.

Sometimes a composer will use only a segment of a mode or scale, as Bartók does in the piano piece shown in Example 5.20. In that case, the melody will inevitably feature characteristic sounds of the mode. Here, the **Lydian** mode (which sounds like a major scale but with ♯4̂) is identified in the title, and the melody, with F as the tonic, features a prominent downbeat on B♮ (♯4̂) in measures 2 and 5.

EXAMPLE 5.20: Bartók, "In Lydian Mode," mm. 1–8 🎧

The "Relative" Identification of Modes

There are six traditional **diatonic modes**, sometimes called the "church" modes because of their association with early plainsong chants sung in the Christian church. These modes share the same diatonic collection as a major (or natural minor) scale, but each begins on a different pitch. Sing or play the six "rotations" shown in Example 5.21, and listen to how the new arrangement of whole and half steps gives each mode a distinctive sound.

KEY CONCEPT The diatonic collection of pitches from C to C may be rotated to begin with any pitch. Each rotation forms a diatonic mode. These are (in order, from C): Ionian, Dorian, Phrygian, Lydian, Mixolydian, and Aeolian. (As a shortcut to learning their names, think of a sentence with the first letter of each mode in order, like "I don't particularly like magic acts.")

To identify a mode with the "relative" method, think of the major key associated with the work's key signature (for example, C major, as below).

- If the melody rests on 1̂ as its most stable pitch, it is Ionian (major).
- If it rests on 2̂: Dorian.
- If it rests on 3̂: Phrygian.
- If it rests on 4̂: Lydian.
- If it rests on 5̂: Mixolydian.
- If it rests on 6̂: Aeolian (natural minor).

EXAMPLE 5.21: Modes as rotations of the C major diatonic collection

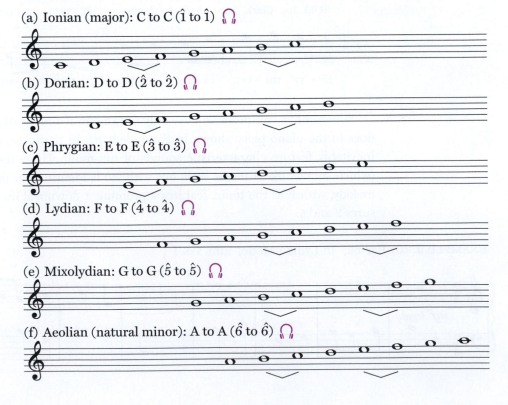

(a) Ionian (major): C to C (1̂ to 1̂)

(b) Dorian: D to D (2̂ to 2̂)

(c) Phrygian: E to E (3̂ to 3̂)

(d) Lydian: F to F (4̂ to 4̂)

(e) Mixolydian: G to G (5̂ to 5̂)

(f) Aeolian (natural minor): A to A (6̂ to 6̂)

The "Parallel" Identification of Modes

Because our twenty-first-century ears are accustomed to the major and minor scales, we sometimes hear the modes as alterations of these more familiar scales. We can therefore group the modes into two families, according to whether their third scale degree comes from the major or minor pentachord. Example 5.22 summarizes this approach, with each mode beginning on C.

EXAMPLE 5.22: Modes grouped by families (on C)

(a) Based on major pentachord ($\hat{3}$) 🎧

Ionian (major)

Mixolydian ($\flat\hat{7}$)

Lydian ($\sharp\hat{4}$)

(b) Based on minor pentachord ($\flat\hat{3}$) 🎧

Aeolian (natural minor)

Dorian ($\sharp\hat{6}$)

Phrygian ($\flat\hat{2}$)

Spelling Modal Scales

Now you can spell a mode from any given starting note by using either the relative or parallel method, as described below.

KEY CONCEPT To write a Dorian scale beginning on G:

Relative method (Example 5.23a):

1. Write note heads on the staff from G to G.

2. Remember that Dorian begins on $\hat{2}$ of a major scale; G is $\hat{2}$ in the scale of F major.

3. The key signature of F major has one flat, so add a flat to B.

Parallel method (part b):

1. Remember that Dorian sounds like natural minor, with a raised sixth scale degree.

2. Write a G natural-minor scale, with two flats (B♭ and E♭).

3. Raise $\flat\hat{6}$ by changing E♭ to E♮.

EXAMPLE 5.23: Two ways to write G Dorian

(a) Relative method

1. and 2. Write pitches G to G, and think of the scale (F major) in which G is $\hat{2}$.

3. Add accidentals from key signature of F major.

(b) Parallel method

1. and 2. Write pitches and accidentals for G natural minor.

3. Raise ♭$\hat{6}$ to $\hat{6}$.

Try it #9

Use one of the methods described above to write each of the following modes.

(a) E Dorian   (b) B♭ Lydian

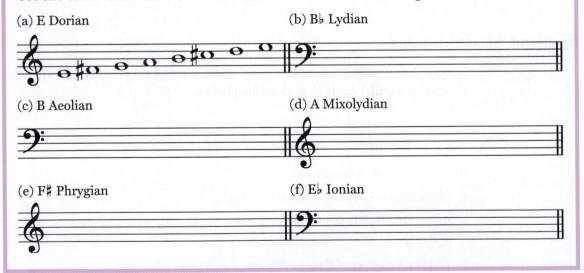

(c) B Aeolian   (d) A Mixolydian

(e) F♯ Phrygian   (f) E♭ Ionian

Twentieth-Century and Contemporary Modal Practice

After years of neglect in the late eighteenth and nineteenth centuries (outside of folk music), the diatonic modes received renewed interest in the twentieth century as jazz and popular musicians—as well as classical composers—rediscovered their beauty. In modern use, even though the six diatonic modes can be transposed to begin on any pitch class, they are most often seen in their white-key versions, or with one flat or one sharp. Musicians occasionally draw on a seventh diatonic mode as well—the **Locrian**, or B to B.

Just as composers mix major and minor for expressive effect, musical passages may express one mode, then shift to another. For example, consider Lennon and McCartney's "Eleanor Rigby" (Example 5.24). Its key signature of one sharp and repeated Es in the cello and second violin suggest E minor. Yet the melody of measures 9–12 features a C♯ alteration—a $\hat{6}$ that temporarily invokes the Dorian mode.

EXAMPLE 5.24: Lennon and McCartney, "Eleanor Rigby," mm. 9–12

Did You Know?

In the early eighteenth century (during the lifetimes of Johann Sebastian Bach, George Frideric Handel, and Joseph Haydn), writers argued over whether the old modes should be taught or be replaced by the more modern major and minor scales. Those preferring to retain the modes lamented the possible loss of their beauty and richness; those in favor of major and minor observed that the scales worked better with the functional harmonies of tonal music. You may be surprised to learn that to these writers, the model minor scale was not Aeolian (or natural minor) but Dorian. Manuscripts of music in minor from that time often show one fewer flat in the key signature than we would expect; the extra flat (for the sixth scale degree) was carefully written in every time that pitch class appeared in the music. For example, Bach's Minuet II from the Cello Suite No. 1, shown here, is in G minor (note the F♯ leading tone), yet the key signature shows only one flat. The other flat, E♭, is added as an accidental in measures 25, 27, and 29.

TERMS YOU SHOULD KNOW

diatonic modes
- Aeolian
- Dorian
- Ionian
- Locrian
- Lydian
- Mixolydian
- Phrygian

major pentachord
minor pentachord
minor scale
- harmonic
- melodic
- natural
modal scale degree
mode

parallel major
parallel minor
pentatonic scale
- major pentatonic
- minor pentatonic
raised submediant
relative major
relative minor

subtonic
tetrachord
- major
- harmonic minor
- natural minor

QUESTIONS FOR REVIEW

1. What similarities do relative and parallel minor share with major? How do relative and parallel minor differ from each other?
2. What are the differences between the three minor scale types? How are these differences reflected in the scale-degree names?
3. Given a key signature, how do you know which minor key it represents?
4. Given a minor key, how do you find the relative major?
5. How do the diatonic modes differ from major and minor scales? Describe the relative and parallel methods for identifying and spelling modes.
6. Given a pitch and a mode to build on it, what steps should you follow?
7. Find a piece, in your own repertoire if possible, with two movements related by relative or parallel keys. Find a piece written in one of the diatonic modes.

Know It? Show It!

Focus by working through the tutorials.

Learn with InQuizitive.

Apply what you've learned to complete the workbook assignments.

6

Intervals

Overview

In this chapter, we combine pitches to form intervals. We also examine how composers use intervals to write music in different styles.

Repertoire

"The Ash Grove"

Johann Sebastian Bach, Invention in D Minor

George Frideric Handel, Chaconne in G Major

Wolfgang Amadeus Mozart, *Variations on "Ah, vous dirai-je Maman"*

John Philip Sousa, "The Stars and Stripes Forever"

Anton Webern, *Symphonie*, Op. 21, mvt. 1

Outline

Combining pitches
- Interval size
- Melodic and harmonic intervals
- Compound intervals

Interval quality
- Major, minor, and perfect intervals
- Inverting intervals

Spelling intervals
- Smaller intervals: 2, 3, and 4
- Larger intervals: 5, 6, and 7
- Semitones and interval size
- Augmented and diminished intervals
- Enharmonically equivalent intervals

Consonant and dissonant intervals
- Analyzing intervals in music

Combining Pitches

Interval Size

Listen to Example 6.1, a passage from a keyboard composition by Handel, while focusing on the treble-clef melody. Several pairs of pitches are bracketed in the first three measures: these are examples of intervals.

> **KEY CONCEPT** An **interval** measures the musical space between two pitches. Intervals are identified by their size (typically a number between 1 and 8) and quality (such as major or minor).

EXAMPLE 6.1: Handel, Chaconne in G Major, Variation 5, mm. 57-64

Some intervals bracketed in the example are whole (W) and half (H) steps; these are all seconds (2). Several other intervals are bracketed as well: in measure 57, an ascending third (3: B-C-D) and fifth (5: G-A-B-C-D); and in measure 58, a descending seventh (7: D-C-B-A-G-F-E) and an octave.

> **KEY CONCEPT** When naming intervals, always count the first and last letter names. For example, from A up to D is a fourth (A-B-C-D); *any* A up to *any* D is some kind of fourth, no matter what the accidental. Similarly, from A down to D is a fifth (A-G-F-E-D).

If two parts play the exact same pitch, this "interval"—which spans no actual space—is a **unison** (from the Latin *unus*, or "one"), abbreviated U (or 1). The term may be familiar from choral singing: when all women or all men sing a line together, they are singing "in unison." (When women and men sing together, however, they usually sing in octaves.)

Melodic and Harmonic Intervals

Intervals between successive pitches, like those in the treble clef of Example 6.1, are **melodic intervals**. In the bass-clef part of measure 61, two pitches on beat 1 sound at once: G3 and B3 (a third). Intervals between two pitches sounding simultaneously are **harmonic intervals**. Name them the same way as melodic intervals—by counting the letter names encompassed by the interval. Handel's bass-clef part, in fact, features harmonic intervals in every measure.

KEY CONCEPT Melodic intervals are formed between two successive pitches in a melodic line. Harmonic intervals are formed between two pitches sounding at the same time.

Learning to identify interval sizes quickly and accurately by eye and by ear is an essential step in reading music fluently. Example 6.2 shows all the interval sizes up to an octave. When you write harmonic intervals (part b), align the two note heads with one directly above the other; for unisons and seconds, though, you must write the note heads side by side with the lower note on the left, unless each note gets a separate stem (part c).

EXAMPLE 6.2: Interval sizes up to the octave

(a) Melodic intervals

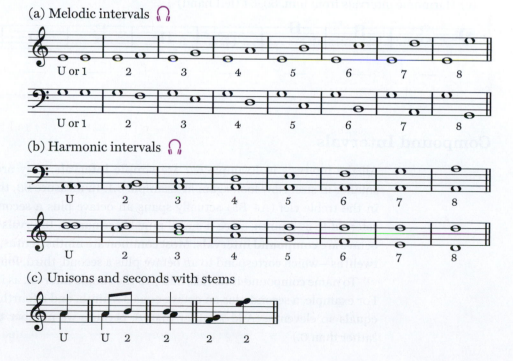

(b) Harmonic intervals

(c) Unisons and seconds with stems

KEY CONCEPT Learn these visual landmarks to identify interval sizes quickly.

Thirds, fifths, and sevenths always have both pitches on lines or both on spaces.

- For thirds, the lines or spaces are adjacent.
- For fifths, skip one line or space.
- For sevenths, skip two spaces or lines.

Seconds, fourths, sixths, and octaves always have one pitch on a line and one on a space.

Try it #1

The intervals notated below are from measures 60–64 of Example 6.1. Write the size of each interval in the blank, as quickly as possible.

(a) Melodic intervals from mm. 60–61 (right hand) 🎧

(b) Melodic intervals from mm. 61–62 (right hand) 🎧

(c) Harmonic intervals from mm. 60–64 (left hand) 🎧

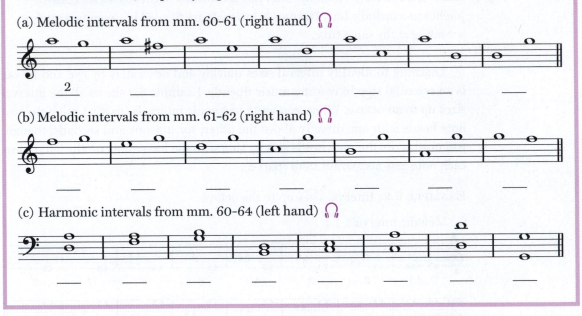

Compound Intervals

All the intervals in Example 6.2 are **simple intervals**: they are an octave or smaller in size. Now look again at Example 6.1. In measure 63, the first interval in the treble clef (A4–B5) actually spans an octave plus a second—sometimes referred to as a ninth, since it spans nine letter names. Intervals larger than an octave are **compound intervals**. Most common are ninths, tenths, elevenths, and twelfths—which correspond to an octave plus a second, third, fourth, and fifth.

To name compound intervals, add 7 to the simple interval, as in Example 6.3. For example, a second plus an octave equals a ninth, and a fourth plus an octave equals an eleventh. (Add 7 rather than 8, because we number the unison as 1 rather than 0.)

EXAMPLE 6.3: Naming compound intervals

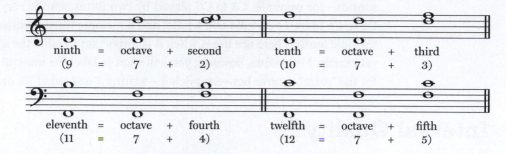

ninth	=	octave	+	second	tenth	=	octave	+	third
(9	=	7	+	2)	(10	=	7	+	3)

eleventh	=	octave	+	fourth	twelfth	=	octave	+	fifth
(11	=	7	+	4)	(12	=	7	+	5)

Though most melodies feature intervals smaller than an octave, some twentieth-century composers are more liberal with compound intervals in melodic lines. Example 6.4, from Webern's *Symphonie*, shows large intervals characteristic of this composer's style. (Parenthetical numbers and shading in the score refer to *Try it #2*.)

EXAMPLE 6.4: Webern, *Symphonie*, mvt. 2, mm. 12–17

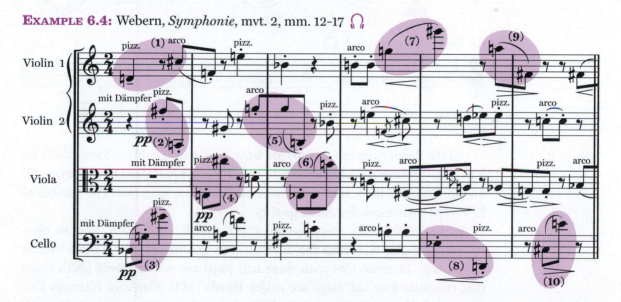

Try it #2

For each shaded interval (simple or compound) in Example 6.4, write the interval size in the corresponding blank below. If the interval is compound, also write the simple-interval equivalent in parentheses.

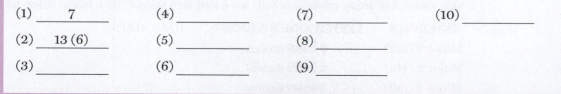

(1) ____7____   (4) _____   (7) _____   (10) _____

(2) __13 (6)__   (5) _____   (8) _____

(3) _____   (6) _____   (9) _____

The exact musical space spanned by an interval is important to the way it sounds—for example, C5 to C6 played by two flutes sounds very different from C2 to C6 played by a tuba and a flute, and a melodic third is easier to sing than a melodic tenth. There are times when it is important to label the span of an interval exactly. More often, however, you will want to label the interval without regard for the "extra" octaves between pitches—writing 3 instead of 10, or 5 instead of 12.

Interval Quality

Listen to the beginning of the folk song shown in Example 6.5a.

EXAMPLE 6.5: "The Ash Grove"

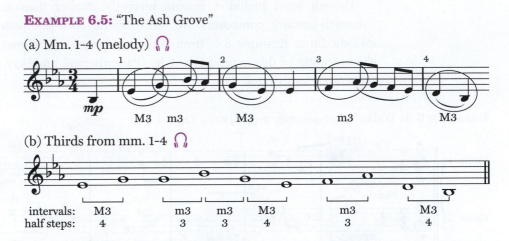

All the thirds from this melody are isolated in part (b). If you locate them on a keyboard (check the key signature!) and count the half steps they span, you'll find that some of them span three half steps and some span four. The number of half steps determines the third's **quality**.

While an interval's size—second, third, fourth, fifth, sixth, and so on—indicates roughly how large the interval is, its quality provides a more precise description. Intervals that span three half steps are **minor thirds** (m3); those that comprise four half steps are **major thirds** (M3). Similarly, intervals that span one half step are **minor seconds** (m2), and those that encompass two half steps are **major seconds** (M2).

KEY CONCEPT When two intervals share the same interval size but not the same number of half steps, they differ in quality. To find the quality of small intervals, count half steps: minor intervals are a half step smaller than major intervals.

INTERVALS	LETTER NAMES SPANNED	HALF STEPS
Minor 2 (m2)	2 letter names	1
Major 2 (M2)	2 letter names	2
Minor 3 (m3)	3 letter names	3
Major 3 (M3)	3 letter names	4

Major, Minor, and Perfect Intervals

The F major scale and its parallel minor, F minor, are given in Example 6.6. You'll see that scale degrees $\hat{1}$, $\hat{4}$, $\hat{5}$, and $\hat{8}$ in the two scales are exactly the same. The interval from $\hat{1}$ to $\hat{4}$ is a **perfect fourth** (abbreviated P4), from $\hat{1}$ to $\hat{5}$ is a **perfect fifth** (P5), and from $\hat{1}$ to $\hat{8}$ is a **perfect octave** (P8). The interval from $\hat{1}$ to itself is a **perfect unison** (PU). From the time of the earliest writings about music, around the fifth century BCE, these intervals were considered the purest, hence the term "perfect."

EXAMPLE 6.6: Perfect intervals in major and minor scales

(a) F major

(b) F minor

KEY CONCEPT Perfect intervals, which share identical pitches in parallel major and minor keys, are never major or minor. Memorize these labels: PU, P4, P5, P8.

Now look at Example 6.7 to compare the intervals between $\hat{1}$ and $\hat{3}$, $\hat{1}$ and $\hat{6}$, and $\hat{1}$ and $\hat{7}$. In the major scale (part a), these form a major third (M3), major sixth (M6), and major seventh (M7), respectively. In the minor scale (part b), they are a minor third (m3), minor sixth (m6), and minor seventh (m7). You may recall (from Chapter 5) that scale degrees $\hat{3}$, $\hat{6}$, and $\hat{7}$ are often referred to as the modal scale degrees; the intervals they form above the tonic help give major and minor keys their characteristic sound.

KEY CONCEPT Major intervals 3, 6, and 7 (built above the tonic of a major scale) are a half step larger than the corresponding minor intervals 3, 6, and 7 (built above the tonic in a minor scale). The interval between $\hat{1}$ and $\hat{2}$ is always a M2.

EXAMPLE 6.7: Major and minor intervals within scales

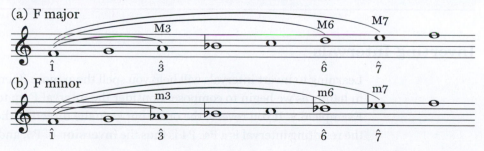

(a) F major

(b) F minor

Try it #3

(a) Identify the size and quality of each melodic interval in the keys below. 🎧

A♭ major

P5

G minor

(b) Write each melodic interval in the key of E major. First write the note head for the correct interval size, then add accidentals (if needed) from the key signature of E major.

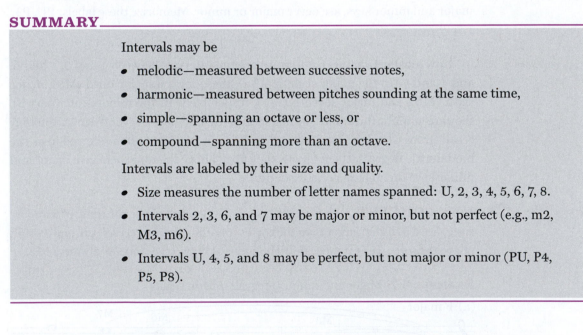

M6   P5   M7   PU   M3   P4   M2

SUMMARY

Intervals may be

- melodic—measured between successive notes,
- harmonic—measured between pitches sounding at the same time,
- simple—spanning an octave or less, or
- compound—spanning more than an octave.

Intervals are labeled by their size and quality.

- Size measures the number of letter names spanned: U, 2, 3, 4, 5, 6, 7, 8.
- Intervals 2, 3, 6, and 7 may be major or minor, but not perfect (e.g., m2, M3, m6).
- Intervals U, 4, 5, and 8 may be perfect, but not major or minor (PU, P4, P5, P8).

Inverting Intervals

Learning to invert intervals will help you spell them more fluently and will come in handy as we begin to compose. Consider the interval F up to C (P5) shown in Example 6.8. If you reverse the order but keep the direction the same, C up to F, the resulting interval is a P4. P4 is thus the **inversion** of P5, and pairs of intervals like these, made from the same pitch classes but with the order reversed, are **inversionally related**. As the example shows, perfect intervals remain perfect when they are inverted. But a major interval inverts to a minor interval—for example, a M3 inverts to a m6 (part b); and a minor interval inverts to a major interval—a m2 inverts to a M7 (part c).

EXAMPLE 6.8: Inversionally related intervals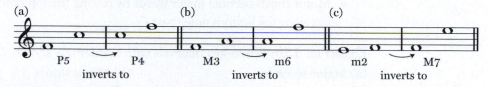

> **KEY CONCEPT** When intervals are inverted,
> - perfect intervals remain perfect;
> - major intervals invert to minor;
> - minor intervals invert to major;
> - and the two interval sizes always sum to 9 (e.g., 1 inverts to 8, 3 inverts to 6, 4 inverts to 5).

Spelling Intervals

Smaller Intervals: 2, 3, and 4

There are several different methods for identifying and spelling intervals. Some musicians find it easiest to memorize the size (major or minor) of the white-key intervals on a keyboard, beginning with seconds, thirds, and fourths (Example 6.9).

EXAMPLE 6.9: White-key interval qualities

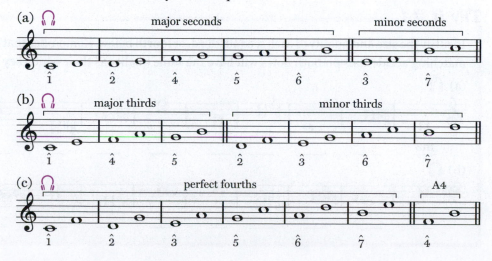

Once you know these interval qualities, all others may be calculated in relation to them, as illustrated in Example 6.10.

- An interval with matching accidentals (both sharps or both flats) has the same quality as the white-key interval (parts a and b).
- Major seconds become minor seconds by lowering the top note (part c) or by raising the bottom note (part e).
- Minor thirds become major thirds by raising the top note (part d) or by lowering the bottom note (part f).

EXAMPLE 6.10: White-key intervals with accidentals added

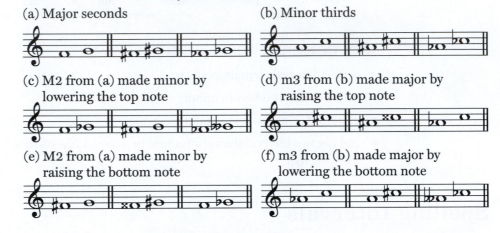

(a) Major seconds   (b) Minor thirds

(c) M2 from (a) made minor by lowering the top note

(d) m3 from (b) made major by raising the top note

(e) M2 from (a) made minor by raising the bottom note

(f) m3 from (b) made major by lowering the bottom note

SUMMARY

- A major interval made one chromatic half step smaller becomes minor.
- A minor interval made one chromatic half step larger becomes major.
- Chromatic half steps don't change the letter name of either note.
- Perfect intervals can't be made major or minor.

Try it #4

Identify the size and quality of each second, third, or fourth below. Remember that intervals with matching accidentals on both notes will have the same quality as their white-key counterparts.

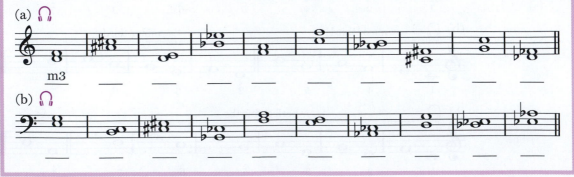

(a)

m3 ___   ___   ___   ___   ___   ___   ___

(b)

___   ___   ___   ___   ___   ___   ___   ___

To write an interval (Example 6.11):

- Write the note heads for the correct interval size on the staff without accidentals (part a) or with matching accidentals (part b).

- If the quality of the interval is not correct, adjust by adding a flat, sharp, or natural to raise or lower the upper note.

- Either note of the interval can be adjusted, as shown in part (c).

If asked to write an interval up or down from a given note, however, never change the given note; make the adjustment for quality on the other note.

EXAMPLE 6.11: Changing the quality of intervals

(a) Altering the upper note of a white-key interval

(b) Altering the upper note of an interval with matching accidentals

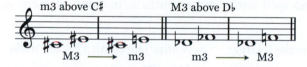

(c) Altering the lower note

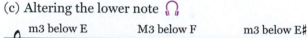

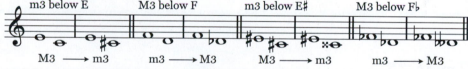

Larger Intervals: 5, 6, and 7

The smaller intervals (2, 3, and 4) can help you identify and spell their inversions (7, 6, and 5). To identify the quality of a seventh, for example, think of the quality of its inversion: if the inversion is a m2, the seventh is a M7. The process is illustrated in Example 6.12.

- To identify the interval D up to C, think about its inversion, C-D (part a).

- Since C-D is a M2, D-C is a m7.

- This process also works if there are matching accidentals: since C♯-D♯ is a major second, D♯-C♯ is a minor seventh.

- Follow parts (b) and (c) to see the procedure for sixths and fifths.

EXAMPLE 6.12: Identifying larger intervals from their inversions

(a) Identifying sevenths by the quality of seconds

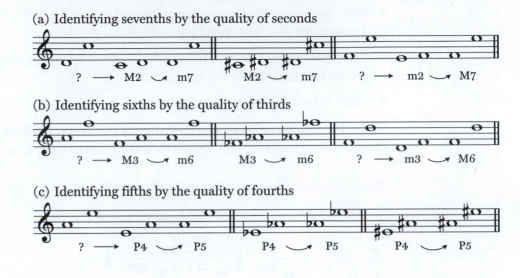

(b) Identifying sixths by the quality of thirds

(c) Identifying fifths by the quality of fourths

Another Way

Another way to identify and spell sixths and sevenths is to compare them with the closest perfect interval: P5 or P8.

Sixths: start with a P5 and make it larger.   Sevenths: start with a P8 and make it smaller.

- M6 = P5 + M2   - M7 = P8 - m2
- m6 = P5 + m2   - m7 = P8 - M2

Try it #5

(a) Name the interval formed by each pair of pitches below. Then write the inversion, and name the new interval.

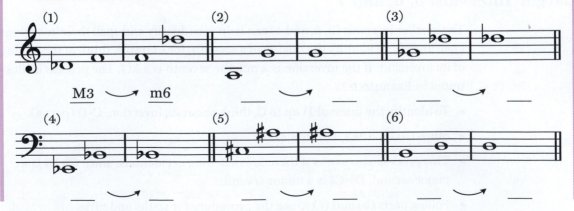

(1)   M3 ⌣ m6

(2)   ___ ⌣ ___

(3)   ___ ⌣ ___

(4)   ___ ⌣ ___

(5)   ___ ⌣ ___

(6)   ___ ⌣ ___

(b) Write harmonic intervals above the pitches given. To check your spelling, imagine the interval's inversion.

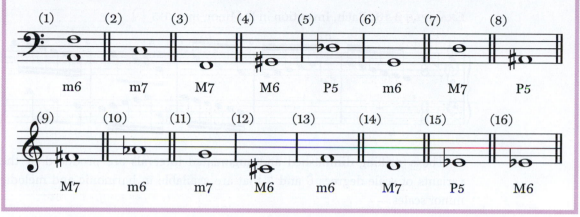

Semitones and Interval Size

You can also spell intervals by counting the scale steps from the first pitch to the second, then counting the half steps (semitones) between them; Figure 6.1 summarizes this information. Be sure to count the number of scale steps to match the interval size. (This system can be slower, especially for large intervals, and counting half steps may lead to spelling errors.)

FIGURE 6.1: Intervals as scale steps plus semitones

INTERVAL	SCALE STEPS	HALF STEPS	INTERVAL	SCALE STEPS	HALF STEPS
unison	1	0	P5	5	7
m2	2	1	m6	6	8
M2	2	2	M6	6	9
m3	3	3	m7	7	10
M3	3	4	M7	7	11
P4	4	5	P8	8	12
A4 or d5	4 or 5	6			

Augmented and Diminished Intervals

In Chapter 5, we saw how Bach, in his D Minor Invention (Example 6.13), made a dramatic leap from B♭4 down to C♯4 and back up in measures 1-2 to avoid the melodic augmented second (A2). We will now learn how to name this interval (B♭–C♯) and one other new type shaded in the example: the G4 to C♯5 in measure 4.

- If the B♭ in measure 1 went down to a C♮ instead of C♯, it would be a minor seventh (m7). The interval Bach has written is a half step smaller than a m7 (but still spans seven letter names): this is a **diminished seventh** (d7).

- If the interval in measure 4 were G4–C5, it would be a perfect fourth (P4); the C♯ makes it a half step larger, an **augmented fourth** (A4).

EXAMPLE 6.13: Bach, Invention in D Minor, mm. 1–5

These striking diminished and augmented intervals are produced by the variants of scale degrees $\hat{6}$ and $\hat{7}$ that are available in harmonic and melodic minor scales.

KEY CONCEPT

- If a major or perfect interval is made one chromatic half step larger, it becomes augmented.
- If a minor or perfect interval is made one chromatic half step smaller, it becomes diminished.
- If a diminished interval is inverted, it becomes augmented (and vice versa).

Spelling Augmented and Diminished Intervals Although any augmented and diminished intervals can be spelled by raising or lowering scale degrees by a half step, only a few—the A2, A4, d5, A6, and d7—are commonly encountered in tonal music. To spell such an interval, first spell a major, minor, or perfect interval, then adjust the quality, as shown in Example 6.14. (Don't change the letter name of either pitch.) For a large interval, you may find it helpful to first spell its smaller inversion (e.g., for A6, spell d3) and then invert.

EXAMPLE 6.14: Spelling augmented and diminished intervals

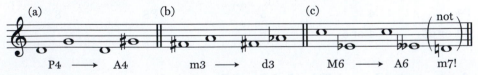

SUMMARY

FOR A	START WITH	ADD AN ACCIDENTAL TO MAKE IT
diminished 2, 3, 6, 7	minor 2, 3, 6, 7	one chromatic half step smaller
diminished 4, 5, 8	perfect 4, 5, 8	one chromatic half step smaller
augmented 2, 3, 6, 7	major 2, 3, 6, 7	one chromatic half step larger
augmented U, 4, 5, 8	perfect U, 4, 5, 8	one chromatic half step larger

If a major or perfect interval is made one whole step larger (without changing letter names), it is **doubly augmented**. Similarly, if a minor or perfect interval is made one whole step smaller (without changing letter names), it is **doubly diminished**. Both types are rare.

The Tritone One interval in the diatonic major scale is neither major, minor, nor perfect: the A4 (or d5), as seen in Example 6.15a. Here the interval between F and B ($\hat{4}$ and $\hat{7}$; *fa* and *ti*) is an augmented fourth (A4) or a **diminished fifth** (abbreviated d5), depending on its position. When $\hat{4}$ is lower than $\hat{7}$ (F-B), the interval is an A4; when $\hat{4}$ is higher than $\hat{7}$ (B-F), it's a d5.

The A4 spans exactly three whole steps, hence its name: **tritone** (from "tri-," meaning "three"). The A4 and d5 are the only inversionally related intervals that are exactly the same size in semitones (six). They sound identical if not heard in a musical context; for this reason, most people use the term "tritone" for both intervals.

EXAMPLE 6.15: The A4 and d5 in C major

(a) In a C major scale

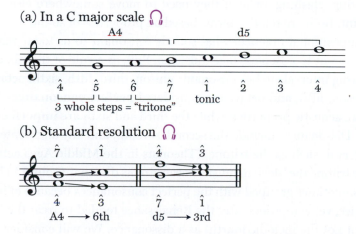

(b) Standard resolution

Because of the tendency of $\hat{7}$ to move to $\hat{1}$, the A4 and d5 **resolve** differently. As part (b) shows, augmented fourths move out, or resolve, to a sixth, while diminished fifths move in (resolve) to a third. We can distinguish between the sounds of the A4 and d5 by the interval to which each resolves.

Enharmonically Equivalent Intervals

Intervals that span the same number of half steps but have different names are **enharmonically equivalent**. For example, the m3 F to A♭ comprises three semitones, as does the A2 F to G♯. Like these, any interval can be spelled in several ways, all of them enharmonic. (Think of enharmonic intervals as similar to homonyms in language: "here" and "hear" sound the same but have completely different meanings in a sentence.) The correct spelling is important: it reveals how the interval functions in the music.

Example 6.16, for instance, shows that an interval spanning ten semitones spelled A♭ to G♭ (a m7) does not resolve the same way as one spelled A♭ to F♯ (an A6); we will learn the reasons why in future chapters. For now, remember that enharmonically equivalent intervals are not really "equivalent" in key contexts. The correct spelling makes the interval easier to read for performers, and avoids confusion that may waste rehearsal time!

EXAMPLE 6.16: Resolutions of m7 and A6

Consonant and Dissonant Intervals

Over the course of music history, intervals have been characterized as **consonant** if they sound pleasing to the ear or tonally stable, and **dissonant** if they sound jarring, clashing, or as if they need to move somewhere else to find a resting point. Both are relative terms based on properties of sound and on the norms of compositional practice: what sounds consonant to us today may have sounded dissonant to a Renaissance musician. Still, as a rule of thumb, consider the following intervals to be consonant: unison, third, fifth, sixth, octave. Of these, the unison, fifth, and octave are considered **perfect consonances** because of their pure acoustic properties, while the third and sixth are **imperfect consonances**.

Dissonances include the second, seventh, and any augmented or diminished interval, such as the tritone. (Theorists in the Middle Ages actually considered the tritone the "devil in music" because of its dissonant sound.) The perfect fourth is sometimes grouped with the perfect consonances because of its acoustic properties, yet composers after the Renaissance tended to treat the harmonic fourth (but not the melodic fourth) as a dissonance. We will consider these properties further in later chapters on counterpoint and harmony.

To hear the difference between consonant and dissonant intervals, listen to the introduction of Sousa's "The Stars and Stripes Forever" (Example 6.17), or play the example slowly. As the introduction progresses, the intervals between the highest and lowest parts become more intense and the music seems to push forward to the chord in measure 4. What harmonic intervals achieve this effect?

EXAMPLE 6.17: Sousa, "The Stars and Stripes Forever," mm. 1–4

The first four harmonic intervals are all octaves—you can consider this passage as a single melody, but with higher and lower instruments playing the melody together (**doubled** in octaves). New harmonic intervals arrive in measure 2, beat 2, where the upper parts have E♭4 and E♭5 and the lower parts sound C3, E♭3, and C4. The simple interval (eliminating the octaves) between the bass part's C and the E♭ above is a m3, a consonant interval. The M6 between E♭3 and C4 is also consonant.

At the end of measure 2, though, the bass's C3 to F4/F5 is a P4, which sounds dissonant—especially because it is accompanied by another dissonant interval, E♭3 to F4/F5, a major ninth. This motion from consonance to dissonance creates forward momentum into the next measure.

In measure 3, consider the intervals between the C♭ in the bass and the G♭, G♮, A♭, and A♮ in the melody: P5 (consonant), A5 (dissonant), M6 (consonant), and A6 (dissonant), respectively. In addition, there is a dissonant tritone (A4) in the last chord in measure 3 between the E♭ and A♮. When the A6 and A4 connect by step to the consonant intervals of measure 4—the A6 (C♭-A♮) moves outward to a P8, and the A4 (E♭-A♮) moves outward to a m6—the tension that has built up over this passage is released. The motion from a dissonant interval to a consonant one, its resolution, provides this release.

One critical element that defines any given musical style is the way composers handle consonant and dissonant intervals. As you heard in earlier examples, the dissonant interval of a seventh resolves to a consonance in the tonal music of Handel (in the first half of the eighteenth century), but does not resolve at all in the nontonal pieces of Webern (in the first half of the twentieth century) and may not resolve in jazz or popular music either.

SUMMARY

- Consonant intervals: unison, 3, 5, 6, 8
- Dissonant intervals: 2, 7, any augmented or diminished interval
- Special case: P4 (usually treated as a consonance melodically and a dissonance harmonically)

Analyzing Intervals in Music

When you are identifying intervals in music with a key signature, always consider both the key signature and any accidentals that appear in a measure. For example, the shaded notes in measures 1-2 of Example 6.18 are D-E♭ (m2) and C-E♭ (m3), not D-E (M2) and C-E (M3). In measure 3, there are accidentals on almost every note: the natural on the second quarter note is necessary to cancel the previous G♭, and the natural on the last quarter note cancels the A♭ of the key signature. This passage ends entirely with melodic half steps—a segment of the chromatic scale.

EXAMPLE 6.18: Sousa, "The Stars and Stripes Forever" (melody), mm. 1-4 🎧

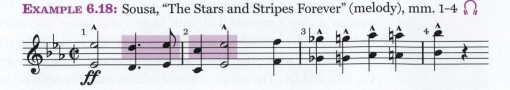

Musical scores sometimes include "courtesy" accidentals that aren't entirely necessary. For example, in measure 203 of Mozart's *Variations* (Example 6.19), a flat sign appears next to the A♭ on beat 2, even though this flat appears in the key signature. The notated flat is not really needed to cancel the A♮ of the previous measure, because the bar line automatically cancels it; this A♭ is a courtesy accidental, there to remind the performer to play the right note. Also in measure 203, the E♭ on beat 2 is tied over to the first beat of measure 204; here the accidental stays in effect through the tie (even though it crosses the bar line).

EXAMPLE 6.19: Mozart, *Variations on "Ah, vous dirai-je Maman,"* Variation 8, mm. 201-208 (right hand only) 🎧

Try it #6

Listen to Variation 8 of Mozart's *Variations on "Ah, vous dirai-je Maman,"* paying particular attention to the harmonic intervals formed in the right hand of measures 201-208. Analyze each shaded interval in Example 6.19, and write its name in the blanks below the staves.

SUMMARY

- Be mindful of the flats or sharps in the key signature plus any accidentals added in the score when determining interval qualities.

- Remember that accidentals normally apply through the end of the measure unless another accidental cancels them.

- If a note with an accidental is tied over a bar line, the accidental continues in effect to the end of the tie. Courtesy accidentals may be included to remind performers that an accidental indicated in the key signature is back in effect.

Did You Know?

Many writers from the Middle Ages (c. 500-1430) and Renaissance (c. 1430-1600) attribute the characterization of "perfect intervals" to the famous Greek mathematician Pythagoras (sixth century BCE), who was said to have discovered mathematical ratios by listening to smiths striking anvils with hammers in a blacksmith's shop and noticing that when the sizes of the hammers were in a ratio of 2:1, an octave sounded. (This oft-repeated legend, though, is not true: the sounds produced would be determined by the size of the anvils, not the hammers.) In any case, from the time of Pythagoras, perfect intervals were considered beautiful because of their mathematical ratios, which could also be demonstrated on a plucked string. The octave described the relationship between a plucked full length of string and a string divided in half (2:1). The fifth described the relationship between the full string and a string two-thirds the original length (3:2). And the fourth resulted when the sound of the full string was compared with that of a string three-fourths its length (4:3). The difference between the ratio numbers in each case is 1 (2-1, 3-2, and 4-3): mathematicians call these "superparticular" ratios. The purity of these intervals' sound and the beauty of their ratios have resulted in our term "perfect" for the octave, fifth, and fourth.

TERMS YOU SHOULD KNOW

compound interval
consonance
- imperfect
- perfect
dissonance
enharmonically related interval
interval
- harmonic
- melodic

interval quality
- major
- minor
- perfect
- augmented
- diminished

interval size
inversionally related interval
melodic interval
tritone
unison

QUESTIONS FOR REVIEW

1. What information is missing when only an interval's size is given?
2. Which interval sizes are considered consonant? dissonant?
3. What is the difference between a major and a minor interval of the same size (for example, M6 and m6)?
4. What is the interval called that is one chromatic half step smaller than a minor interval? one chromatic half step larger than a major interval?
5. What is the interval called that is one chromatic half step smaller than a perfect interval? one chromatic half step larger than a perfect interval?
6. Name as many enharmonically equivalent intervals to C♯-E as you can.
7. Examine the melodic intervals between pitches in a phrase of a piece you perform. Which interval size appears most often? What is the largest interval?

Know It? Show It!

Focus by working through the tutorials.

Learn with InQuizitive.

Apply what you've learned to complete the workbook assignments.

7

Triads

Overview

In this chapter, we combine intervals to form triads. We will identify triad types and learn how they function in musical contexts.

Repertoire

Johann Sebastian Bach, "O Haupt voll Blut und Wunden" ("O Head, Full of Blood and Wounds")

Arcangelo Corelli, Sonata in D Minor, Op. 4, No. 8, Preludio

Barry Gordy, Hall Davis, Willie Hutch, and Bob West, "I'll Be There"

George Frideric Handel, Chaconne in G Major

William "Smokey" Robinson and Ronald White, "My Girl"

"St. George's Windsor" ("Come, Ye Thankful People, Come")

Outline

Chords and triads
- Triad qualities in major keys
- Triad qualities in minor keys

Spelling triads
- By interval
- By the C-major method
- By key signature

Triad inversion

Figured bass

Triads in popular-music notation

Chords and Triads

Listen to Example 7.1, from Handel's Chaconne in G Major. This work is a series of variations, each of which varies the rhythmic patterns, melody, and other features of the first eight measures (the "theme"). The shading in the right hand of Example 7.1 highlights the main topic of this chapter: the triad.

EXAMPLE 7.1: Handel, Chaconne in G Major, Variation 4, mm. 33–36

KEY CONCEPT Two or more intervals sounding together form a **chord.** The pitches in a chord usually sound all at once, but they may also appear in succession. Three-note chords that can be represented as two thirds, one above the other, are called **triads.**

The shaded triad in measure 33, G-B-D, is made of two simultaneous thirds (G-B and B-D), written one above the other. In this particular spacing, you can recognize triads easily by their position on the staff as line-line-line or space-space-space. Example 7.2 shows additional triads stacked in thirds in the left hand of Variation 1: on the downbeats of measures 9 and 11–14. You will also see in the right hand of measures 9, 12, and 13 how the notes of a triad might be spread out, or **arpeggiated,** to form a melody.

EXAMPLE 7.2: Handel, Chaconne, Variation 1, mm. 9-16

⌢ **KEY CONCEPT** When triads are spelled in thirds, the interval between the lowest pitch (the root) and the highest (the **fifth**) is a fifth. The middle pitch, the **third**, lies a third above the root. When the root is in the lowest-sounding voice, the triad is in **root position**.

All chords marked with arrows in Example 7.2 are in root position. We speak of the root, third, and fifth of a triad, though, even when the triad is not arranged in thirds. We will return to the Handel variations later in this chapter to analyze some of these non-root-position chords.

Example 7.3 shows four root-position triads that differ in **quality**. The **major triad** has a M3 between its root and third and a m3 between its third and fifth, while the **minor triad** has the opposite—a m3 between root and third and a M3 on the top. In both major and minor triads, there is a P5 between the root and fifth. The **diminished triad** is made up of two minor thirds and a d5, and the **augmented triad** two major thirds and an A5. Triads, as here, are named by the letter name of their root combined with their quality, or abbreviated so that the capital letter name alone stands for major; an added small "m" (or a lowercase letter) stands for minor; and a ° for diminished and ⁺ for augmented.

EXAMPLE 7.3: Triad quality: Major, minor, diminished and augmented 🎧

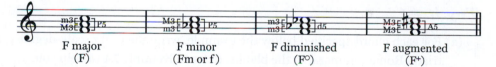

F major   F minor   F diminished   F augmented
(F)   (Fm or f)   (F°)   (F⁺)

Triad Qualities in Major Keys

In Example 7.4, triads are written above each note of the G major scale, along with several ways to label these chords. You can refer to triads in a certain key by the scale degree on which they are built (for example, the triad on 2̂) or by their scale-degree name. ("Tonic," "subdominant," "dominant," and so on refer both to the scale degrees and to the triads built on them.) Note also the Roman numerals below the staff.

⌢ **KEY CONCEPT** Roman numerals are a handy way of labeling both a chord's scale-degree position (I to vii°) and its quality: a capital numeral indicates a major triad (I, IV, V), and a lowercase numeral a minor triad (ii, iii, vi). For diminished triads, add a small raised (superscript) circle to the lowercase numeral (vii°); for augmented triads, add a small ⁺ to the capital numeral (III⁺). When using Roman numerals, always indicate the key to the left (as in Example 7.4), to place the numerals in context. Write a capital letter for major keys and a lowercase letter for minor keys.

EXAMPLE 7.4: Triads above each scale degree in G major

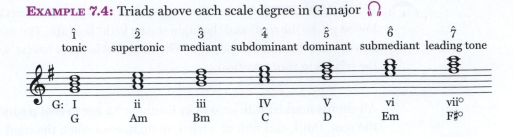

Example 7.5 shows **scale-degree triads**—triads within a certain key context—listed by quality, with the major triads together and minor triads together. Memorize which triads are of which quality in major keys; this will help you write Roman numerals correctly.

EXAMPLE 7.5: Triad qualities in major

(a) Major triads on 1̂, 4̂, and 5̂   (b) Minor triads on 2̂, 3̂, and 6̂   (c) Diminished triad on 7̂

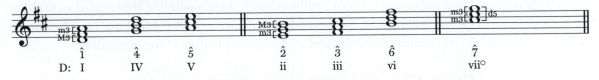

Try it #1

(a) For each chord specified below the example, write the root's scale-degree number and the triad's Roman numeral in the blanks. Refer to Example 7.4 to help you.

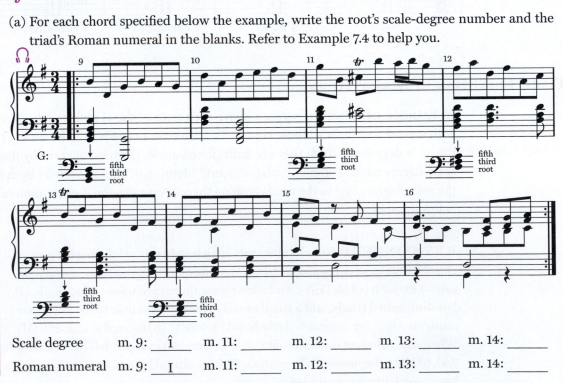

Scale degree   m. 9: _1̂_   m. 11: ____   m. 12: ____   m. 13: ____   m. 14: ____

Roman numeral   m. 9: _I_   m. 11: ____   m. 12: ____   m. 13: ____   m. 14: ____

(b) Complete the E♭ major scale below, and write the appropriate triad above each scale degree. Use whole notes, and add accidentals next to the note as needed. Label each triad's quality in the first row of blanks: M, m, or d. Then write Roman numerals beneath.

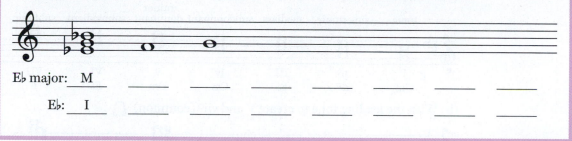

E♭ major: __M__ ___ ___ ___ ___ ___ ___ ___

E♭: __I__ ___ ___ ___ ___ ___ ___ ___

Roman numerals written below the staves of a musical score provide a highly effective way to analyze patterns and the progression of chords in a composition. Those in Example 7.6 show root-position major and minor triads in a hymn texture. When you analyze music, keep in mind that not all triads carry equal structural weight, and some (such as I and V) appear much more often than others. Not all scale-degree triads are equal!

EXAMPLE 7.6: Triads in "St. George's Windsor," mm. 5–6 🎧

Triad Qualities in Minor Keys

Triads built above the scale degrees of a natural minor scale have their own set of qualities, as shown in Example 7.7a. Triads on $\hat{1}$, $\hat{4}$, and $\hat{5}$ are minor, those on ♭$\hat{3}$, ♭$\hat{6}$, and ♭$\hat{7}$ are major, and the triad on $\hat{2}$ is diminished. But when you raise the seventh scale degree to create a leading tone (as you almost always do when writing in a minor key), the triads on $\hat{5}$ and $\hat{7}$ become major and diminished in quality, respectively (part b). Part (c) shows how the leading tone affects the quality of the mediant triad; this usage is rare and you should avoid writing it. Compare Examples 7.4 and 7.7 to see the differences between parallel keys.

EXAMPLE 7.7: Triads above each scale degree in G minor

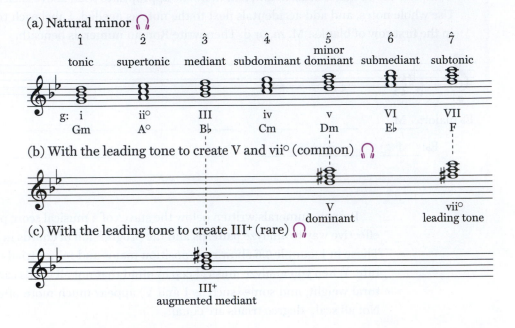

(a) Natural minor

(b) With the leading tone to create V and vii° (common)

(c) With the leading tone to create III⁺ (rare)

III⁺
augmented mediant

SUMMARY

In major keys,

- triads on scale degrees $\hat{1}$, $\hat{4}$, and $\hat{5}$ are major;

- triads on $\hat{2}$, $\hat{3}$, and $\hat{6}$ are minor;

- the triad on $\hat{7}$ is diminished.

In minor keys (harmonic minor),

- triads on $\hat{1}$ and $\hat{4}$ are minor;

- triads on $\hat{5}$ and $\flat\hat{6}$ are major;

- triads on $\hat{2}$ and $\hat{7}$ are diminished;

- the triad on $\flat\hat{3}$ is usually major, featuring the diatonic $\flat\hat{7}$ rather than the leading tone ($\hat{7}$).

Try it #2

Write the appropriate triad above each scale degree in C minor, adding accidentals before each note as needed. On the first staff, write all the triads in natural minor; on the second, add the appropriate accidental to spell a major triad on $\hat{5}$ and a diminished one on $\hat{7}$. Write the triad qualities (M, m, or d) in the blanks provided.

Natural minor:

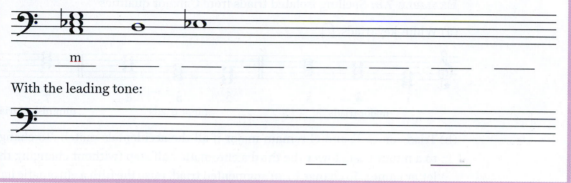

___m___ ___ ___ ___ ___ ___ ___

With the leading tone:

Spelling Triads

By Interval

Example 7.8 summarizes the key points to remember when spelling triads as stacks of intervals. To help you learn to spell and identify triad qualities quickly, we provide other methods below; choose the one that works best for you.

EXAMPLE 7.8: Spelling isolated triads by interval

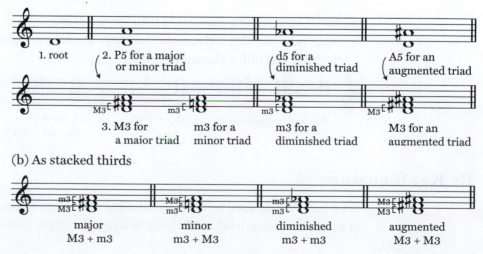

(a) As fifths and thirds

1. root
2. P5 for a major or minor triad   d5 for a diminished triad   A5 for an augmented triad
3. M3 for a major triad   m3 for a minor triad   m3 for a diminished triad   M3 for an augmented triad

(b) As stacked thirds

major
M3 + m3

minor
m3 + M3

diminished
m3 + m3

augmented
M3 + M3

By the C-Major Method

If you like to visualize triads on the keyboard or staff, first memorize the qualities of each triad in C major, as the piano white keys or plain note heads on the staff (Example 7.9a). Then use this information to build the other triad types, as in parts (b–d).

EXAMPLE 7.9: Spelling isolated triads from C major qualities

(a) White-key triads

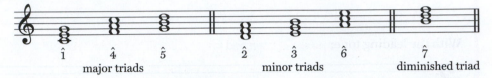

$\hat{1}$　$\hat{4}$　$\hat{5}$　　$\hat{2}$　$\hat{3}$　$\hat{6}$　　$\hat{7}$

major triads　　minor triads　　diminished triad

(b) Triads on C, F, and G remain major if all the accidentals match. To change to a minor triad, lower the third a chromatic half step (without changing the letter name). To change to an augmented triad, raise the fifth a chromatic half step.

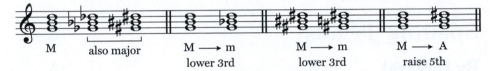

M　also major　　M ⟶ m　　M ⟶ m　　M ⟶ A
　　　　　　　lower 3rd　　lower 3rd　　raise 5th

(c) Triads on D, E, and A remain minor if all the accidentals match. To make a major triad, raise the third a chromatic half step. To change to a diminished triad, lower the fifth a chromatic half step.

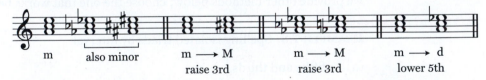

m　also minor　　m ⟶ M　　m ⟶ M　　m ⟶ d
　　　　　　　raise 3rd　　raise 3rd　　lower 5th

(d) Triads on B remain diminished if all the accidentals match. To make a minor triad, raise the fifth a chromatic half step. To make a major triad, raise both the third and fifth a chromatic half step.

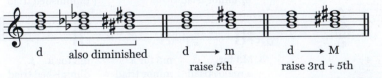

d　also diminished　　d ⟶ m　　d ⟶ M
　　　　　　　　raise 5th　　raise 3rd + 5th

By Key Signature

Yet a third way to spell triads is by thinking of key signatures. Imagine the root of a major or minor triad as the tonic in a key; the upper notes lie in the scale.

- For a major triad, think of the root's major key signature and write $\hat{1}$, $\hat{3}$, and $\hat{5}$.

- For a minor triad, think of the root's minor key signature and write $\hat{1}$, $\flat\hat{3}$, and $\hat{5}$.

- Spell a diminished triad by lowering the fifth of a minor triad a chromatic half step.

- Spell an augmented triad by raising the fifth of a major triad a chromatic half step.

Try it #3

Spell the following triads, by any method you choose.

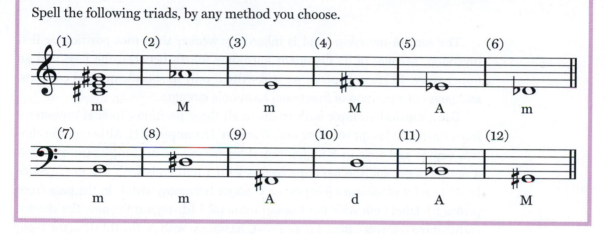

Triad Inversion

Listen again to a passage from the Handel Chaconne (Example 7.10) to hear several triads that are not in root position.

EXAMPLE 7.10: Handel, Chaconne, Variation 1, mm. 13-16

In measure 13, beat 1, the root of the bass-clef triad appears in the bass. On beat 2, the chord tones G-B-D are the same, but now B2, the third, is the lowest voice. This triad—no longer in root position—is **inverted**.

KEY CONCEPT If the root of a triad is the bass (as we have seen), the triad is in **root position**. Otherwise, the triad is in inversion.

- If the third is the bass, the triad is in **first inversion**.
- If the fifth is the bass, the triad is in **second inversion**.

Be careful not to confuse the terms "root" and "bass": any member of a triad—root, third, or fifth—may sound in the bass (lowest) voice.

The second-inversion triad is inherently weaker than root position or first inversion, because of its dissonant harmonic fourth between the bass and an upper voice. In later chapters, we will write it only in specific musical contexts, and never in a position of functional harmonic strength.

For a musical example with triads in all three positions, look at measure 9 from Bach's "O Haupt voll Blut und Wunden" (Example 7.11). Although the chorale begins and ends in F major, this short passage is in C major (every B has a natural sign, and the bass line begins with $\hat{1}$ and ends with $\hat{5}$-$\hat{1}$ in C). Since beats 1 and 2 of measure 9 express a C major harmony, with C in the bass (root position), label both with the Roman numeral I (disregard for now the shaded eighth-note offbeats). Beat 3 is an F-A-C harmony, with A (the third) in the bass: a IV chord in first inversion. Another C major chord appears on beat 4, but this time with the fifth, G, in the bass: the I chord in second inversion.

EXAMPLE 7.11: Bach, "O Haupt voll Blut und Wunden," mm. 9-10

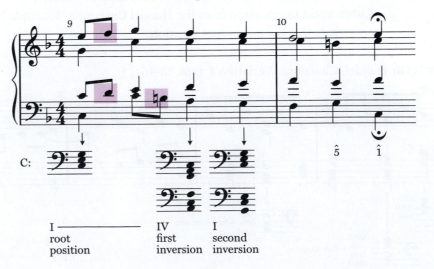

To help identify the root and Roman numeral of an inverted triad, think about how the pitches of the chord would be notated if they were in root position. You might write the pitch classes on a separate staff and stack them in thirds, as in Example 7.11. Eventually, you'll be able to do this quickly in your head.

KEY CONCEPT To identify the root of an inverted chord, look for the interval of a fourth. The upper note of the fourth is the root.

Verify this principle for yourself by looking at the small staves below Example 7.11. In the F-A-C chord (m. 9, beat 3), C is below F; the F (the top of the fourth) is the root of this chord. On beat 4, C-E-G, G appears below C; C (the top of the fourth) is the root.

Try it #4

Identify the Roman numeral and inversion for each left-hand triad specified below. Be sure that the Roman numeral shows the correct chord quality (major, minor, or diminished).

Handel, Chaconne, Variation 3, mm. 29-32

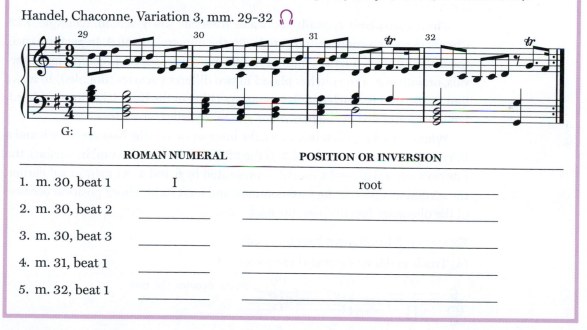

	ROMAN NUMERAL	POSITION OR INVERSION
1. m. 30, beat 1	I	root
2. m. 30, beat 2		
3. m. 30, beat 3		
4. m. 31, beat 1		
5. m. 32, beat 1		

Figured Bass

The music shown in Example 7.12 comes from a Baroque-era chamber work for two violins and **basso continuo**—a keyboard accompaniment notated with figures below its bass line, which is doubled by a cello or another low instrument. Although the right-hand part is written out here, in Baroque practice these upper voices would normally be improvised by the performer from the figures below the bass line—the figured bass.

EXAMPLE 7.12: Corelli, Preludio, from Sonata in D Minor, mm. 1–7 🎧

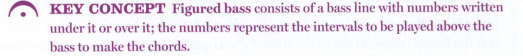

🔵 **KEY CONCEPT** **Figured bass** consists of a bass line with numbers written under it or over it; the numbers represent the intervals to be played above the bass to make the chords.

The figured-bass symbols for these intervals are given in Example 7.13. Chords in root position are indicated with the numerals 5 and 3. In performance, the fifth and third might be played in various ways: spaced as compound intervals, or with one of the pitches played in two different octaves (doubled) to make four parts (part b). Such details are not specified in the basic label for the chord, but are determined by the performer and by stylistic conventions.

When a triad is in first inversion, the intervals above the bass are a sixth and a third, represented with a 6 and 3. If the fifth is in the bass (second inversion), the intervals are a sixth and a fourth, represented by 6 and 4. As mentioned earlier, the second inversion is the least common and least stable chord position because of the dissonant fourth above the bass.

EXAMPLE 7.13: Figured bass for triads

(a) Triads and inversions in three voices 🎧

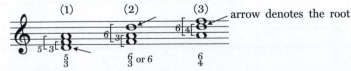

(b) Triads and inversions in four voices (keyboard style) 🎧

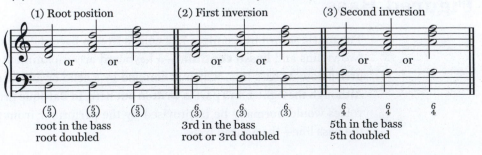

Because Baroque keyboard players needed to read the bass line and figures quickly to know which intervals (and therefore chords) to play, the figures were made simple. For example, since the $\frac{5}{3}$ figure was the most common, it was often left out; when performers saw a bass note without a figure (or with just 5), they assumed $\frac{5}{3}$. The figure $\frac{6}{3}$ was frequently shortened to just 6 (with 3 understood to be the remaining interval). For the less-usual second inversion, though ($\frac{6}{4}$), the full figure was given to avoid confusion with $\frac{6}{3}$.

KEY CONCEPT When playing or writing music from figured bass, use chord tones that are diatonic in the key (that fall within the relevant scale), unless an accidental appears in the figure—either by itself or next to a number (Example 7.14).

- By itself, an accidental always affects the note a third above the bass (not necessarily the third of the chord).

- Next to a number, an accidental tells you to alter that note; e.g., ♯6 means to raise the note a sixth above the bass a chromatic half step; ♭3 means to lower the note a third above the bass a chromatic half step.

- A slash through a number ($\cancel{6}$) means to raise the note (with either a ♯ or ♮ depending on the key).

In part (a) of Example 7.14, for instance, the lone sharp says to raise the third above the bass note A (making a C♯, the leading tone of D minor). In part (b), the player would perform a sixth above the bass (F) plus a raised third (C♯). The figure for part (c) indicates a raised sixth (C♯), with the performer supplying a third (G). Parts (d) and (e) show a single accidental, each of which *lowers* the third above the bass. In all these examples, the bass note has been doubled in an upper voice to create a four-voice texture (we will learn more about doubling in Chapter 12).

EXAMPLE 7.14: Reading figures

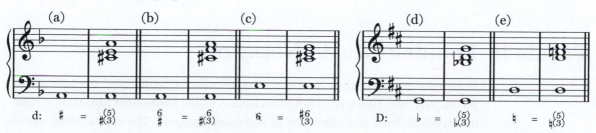

Try it #5

In the treble-clef staff, write the three notes (in whole notes) of the triad indicated by the bass and figures. Write all three notes of the triad (line-line-line or space-space-space) plus any accidentals specified.

(a)   (b)   (c)   (d)   (e)   (f)

You will sometimes use figures the way Baroque musicians did, to represent intervals over a bass line. But you will also often write figures to show the inversion of a chord—$\frac{5}{3}$ (or nothing) for root position, $\frac{6}{3}$ or ^{6} for first inversion, and $\frac{6}{4}$ for second inversion. When these figures are combined with Roman numerals, they identify the chord's scale degree, quality, and inversion—providing a lot of information in one space-saving label. When analyzing Baroque music with a figured bass, consider the figures to be part of the musical score; write your Roman numerals and inversions in a separate layer below them.

Try it #6

The bass line of Example 7.12 is reproduced below, with blanks underneath some of the figures. Write Roman numerals and inversions in the blanks (we will learn about the remaining figures in Chapters 8 and 10).

Key: d   i   ___ ___ ___   ___ ___

Triads in Popular-Music Notation

In popular music, harmonies are commonly notated with chord symbols above the melody line. This type of notation, usually called **lead-sheet notation**, is read by keyboard, bass, and other pop or jazz combo players. The capital letter name of the root is used for all triad types, with added symbols or abbreviations for qualities other than major. For example:

TRIAD TYPE	LEAD-SHEET NOTATION
F major	F
F minor	Fm, Fmin, or F-
F augmented	F$^+$ or F($\sharp$5)
F diminished	F$^\circ$ or Fdim

Often a lead sheet will show both the chord type and a fretboard diagram, which indicates guitar fingerings: the vertical lines represent guitar strings, the horizontal lines show the frets, and the black dots indicate where to place your fingers. Compare the accompaniment in Example 7.15, from Smokey Robinson's "My Girl," with the chord symbols and fretboard diagrams.

EXAMPLE 7.15: Robinson and White, "My Girl," mm. 27-30

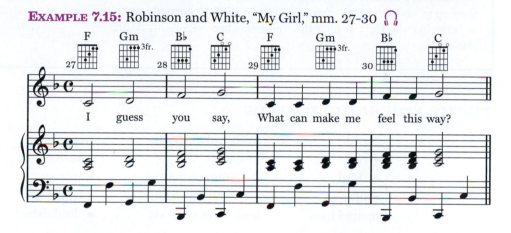

Inverted triads are indicated with the triad type followed by a slash, then the letter name of the pitch that appears in the bass. Example 7.16 features first-inversion triads on alternate measures to create a bass line that descends by scale step. Here, a first-inversion C major triad (m. 6) is notated C/E, and a first-inversion A minor triad (m. 8) as Am/C. "Slash notation" can also be used when a note outside the triad appears in the bass, such as G/C: a G major chord with a C in the bass.

EXAMPLE 7.16: Gordy, Davis, Hutch, and West, "I'll Be There," mm. 5-8

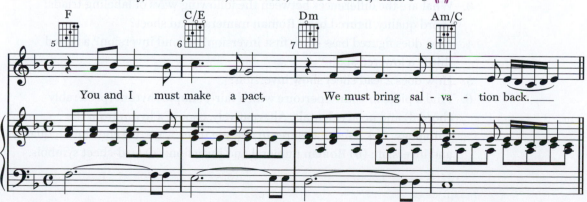

Did You Know?

The idea of the invertible triad, with its three forms—root position, first inversion, and second inversion—first appears in writings about music in the early seventeenth century (the early Baroque era), but was not widely accepted among musicians until the mid-eighteenth century (at the end of the Baroque and beginning of the Classical era). The invertible triad was described by Otto Siegfried Harnish (c. 1568-1623) in 1608, and the term *trias harmonica* (harmonic triad) was used by Johannes Lippius (1585-1612) in 1610. Lippius, a Christian theologian and musician, characterized the triad as being like the Holy Trinity: three elements but also one.

The French composer Jean-Philippe Rameau (1683-1764) is often credited with the idea of chord inversion, because his controversial writings (published between 1722 and 1760) brought this idea to the forefront at a time when the music being composed was increasingly built on chords rather than independent lines. Rameau labeled the chords with a separate bass-clef staff underneath the music, where he wrote in the roots of each chord; this practice was called "fundamental bass," not to be confused with figured bass. Roman numerals were not used for analysis until after Rameau's death.

TERMS YOU SHOULD KNOW

chord
- root
- third
- fifth

figured bass

fretboard diagram

inversion
- first inversion
- second inversion

lead-sheet notation

triad
- major
- minor
- augmented
- diminished

QUESTIONS FOR REVIEW

1. Describe two different ways of spelling each of these triad types from a given root: major, minor, diminished, and augmented.
2. Given the same root, which interval or intervals differ in the following pairs of triads: major and minor, major and augmented, minor and diminished, minor and augmented?
3. What are the differences between the following ways of labeling triads: chord quality, figured bass, Roman numeral, lead sheet?
4. How does figured bass show first inversion? second inversion? a raised third? a lowered sixth?
5. How does a lead sheet show inversion?
6. Find a piece in your repertoire with a fairly simple rhythm (preferably chordal) and no accidentals. Alternatively, choose a hymn from the anthology. Pick a few measures to analyze three ways: (a) chord root, quality, and inversion; (b) Roman numeral and inversion; (c) lead-sheet symbols.

Know It? Show It!

Focus by working through the tutorials.

Learn with InQuizitive.

Apply what you've learned to complete the workbook assignments.

8

Seventh Chords

Outline

Seventh chords

- Diatonic seventh chords in major keys
- Seventh chords in inversion
- Diatonic seventh chords in minor keys
- Spelling seventh chords

Seventh chords in popular styles

- Less common seventh chords

Triads and seventh chords in musical textures

- Arpeggiated triads and seventh chords
- Triads and seventh chords in transposing scores
- Seventh chords and musical style

Overview

This chapter explains how to spell and label seventh chords. We consider different musical contexts for seventh chords, look at how triads and seventh chords are arpeggiated, and learn to read them in transposing scores.

Repertoire

Johann Sebastian Bach, Prelude in C Major, from *The Well-Tempered Clavier*, Book 1

Gerry Goffin and Michael Masser, "Saving All My Love for You"

Joseph Haydn, Concerto in D Major for Horn and Orchestra, mvt. 1

Edward Heyman and Victor Young, "When I Fall in Love"

Wolfgang Amadeus Mozart
    Piano Sonata in C Major, K. 545, mvt. 1
    "Voi, che sapete" ("You who know"), from *The Marriage of Figaro*

Seventh Chords

Listen to Example 8.1a, the opening measures of a prelude for keyboard by J. S. Bach. The beauty of this piece comes from the ordering of its triads and seventh chords, the artful way they are connected, and the delicate manner in which individual notes are brought out in the texture. Each measure consists of only one type of chord (notated in root position in part b).

EXAMPLE 8.1: Bach, Prelude in C Major

(a) Mm. 1–11

(b) Root-position chords in mm. 1–11

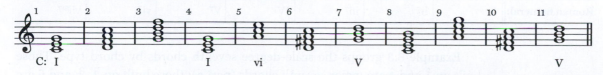

The triads in measures 1, 4, 5, 7, and 11 should be familiar: they are C major, A minor, and G major triads, or the tonic, submediant, and dominant chords in the key of C major. The other chords (without Roman numerals) contain four pitches—an additional third has been added on top of the triad. These are called seventh chords, because the distance from the root to the top note is a seventh.

KEY CONCEPT **Seventh chords** consist of four notes—a root, third, fifth, and seventh—and are named by the quality of the triad plus the quality of the seventh measured from the root. For example, a **major-major seventh** chord (**MM7**), or **major seventh** for short, has a major triad and a major seventh.

There are several qualities of seventh chords in the Bach passage. The chord in measure 2 consists of a D minor triad plus a C, which forms a minor seventh from the root (D-C)—making a **minor-minor seventh** chord (**mm7**), or **minor seventh** for short. In measure 3, the G major triad plus an F, a combination of major triad and minor seventh (G-F), makes a **major-minor seventh** chord, usually called a **dominant seventh** (Mm7).

Diatonic Seventh Chords in Major Keys

You can build a seventh chord above each note in a major or minor scale by adding a third above the scale-degree triad. Example 8.2 shows all the possibilities in the key of G major.

EXAMPLE 8.2: Seventh chords built above the G major scale

	$\hat{1}$	$\hat{2}$	$\hat{3}$	$\hat{4}$	$\hat{5}$	$\hat{6}$	$\hat{7}$
Triad quality:	M	m	m	M	M	m	d
7th quality:	M	m	m	M	m	m	m
Full name:	major-major 7th	minor-minor 7th	minor-minor 7th	major-major 7th	major-minor 7th	minor-minor 7th	diminished-minor 7th
Common name:	major 7th	minor 7th	minor 7th	major 7th	dominant 7th	minor 7th	half-diminished 7th
Abbreviation:	MM7	mm7	mm7	MM7	Mm7	mm7	ø7
Roman numeral:	I7	ii7	iii7	IV7	V7	vi7	viiø7

Example 8.3 groups the scale-degree seventh chords by chord type. Those built on $\hat{1}$ and $\hat{4}$ are major seventh chords (part a); those built on $\hat{2}$, $\hat{3}$, and $\hat{6}$ are minor seventh chords (part b). The chord built on $\hat{5}$ (part c) is the only seventh with a major triad and a minor seventh: the dominant seventh chord, so called because it is built on the dominant scale degree.

EXAMPLE 8.3: Scale-degree seventh chords in major keys 🎧

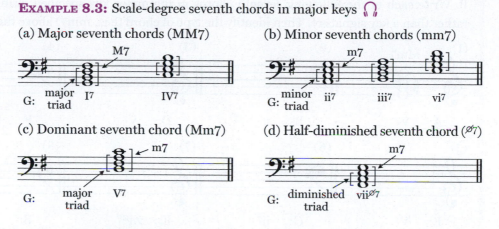

(a) Major seventh chords (MM7)

G: major triad   I7   IV7

(b) Minor seventh chords (mm7)

G: minor triad   ii7   iii7   vi7

(c) Dominant seventh chord (Mm7)

G: major triad   V7

(d) Half-diminished seventh chord (ø7)

G: diminished triad   viiø7

The remaining chord to consider in major keys is built on the leading tone (part d): a diminished triad and a minor seventh, called a **diminished-minor** or **half-diminished seventh** chord ("half" because there is a diminished triad but no diminished seventh). This is abbreviated with a small circle with a slash through it (ø7). As Examples 8.2 and 8.3 show, seventh chords are often labeled with Roman numerals to indicate their scale-degree placement (and function) in the key. For example, the dominant seventh chord on $\hat{5}$ is labeled V7, and the leading-tone seventh chord viiø7.

SUMMARY

In major keys:

- Seventh chords on $\hat{1}$ and $\hat{4}$ are major sevenths (MM7)—I7 and IV7.
- Seventh chords on $\hat{2}$, $\hat{3}$, and $\hat{6}$ are minor sevenths (mm7)—ii7, iii7, and vi7.
- The seventh chord on $\hat{5}$ is a dominant seventh (Mm7)—V7.
- The seventh chord on $\hat{7}$ is half diminished (ø7)—viiø7.

Try it #1

A. Label each seventh chord with its appropriate Roman numeral. 🎧

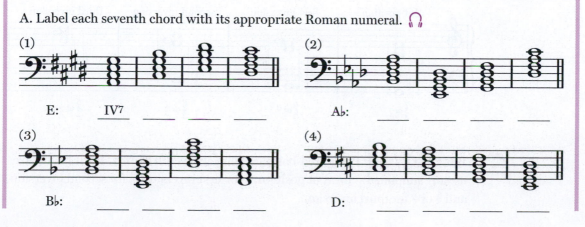

(1)

E: IV7   _____   _____   _____

(2)

Ab: _____   _____   _____   _____

(3)

Bb: _____   _____   _____   _____

(4)

D: _____   _____   _____   _____

B. Write each of the following seventh chords in the major key specified, using accidentals rather than a key signature. Then identify the type of chord (e.g., mm7) above the staff.

Seventh Chords in Inversion

Like triads, seventh chords can be written in an inversion as well as in root position. Example 8.4 gives the figured-bass symbols (both the complete figures and the standard abbreviated versions) for inverted seventh chords, measured as intervals above the bass. Abbreviated figures always show the location of the second: to locate the root of an inverted seventh chord (marked with an arrow in the example), find the upper note of the second.

EXAMPLE 8.4: Figured bass for seventh chords

(a) A seventh chord and its inversions on the treble staff (arrow marks the root)

(b) A seventh chord and its inversions on the grand staff

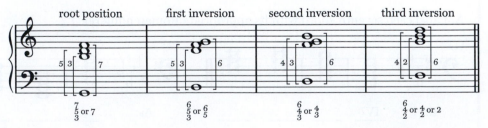

KEY CONCEPT Figured-bass symbols for seventh chords, as for triads, are usually simplified: 7 for root position, $\frac{6}{5}$ for first inversion, $\frac{4}{3}$ for second inversion, and $\frac{4}{2}$ or 2 for third inversion.

Try it #2

A. On the chart below the score, circle the correct seventh-chord quality in the indicated measure; then circle the word and figures that identify which chord member is in the bass.

Bach, Prelude in C Major, mm. 1-6

	QUALITY				BASS AND FIGURES		
m. 2	MM7	mm7	Mm7	ø7	third ($^6_5$)	fifth ($^4_3$)	seventh ($^4_2$)
m. 3	MM7	mm7	Mm7	ø7	third ($^6_5$)	fifth ($^4_3$)	seventh ($^4_2$)
m. 6	MM7	mm7	Mm7	ø7	third ($^6_5$)	fifth ($^4_3$)	seventh ($^4_2$)

B. For each key and chord below, write the key signature and then the seventh chord in root position and inversion, as specified by the figures.

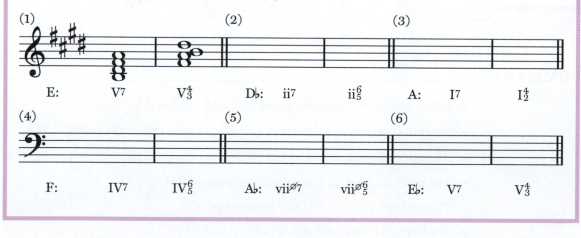

(1) E: V7 V$^4_3$ (2) D♭: ii7 ii$^6_5$ (3) A: I7 I$^4_2$

(4) F: IV7 IV$^6_5$ (5) A♭: vii°7 vii°$^6_5$ (6) E♭: V7 V$^4_3$

Diatonic Seventh Chords in Minor Keys

Now look at Example 8.5, seventh chords built from the G minor scale. Since scale degree ♭$\hat{7}$ is typically raised in minor to make a leading tone, the chords on $\hat{5}$ and $\hat{7}$ are written here with an F♯. The seventh chord built on this leading tone introduces another type, a diminished triad plus a diminished seventh: called a **fully diminished seventh** chord, or **diminished seventh** for short, and labeled vii°7. In minor keys, then, you will find both half-diminished and fully diminished sevenths: ii⌀7 and vii°7. Together, Examples 8.2 and 8.5 present all the diatonic seventh chords you are likely to encounter.

EXAMPLE 8.5: Seventh chords built above the G minor scale

	$\hat{1}$	$\hat{2}$	♭$\hat{3}$	$\hat{4}$	$\hat{5}$	♭$\hat{6}$	$\hat{7}$
Triad quality:	m	d	M	m	M	M	d
7th quality:	m	m	M	m	m	M	d
Full name:	minor-minor 7th	diminished-minor 7th	major-major 7th	minor-minor 7th	major-minor 7th	major-major 7th	fully diminished 7th
Common name:	minor 7th	half-diminished 7th	major 7th	minor 7th	dominant 7th	major 7th	diminished 7th
Abbreviation:	mm7	⌀7	MM7	mm7	Mm7	MM7	°7
Roman numeral:	i7	ii⌀7	III7	iv7	V7	VI7	vii°7

SUMMARY

In minor keys (with the leading tone in chords on $\hat{5}$ and $\hat{7}$):

- Seventh chords on scale degrees $\hat{1}$ and $\hat{4}$ are minor sevenths (mm7).

- Seventh chords on ♭$\hat{3}$ and ♭$\hat{6}$ are major sevenths (MM7).

- The seventh chord on $\hat{5}$ is a dominant seventh (Mm7).

- The seventh chord on $\hat{2}$ is half diminished (⌀7).

- The seventh chord on $\hat{7}$ is fully diminished (°7).

Try it #3

Spell each of the following seventh chords in the given minor key, including the leading tone in chords on $\hat{5}$ and $\hat{7}$. First write the key signature, then write the chord and identify its type above the staff.

(1) mm7   b: iv7

(2)   c♯: ii⌀7

(3)   a: V7

(4)   f: i7

(5)   c: vii°7

(6)   f♯: ii⌀7

(7)   g: vii°7

(8)   e: i7

Spelling Seventh Chords

KEY CONCEPT To spell seventh chords above a given root, first spell the correct-quality triad and then add the proper seventh.

For example, to write a minor seventh chord (mm7) above F:

1. Spell the minor triad: F–A♭–C (Example 8.6a).

2. Add the seventh, a third above the triad's fifth (E).

3. Check the interval quality between the root and seventh. Since F to E is a major seventh, add a flat to the E to make a minor seventh.

EXAMPLE 8.6: Spelling a minor seventh chord (mm7)

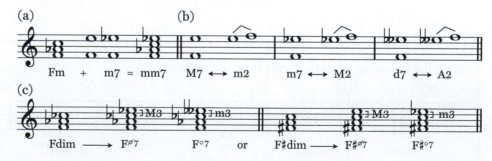

(a) Fm + m7 = mm7   M7 ⟷ m2

(b)   m7 ⟷ M2   d7 ⟷ A2

(c) Fdim ⟶ F⌀7   F°7 or F♯dim ⟶ F♯⌀7   F♯°7

You may find it easier to check the quality of the seventh by inverting it (part b). Imagine the root of the seventh up an octave, making a second. If the second is minor (half step), the seventh is major; if the second is major (whole step), the seventh is minor; if the second is augmented, the seventh is diminished.

To make a diminished seventh chord (part c), write a diminished triad first, then add a third on top: for a half-diminished seventh, the third is major; for a fully diminished seventh, the third is minor. In fact, all thirds in the fully diminished seventh are minor.

SUMMARY

To spell seventh chords outside of a key context:

(1) Write three thirds on the staff (line-line-line-line or space-space-space-space).

(2) Check the quality of the triad, and add accidentals as needed:
- MM7 and Mm7 have major triads,
- mm7 has a minor triad,
- °7 and ⌀7 have diminished triads.

(3) Check the quality of the seventh, and add accidentals as needed:
- MM7 has a major seventh,
- Mm7, mm7, and ⌀7 have a minor seventh,
- °7 has a diminished seventh.

Another Way

You could also think of seventh chords as a triad with an additional third on top:

- MM7 = major triad + M3
- Mm7 = major triad + m3
- mm7 = minor triad + m3

- ⌀7 = diminished triad + M3
- °7 = diminished triad + m3

Try it #4

Spell the following seventh chords from the roots provided.

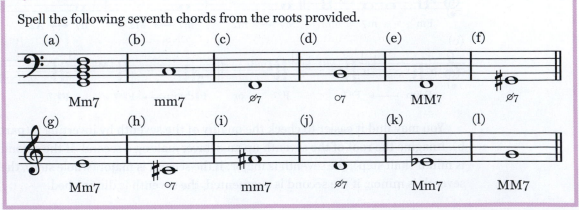

(a) Mm7 (b) mm7 (c) ⌀7 (d) °7 (e) MM7 (f) ⌀7

(g) Mm7 (h) °7 (i) mm7 (j) ⌀7 (k) Mm7 (l) MM7

Seventh Chords in Popular Styles

If you play in studio, rock, or jazz bands, you may be familiar with another way of labeling seventh chords. This system is found in lead sheets and may be combined with guitar fretboard diagrams—as in Example 8.7, a melody harmonized almost entirely with seventh chords.

EXAMPLE 8.7: Goffin and Masser, "Saving All My Love for You," mm. 44-48 🎧

The Dmaj7 chord in measure 45 is a D major seventh (D-F♯-A-C♯); it could also be labeled, D△7, DM7, or D+7 (the system is not completely standardized, and these symbols are used interchangeably). The next two chords are minor sevenths built on C♯ (C♯-E-G♯-B) and B (B-D-F♯-A). This three-chord pattern appears three times in the passage (for variety, the piano arrangement slightly changes the C♯m7 in m. 46), before closing with D/E (a D major triad with an E in the bass) and an arrival on Amaj7 (A-C♯-E-G♯).

Example 8.8 shows various seventh chords in C major and C minor, with some of their possible labels. Half-diminished seventh chords are often notated (as in part a) as minor sevenths with a ♭5.

EXAMPLE 8.8: Seventh chords in C major and C minor, with lead-sheet labels

(a) C major

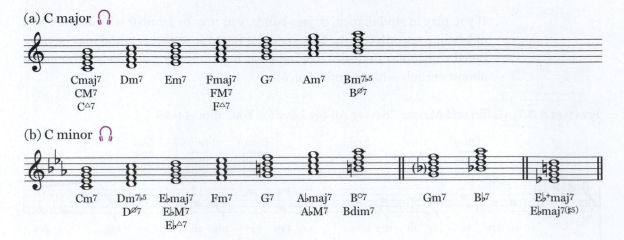

Cmaj7   Dm7   Em7   Fmaj7   G7   Am7   Bm7♭5
CM7   FM7   B∅7
C△7   F△7

(b) C minor

Cm7   Dm7♭5   E♭maj7   Fm7   G7   A♭maj7   B°7   Gm7   B♭7   E♭+maj7
        D∅7   E♭M7   A♭M7   Bdim7   E♭maj7(♯5)
                  E♭△7

Less Common Seventh Chords

You may have noticed that Examples 8.2 and 8.5 don't exhaust *all* the possible combinations of triads and sevenths. For example, you could write an augmented triad with a major or minor seventh, or a minor triad with a major seventh. Although these chords are not a regular feature of common-practice tonal music, they add harmonic richness in jazz and popular styles as substitutes for diatonic seventh chords. As an illustration, listen to Example 8.9, from "When I Fall in Love." In measure 8, the B♭7 indicates a dominant seventh (which sounds on beat 2, B♭-D-F-A♭), while the C7+5 in measure 10 is an augmented triad with minor seventh, C-E♮-G♯-B♭ (the G♯ is spelled A♭). The excerpt closes with an Fm7 (F-A♭-C-E♭).

EXAMPLE 8.9: Heyman and Young, "When I Fall in Love," mm. 5–11

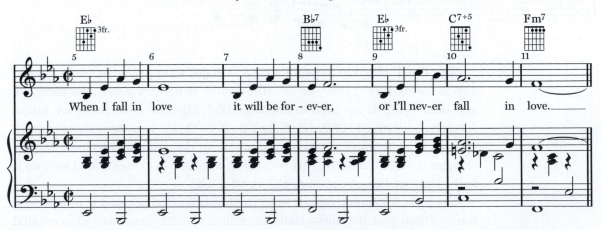

Try it #5

On the staves below, write the seventh chords requested. Write in all the accidentals (rather than a key signature) for practice spelling these chords.

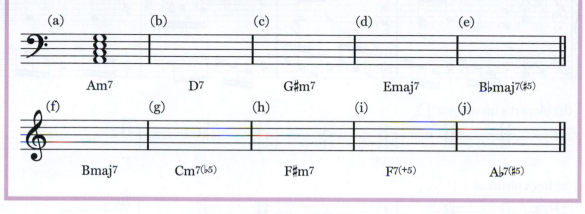

(a)   (b)   (c)   (d)   (e)

Am⁷   D⁷   G♯m⁷   Emaj⁷   B♭maj⁷⁽♯⁵⁾

(f)   (g)   (h)   (i)   (j)

Bmaj⁷   Cm⁷⁽♭⁵⁾   F♯m⁷   F⁷⁽⁺⁵⁾   A♭⁷⁽♯⁵⁾

Triads and Seventh Chords in Musical Textures

Arpeggiated Triads and Seventh Chords

In "When I Fall in Love," all members of each chord sound at the same time. But sometimes a chord may be **arpeggiated**—played one pitch at a time—as in the Bach Prelude (Example 8.1) and the bass-clef part of Mozart's "Voi, che sapete," shown in Example 8.10a. (Mozart probably chose to arpeggiate the chords here because a character onstage is pretending to accompany the singer on a guitar, which the arpeggiated chords can mimic.) To analyze the left-hand chords in this B♭ major passage:

- write the pitches for the whole chord in Mozart's inversion (part b);

- rearrange the notes in root position to identify the chord root and Roman numeral (part c);

- add the correct inversion (from part b) to your Roman numerals.

In the first measure, a B♭ major triad is played one chord member at a time, while in the following measure an F major chord (V⁶) is arpeggiated A-C-F-A. Mozart likely used a first-inversion chord here (with the A in the bass instead of the root F) to make a smooth connection between the B♭s of measures 1 and 3. The remaining chords include a ii$^6_5$ (E♭-G-B♭-C; disregard the shaded D5 in the right-hand part) and V (F-A-C).

EXAMPLE 8.10: Mozart, "Voi, che sapete"

(a) Mm. 1–4

(b) Mozart's inversions

B♭:   I   V⁶₅   I   ii⁶₅   V

(c) Root position

B♭:   I   V7   I   ii7   V

For another familiar accompaniment pattern from the Classical period, listen to the passage in Example 8.11, from a piano sonata by Mozart. The left-hand accompanimental pattern arpeggiates the harmony with a "low-up-down-up" contour that is typical of an **Alberti bass**. In this kind of writing, the low pitches that begin each arpeggiated pattern are considered the bass notes of the chord (not necessarily the root) and form a bass line: here, $\hat{1}$-$\hat{2}$-$\hat{1}$-$\hat{1}$-$\hat{7}$-$\hat{1}$ (shaded in the example), with a dominant seventh chord harmonizing $\hat{2}$ and $\hat{7}$.

EXAMPLE 8.11: Mozart, Piano Sonata in C Major, mvt. 1, mm. 1–4

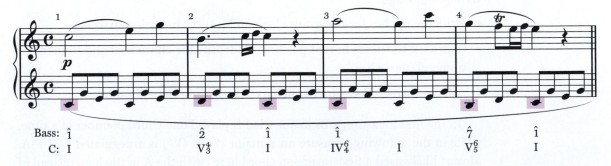

Bass: $\hat{1}$ $\hat{2}$ $\hat{1}$ $\hat{1}$ $\hat{7}$ $\hat{1}$
C: I   V⁴₃   I   IV⁶₄   I   V⁶₅   I

The Mozart examples represent only two possible arpeggiation patterns; the Bach Prelude in Example 8.1 is another. When you encounter any arpeggiated accompaniment, stack the chords in thirds to identify the root and quality.

Triads and Seventh Chords in Transposing Scores

Look at Example 8.12, from a horn concerto by Haydn, to identify triads and seventh chords in a fuller musical texture. At first glance, it seems that the first violin and horn soloist are playing in seconds (G against F, followed by B against A). But the label to the left of the horn's line includes a "(D)," which means that this instrument is a transposing one: a horn in D.

EXAMPLE 8.12: Haydn, Horn Concerto in D Major, mvt. 1, mm. 42–44

KEY CONCEPT For many instruments, called **C instruments** (or **concert-pitch instruments**), the pitch you see notated is the pitch you hear; these include the piano, flute, oboe, bassoon, trombone, tuba, harp, and most of the string family. (Some C instruments sound in a different octave from their notation: the piccolo and xylophone sound an octave higher than notated; guitar, string bass, and contrabassoon sound an octave lower than notated.) But for some wind and brass instruments, called **transposing instruments**, the pitch you see notated is not the pitch you hear.

The horn is one such transposing instrument, and the Haydn concerto excerpt—showing the notes the instrument plays rather than the sounding pitches—is an example of a **transposed score**. You can identify a transposed score by key signatures that are not the same in all instruments, as here. Sometimes, on the other hand, the score for a band or orchestral work will show the sounding pitches for transposing instruments; this is called a **C score**, and can be recognized by all parts having the same key signature.

In the fairly populous category of B♭ instruments—B♭ trumpet, B♭ clarinet, bass clarinet, and tenor saxophone, among others—when the performer plays a notated pitch, the sound is a whole step lower than the notated pitch (or, in the case of bass clarinet and tenor saxophone, a whole step plus an octave lower). When you write for B♭ instruments, you therefore need to write the pitches a whole step *higher* (and use a key signature a whole step higher). In the Haydn example, the horn in D transposes by whole step as well, but in this case the sounding pitch is a whole step higher than notated, so the part is notated a whole step *lower*: the horn actually doubles the first violin part.

Try it #6

Write Roman numerals for the triads and seventh chords of Example 8.12 in the blanks below (the blanks indicate where the chords or inversions change). Remember that the transposing horn part is playing the same notes as the first violin.

D: IV⁶ ___ ___   ___ ___ ___   ___ ___ ___ ___

KEY CONCEPT What you see is the notated pitch; what you hear is the concert pitch. To remember how to read notes for transposing instruments (on a transposing score), imagine that a C is notated. When the performer reads a C, the resulting **sounding pitch** (or **concert pitch**) is usually associated with the name of the instrument: a notated C played by a B♭ clarinet sounds B♭; a notated C played by a D trumpet or horn sounds D.

Assigning specific pitches, chords, or melodies to particular instruments is called **arranging**; doing the same for larger ensembles is called **orchestration**. Appendix 5 summarizes the ranges and transpositions of most orchestral and band instruments, but the most common transpositions are listed below.

KEY CONCEPT

B♭ instruments: the notated key is a whole step above the concert-pitch key.

- To write for a B♭ instrument, transpose the concert part up a whole step.

- To read from a transposed part, remember that concert pitches sound a whole step lower than the notation.

- The B♭ tenor saxophone and B♭ euphonium are written in the treble clef, but sound in the bass clef; transpose up a whole step plus an octave, or a major ninth.

E♭ instruments: the notated key is a minor third below the concert-pitch key.

- To write for an E♭ clarinet, transpose the concert part down a minor third.
- To read from a transposed part, remember that concert pitches sound up a minor third from the notation.
- To write for an E♭ alto saxophone or E♭ horn, transpose the concert part up a major sixth; concert pitches sound a major sixth lower than the notation.
- The E♭ baritone (bari) saxophone is written in the treble clef, but sounds in the bass clef; transpose up a major sixth plus an octave.

F instruments: the notated key is a perfect fifth above the concert-pitch key.

- To write for F horn or English horn, transpose the concert part up a perfect fifth; concert pitches sound a perfect fifth lower than the notation.

A instruments: the notated key is a minor third above the concert-pitch key.

- To write for an A clarinet, transpose the concert part up a minor third; concert pitches sound a minor third lower than the notation.

SUMMARY

To label triads or seventh chords correctly from a score with transposing instruments:

- Be sure to include the sounding (concert) pitch in your chord calculation instead of the notated pitch.
- Be careful with instruments that transpose down, especially those that could be playing the lowest bass notes, to get the correct inversion.
- To make an arrangement for transposing instruments, start with the notation in concert pitch, then transpose as necessary for your performers.

Try it #7

Given the concert key. write the key of the transposed part for each instrument listed below.

CONCERT KEY	INSTRUMENT TYPE	KEY OF TRANPOSED PART
E♭	B♭ instrument	F
C	F instrument	
B♭	E♭ instrument	
G	A instrument	
F	F instrument	
C	B♭ instrument	
E♭	F instrument	
C	E♭ instrument	

Seventh Chords and Musical Style

The treatment of seventh chords is an important aspect of musical style. For example, only sevenths built on scale degrees $\hat{2}$, $\hat{5}$, and $\hat{7}$ appear frequently in Classical-period music; yet we find seventh chords on all scale degrees in Romantic music, jazz, and popular styles. In some styles, the dissonant interval of a seventh must be approached and resolved down by step; in others, the seventh may be left unresolved altogether for dramatic effect, or the entire chord may simply slide up or down to another seventh chord. In common-practice tonal music, for example, composers would not normally end a piece with a I7 or i7, yet tonic chords at the end of a jazz standard often do feature an unresolved seventh. As you identify seventh chords in music you are playing, consider what type of seventh each chord is, and how the chord is connected to those around it. Later chapters will explore other facets of these indispensable chords.

Did You Know?

The Alberti bass is named for Domenico Alberti, an Italian singer, keyboard player, and composer who was born in Venice around 1710 and died in Rome at only thirty. Alberti was one of the first to use the left-hand arpeggiation pattern that has become associated with his name, often found accompanying a right-hand melody in keyboard music of the Classical era. As few of Alberti's own compositions are performed today, the pattern has largely become associated with keyboard works by Mozart—such as the second movement of the Piano Sonata in C Major, K. 545, shown below.

TERMS YOU SHOULD KNOW

Alberti bass
arpeggiated chord
arranging, arrangement
B♭ instruments
C instruments, concert instruments
C score, concert-pitch score
concert key, concert pitch
E♭ instruments
F instruments
seventh chords
- first inversion
- second inversion
- third inversion

seventh-chord qualities
- dominant seventh (Mm7)
- fully diminished seventh (^{o}7)
- half-diminished seventh (^{ø}7)
- major seventh (MM7)
- minor seventh (mm7)
orchestration
transposing instruments
transposed score

QUESTIONS FOR REVIEW

1. In major keys, which scale-degree seventh chords are MM7? Which are mm7? Which are Mm7? Which are ^{ø}7 or ^{o}7?

2. In minor keys (using the natural minor scale), which scale-degree seventh chords are MM7? mm7? Mm7? or ^{ø}7 or ^{o}7?

3. When the leading tone is added in minor keys, which seventh chords are usually altered? How does their quality change?

4. In the key of C minor, label each of the following sonorities with chord quality, Roman numeral, and lead-sheet symbol:
   - F–A♭–C–E♭
   - B–D–F–A♭
   - E♭–G–B♭–D

5. Describe the steps you take to spell a seventh chord. How can the principle of interval inversion help?

6. What are the figures for seventh chords in each inversion?

7. How is an Alberti bass constructed?

8. What is the difference between a concert-pitch score (C score) and a transposed score? How can you determine if an orchestral or band score is a C score or transposed score?

9. How do you find the concert pitch in a transposed score for B♭ clarinet? E♭ clarinet? F horn? piccolo?

Know It? Show It!

Focus by working through the tutorials.

Learn with InQuizitive.

Apply what you've learned to complete the workbook assignments.

9

Connecting Intervals in Note-to-Note Counterpoint

Overview

In this chapter, we learn how to connect melodic and harmonic intervals to make two-part, note-to-note counterpoint in strict species.

Repertoire

Cantus firmi by
    Johann Joseph Fux (1660–1741)
    Knud Jeppesen (1892–1974)
    Heinrich Schenker (1868–1935)

Outline

Species counterpoint

Connecting melodic intervals

Connecting harmonic intervals
- Four types of contrapuntal motion
- Consonant harmonic intervals

Writing note-to-note counterpoint in strict style
- Beginning and ending a first-species counterpoint
- Completing the middle

Species Counterpoint

Chapters 6-8 laid the basic building blocks for tonal music: melodic and harmonic intervals, triads, and seventh chords. Here, we make the two dimensions of melody and harmony work together to form counterpoint.

KEY CONCEPT **Counterpoint** is created when two or more different melodic lines are combined so that the lines form harmonies, or when individual voices in a succession of harmonies make good melodic lines. The process of connecting harmonic and melodic intervals is called **voice-leading**.

Composers of the eighteenth and nineteenth centuries—such as Bach, Handel, Mozart, Beethoven, and Brahms—considered counterpoint a foundation of their musical art, but the tradition of studying counterpoint stretches back hundreds of years, and continues as a valued component of musicians' training today. In the Baroque era (1600-1750), beginners would learn counterpoint in steps—by the **species** method—beginning with the simplest style in two parts and adding complexity until they were writing in four or more parts. We will do the same: first learn how to connect intervals in two parts (here and in Chapter 10), and consider the connections between species counterpoint and music literature more fully in Chapter 11.

The study of counterpoint will prove invaluable as you continue your music studies. To compose music, you might begin with a simple framework and add elaboration; to analyze music, you can use your knowledge of counterpoint to discover this underlying framework and see how it is embellished. Though a detailed consideration of note-to-note connections may seem abstract or removed from the context of music literature, the principles involved are actually the basis of all tonal composition.

Aspiring composers and musicians traditionally begin two-voice counterpoint with a "given line"—called a **cantus firmus** (CF, or cantus, for short), a line that is not to be changed. The student then writes another voice above or below it. The simplest type of counterpoint, called **first species** ("species" simply means "type of"), matches each note of the cantus with a note of the same duration. First-species counterpoint is also called "note-to-note," or 1:1, because both parts move at the same time to the next harmonic interval. While in traditional first-species exercises the cantus is notated in whole notes and the student provides a counterpoint in whole notes, any duration may be used as long as it is the same in both voices.

Connecting Melodic Intervals

Sing or play Example 9.1, a first-species counterpoint, to hear how each harmonic interval connects to the next. In this example, the cantus firmus is the lower part (labeled CF1), the counterpoint the upper part (CPT). This cantus is by Johann Joseph Fux, whose counterpoint treatise was widely studied in the eighteenth century. Each of the cantus lines in this chapter is taken from traditional counterpoint teaching.

EXAMPLE 9.1: Cantus firmus 1 (Fux, adapted) in a first-species setting

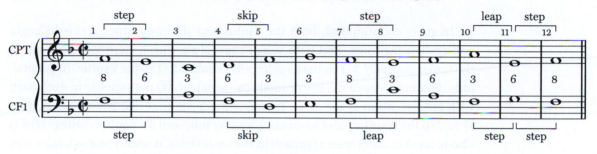

KEY CONCEPT Melodic intervals are connected by step, skip, or leap. Consider a half or whole step as a **step**, a third as a **skip** (it "skips" between adjacent triad members), and a fourth, fifth, or larger as a **leap** (it "leaps" over members of a triad). A melodic line that moves primarily by step is **conjunct**; one that moves primarily by skip or leap is **disjunct**.

To write a good contrapuntal line in strict style, use primarily conjunct motion, with a few skips or a leap for variety, as in Example 9.1. The melodic skips or leaps should be consonant: m3, M3, P4, P5, m6, M6, and P8. Dissonant melodic intervals larger than a M2, such as a m7, M7, d5, A4, or A2 (in minor), are not permitted in this style. Aim for a line with a good shape, with one or two high or low points, and avoid repeating one or two notes excessively.

Larger intervals create a dramatic effect and for this reason must be treated carefully. For instance, in Example 9.1 the leap from F3 to C4 in CF1 (mm. 7-8) emphasizes the climax of this melodic line.

KEY CONCEPT You may include one leap larger than a fourth in a first-species counterpoint melody. Where possible, approach the leap by step in the opposite direction (for example, approach an ascending leap with descending stepwise motion); after the leap, change direction again and fill in the space with smaller intervals.

The leap in Example 9.1's CF1, for instance, is followed by a change of direction that fills in the leap with thirds (mm. 9-10). In CF2 of Example 9.2 (below), the leap in measures 1-2 is filled in by step.

The upper line in Example 9.1 also includes a leap, the P4 in measures 10-11. This downward leap is approached by ascending motion and followed by an ascending step, balancing the line and constraining its range. To create a strong melodic line, avoid

- leaps preceded or followed by a skip in the same direction, and

- more than two skips or leaps in a row.

In strict counterpoint, both the cantus and the counterpoint should begin and end on the tonic, and both voices must close with a stepwise approach to the tonic: normally $\hat{7}$-$\hat{1}$ in the counterpoint against $\hat{2}$-$\hat{1}$ in the cantus. In general, only diatonic notes of the key or mode (no accidentals) may appear in each part, with one exception at the close: in minor-mode settings like Example 9.2, raise $\flat\hat{7}$ to $\hat{7}$ in the counterpoint to create a leading tone and a stronger ending. If $\flat\hat{6}$ is also present in a stepwise approach to the tonic (here, it would be B♭4), raise it as well (to $\hat{6}$, as in melodic minor), to avoid creating a melodic A2 with the leading tone. Be sure to consider the harmonic intervals that a $\flat\hat{6}$ or $\hat{6}$ would form with the cantus: neither can appear in measure 7, as each would make a dissonance with F3 in the cantus (a P4 for B♭ and an A4 for B♮), harmonic intervals not permitted in strict style.

EXAMPLE 9.2: Cantus firmus 2 (Jeppesen) in a first-species setting 🎧

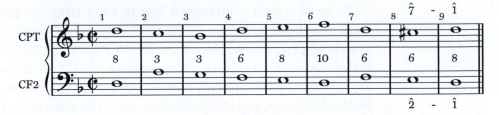

If $\flat\hat{6}$ and $\flat\hat{7}$ from natural minor appear in the cantus near the close, there is the possibility of a clash between these scale degrees and $\hat{6}$ and $\hat{7}$ in the counterpoint. This clash, called a **cross relation** (Example 9.3a), should be avoided. In addition, avoid following $\flat\hat{6}$ by $\hat{6}$ in the same part (part b); a chromatic half step is unacceptable in this style. A good approach to $\hat{6}$ and $\hat{7}$ is shown in part (c).

EXAMPLE 9.3: Treatment of the sixth and seventh scale degrees in minor keys

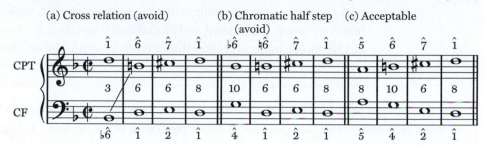

SUMMARY

Guidelines for writing a good melodic line (in any species):

- Melodic intervals larger than steps must be consonant; don't use the intervals m7, M7, d5, A4, or A2.

- Create a pleasing shape, with one or two high or low points and at most one immediately repeated note; avoid too many reappearances of a single note.

- Write primarily steps and skips; normally, each line should include no more than one leap.

- Precede and follow a leap with motion in the opposite direction, stepwise where possible.

- Begin and end on $\hat{1}$, and approach $\hat{1}$ at the cadence by step.

- At the cadence in minor, raise $\flat\hat{7}$ to $\hat{7}$, but avoid a melodic A2, a cross relation, or a chromatic half step.

Connecting Harmonic Intervals

Each time you write a counterpoint exercise, label the harmonic interval sizes between the staves, as in Examples 9.1-9.3. For intervals larger than a tenth, use the simple rather than the compound number (4 rather than 11). In first species, the distance between the two parts is normally no larger than a tenth (which may be indicated as either 10 or 3); the voices may occasionally move farther apart, but not for long. (Some examples in this chapter will show slightly wider spacing between the parts to allow the cantus and counterpoint to fit on the bass and treble staves without ledger lines.)

KEY CONCEPT To analyze harmonic intervals between the upper and lower parts, write interval sizes only, without specifying perfect, major, or minor; do, however, specify augmented and diminished intervals (e.g., A4 or d5). Reduce any harmonic interval greater than a tenth to within the octave (write 4, not 11).

Try it #1

On the example below, (1) label the harmonic intervals between the staves; (2) label any skips or leaps between two melody pitches (in either part) with brackets; and (3) beneath the score, circle the appropriate word that describes the predominant type of motion for each part.

Cantus firmus 3 (Schenker) in a first-species setting

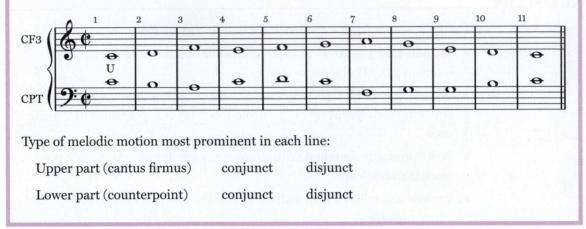

Type of melodic motion most prominent in each line:

Upper part (cantus firmus)   conjunct   disjunct

Lower part (counterpoint)   conjunct   disjunct

Four Types of Contrapuntal Motion

In writing or analyzing counterpoint, one important aspect to consider is how the voices of each harmonic interval make a linear connection with the next harmonic interval.

KEY CONCEPT There are four types of contrapuntal motion between pairs of voices.

Contrary motion (C): The two parts move in opposite directions. This is the preferred type of motion because it gives voices the most independence and balance.

Parallel motion (P): Both parts move in the same direction by the same interval; this is allowed between imperfect consonances, but not between perfect consonances.

Similar motion (S): Both parts move in the same direction, but not by the same interval. Similar motion may be used freely except when approaching a perfect interval, where it is acceptable only if the upper part moves by step.

Oblique motion (O):   One part repeats or sustains a single pitch, the other moves by leap, skip, or step. Because oblique motion requires one part to be static, this type, though acceptable, is not as desirable.

The counterpoint from Examples 9.1 and 9.2 prominently features contrary motion; the only exceptions are parallel motion between thirds (9.1, mm. 5-6; 9.2, mm. 2-3) and sixths (9.2, mm. 7-8). Example 9.4 also features contrary motion (C) but includes parallel motion (P) twice and oblique motion (O) just before the close.

EXAMPLE 9.4: Cantus firmus 3 (Schenker) in a first-species setting 🎧

Try it #2

In the example below, write the harmonic interval numbers between the staves. Then identify the motion between these intervals as C (contrary), S (similar), O (oblique), or P (parallel) by writing the appropriate letter below the staff, between adjacent notes.

Cantus firmus 7 (Fux) in a first-species setting

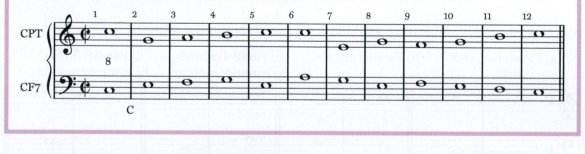

Consonant Harmonic Intervals

As noted in Chapter 6, the consonant intervals include the PU, P5, and P8 (perfect consonances) and the M3, m3, M6, and m6 (imperfect consonances). The perfect fourth is a special case.

KEY CONCEPT The P4 is treated as a dissonance when it appears harmonically between the lowest voice and any upper voice. But it is considered a consonant melodic interval, and a consonant harmonic interval between upper voices when there are three or more parts. When writing counterpoint in only two parts, treat the harmonic P4 as a dissonance.

Perfect Consonances: PU, P5, P8 Because of their stability and tendency to sound open, perfect intervals must be treated carefully in contrapuntal settings. Of the consonant intervals, the PU is the most consonant and most stable; it therefore appears only at the beginning or end of an exercise, as in Example 9.4, not in the middle. More frequent unisons cause two parts to sound like only one, and stop the sense of forward motion.

The P8 is likewise very stable, and may be found at the beginning or end, but it may also occasionally be employed in the middle, since it does not have as strong a tendency to delay the forward motion. However, the P8 also sounds hollow; avoid writing it too often in a single exercise because of its open sound and relative stability.

The P5 creates a sense of stability as well, but less so than the P8 or PU. It implies a triad, although the quality of triad is unclear since there is no third. The P5 also has a hollow sound, and tends to stand out unless approached properly in both parts.

KEY CONCEPT Moving from one perfect interval to another of the same size is prohibited in first-species counterpoint (Example 9.5). If the motion is in the same direction, it results in **parallel octaves** (P8-P8; part a), **parallel fifths** (P5-P5; part b), or **parallel unisons** (PU-PU). Contrary motion between two perfect intervals of the *same size* is likewise not acceptable (known as parallel octaves or fifths by contrary motion, or contrary octaves or fifths; parts c-d).

EXAMPLE 9.5: Parallel, contrary, and hidden (or direct) octaves and fifths

A perfect harmonic interval is normally approached by contrary motion. Often the upper voice will lead into a perfect interval by step, while the lower part may step or skip. Leaps in one or both parts into a perfect interval are not recommended, as they make the interval stand out from the surrounding counterpoint. Also avoid approaches to perfect intervals by similar motion, because the motion *implies* parallel fifths or octaves, as illustrated in Example 9.5e–f (an approach called hidden fifths or octaves, sometimes direct fifths or octaves). Only when the *upper* voice moves by step is similar motion to a perfect interval acceptable.

Try it #3

The counterpoint below includes some common errors. Write the harmonic interval numbers between the staves, then circle any parallel perfect intervals.

Cantus firmus 3 (Schenker)

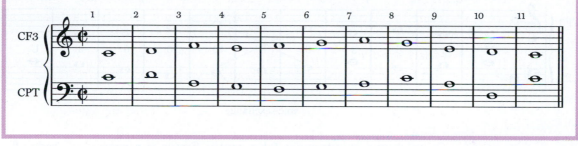

Imperfect Consonances: M3, m3, M6, m6 Imperfect consonances sound warm and blending, less open than perfect consonances, and provide more sense of forward direction; they may connect to either imperfect or perfect consonances. In strict style, most of the harmonic intervals other than those at the opening and close will be thirds and sixths, with occasional perfect intervals providing contrast. Although imperfect consonances may connect to a same-size interval, making parallel thirds or sixths, such a succession should be limited to three in a row to avoid monotony and a loss of independent lines.

Example 9.6 moves mostly in contrary motion, where seven of the eleven intervals are imperfect consonances and four are perfect.

EXAMPLE 9.6: Cantus firmus 3 (Schenker)

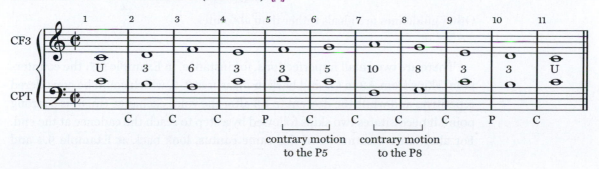

Here the perfect consonances in measures 6 and 8 are approached (by step in both voices, with contrary motion) and left carefully to blend gracefully into the counterpoint. Still, although this setting is strong overall, the repetition of C4 in the counterpoint (five of the eleven notes) is a weakness.

Yet another setting of CF3 in Example 9.7 gives the same opening intervals, but sets pitches 5 to 7 of the cantus with stepwise contrary motion. This procedure has a special name, the **voice exchange**: the pitch classes F-G-A in the upper voice change positions with A-G-F in the lower voice. Such an intervallic pattern (6-8-10) and the melodic voice exchange, characteristic in this style, are highly desirable because of the way the perfect consonance (8) is treated: approached by step in each voice, with contrary motion.

EXAMPLE 9.7: Cantus firmus 3 (Schenker) in another first-species setting 🎧

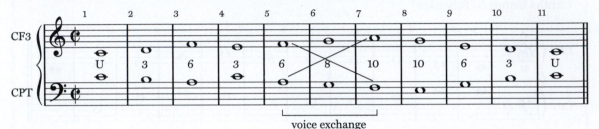

voice exchange

Completing a counterpoint for a cantus firmus is a process of trade-offs: choices that make an excellent setting for one portion may create challenges in others, and most good settings will include something that could be criticized. Part of the learning process in writing counterpoint is trying out different combinations to hear their effect, while striving for a technically perfect setting.

🎧 **KEY CONCEPT** First-species settings should follow these most essential guidelines:

- Write the proper opening and closing gestures.
- Watch for parallel fifths and octaves.
- Write only consonant harmonic intervals.
- Avoid dissonant melodic intervals larger than a step.

Other guidelines are ideals rather than absolutes.

There are two small imperfections, for instance, in Example 9.7: the counterpoint skips from A3 to C4 and back in measures 3-5, which could be considered repetitive; and while the descent to E3 after the voice exchange (m. 8) is a strong point, it necessitates two skips followed by a step to reach the cadence at the end. For alternative treatments of this same cantus, look back at Example 9.4 and

Try it #1. A weakness of Example 9.4 is the contour: essentially down then up, with no other changes of direction. *Try it #1* includes a little segment, C4-D4-C4 (mm. 4-6), separated by a skip on one side and a leap on the other, which breaks up the line into three distinct sections (mm. 1-3, 4-6, 7-11); the strongest lines will exhibit a flowing contour from beginning to end without any discrete segments.

Writing Note-to-Note Counterpoint in Strict Style
Beginning and Ending a First-Species Counterpoint

As a first step in writing a complete counterpoint to a given cantus firmus, set a PU or P8 against the first note of the cantus. A P5 is possible only if the cantus is the lower part (scale degree $\hat{1}$ should always be in the bass). To decide which opening interval to use,

- examine the contour of the cantus, then choose a starting interval that will allow your counterpoint to stay within a tenth of the cantus, while leaving space for the lines to flow without colliding or crossing.

- If the cantus is the lower part and moves down (or if it's the upper part and moves up), a unison opening could work well, allowing the lines to start together, then diverge without moving too far apart (see Example 9.4).

- If the cantus is the upper part and moves down, or the lower part and moves up (toward the part you will be writing, as in Examples 9.1 and 9.2), use a P8.

Now decide on the intervals at the close. The only ones employed in strict style are 6-8 and 3-U (or 10-8). If the cantus descends to the final note (as most do), the counterpoint should ascend. As mentioned previously, if the cantus implies scale degrees $\hat{2}$-$\hat{1}$ in a minor mode, $\flat\hat{7}$ in the counterpoint line should be raised to make the leading tone. And if the leading tone is preceded by $\flat\hat{6}$, then both $\flat\hat{6}$ and $\flat\hat{7}$ must be raised, as in melodic minor—but take care that these alterations do not create cross relations or chromatic half steps.

Completing the Middle

After selecting the opening and closing intervals, sing through the cantus to consider the middle—this portion will need some planning to achieve an appealing result. Take a close look at the shape of the given line: Where are the steps and skips? Is there a leap? The contour of a successful counterpoint will complement the cantus and provide contrary motion where possible.

KEY CONCEPT Set intervals as follows:

CANTUS	COUNTERPOINT
Leap	Set with a step, in contrary motion.
Steps	May incorporate a skip or leap (as well as step).
Skip	Set with either a step (preferred) or a skip.

Simultaneous skips that exchange pitch classes (e.g., an ascending E–G in the cantus, a descending G–E in the counterpoint) normally sound good as long as there are steps around them. Also, consider the overall shape of your contrapuntal line. If you use oblique motion, limit it to one or two instances (in longer CFs), only one of which involves the tonic.

Try for a mix of perfect and imperfect harmonic consonances, with more imperfect than perfect. At least one P5 or P8 should appear somewhere in the middle. Because perfect intervals are best approached and left by contrary motion, one typical interval sequence is 6-8-10 (or 10-8-6), making a voice exchange (as in Example 9.7). Other possible approaches to P8 and P5 are shown in Example 9.6. All previous guidelines for writing perfect intervals still apply (see Example 9.5).

As you complete your counterpoint, be sure that the lines generally stay within a tenth of each other, without crossing. This particular problem, **crossed voices**, can be seen in Example 9.8a, measure 2, where the lower voice on E4 is positioned above the upper voice's C4. In part (b), the violation of range known as **overlapping** occurs: in measure 2, the E4 in the lower voice is higher than measure 1's D4 in the upper voice. Similarly, in part (c), the lower voice in measure 1 is higher than the upper voice in measure 2.

Crossed or overlapping voices often appear in combination with other errors, such as the unison in part (a), or inappropriate leaps in parts (b) and (c). Also remember to avoid any melodic or harmonic dissonances (watch out for the harmonic P4!) or accidentals in the middle of the counterpoint (add an accidental only at the cadence in minor).

EXAMPLE 9.8: Crossed voices and overlapping 🎧

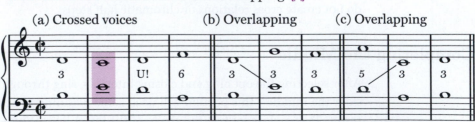

(a) Crossed voices   (b) Overlapping   (c) Overlapping

SUMMARY

Guidelines for writing first-species counterpoint:

- For the opening harmonic interval, write P8, PU, or P5 (the latter only with the cantus in the lower voice).

- For the closing harmonic intervals, write 6-8 or 3-U (10-8). In minor, raise ♭$\hat{7}$, and raise ♭$\hat{6}$ if it precedes $\hat{7}$ (to avoid an A2); but watch out for cross relations.

- Write mostly contrary motion between the parts.

- Avoid parallel octaves or fifths (by parallel *or* contrary motion).

- Approach perfect intervals by contrary motion, or in similar motion with a stepwise upper voice.

- Don't write more than three parallel imperfect consonances (3 or 6) in a row.

- Include a mix of perfect and imperfect consonances, with more imperfect than perfect.

- Avoid dissonant harmonic intervals (including P4); don't add accidentals except at the cadence in minor.

- Avoid dissonant melodic intervals (e.g., m7, M7, d5, A4, or A2 in minor).

- Write leaps sparingly; approach and leave them by step in contrary motion if possible; and set them with a step in the other part (preferably in contrary motion to the leap). Don't set a leap in one voice against a leap in the other.

- Give your melodic line an interesting contour; it should not be static, repeating notes or circling around one note. Keep the ranges of the lines distinct: don't overlap or cross voices.

- Aim for primarily stepwise motion, with no more than two skips or leaps in a row.

To help you choose among the many possibilities for the middle of your counterpoint, try making a table like the one in Example 9.9. First, fill in the bottom row with the cantus letter names. Then look at the column at the far left, and in the remaining boxes write the note names of the third, fifth, and sixth above each cantus note. If the cantus is the upper line, write the letter names in the top row, then (top to bottom) 8, 3, 5, and 6.

EXAMPLE 9.9: Cantus firmus 2 (Jeppesen) in a first-species setting 🎧

6	B♭	F	E	D	C	B♭	D	C♯ (LT)	B♭
5	A	E						B♭ (d5!)	A
3	F	C						G	F
8	D	A	G	F	E	D	F	E	D

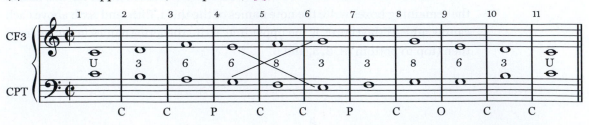

CPT · · · ♯o o
8 · · · · · · 6 8
CF2 · · · · · · · · ·

Shade or cross out letter names that should not be used, such as the dissonant d5 in the eighth box. Since the first note D3 should be set with an octave, all choices but the D have been shaded; and because this is a minor-mode cantus, the C♯ has been selected (m. 8) to approach the cadence on D. Continue to eliminate other potential intervals as you make selections, such as any that would create parallel octaves or fifths (like A in the second box). Don't change the cantus, no matter how tempting it is to correct problems that way!

Try it #4

Complete the table and counterpoint in Example 9.9. Include at least one perfect interval in the middle of the setting. Write the harmonic interval numbers between the staves.

Since the cantus may be either the upper or lower part in strict species, this feature creates the possibility for **invertible counterpoint**, where the two lines may be reversed in register (e.g., the upper counterpoint may be transposed to sound below the cantus). Example 9.10 shows invertible counterpoint based on Example 9.4 (repeated here for comparison).

EXAMPLE 9.10: Cantus firmus 3 (Schenker) in invertible counterpoint

(a) CF 3 in the upper voice (Example 9.4) 🎧

CF3
1   2   3   4   5   6   7   8   9   10   11
U   3   6   6   8   3   3   8   6   3   U
CPT
C   C   P   C   C   P   C   O   C   C

(b) CF3 in the lower voice 🎧

The intervals are inverted in the two examples as well: U becomes 8, 3 becomes 6, and so on (inverted intervals sum to 9). A P5, however, may not be used in invertible counterpoint, because the inversion is a P4. The 6-8-3 voice exchange between E and G in part (a) remains a voice exchange in (b), now with the intervals 3-8-6. In the eighteenth century, counterpoint exercises were often written with the cantus notated in the middle staff of three—with one counterpoint written above and another below—to explore where invertible counterpoint worked and where it didn't. Invertible counterpoint became a key element of inventions and fugues (as we'll see in Chapter 24).

Did You Know?

The word "counterpoint" came into use around the twelfth century; the "punctus," or point, referred to a written musical note that later became the breve (analogous to the whole note). The practice of counterpoint as a compositional technique, however, predates the term—the earliest written account is an anonymous treatise called *Musica enchiriadis* (from around 900 CE). This textbook for musicians describes adding counterpoint to a preexisting cantus firmus by doubling the melody at a fifth to make two parts, then doubling each of those parts at the octave to get four—a practice also known as organum. In the twelfth century, note-against-note (punctus to punctus) counterpoint gave way to florid organum, with many notes to one of the slow-moving cantus. Counterpoint served as the primary compositional technique in the late Middle Ages (c. 900-1430) and Renaissance (1430-1600), and its fundamental principles remain the foundation of tonal practice to this day.

TERMS YOU SHOULD KNOW

cantus firmus (or cantus)	first species	parallel motion
conjunct	hidden fifths	• parallel fifths
consonant	hidden octaves	• parallel octaves
contrary motion	invertible counterpoint	similar motion
counterpoint	leap	skip
cross relation	note-to-note (1:1)	species
crossed voices	oblique motion	step
disjunct	overlapping voices	voice crossing
		voice exchange
		voice-leading

QUESTIONS FOR REVIEW

1. Why is it important to learn counterpoint?
2. What sizes of melodic intervals are called steps? skips? leaps?
3. What are the four types of contrapuntal motion between pairs of voices?
4. What are the basic guidelines for composing note-to-note (1:1) counterpoint?
5. What special considerations should you keep in mind when writing perfect consonances?
6. How do you write a cadence in strict style? What additional considerations apply to minor-mode cadences?

Know It? Show It!

Focus by working through the tutorials.

Learn with InQuizitive.

Apply what you've learned to complete the workbook assignments.

10

Melodic and Rhythmic Embellishment in Two-Voice Composition

Overview

In this chapter, we embellish two-voice note-to-note counterpoint with passing tones, neighbor tones, consonant skips, and suspensions in strict second-, third-, and fourth-species style. We also combine these embellishment types in fifth species, and examine a Renaissance piece to see how the species practice of the eighteenth century is evident in older compositional styles as well.

Repertoire

Cantus firmi by
    Johann Joseph Fux (1660–1741)
    Knud Jeppesen (1892–1974)
    Johann Philipp Kirnberger (1721–1783)
Tomás Luis de Victoria, "O magnum mysterium" ("O Great Mystery")

Outline

Melodic embellishment in second-species (2:1) counterpoint
- Passing tones
- Consonant skips
- Neighbor tones

Writing 2:1 counterpoint
- Opening and closing patterns
- Melodic considerations
- Harmonic considerations

Further melodic embellishment in third-species (4:1) counterpoint

Writing 4:1 counterpoint

Rhythmic displacement in fourth-species counterpoint
- Types of suspensions
- Rhythmic character of fourth species
- Breaking species and tying consonances
- Chains of suspensions

Writing fourth-species counterpoint

Fifth species and free counterpoint

Melodic Embellishment in Second-Species (2:1) Counterpoint

Play or listen to the counterpoint in Example 10.1; listen particularly for the consonances and dissonances.

EXAMPLE 10.1: Cantus firmus 4 (Fux) in a second-species setting

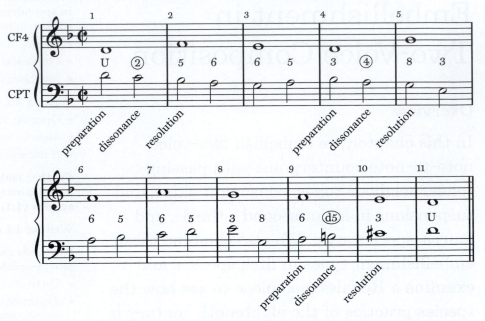

👂 **KEY CONCEPT** In strict second species (2:1), there are two half notes in the counterpoint for each whole note of the cantus.

Second species introduces the concept of **metric accent**, since the two half notes in a measure do not carry the same "weight," or emphasis. You can consider each measure as having only one beat that's divided into two, where the first half note ("on the beat") is accented and the second (the "offbeat") is unaccented; or as having two beats (a downbeat and an upbeat). With either approach, the first half note in the measure, which corresponds with the cantus note, receives a stronger accent than the second. The unaccented notes are sometimes called diminutions because they divide the duration of the original first-species framework in half.

Second species also introduces the dissonant harmonic intervals 2, 4, A4, d5, 7, and 9 (these are circled in examples throughout).

⌢ **KEY CONCEPT** A dissonant harmonic interval in second-species counterpoint must fall on the unaccented second half of the measure. It is approached by step from a consonant harmonic interval (the "preparation") on the downbeat and must connect by step to a consonant harmonic interval on the following downbeat (the "resolution"). In general, a resolution is motion from a harmonic dissonance to a consonance.

You can also set two consonances against a cantus note, either by skip or leap (see Example 10.1, mm. 5 and 8), or by step with 5-6 or 6-5 intervals (mm. 2, 3, 6, and 7). Within each measure, the second half note's entry automatically creates oblique motion; connections over the bar line will feature contrary, parallel, or similar motion.

SUMMARY

Second species (2:1) introduces the following concepts:

- accented and unaccented notes in the measure;
- dissonance created by the harmonic intervals 2, 4, A4, d5, 7, and 9 in unaccented positions;
- consonant skips or leaps, and steps, with harmonic intervals 5-6 or 6-5.

Passing Tones

The most common type of melodically generated dissonance in 2:1 counterpoint is the passing tone.

⌢ **KEY CONCEPT** A passing tone (labeled P) is a melodic embellishment that fills in a skip by stepwise motion; it is approached by step and left by step in the same direction. Passing tones introduce the harmonic dissonance of 2, 4, or 7 on the unaccented part of the measure.

If you look back at Example 10.1, you will see dissonant passing tones in measures 1, 4, and 9. The dissonant intervals A4 (resolves to 6) and d5 (resolves to 3) may be used as passing tones only if they are followed by the appropriate interval of resolution, as in measures 9-10. Consonant passing tones with the intervals 5-6 or 6-5 are also possible (as in mm. 2, 3, 6, and 7), but because embellishing tones are analyzed mostly to examine the treatment of dissonant intervals, these consonant passing tones are usually not labeled.

More passing tones can be seen in Example 10.2 (in mm. 2, 4, and 7).

EXAMPLE 10.2: Cantus firmus 5 (Kirnberger) in a second-species setting 🎧

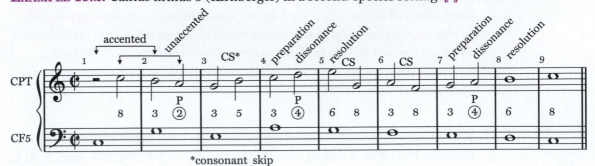

*consonant skip

Consonant Skips

A second melodic embellishment introduced in second species is the consonant skip (mm. 3, 5, and 6 of Example 10.2).

KEY CONCEPT Consonant skips (CS) or **leaps** are melodic embellishments made when both half notes of the skip or leap form a consonant harmonic interval with the cantus.

These are also referred to as "chordal skips," even though the melodic interval traversed may be a skip or a leap and the notes may not imply chords. Consonant skips and leaps are employed, along with passing tones, to provide a mix of consonant and dissonant harmonic intervals; to balance the steps, skips, and leaps in the cantus; and to make a pleasing shape for the contrapuntal line. Avoid using too many passing tones or consonant skips in a row, or the line will be too conjunct (P) or disjunct (CS) and therefore lacking in variety.

Neighbor Tones

A third melodic embellishment introduced in second species is the neighbor tone (Example 10.3.)

KEY CONCEPT A neighbor tone (N) is a melodic embellishment on an unaccented part of a measure that decorates a melody note by stepping to the note above or below it, then returning to the original note. Neighbor tones are approached (prepared) and left (resolved) by step, in opposite directions.

A neighbor tone that moves up by step is called an **upper neighbor** (UN), while a neighbor tone that moves down is a **lower neighbor** (LN). Neighbor tones temporarily displace the pitch they decorate, and may form consonant or dissonant intervals with the cantus. Some teachers of counterpoint restrict neighbor tones in second species to consonant intervals, while others allow dissonant ones when they help to improve the shape of the counterpoint line. We include both types, in preparation for writing in eighteenth-century style.

EXAMPLE 10.3: Cantus firmus 6 (Kirnberger) in a second-species setting 🎧

Neighbor tones are used sparingly in second-species counterpoint, and their placement requires careful consideration. Because they return to the same note they left, too many will make a line static.

Try it #1

Analyze the harmonic intervals of the counterpoint below by writing the interval numbers between the staves and circling the ones that are dissonances. Locate and label one additional dissonant passing tone (P), two consonant passing tones, two neighbor tones (N), and four consonant skips or leaps (CS).

Cantus firmus 4 (Fux) in a second-species setting 🎧

Writing 2:1 Counterpoint

Opening and Closing Patterns

To write second-species counterpoint, follow the same general procedures as in first species: compose the opening and closing measures first to ensure that they make good harmonic and contrapuntal sense, then fill in the middle section. As in first species, the opening harmonic interval must be a P8 or PU (or P5 if the counterpoint is in the upper part). Rhythmically, the first note of the counterpoint may appear on the downbeat (Example 10.1) *or* on the upbeat to measure 2, preceded by a half rest (Examples 10.2 and 10.3). Starting with the half-measure rest is the preferred method, to allow the voices more independence.

Example 10.4 illustrates some typical closing patterns. As in first species, the final note of the counterpoint is a whole note PU or P8, and the penultimate measure may be filled with either two half notes or a whole note. In parts (a) to (c), the 3–8 or 6–8 closing gesture begins on the second half note of the penultimate measure, preceded by a 5. If the penultimate measure is a whole note, as in (d) and (e), the exercise ends as in first species. And as in first species, raise both the sixth and seventh scale degrees in minor as you approach 1̂; the resulting d5 and A4 in (d) and (e) are treated as dissonant passing tones.

EXAMPLE 10.4: Closing patterns in second species

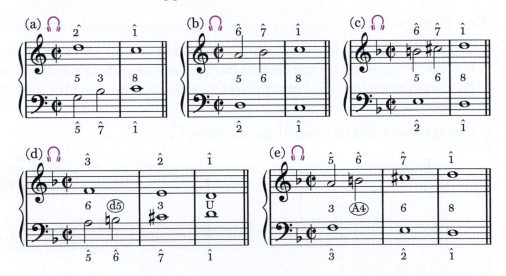

> **KEY CONCEPT** Other than the first measure (which may begin with a rest) and the closing one or two measures, second-species counterpoint will feature two half notes per whole note of the cantus firmus. Pitches may not be immediately repeated, whether within a measure or over a bar line.

Try it #2

Write a counterpoint for the following closing patterns. Use 2:1 motion in the first measure of each, and whole notes in the other measures. Label scale degrees and harmonic intervals.

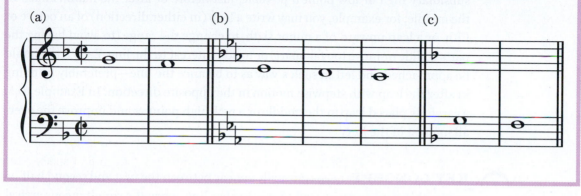

(a)   (b)   (c)

Melodic Considerations

In the middle section of the counterpoint, the embellishments most characteristic of second species are dissonant passing tones and consonant skips—although consonant passing tones, neighbor tones, and an occasional leap (as described below) may also be included to make a better line. Consider a span of at least three half notes—ideally, consider two or three measures at a time—and plan the consonant downbeats, offbeat embellishments, and contour direction for this longer stretch. As dissonant passing tones are emblematic of second species (in fact, their absence is considered an error), you may want to plan several of these as you make initial choices.

One of the challenges in writing a strong second-species setting is attending to such local details as individual passing tones and consonant skips while creating a line with an interesting and coherent overall shape. Consider Example 10.5, another setting of CF5. The opening (mm. 1–2) and close (mm. 7–9) are correctly executed, and the counterpoint in measures 1–7 is quite good if we examine two- or three-measure segments: there are consonant skips, prepared and resolved dissonant passing tones, consonant passing tones (5–6), and mostly conjunct motion against the cantus leaps. Overall, though, the line lacks a single high point or climax, and it obsessively repeats the same few pitches: B4, C5, D5, and E5.

EXAMPLE 10.5: Cantus firmus 5 (Kirnberger) in a second-species setting 🎧

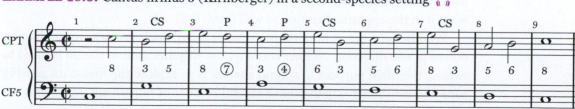

Since there *is* a tendency for second species melodies to circle around a few pitches for too long, allow your line a wider range overall than first species—spanning an octave or tenth between its highest and lowest point—and plan a subsidiary high or low point if possible, just before or after the main climax. In the middle, for example, you may write a leap (in either direction) of an octave or fifth, or a leap upward of a minor sixth, to change the range (to avoid having the parts collide or move too far apart) or to add interest to the line. Each leap should be approached and left in such a way as to balance the line—preferably by filling in after the leap with stepwise motion in the opposite direction. In Example 10.5, a carefully placed leap in the middle or a new high point would improve the overall interest of the line.

KEY CONCEPT Leaps normally appear between the first and second half note within a measure instead of over the bar line, when the simultaneous arrival of the new cantus note would give the disjunct motion added prominence. Where possible, skip or leap within the bar lines, but step over them.

Example 10.6 illustrates this principle. If you plan thirds on the downbeats of measures 3 and 4, there will be a melodic fourth between these accented beats, with no possibility of a stepwise connection. A consonant skip within measure 3 and a step over the bar will connect the beats nicely.

EXAMPLE 10.6: Cantus firmus 5 (Kirnberger) in a second-species setting 🎧

Where there is too much stepwise motion in one direction or a static line, a P4 or P5 leap within a measure may substitute for a consonant skip of a third. Two consonant skips or a skip followed by a small leap (P4) in the same direction are also acceptable (as in mm. 4–5); they are treated as the equivalent of a leap of a fifth or sixth from downbeat to downbeat in first species. Ideally, approach any leap (or combination of skips equating to a leap) from the opposite direction, and leave it in the opposite direction as well (mm. 4–5).

Whether you are writing steps, skips, or leaps, don't progress more than an octave in one direction. Neither conjunct nor disjunct motion should be used to excess: the main purpose of second species is to explore the dissonant passing tone and consonant skip through a careful balance of skips, leaps, and steps.

SUMMARY

To write a good contrapuntal line in second species:

- Use a wider range than in first species, with steps, skips, and leaps.
- Create one high point to the line, and a subsidiary one if possible.
- Include a leap, on the offbeat, to change the range or create melodic interest.
- Consider two skips, or a skip plus small leap (P4), as equivalent to a leap.
- Ideally, after a leap, follow with motion in the opposite direction.

Harmonic Considerations

The primary harmonic consideration in second species is that the interval on the first half note of each measure must be a perfect or imperfect consonance; write dissonant passing or neighbor tones only on the second half note. Unisons are likewise allowed only on the upbeat, and must be left by motion contrary to their approach (alternatively, move the counterpoint line up or down an octave to avoid them). As in first species, treat perfect intervals with special care.

KEY CONCEPT To avoid hidden (or direct) fifths and octaves, approach intervals P5 and P8 by step in the upper part, ideally in contrary motion. Don't approach either one in similar motion with a skip or leap in the upper voice.

With the addition of melodic embellishments in 2:1 counterpoint, you have new opportunities for forbidden parallel motion between perfect intervals. For this reason, you should evaluate the harmonic intervals in two ways: from the downbeat of one measure to the downbeat of the next and from each note to the next. The motion from downbeat to downbeat should follow first-species guidelines. For example, perfect consonances of the same size from downbeat to downbeat will create parallel fifths or octaves (prohibited), no matter what the intervening note on the offbeat is. No more than three consecutive downbeats should have the same imperfect consonance (3-3-3 or 6-6-6).

KEY CONCEPT Always double-check your counterpoint for parallel perfect intervals not only from downbeat to downbeat (as in 1:1, "downbeat-to-downbeat parallels"), but also from upbeat to downbeat over the bar line ("adjacency parallels").

Example 10.7 includes both kinds of prohibited motion: downbeat-to-downbeat parallels in measures 3-4 and 8-9 and adjacency parallels in 1-2 and 7-8. Perfect intervals on the upbeats of two consecutive measures *are* permitted (as in mm. 4-5), but not more than two in a row of the same type, as they will attract attention. Overall, the counterpoint in Example 10.7 includes too many perfect intervals, with only two dissonant passing tones. (Still, mm. 4-7 could work with a revised opening and closing, and mm. 6-7 illustrate the correct resolution of the dissonant passing tone A4 to a 6.) When you have finished your counterpoint, perform it (at the keyboard or with a partner) to check for parallel perfect intervals, inappropriate dissonances, or other errors.

EXAMPLE 10.7: Prohibited parallel motion in second-species counterpoint

SUMMARY

To write a 2:1 counterpoint in strict style:

1. Start with either a half rest or half note on the downbeat of the first measure; the first harmonic interval should be an 8 or U (or 5 if the counterpoint is the upper part).

2. End with a whole note in the last measure and the harmonic intervals 5-6-8 or 5-3-8 (or U) in the last two measures; or make the last two notes whole notes 6-8 or 3-8 (U), as in first species.

3. Other than at the beginning and close, use half notes for the counterpoint; don't immediately repeat the same pitch.

4. Write consonant harmonic intervals on the beat; they may also appear on the upbeats, approached as steps, consonant skips, or consonant leaps.

5. Include dissonant harmonic intervals (2, 4, 7, 9, and d5 and A4 if resolved correctly) on the upbeats as passing or (more rarely) neighbor tones.

6. Check from one downbeat to the next and from an upbeat to the next downbeat for parallel fifths or octaves; perfect fifths and octaves are allowed from one upbeat to the next, but no more than two in a row.

7. Intervals on the downbeat are normally approached by step (preferred) or skip; avoid similar motion into a P8 or P5 over the bar line unless the upper voice moves by step.

8. Use no accidentals except to raise $\hat{7}$ (and $\hat{6}$ if necessary) at the close in minor.

9. Continue to follow the guidelines for 1:1 counterpoint with respect to the overall motion between the parts (contrary, parallel, similar, oblique) and principles of good melodic writing.

Further Melodic Embellishment in Third-Species (4:1) Counterpoint

In **third-species** (4:1) counterpoint, the cantus whole note is set with four quarter notes, as in Example 10.8. Third species is thus a further rhythmic diminution of second species: each half note of second species is divided in two to make quarter notes. Again, the strongest accent falls on the first of the four quarter notes (the beat, or downbeat), which enters with the cantus note. The third quarter note (upbeat, analogous to the second half note in second species) takes a lesser accent, while the second and fourth quarter notes are unaccented. In third species, our main concern is to incorporate more elaborate embellishments—passing and neighbor tones, consonant skips—while maintaining a good balance between the voices and a pleasing overall contour.

EXAMPLE 10.8: Cantus firmus 5 (Kirnberger) in a third-species setting 🎧

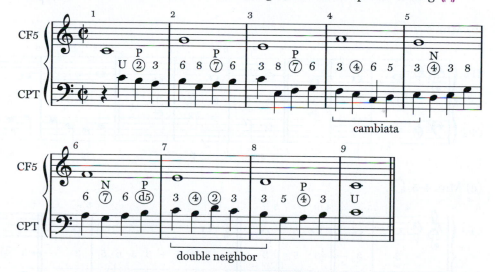

As you can see in Example 10.8, consonant skips (especially two or more in a row) are less common in third species than in second. While leaps occasionally appear in the middle of a measure to improve the distance between the lines (as in m. 3) or for variety, the emphasis is on passing and neighbor tones creating a smooth, flowing, conjunct counterpoint. To help achieve this, connections from the fourth quarter note to the first over the bar will normally be by step.

As should also be clear from Example 10.8, third species offers many possibilities for embellishments. Example 10.9 illustrates how some embellishments from Example 10.8 relate back to 1:1 and 2:1 frameworks. In parts (a) and (b), a first-species model is elaborated in two stages. Part (c) introduces a new embellishment: the **cambiata**, which combines passing and neighboring tones to make a figure with an apparent skip from a dissonance on the second quarter note (E3 in m. 4). This E3, a passing tone, resolves on the fourth note (D3). Another new embellishment, the **double neighbor** (DN, part d), combines successive upper and lower neighbors (in either order) around the same main pitch (here, C4). The second neighbor (D4) must resolve (to C4), and the figure must continue to the next beat in the same direction as the resolution (to B3) to complete the pattern.

EXAMPLE 10.9: Building third-species embellishments from a 1:1 or 2:1 framework

(a) Mm. 1-2

(b) Mm. 5-7

(c) Mm. 4-5

(d) Mm. 7-8

Try it #3

For each of the given 4:1 segments below, label the harmonic intervals between the parts, circle the dissonant intervals, and label them as P or N. Then identify a possible underlying note-to-note or 2:1 framework and write it in the blank treble staff to the right.

Most of the guidelines for second species apply to third as well: the harmonic interval on the first quarter note of each measure must be consonant; those for the other quarter notes may be either consonant or dissonant. Avoid down-beat-to-downbeat, upbeat-to-downbeat, and adjacency parallels over the bar line (see Example 10.10). Parallel perfect intervals from the second quarter note of one measure to any part of the following measure are acceptable, as are those from the third or fourth quarter note of a measure to any part of the following measure after the downbeat. Look back at your answers to *Try it #3*, and check to see if you incorporated parallels.

EXAMPLE 10.10: Parallel octaves and fifths in third species

(a) Downbeat-to-downbeat parallels

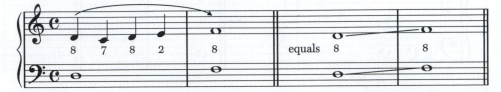

(b) Upbeat-to-downbeat parallels

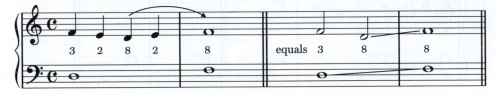

(c) Adjacency parallels

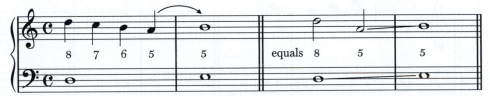

Writing 4:1 Counterpoint

As in first and second species, compose the opening and closing measures first, then fill in the middle section; the opening harmonic interval, again, is a P8 or PU (or P5 if the counterpoint is in the upper part). Rhythmically, the first note of the counterpoint may appear on the downbeat (Example 10.11), making four quarter notes in the measure, or as the second quarter note, preceded by a quarter rest (Example 10.8). While starting with the quarter rest is preferred, starting on the downbeat sometimes provides a smoother connection to the downbeat of the second measure or a better contour.

As in first species, the final note of the counterpoint is a whole note PU or P8, but it is preceded by four quarter notes in the penultimate measure (see Examples 10.8 and 10.11). In minor, raise both the sixth and seventh scale degrees as you approach 1̂ (Example 10.11).

EXAMPLE 10.11: Cantus firmus 2 (Fux) in a third-species setting 🎧

In planning your counterpoint, consider both the overall contour (as always) and where you can incorporate dissonant intervals. The downbeat quarter notes must all be consonances, but any other quarter note may be a dissonant passing or neighbor tone (every measure of Example 10.11 except the last has at least one). You may start with a soprano/bass framework as for first or second species, but may also plan a dramatic leap within a measure (such as that in Example 10.11, m. 4), to make a soaring line. Compare the excerpts in *Try it #3* (which are taken from Example 10.11) to see how these two-measure segments relate to first or second species, and how the leap was created.

🎧 **KEY CONCEPT** To write a 4:1 counterpoint:

1. **Think in groups of five rather than four.** Connect each group of four quarter notes smoothly to the next beat, "stepping over the bar." Avoid the same melodic shape in two consecutive measures.

2. **Use consonant skips.** Starting with a note-to-note framework, add a skip to a consonance and back, then fill in one of the skips with a passing tone (Example 10.9a). Avoid too many skips in one direction (two are usually enough) and isolating pitches by skipping (or leaping) both into and out of them.

3. **Use passing tones.** Fill in consonant skips with passing tones (Example 10.11, m. 1), or plan a stepwise line from one downbeat to the next.

4. **Use neighbor tones.** Neighbor tones may decorate a repeated pitch, or a double neighbor may turn one beat of note-against-note into 4:1 (Example 10.9d); too many double neighbors, though, will create a "circular" melodic line. Combine a neighbor pattern with a passing tone (in either order) to fill in a skip (Example 10.9b, m. 6; Example 10.11, m. 6).

5. **Every dissonant interval should be a passing or neighbor tone,** unless it is part of a cambiata or double neighbor. Make sure the dissonant pitch "passes" or "neighbors" correctly!

6. **Watch for forbidden parallels.** Check each pair of measures for parallel octaves or fifths in three places: on consecutive beats (downbeat-to-downbeat parallels), from the third quarter (upbeat) to the next downbeat, and from the fourth quarter to the next downbeat (adjacency parallels). Example 10.10 shows all three types of parallels.

7. **Write interval numbers between the lines** to check for the correct use of dissonance and for parallels.

8. **Check the contour.** Make sure your counterpoint has an interesting melodic contour, rising to a single high point, ideally with a subsidiary high point as well. The line should not proceed more than an octave in a single direction.

9. **Listen.** Always sing or play your counterpoint—each line separately and the two lines together—to check your work. If it sounds wrong, it probably is. (The reverse—if it sounds right, it usually is—does not always work, but as you learn more about counterpoint, your ability to hear correct and incorrect progressions will improve.)

Try it #4

The counterpoint below incorporates some common errors in third-species writing. Start by writing the harmonic interval numbers between the lines, then circle any dissonant intervals and label their type (P, N). Identify the measure(s) where you find the following errors (for parallels, indicate the measure where they "land").

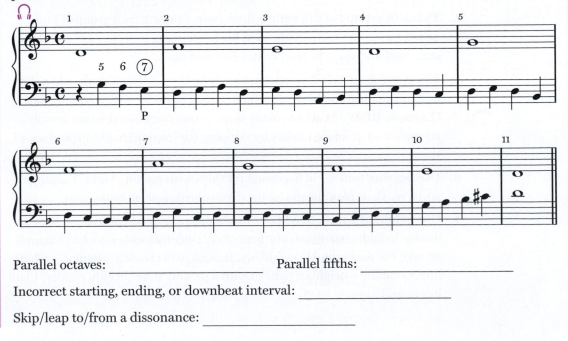

Parallel octaves: _____   Parallel fifths: _____

Incorrect starting, ending, or downbeat interval: _____

Skip/leap to/from a dissonance: _____

Inappropriate melodic interval: _____

Static line: _____

Incorrectly executed cambiata or double neighbor: _____

Rhythmic Displacement in Fourth-Species Counterpoint

In the species we have considered so far, the basic note-to-note framework has been elaborated by adding pitches to the counterpoint to create consonant or dissonant harmonic intervals and provide melodic motion. Now we learn a second general category of elaboration—rhythmic displacement—where consonant pitches are shifted in time to create dissonant harmonic intervals, which then resolve. The most common type of rhythmic displacement is the suspension, studied in **fourth species** (Example 10.12).

EXAMPLE 10.12: Cantus firmus 2 (Jeppesen) in a fourth-species setting 🎧

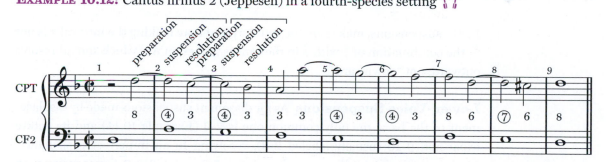

KEY CONCEPT A suspension is a rhythmic embellishment created when a consonant pitch is held over (suspended) to the first beat of the next measure, forming a harmonic dissonance until the suspended voice moves down by step. Suspensions consist of three parts (marked on Example 10.12):

- a consonant harmonic interval (the preparation) on the second half of the measure;

- the consonant pitch held over to the first half of the next measure to make an accented dissonant interval (the suspension);

- the resolution of that dissonance down by step on the second half of the measure to a consonant interval (the resolution), which may itself serve as the preparation for the next suspension.

Types of Suspensions

Upper-Voice Suspensions There are only three types of dissonant upper-voice suspensions, as labeled in Example 10.13.

🎧 **KEY CONCEPT** Suspensions are named by the numbers of the dissonant harmonic interval and its resolution. The most familiar upper-voice suspensions are 4-3 (part a) and 7-6 (part b); both resolve to imperfect consonances, and both appear in Examples 10.12 and 10.13. The 9-8 suspension (Example 10.13c) may appear in an upper voice as well, but is less satisfactory because it resolves to a perfect consonance.

EXAMPLE 10.13: Suspension types in the upper part 🎧

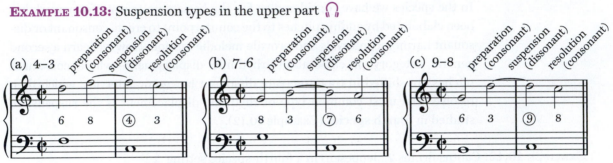

In 4-3 suspensions, make sure the counterpoint note making the interval 4 is not $\hat{7}$; the combination of $\hat{7}$ with $\hat{4}$ in the cantus makes an A4, which should resolve outward, not "downward."

Lower-Voice Suspensions As for dissonant suspensions made by displacement of the bass, the only common one is 2-3 (Example 10.14) and its octave expansion 9-10 (usually labeled 2-3), resolving to an imperfect consonance. Don't write the intervallic successions 4-5 or 7-8, or a 4-3 or 7-6 suspension with the dissonance resolving up (no matter how tempting!); these are not acceptable suspensions in the lower part.

EXAMPLE 10.14: Suspension types in the lower part (2-3) 🎧

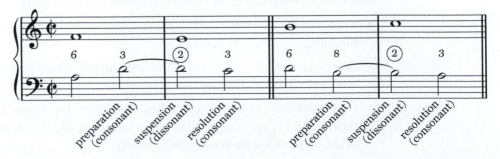

Rhythmic Character of Fourth Species

Because of these pervasive suspensions, one of the immediately recognizable aspects of fourth species is its rhythmic character: two half notes are set against a whole note (as in second species), but the second half note in most measures is tied over to the following downbeat. The parts sound in alternation, with the new cantus notes entering on the downbeat and the new counterpoint notes primarily on the upbeats. You could think of suspensions as consonant intervals of a note-to-note first species that, rather than moving to the next pitch on time, are held so that the next pitch arrives late—a rhythmic displacement. In traditional fourth-species counterpoint, it is essential to maintain the rhythmic displacement almost exclusively throughout the setting, employing suspensions as much as possible.

As in Examples 10.12 above and 10.15 below, the counterpoint line begins with a half rest to start the rhythmic alternation of the parts; and the series of ties ends in the penultimate measure, whose second half note (the leading tone) is never tied over in strict style, but resolves to the octave or unison as in previous species. This works well with stepwise, descending portions of the cantus, as in measures 7-11 of Example 10.15.

EXAMPLE 10.15: Cantus firmus 6 (Kirnberger) in a fourth-species setting

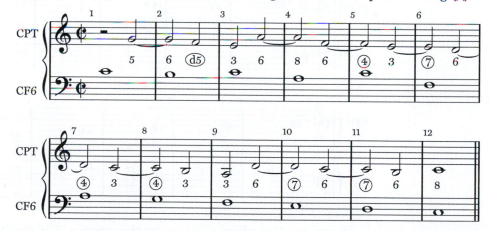

Breaking Species and Tying Consonances

Though the main objective of fourth species is to learn to write dissonant suspensions, a consonant interval may sometimes be tied over to another consonance (Example 10.15, mm. 3-4); or there may be a disruption of the series, called **breaking species** (mm. 2-3 and 8-9). Since suspensions always resolve down, fourth-species counterpoints tend to "go downhill"; a leap upward allows the suspensions to start down again. In strict style, composers break species as little as possible, but will use this technique after three suspensions in a row of the same type to make the line less repetitive. They may also break species when there is no consonance available to tie over (Example 10.15, mm. 2-3), or to set up a particular suspension figure, especially approaching the close (e.g., mm. 8-9, setting up a pair of 7-6 suspensions).

Breaking species, then, means that a short span of the exercise will be written as if in second species. The disjunct first half of the cantus in Example 10.15 makes it difficult to set measures 1-6 without breaking species somewhere. Fourth-species settings work best with stepwise, descending sections of the cantus; cantus lines with skips or leaps or ascending steps are more challenging.

Since there are fewer dissonant suspension options in the bass (only 2-3), preparing a good counterpoint when the cantus is in the upper part is challenging: such settings will require (1) consonances tied across the bar against the skips and leap in the cantus (Example 10.16, mm. 4-7), and (2) breaking species (as in mm. 1-2 and 8-9). When tying a consonance on the upbeat to a consonance on the downbeat, the downbeat consonance does not have to resolve because it is not a dissonance; it may connect by step, skip, or leap to the next consonance. Tying over a consonance is preferred to breaking species because it retains the rhythmic character of this species.

EXAMPLE 10.16: Cantus firmus 6 (Kirnberger) in a fourth-species setting 🎧

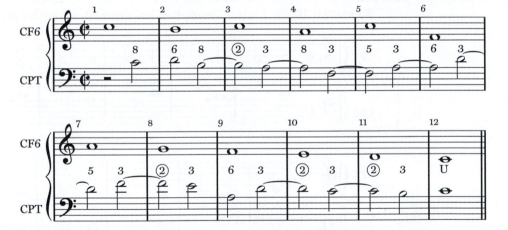

Some teachers allow a unison in this species if it results from a consonance-to-consonance tie (at either end of it) and does not fall in an area where species is broken. Although we prefer that the voices are moved wider apart to make what was a unison an octave, the choice depends on which is considered a more serious error—unison or wider spacing.

Chains of Suspensions

When the cantus features a stepwise descending line, you may want to follow one suspension in the counterpoint with another of the same type, creating a **chain of suspensions**. Such a chain is actually a rhythmic displacement of a note-to-note series of descending parallel thirds or sixths, as shown in Example 10.17. Only 4-3, 7-6, and 2-3 suspensions are used in chains, as 9-8 or 5-6 or 6-5 chains would imply parallel octaves or fifths.

EXAMPLE 10.17: Chains of suspensions

(a) Note-to-note parallel thirds and sixths 🎧

(b) Chain in the upper part 🎧

(c) Chain in the lower part 🎧

Writing Fourth-Species Counterpoint

When writing a fourth-species counterpoint, first complete the opening and closing patterns, then consider the cantus to determine where you can place dissonant suspensions. The opening harmonic interval is either a P8 or P5 when the counterpoint is in the upper voice, a P8 or PU when in the lower voice.

Although the counterpoint usually begins with a half rest followed by a half note, as we have seen, a half note followed by a half note (which is then tied over) is also allowed. The required ending is a 7-6 suspension if the counterpoint is in the upper voice, or a 2-3 (or 9-10) if in the lower voice, leading to the final whole note P8 or U; the last note in the penultimate measure is not tied over to the final measure. In minor-mode settings, raise ♭7 to make the leading tone at the cadence, as in Example 10.12.

SUMMARY

In fourth species, use dissonant suspensions as much as possible. The acceptable dissonant suspensions are 7-6, 4-3, and 9-8 when the counterpoint is in the upper part, and 2-3 when in the lower part. Include consonant suspensions or break species as necessary, for the following reasons:

- when there are skips, leaps, or ascending steps in the cantus and dissonant suspensions are not possible;

- to make a more interesting line;

- to reestablish a proper distance between the parts if they are about to cross;

- to conclude a suspension chain after three statements;

- to prevent counterpoint errors;

- to solve difficult places in the cantus where a dissonant suspension (or even any type of tie over the bar) is not available.

Try it #5

The following counterpoint is chock full of errors. Start by writing in the harmonic interval numbers, then check the suspensions. In the box above each measure, mark those that are good with a check, and those that are flawed with an X. Identify what type of error you find in each measure marked with X.

Cantus firmus 3 (Schenker) in a flawed fourth-species setting

Fifth Species and Free Counterpoint

After learning fourth species, the next step for eighteenth-century music students was to create a counterpoint with varied rhythm called **fifth species**, which may include quarter notes (from third species), half notes (second species), half notes tied over the bar (fourth species), and whole notes (first species) mixed together. The counterpoint in Example 10.18, in Dorian mode (from Fux's *Gradus ad Parnassum*), is one that eighteenth-century musicians would have known. Play through or sing it with your class, then evaluate the intervals between the voices.

EXAMPLE 10.18: An example of fifth species from *Gradus ad Parnassum* 🎧

Try it #6

Write the harmonic interval numbers between the staves of Example 10.18. Circle the number for any dissonant interval, and label any passing or neighbor tones, consonant skips, or suspensions; for now, disregard Fux's eighth notes in measure 8.

The opening and close of Fux's counterpoint are standard from fourth species, while measures 2-6 are based on third species. As is customary in fifth species, the 7-6 suspensions in measures 8-9 are "ornamented"—first by a pair of eighth notes, then by a leap away to a consonance—before the dissonance resolves; the dissonant suspension and any embellishment total a half note's duration, with the resolution on the third quarter note. In measure 8, the D5 eighth note may at first glance seem to be a neighbor tone, but that would imply an early arrival of the suspension's resolution; instead, there is a skip to a consonance from F5 to D5, filled in with a passing tone (E5). All tied notes in measures 1-7 are consonant suspensions.

Eighth notes may appear only on the second or fourth quarter note and must be approached and left by step; they usually embellish a suspension, as here. There are four places in measures 2-5 where the voices cross or touch to make a unison (Fux's guidelines allow voice crossings and unisons, although modern counterpoint guidelines do not, as they cloud the distinction between parts); dropping the entire cantus (lower part) an octave into the bass clef would solve these issues, but moves the voices farther apart than Fux preferred.

In most tonal music, unlike counterpoint exercises, melodic and rhythmic embellishments are not isolated in one voice—the species are mixed together in all the parts, a technique sometimes called "free counterpoint." The term may be misleading, though. It does not mean you can do just anything with dissonances; instead, you are free to choose where, how, and with what note values you employ them.

To conclude this chapter, we turn to a beautiful piece of sixteenth-century music—"O magnum mysterium," by Tomás Luis de Victoria. Like other works from that era, this one begins with the voices entering one at a time, each with the same melodic idea—a compositional technique called a **point of imitation**. Instead of a preexisting line or cantus firmus, these two parts are based on the same melodic idea, beginning with a distinctive P5 leap (Example 10.19). When the second part (alto) enters, making two-voice counterpoint, it has the same melodic intervals, rhythmic durations, and contour as the first part (soprano), transposed down a P5. A point of imitation may encompass only the first few notes of the melody or may include almost all of it, as here. Only as the text phrase nears the end in measures 8-9 does the imitation end. We will consider imitative counterpoint in more detail in Chapter 24.

EXAMPLE 10.19: Victoria, "O magnum mysterium," mm. 1-9 (soprano and alto parts) 🎧

Translation: O great mystery and wondrous sacrament.

Now let's consider the counterpoint. Measures 2-6 are essentially note-to-note—some notes are repeated to accommodate the text, and durations vary;

measure 7 shows 4:1 followed by 2:1, and measure 8 a 2-3 suspension, as marked on the example. Following this passage, the tenor and bass voices enter with the same counterpoint in measures 8-11, in another point of imitation transposed down an octave from the soprano part. (The opening leap of a P5 down and back up makes this melody easy to hear each time it appears.) Both upper parts now introduce new counterpoint that combines with the tenor and bass to make a four-voice texture and full triads.

Compared with Example 10.18, this counterpoint is "freer": it freely mixes the different species and a variety of durations, and includes more P8 and P5 than normally appear in species settings. And when all four parts enter, we hear full chords and harmonic progressions, topics we turn to in the next two chapters.

Did You Know?

The most famous counterpoint treatise from the seventeenth and eighteenth centuries is Johann Joseph Fux's *Gradus ad Parnassum* (*Steps to Parnassus*). Although Fux's approach was modeled on sixteenth-century music, this treatise was a "best-seller" in its day, studied by countless eighteenth-century musicians. Fux taught counterpoint beginning with note-to-note and ending with fifth species, intended to approximate the use of dissonance in real music. His examples are notated with movable C-clefs, which sometimes correspond to both parts in the treble clef or both in the bass clef, whereas we have modeled soprano/bass pairings in a treble and bass clef. When musicians refer to species counterpoint today, Fux's method is what they are talking about. Portions of *Gradus ad Parnassum* are readily available in an English translation—*The Study of Counterpoint from Johann Joseph Fux's "Gradus ad Parnassum,"* trans. Alfred Mann (New York: Norton, 1943; reprinted 1965). Read this best-seller for yourself!

TERMS YOU SHOULD KNOW

cambiata	double neighbor	neighbor tone	second species (2:1)
chains of suspensions	fifth species	passing tone	suspension
consonant skip	fourth species	preparation	third species (4:1)
diminution	metric accent	resolution	

QUESTIONS FOR REVIEW

1. Which dissonances are explored in 2:1 counterpoint?
2. What types of intervals may be used in 2:1 in the first half of the measure? in the second half?
3. How is a passing tone approached and resolved? a neighbor tone?
4. What types of embellishments are introduced in third species?
5. What types of suspensions are used in fourth species? Which appear in the upper part? in the lower part?

6. Name the three parts of a suspension.

7. Which suspensions can be used in chains? Which are not found in chains, and why aren't they?

8. What types of embellishments may be found in fifth species?

Know It? Show It!

Focus by working through the tutorials.

Learn with InQuizitive.

Apply what you've learned to complete the workbook assignments.

Diatonic Harmony and Tonicization

From Species to Chorale Style: Soprano and Bass Lines

Outline

Note-to-note counterpoint in chorale style

- Contrapuntal motion
- Chordal dissonance
- Characteristics of bass and melody lines
- Writing counterpoint with a given line

Melodic embellishment in chorale textures

- Passing tones, neighbor tones, and consonant skips
- Suspensions

Overview

In Baroque-era music and after, note-to-note counterpoint incorporates dissonances made from seventh chords and features a bass line that implies tonal harmonic progressions. Here, we learn to write tonal cadences and melodic embellishments in two-part chorale textures.

Repertoire

Johann Sebastian Bach, "Wachet auf" ("Awake," Chorale No. 197)

Traditional hymn settings

"Chartres" (fifteenth-century French melody, harmonization by Charles Wood)

"Ein feste Burg" ("A Mighty Fortress," melody by Martin Luther, 1529; harmonization by J. S. Bach)

"My Country, 'Tis of Thee" ("America") (*Thesaurus Musicus*, 1740)

"Old Hundredth" (harmonization by Louis Bourgeois, 1551)

"Rosa Mystica" (traditional melody, harmonization by Michael Praetorius, 1609)

"St. George's Windsor" (harmonization by George J. Elvey, 1858)

Note-to-Note Counterpoint in Chorale Style

Although the principles of species counterpoint underlie much of tonal music, very few pieces are written exclusively in strict style. Instead, in the Baroque and subsequent eras, the intervallic connections of species counterpoint were combined with an emerging sense of harmony and functional tonality to create tonal counterpoint.

Hymns or patriotic songs are a good place to start. While hymns are often set for four parts, pairs of voices—such as the soprano and the bass—form two-part note-to-note counterpoint: the soprano normally carries the traditional melody (which may have been written as early as the fifteenth century), and the bass line supplies the tonal foundation of the harmonic progression. In these settings, the familiar melody serves as a "cantus firmus," as it cannot be changed. Though we focus on two-voice pairs in this chapter, listen to each hymn while following the anthology score to become familiar with the four-part settings.

Eighteenth-century note-to-note counterpoint differs from strict-species style in several ways. In first-species exercises:

- The species is immediately recognizable by its whole-note durations in both parts, harking back to Renaissance settings.

- Because first species features only consonant intervals, there is usually no strong forward momentum; only at the close is there a sense of arrival.

- The voices are equal: the cantus can be the top or bottom part, and often the counterpoint is invertible (the same counterpoint works either above or below the cantus).

In contrast, in eighteenth-century style:

- The durations are normally half and quarter notes, or quarter and eighth notes.

- Pitches may be immediately repeated, adding more oblique motion, though pitch repetitions are more common within a measure than across a bar line.

- Composers include both consonant and dissonant harmonic intervals drawn from seventh chords to create forward motion.

- The voices are not equal: the lowest part—the bass line—takes on a special role as the foundation of the harmonic progressions, with the melody in the soprano; these roles are usually not invertible.

In hymn settings, don't be surprised by an occasional deviation from the species guidelines, particularly with regard to dissonance. Nevertheless, the basic principles of counterpoint, including the balance between linear and harmonic motion, are the same in both styles.

Contrapuntal Motion

In Example 11.1, note-to-note counterpoint from "St. George's Windsor," each bass note corresponds to a single soprano note in the same rhythm—making a **homorhythmic** texture, meaning "same rhythm" in all parts. As in first-species counterpoint, the intervals are a mix of perfect and imperfect consonances, the voices employ mostly contrary motion (C), and the last two intervals are 6 and 8. Unlike in strict style, however, notes are repeated in measures 1 and 3 (marked R) and across the bar line in measures 2–3, resulting from repeated notes in the existing hymn melody.

EXAMPLE 11.1: "St. George's Windsor," mm. 1–4 (soprano/bass)

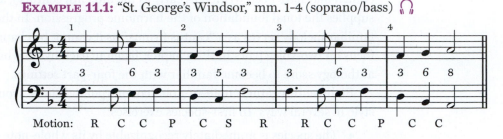

Motion: R   C   C   P   C   S   R   R   C   C   P   C   C

Hymns feature oblique motion more often than strict style does, to accommodate repeated notes in the melody or bass, as in Example 11.2. This example also shows a strong tonal cadence typical of eighteenth-century style: scale degrees $\hat{5}$–$\hat{1}$ in the bass and $\hat{7}$–$\hat{1}$ in the soprano.

EXAMPLE 11.2: "My Country, 'Tis of Thee," mm. 1–6 (soprano/bass)

Motion: O

Try it #1

In the blanks below Example 11.2, label the motion between each pair of harmonic intervals as C (contrary), O (oblique), P (parallel), S (similar), or R (repetition).

KEY CONCEPT In tonal music, a unit of musical thought that ends with a point of closure or repose is called a **phrase.** The combination of melodic, harmonic, and rhythmic elements that create a sense of closure at the end of a phrase is called a **cadence.**

The bass $\hat{5}$-$\hat{1}$ implies harmonic motion from root-position V to I. When combined with either of the usual upper-voice closing gestures from strict species, $\hat{2}$-$\hat{1}$ or $\hat{7}$-$\hat{1}$, this motion represents the strongest type of tonal cadence (Example 11.3).

EXAMPLE 11.3: Cadences from species counterpoint and eighteenth-century style

A slightly different type of cadence is seen in the first phrase of "Old Hundredth" (Example 11.4). Again there is strong $\hat{5}$-$\hat{1}$ bass motion—implying root position V–I in G major—but $\hat{2}$-$\hat{3}$ in the soprano (we will return to such cadence types later in the chapter).

EXAMPLE 11.4: "Old Hundredth," mm. 1-3

SUMMARY

Note-to-note counterpoint in eighteenth-century style generally follows the conventions of species counterpoint in regard to contrapuntal motion and the connection of consonant intervals. Differences include

- more oblique motion, to accommodate repeated notes in a chorale melody;
- new cadence intervals;
- a bass that implies stronger harmonic motion.

Chordal Dissonance

In strict counterpoint, dissonant harmonic intervals are created by melodic embellishments in second and third species and by rhythmic displacement in fourth species. Now we meet an additional type of dissonant interval that is essential to eighteenth-century style: **chordal dissonance**, arising from seventh chords.

KEY CONCEPT Although consonant harmonic intervals in eighteenth-century style may move either to another consonance or to a dissonance, dissonant harmonic intervals are treated more carefully. They are traditionally approached by step in one or both voices, and must resolve to a consonant interval.

Example 11.5 shows the most significant source of chordal dissonances: the dominant seventh chord. The root and seventh of this chord form a m7 and its inversion (M2), while the third and seventh form a d5 and its inversion (A4).

EXAMPLE 11.5: Dissonant intervals of the V7 chord

(a) Harmonic dissonances

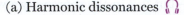

(b) Resolutions (D = dissonant; C = consonant)

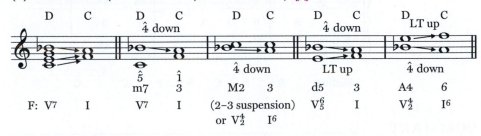

As shown in part (b), the root and seventh normally resolve in to a third to imply dominant-tonic motion. Its inversion, the M2, also resolves to a third, though we don't usually see this in two-voice counterpoint except as a 2-3 bass suspension. When the dissonant tritone between the third and seventh of the chord is spelled as a d5, it resolves in to a third; when spelled as an A4, it resolves out to a sixth. These are the same resolutions employed in third-species counterpoint; in tonal harmonic contexts, they allow $\hat{7}$ to move properly up to $\hat{1}$, and $\hat{4}$ (the chordal seventh) to resolve down. As was also the case in third species, this resolution often occurs over a bar line, from a relatively weak metrical position to a strong one.

KEY CONCEPT In the dominant seventh harmony, the chordal seventh ($\hat{4}$) and the leading tone ($\hat{7}$) are **tendency tones**. Always resolve the chordal seventh down ($\hat{4}$ to $\hat{3}$) and the leading tone up ($\hat{7}$ to $\hat{1}$).

You can see the dominant seventh intervals in context in Example 11.6. Part (b) gives the full harmonic setting, with the two A4 intervals (from mm. 9 and 11) resolving outward to a sixth: the seventh of the chord moves down, and the third (the leading tone of the key, LT) moves up. When the seventh is in the bass, as here, the chord is a $^4_2$ inversion, and the implied harmonies are V$^4_2$ to I^6. The outer-voice A4 and d5 usually fall in the middle of a phrase instead of at the end, where an implied root-position V7-I provides a stronger cadence (not shown here). Part (c) summarizes the voice-leading for these chords.

EXAMPLE 11.6: "St. George's Windsor," mm. 9–12 (soprano and bass)

(a) Soprano-bass pair

(b) Full SATB context

(c) Interval resolutions

KEY CONCEPT The dissonant harmonic intervals of a dominant seventh chord are resolved as follows:

DISSONANT INTERVAL	MOVES . . .	CHORDS IMPLIED
m7	In to a third with a leap from $\hat{5}$ to $\hat{1}$ in the bass.	V^7 to I
d5	In by contrary motion to a third, with $\hat{7}$ resolving up to $\hat{1}$ in the bass.	V^6_5 to I
A4	Out by contrary motion to a sixth, with the chordal seventh resolving down a third in the bass ($\hat{4}$ to $\hat{3}$).	V^4_2 to I^6

Try it #2

Identify and resolve the following chordal dissonances. Label each interval and circle the dissonant one, then write the implied harmonies (tonic or dominant) under the staff, providing both the Roman numeral and inversion.

Characteristics of Bass and Melody Lines

In eighteenth-century style, the melody and bass lines should make good two-voice counterpoint, but each line also conveys a tonal function, especially at the beginning and end of a phrase.

KEY CONCEPT Scale degrees chosen for the melody and bass line imply particular harmonies: V or V^7 ($\hat{5}$, $\hat{7}$, $\hat{2}$, and $\hat{4}$) and I ($\hat{1}$ and $\hat{3}$).

Ending the Counterpoint Typical bass lines implying tonic (I or i) and dominant (V or V7) harmonies are given in Example 11.7 in D major and D minor. These are not all equally conclusive or strong, and some connections make better phrase endings than others. The bass lines in part (a) can all be used as a final cadence; those in part (b) are more often found within a phrase, but in some styles of music may appear at the end as well, making a less conclusive cadence. The patterns in part (c) are used to end a phrase on an implied V chord, making an inconclusive cadence. Example 11.8 shows bass lines for conclusive cadences in three hymns.

EXAMPLE 11.7: Bass lines implying V(7) and I or i in D major and D minor

(a) Conclusive

(b) Less conclusive

(c) Inconclusive: Ending on the dominant

EXAMPLE 11.8: Hymn bass lines

(a) "St. George's Windsor," mm. 1–2

(b) "Old Hundredth," mm. 1–3

(c) "Rosa Mystica," mm. 1–4

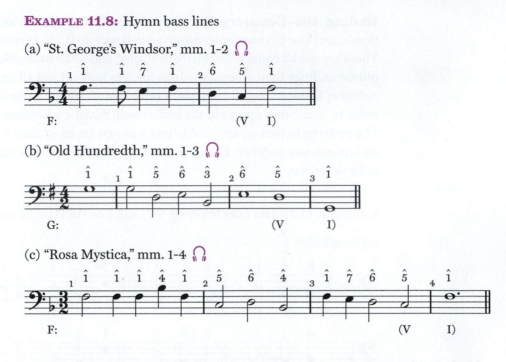

Remember that in minor keys, the dominant harmony (V or V7) includes the leading tone; when the bass line moves from $\hat{7}$ to $\hat{1}$, write the correct accidental for the leading tone. If the bass line ascends by step from $\hat{5}$ up to $\hat{1}$, use the ascending melodic minor ($\hat{6}$ and $\hat{7}$); if it descends from $\hat{1}$ down to $\hat{5}$, use the descending form of melodic minor ($\flat\hat{7}$ and $\flat\hat{6}$).

SUMMARY

Typical closing scale-degree patterns for bass lines:

- Conclusive: $\hat{5}$-$\hat{1}$, usually approached by $\hat{1}$, $\hat{2}$, $\hat{4}$, $\hat{6}$, or $\flat\hat{6}$ in minor (Example 11.7a)

- Less conclusive, used mid-phrase or as a close in some styles: $\hat{7}$-$\hat{1}$, usually approached by $\hat{1}$, $\hat{6}$, or $\hat{5}$ (part b)

- Inconclusive, ending with $\hat{5}$: usually approached by $\hat{1}$, $\hat{4}$, $\hat{6}$, or $\flat\hat{6}$ in minor (part c)

The soprano line is normally more conjunct than the bass, but it, too, contributes to the cadence at the end of a phrase. While the strongest cadences are made from $\hat{2}$-$\hat{1}$ or $\hat{7}$-$\hat{1}$ in the melody and $\hat{5}$-$\hat{1}$ in the bass, melodies also may close on $\hat{3}$ (or $\flat\hat{3}$) for a less conclusive ending on the tonic, or on $\hat{5}$, $\hat{2}$, or $\hat{7}$ for inconclusive endings on the dominant harmony, as in Example 11.9.

EXAMPLE 11.9: Melodic cadential patterns in D major and D minor

(a) Conclusive

(b) Less conclusive

(c) Inconclusive: Ending on V

SUMMARY

Typical closing scale-degree patterns for soprano lines in major keys (substitute ♭$\hat{3}$ in minor):

- Conclusive, ending on $\hat{1}$: $\hat{3}$-$\hat{2}$-$\hat{1}$, $\hat{2}$-$\hat{7}$-$\hat{1}$, $\hat{6}$-$\hat{7}$-$\hat{1}$, $\hat{2}$-$\hat{2}$-$\hat{1}$ (Example 11.9a).
- Less conclusive, ending on $\hat{3}$: $\hat{5}$-$\hat{4}$-$\hat{3}$, $\hat{2}$-$\hat{3}$ (part b).
- Inconclusive, ending on $\hat{5}$, $\hat{2}$, or $\hat{7}$: $\hat{6}$-$\hat{5}$ (♭$\hat{6}$-$\hat{5}$ in minor), $\hat{4}$-$\hat{3}$-$\hat{2}$, $\hat{2}$-$\hat{1}$-$\hat{7}$ (part c).

Example 11.10 summarizes common root-position cadential patterns in two voices: part (a) shows the strongest cadence, $\hat{2}$-$\hat{1}$ in the soprano against $\hat{5}$-$\hat{1}$ in the bass, while part (b) substitutes $\hat{7}$-$\hat{1}$ in the melody. Parts (c) and (d) illustrate two weaker endings, $\hat{5}$ to $\hat{1}$ in the bass accompanied by $\hat{4}$-$\hat{3}$ or $\hat{2}$-$\hat{3}$ in the melody. Parts (e) and (f) show familiar cadences from strict species, also used in tonal music within a phrase and at weak cadences in some styles. All these cadences are common in minor keys as well; in (b), (e), and (f), F would be raised to F♯ to make the leading tone.

EXAMPLE 11.10: Cadences in two voices 🎧

Look now at the final hymn cadences in Example 11.11 to see how their soprano-bass pairs imply V(7) and I. In each, the melodic notes are $\hat{3}$-$\hat{2}$-$\hat{1}$, accompanied by $\hat{5}$-$\hat{5}$-$\hat{1}$ in the bass, making the harmonic intervals 6-5-8.

EXAMPLE 11.11: Final cadences (soprano and bass)

(a) "Old Hundredth," mm. 11-12 🎧

(b) "St. George's Windsor," m. 16 🎧

(c) "My Country," mm. 13-14 🎧

Try it #3

In the examples below, label (1) scale-degree numbers for each note (above the melody and below the bass); (2) harmonic intervals between the parts; and (3) Roman numerals and figures for the implied chords, in the blanks underneath.

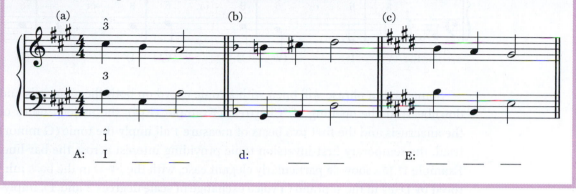

A: I ___ ___ ___   d: ___ ___ ___   E: ___ ___ ___

Opening the Counterpoint Melodic openings are more varied than cadences. A tonal melody often begins on î or ê, implying a tonic harmony, as in Example 11.12a–c. Less common are soprano-bass pairings of ĵ and î, or ĵ and ê, because the harmony is ambiguous: the implied triad could be major or minor (part d); or the notes could be the third and fifth of a major chord (D major), or the root and third of a minor chord (F♯ minor, part e).

EXAMPLE 11.12: Opening intervals implying tonic harmony

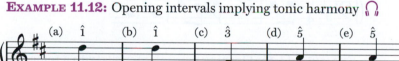

In pieces that begin with an anacrusis, the anacrusis usually implies the dominant, while the first downbeat interval establishes the tonic harmony. Some common settings are shown in Example 11.13. These parts could be exchanged: for example, the B♭–E♭ (ĵ–î) of part (a) could be in the bass, with B♭–G (ĵ–ê) in the soprano.

EXAMPLE 11.13: Opening intervals with an anacrusis

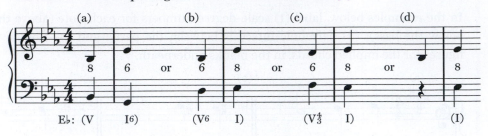

Sometimes a phrase will open with a tonic chord on both the anacrusis and downbeat; at the opening of "Chartres" (Example 11.14), the melody notes of the anacrusis and the first two beats of measure 1 all imply the tonic (G minor) triad, the temporary first-inversion tonic providing interest across the bar line. Example 11.15a shows a particularly elegant case, with the F♯–D in the bass mirrored by D–F♯ in the soprano (a voice exchange of scale degrees $\hat{3}$ and $\hat{1}$), implying I⁶–I. In parts (b) and (c), the anacrusis is ambiguous, with the third and fifth of the tonic triad in (b) and only the root in (c); but the arrival of the second interval clarifies that each anacrusis implies the tonic chord.

EXAMPLE 11.14: "Chartres," mm. 1-2 (soprano and bass) with tonic anacrusis

EXAMPLE 11.15: Opening pairs of intervals with a tonic anacrusis

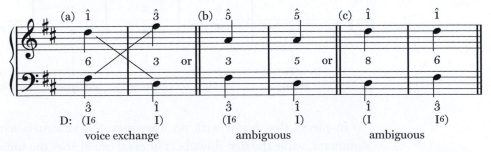

Writing Counterpoint with a Given Line

Composers in the eighteenth century often wrote counterpoint for a preexisting soprano or bass line, making new settings of hymn or chorale melodies or reusing a standard bass line as the starting point for creating a new melody. Follow this general procedure to write your own settings with a given melody or bass line.

1. Start by identifying the key and mode, then write the scale degree over each note. Sing or play the given line.

2. Look at the beginning and end of the given line to determine where it implies a I or V(7) chord. Then choose scale degrees for the contrapuntal line that match the implied harmonies at the beginning and make an appropriate cadence at the end. Fill in the first few and last few notes, and write in the intervals and implied Roman numerals.

3. Examine the shape of the middle portion of the given part. Where there are several steps in a row, plan to include a skip or leap in your line; where there are skips or leaps, write steps in your line.

4. Think about the contour of the given line, and how you want the contour of your melody to balance it. Choose a possible high point, with an interval that is consonant with the given line's note. Sketch out a general shape for your line.

5. Begin filling in the middle, considering both the harmonic intervals between the two parts and the shape of your line. Label the intervals, and check every perfect interval for parallels and for the type of approach (e.g., contrary or oblique motion, or similar motion with stepwise soprano). For now, you do not need to be concerned about the harmonic implications of the middle other than those implying tonic or dominant harmonies. Revise as necessary to make good contrapuntal and melodic sense.

KEY CONCEPT Always check the counterpoint you have written, to make sure it

- opens with either an implied tonic harmony or a V-I anacrusis;
- closes with one of the standard types of cadences;
- forms consonant harmonic intervals or chordal dissonances (from V7) with the given line;
- resolves tendency tones (from V7) correctly;
- includes both perfect and imperfect consonances, with more of the latter;
- avoids parallel octaves and fifths (by approaching perfect consonances with contrary motion, similar motion with a stepwise upper line, or oblique motion);
- shows a pleasing overall contour that coordinates well with the shape of the given line.

Examine the opening and closing patterns in Example 11.16, and consider how you would write a well-balanced melody, following the guidelines above. The bass line begins with an anacrusis ($\hat{5}$–$\hat{1}$ in D minor) and ends with $\hat{5}$–$\hat{5}$–$\hat{1}$.

EXAMPLE 11.16: A typical bass line in eighteenth-century style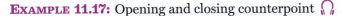

Example 11.17 shows one possible setting: a $\hat{5}$–♭$\hat{3}$ opening and $\hat{5}$–$\hat{4}$–♭$\hat{3}$ conclusion. In measure 1, the bass line's $\hat{1}$–$\hat{7}$–$\hat{1}$ is set in contrary motion with ♭$\hat{3}$–$\hat{4}$–♭$\hat{3}$ to imply a i–V$^6_5$–i progression; and the dissonant d5 resolves correctly to a third.

EXAMPLE 11.17: Opening and closing counterpoint

Starting on beat 3 of measure 1, the bass's D3–E3–F3 could be set with a voice exchange F4–E4–D4 in the soprano to make the pattern 3-8-6 (Example 11.18)—a strong contrapuntal gesture because it employs both imperfect and perfect consonances, and approaches and leaves the P8 stepwise in contrary motion.

EXAMPLE 11.18: A possible note-to-note setting

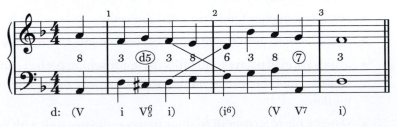

We have set the bass-line step F3–G3 in measure 2 with an upward leap, D4 to B♭4, adding interest to the melody and providing a distinctive high point. The leap is both approached and left by steps in the opposite direction. Overall, then, the contour of the soprano melody provides contrary motion, and a good balance, with the bass.

Try it #4

Example 11.18 is only one possible setting for this bass line; try another option using the hints below. Refer to the guidelines above, and be sure to sing or play through your counterpoint when complete. 🎧

Hints: The cadence may be set with intervals 3-3-8, 3-5-8, or 5-3-8 (don't forget to use the leading tone C♯). Explore various opening intervals: 3-8 (again, with C♯), 5-3, or 8-5. The bass's C♯3-D3-E3 in measure 1 may be set with a voice exchange, E4-D4-C♯4 (resolving to D in m. 2), as can the F3-G3-A3 in measure 2.

Melodic Embellishment in Chorale Textures

Passing Tones, Neighbor Tones, and Consonant Skips

Melodic embellishments, particularly unaccented passing and neighbor tones and consonant skips, are prevalent in eighteenth-century two-voice counterpoint. But unlike species style, these embellishments may appear in different voices on different beats, creating rhythmic variety between the two lines. For an example, listen to the first phrase of "Ein feste Burg" (Example 11.19); pay close attention to any passing tones.

EXAMPLE 11.19: Bach, "Ein feste Burg," mm. 1-4 (soprano and bass) 🎧

KEY CONCEPT   Three types of passing tones are permitted in eighteenth-century style: the dissonant passing tone in either an unaccented or accented position, and the unaccented consonant passing tone. (It is possible to have two dissonant passing tones in a row, one unaccented and one accented.) The dissonant unaccented passing tone is by far the most common.

The passing tones labeled in Example 11.19 are dissonant unaccented (anacrusis), dissonant accented (m. 1), and consonant (m. 3). In the places where both voices move together rhythmically, on beats with no embellishments, the guidelines of 1:1 counterpoint apply. If we eliminate the second note of each pair of eighth notes, for example, and adjust for accented passing tones (leave out the bass's accented passing tone A3 in m. 1 and keep the G3), the principles of good counterpoint are followed from beat to beat.

Try it #5

In Example 11.19, the intervals between the voices are labeled (dissonant intervals are circled), along with three passing tones. Which of the remaining offbeat eighth notes also make dissonant passing tones? Circle and label them.

Both consonant and dissonant neighbor tones are also typical embellishments in this style, as are consonant skips. Listen to the soprano and bass lines of Bach's "Wachet auf," given in Example 11.20.

EXAMPLE 11.20: Bach, "Wachet auf," mm. 32–36 (soprano and bass)

In measure 33, the bass-line F3 on beat 2 is a dissonant neighbor tone. As in species style, it appears in an unaccented position and moves away from and returns to a consonance by step: 6-7-3. Where melody and bass lines imply harmonic progressions, a consonant skip like that on beat 4 may also be referred to as a **chordal skip** if it spans members of the same implied harmony (here, E♭ major).

Suspensions

Unlike fourth species, suspensions in eighteenth-century counterpoint are mixed with other types of embellishments or reserved to highlight a cadence. The available dissonant suspensions are the same as in strict style: 4-3, 7-6, and 9-8 in the upper part and 2-3 (or 9-10) in the lower. For an example, listen to the first part of "Rosa Mystica" (soprano and bass lines are shown in Example 11.21), and focus on the intervals approaching the cadence in measures 3-4.

EXAMPLE 11.21: "Rosa Mystica," mm. 1-4 (soprano and bass)

In eighteenth-century style, suspensions may be connected to their consonant preparation by a tie, or by a longer duration. In measure 3, for example, the half notes G4 and F4 replace tied quarter notes for the preparation and suspension components of this 4-3 chain. Since this example is primarily note-to-note, the rhythmic interest and dissonance provided by the suspensions prove even more striking.

While we have focused primarily on soprano and bass voices in this chapter, the principles of good counterpoint also apply between the bass and each of the upper parts. In Example 11.22, for instance, the alto and bass parts from "Wachet auf," the texture is primarily 2:1, with dissonant passing tones in measures 8 and 9 (including two in a row), and a neighbor tone in measure 7. Here, the cadence is approached through a suspension chain in measure 10; when the suspended note is not tied to its preparation (the C5 in mm. 9-10), the dissonance figure is called a **rearticulated suspension**.

EXAMPLE 11.22: Bach, "Wachet auf," mm. 6-11 (alto and bass)

As in Examples 11.21 and 11.22, suspensions must arrive *on* the beat. They normally resolve on the following beat, but may also resolve on the unaccented part of the same beat. In performance, musicians tend to *crescendo* slightly into the accented dissonance and pull away from the resolution; try this (subtly!) for a more expressive performance.

KEY CONCEPT Suspensions in eighteenth-century style, like those in strict style, consist of three parts:

(1) a consonance (the preparation), which is held over to the next beat to make

(2) an accented dissonance (the suspension), which then resolves down by step to

(3) a consonance (the resolution).

The preparation may be connected to the suspension by a tie as in strict style; the preparation and suspension may be a single note of longer duration if they are in the same measure; or the tie may be missing altogether for a rearticulated suspension. Although the suspension must fall on an accented note (on the beat), the preparation and resolution may fall on the beat or offbeat.

Recognizing and labeling harmonic patterns in phrase openings and cadences, as we have done in this chapter, is the first step in learning music analysis. Be sure to identify melodic embellishments—passing tones, neighbor tones, consonant skips—and suspensions as well: they will help you understand other elements of the counterpoint.

SUMMARY

When writing eighteenth-century 2:1 counterpoint:

1. Continue to follow the guidelines for 1:1 counterpoint with respect to types of motion (contrary, similar, oblique, and parallel) and principles of good melodic writing. Phrase beginnings and endings will imply tonic and dominant (seventh) harmonies.

2. Incorporate chordal skips, dissonant passing tones, and neighbor tones on the offbeats, and occasionally passing and neighbor tones on the beat.

3. Treat the P4 as a dissonance—as a passing or neighbor tone or in a 4-3 suspension.

4. Avoid similar motion into perfect intervals unless the upper voice moves by step.

5. Avoid parallel perfect consonances (P5-P5, P8-P8) from offbeat to beat or on consecutive beats.

6. Occasionally include dissonant suspensions, especially approaching a cadence.

Did You Know?

The melodies of hymns were often composed long before the familiar SATB settings that are sung now; they also appear with different harmonizations and texts appropriate to different occasions. For example, the tune "Chartres" is a fifteenth-century French melody, but the four-part harmonization included here is by Irish composer Charles Wood, written in the nineteenth century. Our harmonization of "Old Hundredth" is by Louis Bourgeois, from the sixteenth century; one text that is often sung with this melody today is the "Doxology." The melody "St. George's Windsor," here in a nineteenth-century harmonization by George J. Elvey, is associated in the United States with the Thanksgiving hymn "Come, ye thankful people, come." These harmonizations come from the *Episcopal Hymnal* of 1940.

TERMS YOU SHOULD KNOW

accented passing tone	chordal dissonance	homorhythmic
cadence	chordal skip	rearticulated suspension
		phrase

QUESTIONS FOR REVIEW

1. What are some differences between strict first-species counterpoint and note-to-note eighteenth-century counterpoint?
2. What dissonant intervals are components of a dominant seventh chord? How should each of these dissonances resolve?
3. What types of motion are allowed when approaching a perfect interval?
4. What are typical soprano-bass patterns for openings with an anacrusis?
5. What types of conclusive cadences are used in two-part eighteenth-century style? What are the characteristic scale degrees in each part?
6. What is different about the use of passing tones, neighbor tones, and suspensions in eighteenth-century style as opposed to species style?
7. What steps should you follow to harmonize a melody in eighteenth-century style?

Know It? Show It!

Focus by working through the tutorials.

Learn with InQuizitive.

Apply what you've learned to complete the workbook assignments.

The Basic Phrase in SATB Style

Outline

The basic phrase
- Defining the phrase model: T–D–T
- Establishing the tonic area
- Cadential area and cadence types

The notation of four-part harmony
- Writing for voices: SATB

Connecting the dominant and tonic areas
- Resolving the leading tone in V and V^6
- Perfect consonances

Melody and accompaniment
- Writing for keyboard
- Harmonizing a melody
- Creating an accompaniment

Overview

This chapter introduces the basic phrase— the harmonic foundation for most tonal music, from short phrases to entire movements. We arrange its harmonic pillars, I and V, in SATB and keyboard styles, and harmonize a melody with keyboard accompaniment.

Repertoire

Johann Sebastian Bach
  "Ach Gott, vom Himmel sieh' darein" ("O God, Look Down on Us from Heaven," Chorale No. 253)
  "Wachet auf" ("Awake," Chorale No. 197)

Ludwig van Beethoven
  Piano Sonata in D Minor, Op. 31, No. 2 (*Tempest*), mvt. 3
  Sonatina in F Major, Op. Posth., mvt. 2

Muzio Clementi, Sonatina in C Major, Op. 36, No. 1, mvt. 1

"Clementine" (folk tune)

Joseph Haydn, Piano Sonata No. 9 in F Major, Scherzo

"Merrily We Roll Along"

Wolfgang Amadeus Mozart, Piano Sonata in C Major, K. 545, mvt. 1

"My Country, 'Tis of Thee"

The Basic Phrase

A **phrase**, as we learned in Chapter 11, is a basic unit of musical thought, and its end is marked by a cadence: the harmonic, melodic, and rhythmic features that make a phrase sound like a discrete thought. Phrases may end conclusively (like a sentence punctuated with a period) or inconclusively (like a clause punctuated with a comma or semicolon).

Listen to the Haydn Scherzo and Clementi Sonatina excerpts in Examples 12.1 and 12.2. The Haydn passage consists of two complete four-measure phrases, the Clementi excerpt just one phrase.

KEY CONCEPT In Classical-era compositions, phrases are typically four or eight measures long. Phrases of equal duration tend to follow one another in succession: 4 + 4 or 8 + 8. This regularity differentiates Classical from Baroque style, where lengths frequently differ from phrase to phrase.

EXAMPLE 12.1: Haydn, Piano Sonata No. 9 in F Major, Scherzo, mm. 1-8 🎧

EXAMPLE 12.2: Clementi, Sonatina in C Major, mvt. 1, mm. 1-4 🎧

Which of the Haydn and Clementi phrases sounds most conclusive (as a complete musical thought) and which the least conclusive (as though the music must continue)? To answer this question, listen for the melodic scale degree with which each phrase ends, as well as its harmonic support. Conclusive cadences, like the final cadence of the Haydn excerpt, sound finished. They generally end on $\hat{1}$ (here, F) in both the soprano and bass. In addition, the bass motion from $\hat{5}$ to $\hat{1}$ (C to F) provides strong closure. While the first cadence, in measures 3–4, sounds *somewhat* conclusive—it ends with $\hat{5}$ to $\hat{1}$ in the bass—it is weaker than the final cadence because its soprano ends on $\hat{3}$ (A) rather than $\hat{1}$ (F). The cadence in Example 12.2 (Clementi) sounds the most inconclusive, as though the music needs to continue; it does not end with $\hat{1}$ in either the soprano or the bass.

Recognizing conclusive and inconclusive phrase types can help you shape a musical performance—by using expressive timing techniques (rubato), for example, to emphasize the arrival on the tonic in a conclusive phrase.

Defining the Phrase Model: T–D–T

Conclusive phrases include at least three tonal areas, which form the harmonic structure of the **basic phrase**: an opening tonic area (T), a dominant area (D), and tonic closure (T) at the cadence (these areas are marked in Examples 12.1 and 12.2 as a lower analytical layer). The T–D–T basic phrase governs both large- and small-scale harmonic motion in much tonal music. Inconclusive phrases like the one in Example 12.2 begin with the tonic area and then cadence in the dominant area, T–D, rather than completing the full pattern.

KEY CONCEPT In two-level analyses, the top level gives Roman numerals for each chord. The lower level supplies the **contextual analysis**—indicating how these harmonies function within the basic phrase model.

Establishing the Tonic Area

The tonic area at the beginning of the basic phrase establishes a stable home base. Typically, a root-position tonic triad begins the phrase, then the tonic area is expanded by

- repeating or arpeggiating the tonic triad,
- combining root-position and inverted tonic triads, or
- adding passing tones and/or neighbor tones between chord members.

Both Examples 12.1 and 12.2 feature arpeggiation of the tonic and passing tones to extend the tonic area. So does Example 12.3, from a Beethoven sonata.

EXAMPLE 12.3: Beethoven, *Tempest* Sonata, mvt. 3, mm. 1-3

Example 12.4, from Bach's setting of a chorale melody, expands the tonic by moving to first inversion and back. In writing the analysis, you need not repeat the Roman numeral I in measure 33, but may simply show the change in inversion. Passing and neighbor tones in parallel tenths between the bass and alto voices add contrapuntal interest.

EXAMPLE 12.4: Bach, "Wachet auf," mm. 32-33

At the beginning of a basic phrase, dominant chords can also be used to expand the tonic area in one or more of these contexts:

- on weak beats (e.g., I–V–I, with V on the weak beat);
- in inversion, which weakens their harmonic strength;
- with bass-line passing or neighboring motion between two tonic triads; or
- as an anacrusis to the opening tonic triad.

Example 12.5 shows each of these contexts. Bach's chorale begins with a weak-beat dominant anacrusis; in the contextual analysis, delay the T label until the arrival of the tonic triad. With its tendency tones (the leading tone and chordal seventh), this chord actually has the effect of strengthening the initial tonic. In measures 5–6, each dominant chord appears in inversion; the first on a weak beat and in a passing context (P) and the second in a neighboring context (N). Both chords expand the tonic area until the cadence on the dominant—marked here by a **fermata**, or pause (⌢).

EXAMPLE 12.5: Bach, "Ach Gott, vom Himmel sieh' darein," mm. 5-6

g: V   i   V$^6_4$ i^6 i   V$^6_5$ i   V
            (P)   (N)

Contextual: T —————————————————————————————————— D

SUMMARY

To complete a contextual analysis:

- First write a complete first-level Roman numeral analysis below the score.

- Below the opening tonic chord, write T; no label is needed for a dominant anacrusis, if present.

- Find the cadence: if the phrase ends with V-I, label the concluding chords as D–T. If it ends on V, mark the final chord as D.

- Now consider how the tonic area is expanded: look for weak-beat root-position V chords, inverted V chords, or passing motion between inversions of I. Draw a line from the initial T as long as the tonic area continues.

Cadential Area and Cadence Types

Look back at the two phrases from Haydn's sonata in Example 12.1: both end with V7-I cadences, but (as is usual in paired phrases) the first cadence is weaker than the more conclusive second.

Authentic Cadences The cadential area of a T-D-T phrase is its dominant-to-tonic ending. Two types of cadences may conclude such phrases, both known as authentic cadences.

KEY CONCEPT An authentic cadence (AC) is formed when V moves to I to end a phrase. It is most definitive when the harmonies are in root position and the soprano line moves from $\hat{7}$ to $\hat{1}$ or $\hat{2}$ to $\hat{1}$ (Example 12.6a and b), making a **perfect authentic cadence** (PAC). An **imperfect authentic cadence** (IAC) occurs when one of these factors is weakened; the most common IAC ends with $\hat{4}$–$\hat{3}$ in the soprano (part c).

"Authentic" refers to the progression V–I, and "perfect" indicates that the soprano and bass are in their strongest positions: root-position harmonies ending with $\hat{1}$ in the soprano. Because motion between root-position V or V7 and I has such a pronounced cadential sound, this chord sequence is often reserved for final cadences and used less often mid-phrase, where inverted dominant harmonies help expand the tonic area.

EXAMPLE 12.6: Authentic cadence types in four voices

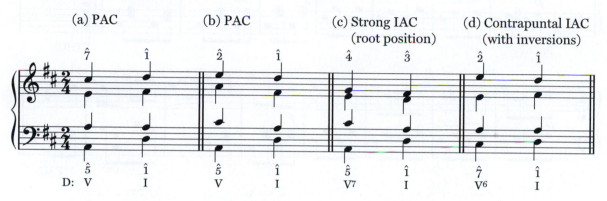

A strong IAC, as in part (c), makes a less conclusive cadence than a PAC would; it appears in a wide variety of styles of music at locations where a less conclusive cadence is desirable. The progression V6 to I in part (d), with an inverted dominant harmony, often appears earlier within a phrase as part of the initial tonic (T) area. If it comes at the end of a phrase, we call it a **contrapuntal IAC**. If you are considering labeling a cadence with an inverted dominant harmony, first determine whether this is a true phrase ending or an expansion of the tonic area. A true phrase ending requires more contextual support in the form of other features (slowing down, longer note values, end of a line of text).

Half Cadence   An inconclusive cadence that ends on V, as in Example 12.2 or 12.5, is called a **half cadence** (HC). Here the basic phrase model is incomplete or interrupted (T–D); the phrase ends in the dominant area without moving on to the tonic.

KEY CONCEPT Authentic cadences are defined by two chords (V–I), but half cadences are identified only by their final chord; the chord that precedes the V could be one of several possibilities. Half cadences usually end on a root-position dominant triad, and often (though not always) feature $\hat{2}$ in the soprano. Although not common in Baroque or Classical styles, a half cadence ending on V7 is also a possibility, especially in folk or popular styles.

Half cadences often function like a comma in a sentence, where an inconclusive phrase ending (HC) is followed by a conclusive one (AC), as in Example 12.7.

EXAMPLE 12.7: Beethoven, Sonatina in F Major, mvt. 2, mm. 1-8

Listen to these two phrases. At measure 8, the melody pauses briefly on an eighth-note $\hat{2}$ (G5) before launching into a sixteenth-note flourish that links to phrase 2; for its part, the harmony comes to rest on a quarter-note V chord. Measure 9 initiates a new phrase, with music almost identical to measure 1. Therefore, although V (m. 8) does move on to I (in m. 9), it does not create an authentic cadence here—rather, harmonic, melodic, and rhythmic factors divide the music into two distinct eight-measure phrases, each with its own cadence: a HC at measure 8 and a PAC at measure 16.

SUMMARY

The musical role of a phrase is defined in part by its cadence.

- A perfect authentic cadence (PAC) ends with root-position V-I and the melody ending $\hat{2}$-$\hat{1}$ or $\hat{7}$-$\hat{1}$; this is the strongest phrase ending.

- An imperfect authentic cadence (IAC) also ends with V-I, but the melody ends on $\hat{3}$ or $\hat{5}$ for a less conclusive phrase ending. A strong IAC has root-position harmonies; a contrapuntal IAC includes inversions.

- A half cadence (HC) ends on V, with the melody often on $\hat{2}$; an inconclusive phrase ending.

Try it #1

A. Listen to an excerpt from Brahms's *Variations on a Theme by Haydn*. Identify the measure numbers of one HC and one PAC. Analyze the cadential harmonies with Roman numerals.

HC: _____   PAC: _____

B. How do Brahms's phrase lengths differ from the Classical-era works we have studied so far?

The Notation of Four-Part Harmony

In Chapter 11, we saw how familiar principles of two-voice species counterpoint may be found in eighteenth-century style, specifically in the outer voices of hymns. We turn now to writing in four voices, or **SATB** style (so named from the voices—high to low—soprano, alto, tenor, bass). In SATB settings, individual members of triads and seventh chords are assigned to particular octaves; these chords, as we have seen, are not always in root position but are voiced in different inversions to create a smooth bass melody.

Writing for Voices: SATB

Listen to "My Country, 'Tis of Thee" (Example 12.8), and focus on the spacing and registers (highness or lowness) that characterize the four distinct vocal parts.

EXAMPLE 12.8: "My Country, 'Tis of Thee," mm. 1–6

To write a good SATB setting that is easy to sing, keep five basic concepts in mind: (1) clear notation, (2) comfortable vocal ranges, (3) spacing that allows the voices to blend well, (4) independent melodic lines, and (5) appropriate chordal doublings. We will consider each in turn.

Staff, Clefs, and Stems   On a grand staff, notate the soprano and alto voices on the treble staff and the bass and tenor voices on the bass staff.

KEY CONCEPT   The direction of stems, combined with the clef, indicates which notes each voice part sings (Example 12.8):

- soprano: treble staff, stems up

- alto: treble staff, stems down

- tenor: bass staff, stems up

- bass: bass staff, stems down

Sing or play each voice part in Example 12.8 as a melody. If the soprano and alto sing the same note at the same time, the note will have two stems: one up for soprano and one down for alto (as in m. 4, beat 3). This is true for the tenor and bass as well (see Example 12.9a). When alto and tenor sing in unison, however, each voice receives its own note—one for each staff (part b). When either soprano and alto or tenor and bass sing unison whole notes, write two whole notes right next to each other (part c).

EXAMPLE 12.9: Notating unisons in SATB style

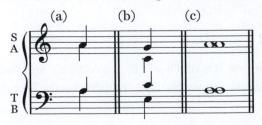

Range The pitches in each vocal part should fall within a comfortable singing range for the performers, as shown in Example 12.10. These ranges are somewhat flexible—they will vary depending on the age and experience of the singer and the style of music being performed—but in general you should stay within these guidelines.

EXAMPLE 12.10: SATB vocal ranges

Spacing Four-part chords sound best if the interval between adjacent pairs of the upper parts (SAT) is an octave or less, to allow the parts to blend well. The distance between tenor and bass may be wider; these voices can sound muddy if written too close together in a low octave. This spacing principle is based on the overtone series (Appendix 3), in which the lowest tones above the fundamental (lowest note) are more widely spaced than the upper tones.

Example 12.11 provides some examples of good and poor spacing. In part (a), all chords except the second are in **close position**: the upper three voices are as close together as possible. The second chord is in **open position**: the soprano and alto E5 and G4 skip over a potential chord tone, C5, and the alto and tenor G4 and C4 skip over the chord tone E4. Still, all four triads show good spacing choices. In part (b), the poor voicing between alto and tenor (first chord) can be hard to see on the grand staff.

EXAMPLE 12.11: Spacing guidelines

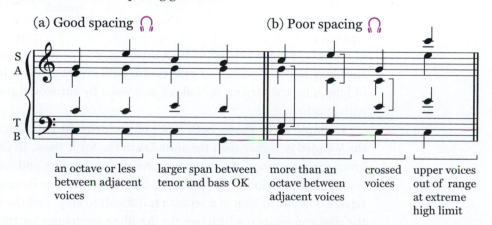

SUMMARY

In SATB style:

- The interval between the soprano and alto and between the alto and tenor is an octave or less.
- The interval between the tenor and bass may exceed an octave, but usually remains within a twelfth.

Independent Melodic Lines   In strict SATB style, each voice should fall within its own range, and **voice crossings** should be avoided: one voice should not be higher than the part above it or lower than the part below it within a chord (see Example 12.11b, third chord). In Bach chorale settings, however, the composer sometimes writes voice crossings to create a more interesting melodic line, as in measure 19 of Example 12.12; here the tenor line soars upward above the alto, which drops to move in parallel thirds with the bass. When you find voice crossings like these, or any other departures from the basic guidelines, in music you are studying, consider which concerns may have motivated the composer's choices.

EXAMPLE 12.12: Bach, "Wachet auf" (chorale), mm. 17–20

crossed
voices

Overlapping is related to voice crossing, except that it occurs between two chords rather than within a single chord. Both errors result in less independence of line: a listener trying to "follow" one voice by ear would probably confuse it with another.

Example 12.13 shows both types of problem. In part (a), the tenor's E5 in the V chord is higher than the alto's D4 in the tonic triad. In (b), the alto's D4 is lower than the tenor's F4 in the tonic triad. Overlapping and voice crossing often occur in conjunction with other voice-leading errors. For instance, in part (a), the tenor's downward leap of a seventh is difficult to sing, and the tonic triad triples the root and omits the fifth (see the doubling guidelines for triads on p. 240). In part (b), the tonic likewise has no fifth and the alto-bass voice-leading moves in contrary octaves. In both examples, the alto A4 leaps down by fifth, when it could skip by third to F4.

EXAMPLE 12.13: Overlapping and voice crossing

(a) Overlapping   (b) Voice crossing

d: V   i   V   i

Try it #2

Evaluate the range and spacing of each SATB chord below. In the blanks, write the chord's root, quality, and figure, and the letter from the list below (A–E) that best describes the chord's voicing.

   A. Proper range and spacing.

   B. A vocal range extends beyond the recommended guidelines.

   C. Spacing between soprano and alto exceeds an octave.

   D. Spacing between alto and tenor exceeds an octave.

   E. Voices are crossed.

	(1)	(2)	(3)	(4)	(5)	(6)	(7)	(8)
Root:	A♭							
Quality:	maj							
Figure:	$^6_3$							
Voicing:	E							

Doubling Because triads consist of only three chord members, one of them must be represented twice, or doubled, to make four parts. Following are general guidelines for doubling, but you will find exceptions in some pieces, where the doubling differs because of the musical context. Where two possibilities are available for doubling, use the one that produces the smoother connection between chords and a more independent vocal line.

KEY CONCEPT Doubling guidelines for triads:

1. Never double a note with an accidental or a **tendency tone**: a scale degree or chord member that must be resolved, such as the leading tone ($\hat{7}$).

2. In root position (major or minor quality), usually the bass (root) is doubled.

3. For first inversion, you can double any chord member that does not have an added accidental and is not a tendency tone. Doubling the soprano is one common strategy for major or minor triads; doubling the bass is another.

4. For second inversion, always double the bass.

5. For diminished triads (which often appear in first inversion), double the bass (the third of the chord). Occasionally, the fifth may be doubled. Doubling the root emphasizes the dissonance and will cause voice-leading problems when you resolve the chord's d5.

Example 12.14 shows "My Country" with chord positions and doubling indicated. (Remember, the absence of figures means root position. For now, disregard the circled passing tones in m. 2.) In every root-position triad except one, the bass (the root) is doubled to make four parts (guideline 2); for that one exception (m. 4, on "-ty"), the third has been doubled at the unison. In both second-inversion triads (mm. 4–5), the bass is doubled (guideline 4). The guideline with the most variability is guideline 3, for first-inversion triads, where you can double any note as long as it is not a tendency tone. Here, each first-inversion triad doubles the bass, the third of the chord. Finally, the single seventh chord in this example (m. 4) includes all four chord members, so needs no doubling.

EXAMPLE 12.14: Doubling in "My Country, 'Tis of Thee," mm. 1-6

Try it #3

A. For each triad and inversion specified, write an SATB chord with the proper doubling.

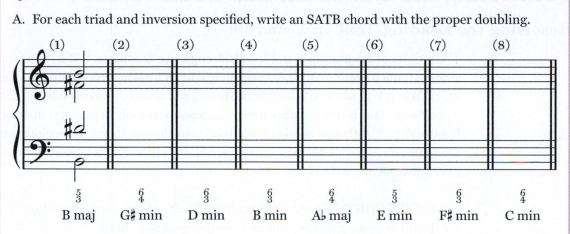

B. Now write an SATB chord with the proper doubling for each bass note and figured bass symbol. Remember, an accidental with no number applies to the third above the bass, and a slash through a number raises that pitch (the same as a ♯).

SUMMARY

To write a good SATB setting, keep three basic goals in mind:

1. Voices should blend together with appropriate doubling and spacing.

2. Each vocal part should maintain an independent melodic line.

3. All parts should be easy to read and sing.

Connecting the Dominant and Tonic Areas

Resolving the Leading Tone in V and V⁶

The process of connecting V and I, with strong voice-leading in SATB style, provides in a microcosm many concepts you will draw on when composing in freer styles. When V resolves to I, the leading tone $\hat{7}$ will almost always resolve up to $\hat{1}$ by half step. This is true whether the key is major or minor: in minor, remember to raise $\flat\hat{7}$ to $\hat{7}$. Although the dominant triad provides the strongest resolution to the tonic when in root position, first inversion (V⁶) is common as well, with the bass line resolving $\hat{7}$-$\hat{1}$.

KEY CONCEPT Minor-key authentic and half cadences always need an accidental to create a leading tone and a major-quality V chord.

Example 12.15 shows different resolutions of V-I in D major and D minor. Memorize the voice-leading of each part to write this chord connection correctly.

- $\hat{7}$ resolves up by half step to $\hat{1}$ (C♯ to D), whether in an upper voice (parts a, c) or the bass (parts b, d).
- $\hat{2}$ moves by step, either to $\hat{3}$ (parts a, c) or $\hat{1}$ (parts b, d).
- Because I and V share one note ($\hat{5}$), this pitch is often retained as a common tone in the same upper voice: here, the A is kept in either the alto or tenor. It may also drop to $\hat{3}$ to complete the triad (the alto in parts b, d).

EXAMPLE 12.15: Resolution of V-I (i) and V6-I (i)

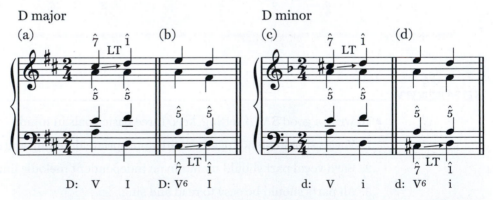

These voice-leading guidelines are based on the following general principles.

- In the upper three voices, move the smallest possible distance to another chord tone, generally by step or skip of a third. Avoid larger leaps.
- The leading tone should resolve up to $\hat{1}$.
- No voice should move by a melodic interval that would be difficult to sing, such as an A2, A4, or d5 (which may arise in minor keys).

Perfect Consonances

In SATB style, the principles of chord connection—connecting melodic lines in four voices—are intimately related to those for writing counterpoint in two voices.

- In both two- and four-voice writing, parallel motion between imperfect consonances—6 to 6, or 3 to 3—is fine (Example 12.16a), provided that it does not continue so long that the voices lose their independence.

- Parallel octaves or fifths are avoided (parts b and c) because they work against the principle of independent voices. (Parallel fifths may appear as a doubling of the melody in rock and folk music, though, and in some early twentieth-century music.)

- A simple repetition of fifths or octaves is common (part d).

- As in species counterpoint, **contrary octaves** (part e) and **contrary fifths** (part f) are not allowed in strict SATB style.

EXAMPLE 12.16: V–I voice-leading guidelines

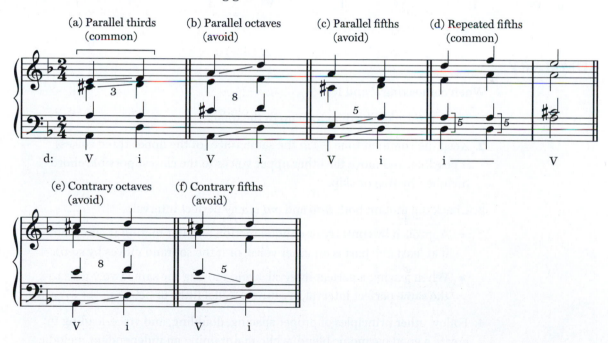

KEY CONCEPT Any perfect interval should be approached by contrary or oblique motion. Similar motion into a P8 or P5—direct, or hidden, fifths or octaves—is prohibited in the bass-soprano outer voices (unless the soprano moves by step), just as in species counterpoint (Chapter 9, Example 9.5), but allowed if at least one of the parts is an inner voice.

Direct octaves or fifths in the outer voices may sound as though the soprano has taken on the role of a bass line, as in Example 12.17a and c, where the soprano's leap of a fourth mimics bass motion and emphasizes the "hollow" sound of the octave or fifth. Rewrite the soprano line so that it approaches the octave or fifth by step or common tone, and check the doubling (in part a, the fifth of the tonic triad is doubled).

EXAMPLE 12.17: Direct, or hidden, fifths and octaves

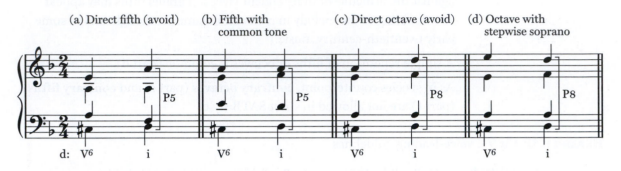

SUMMARY

When connecting V and I:

1. First, resolve the leading tone up to the tonic.

2. Keep the common tone ($\hat{5}$) in the same voice (of the upper three voices) if possible, and move the other upper voices to the closest possible chord member, by step or skip.

3. Check the motion both *into* and *out of* any perfect interval.

   • Approach by contrary or oblique motion (similar motion is acceptable if at least one part is an inner voice, or if the soprano moves by step).

   • When leaving a perfect interval, avoid moving the same two voices to the same perfect interval, creating parallel fifths or octaves.

4. Follow other principles of proper spacing, doubling, and voice-leading to create a good harmonic blend, while maintaining an independent melodic line for each voice.

Try it #4

A. Write the key and Roman numerals for each V–I (or V–i) chord connection below. In the blanks below the staff, write the letter that best describes the voice-leading between chords.

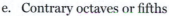

    a. Proper voice-leading   d. Unresolved leading tone

    b. Parallel fifths   e. Contrary octaves or fifths

    c. Parallel octaves

B. Connect V to I with proper voice-leading in each of the keys specified.

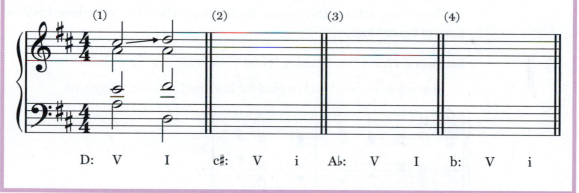

Melody and Accompaniment

Writing for Keyboard

When you write for the keyboard rather than voices, you can take advantage of ten fingers and wider ranges. Numerous types of settings are possible, some with more than four voices. We will examine a wide variety of keyboard styles and textures in future chapters, but for now we will concentrate on assigning the four voices to two hands.

KEY CONCEPT **Texture** refers to the number and alignment of individual voices or instrumental lines in a composition. You are already familiar with three types.

- **Contrapuntal** textures combine independent melodic lines to create harmonic intervals (as in species counterpoint).
- **Homophonic** textures are chordal, with most voices moving together homorhythmically and harmonies connected by voice-leading (as in SATB or hymn-style writing).
- **Melody-and-accompaniment** textures feature a rhythmically independent melody plus its harmonic support, which may include chordal arpeggiation or other types of figuration.

The last two textures concern us here.

Homophonic texture Four-part homophonic textures written specifically for keyboard either stem the two parts on each staff together (Example 12.18a), or place the upper three voices in the right hand (part b). The upper three voices usually stay within an octave of one another so that the pitches fit comfortably in one hand. You will see this texture frequently, particularly in keyboard realizations of figured bass.

EXAMPLE 12.18: "My Country, 'Tis of Thee," mm. 1–2

(a) Two voices in each hand (typical for keyboard notation of hymns)

(b) Three voices in the right hand, one in the left (typical for figured bass)

When you assign pitches to each hand, be sure they fall within a hand's reach—usually an octave. Limit the number of pitches per hand to three (possibly four) to allow the player a comfortable hand position and simultaneous attack. Avoid a large space between the hands (e.g., more than a tenth between the lowest pitch in the right hand and the highest in the left). Such a spacing would create the effect of two different chords, one in each hand, rather than a single chord.

Melody-and-accompaniment texture   One additional distribution of voices appears frequently in accompanied melodies—three voices in the left hand and one in the right. This voicing, often taught in keyboard harmony classes, may be used to accompany a right-hand melody, as in Example 12.19.

EXAMPLE 12.19: "Merrily We Roll Along," mm. 1-4

Left-hand chords also serve as a basis for arpeggiated accompaniments, such as Alberti bass. Listen to the passage shown in Example 12.20a, the opening measures of a Mozart sonata. This Alberti-bass accompaniment, with its low-high-mid-high contour, is based on the underlying chordal model shown in part (b).

EXAMPLE 12.20: Mozart, Piano Sonata in C Major, mvt. 1

(a) Mm. 1-4

(b) Reduction of mm. 1-4, left-hand part

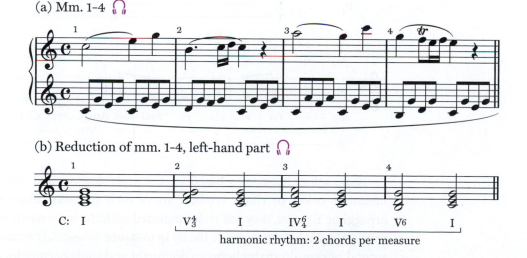

Harmonizing a Melody

When selecting harmonies for a melody of any type, first determine what the **harmonic rhythm** should be: how quickly the harmony needs to change to fit with the melody. This is an important element of musical style. In folk songs and some dance forms, for example, a typical harmonic rhythm is one chord per measure; pitches that do not belong to the harmony of the measure may be interpreted as passing, neighbor, or other embellishing tones. In Example 12.20, the harmonic rhythm is primarily two chords per measure. Once you have established a harmonic rhythm, keep it fairly consistent throughout. The one exception is at the cadence, where the harmonic rhythm often speeds up (more harmonies per measure), then comes to rest with a longer duration on the final chord.

Many simple folk songs, such as "Clementine" (Example 12.21), may be harmonized with just the tonic and dominant chords, following the basic phrase model. To write an accompaniment to this melody, identify the key and mode, then sing the melody with scale-degree numbers or solfège syllables. Let the numbers or syllables guide decisions about which phrases should end on I and which on V. In this example, phrase 1 ends in measure 4 on $\hat{2}$ ("mine") and implies a HC: a C major chord (V in the key of F major). Phrase 2 ends in measure 8 on $\hat{1}$ ("-tine"), implying a PAC. In two-phrase pairs, like this one, the first will often end on V, while the second completes the T–D–T basic phrase.

EXAMPLE 12.21: "Clementine" (melody), mm. 1–8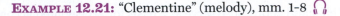

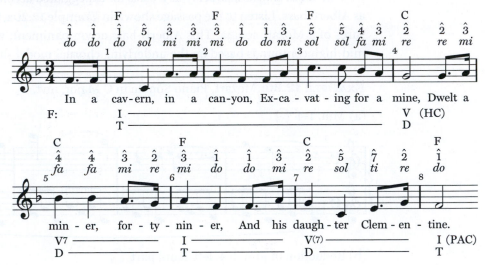

Next, select harmonies based on the scale degrees and write the Roman numerals below or chord symbols above each measure. Since measures 1–3 arpeggiate F major, they will be harmonized with the tonic triad, moving toward the half cadence in measure 4; the B♭ in measure 3, beat 3, is a passing tone. The second phrase alternates between dominant and tonic harmonies, with the A in measures 4 and 5 additional passing tones. What remains now is to create an idiomatic keyboard accompaniment.

Creating an Accompaniment

One way to begin is to write a good SATB harmonization, and then add rhythmic figuration. Listen to the first phrase of "Merrily We Roll Along" as shown in Example 12.22, with an SATB harmonization below the melody.

EXAMPLE 12.22: "Merrily We Roll Along," mm. 1-4, with SATB accompaniment 🎧

Example 12.23 illustrates five different keyboard textures that can be derived from this SATB model. Part (a) is a chordal pattern with the roots in the bass on the downbeat, and the other parts in the right hand delayed to beat 2. Part (b) is a rhythmic variant, where the upper parts come on the offbeats and beat 2 of each bar sounds $\hat{5}$ in the bass—similar to a Sousa march. The next three patterns are arpeggiated accompaniments, often chosen for lyrical settings. In part (c), the block chords of (a) are arpeggiated as even eighth notes, and in (d) as sixteenths. Part (e) doubles the melody in the right hand and realizes the chords as an Alberti bass in the left hand, changing V to V^6 for a smoother left-hand pattern.

For a triple-meter melody, try a waltz bass—follow pattern (a), with the bass note on the downbeat and upper-voice chords on beats 2 and 3. Play or listen to each of these to see what a different effect the accompaniment has on the character of the setting.

EXAMPLE 12.23: "Merrily We Roll Along," mm. 1-4, with keyboard accompaniment patterns

(a) With chords displaced to beat 2 🎧

(b) With Sousa-style accompaniment

(c) With eighth-note arpeggiated accompaniment

(d) With sixteenth-note arpeggiated accompaniment

(e) With Alberti bass

As you can see in Example 12.24, the T-D-T phrase model captures the principles of harmonic progression we have studied thus far. The left-hand columns show three different ways to expand the tonic area: by simple reiteration, by motion to an inversion, or by bass-line neighboring motion with V^6. Any of these patterns can then move to V and back to I to complete the basic phrase. In the coming chapters, we will let principles of contrapuntal writing continue to guide our compositional choices as we add more harmonies to our musical palette.

EXAMPLE 12.24: Basic phrase model T-D-T

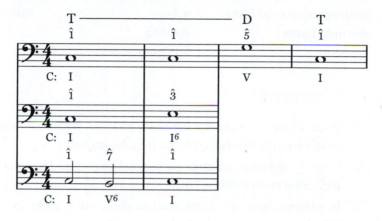

Did You Know?

The melody that we know as "My Country, 'Tis of Thee," or "America," is also sung in England as "God Save the Queen" (or "King," depending on the current monarch). The origin of the melody is a mystery. It was first published in England in 1744, and became popular after a version of the song with words by Thomas Arne was performed in the Drury Lane and Covent Garden Theaters in London the following year. Arne's lyrics rallied support for King George II and decried the Scots, led by "Bonnie Prince Charlie," George's Stuart rival for the throne. Both Beethoven (see anthology) and Haydn incorporated the melody into their own compositions.

Several different politically oriented lyrics were set to this tune in the American colonies and in the early days after the Revolution. The text beginning "My country, 'tis of thee" was written by Samuel Francis Smith, and was first performed with the tune on July 4, 1831. On August 28, 1963, Martin Luther King quoted Smith's lyrics in his "I have a dream" speech from the steps of the Lincoln Memorial, as he called on the nation to "let freedom ring."

TERMS YOU SHOULD KNOW

basic phrase (T–D–T)
cadence
- half (HC)
- imperfect authentic (IAC)
  - contrapuntal IAC
  - strong IAC
- perfect authentic (PAC)

contextual analysis
contrary octaves or fifths
dominant area
doubling

harmonic rhythm
keyboard spacing
parallel octaves or fifths
resolution
SATB
- soprano
- alto
- tenor
- bass

spacing
tendency tones

texture
- contrapuntal
- homophonic
- melody and
  accompaniment

tonic area
tonic closure
vocal range
voice crossing

QUESTIONS FOR REVIEW

1. What elements make up the basic phrase? Name and define the possible cadences with which the phrase might conclude.

2. How do cadences differ in their tonal strength? How does a contrapuntal IAC differ from a strong IAC?

3. In general, how are stems used to show voice parts in an SATB setting? Which stems go up and which go down?

3. What is the standard range for soprano voices? alto? tenor? bass? When can you exceed these ranges?

4. What are some guidelines that govern spacing between adjacent voices in SATB settings? How does this differ from keyboard spacing?

5. What chord member is usually doubled in a triad in root position? in first inversion? in second inversion? What might influence you to double a different note?

6. Within the dominant area, how do you treat the leading tone when doubling? when resolving? What must you remember about the seventh scale degree in minor keys?

7. What principles of species counterpoint come into play when you approach perfect fifths or octaves?

8. What are the steps for harmonizing a folk melody?

9. How is an SATB harmonization converted into a keyboard accompaniment?

10. In music for your own instrument, find at least one example of each cadence type considered in this chapter.

Know It? Show It!

Focus by working through the tutorials.

Learn with InQuizitive.

Apply what you've learned to complete the workbook assignments.

Dominant Sevenths, the Predominant Area, and Chorale Harmonization

Outline

Writing V⁷ and its inversions

- Resolving the leading tone and chordal seventh
- Approaching perfect intervals

Expanding the basic phrase: T–PD–D–T

- Predominant function: Subdominant and supertonic chords
- Voice-leading from predominant to dominant
- Predominant seventh chords
- Harmonic function and principles of progression

Realizing figured bass

Harmonizing chorale melodies

- Soprano-bass counterpoint and chord choice
- Completing the inner voices

Overview

In this chapter, we add sevenths to dominant chords, and expand the basic phrase model to include predominant harmonies: T–PD–D–T. We learn how to resolve dominant sevenths and to connect the predominant and dominant areas in SATB style. Then we apply this knowledge to realize a figured bass and harmonize a chorale melody.

Repertoire

Johann Sebastian Bach
    "Ach Gott, vom Himmel sieh' darein" ("O God, Look Down on Us from Heaven," Chorale No. 253)
    "Aus meines Herzens Grunde" ("From My Inmost Heart," Chorale No. 1)
 Arcangelo Corelli, Sonata in D Minor, Op. 4, No. 8, Preludio
Joseph Haydn, Piano Sonata No. 9 in F Major, mvt. 3
Wolfgang Amadeus Mozart
    Piano Sonata in C Major, K. 545, mvt. 1
    "Voi, che sapete" ("You who know"), from *The Marriage of Figaro*

Writing V⁷ and Its Inversions

Listen to Example 13.1, the concluding measures of a Mozart sonata. Here, the dramatic trill in the right hand of measure 70 signals the end of the final phrase, with a V7-I perfect authentic cadence—an even stronger cadence than V-I. The remaining measures reiterate the V7-I motion twice more with cadential flourishes, expanding the final tonic harmony and bringing this movement to an exuberant end.

EXAMPLE 13.1: Mozart, Piano Sonata in C Major, mvt. 1, mm. 70-73 🎧

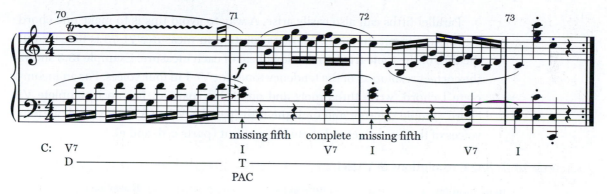

Resolving the Leading Tone and Chordal Seventh

When you add a seventh to the dominant chord, as in measure 70 (G-B-D-F), two new voice-leading considerations arise. First, the chordal seventh (scale degree $\hat{4}$; here, F4 in the left hand) creates a dissonance with the chord's root (G3); in common-practice style, it almost always resolves down by step—as here, F4 to E4. Second, as we know, the leading tone, $\hat{7}$, resolves up to $\hat{1}$.

🎵 **KEY CONCEPT** When V⁷ moves to I, two tendency tones resolve stepwise: the chordal seventh resolves down ($\hat{4}$-$\hat{3}$), and the leading tone resolves up ($\hat{7}$-$\hat{1}$). When $\hat{7}$ and $\hat{4}$ are voiced as a d5, they contract inward to a third; when $\hat{4}$ and $\hat{7}$ are arranged as an A4, they expand outward to a sixth.

When resolving V⁷ to I, you already know not to double the leading tone in the dominant harmony, because of its function as a tendency tone. Example 13.2 illustrates the two voice-leading problems that would result: either (a) both leading tones (C♯) will resolve correctly, resulting in parallel octaves (labeled ||8); or (b) one of the leading tones will resolve incorrectly.

EXAMPLE 13.2: Voice-leading problems caused by incorrect doubling

D: V7   I   V7   I
Two LTs   One LT resolves
resolve = ‖ 8.   incorrectly.

Parallel fifths can also easily arise. A way to avoid this is to make one chord incomplete (omit the fifth); Mozart's solution in measures 71-73 is to leave out the fifth of the tonic triad on the downbeat of each measure. Example 13.3 shows the correct resolution of the tendency tones for V7-I in four voices. For an incomplete I chord, write three roots and one third (part a). For an incomplete V7 chord, double the root and omit the fifth (part b). When V7 is inverted, all four voices of the seventh chord should be present (parts c, d, and e).

EXAMPLE 13.3: SATB resolutions of V7 to I

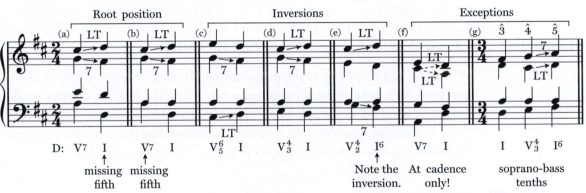

D: V7   I   V7   I   V$_5^6$ I   V$_3^4$ I   V$_2^4$ I⁶   V7   I   I   V$_3^4$ I⁶
     missing missing   Note the   At cadence   soprano-bass
     fifth   fifth   inversion. only!   tenths

Although V7 may appear in any inversion, a root-position V7 creates the strongest progression, and V$_5^6$ the next strongest. Use second and third inversions when you want to write weaker dominants—for example, to expand the tonic area at the beginning of a phrase. Part (e) shows the only correct resolution of V$_2^4$: to a I⁶. Since the chordal seventh ($\hat{4}$) is in the bass, its resolution down to $\hat{3}$ creates a first-inversion tonic triad.

Two common "exceptions" to these guidelines are given in parts (f) and (g).

- In part (f), $\hat{7}$ (C♯) does not resolve to 1 but instead skips down to $\hat{5}$ to produce a complete tonic triad. Use this type of resolution only at a cadence where complete chords are desired and only when $\hat{7}$ appears in an inner voice. (It works in part because we hear the $\hat{7}$ in the alto resolving up to $\hat{1}$ in the soprano.)

- In part (g), V$^4_3$ functions as a passing chord between I and I⁶, with the soprano and bass moving in parallel tenths—a common expansion strategy for the tonic area. The contrapuntal motion of the rising parallel tenths overrides the tendency of the chordal seventh to resolve down. (Chapter 14 will delve further into tonic expansions from I to I⁶.)

Try it #1

Provide a key signature and SATB voice parts (in half notes) for each root-position V7-I (or V7-i). Where a harmony is marked with an asterisk, write an incomplete chord (omit the fifth). Draw arrows to show the resolution of the leading tone up and chordal seventh down.

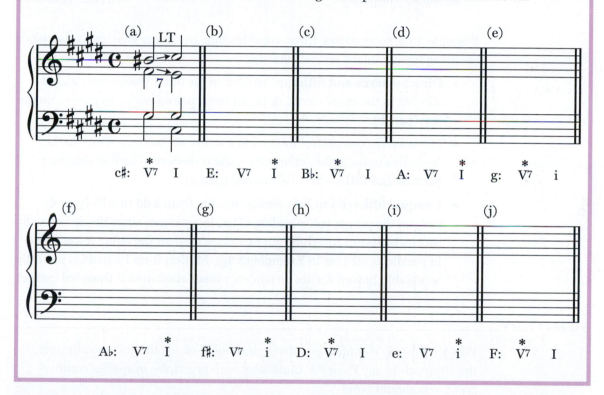

Approaching Perfect Intervals

When you resolve dominant sevenths in SATB style, watch for the voice-leading problems shown in Example 13.4a, c, and d. To avoid them, you could change a chord's doubling or spacing, or revise the soprano line to create stepwise motion into the octave or fifth. A new concern with the V⁷ chord is created by the d5 or A4 between scale degrees $\hat{7}$ and $\hat{4}$, as shown in parts (d) and (e).

EXAMPLE 13.4: Resolving the V7: Motion into perfect intervals 🎧

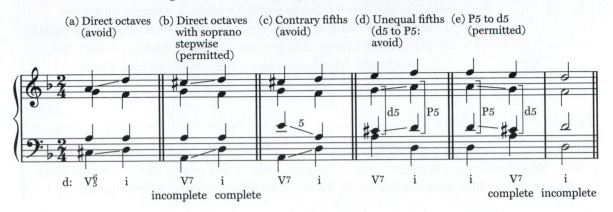

Example 13.4 summarizes three voice-leading problems that can arise when resolving the dominant seventh chord.

- **Direct octaves and fifths** are avoided in the outer voices (part a), but allowed in the inner voices, or in any voice paired with a *stepwise* soprano line (part b).

- Motion from one perfect interval to another of the same size, whether the voices move in the same or opposite directions—such as **contrary octaves and fifths**—are also avoided (part c).

- **Unequal fifths (d5 to P5):** Similar motion from a d5 to a P5 (part d) violates the proper voice-leading of tendency tones, since the d5 normally contracts inward to a third. An exception is when the outer voices move in parallel tenths (as in Example 13.3g). Motion from P5 to d5 is perfectly acceptable, however, since no tendency tone's resolution is thwarted (part e).

SUMMARY

When writing in common-practice style, double-check the voice-leading on the approach to any P5 or P8. Consistent with principles of species counterpoint, you should avoid

1. parallel octaves or fifths;

2. direct octaves or fifths—similar motion into a P5 or P8 between the soprano and bass (unless the soprano moves by step);

3. contrary octaves or fifths;

4. unequal fifths—motion from d5 to P5, especially between the soprano and bass (unless these outer voices move in parallel tenths).

Also, avoid the errors of overlapping and voice crossing illustrated in Example 13.5 (parts a and b), which violate the principle of independence of lines. Parts (c) and (d) are a reminder of one last voice-leading principle that should be familiar from species counterpoint: avoid writing melodic augmented or diminished intervals, which are difficult to sing in tune. A2s arise in minor keys between $\flat\hat{6}$ and $\hat{7}$, d5s and A4s between $\hat{7}$ and $\hat{4}$ in either major or minor.

EXAMPLE 13.5: Some voice-leading problems to avoid 🎧

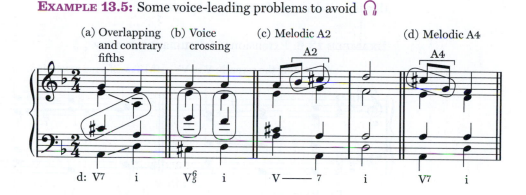

(a) Overlapping and contrary fifths   (b) Voice crossing   (c) Melodic A2   (d) Melodic A4

d: V⁷   i   V⁶₅   i   V ——— 7   i   V⁷   i

Try it #2

Check your understanding of voice-leading guidelines by examining the chorale phrase below. Sing or play through the phrase, circle and label the (numerous) mistakes, and then rewrite the phrase with correct voice-leading. 🎧

c: i   V⁶   i— 6   V—7   i
      T —————————   D   T

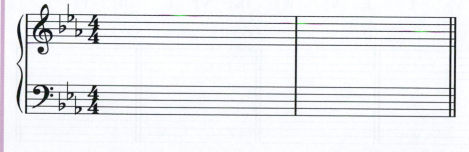

When you write harmonic progressions, you may include more than one dominant chord in a row (Example 13.6) in different inversions and spacing, to maintain musical interest. Place the strongest dominant chord (usually root-position V7) just before the resolution to tonic harmony. When V moves to V7 (part a), the added seventh often acts like a passing tone, creating 8-7 motion above the bass (labeled V8-7). When you extend the harmony by changing inversion (part b), a tendency tone (C♯) may move from one voice to another before it resolves; this is called a **transferred resolution**.

EXAMPLE 13.6: Extensions of dominant harmony

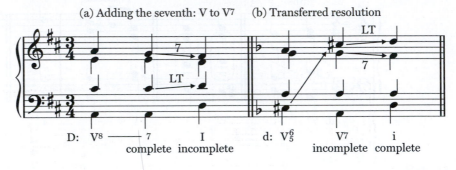

Try it #3

Write the following progressions in SATB voicing with half notes. Provide the appropriate key signatures, and add accidentals as needed. Draw arrows to show the resolution of leading tones up and chordal sevenths down.

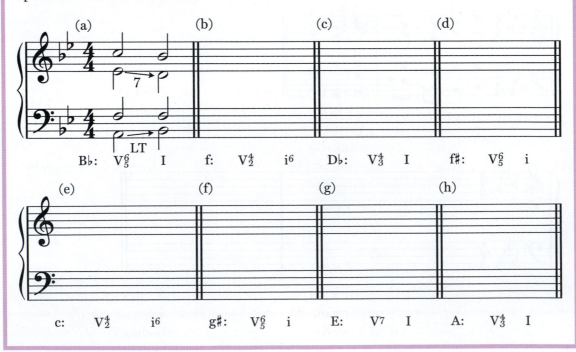

Expanding the Basic Phrase: T–PD–D–T

Predominant Function: Subdominant and Supertonic Chords

Having considered the D-T motion that completes the basic phrase, we now turn to the tonal area that typically precedes the dominant: the predominant area (PD). We will examine a number of predominant chords in future chapters, but for now will focus on the subdominant triad and supertonic triads and sevenths—any of which may lead to V or V7. In Example 13.7, the tonic area is expanded for two measures by repetition and arpeggiation. It moves to a ii6 in the penultimate measure to prepare the PAC.

EXAMPLE 13.7: Haydn, Piano Sonata in F major, mvt. 3, mm. 21-24 🎧

KEY CONCEPT Predominant harmonies—ii and IV (and their minor-key equivalents)—are so named because they lead to the dominant. Predominant triads share scale degrees $\hat{4}$ and $\hat{6}$.

The predominant area (sometimes called the "dominant preparation area" or "subdominant area") expands the basic phrase model to four parts: T-PD-D-T. This type of phrase is even more common than T-D-T, and its many possible variations shape most of common-practice tonal music. You should memorize the chord progressions employed in each functional area—to serve as a handy template for choosing chords when you write your own progressions, harmonize a melody, or compose music on your own. Following are typical Roman numerals for the T-PD-D-T basic phrase.

- In major keys: I ——— (IV, ii6, or ii) —— (V or V7) —— I
  T ——— PD ——————— D ————— T

- In minor keys: i ——— (iv or ii°6) ——— (V or V7) —— i
  T ——— PD ——————— D ————— T

In minor keys, the diminished triad ii°—like vii° in major keys—generally appears in first inversion. Remember that the tonic area is often expanded, so that T forms the longest part of the phrase; the concluding PD-D-T will occur in closer succession, at or near the final cadence.

> **KEY CONCEPT** When two predominant harmonies appear in succession before moving to V, they do so in a falling-third root progression: IV to ii (and not the other way around).

Voice-Leading from Predominant to Dominant

Example 13.8 illustrates how the predominant and dominant connect in SATB texture. The same progression appears in parts (a) and (c), but with IV in (a) and ii^6 in (c). These two chords differ by only one note (here, F or G in the alto) and can substitute for each other: they both have $\hat{4}$ in the bass, which accounts in part for the frequency with which the ii chord appears in first inversion and for the doubling in the ii^6—usually $\hat{4}$, as here. In both progressions (a) and (c), when the predominant moves to dominant, all three of the upper voices move down to the closest possible chord tone, while the bass moves up by step from $\hat{4}$ to $\hat{5}$. In minor keys, iv is minor (part b) and ii$^{\circ 6}$ diminished (part d). For ii$^{\circ 6}$, the normal doubling is the third of the chord, so that the dissonant interval (G-D♭) is not emphasized.

EXAMPLE 13.8: Predominant to dominant: Upper voices in contrary motion to the bass 🎧

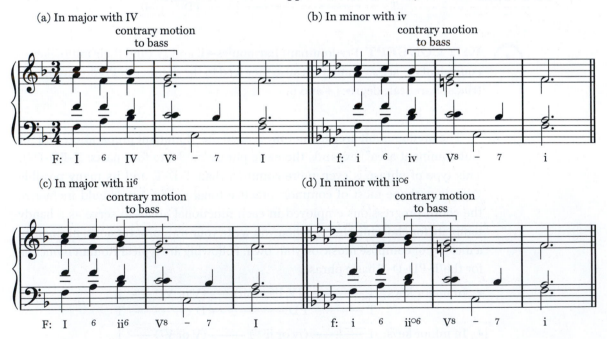

> **KEY CONCEPT** When root-position IV moves to root-position V, write the upper voices in contrary motion with the bass to avoid parallel fifths or octaves.

Try it #4

Write the following progressions in SATB voicing, with half notes. Provide the appropriate key signatures, and add accidentals as needed. Move the upper three voices in contrary motion to the bass where possible.

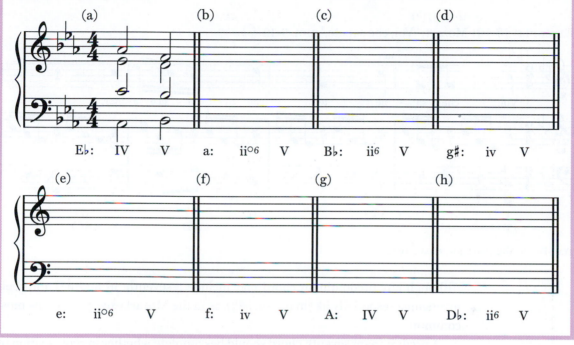

(a)   (b)   (c)   (d)

Eb: IV V   a: ii°6 V   Bb: ii6 V   g#: iv V

(e)   (f)   (g)   (h)

e: ii°6 V   f: iv V   A: IV V   Db: ii6 V

When the predominant moves to a V7 chord, additional voice-leading factors arise. Among the most important is how to prepare the chordal seventh—a dissonance that should be approached by common tone or step. Preparation by common tone is possible because both predominants include $\hat{4}$ (the seventh of V7); Example 13.9 retains this pitch in the tenor (Bb). When IV moves to V7, move the upper voices in contrary motion to the stepwise bass; otherwise parallel fifths will result (part a). You may omit the fifth in the V7, as in part (b). If you want a complete V7, choose a ii6 or ii chord as predominant; this chord allows for two common tones with V7 (parts c and d, here Bb and G).

EXAMPLE 13.9: Predominant to V7: Preparation of the chordal seventh

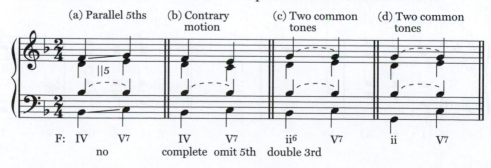

(a) Parallel 5ths   (b) Contrary motion   (c) Two common tones   (d) Two common tones

F: IV V7   IV V7   ii6 V7   ii V7
      no   complete omit 5th double 3rd

Predominant Seventh Chords

Thus far, the only seventh chord included in the basic phrase has been the dominant seventh, but you may also find predominant sevenths—like the one in measure 11 of Example 13.10.

EXAMPLE 13.10: Mozart, "Voi, che sapete," mm. 9-12

Translation: You who know what love is.

Although any predominant chord may include a seventh, ii7 and ii∅7 and their inversions—especially ii$\frac{6}{5}$ (in minor, ii∅$\frac{6}{5}$), as in the Mozart excerpt—are the most common.

A predominant seventh chord should be complete whether in root position or in inversion (unless it appears in a sequence, as we will see in Chapter 19). And the usual guidelines for treating the dissonance still apply: the chordal seventh should be prepared by common tone or step, and should resolve down by step.

Example 13.11 is a variant of Example 13.8c and d, substituting a ii$\frac{6}{5}$ in place of the ii6. Here, two voices move in contrary motion to the bass from ii$\frac{6}{5}$ to V, with $\hat{2}$ (G) held as a common tone. Within the ii$\frac{6}{5}$ chord, its chordal seventh (F, in the tenor) is prepared by common tone with the preceding tonic, and resolves down by step. Other predominant sevenths are possible as well, as in the progression I-ii$\frac{4}{3}$-V$\frac{6}{5}$-I.

EXAMPLE 13.11: Writing a predominant seventh chord

Harmonic Function and Principles of Progression

Now that the phrase model T-PD-D-T is complete, we have a variety of chord progressions to choose from. One way to think about these progressions is as a combination of bass-line patterns paired with the harmonies we have studied so far: I, ii, IV, and V (in minor i, ii°, iv, V). Example 13.12 shows the various chord choices available at this stage of our studies—organized by functional category, T-PD-D-T—to expand the basic phrase model.

EXAMPLE 13.12: Chord choices from the basic phrase model

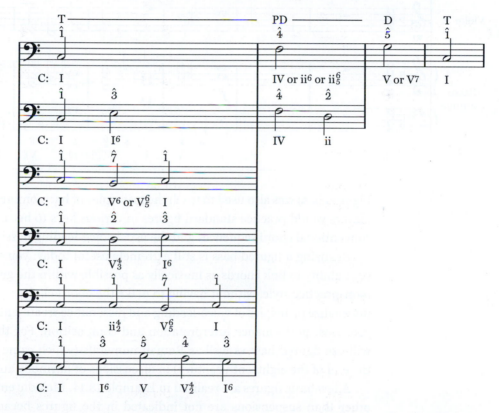

In each functional category (T, PD, D, or T), choose a progression from the measures below it. For example, the tonic area in a phrase might be expanded by bass-line neighboring harmonies I-V6-I or I-V$^6_5$-I, as well as bass-line passing harmonies like I-V$^4_3$-I6. A bass-line pattern of $\hat{1}$-$\hat{1}$-$\hat{7}$-$\hat{1}$ can be beautifully harmonized with the basic-phrase pattern I-ii$^4_2$-V$^6_5$-I. Following the tonic expansion, conclude the phrase with the PD-D-T harmonies of your choice.

Realizing Figured Bass

In the Baroque and Classical eras, performers on keyboards, lutes, and other harmony instruments were expected to improvise harmonic progressions from a given bass line—to **realize** a figured bass, like the one shown in Example 13.13.

EXAMPLE 13.13: Corelli, Preludio, from Sonata in D Minor, mm. 1-7 🎧

Figured bass was also used to teach the principles of harmony and voice-leading: players would practice standard figures in various keys to become familiar with conventional chord sequences and the usual voice-leading possibilities.

Realizing a figured bass is still extremely useful today; you can demonstrate your ability to link chords as musically as possible within the guidelines of common-practice style, without having to make the chord choices yourself. You also internalize principles of voice-leading and dissonance treatment that can inform your own performance interpretation and composition. For these reasons, we will use figured bass as well as Roman numerals (which came into use only at the end of the eighteenth century) in discussions of harmony and voice-leading.

A few basic figures are realized in Example 13.14. Melodic embellishing tones other than suspensions are not indicated in the figures because they are not part of the main harmonic framework. Musicians realizing the bass would be expected to add them according to their taste.

EXAMPLE 13.14: Realization of common figures 🎧

KEY CONCEPT When realizing a figured bass:

- Sing the given line(s) with scale-degree numbers or solfège.
- If there is an accidental next to a number, raise or lower the pitch that lies that interval above the bass by one chromatic half step; if there's a slash through a number, raise the pitch a half step (part a).
- If you see an accidental by itself, raise or lower the third above the bass (part b)—not necessarily the third of the chord.
- Place pitches above the bass in an appropriate octave (of your choosing) based on the intervals indicated in the figures (part c).
- Use pitches diatonic in the key (part d), unless an accidental is specified.
- If there is a dash between two numbers (or between a number and an accidental), those intervals should be in the same voice-leading strand, as in a 4-3 suspension (part e).
- Remember that accidentals in the figure apply only to that single chord, and that figured bass does not list *all* intervals above the bass—some, like octaves and thirds, may be implied.
- Follow doubling and voice-leading guidelines for the style when voicing or connecting chords; these are not specified by the figures.

The melody and bass of one of Bach's chorale hamonizations is given in Example 13.15 (the melody was written in 1524 by German Protestant reformer Martin Luther), with the figured bass below.

EXAMPLE 13.15: Bach, "Ach Gott, vom Himmel sieh' darein," mm. 1-2, melody and figured bass (adapted)

To realize the figured bass, first sing through the soprano and bass lines on solfège or scale-degree numbers, and examine the counterpoint. This phrase ends on a half cadence, and its soprano-bass counterpoint features beautiful contrary motion (and a voice exchange) in the first full measure. Now consider the figures. The ♯ below the first and last bass notes indicates that the third above the bass is to be raised (from F to F♯)—this figure supplies the leading tone for the dominant harmonies. We will voice the opening chord in close position, since the bass line rises in the first complete measure and we need to keep the tenor in a higher register so that the bass line does not overlap its range. A good voicing for the first chord would be F♯4 in the alto and D4 in the tenor (doubling the root). The F♯ resolves up to G in measure 1, and the tenor's D remains as a common tone. (Remember that the absence of other figures implies a $\frac{5}{3}$ chord.)

The second chord of measure 1 specifies a sixth and fourth (F and D) above this bass note, and we raise the sixth to F♯ because of the slash in the figure. The figure ^{6} for the third chord implies $\frac{6}{3}$; place a sixth and third (G and D) above this pitch. Because the sixth is also the melody note (and the root of the triad), we double it in the alto by drawing stems above and below the G4. Example 13.16 shows a complete realization of this chorale phrase.

EXAMPLE 13.16: Bach, "Ach Gott, vom Himmel sieh' darein," mm. 1-2, SATB realization (adapted)

As in Example 13.15, write your Roman numeral analysis on a separate line below the figures (the figured bass is part of the music itself, not an analysis). You will see slight variations between the figures and the Roman numeral inversion symbols, since figures also indicate chromatic alterations and may specify suspensions or other voice-leading above the bass. The contextual analysis, below the Roman numerals, shows how the tonic area may be extended by the dominant. In this example, dominant harmonies in measures 1 and 2 are inverted, which weakens their harmonic function and strengthens their contrapuntal role. Follow the bass line to see how they function: the first dominant passes between the root position and inverted tonic (P), and the second plays a neighboring role (N). (We will return to this idea in Chapter 14.)

Harmonizing Chorale Melodies

You can harmonize many chorale melodies with the tonic, dominant, and predominant harmonies discussed in this chapter. Follow the general procedure for harmonizing a melody from Chapter 11: select an appropriate cadence, and compose a bass line that makes good counterpoint with the melody. Be sure to consult Example 13.12 for T-PD-D-T progressions that will work well with the bass line. For chorale melodies, the harmonic rhythm is usually one chord per beat; if the same chord is needed for two or more beats, you might change the soprano note or bass inversion of the chord to provide melodic or harmonic variety. After selecting the harmonic progression, complete the inner parts to make an SATB setting.

Soprano-Bass Counterpoint and Chord Choice

To demonstrate, we will harmonize the melody in Example 13.17. Begin by singing through the melody on scale-degree numbers or solfège (or thinking of these): $\hat{3}$-$\hat{5}$-$\hat{4}$-$\hat{3}$-$\hat{2}$-$\hat{1}$, or *mi-sol-fa-mi-re-do*. Use this information to plan the harmonies, with mostly an even quarter-note rhythm. Because the melody ends with $\hat{2}$-$\hat{1}$, plan a perfect authentic cadence: D3 to G2 in the bass and Roman numerals V (or V7) to I.

Now examine the beginning of the phrase, $\hat{3}$-$\hat{5}$; you could harmonize both with a tonic triad, or with I moving to V. Choose the latter because of the anacrusis: a change of harmony over the bar line articulates the rhythm well.

EXAMPLE 13.17: Bach, "Aus meines Herzens Grunde," mm. 5-7 (melody)

KEY CONCEPT When you write a bass line and select harmonies for a given melody, you need not work "left to right." One effective way is to start with the cadence, then go back to the beginning to write the tonic opening. Finally, fill in the middle of the phrase.

Next, write a good bass line in counterpoint with the melody—one that supports the harmonies chosen thus far, completes a good basic-phrase progression, and includes inversions to create a singable line. Beginning with the tonic harmony on the anacrusis, choose the low G2 to allow the bass line to rise in measures 5-6 in counterpoint with the soprano line. This dominant harmony could extend for all of measure 5, with the melody's $\hat{5}$-$\hat{4}$ moving to the seventh of a V7 chord. For variety and for stepwise contrary motion with the soprano, begin with V6 on the downbeat, moving up by step to a $\frac{4}{3}$ inversion at the end of the bar and saving the stronger root-position V for the cadence.

In measure 6, which prepares the cadence, we have an opportunity to use a predominant harmony to complete the T-PD-D-T basic phrase. Scale-degree $\hat{3}$ (B4) on the downbeat implies a tonic harmony, and $\hat{2}$ (A4) on beat 2 will support a predominant (the supertonic) as well as the dominant on the following beat. Since the melody descends by step to the cadence, we will craft a bass line that moves first in contrary motion before its cadential descent. The complete bass line (Bach's own, as it happens) is shown in Example 13.18. Roman numerals are given for one possible harmonization below the staff.

EXAMPLE 13.18: Bach, "Aus meines Herzens Grunde," mm. 5-7 (soprano and bass) 🎧

KEY CONCEPT Write the soprano-bass counterpoint first before filling in the inner voices. Make sure both parts have singable melodic lines, and that they make good contrapuntal and harmonic sense, following the T-PD-D-T phrase model.

Completing the Inner Voices

Before adding the alto and tenor lines, scan the soprano-bass counterpoint to see whether there are places that might present special challenges (for example, places where the outer voices are particularly close together, or where they form fifths or octaves). In measure 6, we have an octave on the downbeat, followed by a chord with a seventh to prepare and resolve. For this reason, it would be good to begin part-writing near the cadence, and then fill in the beginning of the phrase.

At the downbeat of measure 6, there are only two notes left to complete the I⁶ chord (G and D), and either voicing is possible: G3 in tenor and D4 in alto, or D4 in tenor and G4 in alto. For now, pick the higher register, to allow the voices to move downward in contrary motion with the bass if so desired.

KEY CONCEPT Before voicing the first chord in a progression, scan the soprano and bass lines for motion up or down, and plan the chord's spacing with this motion in mind. For example, if the bass moves up, place the other voices in a higher register to allow them room to move down in contrary motion.

For the second chord in measure 6, the alto G4 can remain as a common tone between the I⁶ (G-B-D) and ii₅⁶ (A-C-E-G) to prepare the chordal seventh. The only remaining pitch, E, is left for the tenor, moving stepwise from the downbeat in parallel tenths with the bass and contrary motion with the soprano. Now we connect the predominant and dominant areas (beats 2-3) with contrary motion against the $\hat{4}$-$\hat{5}$ bass: A remains in the soprano, and the other two voices move down.

Example 13.19 shows Bach's solution; he adds ⁸⁻⁷ motion above the dominant for a stepwise tenor line, which resolves down as chordal sevenths should. He also makes the final I chord a complete triad, with the alto skipping from the leading tone (F♯) down to the fifth of the tonic (D) rather than resolving upward. This is his solution in most chorales, and is a good choice for our writing as well—but only at cadences. Now listen to this harmonization of the chorale phrase.

EXAMPLE 13.19: Bach, "Aus meines Herzens Grunde," mm. 5-7 (adapted) 🎧

When you harmonize a melody or realize a figured bass, always go back and proofread your work. One of the easiest ways to do this is at a keyboard (or using the playback feature of a music notation program)—often your ear will pick out mistakes that your eye may not. Play through your work slowly, and listen and look for specific types of errors.

- Scan through once for the resolution of every tendency tone (leading tone and chordal seventh). You might want to label the tendency tones with arrows (up for leading tones, down for chordal sevenths) as a reminder.

- When writing in a minor key, be sure that ♭$\hat{7}$ is raised to make a leading tone. If it is preceded by $\hat{6}$, raise that as well; otherwise a melodic A2 will result.

- Locate each perfect fifth or octave, and check the voice-leading into and out of it for any parallel motion.

- Sing each line to yourself on scale degrees or solfège to check again for the resolution of tendency tones, for awkward leaps, and for a musical line.

SUMMARY

Keep in mind the following guidelines when connecting SATB chords.

1. Above all, write musically:
   - Listen to what you write, by playing or singing each line.
   - Avoid static harmonic progressions; create interest over an unchanging harmony by changing the soprano pitch, the inversion, and/or the spacing of the chord.
   - Write melodies with stepwise motion and skips between chord members; avoid large leaps (except in the bass) and augmented or diminished melodic intervals.
   - Write passing or neighbor tones to create a smooth line and add melodic interest.

2. Work to achieve smooth voice-leading:
   - Resolve tendency tones correctly, and never double them.
   - If two chords share a common tone, keep that common tone in the same voice if possible.
   - Move each voice to the closest possible member of the following chord (without creating parallel perfect intervals).
   - Approach chordal sevenths by common tone or step, or from below by skip.

3. Aim for independence of the four voices:
   - Keep each voice within its own characteristic range. No pitch in one part should cross above or below that of an adjacent part—either within a single chord (voice-crossing) or between two consecutive chords (overlapping).
   - Balance parallel or similar motion with contrary and oblique motion. Avoid moving all four voices in the same direction.
   - Write in contrary or oblique motion when you approach and leave any perfect interval to avoid parallel fifths, octaves, or unisons.

Although this chapter has focused on the simplified texture of chorales, you might be surprised to discover how many composers of different genres and eras have followed the principles for good chorale-style writing to control their use of dissonance, make harmonic choices, plan voice-leading, and compose pleasing melodies and bass lines. Such common features between musical styles will be pointed out in later chapters as they arise.

Did You Know?

Composers and performers in the Renaissance (1430-1600) did not think of chords as invertible harmonies stacked in thirds above a root as we do today. Instead, they described music by the way the intervals were prepared and resolved. At first, the interval of a seventh appeared only on the offbeats, approached by a perfect octave and resolving down by step on the next beat. Some composers of the early Baroque era (1600-1750) liked the dramatic sound made when the chordal seventh was placed in an accented position, but that treatment was not permitted in the strict style of church music, and was deemed appropriate only for theatrical or dramatic music, like opera. Over time, the seventh began to be accepted as a dissonance that could appear on the beat as a complete V7, instead of entering as 8-7 motion. It continued to resolve down by step in common-practice tonal music, but in the twentieth century and more recent popular styles the seventh can simply be considered part of a sonority and remain unresolved.

TERMS YOU SHOULD KNOW

contrary motion

direct octaves and fifths

overlapping

predominant area

realization

tendency tones

T-PD-D-T phrase

transferred resolution

unequal fifths

QUESTIONS FOR REVIEW

1. What tendency tones in a V7 must resolve? Do they resolve differently when the dominant appears in an inversion? If so, how? Do they resolve differently at the cadence? If so, how?

2. What principles of species counterpoint come into play when a progression approaches perfect fifths or octaves?

3. Name several chords that might appear in the predominant area of the basic phrase. Are particular inversions more typical than others? Why or why not?

4. Which is the most common predominant seventh chord (and inversion)? What principles should be followed when preparing and resolving such chords?

5. What voice-leading principle must be kept in mind when moving between root-position IV and V?

6. What are the steps for harmonizing a chorale melody?

Know It? Show It!

🖥 **Focus** by working through the tutorials.

🐭 **Learn** with InQuizitive.

✍ **Apply** what you've learned to complete the workbook assignments.

14

Expanding the Basic Phrase

Overview

This chapter explores some ways the tonic, dominant, and predominant areas may be expanded within the basic phrase. We consider four types of $\frac{6}{4}$ chords and contexts for the submediant triad.

Repertoire

Johannes Brahms, *Variations on a Theme by Haydn*

Wolfgang Amadeus Mozart
  Piano Sonata in B♭ Major, K. 333, mvt. 1
  Piano Sonata in C Major, K. 545, mvts. 1 and 2
  Piano Sonata in D Major, K. 284, mvt. 3
  Sonata for Violin and Piano, K. 296, mvt. 2

"My Country, 'Tis of Thee"

Franz Schubert, "Morgengruss" ("Morning Greeting"), from *Die schöne Müllerin* (*The Fair Maid of the Mill*)

John Philip Sousa, "The Stars and Stripes Forever"

"St. George's Windsor"

"Wayfaring Stranger" (arranged by Norman Lloyd)

Outline

Expanding harmonic areas with $\frac{6}{4}$ chords
- The cadential $\frac{6}{4}$
- The pedal or neighboring $\frac{6}{4}$
- The arpeggiating $\frac{6}{4}$
- The passing $\frac{6}{4}$
- The four $\frac{6}{4}$ types

Other expansions of the tonic area
- The subdominant in tonic expansions
- The dominant in tonic expansions
- Contexts for the submediant
- Embedding PD–D–T within the tonic area
- Extending the final tonic area

Expanding Harmonic Areas with $\frac{6}{4}$ Chords

Looking at how composers expand the basic phrase model T–PD–D–T provides valuable insight into their compositional styles and into the features that make their works uniquely beautiful. When functional areas are expanded, diatonic triads may lose their usual functions and work in quite different ways; for example, IV may no longer serve as a predominant, but instead become an extension of the tonic. A good place to begin is with $\frac{6}{4}$ chords.

The Cadential $\frac{6}{4}$

In the Classical style—the music of Mozart, for example—many cadences include a brief expansion of the dominant area by a **cadential $\frac{6}{4}$**. Listen to the opening of the third movement of Mozart's Piano Sonata in D Major (Example 14.1), which features this voice-leading chord.

EXAMPLE 14.1: Mozart, Piano Sonata in D Major, mvt. 3, mm. 1-4 🎧

D: ii⁶   V$_{4-3}^{6-5}$
                                                          PD   D
                                                                     (HC)

In this familiar-sounding Mozart cadence (m. 4), the dominant triad (A-C♯-E) is preceded by what appears to be a tonic harmony in second inversion, A-D-F♯. This chord, however, does not *function* as the tonic; rather, it displaces and embellishes the V chord by simultaneous 6-5 (F♯ to E) and 4-3 (D to C♯) motion above the sustained bass note A, the root of the dominant. You could think of this voice-leading like a consonant 6–5 and a dissonant 4–3 suspension (but without the suspension's preparation). Also like a suspension, the cadential $\frac{6}{4}$ is written on a strong beat and resolved on a weak beat. The F5 and D4 of Mozart's cadential $\frac{6}{4}$ are approached by step from the previous chord, a ii⁶— standard voice-leading for this harmony.

🎧 **KEY CONCEPT** The cadential $\frac{6}{4}$ has a dominant function, even though it is built of tones from the tonic triad. Its $\frac{6}{4}$–$\frac{5}{3}$ motion expands the dominant area of the basic phrase, with the dissonant $\frac{6}{4}$ on the strong beat and its resolution on a weaker beat. In four voices, the bass of the $^6_4$ chord is doubled, to reinforce its dominant function.

Don't write V$^6_4$ alone as a symbol for the cadential $^6_4$, since that notation implies a second-inversion dominant triad. Think instead of V$^{6-5}_{4-3}$ as a single analytical symbol that shows voice-leading above a dominant harmony. Likewise, it's best not to write I$^6_4$ for the first chord, even though many older textbooks do; while I$^6_4$ reflects the pitch content above the bass, it obscures the chord's dominant function and does not reflect its characteristic voice-leading. If you doubt the dominant function of the cadential $^6_4$, try singing the chord roots as you listen to Example 14.1. Chances are, you will sing $\hat{5}$ on both beats of measure 4.

Cadential $^6_4$s are found in many styles of tonal music. In "My Country, 'Tis of Thee" (Example 14.2), for instance, the first full phrase includes two cadential $^6_4$s: the one marked in measure 5 moves to a decisive PAC cadence (m. 6), but the one in measure 4 resolves evasively to vi (more about this Chapter 15). Both $^6_4$ chords double the bass's C, and both are preceded by ii^6 chords. The $^6_4$ in measure 4 is labeled V$^{8-7}_{6-3}$ to account for the octave C in the tenor moving down to the chordal seventh, B♭.

EXAMPLE 14.2: "My Country, 'Tis of Thee," mm. 1–6

Like most embellishing chords, the cadential $^6_4$ could be removed from the cadence without changing the general harmonic plan of the phrase, but it provides smooth voice-leading from the predominant area. Cadential $^6_4$s are almost always preceded by a predominant harmony (as in Examples 14.1 and 14.2), rarely by the tonic harmony. For now, approach them with ii, ii^6, ii^7, or IV (in minor, ii^{o6}, ii^{ø7}, or iv) or other inversions of these chords.

Writing Cadential $^6_4$ Chords Typical progressions with a cadential $^6_4$ chord are given in Example 14.3. The voice-leading for all of these is the same in the parallel minor (part b), but raise ♭$\hat{7}$ to create a leading tone in the V or V^7.

EXAMPLE 14.3: Resolutions of the cadential $^6_4$

KEY CONCEPT To write a cadential $^6_4$:

1. Always double the bass, which reinforces the dominant function. Any other doubling will result in voice-leading problems and won't be idiomatic.

2. Approach the cadential $^6_4$ from a predominant harmony: usually ii6, ii7, or IV (iiº6, iiØ7, or iv in minor) or other inversions. Keep common tones, if any, between the predominant chord and the $^6_4$, and move other voices the shortest distance.

3. Write the $^6_4$ chord on a strong beat in the measure; it displaces the V or V7, which would normally occupy a strong beat. In triple meter, the cadential $^6_4$ sometimes appears on beat 2, resolving to V or V7 on beat 3.

4. Resolve the "suspended" tones of the $^6_4$ downward: the sixth above the bass moves to a fifth, and the fourth moves to a third ($^{6-5}_{4-3}$).

5. Typical soprano parts are $\hat{1}$-$\hat{7}$-$\hat{1}$ (Example 14.3a-c) or $\hat{3}$-$\hat{2}$-$\hat{1}$ (parts d and e) over the bass $\hat{5}$-$\hat{1}$, creating a PAC.

6. If the cadential $^6_4$ resolves to a dominant seventh, the doubled bass note (in one of the upper voices) moves to the seventh of the V7 chord ($\hat{4}$), making an 8-7 motion above the bass (parts d and e).

Try it #1

Complete the authentic cadences indicated by the Roman numerals below. Write the melody notes as $\hat{4}$-$\hat{3}$-$\hat{2}$-$\hat{1}$. Use quarter notes and, for the final chord, half notes.

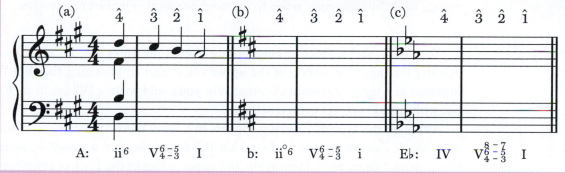

A: ii^6 V$^{6-5}_{4-3}$ I   b: ii$^{\circ 6}$ V$^{6-5}_{4-3}$ i   E♭: IV   V$^{8-7}_{6-\,\,5}_{4-3}$ I

The Pedal or Neighboring $\frac{6}{4}$

Now listen to Example 14.4 to hear another type of $\frac{6}{4}$. At the beginning of each of the two phrases in this example (mm. 1–2 and 5–6), the opening tonic is expanded in the triplets of the piano left hand by neighboring motion, A-B♭-A and C-D-C above a static F3 in the bass. This voicing takes advantage of the common tone between I and IV, F, by holding it in the bass as a pedal point and placing the IV chord briefly in the position (F-B♭-D).

EXAMPLE 14.4: Mozart, Sonata for Violin and Piano, K. 296, mvt. 2, mm. 1–8

> **KEY CONCEPT** A $^6_4$ chord created by two simultaneous upper neighbors above a common-tone pedal in the bass is known as a **pedal** or **neighboring** $^6_4$. The "pedal" label refers to the sustained or repeated bass note (like a low organ pedal), while "neighboring" refers to the neighbor motion in the upper voices.

You could label a pedal or neighboring $^6_4$ as in measures 1-2, I^{5-6-5}_{3-4-3}, highlighting the neighbor motion of the upper voices and emphasizing the chord's function as a tonic expansion. Alternatively, you could write a IV^6_4 (as in m. 5), but with (ped $^6_4$) or (N$^6_4$) written below.

Although this type of $^6_4$ usually appears in a weak metric position, as in the example, it can sometimes be found on the strong beat of a measure, as in Example 14.5 (mm. 2–3). Here again, the upper voices of the $^6_4$ act as neighbors to the tonic chord tones, with the characteristic pedal point in the bass. Because it expands the tonic and does not proceed to V, this type of IV^6_4 does not carry the PD label, and the phrase expresses T-D-T only.

EXAMPLE 14.5: Mozart, Piano Sonata in C Major, mvt. 1, mm. 1-4

SUMMARY

The pedal or neighboring $^6_4$

- embellishes and prolongs a root-position triad;
- is usually metrically unaccented;
- shares its bass note with the harmony it embellishes, while two upper voices move in stepwise neighbor motion above that bass.

The same technique may be applied to a root-position triad or seventh chord in the dominant area, as in the Schubert song shown in Example 14.6. Here, the dominant harmony of the half cadence (mm. 9–10) is extended for an additional measure with a pedal I^6_4. (For now, disregard the circled embellishing tones.)

EXAMPLE 14.6: Schubert, "Morgengruss," mm. 5–10

Translation: Good morning, beautiful miller maid! Why did you immediately hide your little head as if something had happened to you?

Example 14.7 shows $\frac{6}{4}$ chords expanding the tonic and dominant areas in an SATB context; they may be found in the predominant area as well, but are less common there.

EXAMPLE 14.7: Expanding the tonic and dominant areas

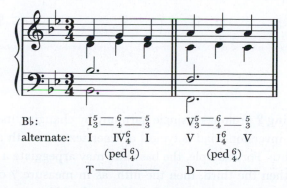

KEY CONCEPT To write a pedal (neighboring) $^6_4$:

1. Decide which harmony you want to prolong (T, D, or PD). Write that chord in root position twice with the same voicing, leaving a space between chords for the neighbor tones (Example 14.8a).

2. Fill in the bass of the $^6_4$ chord first—the same bass as the chords on either side—and double it in the same voice as the other chords (part b).

3. Write upper neighbors to decorate the other two voices (part c).

EXAMPLE 14.8: Steps in writing a pedal (neighboring) $^6_4$ chord

Try it #2

Write a pedal (neighboring) $^6_4$ between the two tonic triads given.

The Arpeggiating $^6_4$

The **arpeggiating** $^6_4$ prolongs a single harmony by changing its bass note. This type of second-inversion triad is typical of freer textures with a relatively slow harmonic rhythm. For example, the bass line may arpeggiate a triad, sounding first the root, then the third, then the fifth, as in measure 7 of "My Country" (Example 14.9). When the bass reaches the triad's fifth, an arpeggiating $^6_4$ has been created.

EXAMPLE 14.9: "My Country, 'Tis of Thee," mm. 7-10 🎧

A bass instrument may create an arpeggiating $^6_4$ by alternating between a chordal root and fifth, as in Sousa's "Stars and Stripes Forever" (Example 14.10). In this kind of root-fifth alternation, also found in rags, waltzes, and some popular songs, the $^6_4$s are ephemeral: the bass line quickly returns to the root.

EXAMPLE 14.10: Sousa, "The Stars and Stripes Forever," Trio, mm. 37–40 🎧

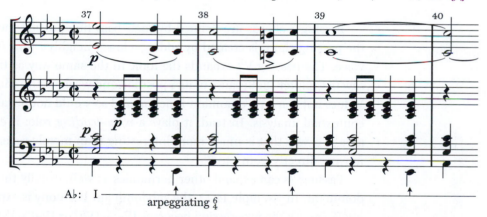

There are no special voice-leading rules for writing an arpeggiating $^6_4$, other than the recommendation that it be placed on a weak beat. When analyzing with Roman numerals, consider what the main bass note of the measure is—usually the lowest-sounding chord tone—and examine the progression with that note in mind. Label the chord with (arp) or (arpeggiating) written beneath the $^6_4$, as in Examples 14.9 and 14.10.

The Passing $^6_4$

A common strategy for expanding the tonic area is to move from root-position I to I⁶ or the reverse, which may involve a voice exchange between $\hat{1}$ and $\hat{3}$. Example 14.11 shows a soprano-bass voice exchange similar to those in first-species style.

In part (a), F#5–D5 in the soprano changes places with D3–F#3 in the bass. Part (b) shows the same exchange embellished with unaccented passing tones, producing counterpoint in contrary motion: $\hat{1}$-$\hat{2}$-$\hat{3}$ in the bass and $\hat{3}$-$\hat{2}$-$\hat{1}$ in the soprano. The passing tone here can be harmonized, as in part (c), with a **passing $^6_4$** chord, labeled (P$^6_4$).

EXAMPLE 14.11: Voice exchanges between I and I⁶ that expand the tonic area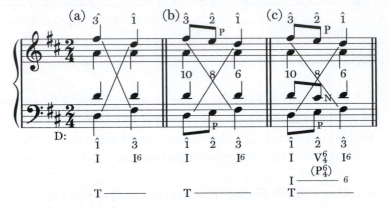

Passing $^6_4$ chords are defined by their bass-line passing motion. In part (c), the passing chord is created by adding a lower neighbor tone (C#4) to the tenor voice. The passing V$^6_4$ expands the tonic in the same way as the passing V$^4_3$ we saw in Chapter 13. Because of its $^6_4$ position and weak metric context, this passing V does not convey a dominant function and so would not be labeled with a D in contextual analysis. Instead, it plays a *voice-leading* role: it expands the tonic area in a way that is much more interesting than merely repeating the tonic or moving directly from I to I⁶.

Passing $^6_4$s can expand other harmonies as well, usually the subdominant or dominant. In Example 14.12, the subdominant harmony is expanded by a passing I$^6_4$ (m. 2); the progression becomes IV-I$^6_4$-IV⁶ (or IV-P$^6_4$-IV⁶).

EXAMPLE 14.12: Subdominant prolonged with a passing $^6_4$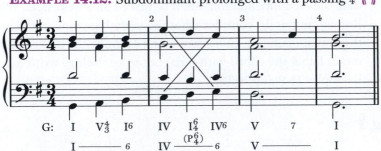

Progressions featuring passing $^6_4$s are usually "reversible": the root-position harmony can come first or last. Unlike cadential $^6_4$s, passing $^6_4$s typically occur on unaccented positions in the measure. Analyze with a P$^6_4$ beneath the chord, and in the contextual analysis simply write a long dash after the functional label (e.g., T or PD), as in Example 14.12.

The passing $^6_4$ may also connect two different chords as long as the chords belong to the same functional area. For example, in the progression IV⁶-I$^6_4$-IV, the last chord may be replaced with ii⁶—a triad with the same function and the same bass as the IV chord (Example 14.13, m. 2). This type of progression, sometimes with chromatic chords substituted for the diatonic ones, is a mainstay of Romantic-era harmony, as we will see in later chapters.

EXAMPLE 14.13: Passing $^6_4$: IV⁶-I$^6_4$-ii⁶

G: I   IV⁶ I$^6_4$ ii⁶   V⁷ ——————   I
                 (P$^6_4$)
    T   PD ——————   D ——————   T

KEY CONCEPT To write passing $^6_4$s:

1. Decide which harmony you want to prolong (normally tonic, dominant, or subdominant).

2. Set up root-position and first-inversion chords of that harmony, with a voice exchange between the bass and one of the upper parts, often the soprano (Example 14.14a).

3. Fill in the skips of a third with stepwise motion in both voices; this automatically doubles the fifth of the $^6_4$, the correct doubling (part b).

4. Complete the other voices. All parts should connect by common tone or by step.

EXAMPLE 14.14: Steps in writing a passing $^6_4$

(a)   (b)   (c)   P
                                                         CT
                                                         N
                                                         P
G: IV ——— 6   IV ——— 6 $^6_4$ 6
                                               (P$^6_4$)   6
                                           IV ———

Try it #3

Fill in the space between the I and I^6 (or i and i^6) with a passing $^6_4$, from the bass and figures provided. Include a voice exchange with the soprano, and write a Roman numeral analysis.

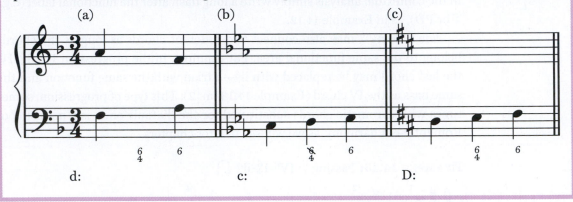

The Four $^6_4$ Types

When a root-position chord is replaced with a first-inversion chord, the general function of the progression stays the same. We might infer that triads in $^6_4$ position are also interchangeable with other inversions. But $^6_4$ chords have always been treated specially in tonal music: they are used only in a few specific contexts, usually to expand one of the functional areas of the basic phrase.

KEY CONCEPT Each $^6_4$ chord you write must be one of the following types:

- cadential $^6_4$
- pedal or neighboring $^6_4$
- passing $^6_4$
- arpeggiating $^6_4$

Further, be sure any $^6_4$ you write lies within the T, PD, or D area (e.g., don't write a iii$^6_4$ or vi$^6_4$). Although $^6_4$ chords can be left out without changing the underlying organization of a phrase, this does not mean they are unimportant: second inversions are an essential voice-leading strategy in many genres of tonal music and can be a significant indication of musical style.

SUMMARY

To review, when writing $^6_4$ chords:

- Always double the bass.
- Be sure you can name the type of $^6_4$. (If you can't name it, it probably doesn't belong there.)
- In all $^6_4$s except arpeggiating, all voices should approach and leave chord members by step (forming neighbor or passing tones) or by common tone.
- Arpeggiating $^6_4$s feature chordal skips within the expanded harmony, but must resolve correctly to the next harmony.

Other Expansions of the Tonic Area

The Subdominant in Tonic Expansions

As we have seen, when the subdominant, in any inversion, appears between two tonic chords, it does not serve a predominant function because it does not progress to a dominant harmony. Example 14.15, showing i–iv–i in a folk style, illustrates this principle. (Circled notes are embellishing tones.)

EXAMPLE 14.15: "Wayfaring Stranger," mm. 1–4

Measures 1-2 of Example 14.16 feature a tonic expansion with root-position I–IV–I chords; these same chords appear in measure 1, but with the IV as a neighboring $^6_4$ lasting only one sixteenth note. The repetition of the same gesture in measure 2 with the root of the IV (E♭) in the bass draws the listener's attention to both statements.

EXAMPLE 14.16: Brahms, *Variations on a Theme by Haydn*, mm. 1–5

The Dominant in Tonic Expansions

When the tonic area is expanded by dominant triads and seventh chords, there are several outer-voice patterns that work well and fit within the guidelines of species counterpoint. In Example 14.17, for instance, neighbor and passing motion in the soprano and/or bass produces the outer-voice intervals 8-6-8 and 10-10-10.

EXAMPLE 14.17: Tonic expansions with neighbor and passing motion

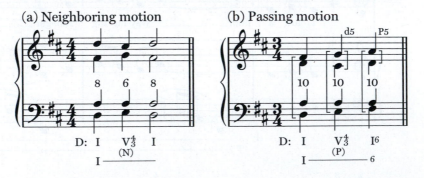

(a) Neighboring motion

(b) Passing motion

In part (b), the passing dominant is analogous to the passing $^6_4$, and this voice-leading pattern (10-10-10) overrides the normal resolution of the chordal seventh (G4) down.

KEY CONCEPT When the soprano moves $\hat{3}$-$\hat{4}$-$\hat{5}$ against a bass line of $\hat{1}$-$\hat{2}$-$\hat{3}$, the outer voices move in parallel tenths. The chordal seventh of the V$^4_3$ moves upward ($\hat{4}$ to $\hat{5}$ in the soprano), and the d5 may move to a P5.

Outer-voice patterns that imply a tonic expansion include

- stepwise motion between members of the tonic triad
  (e.g., $\hat{1}$-$\hat{2}$-$\hat{3}$, $\hat{3}$-$\hat{2}$-$\hat{1}$, $\hat{3}$-$\hat{4}$-$\hat{5}$, or $\hat{5}$-$\hat{4}$-$\hat{3}$ in either soprano or bass), or

- neighboring motion above or below a member of the tonic triad
  (e.g., $\hat{1}$-$\hat{2}$-$\hat{1}$, $\hat{1}$-$\hat{7}$-$\hat{1}$, $\hat{3}$-$\hat{2}$-$\hat{3}$, $\hat{3}$-$\hat{4}$-$\hat{3}$, or $\hat{5}$-$\hat{4}$-$\hat{5}$).

Combine these patterns with contrary motion in the other voice, or with parallel motion between voices in tenths. You may also combine passing motion in one voice with neighbor motion in the other. As always, avoid soprano-bass patterns that result in parallel perfect intervals or a poor resolution of tendency tones.

Although we have focused on stepwise motion, bass-soprano combinations that include a bass-line skip are also possible. For example, the bass might skip from a member of the tonic triad to an inverted dominant chord before resolving, as in Example 14.18a and b. The bass note G3 in part (a) could have been approached by step from the chord tone F♯, had the initial tonic chord been in first inversion; this implied stepwise connection is what makes the bass line work.

In part (b), the bass line skips a diminished fourth; although such a skip is normally avoided in common-practice voice-leading, here it makes sense because of the stepwise connection that would have been made had the first chord been in root position. Motion of this sort in the bass can be expressive and beautiful, especially skips to the leading tone in minor. Write skips like this only in the bass, and only where the function of the skip (here, as a tonic expansion) is clear.

Double neighbor tones are another possibility for the bass (part c): the bass line skips from one inversion of the dominant to another, as in the progression I-V$^4_3$-V$^6_5$-I (shown here), or I-V$^6_5$-V$^4_3$-I.

EXAMPLE 14.18: Tonic expansions with skips in the bass line 🎧

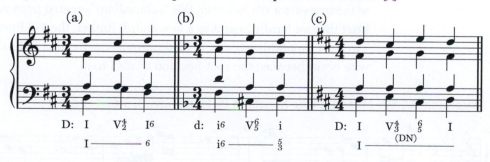

Try it #4

Determine which three chords best harmonize the following outer-voice patterns. Notate the chords on the staves, and write the Roman numerals below.

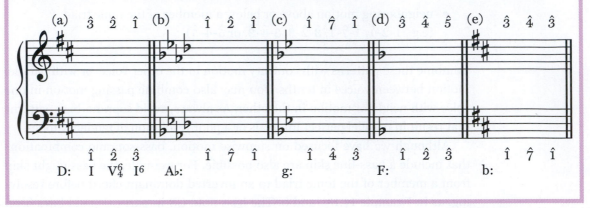

(a) $\hat{3}$ $\hat{2}$ $\hat{1}$ (b) $\hat{1}$ $\hat{2}$ $\hat{1}$ (c) $\hat{1}$ $\hat{7}$ $\hat{1}$ (d) $\hat{3}$ $\hat{4}$ $\hat{5}$ (e) $\hat{3}$ $\hat{4}$ $\hat{3}$

$\hat{1}$ $\hat{2}$ $\hat{3}$ $\hat{1}$ $\hat{7}$ $\hat{1}$ $\hat{1}$ $\hat{4}$ $\hat{3}$ $\hat{1}$ $\hat{2}$ $\hat{3}$ $\hat{1}$ $\hat{7}$ $\hat{1}$

D: I V_4^6 I^6 A♭:   g: F: b:

Contexts for the Submediant

Since the submediant triad shares two scale degrees with the tonic triad ($\hat{1}$ and $\hat{3}$), it often serves as a tonic expansion or substitute. The two types of tonic expansions presented here—by 5-6 motion and the progression I-vi (or i-VI in minor)—usually appear at phrase beginnings.

With 5-6 Motion Consider the first phrase from Mozart's B♭ Major Sonata (Example 14.19), where the tonic chord in the first half of measure 1, arpeggiated in the left hand, is subtly transformed in the second half of the measure as F4 moves to G4 (G5 appears in the right-hand melody as well). Since this F-G motion above the bass, B♭3, forms the intervals 5-6, you could label the last beat of the measure a vi⁶; however, this "submediant" created from voice-leading is so brief that we hardly hear it as a new chord. Rather, the 5-6 linear motion allows I to move smoothly to ii (m. 2), and prevents the parallel fifths that would otherwise occur between the root-position triads I to ii.

EXAMPLE 14.19: Mozart, Piano Sonata in B♭ Major, mvt. 1, mm. 1-4

B♭: I 5————————6 ii ———————————— V⁷———————— I ————
     T ————————————   PD ——————————   D ————————   T ————

KEY CONCEPT The tonic area may be expanded by 5-6 intervallic motion above scale degree $\hat{1}$. This motion is generally labeled I5-6 rather than I-vi⁶, though either is correct.

I-vi (i-VI in Minor) A phrase that begins with tonic and submediant harmonies creates an effect similar to the linear 5-6, but the bass movement down a third adds emphasis to the change of chord color: from major to minor (I-vi) in major keys, and from minor to major (i-VI) in minor keys. The progression I–vi–IV–V is a standard context for the submediant; you probably know it well from the "Heart and Soul" piano duet. This expansion of the tonic area is usually labeled with separate Roman numerals, as in "My Country" (Example 14.20).

EXAMPLE 14.20: "My Country, 'Tis of Thee," mm. 1-6

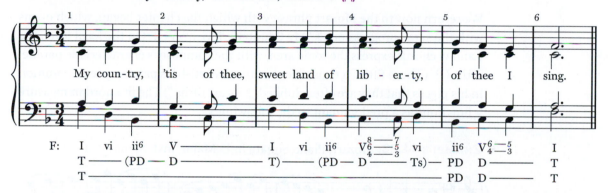

In the upper-level contextual analysis given here, we show that the vi chord expands the tonic area (in mm. 1 and 3) by drawing a line from T until the harmonic function changes (on beat 3). In measure 4, the context for the submediant is slightly different: it follows V, not I. Rather than expanding the tonic, it serves instead as a tonic substitute, supplying a **deceptive resolution** to V (we will learn more about this in Chapter 15). Label this type of vi chord as a Ts (tonic substitute) in keeping with the basic phrase model (D resolves to T).

Now look at the voice-leading for I to vi in measures 1 and 3. To connect the tonic and submediant harmonies:

- hold the common tones ($\hat{1}$ and $\hat{3}$) in two parts,
- move $\hat{5}$ to $\hat{6}$,
- move the bass down a third from $\hat{1}$ to $\hat{6}$.
- The root of the vi chord will be doubled.

In phrases without the standard predominants—ii⁶, ii⁶₅, or IV (or their minor-key equivalents)—the vi chord can also play a weak predominant role, as shown in the hymn in Example 14.21. Here, because of its position on a strong beat, moving to the cadential V, the submediant functions more as cadential preparation than tonic expansion. (Contrast this with Example 14.20, where the vi chord appears on a weak beat and moves to ii⁶.)

EXAMPLE 14.21: "St. George's Windsor," mm. 1-2

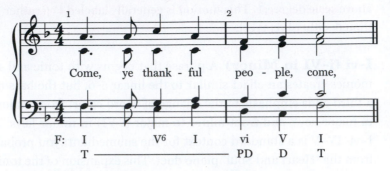

Embedding PD–D–T Within the Tonic Area

We return now to the Mozart phrase with which the chapter began, which opens with the same progression as "My Country": I-vi-ii⁶-V⁷-I. On the local level, the I and vi chords express the tonic area, with the composer's characteristic parallel fifths (!). (These fifths, a consequent of the Alberti-bass pattern, are so common in his pieces that they are often dubbed "Mozart fifths.") The ii⁶ chord in measure 2 functions as a predominant to the following V⁷.

EXAMPLE 14.22: Mozart, Piano Sonata in D Major, mvt. 3, mm. 1-4

Let's consider how this progression functions in terms of the phrase as a whole. Although the V⁷ in measure 2 moves to I, it does not create a phrase-ending cadence here. While the left hand sets up what seems to be cadential motion (root motion $\hat{5}$ to $\hat{1}$), the melody refuses to cooperate—it comes to a resting place only in measure 4 at the half cadence. We can therefore interpret the opening two-and-a-half measures as a tonic expansion, followed by predominant (ii⁶) and dominant harmonies at the cadence (mm. 3–4), expanded by a cadential $^6_4$. The two-level contextual analysis here and under Example 14.20 shows how an embedded PD-D-T (in parentheses, upper level) can expand the tonic area, while the lower level indicates how long the opening tonic expansion actually lasts (usually until the cadential PD-D-T).

KEY CONCEPT Not every dominant-tonic progression makes a cadence. All the musical elements—melody, rhythm, and harmony—must cooperate to create a sense of finality. When small-scale D-T or PD-D-T progressions are embedded within a larger phrase, they serve to prolong the tonic area.

Try it #5

Provide a Roman numeral and contextual analysis for the short progression below, using Example 14.22 as your model.

Extending the Final Tonic Area

For an example of a tonic expansion at the end of the phrase model, listen to the end of the second movement of the Mozart sonata shown in Example 14.23. Here, after an extended final, lyrical phrase (not shown), the cadential $^6_4$ ushers in a conclusive PAC in measures 71–72. Yet this is not the end of the movement: Mozart twice reiterates a V7–I progression that extends the final tonic area. This type of cadential extension, sometimes called a **codetta**, can also be created by repeating IV–I, IV–I. When writing a contextual analysis, look for the end of a four- or eight-bar melodic-harmonic unit as the end of the basic phrase (D–T); any cadential flourishes or repeated V–I chords that follow are extensions of the tonic.

EXAMPLE 14.23: Mozart, Piano Sonata in C Major, mvt. 2, mm. 71–74 🎧

Finally, we can add to the list of basic phrase progressions those studied in this chapter. Read Example 14.24 like a menu—choose one pattern from each column to create an idiomatic progression (the PD column is optional). You now have a vocabulary of chords and progressions that will take you far in analyzing the music you hear and perform.

EXAMPLE 14.24: Basic phrase progressions with T, PD, and D expansions and extensions

T	PD	D	T
C: I_3^5 – $_4^6$ – $_3^5$ (I IV$_4^6$ I)	IV or ii$_5^6$	V$_4^6$ – $_3^5$	I
C: I I^6 I$_4^6$ I	vi or IV^6	V$_{4-3}^{8-7}_{6-5}$	I
C: I V$_4^6$ I^6	IV I$_4^6$ IV^6	V$_3^5$ – $_4^6$ – $_3^5$ (V I$_4^6$ V)	I
C: I IV I	IV^6 I$_4^6$ ii$_{(5)}^6$	V or V^7	I
C: I V$_2^4$ I^6			
C: I^6 V$_5^6$ I			
C: I V$_3^4$ V$_5^6$ I			
C: I vi			
C: I$^{5-6}$			
C: I vi ii^6 V I T —— (PD D T)			

Did You Know?

Johannes Brahms's *Variations on a Theme by Haydn*, consisting of a theme in B♭ major, eight variations, and a finale, was composed in 1873 and published in two versions: for two pianos (written first but designated Op. 56b) and for orchestra (Op. 56a). Recent scholarship, however, has revealed that the theme is not likely by Haydn after all. In 1870, Brahms's friend Carl Ferdinand Pohl, librarian of the Vienna Philharmonic Society and a Haydn biographer, showed the composer a transcription he had made of a piece attributed to Haydn. The second movement was titled "St. Anthony Chorale," and this is the theme Brahms appropriated. It turns out that Pohl's piece was not by Haydn, however, and while current usage still prefers the original title, *Variations on the St. Anthony Chorale* is the name favored by those who object to perpetuating a misattribution. Even that name tells us very little, though: to date, no other mention of the so-called St. Anthony Chorale has been found.

Just before the end of the piece, in the coda of the finale, Brahms quotes a short passage that really is by Haydn—the cello line from a measure of his *Clock* Symphony (second movement), one of the finest examples of his pioneering work in the symphonic variation form. This fragmentary allusion may be the music's sole remaining link to Haydn.

TERMS YOU SHOULD KNOW

5-6 motion	embedded PD-D-T	tonic expansion
arpeggiating $^6_4$	passing $^6_4$	tonic substitute (Ts)
cadential $^6_4$	pedal or neighboring $^6_4$	voice exchange
dominant expansion	pedal point	

QUESTIONS FOR REVIEW

1. Why are cadential $^6_4$s labeled V$^{6-5}_{4-3}$? Discuss the pros and cons of other possible labeling systems.
2. What is the function of a pedal or neighboring $^6_4$? Where is it found?
3. What is the function of an arpeggiating $^6_4$? Where is it found?
4. What type of $^6_4$ is associated with a voice exchange?
5. What chords (in inversions) typically pass between I and I[6]?
6. In music for your own instrument, find an example of three of the four $^6_4$ types.
7. Under what circumstances do the tendency tones of a passing dominant chord not resolve as usual?
8. What are two ways in which a submediant triad may expand the tonic area?
9. In a contextual analysis, how do you show brief T-D-T or T-PD-D-T progressions that prolong the tonic at the beginning of a phrase?

Know It? Show It!

Focus by working through the tutorials.

Learn with InQuizitive.

Apply what you've learned to complete the workbook assignments.

15

New Cadence Types and Diatonic Root Progressions

Overview

This chapter introduces three additional cadence types and voice-leading for specific root progressions. We also consider uses of the mediant and minor dominant triads.

Repertoire

Johann Sebastian Bach
  Chaconne, from Violin Partita No. 2 in D Minor
  Invention in D Minor
  "Wachet auf" ("Awake," Chorale No. 197)

Arcangelo Corelli, Sonata in D Minor, Op. 4, No. 8, Preludio

George Frideric Handel, "Hallelujah!" from *Messiah*

John Lennon and Paul McCartney, "Nowhere Man," from *Rubber Soul*

Don McLean, "Vincent"

Wolfgang Amadeus Mozart, Piano Sonata in D Major, K. 284, mvt. 3

"My Country, 'Tis of Thee"

"Old Hundredth"

Joel Phillips, "Blues for Norton"

Purcell, "Dido's Lament," from *Dido and Aeneas*

"Wayfaring Stranger" (arranged by Norman Lloyd)

Outline

New cadence types
- The deceptive cadence and resolution: V–vi (or V–VI)
- The plagal cadence and extension: IV–I (or iv–i)
- The Phrygian cadence: iv^6–V

Basic root progressions
- Root motion by descending fifth
- Root motion by descending third
- Root motion by second

Other diatonic harmonies
- About mediant triads
- The mediant and minor dominant in minor keys
- Parallel $^6_3$ chords

New Cadence Types

The Deceptive Cadence and Resolution: V–vi (or V–VI)

Thus far, we have considered how to end phrases with a half cadence (HC), an imperfect authentic cadence (IAC), and a perfect authentic cadence (PAC). Listen to two phrases from Bach's chorale "Wachet auf" (Example 15.1) to hear another option. The melody is the same in each phrase, but the two cadences are quite different.

EXAMPLE 15.1: Bach, "Wachet auf," mm. 18-24 🎧

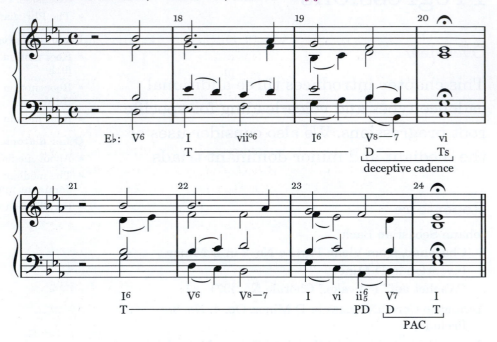

At the end of the first phrase (m. 20), Bach replaces the expected final tonic harmony with a tonic substitute (Ts), the submediant triad, to make a **deceptive cadence**: V7-vi. The name is appropriate, since the drama of this harmonic "deception" can be striking.

Sometimes a V-vi motion that sounds deceptive will appear in the middle of a phrase rather than at the end; this is called a **deceptive resolution**, and we have already seen one example, in "My Country, 'Tis of Thee." Listen again to Example 15.2. In measure 4, the V7 on beat 2 is followed by a vi (a deceptive resolution), preventing the phrase from ending on "liberty"; the cadence in measures 5-6 then concludes on the tonic. When connecting V or V7 to vi or VI in the middle of a phrase, you may want to weaken the dominant chord by inverting it or by placing it in a weaker metrical position to make the progression less likely to sound like a firm cadence.

EXAMPLE 15.2: "My Country, 'Tis of Thee," mm. 1-6

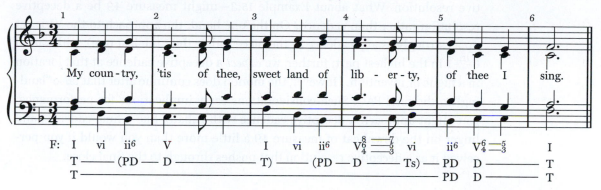

Deceptive cadences in general are fairly rare, but in Baroque music you might find one toward the end of a fugue or invention, as in Example 15.3. These contrapuntal pieces tend to build up forward momentum until a "false ending" briefly slows the momentum in preparation for the final cadence. The deceptive cadence (in m. 49) is set up just like a definitive final PAC except that the bass resolves up by step instead of down a fifth. Then the remainder of the phrase completes the thought that was interrupted by the deception. Though the harmonic rhythm overall is one or two chords per measure, in measures 48 and 51 it accelerates before the cadence, also typical of Baroque style.

EXAMPLE 15.3: Bach, Invention in D Minor, mm. 45-52

While you may occasionally encounter a "true" deceptive cadence like that in Example 15.1, where it's accompanied by a fermata and a rhythmic context that marks the end of the phrase, you will more often find V–vi employed as a deceptive resolution. What about Example 15.3—might measure 49 be a deceptive resolution rather than cadence? On the one hand, the approach to the VI is set up as strongly as any cadence in the piece (other than the last one), with raised $\hat{6}$-$\hat{7}$-$\hat{1}$ in the highest part; further, we *expect* a deceptive cadence at that location in a fugue or invention. However, the motion does continue after that false "landing" to the final PAC. Such considerations carry implications for performance: you might approach a deceptive cadence with rubato, like a final cadence, and linger on the downbeat of measure 49 a little more than you would if you perceived it as a deceptive resolution that pushes through to the final close.

KEY CONCEPT The most effective deceptive cadences are voiced just like PACs (see Example 15.4):

- Use root position for both the V (V7) and vi (VI) chords, with $\hat{5}$-$\hat{6}$ in the bass.

- The upper parts resolve the V or V7 normally, with $\hat{7}$ moving up to $\hat{1}$ and the remaining voices moving in contrary motion to the bass (parts a-b).

- $\hat{7}$-$\hat{1}$ or $\hat{2}$-$\hat{1}$ often appear in the highest part, as in a PAC V$^{(7)}$–I (parts c-d).

- Correct voice-leading results in a doubled third ($\hat{1}$) in the vi (or VI) chord—an exception to the "double the root in root-position triads" guideline.

EXAMPLE 15.4: Deceptive cadence model (D–Ts)

If you attempt to resolve V to vi (or VI) without doubling the third ($\hat{1}$) in the vi (VI), you will end up with parallel everything: parallel octaves *and* fifths between the bass and an upper part (part e). Also recall that in minor keys, the $\flat\hat{7}$ must be raised to $\hat{7}$ (part d); omitting that accidental is a common error (part e). Although the deceptive cadence with the submediant is the most typical, resolutions such as V–IV6 (or other chords that share scale degrees with I or vi) can create a similar effect.

The Plagal Cadence and Extension: IV–I (or iv–i)

Now listen to the final measures of the hymn "Old Hundredth" (Example 15.5). This setting, like many American hymns, includes an "Amen" at the end, set with the root-position chords IV-I; these chords form a **plagal cadence**. Because of their association with hymns, plagal cadences are sometimes even called "Amen" cadences. Measure 13 provides the standard voice-leading, holding the common tone and moving the other upper voices down by step. Though any of the three upper parts may be used as the soprano line, $\hat{4}$–$\hat{3}$ and $\hat{1}$–$\hat{1}$ are especially common.

EXAMPLE 15.5: "Old Hundredth," mm. 9-13

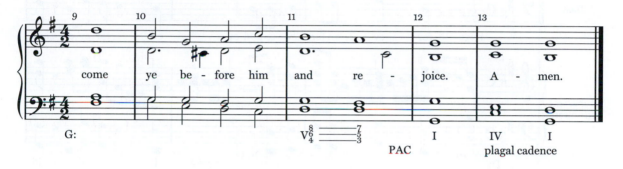

We know from earlier chapters that the progression I-IV-I prolongs the tonic area; plagal motion after a piece's concluding dominant-tonic cadence can also be interpreted as an expansion of the final tonic (some musicians speak of a "plagal resolution" or "plagal expansion of the tonic" rather than "cadence"). A famous instance is shown in Example 15.6, from the end of Handel's "Hallelujah Chorus." The final PAC arrives in measures 87-88, but the choir continues to sing I-IV-I repeatedly in a closing section that ends with a forceful plagal cadence on the final "Hallelujah!" Some conductors interpret this structure musically with a sense of arrival in measure 88, before launching into the plagal extension. The extension allows the rhythmic energy of the piece to unwind while reaffirming the tonic with the repeated D5s in the soprano.

EXAMPLE 15.6: Handel, "Hallelujah!," mm. 86-94 (plagal extension) 🎧

plagal cadence

In some rock and blues styles, the progression I-V-IV-I is a basic ingredient of the harmonic structure. Take the opening of Lennon and McCartney's "Nowhere Man" (Example 15.7), for instance. You might hear the first four measures (chord symbols E-B-A-E, or I-V-IV-I) as prolonging the tonic; measures 5-7 then end with a plagal cadence (iv-I). The use of the progression ii-iv, not standard in common-practice music, and the minor iv (instead of major) lend a fittingly lonely sound to depict this "nowhere" man.

EXAMPLE 15.7: Lennon and McCartney, "Nowhere Man," mm. 1-9

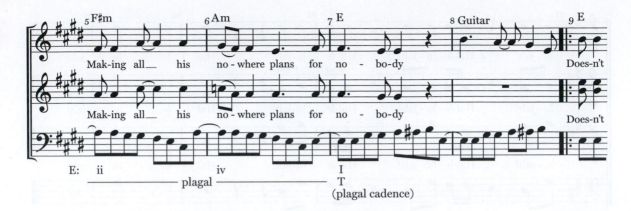

The progression I-V-IV-I came into use in the mid-twentieth century through the blues, an American style that originated early in the twentieth century. The twelve-bar blues shown in Example 15.8 (mm. 2-13) ends with this I-V-IV-I progression, with sevenths added to the chords (as in most blues). Still, although plagal cadences may be used freely in a contemporary or popular style, when composing in common-practice style, write an authentic cadence first, and then expand the final tonic with plagal motion.

EXAMPLE 15.8: Phillips, "Blues for Norton," mm. 1-13 (plagal cadence) 🎧

The Phrygian Cadence: iv⁶–V

Another type of half cadence found in Baroque-era music features a iv⁶ chord in a minor key as the predominant to V.

KEY CONCEPT The **Phrygian cadence**, always iv⁶-V in minor, is named for its characteristic bass line: the half-step descent from ♭$\hat{6}$ to $\hat{5}$ (Example 15.9a). (Such a descent evokes the Phrygian mode, with its half step from ♭$\hat{2}$ to $\hat{1}$.) In addition:

- The highest part normally moves $\hat{4}$-$\hat{5}$ (a whole step), approaching $\hat{5}$ in contrary motion.
- $\hat{1}$ is doubled in the iv⁶; don't double ♭$\hat{6}$, as this leads to an A2 from ♭$\hat{6}$ to $\hat{7}$ (part b, tenor voice) or parallel octaves (part c, bass and tenor).

EXAMPLE 15.9: Part-writing the Phrygian cadence

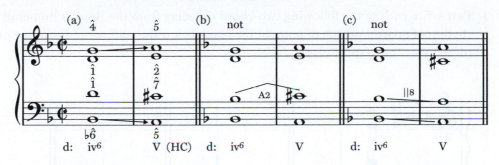

Listen to Example 15.10, from Corelli's Preludio. The expressive opening of this D minor movement features 9-8 suspensions and a Phrygian cadence in measures 6-7, iv6-V. The prelude also ends with a Phrygian cadence (anthology)—an inconclusive "conclusion" that sets up expectations on the part of the listener for the lively second movement.

EXAMPLE 15.10: Corelli, Preludio from Sonata in D Minor, mm. 1-7

SUMMARY

New cadence types:

- The deceptive cadence (V-vi or V-VI) avoids the expected tonic resolution.

- The plagal cadence (IV-I or iv-i; "Amen" cadence) prolongs the tonic area.

- The Phrygian cadence (iv6-V) is a special type of half cadence.

Try it #1

Part-write each of the following two-chord cadences from the Roman numerals given. Use a rhythm of quarter note, half note. In the blank below the staff, write the name of the cadence (deceptive, Phrygian, or plagal).

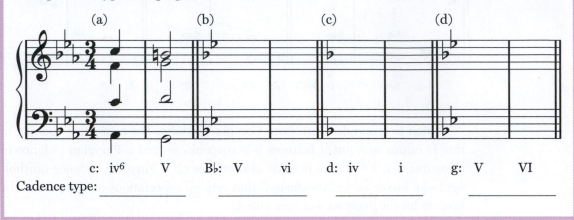

	(a)	(b)		(c)		(d)	
	c: iv⁶ V	B♭: V	vi	d: iv	i	g: V	VI

Cadence type: _____   _____   _____   _____

Basic Root Progressions

In tonal music, most of the connections between chords involve one of three basic root movements.

- **Descending fifth**: authentic cadences (V to I or i), for example, show a root motion from $\hat{5}$ to $\hat{1}$; even though the roots of these chords may not necessarily be in the bass, authentic cadences as a group can be thought of as descending-fifth root progressions.

- **Descending third**: we have seen this root progression in the tonic expansion I to vi, but it may be found in the predominant area of a phrase as well (IV to ii).

- **Ascending second**: connections between I and ii, IV and V, and V and vi are examples of this root progression, which typically connects two functional areas—tonic and predominant or predominant and dominant, for example.

Root Motion by Descending Fifth

The strongest root motion in tonal music is by descending fifth (or ascending fourth—you can think of those as interchangeable); it underlies the cadences introduced in Chapter 12 and many other standard progressions.

🎧 **KEY CONCEPT** The descending-fifth root progression may connect two chords, may form a chain of three or four chords, or may circle through all the diatonic chords in a key:

I-IV-vii°-iii-vi-ii-V-I in major keys,

i-iv-vii° (or VII)-III-VI-ii°-V-I in minor.

All the fifths between the roots of chords in the major-key chain are perfect except the one between IV and vii°, a diminished fifth (scale degrees $\hat{4}$ and $\hat{7}$). (Root position vii° usually occurs only in descending-fifth progressions.) In minor keys, there are two possible diminished fifths because of the variable forms of $\hat{6}$ and $\hat{7}$: between iv and vii° and between VI and ii°.

Listen to part of this chain in action in Example 15.11, a passage from a Mozart sonata. Beginning on the second beat of measure 1, Mozart employs the progression vi-ii6-V7-I, a four-chord segment from the end of the chain: here, the descending fifths form an embedded PD-D-T within the tonic area.

EXAMPLE 15.11: Mozart, Piano Sonata in D Major, mvt. 3, mm. 1-4 🎧

Not all the links in the descending-fifth chain are equally strong: for example, connections involving either the leading-tone or mediant triad rarely appear without the rest of the chain. Other than in sequences (Chapter 19), we don't normally find root motion by *ascending* fifth in tonal music, other than between the tonic and dominant.

🎧 **KEY CONCEPT** Here are some of the most common descending-fifth progressions, and where they appear in the basic phrase model. These progressions are ubiquitous in all styles of tonal music.

I-IV (or i-iv)   T-PD, or T expansion (the beginning or end of a phrase)

vi-ii (or VI-ii°)   PD area, with vi sometimes as a T expansion leading into PD

ii-V (or ii°-V)   PD-D

V-I (or V-i)   D-T (or as a T expansion)

Part-Writing Triads with roots a fifth apart share one chord member; for example, G-B-D and C-E-G share pitch class G. Example 15.12 illustrates how to connect these two chords. They could be functioning as V-I in the key of C major, as here, but they could also be I-IV in G major: the basic voice-leading connections are the same.

EXAMPLE 15.12: Connecting chords a fifth apart 🎧

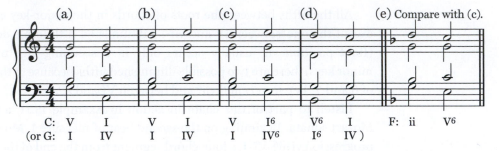

(a)		(b)		(c)		(d)			(e) Compare with (c).	
C: V	I	V	I	V	I⁶	V⁶	I		F: ii	V⁶
(or G: I	IV	I	IV	I	IV⁶	I⁶	IV)			

If we added a B♭ to the key signature to make the key of F major, the same voice-leading and doubling would apply for ii-V (G minor to C major) except in part (c), where there is a first-inversion C major chord; doubling the E would mean doubling the leading tone in F major (see part e). As always, observe the guidelines for doubling and resolving tendency tones within the key.

KEY CONCEPT A standard method of connecting triads with roots a fifth apart is to hold the common tone in the same voice and move all the other parts to the closest possible chord member.

In some descending-fifth progressions, seventh chords may substitute for some of the triads: ii⁷ (or ii⁰⁷) and its inversions instead of ii (or ii°), or V⁷ and its inversions instead of V—as in Example 15.13.

EXAMPLE 15.13: Descending-fifth progressions with seventh chords
(I = incomplete; C = complete)

F: vi	ii⁷	V⁷	I	f: VI	ii⁰⁷	V⁷	i

missing fifth   missing fifth

Though it is possible to substitute IV7 or vi7 (iv7 or VI7 in minor) in place of their triads, these chords are much less prevalent in eighteenth- and nineteenth-century music outside of descending-fifth chains or sequences (Chapter 19). When part-writing any nondominant seventh chord (such as ii7, IV7, and vi7), remember that the chordal seventh should be approached by common tone or by step, and resolve down. Also remember that when root-position V7 moves to I (i), one chord must be incomplete and the other complete.

Root Motion by Descending Third

While root motion by fifth occurs almost exclusively in descending progressions, root motion by third is possible both ascending and descending, with the latter the most typical. In these progressions, however, you don't usually find seventh chords.

KEY CONCEPT The descending-third root progression can also form a chain:

I-vi-IV-ii-vii°-V-iii-I in major keys,

i-VI-iv-ii°-vii° (or VII)-V-III-i in minor.

Common root motion by thirds:

I-vi-IV	T expansion or T-PD
vi-IV-ii	PD area
ii-vii°6	PD to weak D

In Example 15.14, from the beginning of his Chaconne in D Minor, Bach includes the first three chords of the chain.

EXAMPLE 15.14: Bach, Chaconne in D Minor, mm. 3-4

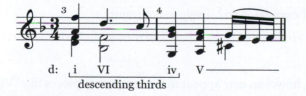

d: i   VI   iv   V ————————
      descending thirds

The last parts of the chain (vii°-V-iii-I) are rarely heard in common-practice progressions: instead, when the phrase reaches the dominant area, a cadence usually follows. The progression vii°-V is likewise rarely found if the texture of the music is chordal and the harmony changes on each chord. In pieces with a freer texture, though, you may encounter a dominant area that begins with vii° (or viiø7 or vii°7), then brings in $\hat{5}$ to make V or V7. If all members of vii°7 and V7 are present, the result is a V7 with an additional third on top—a V9 chord. In that case, the entire dominant area may be given one label: V7 or V9, as appropriate.

Part-Writing Triads whose roots are a third apart share two pitch classes; for example, C-E-G and A-C-E share C and E. Third progressions are usually voiced with the root of the chord doubled in the bass and in an upper part to maximize the common tones between each pair, as in Example 15.15.

EXAMPLE 15.15: Connecting chords by thirds 🎧

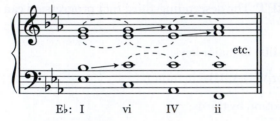

Eb: I   vi   IV   ii

KEY CONCEPT When connecting chords with roots a third apart, hold the common tones and move the other parts to the next-nearest chord member. The chains made by ascending-third motion are:

- I-iii-V-vii°-ii-IV-vi-I in major keys,
- i-III-V-vii° (or VII)-ii°-iv-VI-i in minor.

Only a few of these connections are found in tonal music, and each plays a special role:

- I-iii   T expansion (discussed later in the chapter)
- vi-I   T expansion (relatively uncommon)
- V-vii°   D in freer textures where the root of the V drops out temporarily

The others, however, may appear in contemporary pieces like "Vincent" (Example 15.16), whose verse expands the predominant area with the rising third ii to IV.

EXAMPLE 15.16: McLean, "Vincent," mm. 4–11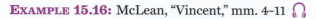

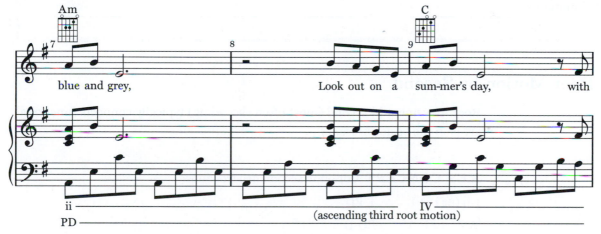

Try it #2

Part-write each of the two-chord pairs below using quarter notes. Label the root-motion type (desc. 5th or desc. 3rd), then circle the common tones between chords: one common tone for descending fifth, two for descending third.

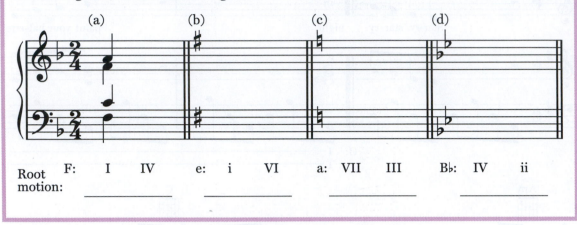

Root
motion:

	(a) F:	I	IV	(b) e:	i	VI	(c) a:	VII	III	(d) B♭:	IV	ii

Root Motion by Second

Root movement by second (most often ascending) typically connects functional areas in the basic phrase.

> **KEY CONCEPT** Common second progressions:
>
> I–ii (or i–ii°)   T–PD
>
> IV–V (or iv–V)   PD–D
>
> I–vii° (or i–vii°)   T–D (with a dominant substitute)
>
> vii°–I (or vii°–i)   D–T (with a dominant substitute)
>
> V–vi (or V–VI)   D–T (with a tonic substitute)

The most direct way to connect chords with roots a second apart would be simply to shift the entire chord up or down a step. While this type of connection is sometimes found in twentieth-century music, folk-style accompaniments, and popular music, common-practice composers usually avoided it because of the parallel fifths and octaves that would result (Example 15.17a). With these parallels, you may possibly hear only one melodic line, doubled by triads, rather than four fully independent voice-leading strands.

EXAMPLE 15.17: Chord progressions with roots a second apart 🎧

(a) Parallel motion (avoid)

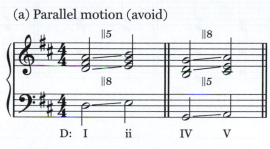

D: I   ii   IV   V

(b) Contrary motion (good)

D: I   ii   IV   V

🔵 **KEY CONCEPT** Chords with roots a second apart are responsible for most parallel-fifth and parallel-octave errors in part-writing. Move the upper parts in contrary motion to the bass line (Example 15.17b) to avoid them.

You could also invert one or more of the chords, but check the voice-leading carefully. If there are still parallels in a progression with inversions, changing the doubling in one of the chords may correct the problem.

Try it #3

Provide Roman numerals and figures for the two-chord pairs below, and identify the root motion in the blanks. Below the blanks, add a contextual analysis showing the function of the submediant in each pair: tonic (T), tonic substitute (Ts), or predominant (PD).

A. 🎧

A: I   vi

Root motion: desc.   3rd   _____   _____   _____

                T ———————

B♭:
Root motion: _____   _____   _____   _____

Other Diatonic Harmonies

About Mediant Triads

The mediant triad, consisting of $\hat{3}$, $\hat{5}$, and $\hat{7}$, shares two scale degrees with the tonic ($\hat{3}$ and $\hat{5}$) and two with the dominant ($\hat{5}$ and $\hat{7}$). Because they sound a little like both chords, mediant triads don't fit cleanly into either the tonic- or dominant-function areas. Root progressions connecting a mediant triad to a dominant-function chord ($V7$ or $vii°$) are rare. If sometimes you come across what seems to be one of these progressions, closer inspection usually reveals that the apparent mediant triad is not a "real" chord, but a dominant-function harmony where not all the chord tones sound at the same time.

Look at the opening of Bach's Chaconne in Example 15.18. All the chords except for one are readily accounted for. In measures 0-1 and 4-5, the i to $ii°^4_2$ is a root progression by ascending second. The $ii°^4_2$-V^6_5-i (mm. 1-2, 5-6) then progresses by descending fifth. Within a slightly larger context, the opening i-$ii°^4_2$-V^6_5-i can be considered an expansion of the tonic, with an embedded PD-D-T; the inversions give these chords a linear function. The i-VI-iv (mm. 2-3) is by descending third.

The chord on beat 2 in measure 3 may seem at first to be a III, progressing to $vii°$ on the next beat. But a consideration of the context reveals otherwise: this piece is based on a four-measure repeating harmonic pattern that starts with an anacrusis (a chaconne always involves a repeated harmonic progression). If you compare the corresponding measures 3 and 7, it becomes clear that the apparent III-$vii°$ is really a $V7$ in which all the chord members simply arrive at different times. Some listeners may also hear beat 2 in measure 3 as a cadential $^6_4$ (without scale degree $\hat{1}$).

EXAMPLE 15.18: Bach, Chaconne in D Minor, mm. 1-8

The mediant may serve as part of a tonic expansion at the beginning of a phrase (I-iii or i-III), though it is less effective as a tonic substitute than the submediant, which shares $\hat{1}$ with the tonic. The progression I-iii may be considered a variation of I-I⁶ (Example 15.19a); here the mediant triad results from linear motion from $\hat{1}$ to $\hat{7}$ in the top part, where the tonic note "disappears" temporarily. Any predominant chord that can follow a I⁶ may follow the apparent iii, but take care to avoid parallel octaves or fifths (as the example does); the most frequently used version of this progression in major keys, which is still rare, is shown in part (b), the opening progression of Peter, Paul and Mary's "Puff the Magic Dragon": I-iii-IV.

EXAMPLE 15.19: Voice-leading for I-iii-IV

(a)   (b)

C: I I⁶   IV   C: I   iii   IV

KEY CONCEPT In general, when tempted to part-write or analyze a chord in common-practice music as iii (in major), give the context further thought. Most likely what you need or hear is either a I or a V chord. The only place where you find iii is in a I-iii-IV progression at the beginning of a phrase, setting a $\hat{1}$-$\hat{7}$-$\hat{6}$ soprano line, or in a sequence (see Chapter 19).

The chart in Example 15.20 summarizes the progressions in major that have been discussed in this chapter, and how they fit into the basic phrase model. Any chord(s) in the first T column may move on to any in the PD column, then to the cadential D-T columns.

EXAMPLE 15.20: Basic phrase model chart for root progressions and the mediant

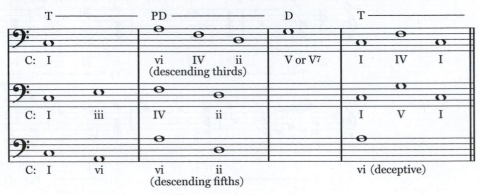

The Mediant and Minor Dominant in Minor Keys

In minor keys, III forms a special relationship with VI (submediant) and VII (subtonic): these three chords possess the same qualities as I, IV, and V in the relative major key (for example, in A minor, the triads on C, F, and G sound like I, IV, V in C major). They are sometimes combined in progressions that temporarily evoke the relative major key; in particular, VII-III sounds like V-I in the relative major. (We will consider these further in Chapters 21 and 22.)

The descending-fifth progression III-VI appears in the modal folk tune "Wayfaring Stranger," which also features another harmonic possibility for this style: the minor dominant. Listen to Example 15.21, and examine the Roman numeral analysis. The first four measures express a i-iv-i tonic expansion, while the cadence (mm. 7-8) enlists the minor dominant. The III-VI in measures 5-6 echoes the i-iv transposed up a third (or in the relative major).

EXAMPLE 15.21: "Wayfaring Stranger," mm. 1-8

through_____ this world of woe;_____ Yet there's no sick - - ness, toil or

iv   i   III

dan-ger_____ In that bright world   to which   I   go._____

VI   iv   v   i
            PD   D   T

Another place you are likely to encounter the minor v is in the **lament bass** progression, shown in both a diatonic and chromatic version in Example 15.22; the chromatic version (part b) incorporates both passing chromatic notes in the bass and 7-6 suspensions in the melody. This progression, dating back to the seventeenth century, has appeared in works from Purcell's "Dido's Lament" (1689) to such popular songs as Kanye West's "Stronger" (2007) and The White Stripes' "Dead Leaves and the Dirty Ground" (2002). In "Dido's Lament" (Example 15.23), the progression includes harmonized chromatic passing tones in the bass that yield first V$^6_5$ then v^6, IV^6 then iv^6 before reaching the dominant at the Phrygian cadence in measure 27.

EXAMPLE 15.22: The lament bass progression 🎧

(a) Diatonic   (b) Chromatic

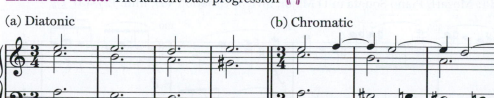

a: i   v^6 iv^6 V   a: i^5 —— 6   V^6 v^6 IV^6 iv^6 V7

EXAMPLE 15.23: Purcell, "Dido's Lament," mm. 22-27 🎧

When I am laid,___ am laid_____ in earth,

g: i   V$_5^6$ v^6 IV^6 iv^6 V^7

Phrygian cadence

KEY CONCEPT   Minor dominant chords (v) are used in three different contexts:

- In folk songs or popular styles with a modal or folk sound, minor v can appear throughout, even at a cadence, instead of V.
- In common-practice music, they are occasionally found at the beginning or in the middle of a phrase in minor keys, where minor v temporarily evokes the sounds of modal composition, but not at cadences, where the leading tone is a necessary ingredient.
- In the lament bass, the progression i-v^6-iv^6-V is the foundational progression for diatonic and chromaticized versions.

Parallel $^6_3$ Chords

Another way that the minor dominant and mediant triads may appear in music literature is in a stream of parallel $^6_3$ chords. In passages like these, the contrapuntal motion of parallel sixths and thirds, rather than principles of root motion, controls the chord succession. Example 15.24 (m. 129) shows an example of the mediant in a stepwise descent of $^6_3$ chords (the ♭II^6 chord will be discussed in Chapter 27 in connection with chromatic harmony).

EXAMPLE 15.24: Mozart, Piano Sonata in D Major, mvt. 3, Variation VII, mm. 127-131 🎧

d: i^6 iv^6 III^6 ♭II^6 i^6 vii°^{6} i^6 V

                      i^6 —————— parallel $^6_3$ chords —————— i^6 V

Minor-key parallel $\frac{6}{3}$ chord successions including the minor dominant are i-v⁶-iv⁶-III⁶ and i-v⁶-iv⁶-V, where V replaces III⁶ (see Example 15.22a). Both harmonize the bass line $\hat{1}$-$\flat\hat{7}$-$\flat\hat{6}$-$\hat{5}$ of the descending melodic and natural minor scales. To analyze a passage with parallel $\frac{6}{3}$ chords, assign Roman numerals only to the beginning and end of the chord succession and write $\frac{6}{3}$ figures in between, rather than giving each chord a Roman numeral. Parallel $\frac{6}{3}$ chords are also used in major keys, where V⁶-IV⁶ is typically followed by V instead of iii⁶.

Did You Know?

Musicians first began describing chord connections by root motion in the mid-eighteenth century. Jean-Philippe Rameau (1683-1764), who brought the ideas of the invertible triad and seventh chord to the fore, also had a theory of how chords were connected. He thought of all chords as being connected in "cadences" by the root motion of a fifth, like our authentic cadences. But he did not limit the idea of cadence to the ends of phrases: all chord connections with roots a fifth apart were cadences to Rameau. When a chord connection did not fit his model—for example, the connection between I and ii⁶—he theorized that the $\hat{4}$ in the bass of the ii⁶ was the "real" root, and that the connection was a descending fifth from $\hat{1}$ to $\hat{4}$. From Rameau's attempts to make all progressions conform to the strong descending-fifth root motion, later theorists such as Hugo Riemann developed the idea of chord substitutes—for example, the idea that ii⁶ can substitute for IV.

TERMS YOU SHOULD KNOW

ascending-second progression	dominant substitute (Ds)
deceptive cadence	parallel $\frac{6}{3}$ chords
deceptive resolution	Phrygian (half) cadence
descending-fifth progression	plagal cadence
descending-third progression	root progression

QUESTIONS FOR REVIEW

1. Where are deceptive cadences typically found? How do they differ from deceptive resolutions? What type of effect do they create?
2. Where are plagal cadences typically found? What type of effect do they create?
3. How does a Phrygian cadence differ from other types of half cadences? What gives it its distinctive sound (and name)?
4. What are the chords in a descending-fifth chain? Where are the "weak links"?
5. What are the chords in a descending-third chain? Where are the "weak links"?

6. Why are root progressions by second not generally found in chains? Where might you see them?

7. What part-writing guidelines should you follow for descending-fifth progressions? descending-third? ascending-second?

8. How are mediant triads used? How can you distinguish an apparent mediant from a real one?

9. In what contexts may minor dominant chords appear in common-practice style? In what other styles might you hear them?

Know It? Show It!

Focus by working through the tutorials.

Learn with InQuizitive.

Apply what you've learned to complete the workbook assignments.

16

Embellishing Tones

Overview

Here, we revisit embellishing tones to adapt concepts learned in species counterpoint to three- and four-part writing. We also explore chromatic versions of familiar embellishments and learn several new types.

Repertoire

Johann Sebastian Bach
"Aus meines Herzens Grunde" ("From My Inmost Heart," Chorale No. 1)
"Christ ist erstanden" ("Christ Is Risen," Chorale No. 197)
"Heut' ist, o Mensch" ("This Day, O Mankind," Chorale No. 168)
"Liebster Jesu" ("Dearest Jesus," Chorale No. 131)
"O Haupt voll Blut und Wunden" ("O Head Full of Blood and Wounds," Chorale No. 74)
Invention in D Minor
Prelude in C Major, from *The Well-Tempered Clavier*, Book I
Prelude in E-flat Major for Organ (*St. Anne*)
John Bettis and Jon Lind, "Crazy for You"
Johannes Brahms, *Variations on a Theme by Haydn*
George Frideric Handel, Chaconne in G Major
Freddie Mercury, "Bohemian Rhapsody"
Wolfgang Amadeus Mozart
Minuet in F Major, K. 2
Piano Sonata in D Major, K. 284, mvt. 3
Variations on "Ah, vous dirai-je Maman"
Henry Purcell, "Music for a While"

Outline

Embellishing a harmonic framework
- Passing and neighbor tones in chorale textures

More on suspensions
- Suspensions in four parts
- Suspensions with change of bass
- Combining suspensions
- Embellishing suspensions
- Retardations

More on neighbor and passing tones
- Chromatic neighbor and passing tones
- Incomplete neighbors
- Double neighbors
- Passing tones, chordal skips, and scales

Other types of embellishments
- Anticipations
- Pedal points

Embellishing tones in popular music

Embellishing a Harmonic Framework

While focusing on simple chordal textures is the clearest way to learn about four-part harmony, very few pieces rely solely on a succession of block chords. Much of the beauty and inventiveness of musical composition lies in how composers embellish melodic lines or chord successions. Because the pitches that embellish a musical line are usually not members of the underlying harmony, some textbooks call them "nonharmonic" or "nonchord" tones. The term "embellishing tone," on the other hand, highlights their musical function.

KEY CONCEPT As we have seen, **embellishing tones**, pitches from outside the underlying harmony, decorate chord tones in specific ways (e.g., as passing tones, neighbor tones, or suspensions). Though they may be consonant or dissonant, the majority are dissonant, adding flavor and interest to the consonant intervals in the chords.

Embellishing tones have expressive potential for performance: you can add accents or subtle changes in timing, for example, to emphasize the tension of a dissonant embellishment and its resolution to a more stable consonance. Identifying them can also clarify a harmonic analysis: you may otherwise find it difficult to supply a Roman numeral to a harmony that includes unexplained extra pitches. Indeed, some "chords" are simply collections of embellishing tones. For this reason, beware of analyzing harmonies by taking vertical "snapshots" of each beat, stacking the pitches in thirds and then applying a Roman numeral; besides being misleading, this procedure is not very musical. Instead, spend some time listening to the passage to decide which pitches are structural and which are embellishing. If in doubt, leave out the pitch in question to see if the chord makes sense within the phrase.

Listen now to the last two vocal phrases of Bach's chorale "Aus meines Herzens Grunde" (Example 16.1), and examine the circled embellishing tones: passing tones, neighbor tones, and suspensions.

EXAMPLE 16.1: Bach, "Aus meines Herzens Grunde," mm. 14–21

Sometimes only one voice at a time includes an embellishing tone (as in mm. 19 and 20); in such cases, the harmonic progression is clear and the embellishments are relatively easy to identify. In other cases, embellishments may be active in more than once voice. In measure 17, for example:

- The first chord is a vi (E-G-B), but the alto has an F♯ tied over from the previous beat to make a 9-8 suspension.
- The chord on beat 2 is a IV (C-E-G), with unaccented passing tones on the second half of the beat in the soprano, alto, and bass connecting to the tonic chord (G-B-D) on beat 3. The upper two parts move here as simultaneous passing tones in parallel thirds (following the principles of good counterpoint), while the bass travels in contrary motion from C3 (the root of the IV chord) down to G2 (the root of the I chord), requiring an *accented* passing tone on beat 3.

It may take a little detective work to identify other embellishing tones. For instance:

- In measure 15, the D4 in the tenor on beat 1 is repeated from the previous chord; it might at first look like a rearticulated suspension, which resolves downward to C4.
- Alternatively, the C4 might be a passing tone.
- Yet a consideration of the harmonic context indicates that both the D and C are part of the chord, a V$^6_5$ in G major, where the seventh enters after the beat.

The following chord (m. 15, beat 2) is a I (G-B-D), with an alto A4 hanging over from beat 1, making a 9-8 suspension. The rhythmic pattern in measure 20, beats 2 and 3, might similarly suggest a pair of suspensions—but all these notes are chord members. If you are unsure of an embellishing tone in analysis, try playing through (or listening to) the passage; your ear is your best guide.

Passing and Neighbor Tones in Chorale Textures

The most important step in writing passing tones, neighbor tones, and suspensions does not involve the embellishments at all. It is rather establishing a strong and well-conceived harmonic framework: appropriate chord progressions, following the basic phrase model and standard expansions of tonal areas, and good voice-leading in each part. Adding embellishments will not correct a faulty framework. Conversely, poorly chosen embellishing tones can create harmonic or voice-leading problems even if the original framework is sturdy.

As in species counterpoint, most passing and neighbor tones in chorale textures are unaccented: they provide rhythmic interest and a temporary element of dissonance. Those that are accented have a stronger, harsher sound, and may obscure the chord progression if not placed properly. An accented passing tone usually follows an unaccented one to fill in a skip of a fourth—as in Example 16.1, measure 17, where the bass's A2 (accented) on beat 3 together with the preceding

B2 fills in the fourth from C3 to G2. This type of accented passing tone usually appears later in a measure rather than on the downbeat.

KEY CONCEPT Passing and neighbor tones can be written in any voice and are usually unaccented, but four-voice textures offer opportunities for accented passing or neighbor tones as well.

Passing or neighbor tones may appear at the same time in two voices in parallel sixths or thirds, as in measure 3 of Example 16.2, where there are also simultaneous passing tones in contrary motion near the end of the measure (soprano-alto-bass). The F♯-A-C in measure 3 on the "and" of beat 2 could be heard as a vii°6—as a harmony lasting only one eighth note (in the progression IV-vii°6-I)—or simply labeled as linear embellishments (an "embellishing chord") leading to the tonic that precedes the half cadence. We show it here as passing because of the prevailing quarter-note harmonic rhythm. Consider the harmonic rhythm and whether the proposed Roman numeral fits into a stylistically appropriate chord progression when you label such "chords."

EXAMPLE 16.2: Bach, "Aus meines Herzens Grunde," mm. 1-4

Before adding embellishing tones to a progression, first make sure the part-writing, doubling, and spacing are correct in the progression. Then examine the voice-leading in each part. Where you see a

- skip of a third, consider adding a passing tone;

- skip of a fourth, consider adding two passing tones—one unaccented and one accented;.

- repeated pitch, consider adding a neighbor tone;

- descending step, you may be able to add a suspension.

- Check the intervals made by any embellishing tone to confirm that its addition does not create voice-leading problems, such as parallel fifths or octaves, or inappropriate melodic or harmonic intervals (melodic A2 or d5, or unresolved A4).

In Example 16.3a, for example, there is a fourth in the bass line; in part (b), we have added two passing tones, one unaccented and one accented. Another alternative, in part (c), is to add a neighbor tone to the soprano. Part (d), though, shows what happens if you try to combine these two embellishments: parallel octaves between soprano and bass. More problems arise in part (e), where the passing tone creates parallel fifths between bass and tenor, and in (f), where the passing tone creates an A2 in the soprano.

EXAMPLE 16.3: Adding passing and neighbor tones

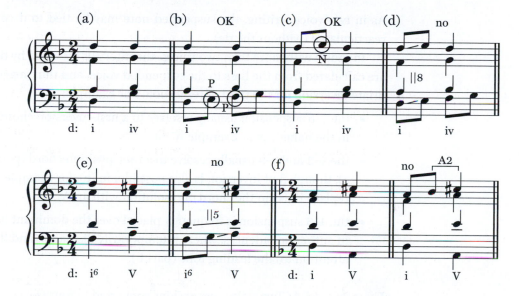

Try it #1

Circle and label all embellishing tones in the chorale excerpt below. Then provide a Roman numeral and contextual analysis below. Label the cadence.

Bach, "Aus meines Herzens Grunde," mm. 8-10

More on Suspensions

Suspensions in Four Parts

Many of the guidelines for suspensions in two-voice species counterpoint apply in fuller textures as well, including the three-step process for writing them:

(1) write a consonant preparation of the tone to be suspended;

(2) retain that tone as a dissonance on a strong beat; and

(3) resolve the suspended tone down by step to a consonant interval.

As in two-voice writing, the suspended note may be tied to its preparation or rearticulated (without the tie).

In music with more than two voices, the intervals specified by the suspension are calculated from the bass to the suspended voice, and thus suggest the appropriate inversion for the triad of resolution. For example:

- the 7-6 suspension usually resolves to a first-inversion chord (hence the 6 in the name), as in Example 16.4a;

- the 4-3 and 9-8 usually resolve to a root-position chord (parts b and c), though first inversion is also possible; in (c), for example, you could replace the G in the chord of resolution with an A);

- the 4-3 suspension is frequently placed over the dominant harmony in authentic cadences, where it temporarily displaces (and thus draws attention to) the leading tone (part b).

EXAMPLE 16.4: Two-voice suspensions converted to four voices

(a) 7-6 suspensions resolve to a first-inversion triad.

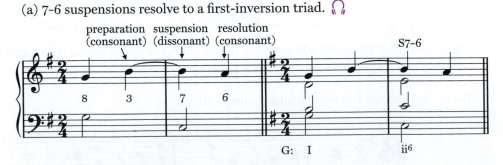

(b) 4-3 suspensions usually resolve to a root-position triad.

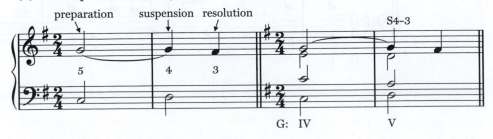

(c) 9-8 suspensions usually resolve to a root-position triad. 🎧

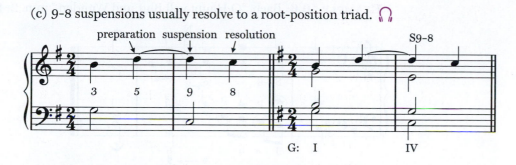

As Example 16.4 shows, in 7-6 and 4-3 suspensions, the note of resolution (the 6 or 3) is not included elsewhere in the chord (e.g., in a 4-3, the third above the bass does not appear elsewhere in the chord—this is especially important when that note is the leading tone!). With the 9-8, however, the note of resolution (the 8) will be doubled in the bass.

KEY CONCEPT When writing a suspension in three or more voices, plan the doubling in the chord of resolution first, so that the resolved note is not doubled in that chord (except in the 9-8 suspension).

In most dissonant suspensions, one of the upper voices is suspended, but the opposite is also possible: the bass may be suspended against the upper voices of a chord. The bass suspension 2-3 (or 9-10) (Example 16.5) resolves to either a first-inversion or root-position triad.

EXAMPLE 16.5: Bass suspension in four voices 🎧

Finally, although our focus is on dissonant suspensions, consonant suspensions above the bass, such as the 6-5, may also be found in four voices. In such cases, analyze with the Roman numeral of the triad of resolution (the 6 is not a chord member).

Suspensions with Change of Bass

In Baroque-era compositions with an active bass line, sometimes the bass note changes before a suspension in an upper part resolves. Listen to Example 16.6, paying close attention to the tenor part in the first two beats of measure 3.

EXAMPLE 16.6: Bach, "O Haupt voll Blut und Wunden," mm. 2-4

The tenor's E4 in the dominant anacrusis is suspended into the tonic harmony on the downbeat of measure 3. On beat 2, when this 9-8 suspension resolves, the tonic harmony changes inversion as the bass moves from D3 via passing tone to F3. The tone of resolution is present in the bass on beat 1 (D3), which is typical of 9-8 suspensions, but the change of bass results in a doubled third in the actual chord of resolution and the interval of a 6 instead of 8 between tenor and bass. The figures 9 6 should be read as one unit: a 9-8 suspension with change of bass (not a ninth chord followed by a triad). The change of bass, while making a more interesting bass line, does not disrupt the effect of the suspension.

Combining Suspensions

The opening of Bach's *St. Anne* Prelude is characterized by dotted rhythms and prominent suspensions, as you can see from Example 16.7.

EXAMPLE 16.7: Bach, *St. Anne* Prelude, mm. 1-4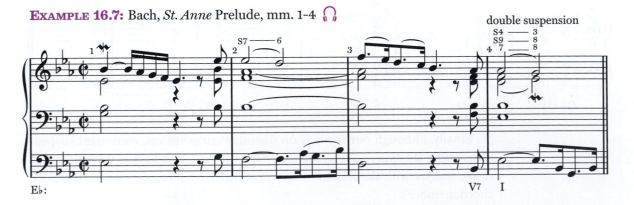

The accented dissonance at the cadence in measure 4 results from simultaneous 9-8 and 4-3 suspensions. In fact, the 9-8 may appear in combination with either the 4-3 or 7-6 in a **double suspension**; the suspended pitches will move in parallel sixths or thirds above the bass. In the Bach cadence, the double suspension is combined with a third dissonance, marked 7-8: a retardation, to which we return later in the chapter. We could hear the tonic as embellished by an entire dominant seventh harmony suspended over $\hat{1}$ in the bass, before resolving on beat 2—a type of suspension particularly favored by Mozart.

You may sometimes find suspensions combined in chains, as in Variation 9 of Handel's Chaconne (Example 16.8). In measures 74-75, the tenor and bass voices present two successive 7-6 suspensions. This type of suspension chain, along with the chain that alternates 4-3 with 9-8 suspensions (Example 16.9), between bass and alto), are the most common.

EXAMPLE 16.8: Handel, Chaconne in G Major, Variation 9, mm. 73-76

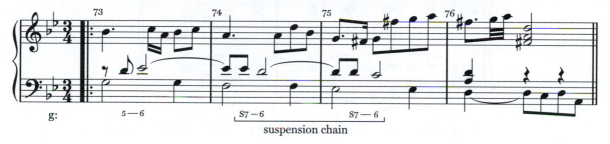

EXAMPLE 16.9: Bach, "Heut' ist, o Mensch," mm. 4-6

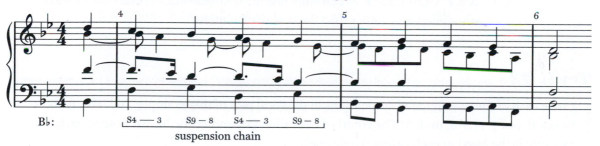

Embellishing Suspensions

Some suspensions are embellished before their resolution, as in Example 16.10, from one of many Bach chorales with a 4-3 suspension above the dominant harmony at the cadence. In measure 14, Bach embellishes the suspended tone, G4 in the alto, by skipping down to E4 before resolving on F♯4.

EXAMPLE 16.10: Bach, "Liebster Jesu," mm. 13-15

The cadence in measures 9-10 of "Christ ist erstanden" (Example 16.11) is highly embellished with suspensions, including a double suspension (m. 10): a dissonant 4-3 in the tenor and a consonant 6-5 in the alto, resulting in parallel thirds between these two voices. The suspended tones resolve on the metrically stronger beat 3, not beat 2, just as they would in fourth-species counterpoint, with the eighths on beat 2 embellishing and intensifying the suspension.

EXAMPLE 16.11: Bach, "Christ ist erstanden," mm. 9-10

> **KEY CONCEPT** When embellishing a suspension, decorate the dissonant suspended tone rather than the tone of resolution.

Try it #2

Circle each of the rearticulated suspensions in the vocal part of this example, and label it above the staff as a 7-6, 9-8, or 4-3. The chord of resolution (assuming the lowest note in each half measure is the bass) in each case is (circle one):

root position   first inversion   second inversion

Purcell, "Music for a While," mm. 12-14

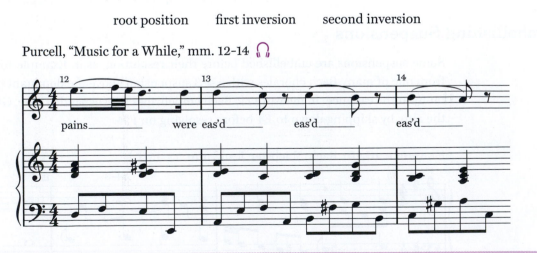

Retardations

In Classical- and some Baroque-era music, you may encounter a rhythmic embellishment that looks and sounds like a suspension, but resolves up by step instead of down.

KEY CONCEPT A **retardation**, like a dissonant suspension, begins with a consonance that is held over—tied or rearticulated—to the next beat, creating a dissonance in the new chord. The dissonance then resolves up by step. The most common retardation is a 7-8, with scale degrees $\hat{7}$ and $\hat{8}$ above $\hat{1}$ in the bass.

Retardations are usually found at an authentic cadence: the tonic arrives in the bass, but part of the dominant harmony is sustained or rearticulated in one or more of the upper voices before resolving to the tonic, as in Mozart's minuet (Example 16.12). Retardations are often combined with a suspension, as in Example 16.13: a 7-8 retardation (m. 205, D4-E♭4) with a 4-3 suspension (A♭3-G3).

EXAMPLE 16.12: Mozart, Minuet in F Major, mm. 21-24 (final cadence)

EXAMPLE 16.13: Bach, *St. Anne* Prelude, mm. 204-205 (final cadence)

More on Neighbor and Passing Tones

Chromatic Neighbor and Passing Tones

Classical-period variations are excellent for the study of melodic and harmonic embellishments, because we know from the theme what the composer considered a starting point. Mozart's *Variations on "Ah, vous dirai-je Maman,"* for example, includes a variety of melodic embellishments and employs several contrapuntal techniques to elaborate the familiar theme. Listen to the second variation (mm. 49-72): the melody in the right hand is based on the "Twinkle, Twinkle, Little Star" tune with added suspensions, while the left-hand accompaniment in rapid sixteenth notes features neighbor tones (Example 16.14).

EXAMPLE 16.14: Mozart, *Variations on "Ah, vous dirai-je Maman,"* mm. 49-56

The circled accidentals in the left hand of measures 53-55 introduce a new type of embellishment. In measure 53, the G♯3 (beat 1) and A♯ (beat 2) are **chromatic neighbor tones**, which neighbor by a half step and require an accidental. You can also write a **chromatic passing tone**, filling in a step with two chromatic half steps—as in Example 16.15 (F to F♯ and F♯ to G). Chromatic neighbor and passing tones stand out more than their diatonic counterparts; but as they are temporary moments of chromaticism, they do not disturb the sense of the key.

EXAMPLE 16.15: Mozart, *Variations on "Ah, vous dirai-je Maman,"* mm. 177-180 🎧

● **KEY CONCEPT** When an accidental is added to create a half-step neighbor or passing tone, the resulting embellishment is called a chromatic neighbor or chromatic passing tone.

Chromatic passing and neighbor tones may be either accented or unaccented. Since accented embellishing tones generally produce a more striking aural effect, performers may sometimes add a slight rhythmic or dynamic stress for heightened expression.

Incomplete Neighbors

The complete neighbor-note patterns we have seen so far comprise the main melody pitch (a consonance), the upper or lower neighbor a step away (usually a dissonance), and the return to the main melody pitch. If one of the consonant elements is left out, the resulting embellishment is called an **incomplete neighbor** (abbreviated IN), and it may take one of two forms:

- it may leap or skip to the dissonance, then resolve like a neighbor tone, by step in the opposite direction (this is sometimes called an **appoggiatura**); or

- it may begin by step, then skip or leap away in the opposite direction (sometimes called an **escape tone** or **échappée**).

In Example 16.16, the ascending C major scale passage in measures 169-170 is followed in measure 171 with an accented passing tone (B5) and chromatic lower neighbor (G♯5). Then the melodic line takes a dramatic leap up to D6, not part of the C major harmony: this is an accented incomplete neighbor to C6—approached by leap and resolved by step in the opposite direction.

EXAMPLE 16.16: Mozart, *Variations on "Ah, vous dirai-je Maman,"* mm. 169-172 🎧

The other type of IN (step-skip or step-leap) is shown in measure 9 of Example 16.17. Here, the C5 in the melody is the chord tone in the predominant harmony. The melody steps up to the dissonant D5, an unaccented IN, then skips to resolve in the cadential V^{6-5}_{4-3}. The final tonic in measure 10 also features accented incomplete neighbors on the downbeat—an embellishment typical of Haydn's style at the cadence.

EXAMPLE 16.17: Brahms, *Variations on a Theme by Haydn*, mm. 6-10 (piano 1) 🎧

🎵 **KEY CONCEPT** To write an incomplete neighbor:

- skip or leap to the dissonant neighbor tone, then resolve to the main melody pitch a step away (usually in the opposite direction); or

- approach the dissonant neighbor tone by step, then leave it by skip or leap in the opposite direction.

Try it #3

Copy each chord pair in the measure to its right, then add Roman numerals and the specified embellishing tones. Circle the embellishing tones.

(a) Add a 7-6 suspension.

(b) Add a chromatic passing tone.

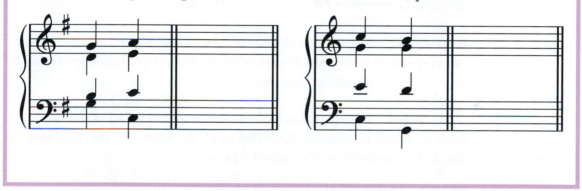

(c) Add an incomplete neighbor.

(d) Add a 4–3 suspension.

Double Neighbors

For one last type of neighbor embellishment, we turn to another Mozart variation set (Example 16.18). In measure 17, A4 is followed first by the upper neighbor B4, then a lower neighbor G#4, before returning to A4. As you recall from third-species counterpoint, this figure is a double neighbor (DN), and it recurs on the downbeat of each of the next two measures.

EXAMPLE 16.18: Mozart, Piano Sonata in D Major, mvt. 3, Variation I, mm. 17-21

KEY CONCEPT The combination of successive upper and lower neighbors (in either order), called a **double neighbor**, typically skips from one neighbor to the other before returning to the chord tone.

A different DN pattern can be seen in Example 16.19. Here, the upper and lower neighbors in measures 49-52 (left hand) are filled in by the chord tone C4. This figuration continues throughout each measure.

EXAMPLE 16.19: Mozart, *Variations on "Ah, vous dirai-je Maman,"* mm. 49-52

Passing Tones, Chordal Skips, and Scales

When a scale appears in a piece of tonal music, it often represents chordal (consonant) skips filled in with passing tones. In Example 16.20a, for instance, the first two measures expand the tonic harmony with a C major scale, which can be considered an arpeggiation of a C major triad that's filled in with passing tones (part b). Sometimes two passing tones are needed to fill in skips of a fourth, as between G4 (m. 169) and C5 (m. 170, beat 1). The slurs in part (b) are simply analytical symbols to show how pitches embellish the triad.

EXAMPLE 16.20: Mozart, *Variations on "Ah, vous dirai-je Maman,"* Variation VII

(a) Mm. 169–170

(b) Reduction, showing arpeggiation with passing tones

The principles observed in writing third-species embellishments from a note-to-note or 2:1 frame also apply in eighteenth-century style, where the durations are normally quarter, eighth, and sixteenth notes. Example 16.21 shows how simple embellishments such as consonant skips, passing tones, and neighbor tones can be combined to make elaborate 4:1 patterns. These are the essential melodic ingredients of the Mozart *Variations*.

EXAMPLE 16.21: Elaborate embellishments created from simple ones

(a) Embellishing a third

(b) Passing tones

(c) Neighbor tones

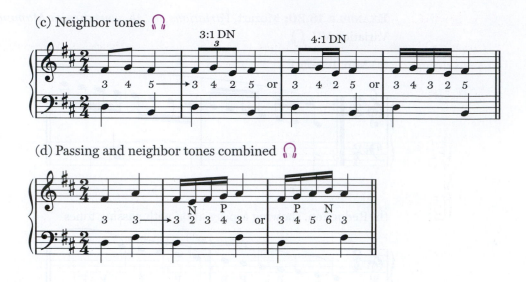

(d) Passing and neighbor tones combined

Other Types of Embellishments

Anticipations

In the case of suspensions and retardations, the embellishment is created when one part of a two-voice framework is delayed and resolves "late." With an **anticipation** (ANT), the opposite happens: one part of the framework arrives "early." Anticipations are unaccented—they appear on the offbeat or a weak beat of a measure—and are usually dissonances. They do not need to resolve in the same way other dissonances do; they are simply repeated on the next beat, where they belong in the counterpoint. Though not included in strict species counterpoint, they are frequently used by eighteenth-century composers to decorate cadences.

Listen to the final measures of Purcell's "Music for a While" to hear anticipations in the vocal line (Example 16.22). When the soprano sings "beguile" (mm. 37-38), she arrives on the A4 tonic pitch one sixteenth note ahead of the tonic chord, anticipating the resolution of $\hat{2}$ to the tonic.

EXAMPLE 16.22: Purcell, "Music for a While," mm. 36-38 (final cadence)

Try it #4

Circle and label all embellishing tones in the chorale excerpt below. Then provide a Roman numeral and contextual analysis.

Bach, "Jesu, der du meine Seele," mm. 1-3 🎧

Pedal Points

Pedal points get their name from passages in organ music, where the organist's foot rests on a single low pedal for measures at a time while the harmonies change above it. Even in music not written for organ, a repeated low tone can mimic the organ pedal's effect, as in Bach's Prelude in C Major (Example 16.23). Here, Bach prolongs the dominant seventh harmony—with dominant pedal point—before the prelude's final four-measure closing. Pedal points do not decorate a musical line in the way that passing or neighbor tones do, but they *are* considered embellishing tones: as the harmonies shift above it, that pedal point will be a "non-chord" tone in relation to some of the harmonies. Like suspensions, pedal points may be sustained or rearticulated.

EXAMPLE 16.23: Bach, Prelude in C Major, mm. 24-31 🎧

V7 _____ °7 (over dominant pedal)*   V$^8_6$$^8_4$

S4 _____

$^7_3$ _____

*More on this harmony in Chapter 20.

When you encounter a pedal point in music, consider carefully the larger context. Most often, the pedal prolongs a single harmony (usually tonic or dominant), as here, and the voices above it are embellishing. Sometimes the upper harmonies are functional and can be analyzed with Roman numerals; other times they can be conveyed with figured-bass numbers (as for a pedal $^6_4$ chord). Because the pedal point sounds below the chords, some analysts omit inversion symbols for these harmonies altogether. Others retain them, opting instead to disregard the "nonharmonic" pedal tone or to note its presence by writing "pedal" with the Roman numerals (as in the Bach analysis above).

Pedal points are not limited to the bass line, as Example 16.24 shows, but may appear in any voice; when in upper voices, they are sometimes called "inverted pedals." With the pedal point in an upper voice, you can label the Roman numerals as usual, and mark the pedal above the upper part.

EXAMPLE 16.24: Bach, Invention in D Minor, mm. 18-23

Embellishing Tones in Popular Music

Some of the guidelines for preparing and resolving embellishing tones are more relaxed in popular music. Suspended tones may be unprepared, and they may add a dissonance that never resolves. In Example 16.25, from "Crazy for You" as sung by Madonna (1985), every chord is labeled "sus 2" or "sus," which gives the simple I-IV-V-I (E-A-B-E) chord progression a rich and lush sound. Some of these "suspensions" connect to chord tones in the following measure—such as the B (the suspended tone in the Asus2 chord, m. 7) that stays for the following Bsus—but none of the suspensions resolve down by step as they would in common-practice style. Yet passing and neighbor tones embellish chord tones in popular styles in the same way they do in other repertoire. For example, the high point of the "Crazy for You" melody is embellished on the word "dark" (m. 9) by a neighbor tone (G♯5).

EXAMPLE 16.25: Bettis and Lind, "Crazy for You," mm. 6-9

In Freddie Mercury's "Bohemian Rhapsody" (sung by Queen, 1975), the humorous quality of the middle section (Example 16.26) is created in part by its chromatic passing and neighbor tones. For example, measure 45 ("I see a little silhouetto") features the chromatic neighbor tone C♯-C♮-C♯ and its accompaniment, E-E♭-E♮. In measures 47-48, the E-E♭-E♮ moves to the voice, with a chromatic passing tone C-C♯-D in the accompaniment. The entire passage is sung over a pedal point, A.

EXAMPLE 16.26: Mercury, "Bohemian Rhapsody," mm. 45-48

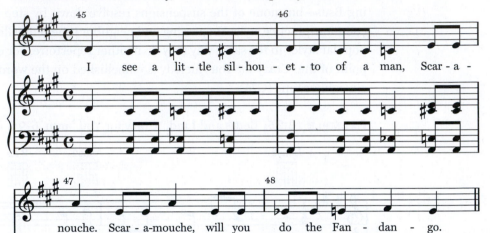

SUMMARY

EMBELLISHMENT	ABBREVIATION	CATEGORY	BRIEF DESCRIPTION
passing tone	P	melodic embellishment	• Dissonance approached by step and left by step in the same direction (up-up or down-down). • Fills in a consonant skip. • May be accented or unaccented; unaccented is more common. • A chromatic passing tone fills in a step.
neighbor tone	N	melodic embellishment	• Dissonance approached by step and left by step in the opposite direction (up-down or down-up). • Decorates a repeated note. • May be accented or unaccented; unaccented is more common. • May be diatonic or chromatic.

EMBELLISHMENT	ABBREVIATION	CATEGORY	BRIEF DESCRIPTION
incomplete neighbor tone	IN	melodic embellishment	• A neighbor figure missing either the approach or resolution. • Skip (leap), then step—or step, then skip (leap)—usually in the opposite direction. • May be accented or unaccented; accented is more common. • May be diatonic or chromatic.
double neighbor	DN (circle both notes)	melodic embellishment	• Combination of upper and lower neighbor. • Step up, skip a third down, step up to the starting point (or the reverse direction). May include the consonant note in the middle as well. • Usually unaccented.
suspension	S or sus (label the type: 4-3, 7-6, 9-8; bass 2-3)	rhythmic displacement	• Prepared by a consonant chord tone. • That tone is held over to make a strong-beat dissonance when the chord changes. • Resolves down by step on the weak part of a beat.
retardation	R	rhythmic displacement	• Prepared by a consonant chord tone. • That tone is held over to make a strong-beat dissonance when the chord changes. • Resolves up by step on the weak part of a beat (usually 7-8).
anticipation	ANT	rhythmic displacement	• One voice arrives early (making a dissonance) before the chord changes. • Dissonance is on a weak beat; repeats on a strong beat as a consonance. • Usually in the highest voice.
pedal point	ped		• Usually in the bass. • Sustained through changing chords.

Did You Know?

Textbooks and analysts differ in how they label embellishing tones. Double neighbors are sometimes called "changing tones." As mentioned in the chapter, an incomplete neighbor may be called an appoggiatura (if it first leaps up, then resolves down by step), or an échappée or escape tone (if approached by a step, then left by a leap). In some traditions, any embellishing tone—other than a chordal skip or suspension—that falls on an accented beat is called an appoggiatura. This term, from the Italian *appoggiare* ("to lean"), accurately describes the tendency to stress or lean on the dissonant pitch in performance. Appoggiaturas may be notated by the composer or added by the performer for expressive purposes. Suspensions also provide an opportunity for expressive interpretation: performers often add a slight *crescendo* from the preparation to the dissonance, and then a relaxation and *diminuendo* into the resolution.

TERMS YOU SHOULD KNOW

anticipation
appoggiatura
chordal (consonant) skip
chromatic neighbor tone
chromatic passing tone
double neighbor tone
double suspension

échappée (escape tone)
incomplete neighbor tone
neighbor tone
• lower neighbor
• upper neighbor
passing tone

pedal point
retardation
suspension
suspension chain
suspension with
   change of bass

QUESTIONS FOR REVIEW

1. What are the three steps necessary to write a suspension? What tone should not be doubled?
2. What are the most common suspension types? How might they be ornamented?
3. What embellishments are available in four voices that are not found in two-voice species counterpoint?
4. Find an example of an ornamented suspension, an anticipation, and a pedal point in music literature that you know.
5. Which intervals above the bass are most typical for retardations?
6. Which embellishing tones appear in chromatic variants?
7. What is "incomplete" about an incomplete neighbor? What are the two IN types?
8. How are pedal points written in lead-sheet notation? How are suspensions?

Know It? Show It!

Focus by working through the tutorials.

Learn with InQuizitive.

Apply what you've learned to complete the workbook assignments.

Voice-Leading Chords: vii°6, vii°7, viiø7, and Others

Outline

Dominant substitutes: Leading-tone chords

- Contexts for the vii°6, viiø7, and vii°7 chords
- Writing and resolving vii°6
- Writing and resolving viiø7, vii°7, and their inversions

Voice-leading $\frac{4}{2}$ chords

Overview

This chapter considers voice-leading patterns that expand the tonic area of the basic phrase with vii°6, vii°7, viiø7, and their inversions, as well as voice-leading $\frac{4}{2}$ chords.

Repertoire

Johann Sebastian Bach

"Aus meines Herzens Grunde" ("From My Inmost Heart," Chorale No. 1)

Cantata No. 140, "Wachet auf," mvts. 4 and 7

"Ein feste Burg ist unser Gott" ("A Mighty Fortress Is Our God," Chorale No. 20)

"O Haupt voll Blut und Wunden" ("O Head Full of Blood and Wounds," Chorale No. 74)

Prelude in C Major, from *The Well-Tempered Clavier*, Book I

Johannes Brahms, "Die Mainacht" ("The May Night")

"St. George's Windsor"

Dominant Substitutes: Leading-Tone Chords

The vii° triad (usually found in first inversion, vii°6) and the seventh chords vii⌀7 and vii°7 are dominant-function chords built on the leading tone. They serve as substitutes for the stronger dominant harmonies V and V7, with which they share scale degrees $\hat{7}$, $\hat{2}$, and $\hat{4}$. As these chords are weaker harmonically, they tend to appear in conjunction with smooth, strong, stepwise voice-leading. In particular, they often expand the tonic area at the beginning or middle of a phrase, just as a V chord can.

Contexts for the vii°6, vii⌀7, and vii°7 chords

To hear several ways these chords are used, listen to Bach's chorale setting "Ein feste Burg ist unser Gott" (anthology), paying particular attention to the excerpts below (Examples 17.1 and 17.2). In measures 1-2 of Example 17.1, the vii°6, appearing mid-phrase, prolongs the tonic harmony (as a passing chord between I6 and I), and participates in a voice-exchange between the tenor and bass—a very strong contrapuntal motion similar to those we have seen with the passing V$_4^6$. The second vii°6 in this example (mm. 3-4) also occurs mid-phrase, this time between IV and I. This vii°6 substitutes where the stronger dominant V would be excessive, creating an embedded PD-D-T before the strong cadential I-V7-I that ends the phrase. This vii°6, as in many chorale settings, is set with a quicker harmonic rhythm than the prevailing quarter-note beat—as if sneaking in a little dominant function where there is no room for an entire beat of it.

EXAMPLE 17.1: Bach, "Ein feste Burg ist unser Gott," mm. 1-4 🎧

In Example 17.2, the same basic progression appears in measures 10-11, again with a quicker eighth-note harmonic rhythm, but here including a vii⌀7 in inversion: IV-vii⌀$_3^4$-I. As with the previous example, most of the voices move completely by step. Another vii° in measure 11 shows a different way this chord is used: here the vii° follows IV6 and arrives on the beat, but (unusually) in root position. A leap in the alto voice then brings in the root of the V7 chord, turning the vii° into a V$_5^6$—the "real" chord on that beat.

EXAMPLE 17.2: Bach, "Ein feste Burg ist unser Gott," mm. 11-12 🎧

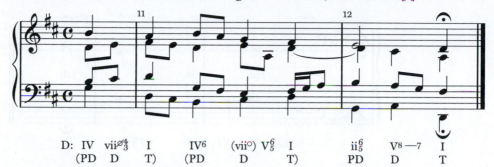

D: IV vii°⁴₃ I   IV⁶   (vii°) V⁶₅ I   ii⁶₅   V⁸—⁷   I
   (PD   D   T)   (PD   D   T)   PD   D   T

🎵 **KEY CONCEPT** These three contexts are typical for leading-tone harmonies:

- as an expansion of the tonic between I and I⁶;
- as a dominant substitute between IV (or ii⁶₅) and I, creating an embedded PD-D-T; and
- as an incomplete V⁷, where the root of the chord appears shortly thereafter.

The vii°⁶ or vii°⁶₅ sometimes appears where you might expect a cadential dominant, especially in hymns and Baroque chorales like "St. George's Windsor" and Bach's "Wachet auf" (Examples 17.3 and 17.4). In "St. George's Windsor," it may appear that there is a cadence in measures 9-10 with the progression I⁶-vii°⁶-I (T-D-T)—the tonic *is* set with a longer duration (♩)—but the larger context shows that the thought in the text is not completed: a similar resting place occurs in measure 12, and the music continues without a conclusive cadence until later in the hymn.

EXAMPLE 17.3: "St. George's Windsor," mm. 9-12 🎧

God, our Ma - ker, doth pro - vide   For   our wants to   be   sup - plied;

          (S7—6)
F: I⁶   vii°⁶   I
    T ————————

Likewise, measure 27 of "Wachet auf" (Example 17.4) is marked by a fermata and a rest following the I-vii°⁶₅-I progression, yet the exclamation of "Hallelujah!" does not feel conclusive, and the chorale does not actually reach a final close until a PAC at the end. Though they carry a dominant function, vii°⁶ and vii°⁷ are not strong enough to create a conclusive cadence.

EXAMPLE 17.4: Bach, Cantata No. 140, mvt. 7, mm. 25–27

Example 17.5, from Bach's "Aus meines Herzens Grunde," shows vii°6 in a slightly more elaborate tonic expansion with embedded PD-D-T. Here, the predominant harmony is ii; this specific progression—an embedded ii-vii°6-I6 expanding the tonic—occurs often in Bach chorales, but can be a little tricky to analyze if you haven't seen it before. If you attempt the maintain the standard chorale harmonic rhythm of one chord per beat and analyze the second beat of measure 8 as vii∅6₅, the seventh of the chord (E4) does not resolve down as expected. And if you were tempted to analyze this progression as I-ii-I6 (T-PD-T), take another look at the F♯4 on beat 2: what at first appears to be a passing tone instead provides the expected dominant function.

The better analysis is ii (A-C-E) to vii°6 (A-C-F♯), which provides both PD and D functions. Note that the voice-leading in this example is based on parallel tenths instead of the voice-exchange. As we have seen, the strong counterpoint of the soprano-bass parallel tenths overrides the tendency of 4̂ (C5) to resolve down to 3̂ (B4) and the d5 to resolve inward to a third.

EXAMPLE 17.5: Bach, "Aus meines Herzens Grunde," mm. 7–10

Example 17.6 shows the same embedded PD-D-T progression (ii-vii°6-I), but with a different voicing that resolves the d5 (E-B♭) to a M3 (F-A).

EXAMPLE 17.6: Bach, "O Haupt voll Blut und Wunden," mm. 11-12

Since a leading-tone harmony can substitute so easily for a dominant harmony, you will often find it as an anacrusis chord before the initial tonic of a phrase in Baroque chorales. For an example, listen to the beginning of "O Haupt voll Blut und Wunden" (Example 17.7), where Bach chooses to harmonize the dominant-function melodic anacrusis $\hat{2}$ with vii°6 instead of V.

EXAMPLE 17.7: Bach, "O Haupt voll Blut und Wunden," mm. 3-4

In minor keys, when the melody ascends through $\hat{5}$, $\hat{6}$, $\hat{7}$, and $\hat{1}$ (as in Example 17.8), the leading-tone chord works well where V or V7 does not. In this setting, i6-IV-vii°6-i provides contrary motion and the outer-voice intervals 10-10-6-8, a strong contrapuntal framework, whereas IV-V would create problems with parallel fifths (here, between bass and alto).

EXAMPLE 17.8: $\hat{5}$-$\hat{6}$-$\hat{7}$-$\hat{1}$ in minor, with vii°6

As with the leading-tone triad, vii⌀7, vii°7, and their inversions resolve to I or I6 (i or i6). Example 17.9 shows a passage from a Brahms song in which vii°$^4_3$ neighbors I6; as the bass line moves back and forth between F♯ and G, the piano right hand has an expressive solo line that (perhaps) imitates the cooing doves of the text. Here, Brahms adds a B♭ to the sonority (so that the diatonic half-diminished seventh is fully diminished), giving the right-hand a poignant diminished seventh leap downward. In later chapters, we will learn about more uses of chromatic chords like this one, with the lowered sixth scale degree from minor changing the quality of vii⌀7 to vii°7.

EXAMPLE 17.9: Brahms, "Die Mainacht," mm. 15-17

Translation: Veiled by leaves, a pair of doves coo.

Writing and Resolving vii°6

Because the leading-tone triad includes the dissonant tritone $\hat{7}$ to $\hat{4}$, you need to pay careful attention to its doubling and inversion. Example 17.10 gives possible SATB arrangements.

KEY CONCEPT In the vii°6, the third (the bass) is usually doubled; less typical but possible is a doubled fifth. Don't double the root, which is the leading tone.

EXAMPLE 17.10: Voicings and spacings for vii°6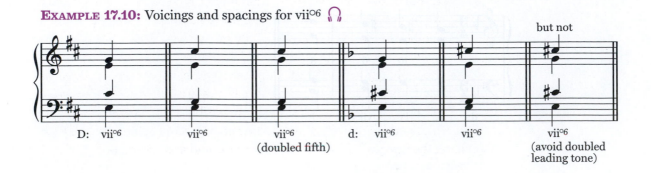

KEY CONCEPT Since V7 and vii°6 share the tendency tones $\hat{7}$ and $\hat{4}$, their normal resolutions follow the same principles:

- $\hat{7}$ resolves up to $\hat{1}$;
- $\hat{4}$ resolves down to $\hat{3}$ or possibly up to $\hat{5}$ (both, if $\hat{4}$ is doubled);
- $\hat{2}$ resolves down to $\hat{1}$ or possibly up to $\hat{3}$ (both, if $\hat{2}$ is doubled).

Example 17.11 gives several correct resolutions: $\hat{7}$ resolves to $\hat{1}$ in each; $\hat{4}$ resolves to $\hat{3}$ in (a) and (b), and to $\hat{5}$ in (c) and (d).

EXAMPLE 17.11: Resolutions of vii°6

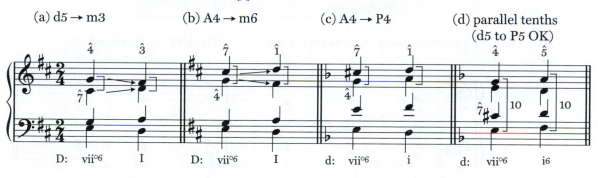

(a) d5 → m3   **(b)** A4 → m6   **(c)** A4 → P4   **(d)** parallel tenths (d5 to P5 OK)

Another Way

When resolving vii°6, it can be helpful to focus on the dissonant tritone (bracketed in Example 17:11):

- If the tritone is spelled as a d5—$\hat{7}$ below $\hat{4}$—it normally resolves inward to a third (part a).
- If the tritone is spelled as an A4—$\hat{4}$ below $\hat{7}$—it resolves outward to a sixth (part b); or it may move in similar motion to a P4 (part c).
- With a d5, $\hat{4}$ resolves up to $\hat{5}$ in one particular context: when the soprano-bass counterpoint moves upward in parallel tenths (part d).

The standard outer-voice patterns for writing vii°6, illustrated in Example 17.12, fit well within the guidelines of species counterpoint. Parts (a) and (b) show a tonic expansion moving from root position to first inversion, featuring a voice exchange in soprano and bass and the outer-voice intervals 10-8-6, first with a V$^6_4$ as the middle chord, then with vii°6. Only one note is different—A4 in part (a), second chord, becomes G4 in part (b). This same progression can also be used with a soprano line of $\hat{1}$-$\hat{7}$-$\hat{1}$ by giving the voice exchange to alto and bass, as in parts (c) and (d). The soprano-bass intervals now are 8-6-6, good outer-voice counterpoint. Both of these progressions are reversible: they can move I-vii°6-I6 or I6-vii°6-I. In parts (e) and (f), the soprano and bass move up in tenths (10-10-10), making the unequal fifths (d5-P5) in soprano and alto acceptable.

EXAMPLE 17.12: Tonic expansions with V⁶₄, V⁴₃, and vii°⁶

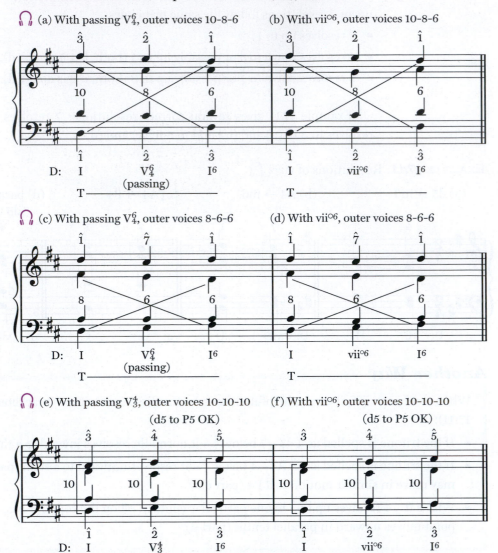

(a) With passing V⁶₄, outer voices 10-8-6

(b) With vii°⁶, outer voices 10-8-6

(c) With passing V⁶₄, outer voices 8-6-6

(d) With vii°⁶, outer voices 8-6-6

(e) With passing V⁴₃, outer voices 10-10-10 (d5 to P5 OK)

(f) With vii°⁶, outer voices 10-10-10 (d5 to P5 OK)

Writing and Resolving vii⌀⁷, vii°⁷, and Their Inversions

The seventh chords vii⌀⁷ and vii°⁷ have the same active ingredients as the diminished triad, but with the added sixth scale degree (Example 17.13); in comparison with the dominant seventh chord, you can think of 6̂ as replacing 5̂. Since 6̂ is one of the modal scale degrees, the quality of the diminished seventh chord will change depending on the form of the scale used. Remember that in a minor key, the root of the leading-tone chord is the raised seventh scale degree—it will require an accidental.

EXAMPLE 17.13: Spelling vii^{ø7} and vii^{o7} in major and minor keys 🎧

(a)   (b)   (c)

D: V$^6_5$ D: vii^{ø7} d: vii^{o7}

Try it #1

For each key given below, write the key signature and leading-tone seventh chord. Check that the chord has the correct quality, and label it as vii^{ø7} or vii^{o7}.

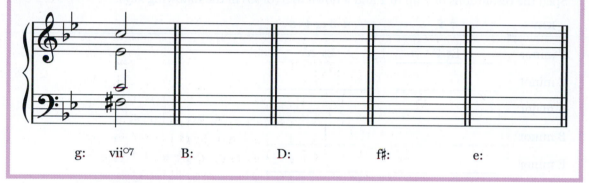

g: vii^{o7} B♭:   D: f♯:   e:

🎵 **KEY CONCEPT** As mentioned earlier, the vii^{ø7} and vii^{o7} are normally written with all four chord members present, in root position or any inversion. Resolve their tendency tones like those of V7:

- Resolve $\hat{7}$ up to $\hat{1}$.
- Resolve $\hat{4}$ down to $\hat{3}$.
- Resolve the chordal seventh down ($\hat{6}$ to $\hat{5}$ or ♭$\hat{6}$ to $\hat{5}$).
- Move $\hat{2}$ to either $\hat{1}$ or $\hat{3}$.
- This voice-leading may result in a tonic triad with doubled third.

Example 17.14a shows a typical resolution of a root-position vii^{o7} to tonic, with $\hat{2}$ moving down to $\hat{1}$ in a complete tonic triad and the other tones resolving by their tendency: $\hat{7}$ up to $\hat{1}$, $\hat{4}$ down to $\hat{3}$, and ♭$\hat{6}$ down to $\hat{5}$. In part (b), all the tendency tones resolve correctly, but $\hat{2}$ moves up to $\hat{3}$: it can't resolve down to $\hat{1}$ when $\hat{6}$ (B) is above it, or parallel fifths would result. Sometimes in major keys, $\hat{6}$ is lowered to ♭$\hat{6}$ (part c), so that the diatonic half-diminished chord is fully diminished (see Example 17.9). In addition to the familiar tritone between $\hat{7}$ and $\hat{4}$, the vii^{o7} (parts c–e) contains a second tritone between $\hat{2}$ and ♭$\hat{6}$ (E and B♭), which introduces the potential for unequal fifths: similar motion from d5 to P5. Where possible, resolve d5 in to a third, especially the d5 that contains the leading tone.

EXAMPLE 17.14: Resolutions of root-position vii°7–i and vii⌀7–I

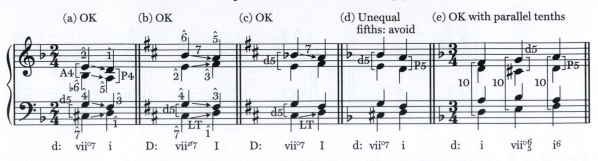

Try it #2

Spell the resolutions of 7̂ up to 1̂ and 4̂ down to 3̂ (or ♭3̂) in the following keys.

KEY	7̂–1̂	4̂–3̂ or 4̂–♭3̂
F minor	E♮–F	B♭–A♭
C minor		
A major		
B minor		
E minor		
A♭ major		

Leading-tone seventh chords are usually found in root position, first inversion, and second inversion; third inversion is rare, as the normal resolution of the tendency tones would result in a second-inversion tonic triad. The vii°7 appears more often in music literature than the vii⌀7, possibly because of the half-step voice-leading between ♭6̂ and 5̂ in the former (see Example 17.15c and d)—even in major keys (as in Example 17.14c). In each part of the example below, note the resolution of the leading tone up and chordal seventh down, as marked; find each d5 and A4 to see how it resolves.

EXAMPLE 17.15: Common resolutions of vii⌀7 and vii°7 in inversion

In the less common third inversion (Example 17.16), because $\hat{6}$ or $\flat\hat{6}$ (the chordal seventh) is in the bass, the bass must resolve down to $\hat{5}$, usually to a second-inversion tonic triad—which then resolves as either a cadential or passing $^6_4$.

EXAMPLE 17.16: Resolutions of vii$^{\varnothing4}_2$ and vii$^{\circ4}_2$ to cadential $^6_4$

Try it #3

A. Resolve each leading-tone seventh chord to the tonic in the keys below.

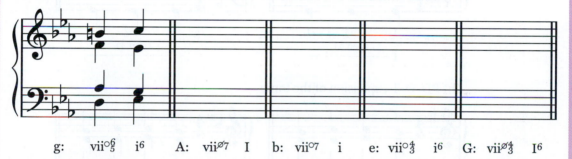

g: vii$^{\circ6}_5$ i^6 A: vii$^{\varnothing7}$ I   b: vii$^{\circ7}$ i   e: vii$^{\circ4}_3$ i^6 G: vii$^{\varnothing4}_3$ I^6

B. A good exercise to prepare for harmonizing melodies is to plan various soprano-bass contrapuntal patterns, then imagine possible Roman numerals for their harmonization. For each soprano-bass pattern below, provide two harmonizations: one that uses V or V7 and its inversions, and one with vii$^{\circ6}$ or vii$^{\circ7}$ and its inversions.

KEY	SOPRANO	BASS	HARMONIZATION 1	HARMONIZATION 2
major	$\hat{3}$-$\hat{2}$-$\hat{1}$	$\hat{1}$-$\hat{2}$-$\hat{3}$	I-V$^6_4$-I^6	I-vii$^{\circ6}$-I^6
major	$\hat{1}$-$\hat{2}$-$\hat{1}$	$\hat{1}$-$\hat{7}$-$\hat{1}$		
minor	$\hat{1}$-$\hat{7}$-$\hat{1}$	$\hat{1}$-$\hat{4}$-$\flat\hat{3}$		
major	$\hat{3}$-$\hat{4}$-$\hat{5}$	$\hat{1}$-$\hat{2}$-$\hat{3}$		
minor	$\flat\hat{3}$-$\hat{4}$-$\flat\hat{3}$	$\hat{1}$-$\hat{7}$-$\hat{1}$		

Voice-Leading $\frac{4}{2}$ Chords

Another chord that can expand the tonic area is the pedal or neighboring ii$\frac{4}{2}$ chord. This expansion may be understood as neighbor tones in all three upper parts above a tonic pedal point (Example 17.17a). That the $\frac{4}{2}$ does not resolve its seventh properly (downward by step) is a clue to its voice-leading role.

EXAMPLE 17.17: The pedal or neighboring ii$\frac{4}{2}$ chord

(a) Neighbor tones above a tonic pedal

(b) PD-D-T expansion of the tonic

The seventh *does* resolve properly (part b) when ii$\frac{4}{2}$ moves to V6 or V$\frac{6}{5}$ in a PD-D-T tonic expansion. The opening of Bach's Prelude in C Major (Example 17.18) provides a beautiful example: the bass line $\hat{1}$-$\hat{1}$-$\hat{7}$-$\hat{1}$ supports the progression I-ii$\frac{4}{2}$-V$\frac{6}{5}$-I, which firmly establishes the tonic at the beginning of the prelude.

EXAMPLE 17.18: Bach, Prelude in C Major, mm. 1-4 🎧

C: I
    T
    T

    ii$\frac{4}{2}$
    (PD

    V$^6_5$
    D
    (T)

    I
    T)

A $\frac{4}{2}$ chord may also have a passing function, such as I–I$\frac{4}{2}$–IV^6 or I–I$\frac{4}{2}$–vi (Example 17.19). These $\frac{4}{2}$ sonorities are created when a passing tone fills in between $\hat{1}$ and $\hat{6}$ in the bass, and are sometimes analyzed with a Roman numeral with $\frac{4}{2}$ inversion as here, especially if they last as long as the chords surrounding them. See also measure 9 of Example 17.20 (the passage is in B♭ major; note the A♮s throughout). In measure 10, you might analyze beat 2 as IV$\frac{4}{2}$ (passing). Alternatively, you could simply circle and label the bass note as passing, without a new Roman numeral, to show the function of this chord as an expansion of the surrounding harmony. Chords like those are generally fairly unstable, and appear where they are supported by sustained or stepwise motion in the bass to create smooth voice-leading between functional harmonies.

EXAMPLE 17.19: Voice-leading for the passing $\frac{4}{2}$ 🎧

E: I   I$\frac{4}{2}$ IV^6
         (passing)

e: i   i$\frac{4}{2}$ iv^6
         (passing)

EXAMPLE 17.20: Bach, Cantata No. 140, mvt. 4, mm. 9-12 🎧

Bach's C Major Prelude makes beautiful use of $\frac{4}{2}$ chords. We saw the opening tonic expansion in Example 17.18. In the later passage shown in Example 17.21, the E3 is held in the bass across the bar line from measure 15 to 16, acting like a bass suspension that resolves down to D3. We have given measure 16 a Roman numeral analysis (IV$\frac{4}{2}$), but we might instead think of this as a voice-leading $\frac{4}{2}$ without Roman numeral.

EXAMPLE 17.21: Bach, Prelude in C Major, mm. 15-19 🎧

Did You Know?

Compositions from the Baroque and Classical eras offer two ways to think of leading-tone triads and seventh chords. During the early eighteenth century (the end of the Baroque era), composers considered harmony from the viewpoint of counterpoint: chords were conceived linearly, made from melodies in each of the SATB parts. Leading-tone chords were frequently used this way, as tonic expansions, in Baroque chorales.

In the late eighteenth century, composers continued to pay careful attention to counterpoint, but some began to think of chords as thirds and fifths above a root, making particular harmonic progressions. Although linear leading-tone chords can be found in Classical compositions, they were less suited to the Alberti bass and slower harmonic rhythm than they were to chorales. Instead,

Classical composers tended to employ leading-tone chords as dominant substitutes.

Some textbooks from the 1940s-70s describe leading-tone triads as dominant seventh chords without a root, labeled $V^{\circ7}$ (see Walter Piston, *Harmony* [New York: Norton, 1941/1987]). While this view led to jokes about whether or not to double the missing root, there is a grain of truth to it—the leading-tone chord often appears in progressions where a V or V^7 could have been used instead. This idea of $vii^{\circ6}$ as a V^7 without a root is an old one, dating back to Jean-Philippe Rameau's theories of chord progressions in the early eighteenth century. When Rameau wrote a "fundamental bass" (an analytical bass line written on a staff under the music's bass line, indicating the roots of each chord), for the vii° chord he designated the root as $\hat{5}$.

TERMS YOU SHOULD KNOW

dominant substitute	half-diminished seventh	neighboring $^4_2$
diminished seventh	leading-tone chord	passing $^4_2$

QUESTIONS FOR REVIEW

1. In what context(s) might a $vii^{\circ6}$ or $vii^{\circ7}$ be written?
2. What chords (and inversions) typically pass between I and I^6?
3. What soprano-bass scale-degree patterns are normally associated with tonic expansions from I to I^6?
4. How does each scale degree in the leading-tone seventh chord usually resolve?
5. How are the d5 and A4 treated when resolving the $vii^{\circ7}$ chord and its inversions?
6. Which leading-tone seventh chord is found more frequently: $vii^{\varnothing7}$ or $vii^{\circ7}$? Why?
7. What outer-voice contrapuntal pattern overrides the tendency of the chordal seventh to resolve down?
8. Where are passing and neighboring $^4_2$ chords used?
9. In music for your own instrument, find an example of a $vii^{\circ7}$ chord and describe its function within the phrase.

Know It? Show It!

Focus by working through the tutorials.

Learn with InQuizitive.

Apply what you've learned to complete the workbook assignments.

18

Phrase Structure and Motivic Analysis

Overview

In this chapter, we consider how phrases may be grouped and expanded, and how motivic and phrase analysis can inform musical interpretation.

Repertoire

Ludwig van Beethoven
  Piano Sonata in C Minor, Op. 13 (*Pathétique*), mvt. 3
  Sonatina in F Major, Op. Posth., mvt. 2
Johannes Brahms, *Variations on a Theme by Haydn*
Muzio Clementi, Sonatina in C Major, Op. 36, No. 1, mvt. 1
Stephen Foster, "Oh! Susanna"
Wolfgang Amadeus Mozart
  Piano Sonata in B♭ Major, K. 333, mvt. 1
  Piano Sonata in C Major, K. 545, mvts. 1 and 2
  Piano Sonata in G Major, K. 283, mvt. 1
  "Voi, che sapete," from *The Marriage of Figaro*
Franz Schubert, Waltz in B Minor, Op. 18, No. 6

Outline

Phrase and motive
- Motives and motivic analysis
- The sentence

Phrases in pairs: The period
- Phrase diagrams
- Parallel and contrasting periods
- Writing parallel and contrasting periods
- Other period types

Phrase rhythm
- Phrase structure and hypermeter
- Linking phrases
- Phrase expansion

Phrase and Motive

In your instrumental or voice lessons, you may have discussed "phrasing" with your teacher. An important part of preparing a piece for performance is determining how it divides up, where the goals are, and how to perform it with directed motion toward these goals. For our purposes, the word "phrase" will not be used as a verb—we will not consider how to "phrase" a melody (at least not in those terms). Instead, the word is used as a noun, one with a distinct meaning.

KEY CONCEPT As we learned in Chapter 11, a phrase is a basic unit of musical thought that ends with a cadence. Phrases are often two, four, or eight measures long, especially in the Classical era, but they may be other lengths as well.

Listen to the opening of a Schubert waltz (Example 18.1) to determine where the phrase or phrases end.

EXAMPLE 18.1: Schubert, Waltz in B Minor, mm. 1-8

You probably heard a strong cadence in measure 8, a PAC in B minor with a stepwise melodic descent to $\hat{1}$. But there is a subsidiary resting point at measure 4, where the melody makes a similar descent to $\hat{2}$ over a V7 harmony. At this point, the entire texture starts again (mm. 5-6 are identical to 1-2), marking a clear division of the passage into two four-bar phrases. The cadence at measure 4 is a HC, on a dominant seventh chord (the half cadences we have seen to this point have concluded with a triad; Romantic and popular styles may include a seventh as well).

Because measure 5 expresses the tonic harmony, you may be tempted to view it as a "resolution" of the V7 in measure 4, rather than a phrase boundary, but a couple of factors work against this interpretation. First, the restatement of the opening material here signals a new beginning. Second, this restatement coincides with the expectation of regular and even measure groupings (in twos and fours) in a waltz style, which would be easier to dance. In performance, the two phrases might be delineated by subtle changes in timing and dynamic shaping, with an ebbing of energy in measure 4 and a tempo resurgence at measure 5.

Motives and Motivic Analysis

The melody of Schubert's waltz is marked by a repeated ♪♩♩ rhythm, which appears (in varied form) in almost every measure.

> **KEY CONCEPT** A motive, the smallest recognizable musical idea, is characterized by its pitches, contour, and/or rhythm; it rarely contains a cadence. For a musical segment to qualify as a motive, it must be repeated either exactly or in varied form (for example, transposed or embellished).

A motive may be purely rhythmic (maintaining its distinctive durations while possibly changing its contour and intervals) or consist simply of a melodic contour (maintaining its shape but changing its intervals and possibly its rhythm). In the Schubert waltz, for example, the opening right-hand motive (♪♩♩) appears first as an ascending triad and then as an ascending third plus step. The first beat of this motive, the ascending third portion, is heard in several transpositions: on B4 (mm. 1, 3, and 5), C♯5 (mm. 2 and 6), and D5, approaching the high point of phrase 2 (m. 7); in measure 4, it appears as a *descending* third from G5.

In music analysis, label motives with numbers or lowercase letters from the end of the alphabet (x, y, z)—we reserve the beginning of the alphabet for phrases and larger formal units—or give them a descriptive name: the scale motive, the arpeggiated motive, the neighbor-note motive, the dotted motive, and so on. For a sample analysis, look at melodic motives from the beginning of a Clementi sonatina (Example 18.2).

EXAMPLE 18.2: Clementi, Sonatina in C Major, mvt. 1, mm. 1–11 🎧

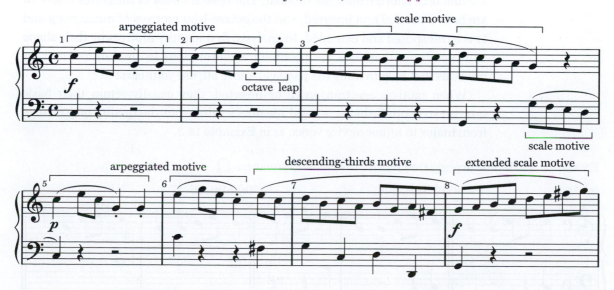

Much of this passage can be interpreted through the lens of a few motives. First, measures 1-2 and 5-6 are related by the same opening ("arpeggiated") motive. Similarly, the five-note descending scale that begins measure 3 ("scale motive") reappears twice in measure 4. The repeated descending-thirds pattern that permeates measure 7 might derive from the second and third pitches of the arpeggiated motive, or measure 7 could be thought of as the scale motive ornamented with descending thirds. Finally, the octave leaps in measures 9 and 11 are an expansion of measure 2's octave leap.

KEY CONCEPT Motives may be varied in a number of ways. They may be

- **transposed** to appear on another scale degree;
- **inverted** so that the direction of each diatonic interval is reversed;
- **extended** by repeating a portion of the motive to make it longer;
- **truncated** by cutting off the end to make it shorter; or
- **fragmented** by taking a small (but recognizable) piece of the original and repeating it with transpositions or other variation.

The arpeggiated motives in measures 2 and 6, then, are truncated, since they are one beat shorter than the original. The scale motives of measures 8 and 10 are both extended and inverted, and the octave-leap motives of measures 9 and 11 are transposed and extended. In analysis, first identify motives by their shape and repetition, then look for possible transformations in rhythm, contour, or intervals that help to unify the passage. Above all, use your ears!

When motives are transposed or inverted, they usually retain their basic interval structure—that is, a third remains a third—but the quality may change from major to minor or vice versa, as in Example 18.3.

EXAMPLE 18.3: The arpeggiated motive in Clementi sonatina 🎧

When Clementi transposes the original motive, its major third (C5-E5) becomes a minor third (E5-G5) in measure 6 (part b). In 16-17 (part c), this initial interval is likewise altered to a minor third; by transposition (16) and by a shift to the minor mode (17). The motive's final interval, originally a perfect fourth, becomes a major third in 6 and 16, but returns to a perfect fourth in 17—all without disrupting the motive's identity. Since this identity rests heavily on contour and rhythm, these slight changes in interval size or quality do not disrupt our recognition of it.

The phrase in measures 28-31 (Example 18.4) begins with the arpeggiated motive, but here its contour is inverted—turned upside down, like a reflection in a mirror. Measure 30 is derived from the descending-thirds motive of 7, but with the thirds stacked harmonically as quarter notes instead of successive eighth notes. And at the end of the phrase, the scale motive from 3-4 is inverted and extended.

EXAMPLE 18.4: Inverted motives in Clementi sonatina, mm. 28-31

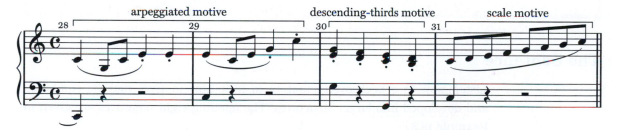

KEY CONCEPT To invert a motive, keep the order of interval sizes the same, but reverse each interval in direction—for example, an ascending third becomes a descending third. To invert a contour motive, reverse the direction of each step, skip, or leap—but you may change the interval size.

In tonal music, inversions are often constructed so their pitches remain within the key or harmony of the passage; the quality of some intervals will change, or their size will be adjusted slightly (such as a P5 to P4). In measure 28 of Example 18.4, for instance, Clementi retains the tonic harmony of the inversion by making the original ascending third a descending *fourth* instead.

Motivic analysis, a topic that has long fascinated music analysts and composers, can reveal remarkable economy and unity, generating complete and satisfying larger forms from a handful of motives. Identifying the primary motives and their transformations can also help you memorize a piece as well as shape a musical and satisfying performance.

Try it #1

Listen to the passage from Mozart's Piano Sonata in D Major shown below. Identify two motives in the right hand; bracket them and label them x and y. In the blanks, describe in a few words how each motive is varied and in which measure.

Mm. 1–4

x: _____   measure: _____

y: _____   measure: _____

The Sentence

Listen now to a Beethoven sonatina to hear how motives may be combined and developed into larger structures. The opening eight measures are given in Example 18.5.

EXAMPLE 18.5: Beethoven, Sonatina in F Major, mvt. 2, mm. 1–8

The passage begins with a chromatic neighbor-tone motive (C5-B♮4-C5) in the right hand, with a tonic pedal in the highest and lowest voices. This motive is repeated a step higher in measures 3–4 (D5-C♯5-D5). Each statement lasts two measures, and they are followed by a four-measure continuation and cadence (mm. 5–8). The first two units share a rhythmic motive (♪♪♪ | ♩.) and staccato articulation. The third unit continues the rhythm and staccato, now over a dominant pedal point, followed by a rhythmic acceleration with sixteenths leading into the cadence. Importantly, the phrase's harmonic motion is incomplete at measure 4 (mm. 1-4 constitute a **subphrase**); all eight measures are needed to complete the phrase. The measure grouping of 2 + 2 + 4 is so common in Classical-era melodies that it has a name.

KEY CONCEPT A sentence generally consists of eight measures in a 2 + 2 + 4 design, or four measures in a 1 + 1 + 2 design. The first two units of the sentence do not end with a cadence, but require the third portion for closure.

- In the first unit, a motive (sometimes called the "basic idea") is stated, typically over tonic harmony.

- In the second unit, the motive is restated, usually varied or transposed, often over a dominant harmony or progression that expands the tonic area.

- In the third unit, the motive is broken up and developed with an accelerated harmonic rhythm as the phrase moves toward the cadence, usually a HC or PAC.

The opening motive plus its restatement are considered the "presentation" phase of the sentence, with the final unit constituting the "continuation" and cadence. This continuation phase typically begins with some element of the introductory motive, such as its rhythm, before moving toward the cadence. Many Classical melodies, like those of Schubert and Clementi we looked at earlier, are composed with elements of the sentence design—such as a repeated one-measure idea that creates a 1 + 1 + 2 grouping. We will reserve the term "sentence," though, for cases where the presentation phase is harmonically incomplete, and the continuation is necessary to reach a true cadence.

For a slightly expanded example of a sentence, listen to the opening of Mozart's G Major Sonata, given in Example 18.6. Here, a ♪♩♪♩ descending-third motive followed by a slurred $\hat{1}$-$\hat{7}$ quarter-note pattern is presented as the basic idea in measures 1-2 and answered in 3-4 by a repeat of the dotted motive up a fifth and quarter-note $\hat{4}$-$\hat{3}$, all within the tonic area of the phrase. The continuation takes the ♪♩ rhythmic motive and develops it by expanding the interval from a second (m. 4) to third (m. 5) to fourth (m. 6), still within the tonic area without a cadence. Mozart continues to avoid strong closure at measures 7-8, but rather adds a scalar flourish that postpones the PD-D-T close until measures 9-10—resulting in a 2 + 2 + 4 (+2 extension) sentence. We will encounter other extended phrases later in the chapter.

EXAMPLE 18.6: Mozart, Piano Sonata in G Major, mvt. 1, mm. 1-10 🎧

Phrases in Pairs: The Period

We now consider how phrases combine to make larger musical structures. Listen to "Oh! Susanna" (Example 18.7), and examine its phrase structure.

EXAMPLE 18.7: Foster, "Oh! Susanna," mm. 1-8 🎧

This melody's harmonic structure is a familiar one, common in music from the Classical era as well as folk and popular songs: I to V or V7 (HC) in the first phrase, followed by I to V–I (PAC) in the second.

KEY CONCEPT When the first in a pair of phrases ends with a harmonically weak cadence (HC or IAC) and the second with a stronger cadence (usually PAC), they form a **period**. The first and second phrases are called the **antecedent** and **consequent**, respectively.

"Oh! Susanna" is a standard period: the first phrase comes to rest on scale degree $\hat{2}$ over a HC (m. 4), and the second concludes with $\hat{2}$-$\hat{1}$ in a PAC (m. 8). Other folk tunes with this melodic structure include "Home on the Range," "Clementine," and "Red River Valley." While some musicians restrict the "antecedent-consequent" label to periods with HC-PAC cadences like "Susanna," our definition focuses on the weak-to-strong relationship of the two cadences to include IAC-PAC and HC-IAC as well. In the latter case, the final cadence must be a strong IAC, with root-position harmonies.

Phrase and period analysis can help in preparing a performance: for example, the arrival on the PAC at the end of the period should be stronger than the arrival on the HC at the end of phrase 1. From the very beginning, you may want to think ahead to the period's end as your first big harmonic and formal goal.

Phrase Diagrams

When analyzing phrases, we generally label them with lowercase letters from the beginning of the alphabet. Phrases that sound different are assigned different letters—**a**, **b**, **c**, and so on—while those identical in every regard take the same letter. Phrases based on the same musical ideas but not exactly identical receive the same alphabet letter with a prime mark ('): **a** and **a′**, for example. When you use a prime mark, be sure to indicate what is alike about the phrases and also what is different. You may also analyze similar phrases with superscripts, as a^1, a^2, a^3, etc.

The chart in Figure 18.1, for the first eight measures of "Oh! Susanna," represents the phrase structure concisely, showing the measures spanned, thematic repetitions, and cadence types.

FIGURE 18.1: Phrase diagram for "Oh! Susanna," mm. 1-8 (parallel period)

```
          a                      a′
m. 1 ⌒  4 mm.  ⌒ 4     5 ⌒  4 mm.  ⌒ 8
D:                 HC                    PAC
```

Parallel and Contrasting Periods

Besides their harmonic and cadence structure, thematic material also shapes periods. When the two phrases begin identically—as in "Oh! Susanna"—or when the second phrase is audibly a variant of the first, the structure is called a **parallel period** (a a′).

When the two phrases begin differently, on the other hand, as in the Beethoven sonata shown in Example 18.8, they form a **contrasting period** (**a b**). The phrases normally share some characteristics—they are not contrasting in every way—but their beginning and overall shape and sound will differ. In this example, the varied return of the bracketed melodic idea from the beginning of phrase 1 at the end of phrase 2 makes an audible connection between the contrasting phrases. Figure 18.2 shows a phrase diagram for this contrasting period.

EXAMPLE 18.8: Beethoven, *Pathétique* Sonata, mvt. 3, mm. 1–8

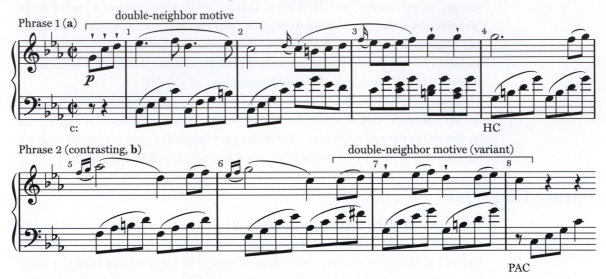

FIGURE 18.2: Phrase diagram for Beethoven sonata, mm. 1–8 (contrasting period)

	a		**b**	
m. 1	4 mm.	4	5	4 mm.	8
c:		HC		PAC

You may also encounter periods in which a sentence structure is embedded. The Beethoven phrase from Example 18.5, in fact, turns out to be the first part of a parallel period, as shown in Example 18.9: the first phrase ends on a HC and the second on a PAC. Each has a 2 + 2 + 4 sentence design, as diagrammed in Figure 18.3.

EXAMPLE 18.9: Beethoven, Sonatina in F Major, mvt. 2, mm. 1–16

I⁵₃ ———— IV⁶₄—I⁵₃— IV⁶₄   V7 ——— I   ii6 V7   I PAC
T ——————————————————   PD   D   T

FIGURE 18.3: Phrase diagram for Beethoven sonatina, mm. 1-16 (parallel period with embedded sentences)

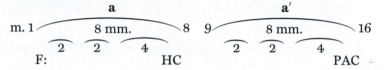

Example 18.10 reproduces measures 1-8 of the Clementi sonatina—another parallel period. The first phrase (mm. 1-4) ends with a half cadence (with the melody on $\hat{5}$); the second (mm. 5-8) begins with a repetition of material from the first, but it changes key, with a PAC (mm. 7-8) in G major. (We will further investigate phrases that change key in later chapters on modulation.) We call this a **modulating period**. The modulation may occur in the first or second phrase, though the latter is more common, and its location can be designated in the formal label—for example, the sonatina's phrases can be labeled "antecedent" and "modulating consequent."

EXAMPLE 18.10 Clementi, Sonatina in C Major, mvt. 1, mm. 1-8

In the periods examined so far, both phrases are the same length—either four or eight measures long—making a period that spans eight or sixteen measures. This is not always the case, however. When the phrases are the same length, the period is called **symmetrical**; when they are different lengths, it is **asymmetrical**.

SUMMARY

A period consists of two successive phrases whose cadences are in the relationship weaker-stronger. The most typical cadence patterns are HC-PAC or IAC-PAC.

- In parallel periods (**a a** or **a a′**), the second phrase often has the character of "starting over," with tonic harmony and thematic material from the opening.

- In contrasting periods (**a b**), the second phrase may begin on the tonic or another harmony, and it features new melodic ideas.

- Phrases that begin with similar but not identical thematic material should be labeled parallel (**a a′**), with a discussion of features that are shared and those that differ.

- A period that changes key is known as a modulating period.

A sentence is a single phrase without a strong internal cadence.

- The measures are grouped by motivic material in the pattern 2 + 2 + 4 (or 1 + 1 + 2).

- The basic idea introduced in the first unit is immediately repeated, usually with slight variation (the presentation).

- The second half of the sentence (the continuation) often develops some motivic feature of the opening idea and then concludes with a cadence.

- Sentences may be embedded within periods.

Writing Parallel and Contrasting Periods

KEY CONCEPT To write a Classical-style antecedent-consequent pair of melodic phrases with a HC-PAC design:

1. Begin by mapping out eight blank measures on two lines of staff paper—four on the top line and four more aligned beneath them on the second line.

2. Sketch a melodic approach to each cadence: $\hat{3}$-$\hat{2}$ at the end of the first line to suggest a HC, and $\hat{2}$-$\hat{1}$ or $\hat{7}$-$\hat{1}$ on the second line for a PAC.

3. Start measure 1 on a member of the tonic triad ($\hat{1}$, $\hat{3}$, or $\hat{5}$). If you want to include an anacrusis, write one that suggests a dominant harmony.

4. In the first four measures, outline a melody that implies an incomplete phrase model (T-PD-D). Plan your progression with a harmonic rhythm of one to two chords per measure, possibly speeding up near the cadence.

5. Now write a melody that expresses your progression by including arpeggiation or passing and neighboring embellishments around chord tones. Create

at least two memorable motives: melodic, rhythmic, or contour. If rhythmic, repeat the rhythm more than once. You may write a sentence as the first half of your period.

6. To make a parallel period, copy one or two measures of your first phrase into the beginning of the second phrase; where possible, continue developing one of the motives as you complete the period. To make a contrasting period, create a different but compatible melodic idea for the start of the second phrase. End either period with a cadence on the tonic.

7. Most melodies feature one high point, or climax. Build yours so that its highest note is stated only once—probably in the second phrase.

Try it #2

Study the following opening phrases in your anthology. In the first two blanks, provide a letter to show the melodic structure of the specified measures, and abbreviation (HC, PAC, IAC) of the cadence type. If IAC, specify whether the cadence is a strong or contrapuntal IAC. In the third blank, name the period type.

EXCERPT	MM. 1–4	MM. 5–8	PERIOD TYPE
(a) Hensel, "Neue Liebe, neues Leben" 🎧	**a** (HC)	_____	_____
(b) "Greensleeves" 🎧	_____	_____	_____
(c) Mozart, Sonata, K. 284, mvt. 3 🎧	_____	_____	_____

What elements make the Mozart example different from the others? What formal ambiguity is present?

Other Period Types

Listen now to the opening of Mozart's aria "Voi, che sapete" (mm. 9-20 are given in Example 18.11), and consider the phrase structure.

EXAMPLE 18.11: Mozart, "Voi, che sapete," mm. 9-20 🎧

Translation: You who know what love is, ladies, see if I have it in my heart.

Here are three phrases that clearly form a unit: the first ends with a half cadence (m. 12); the second prolongs the tonic for two bars and then the dominant for two bars, also ending with a half cadence (V7, m. 16); and the third states the complete basic phrase model (T-PD-D-T) to bring the passage to a close. In addition, the third phrase ends with a cadential motive (♩ ♪.♫.♪ | ♩) that originated in the first (compare mm. 11-12 with 19-20), tying the unit together. Three phrases that belong together, with weak-weak-strong cadences as here, are called a **three-phrase period**, which could be composed variously as **a a b**, **a b b′**, **a b a′**, or **a b c**.

Another type, the **double period**, consists of four phrases in which the only PAC appears at the end, following three inconclusive cadences. Examine Example 18.12 and the phrase diagram (Figure 18.4) below. Though the main key of the movement is B♭ major, this passage is in F major. As you can see, the four cadences make the pattern IAC-HC, IAC-PAC and a thematic design of **a b a′ b′**. Because phrases 1 and 3 are similar, this passage can be labeled a parallel double period; if they were not similar, it would be a contrasting double period. Several other cadential patterns are possible as well, such as HC-IAC and HC-PAC.

EXAMPLE 18.12: Mozart, Piano Sonata in B♭ Major, mvt. 1, mm. 23–38 🎧

FIGURE 18.4: Phrase diagram for Mozart sonata (double period)

m. 23 ⌒ 4 mm. ⌒ 26 27 ⌒ 4 mm. ⌒ 30 31 ⌒ 4 mm. ⌒ 34 35 ⌒ 4 mm. ⌒ 38

   a   **b**   **a′**   **b′**

F: IAC   HC   IAC   PAC

Before labeling a four-part sixteen-measure unit a double period, check the pattern of cadences, since other structures are possible. Four four-measure "phrases" may actually constitute a two-phrase period—if the first and third only expand the tonic and do not conclude with a cadence (if, in other words, they are subphrases).

When two, three, or more phrases group together as a unit but *each* phrase ends with an inconclusive cadence, these comprise a phrase group. Phrase groups often repeat a phrase to create **a b a**, **a a′ b**, **a b b′**, or other pattern, or may be united by shared motives.

Phrase Rhythm

Phrase Structure and Hypermeter

Listen to the opening of the lovely second movement of Mozart's Sonata in C Major, shown in Example 18.13. What exactly defines a phrase and subphrase in this passage, where melodic units seem to form clear two-measure groups? How can pianists give the musical line a direction without making the performance sound choppy?

EXAMPLE 18.13: Mozart, Piano Sonata in C Major, mvt. 2, mm. 1-16 🎧

The initial four measures divide into two two-measure subphrases that prolong the tonic, the first by a I-V$\frac{4}{3}$-I succession and the next by means of a neighboring $\frac{6}{4}$ chord. The first true cadence, a HC, arrives in measure 8, ending this first phrase inconclusively. The next eight measures are then a varied repetition of the first eight, concluding with a PAC. Measures 1-16 therefore constitute a parallel period.

If you were to perform this piece, remember that measures 1-16 form one large unit with two parts; paying too much attention to the shaping of two-measure subphrases could disrupt the perception of the larger design. As for projecting this design, there are two general strategies you could follow. One approach is harmonic: locate the cadences, then move through the harmonies in the middle of the phrase toward the harmonic goal. The other, a metric strategy, requires you to focus on larger hypermetric levels.

Hypermeter, as discussed in Chapter 2, interprets groups of measures as though they were beats within a single measure. Just as you hear four beats as strong-weak-strong-weak within a measure, you can also interpret four measures as strong-weak-strong-weak. Since Classical-era music is often structured from one-, two-, or four-measure units that combine to make four- or eight-measure phrases that then combine into eight-, sixteen-, or thirty-two-measure sections, it is not surprising that some of these larger structures replicate the accent pattern of the smaller ones. This "nesting" of structural units helps give Classical-era music its feeling of balance and unity.

Hypermeter (the regular metric alternation of strong and weak measures) is typically aligned with phrase structure (the harmonies and melodies that conclude with a cadence), as shown in Figure 18.5.

FIGURE 18.5: Phrase and hypermeter in alignment

	a				b		
m. 1			4	5			8
Phrase:			HC				PAC
Hypermeter: 1	2	3	4	1	2	3	4

When analyzing the hypermetric structure of a phrase, first determine whether the music suggests four-measure groups. Then number the measures 1-4 (between the staves), again 1-4, again 1-4, and so on, as in Example 18.13. Here, measures 1-4 are strong-weak-strong-weak, as are 5-8; the phrase ending coincides with the end of the second unit.

The interaction of hypermetric structure with phrase structure is known as **phrase rhythm**. In examining phrase rhythm, consider how harmonic, melodic, and motivic aspects of the phrase fit (or do not fit) within the context of its hypermeter. You might notice, for example, that a phrase has been expanded beyond its four-measure norm, or that measures have been added between phrases. If you are performing the piece, hypermetric analysis might translate into "thinking in one"—one large beat per measure—which can help give your performance a broad sweep and sense of direction. This strategy is particularly helpful for movements in fast tempi, where musicians can get bogged down in all the fast passagework and lose the sense of metrical flow. As you play or sing, try thinking of the strong-weak metric alternation from bar to bar. Don't simply accent the strong bars, though; rather, strive for a gentle ebb and flow of alternating strong and weak, as within a single measure.

Linking Phrases

Adjacent phrases may be linked in various ways. Consider again the opening section of Clementi's sonatina (Example 18.14) for another source of irregular phrase lengths. The first section of this piece spans fifteen measures rather than the sixteen you might expect. Count along while listening to this passage—in four, one beat per bar—to see whether your intuitions about metrically strong and weak measures line up with the conducting pattern.

EXAMPLE 18.14: Clementi, Sonatina in C Major, mvt. 1, mm. 1-11

As we have seen, the sonatina opens with a parallel period (4 + 4 mm.). As the period ends on the downbeat of measure 8, another phrase begins simultaneously—indeed, on the same pitch (G), which does double duty as the end of one phrase and the beginning of the next. This is called **phrase elision** or **overlap**. To diagram elided phrases, draw the end of the first phrase so that it overlaps with the beginning of the next, as in Figure 18.6. Compare this diagram with the anthology score.

Another Way

Some musicians distinguish between elision and overlap. With elision, the end of one phrase and beginning of the next are articulated by the same pitch or pitches, as here.

With overlap, there is more than one musical layer: while one or more parts finish the first phrase, one or more other parts begin another.

FIGURE 18.6: Metric reinterpretation in Clementi sonatina, mm. 1-15

```
              4 mm.          4 mm.                8 mm.
                                            2      2        4

Phrase:                   HC          PAC                    PAC
    m. 1                  4 5          8                      15
Hypermeter: 1   2   3   4  1  2  3    4
                                     = 1   2    3    4  1  2  3  4
```

If you listen for metrically strong and weak bars in the beginning of the sonatina, you will likely be disconcerted at measure 8; it "should" be metrically weak, but the elision reinterprets its role in the phrase, making it the strong initiator of a new four-measure unit. This type of elision, where a disruption of the hypermeter causes a weak measure to become strong, is sometimes called **metric reinterpretation**.

Not all elisions involve metric reinterpretation: for example, if phrase 1 were extended to five measures, its overlap with phrase 2 (Figure 18.7) would not disrupt the strong-weak alternation.

FIGURE 18.7: Elided phrases with no metric reinterpretation

```
                    5 mm.               4 mm.
Phrase:                     IAC                PAC
    m. 1                      5                  8
Hypermeter:  1    2    3    4   1    2    3    4
```

Phrase Expansion

Not all phrases fit into the model of four-bar phrases and hypermeter. Brahms's *Variations on a Theme by Haydn*, for example, begins with a parallel period made up of two five-bar phrases (Example 18.15).

EXAMPLE 18.15: Brahms, *Variations on a Theme by Haydn*, mm. 1-10 (piano I part) 🎧

KEY CONCEPT A phrase that extends beyond a typical phrase length may be viewed as an expansion of an underlying four- or eight-measure phrase. Such phrases may be composed in two ways:

- by **internal expansion**, inserting extra measures in the middle; or

- by **external expansion**, adding measures before the basic phrase begins (as an introduction) or at the end (as a cadential extension or codetta; see Examples 18.18 and 18.19).

In Example 18.15, if we took out measures 3 and 8, the theme would still convey a perfectly coherent melodic and harmonic structure: T-PD-D and T-PD-D-T. These measures are an internal expansion that continues the stepwise melodic descent of the melody.

To find phrase expansions, count four-measure units and determine whether the phrases coincide with them or not. A departure from the four-bar norm is one way listeners can tell that the primary thematic material has ended and a transitional passage or coda has begun. In music of the Baroque era, four-bar hypermeter is much less common than in the Classical; it occurs most frequently in small binary forms and dance movements. (Other Baroque genres employ a technique of "spinning out" that will be covered in Chapter 24.) Melodies from the Romantic era are often much longer.

Sometimes a phrase is preceded by introductory material, an external expansion that may or may not cause a disruption to the hypermeter. Example 18.16 begins with the conclusion of one phrase (on a half cadence in C major, mm. 11-12), ending a four-measure hypermetric unit, and continues with the beginning of the next, in G major. While the second phrase proper begins in measure 14, an inserted measure (13) precedes the theme and delays the hypermetric downbeat; for this reason, the inserted measure, known as a **lead-in**, is given no hypermetric number.

EXAMPLE 18.16: Mozart, Piano Sonata in C Major, mvt. 1, mm. 11–17 🎧

lead-in

Example 18.17 shows a case of a lead-in that does not disrupt the hypermeter. On the downbeat of measure 30, the arrival at a half cadence (in F major) is followed by a flourish of sixteenth notes that fills out the measure and leads to the return of the **a** phrase in measure 31.

EXAMPLE 18.17: Mozart, Piano Sonata in B♭ Major, mvt.1, mm. 27–34 🎧

lead-in

F:

HC

IAC

Expansions at the end of a phrase are known as **cadential extensions**. These sometimes begin with a deceptive resolution of V that leads to an extension, or they may coincide with an elision. In measure 65 of Example 18.18, for instance, Mozart introduces a four-measure phrase that is repeated with alterations in 69-72. Each phrase is introduced by a lead-in (mm. 64 and 68), which does not disrupt the hypermeter. The end of the second phrase, however, is elided with a cadential extension that begins in measure 72 and lasts for three measures. This codetta (a small coda) simply repeats the cadential harmonies V7-I, echoing the PAC of 71-72, disrupting the four-measure hypermeter, and slowing the momentum to end this movement.

EXAMPLE 18.18: Mozart, Piano Sonata in C Major, mvt. 2, mm. 64-74 🎧

🎵 **KEY CONCEPT** A **coda** is a section of music at the end of a movement, generally initiated after a strong cadence in the tonic, that extends the tonic area or the final cadence and brings the work to a close. Codas sometimes consist of energetic cadential flourishes; alternatively, they may dissipate energy and end quietly. A **codetta**, or short coda, lasts only a few measures, or comes at the end of a section rather than the end of a movement.

Listen to the conclusion of the first movement of the same Mozart sonata (Example 18.19), which is similar in construction. In this case, though, the last phrase spills over beyond the four-bar norm, ending in measure 71. This five-measure phrase is an example of phrase expansion, accomplished by drawing out the dominant area for two measures (mm. 69-70). After the cadence on the downbeat of measure 71, a codetta brings the movement to a rousing close.

EXAMPLE 18.19: Mozart, Piano Sonata in C Major, mvt. 1, mm. 67-73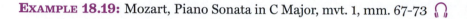

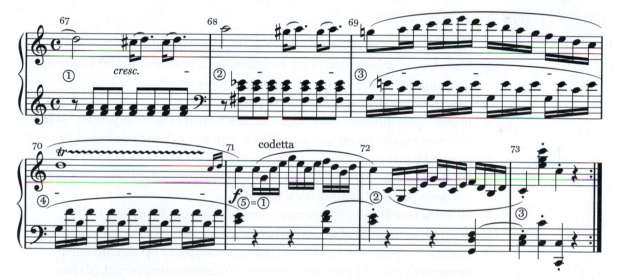

Did You Know?

Perhaps the most famous motives named for their symbolic associations are the leitmotivs used by Richard Wagner (1813-1883) to represent a character, idea, or object in his operas. For example, in the four-opera cycle *Der Ring des Nibelungen* (*The Ring of the Nibelung*), specific motives represent a gold ring, giants, female warriors called Valkyries, a sword, a magic cloak, fire, fate, and Valhalla (residence of the gods), among others. Wagner himself did not coin this term—it was popularized by a friend of his—but it has become closely associated with his music. While locating statements of each leitmotiv is only one part of an analysis of these masterworks, learning to identify them by ear can add greatly to your enjoyment of the operas. To learn more about Wagner's musical style, read the essays in the Norton Critical Score *Prelude and Transfiguration from "Tristan and Isolde,"* edited by Robert Bailey (New York: Norton, 1985). To learn more about Wagner's life, consult Ernest Newman's *Life of Richard Wagner* (London: Cassell, 1933-47; reprinted 1976).

TERMS YOU SHOULD KNOW

cadential extension
coda
codetta
hypermeter
lead-in
metric reinterpretation
modulating period
motive
- contour motive
- rhythmic motive

motivic transformation
- augmentation
- diminution
- fragmentation
period
- contrasting
- parallel
- symmetrical
- asymmetrical
- double

phrase
- antecedent
- consequent
phrase elision
phrase expansion
phrase group
phrase overlap
phrase rhythm
sentence structure
subphrase
truncation

QUESTIONS FOR REVIEW

1. Name three different ways motives may be transformed.
2. What type of information might be gained from phrase analysis? How might this information impact performance interpretations?
3. How do antecedent and consequent phrases differ?
4. In how many different ways might phrases be paired to form periods? What cadences may be found in a period? How can more than two phrases be grouped together?
5. What is the difference between a parallel and a contrasting period? between a symmetrical and asymmetrical period?
6. Describe how elided phrases may or may not disrupt hypermeter.
7. What is the purpose of a coda? Where is a coda located?
8. In music for your own instrument, find an example of (a) an antecedent-consequent pair, (b) a rhythmic motive, (c) a contrasting period, (d) four-measure hypermeter.

Know It? Show It!

Focus by working through the tutorials.

Learn with InQuizitive.

Apply what you've learned to complete the workbook assignments.

19

Diatonic Sequences

Overview

This chapter considers the relationship between harmonic and melodic elements in sequences. We learn how to identify sequence patterns, underlying root progressions, linear-intervallic frameworks, and common bass lines. We also learn how to treat sequences in contextual analysis.

Repertoire

Johann Sebastian Bach
    Invention in D Minor
    Prelude in C Major, BWV 924

Arcangelo Corelli, Trio Sonata in A Minor, Op. 4, No. 5, Allemanda

George Frideric Handel
    Chaconne in G Major
    "Rejoice greatly," from *Messiah*

Fanny Mendelssohn Hensel, "Neue Liebe, neues Leben" ("New Love, New Life")

Jerome Kern and Oscar Hammerstein II, "All the Things You Are," from *Very Warm for May*

Dennis Lambert and Brian Potter, "One Tin Soldier," from *Billy Jack*

Wolfgang Amadeus Mozart, Dies irae, from *Requiem*

Johann Pachelbel, Canon in D

Robert Schumann, "Ich grolle nicht" ("I Bear No Grudge"), from *Dichterliebe* (*The Poet's Love*)

Outline

Sequences

Descending sequences
- Descending-fifth sequence
- Pachelbel sequences
- Descending parallel $^6_3$ chords

Ascending sequences
- Ascending-fifth sequence
- Ascending parallel $^6_3$ chords

Sequences

The phrases we focused on in Chapter 18—composed with regular and predict-able groups of measures (such as 4 + 4, or 2 + 2 + 4) and basic phrase progressions (T-PD-D-T)—create a sense of stability and balance. Yet musical artworks mix moments of stability with instability, and moments of relative stasis with directed progression. Sequences contribute to this mixture of effects by thwarting the expectation of balanced phrases and creating new expectations of their own, through repetition.

KEY CONCEPT A **sequence** is made when a musical idea is expressed, then restated immediately one or more times, with each restatement transposed down or up from the previous one by a consistent interval. The basic musical idea—normally a half or full measure or two measures—is the sequence **pattern**; the interval by which it is transposed is called the **level of transposition**. To label a sequence on a score, mark the pattern and each subsequent transposition with a bracket, and identify the interval of transposition.

For an example, listen to the opening of Bach's Invention in D Minor (Example 19.1). Listen for the moment when a pattern is stated and then immediately repeated, transposed (by an interval other than an octave).

EXAMPLE 19.1: Bach, Invention in D Minor, mm. 1-18 🎧

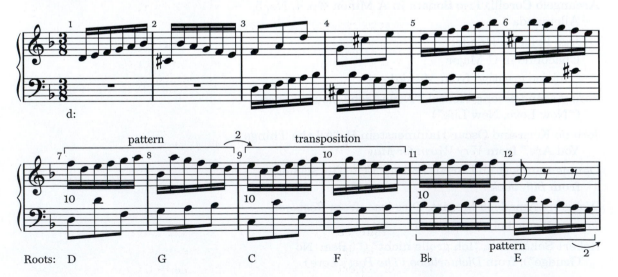

The two-measure pattern in measures 7-8 is transposed down a step in 9-10. It then moves to the left hand in 11-12 to initiate a new sequence, which is transposed down a step in 13-14. This sequence pattern includes both melodic and harmonic elements.

- **Melodic sequence**: The right-hand melodic pattern begins on F5 (m. 7), then is transposed to begin on E5 (m. 9); the left-hand pattern begins on B♭3 (m. 11), then moves to A3 (m. 13).

- **Harmonic sequence**: The roots of the harmonic progression move from D-G (mm. 7-8) down a step to C-F (9-10), while the second root progression is B♭-E (11-12) to A-D (13-14). In this example, the roots of the chords are also the foundation of the bass line. Both bass lines—D3-G3-C3-F3 followed by B♭3-E3-A3-D3—emphasize the descending-fifth progression.

Observe the contrapuntal pattern between voices: the sequences are structured around a series of outer-voice tenths on the downbeats of measures 7, 9, 11, and 13. Such a contrapuntal framework is called a **linear intervallic pattern** (abbreviated **LIP**). While melodic sequences or LIPs may appear on their own, they most often appear in combination: melodic sequence, LIP, bass line, and root progression together, as is the case here.

Now consider the role of these sequences in the opening of this piece. After the presentation of the main subject (motivic idea) three times in measures 1-6, establishing D minor, the sequences create forward momentum toward a new key: a firm PAC in F major in 17-18.

KEY CONCEPT Sequences typically play one of these roles:

- they prolong the tonic area of the phrase; or

- they provide a smooth transition from one key area to another.

In **diatonic sequences**, the interval sizes stay the same when the pattern moves to another pitch level, but the interval qualities may change (for example, major to minor, or perfect to diminished). In Example 19.1, for instance, the initial minor third in the right hand of measure 7 (F5-D5) becomes a major third in measure 9 (E5-C5). In **chromatic sequences**, accidentals are introduced, which may change the quality of the intervals in the pattern and may signal motion to another key; we will learn more about these in Chapter 30.

SUMMARY

A sequence pattern may consist of one of the following:

- a melody only (melodic sequence);

- a soprano-bass contrapuntal framework (LIP)—possibly with inner voices—whose embellishment may or may not be identical in each repetition; or

- a complete texture—melodic sequence, LIP, bass line, root progression— where the pattern is transposed exactly.

Try it #1

Listen to another passage from the Bach invention, and identify two different melodic sequences.

- Draw a bracket over the pattern each time you hear it (even if transposed or varied).

- Compare each pattern with its transposition, label the level of transposition (the interval), and describe any other changes. In what ways does the second sequence differ from the first?

Bach, Invention in D Minor, mm. 18-29

We will consider sequence types in two groups, descending and ascending. Keep in mind, though, that they could be classified by other shared characteristics—such as sequences whose patterns transpose by step, or sequences that display a particular type of bass line. We will point out these correspondences in the descriptions that follow.

KEY CONCEPT When analyzing sequences:

- identify the sequence pattern (a melodic idea, harmonic progression, LIP, or combination of these) and its level of transposition;
- determine the root progression;
- examine the bass-line motion.

Descending Sequences

The three main types of descending sequences have chord progressions derived from the basic root motions we learned in Chapter 15: the descending-fifth sequence is based on the circle of fifths; the Pachelbel sequence is based on descending thirds; and the parallel ⁶₃ sequence is based on descending steps.

Descending-Fifth Sequence

The descending-fifth root progression—where adjacent chords outline segments of the circle of fifths—is by far the most common sequence type; it is well suited to repetitive patterns both in the outer-voice framework and in the entire musical texture. In this type of sequence,

- two fifth-related harmonies make up each pattern, and
- the patterns descend by second.

Example 19.2a reproduces the descending-fifth sequence from Example 19.1. Part (b) provides a chordal reduction: the chord tones from the beginning of each measure minus all embellishing tones. The bass line here consists of the lowest-sounding chord tone of each measure; each two-measure pattern (D-G, C-F) is transposed by a descending second. This example illustrates one of the typical descending-fifth LIPs: 10-8, marked in part (b). Others are shown in Example 19.3.

EXAMPLE 19.2: Bach, Invention in D Minor

(a) Mm. 7-10: melodic pattern descends by second 🎧

Roots: D   G   C   F

(b) Reduction of mm. 7–10: root progression descends by fifth; two-chord pattern descends by second 🎧

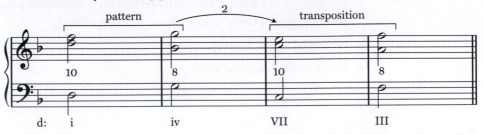

Throughout music of the common-practice era, you will find descending-fifth sequences—the strongest progression in tonal music—in several forms:

- with all root-position triads,
- with alternating root-position and first-inversion triads or sevenths, or
- with all seventh chords (possibly with inversions).

In the root progressions we considered previously, normally no more than three or four chords of the progression would appear successively in the phrase. There were also "weak links," chord connections that tended not to be included, centered around the diminished triad (vii°) and triads whose function is ambiguous (iii). When root-progression chains are found in a sequence, however, these weak harmonic links are supported by the repetition of the pattern and by strong voice-leading, making it possible to travel through the entire chain or at least through long sections of it.

KEY CONCEPT Descending-fifth sequences share the following characteristics:

- The harmonies follow a descending circle-of-fifths root progression or a contiguous segment of it, where each two-chord pair descends by second.
- In major keys, the upper-voice melodic pattern typically aligns with the chords as I-IV, vii°-iii, vi-ii, V-I; or I, IV-vii°, iii-vi, ii-V, I. Both possibilities are bracketed in Example 19.3a.
- The progression is the same in minor keys (i-iv-VII-III-VI-ii°-V-i), with the leading tone usually raised only in the V chord.
- The chords in each pair may appear in different inversions (e.g., $\frac{5}{3}$, $\frac{6}{3}$), making possible a variety of bass lines without changing the root progression.
- Because the transpositions follow the voice-leading of the original two-chord pattern, a root-position vii° chord may appear in major keys with its root doubled (even though it is the leading tone), as can the root-position ii° in minor.
- The outer voices of the chord pairs form a repeated intervallic pattern.

Memorize the Roman numerals in the chain (I-IV-vii°-iii-vi-ii-V-I) and some of the LIPs associated with them, as you will encounter them often. When in root position, the bass line of this sequence will zigzag up and down in order to stay within a reasonable range; this motion contributes to its distinctive sound and highlights the descending-fifth harmonies, while the stepwise melodic pattern contributes smoothness to the descent.

Example 19.3 shows voice-leading frameworks for basic descending-fifth sequences, both root position and with alternating $\frac{6}{3}$ chords. In each framework, any of the upper-voice strands could be the soprano line in an SATB setting; your choice will determine which LIP is created by the soprano and bass. The brackets above the staff indicate the repeated two-chord pattern, which in each case descends by step; and the ties highlight common tones between the chords. Although the examples give the entire course of a sequence, only a portion may appear in a piece—as few as two or three chords.

In the contextual analysis, the ii-V-I at the end plays a dual role: as part of the sequential pattern, but also as the end of a phrase (PD-D-T). If the entire descending-fifth "circle" is employed, starting with the tonic and returning there, the sequence expands the tonic area.

EXAMPLE 19.3: Descending-fifth frameworks

(a) All root position (10-10 LIP)

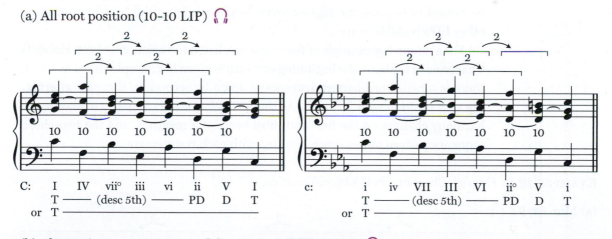

(b) Alternating root position and first inversion (10-6 LIP)

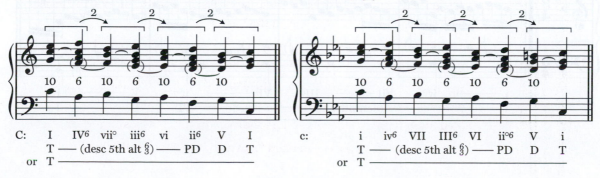

(c) Alternating first inversion and root position (6-10 LIP)

C: I⁶   IV   vii°⁶   iii   vi⁶   ii   V⁶   I
      T —— (desc 5th alt ⁶₃) —— PD   D   T
   or T ————————————————————————————

c: i⁶   iv   VII⁶   III   VI⁶   ii°   V⁶   i
      T —— (desc 5th alt ⁶₃) —— PD   D   T
   or T ————————————————————————————

Bass lines Example 19.3 also illustrates typical bass lines for descending-fifth sequences.

- In root position, bass lines alternate between a descending fifth and an ascending fourth (part a).

- When alternate chords are in ⁶₃ position, the bass line consists of a descending third followed by an ascending second (part b), or vice versa (part c).

One characteristic LIP is shown in each example, but any of the upper parts could be moved to become the highest voice (while retaining the bass line), making other LIPs possible as well.

For a minor-key example of this sequence, listen to Variation 11 from Handel's Chaconne in G Major, the beginning of which is given in Example 19.4a. As usual, there is a two-chord pattern transposed down by second, in this case alternating root position with ⁶₃ chords. As the SATB framework in part (b) shows, the harmony changes on the first and third beats of a measure, and the two-chord sequence pattern moves down one step with each restatement.

EXAMPLE 19.4: Handel, Chaconne in G Major, Variation 11

(a) Mm. 89–92

g: i ———— iv⁶   VII ———— III⁶   VI ———— ii°⁶   V ———— i⁶
      T ———————————— (desc 5th alt ⁶₃) ———————————— PD   D   T
   or T ——

(b) Framework for mm. 89-92

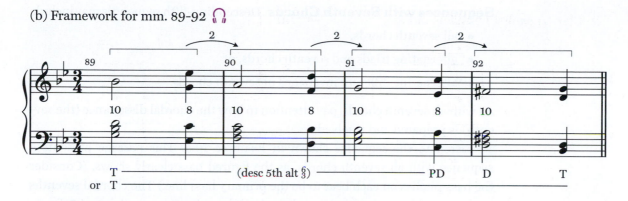

Try it #2

Compare the beginning of Handel's Variation 12 with Variation 11 (Example 19.4). Answer the questions that follow by circling the appropriate words.

Handel, Chaconne in G Major, Variation 12, mm. 97-100

(1) The two passages use (a) the same root progression (b) a different root progression.

(2) The LIP type is (a) 10-10 (b) 10-6 (c) 6-10.

🎵 **KEY CONCEPT** When you write descending-fifth sequences with triads:

- Follow the same part-writing guidelines as for any two chords with roots related by fifth. Plan your voice-leading carefully, since the two-chord pattern will be transposed to form the sequence.
- In most cases, the two-chord pattern will include a common tone. Keep the common tone in the same voice, and move the other voices to the closest chord member.
- Retain the same voice-leading for the two-chord pattern each time it is transposed.
- If the sequence alternates first-inversion triads, the two-chord pattern may or may not have these common-tone connections, depending on what is doubled.
- If the pattern uses root-position triads, the sequence may contain root-position viiº (and iiº in minor); the doubling will be the same throughout, even if that means doubling the leading tone.
- Keep the sequence pattern and LIP consistent as you move through the progression, so its sequential nature is clear to listeners.

Sequences with Seventh Chords Descending-fifth sequences may include

- all seventh chords,
- alternating triads and seventh chords, or
- alternating different inversions of seventh chords.

As with all seventh chords, pay attention to how the chordal dissonance (the seventh) is prepared and resolved.

Listen to the sequence shown in Example 19.5. This passage presents a sequence with all seventh chords, as the figured bass clearly shows. (Consider the bass pitches on each beat to be the primary bass line.) The chordal sevenths are prepared by common tone and resolved down by step as a string of 7-6 suspensions in each two-chord pattern, alternating between first and second violin: for example, the seventh on beat 1 of measure 23, C5, is prepared by a consonant tenth in measure 22 and resolves down by step to B4 on beat 2. These preparations and resolutions of the sevenths are built in to the framework, demonstrating the close link between sequences and the resolution of dissonant intervals in counterpoint.

EXAMPLE 19.5: Corelli, Allemanda, from Trio Sonata in A Minor, mm. 22-24 🎧

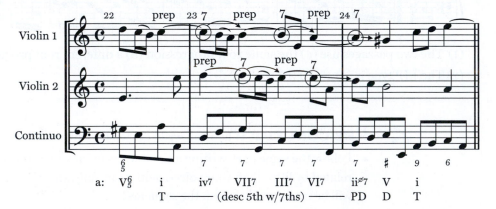

When you write descending-fifth sequences with seventh chords in root position, unacceptable parallels can easily arise unless you vary the doubling of adjacent chords. Look at Example 19.6 to see how this problem can be avoided: in measure 19, the fifth has been omitted from the keyboard accompaniment on beats 2, 3, and 4. A more common solution is to leave out the fifth in alternate chords.

KEY CONCEPT When you write consecutive root-position seventh chords, alternate complete and incomplete chords in the two-chord pattern, omitting the fifth on every other chord.

EXAMPLE 19.6: Handel, "Rejoice greatly," mm. 18-20 (I = incomplete, C = complete)

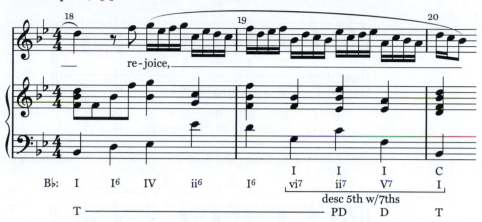

```
Bb:  I      I⁶     IV    ii⁶    I⁶    vi⁷    ii⁷    V⁷    I
                                      I      I      I     C
                                      └── desc 5th w/7ths ──┘
     T ─────────────────────────────── PD     D     T
```

Some basic frameworks for descending-fifth sequences with seventh chords are illustrated in Example 19.7a–d; note their treatment of the chordal seventh.

KEY CONCEPT When you write a descending-fifth sequence in common-practice style:

- Prepare sevenths in each chord by common tone, and resolve down by step.
- In the middle of a sequence, the leading tones need not resolve up, but may be pulled down by a descending voice-leading line.
- In a sequence with all root-position seventh chords, parallel fifths and octaves can easily result. To avoid them, alternate complete (C) and incomplete (I) seventh chords (omit the fifth; Example 19.7a).
- In a sequence with alternating triads and seventh chords (parts b–d), every chord should be complete, with standard doubling.
- Seventh-chord sequences may alternate between two inversions. Inverted seventh chords should be complete in four-part settings (part d).

EXAMPLE 19.7: Frameworks for descending-fifth sequences featuring seventh chords

(a) All root-position chords, alternating complete (C) and incomplete (I) (10-7 LIP)

```
F:  I    IV⁷   vii°⁷  iii⁷   vi⁷   ii⁷   V⁷   I
    T ──── (desc 5th w/7ths) ──── PD    D    T
```

(b) Alternating triads and root-position seventh chords, all complete (10-5 LIP)

F: I   IV7   vii°   iii7   vi   ii7   V7   I
    T ——— (desc 5th alt 7ths) ——— PD   D   T

(c) Alternating triads and first-inversion seventh chords, all complete (10-5 LIP)

F: I⁶   IV   vii°⁶₅   iii   vi⁶₅   ii   V⁶₅   I
    T ——— (desc 5th alt ⁶₅) ——— PD   D   T

(d) Alternating first- and third-inversion seventh chords, all complete (10-9 LIP)

F: I⁶   IV⁴₂   vii°⁶₅   iii⁴₂   vi⁶₅   ii⁴₂   V⁶₅   I
    T ———(desc 5th alt ⁶₅ ⁴₂)——— PD   D   T

Some of the seventh chords shown in Example 19.7—for example, iii7, IV7, vi⁶₅, and iii⁴₂—are rarely found outside of sequences.

Of the characteristic bass lines in descending-fifth sequences with seventh chords, we have already seen two:

- descending fifth, ascending fourth (Example 19.7a and b) and
- alternating thirds and steps (part c).
- A third possibility is a descending stepwise bass (part d).

Use Example 19.7 as a model to write your own variations of the descending-fifth seventh-chord sequence, and look for others in pieces you are performing.

In Popular Music Listen to the first phrase of Kern and Hammerstein's "All the Things You Are" (Example 19.8). This song features chords with a third added above the seventh (**ninth chords**) and harmonies with chromatic alterations. The chord before measure 5 (not shown) is a V7 in F minor, setting up the F minor chord as i. This chord progression should be familiar for the most part: Kern has written seventh and ninth chords to elaborate the root progression i7–iv7–VII$^9_7$–III7–VI7–V7/V (a chromatically altered ii7)–V7. The two-chord sequence pattern is reflected in the melody (A♭4–D♭5, G4–C5, F4–B♮4, E♮4).

EXAMPLE 19.8: Kern and Hammerstein, "All the Things You Are," mm. 5-12 (descending-fifth sequence with seventh chords)

Try it #3

In Example 19.8, there are some differences from the expected diatonic sequence. Circle on the example the chord symbols for the nondiatonic chords. Which diatonic chord does each replace?

Pachelbel Sequences

Listen now to one of the most famous descending sequences of all—Johann Pachelbel's Canon in D (Example 19.9). Chord-to-chord analysis of the continuo part in measures 1-2 reveals a root-progression pattern of down a fourth, then up a second, until just before the cadence: I-V-vi-iii-IV-I-ii⁶₅-V7-I. The two-chord pattern as marked reveals underlying descending thirds: I-vi-IV-ii.

EXAMPLE 19.9: Pachelbel, Canon in D, mm. 1-8

Although the bass line stays the same throughout the piece, as does the harmonic progression (with slight changes in voicing), the upper parts explore the many possible melodic lines that can be generated from these chords, beginning with scalar patterns and becoming increasingly elaborate. As in the example, violin 1 introduces each new strand, which is answered in canon after two measures by violin 2, then two measures later by violin 3.

In music literature, you sometimes find sequences with this same harmonic progression but a stepwise descending bass line. This variation of the Pachelbel sequence alternates root-position chords with first-inversion chords—usually I–V⁶–vi–iii⁶–IV–I⁶–ii, where ii serves as a predominant to prepare the cadence. Here, the underlying descending thirds progression (I–vi–IV–ii) is somewhat concealed; and when V⁶ moves to vi, the leading-tone is pulled down by the voice-leading of the sequence and does not resolve according to its normal tendency.

For an example, listen to the opening of Hensel's "Neue Liebe, neues Leben" (Example 19.10a). The entire texture—melody, bass line, and accompaniment upper voices—follows a sequential pattern, transposed down a third each measure. It breaks off after the third statement of the pattern, just before the half cadence in measures 3–4. Like many sequences, as is clear from part (b), this one expands the tonic before the half cadence.

EXAMPLE 19.10: Hensel, "Neue Liebe, neues Leben"

(a) Mm. 1–4

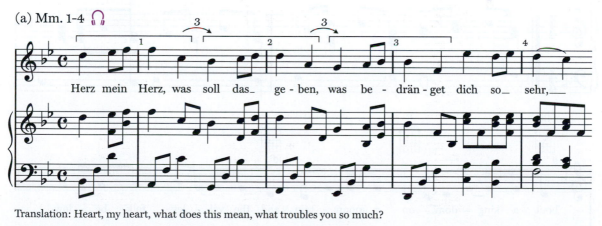

Translation: Heart, my heart, what does this mean, what troubles you so much?

(b) Framework: Pachelbel sequence with stepwise bass

SUMMARY

Characteristic bass lines in Pachelbel sequences may be one of these types:

- descending fourth, ascending step (root-position sequences)
- descending stepwise (alternating root position and first inversion)

Example 19.11 shows another stepwise descending bass line, by the 1970s band Coven. The downbeats of each bar make the descending-third progression clear: F–Dm–Bb–Gm7. You can hear this sequence in many popular songs, performed by artists such as Aerosmith, Green Day, and Avril Lavigne.

EXAMPLE 19.11: Lambert and Potter, "One Tin Soldier," mm. 7–10

SUMMARY

In Pachelbel sequences, the two-chord pattern

- descends by third, so that alternate chords span I-vi-IV-ii;
- has roots that move down a fourth, then up a second: I-V-vi-iii-IV-I-ii;
- may include sevenths on some or all of the chords;
- may include alternating first-inversion chords that result in a stepwise descending bass line.

The two-chord root progression in Example 19.12 descends by third (beginning in m. 5, beat 2: C-F, A-D, F-B) with a stepwise bass line, like the Pachelbel sequence, but it differs in interesting ways. Most striking is the fact that it is comprised of all seventh chords, alternating root position and second inversion. Further, the two-measure melodic pattern in the voice is repeated up a fourth, highlighting the poignant text ("Love lost forever!") in the highest vocal register of the song thus far.

EXAMPLE 19.12: Schumann, "Ich grolle nicht," mm. 5-9

Translation: Eternally lost love, I bear no [grudge].

Descending Parallel $\frac{6}{3}$ Chords

As we have seen, a chain of root progressions by second can easily result in parallel fifths and octaves. While this voice-leading problem is more of a concern in common-practice than popular styles, most root progressions a second apart feature some sort of intervallic pattern to avoid the fifths and octaves—such as a parallel series of $\frac{6}{3}$ chords descending by step, as in Example 19.13. The LIP for this kind of sequence is usually identified 6-6, though the middle voice (a three-voice texture is typical) makes 10-10 (or 3-3) with the bass; both contrapuntal gestures were examined in Chapter 9. This sequence differs from the two previous in that the pattern consists of only one chord instead of two.

EXAMPLE 19.13: Descending parallel $\frac{6}{3}$ chord sequence 🎧

In music literature, parallel $\frac{6}{3}$ chords work more like sequences than like harmonic progressions: they function as a linear succession, spanning harmonic pillars, without a strong sense of root motion. Indeed, a succession of first-inversion triads is more closely related to doubling a melody in thirds and sixths than it is to independent voice-leading. (This compositional strategy was so common in the Renaissance era that it had a name: *fauxbourdon*.) If you analyze with Roman numerals, they will not conform to the familiar phrase or root-progression models; label them as shown above, or analyze with Roman numerals and "(par $\frac{6}{3}$)" below (as in Example 19.14).

Listen to the passage from Mozart's *Requiem* given in Example 19.14. Beginning with the last beat of measure 27, Mozart employs a succession of $\frac{6}{3}$ chords: v6-iv6-III6-♭II6 (first-inversion triads Em-Dm-C-B♭), preceding the half cadence in measure 29. (This altered form of the ii chord will be discussed in Chapter 27.) The progression clearly does not "make sense" according to the principles of harmonic progression presented so far; however, the linear pattern of parallel chords makes it perfectly acceptable, even typical, in common-practice style.

EXAMPLE 19.14: Mozart, Dies irae, from *Requiem*, mm. 27-29

Translation: As foretold by David and the Sibyl.

With 7-6 Motion One way to break up parallel motion when writing a series of $^6_3$ chords is to delay the arrival of one of the chord members with a suspension. We have already observed that descending-fifth sequences may feature linear patterns such as 7-6 suspensions; these same intervals can be used with a series of $^6_3$ chords moving down by step as well, as shown in Examples 19.15 and 19.16. The 7-6 motion creates the effect of two "events" similar to the two-chord pattern of other sequence types.

EXAMPLE 19.15: Descending parallel $^6_3$ chords with 7-6 LIP

Again, if you analyze the "chords" here with Roman numerals, the root progression does not make much sense; the interval succession does, however, because of the resulting linear sequence, which is drawn from contrapuntal rather than harmonic models. If you hear a chain of 7-6 suspensions above a stepwise descending bass, its underlying motion will be parallel $^6_3$ chords.

The chain of 7-6 suspensions is often prepared by a 5-6 motion to set up the first suspension, as in measure 73 of Example 19.16. Listen to this passage to hear how the 7-6 suspensions break up potential parallel motion. As with the other sequences, the 7-6 may appear between the bass and any upper voice—here, the upper voice of the left-hand part.

EXAMPLE 19.16: Handel, Chaconne in G Major, Variation 9, mm. 73-76 🎧

Ascending Sequences

Although ascending sequences are much less common in music literature than descending, you may encounter some of the following types, whose patterns all ascend by step.

Ascending-Fifth Sequence

Example 19.17 shows an ascending-fifth sequence at the beginning of a Bach prelude. The pattern consists of two harmonies and spans one measure, with each pattern transposed up by step (roots C-G, D-A). A lovely detail is the use of 4-3 suspensions embellishing each harmony, alternating in an inner and outer voice in the right hand. As with the descending-fifth sequence, the root progression between adjacent chords alternates ascending fifth and descending fourth.

EXAMPLE 19.17: Bach, Prelude in C Major, BWV 924, mm. 1-4 🎧

Like the descending-fifth sequence, the ascending-fifth may appear with alternate harmonies inverted. Example 19.18 shows the same sequence with the second chord of each pattern inverted. The usual voice-leading is in three parts: one voice in each pattern holds a common tone, while the other two move down a step in parallel tenths. If the cycle of fifths is completed, this sequence prolongs the tonic harmony.

EXAMPLE 19.18: Framework for an ascending-fifth sequence

Ascending Parallel $\frac{6}{3}$ Chords

The LIP for an ascending parallel $\frac{6}{3}$ chord sequence (Example 19.19), as for the descending, is usually identified 6-6, though the middle voice makes 10-10 (or 3-3) with the bass. The sequence is normally written in three voices, without doubling. As before, analyze as shown.

EXAMPLE 19.19: Ascending parallel chords

With 5-6 Motion An ascending sequence based on parallel $\frac{6}{3}$ chords is shown in Example 19.20. Here, a series of first-inversion triads moves up by step, but the arrival of the sixth above the bass is delayed a half beat, making a 5-6 LIP.

EXAMPLE 19.20: Ascending seconds (5-6 LIP)

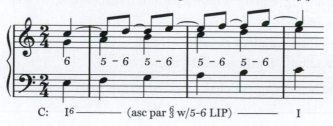

Listen to measures 69-71 of "Neue Liebe, neues Leben" (Example 19.21a) to hear this pattern. Remember that the 5-6 motion may be between the bass and any upper part; here, the upper part is in the left hand of the accompaniment. Ascending sequences like this one, though beautiful, are not frequently found in music literature—they divert the harmonic progression from its traditional goal-directed motion from tonic to dominant.

EXAMPLE 19.21: Hensel, "Neue Liebe, neues Leben"

(a) Mm. 69-71

Translation: Let me go, love!

(b) Reduction of mm. 69-71

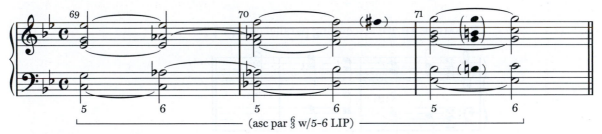

SUMMARY

The following sequences have a pattern transposed down by step:

- descending fifth
- descending parallel §§ chords
- descending 7-6 with parallel §§ chords

The following sequences have a pattern transposed up by step:

- ascending fifth
- ascending parallel §§ chords
- ascending 5-6 with parallel §§ chords

The Pachelbel sequence has a pattern transposed down by thirds.

When you encounter a sequence in a piece of music, write a contextual analysis below the Roman numerals to clarify the harmonic function and goal of the passage. You might replace beat-by-beat Roman numerals with a label on the first and last chord, plus a label that describes the sequence type from among the following.

- descending fifth: "desc 5th" (specify "root," "alt 7ths," or other inversions)

- Pachelbel: "Pach" (specify "alt $\frac{6}{3}$" if present)

- ascending fifth: "asc 5th" (specify "root" or "alt $\frac{6}{3}$")

- parallel $\frac{6}{3}$ chords: "asc par $\frac{6}{3}$" (specify 5-6 if present) or "desc par $\frac{6}{3}$" (specify 7-6 if present)

It may also be helpful to label sequences with brackets and arrows to show the pattern's transposition, and numbers to show the LIP: 6-6, 10-10, 7-6, and so on.

Finally, remember that individual chords within sequences have a weak harmonic function on their own—they are conveyances between stable harmonic areas. Sequences are like subways, buses, or trains: you get on at one location, ride for a while, and get off when you reach your destination. They are usually preceded by a chord or harmonic progression that sets up the tonic and key of the starting location, and they connect at their termination to a progression that reestablishes the key. Some sequences "travel" within one key area, while others move from one key to another.

You could also think of sequences like suspension bridges with pillars at both ends holding up the bridge, but taut cables strung between them supporting the middle. In performance, focus on broad goals and motion between the pillars at the beginning and end.

Did You Know?

The Pachelbel sequence is one that has emerged as a recurrent harmonic foundation of pop and rock songs. In fact, a popular YouTube video by Rob Paravonian ("Pachelbel Rant") describes how he is haunted by this progression in every musical genre he hears—from classical to folk to rock. In addition to Coven's "One Tin Soldier," other songs you may have heard with this progression are Aerosmith's "Cryin'," Green Day's "Basket Case," and Avril Lavigne's "Sk8er Boi." To compare a 1970s and 90s treatment of the Pachelbel sequence, listen to "Go West" (1979) by the Village People, and a cover of the song by the Pet Shop Boys (1993); the latter was nominated for a Best Music Video Grammy in 1995. Listen to any of these while singing along with the bass line, and perhaps Pachelbel will haunt you as well!

TERMS YOU SHOULD KNOW

level of transposition   sequence   sequence pattern
linear intervallic pattern (LIP)   • diatonic
parallel $^6_3$ chords   • chromatic
  • with 5-6 (ascending)   • harmonic
  • with 7-6 (descending)   • melodic
                                                      • ascending fifth
                                                      • descending fifth
                                                      • Pachelbel

QUESTIONS FOR REVIEW

1. What are sequences? Where will you find them?
2. What do you look for in analyzing a sequence pattern?
3. Which root progressions work well in sequence frameworks?
4. What aspects of dissonance resolution must be retained in sequences?
5. What part-writing guidelines are relaxed when you connect chords in a sequence?
6. What steps would you take to write a Pachelbel sequence? How does this sequence type differ from others?
7. What are the LIPs that may be added to parallel $^6_3$ chords to create a sequence?
8. In an embellished sequence, how can you tell which sequence framework (e.g., descending fifth, ascending 5-6) is being used?
9. In music for your own instrument, find two different sequences and label their types.

Know It? Show It!

Focus by working through the tutorials.

Learn with InQuizitive.

Apply what you've learned to complete the workbook assignments.

20

Secondary Dominant and Leading-Tone Chords to V

Overview

This chapter explains how to write and analyze chromatic chords that intensify motion toward the dominant.

Repertoire

Johann Sebastian Bach
   "Ermuntre dich, mein schwacher Geist" ("Take Courage, My Weak Spirit," Chorale No. 102)
   "Wachet auf" ("Awake," Chorale No. 179)
Scott Joplin, "Pine Apple Rag"
Wolfgang Amadeus Mozart
   Piano Sonata in C Major, K. 545, mvt. 1
   Rondo in E♭ Major for Horn and Orchestra, K. 371
Elvis Presley and Vera Matson, "Love Me Tender"

Outline

Intensifying the dominant

Secondary dominants to V
- Spelling secondary dominants
- Tonicization and modulation
- Secondary dominants to V in the basic phrase
- Writing and resolving
- Cross relations

Secondary leading-tone chords to V
- Writing and resolving

Secondary-function chords in dominant expansions

Intensifying the Dominant

Listen to a phrase from Bach's setting of "Wachet auf," given in Example 20.1.

EXAMPLE 20.1: Bach, "Wachet auf," mm. 7-11 🎧

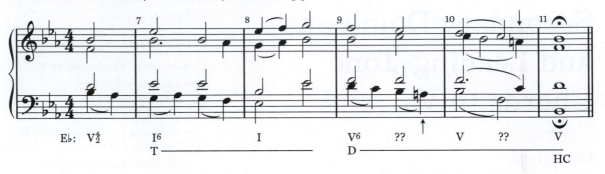

The phrase begins with a prolonged tonic (mm. 7-8) and ends with a half cadence in measure 11. The two A♮s (marked with arrows) in measures 9 and 10 represent a raised 4̂. Write this scale degree as ♯4̂, to symbolize the chromatic inflection of 4̂ up by half step, even in flat keys (as here) where the score notation calls for a natural rather than a sharp.

This ♯4̂ changes the function of the last chord of measure 9: F-A♮-C-E♭ in first inversion (the B♭ on beat 3 is an accented passing tone). Although this chord is built on 2̂ (F) in E♭ major, it is not a ii₅⁶ chord, because its bass is the nondiatonic pitch A♮ instead of A♭. The quality of the chord, a dominant seventh, reveals its local function. Dominant sevenths—whether built on 5̂ or not, whether diatonic or not—generally function like dominants, even if only in a localized way.

If you found this dominant seventh (F-A♮-C-E♭) written without a key context, you could determine its implied tonic in one of two ways:

- count a P5 down (or P4 up) from its root, or
- move a m2 up from the chord's third (A♮, the leading tone).

Both methods reveal that this V7 should resolve to either B♭ major or B♭ minor as its tonic. Indeed, both F-A♮-C-E♭ chords in measures 9-10 resolve to B♭ major (V in E♭) on the next beat; they function like "temporary dominants" to the V chord.

⌒ **KEY CONCEPT** Chords that act like dominants in their spelling and resolution, but resolve to a scale degree and harmony other than the tonic, are called **secondary dominants**. Secondary dominants to V are analyzed as V/V (read "V of V").

Secondary dominants are sometimes called "applied dominants" (a type of **applied chord**, because they are "applied" to a chord other than the tonic) or "secondary-function" chords. In Roman numeral analysis, applied dominants are sometimes notated with arrows that point to their chord of resolution, rather than the "slash" notation used here.

Look again at Example 20.1. We can now provide all the Roman numerals for measures 9 and 10: V^6 V^6_5/V | V V/V, ending with a half cadence on V (m. 11). Each A♮ (#$\hat{4}$) functions as a "temporary" leading tone to $\hat{5}$, intensifying the arrival on the half cadence. Measures 9-11 prolong the dominant harmony. The chorale, however, clearly stays in E♭ major, with the next phrase beginning on the E♭ tonic and concluding with a PAC.

Secondary Dominants to V

Spelling Secondary Dominants

To understand secondary dominants to V, first think of V (v in minor) as a temporary tonic key rather than a chord, and then imagine what the dominant (or dominant seventh) chord would be in that temporary key. For example, for a $V7/V$ in A major (Example 20.2):

- think of the dominant harmony in A major (part a);
- the temporary tonic key would therefore be E major (part b), and
- *its* dominant harmony is B major (part c).
- So $V7/V$ in A major is a B major chord (B-D♯-F♯-A).

The D♯ in E major's key signature is crucial in spelling the secondary dominant correctly. In music literature, though, you are more likely to find secondary dominant seventh chords ($V7/V$) rather than triads, since their Mm7 chord quality marks them unambiguously as having a dominant function (B-D♯-F♯-A). In either case, the music has not left the primary key; the idea of imagining a temporary new tonic is a simple aid in spelling the secondary dominant correctly.

EXAMPLE 20.2: Spelling a secondary dominant to V in A major

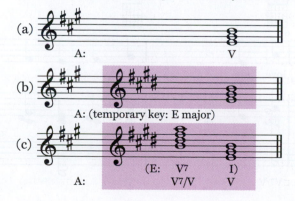

Another Way

You might also think of the secondary dominant in major keys as an altered ii (predominant) chord: raise the third to give it a major or dominant seventh quality (II or II7). (In Example 20.2, the tonic chord is A major; the major supertonic is B major.) The chord quality resulting from this chromatic alteration, together with the voice-leading and resolution of the chord, define it as a secondary dominant (which we will label V/V or V7/V—*not* II or II7).

All V7/V or V/V chords are spelled by raising $\hat{4}$ to $\sharp\hat{4}$, which functions as the leading tone to V. To spell a secondary dominant in a minor key, however, two chromatic alterations are necessary: $\hat{4}$ is raised to $\sharp\hat{4}$, and $\flat\hat{6}$ is raised to $\hat{6}$. Imagine, for example, C minor (three flats) and the temporary minor-dominant key of G minor (two flats). The change in key signature (to G minor) provides the raised $\flat\hat{6}$ (A$\flat$ to A$\natural$), and changing $\hat{4}$ to $\sharp\hat{4}$ (F to F$\sharp$) creates the temporary leading tone and the dominant seventh (Mm7) quality. In sum, V7/V in C minor is spelled D-F$\sharp$-A$\natural$-C, just as in C major.

KEY CONCEPT To spell a secondary dominant to V, double-check that

- the chord is built on $\hat{2}$ (a fifth above $\hat{5}$),
- the triad quality is major (with $\sharp\hat{4}$; in minor, also raise $\flat\hat{6}$ to $\hat{6}$), and
- the chordal seventh (if present) is minor, creating a Mm7 chord.

Secondary dominants to V may be found in many styles. Example 20.3 shows the opening phrase of "Love Me Tender." The dominant seventh chord in measure 7 is intensified by an A7 chord, V7/V, in measure 6; the C$\sharp$ here acts as a temporary leading tone to D, the dominant of G. You can get a snapshot of the harmonic motion from the chord symbols above the staff. The D7sus in m. 7 accounts for the 9-8 and 4-3 suspensions.

EXAMPLE 20.3: Presley and Matson, "Love Me Tender," mm. 5-8

The secondary dominant to V is one of the most common chromatic chords—often found at phrase endings or in other passages where the dominant harmony is prolonged. Practice spelling V7/V in various keys, and look for it in pieces you play (the presence of ♯4̂ is an important clue).

SUMMARY

To spell V7/V in any key:

(a) • Imagine the dominant harmony as a temporary tonic key (in A major, imagine E major as the tonic; in A minor, imagine E minor as the tonic).

     • Using that key signature and key, spell its dominant seventh chord (in E major or minor, V7 is B-D♯-F♯-A).

(b) Or build a dominant seventh chord on 2̂ of the primary key.

With either method, double-check that the chord has the appropriate accidentals to create a Mm7 quality. In minor keys, it will need two accidentals.

Try it #1

For each of the keys below, build a secondary dominant seventh chord by writing first the V chord and then the dominant of this key area. (You can double-check your answer by means of the altered ii chord method.) Write the chords on the staff with accidentals, rather than key signatures.

KEY	V CHORD	V7/V		KEY	V CHORD	V7/V
(a) B♭ major				(f) D major		
(b) E minor				(g) E♭ major		
(c) C minor				(h) B major		
(d) A major				(i) G minor		
(e) A♭ major				(j) F♯ minor		

Tonicization and Modulation

When a secondary dominant resolves, making its chord of resolution seem like a temporary tonic, the effect is called **tonicization**. When a harmony like V is tonicized, the key of the passage does not change except in a very temporary sense. The temporary tonic then returns to its normal functional role in the primary key and progresses as usual.

Tonicizations of greater structural significance are called **modulations**. To identify a modulation, look for such musical indications as

- a continuation of the passage in the new key,

- an authentic cadence in the new key,

- the presence of a predominant harmony in the new key.

Example 20.4 shows another of Bach's chorale settings, an example of tonicization. Phrase 1 ends in measure 4 with V/V (including a 4-3 suspension), tonicizing V (D) at the half cadence. Then immediately after the fermata, phrase 2 begins clearly in G major with a tonic chord. A half cadence preceded by a secondary dominant is called a **tonicized half cadence** (**THC**).

The Roman numerals here illustrate another way to analyze secondary dominants, with "bracket notation": the tonicized chords are labeled briefly as though in the key of V, with a bracket labeled with that Roman numeral. Be careful not to confuse the I chord under the fermata (in the dominant key) with the I chord after the fermata (in the tonic key). Bracket notation is particularly appropriate if there is more than one secondary dominant in a row, or if the V/V is embellished with a cadential $^6_4$ or a suspension, as here.

EXAMPLE 20.4: Bach, "Ermuntre dich, mein schwacher Geist," mm. 1-8

If the secondary dominant is preceded by a vi chord (or vi7), you can think of it as a predominant ii or ii7 within the tonicized area (see m. 4 in Example 20.5). This example meets minimum standards for a modulation, but the effect of V as the tonic is brief; we have labeled it a THC.

EXAMPLE 20.5: Bach, "Wachet auf," mm. 1–5

In contrast, if the music after the tonicized half cadence continues in the dominant key, as in Example 20.6 (from m. 13), then a modulation has occurred, though we do not know that until the beginning of the following phrase.

EXAMPLE 20.6: Mozart, Piano Sonata in C Major, mvt. 1, mm. 8–17

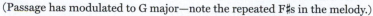

(Passage has modulated to G major—note the repeated F♯s in the melody.)

Secondary Dominants to V in the Basic Phrase

The most common role for V7/V or V/V in the basic phrase is to replace or follow a predominant-function harmony, as in Example 20.7. You could think of V7/V as a supercharged ii7: the raised $\hat{4}$ combined with the descending-fifth root progression (already present between ii7 and V) makes a very strong pull toward V—as though the V7/V were functioning as a predominant.

KEY CONCEPT Because the V7/V "belongs to" the dominant, its temporary key, place it in the dominant area of the basic phrase in your contextual analysis (even though V7/V can be considered an altered predominant).

EXAMPLE 20.7: Typical contexts for a secondary dominant to V

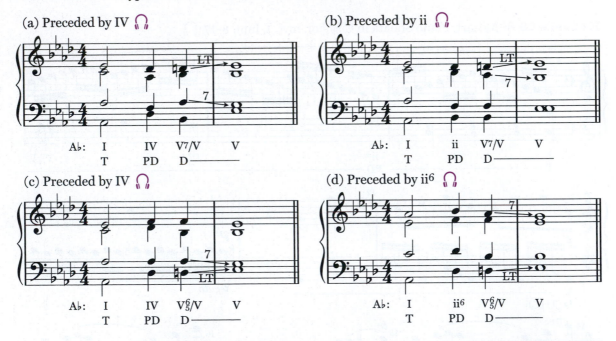

(a) Preceded by IV

Ab: I   IV   V7/V   V
     T   PD   D————

(b) Preceded by ii

Ab: I   ii   V7/V   V
     T   PD   D————

(c) Preceded by IV

Ab: I   IV   V$_5^6$/V   V
     T   PD   D————

(d) Preceded by ii6

Ab: I   ii6   V$_5^6$/V   V
     T   PD   D————

As in progressions from V to I, you can control the strength of the harmonic progression between the secondary dominant and temporary tonic by the choice of inversion and whether to include the seventh. The V$_5^6$/V, for example, is a common inversion choice because it can allow a chromatic ascent to V in the bass line $\hat{4}$-$\#\hat{4}$-$\hat{5}$ (parts c and d).

One way to produce a strong and smooth connection between the predominant harmony and V7/V is by writing a **chromatic voice exchange**. The voice exchange usually occurs between the bass and an inner voice, as in Example 20.8. Part (a) shows a diatonic version of the voice exchange (with $\hat{6}$ and $\hat{4}$), embellished by a passing I$_4^6$ chord. In part (b), the voice exchange is chromatically inflected between $\hat{4}$ (Db) and $\sharp\hat{4}$ (Db). For a voice exchange to be considered chromatic, at least one pitch must appear in both its diatonic form and its chromatically inflected form (here, Db and Db).

EXAMPLE 20.8: Diatonic and chromatic voice exchange 🎧

(a) Diatonic 🎧   (b) Chromatic 🎧

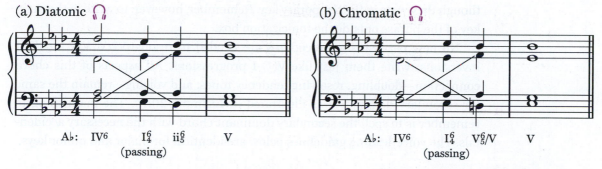

Ab: IV⁶   I⁶₄   ii⁶₅   V   Ab: IV⁶   I⁶₄   V⁶₃/V   V
          (passing)   (passing)

The V7/V may also be expanded by a cadential $^6_4$ in the tonicized key, as in Example 20.9. In measure 11, the voice-leading of the cadential $^6_4$ in the tonicized dominant key (F major) is the same as it would be in the tonic key, and the bracket notation makes this voice-leading clear. The secondary dominant (C–E♮–G–B♭) then resolves to V in measure 12, making a half cadence. This is only a tonicized half cadence and not a modulation to F major, as the phrase that begins in measure 13 starts out the same as the first one, firmly in the key of B♭ major.

EXAMPLE 20.9: Joplin, "Pine Apple Rag," mm. 5-12 🎧

Writing and Resolving

Since you already have written dominant-to-tonic progressions, you may find it helpful to think of the two-chord secondary-dominant progression as being in a temporary key for just those two chords. Imagine that the two chords have a box around them; spell and resolve the chords inside this "tonicization box" as though they were in the temporary key. Remember, however, to write in the main key of the phrase outside the tonicization box.

No new part-writing procedures are needed to resolve V7/V, V/V, or their inversions; write them just like V(7)-I progressions. All aspects of this chord connection—doubling, resolving tendency tones, and voicing—remain the same for secondary dominants, as illustrated in Example 20.10. The main thing to remember is to spell the secondary dominant chord with the necessary accidentals. The voice-leading guidelines below are identical for major and minor keys.

KEY CONCEPT Writing and resolving a V7/V in common-practice style:

- Avoid doubling the #$\hat{4}$ (because of its leading-tone function).
- Resolve the temporary leading tone up (#$\hat{4}$ moves up to $\hat{5}$).
- Resolve the chordal seventh down ($\hat{1}$ moves down to $\hat{7}$).
- When root-position V7/V moves to V or V7, one chord should be complete and the other incomplete in order to avoid unacceptable parallels.

EXAMPLE 20.10: Resolutions of V/V and V7/V

C = complete chord; I = incomplete chord

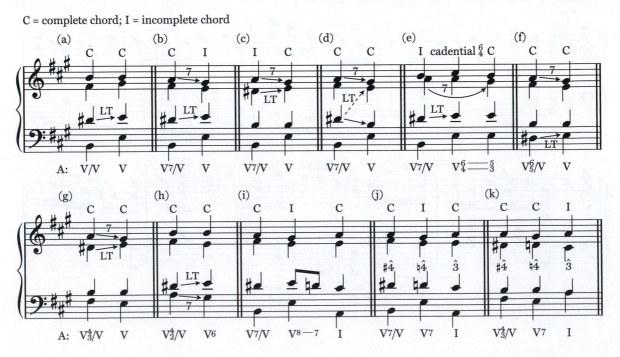

SUMMARY

Resolving secondary dominants (Example 20.10):

1. When moving from a V/V to a V, both chords are complete and resolve normally (part a).

2. When moving from a complete V7/V to V, the V will be incomplete (with three roots and a third) if you resolve all the tendency tones correctly (part b).

3. If you want to resolve a V7/V to a complete V chord, as for a HC,

   - use an incomplete V7/V (missing its fifth; part c); or

   - let the temporary leading tone skip instead to the fifth of the V (part d). The note to which the leading tone *should* resolve is usually in another voice (as shown by the dotted arrow).

4. The V chord may be embellished by a cadential $\frac{6}{4}$ (part e).

5. If the V7/V is inverted, this chord and the V chord should both be complete (parts f-h). Often, the resolution to V is embellished by 8-7 motion before a cadence on I (part i): the $\sharp\hat{4}$ moves to $\hat{5}$ first, then down to $\natural\hat{4}$.

6. When V7/V resolves directly to a V7, one important voice-leading guideline changes: the $\sharp\hat{4}$ shifts downward (not up to $\hat{5}$) to become the seventh of V7 (parts j and k). Here, as the V7 resolves to I, the downward pull of $\sharp\hat{4}$-$\natural\hat{4}$-$\hat{3}$ overcomes the upward tendency of the temporary leading tone.

Cross Relations

When a secondary dominant is preceded by one of the predominant chords, IV or ii, then the chromatic alteration of $\hat{4}$ to $\sharp\hat{4}$ should be handled carefully.

KEY CONCEPT The sudden introduction of $\sharp\hat{4}$ in one voice right after the diatonic $\hat{4}$ sounds in another voice, called a **cross relation** (Example 20.11a), is generally avoided in common-practice music. Keep the chromatically altered pitch in the same voice as the diatonic pitch (part b): $\hat{4}$-$\sharp\hat{4}$-$\hat{5}$.

EXAMPLE 20.11: Possible voice-leading problems 🎧

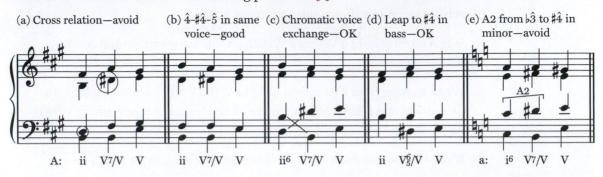

(a) Cross relation—avoid   (b) $\hat{4}$-$\sharp\hat{4}$-$\hat{5}$ in same   (c) Chromatic voice   (d) Leap to $\sharp\hat{4}$ in   (e) A2 from $\flat\hat{3}$ to $\sharp\hat{4}$ in
                              voice—good   exchange—OK   bass—OK   minor—avoid

A: ii   V7/V   V   ii   V7/V   V   ii6   V7/V   V   ii   V$^6_5$/V   V   a: i6   V7/V   V

In eighteenth-century style, there are two permissible contexts for a cross relation. The first is the chromatic voice exchange (part c), which works best with the chromatic note in an inner voice, as here, or with the voice exchange filled in with passing tones (Example 20.7b). The second occurs when the bass leaps to $\sharp\hat{4}$ (part d), as long as the cross relation does not involve the soprano voice. For composers in other styles, cross relations may not seem so objectionable—indeed, they are rather common in some chromatic styles, such as barbershop harmony.

Be careful when you write secondary dominants in minor keys: if V7/V is introduced by i or VI, then scale degrees $\flat\hat{3}$ to $\sharp\hat{4}$ produce a melodic augmented second (part e). You can avoid this by approaching the chromatic tone from above (e.g., $\hat{5}$ to $\sharp\hat{4}$).

Secondary Leading-Tone Chords to V

Since leading-tone chords can substitute for V chords as a dominant function in many progressions, secondary leading-tone chords to V can likewise substitute for secondary dominants to V, in any progression where a weaker sense of the dominant is desired. Most common is the fully diminished vii°7/V and its inversions $^6_5$ and $^4_3$; less common are the vii°6/V and viiø7/V.

KEY CONCEPT To spell a vii°7/V chord in any key (Example 20.12):

1. Imagine the dominant triad (part a), and begin with the pitch a diatonic half step below $\hat{5}$ (on $\sharp\hat{4}$): in the key of A major, this is D♯.

2. Spell a fully diminished seventh chord (all minor thirds above the root, part b). In major keys, be sure to add an accidental to make the seventh of vii°7/V diminished.

EXAMPLE 20.12: Spelling a secondary leading-tone seventh to V in A major

(a)   A: V
                    ($\hat{5}$ is E; $\sharp\hat{4}$ is D$\sharp$)

(b)   A: vii°7/V   V

Try it #2

For each key below, build a vii°7/V chord by first writing the V chord, and then finding the seventh chord built a diatonic half step below it. In major keys, add an accidental to make the vii°7/V diminished. Write the chords with accidentals rather than key signatures.

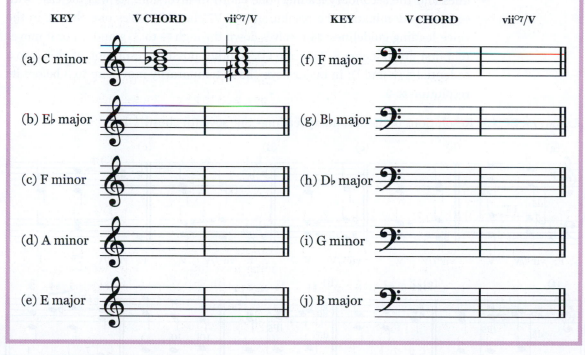

KEY	V CHORD	vii°7/V	KEY	V CHORD	vii°7/V
(a) C minor			(f) F major		
(b) E♭ major			(g) B♭ major		
(c) F minor			(h) D♭ major		
(d) A minor			(i) G minor		
(e) E major			(j) B major		

Writing and Resolving

The secondary leading-tone chord resolves to its temporary tonic (V) exactly as vii°7 does to I. The one element requiring close attention is spelling. Make $\sharp\hat{4}$ (the temporary leading tone) the root of the chord, then be sure that the chord has a fully diminished seventh quality (most typical) or half-diminished quality (used to tonicize major triads only). Spell the secondary vii°7 chord as a stack of minor thirds above $\sharp\hat{4}$ (in major keys, $\hat{3}$ needs to be lowered a half step); for vii°⁷, the top third will be a major third.

KEY CONCEPT When you resolve secondary leading-tone chords to V (Example 20.13):

- Move ♯$\hat{4}$ (the temporary leading tone) up to $\hat{5}$ (parts a–f, i–l).
- Move the chordal seventh down (from $\hat{3}$ or ♭$\hat{3}$ to $\hat{2}$; b–h and j).
- Avoid d5 to P5 unless you can place them in the inner voices (a, f, and h), or unless you can write parallel tenths between the soprano and bass (i); A4 to P4 is also permitted here.
- Be careful not to double the third in the chord of resolution (V)—it is the leading tone in the primary key.

In Example 20.13, part (b) shows the half-diminished version of the seventh chord, while the remaining parts feature the more typical fully diminished version. Parts (e) through (h) give short progressions to the tonic, with stepwise bass lines and the secondary leading-tone chord in inversion. As was the case with secondary dominants, the resolution to a V7 chord involves one change in the voice-leading guidelines: ♯$\hat{4}$ resolves down through ♮$\hat{4}$ to $\hat{3}$ (g and h); or it moves to $\hat{5}$ first, introducing 8–7 motion (j). Another possible resolution of vii°7 is to a cadential $^{6}_{4}$ (k and l); in major keys, the ♭$\hat{3}$ temporarily moves up to $\hat{3}$ before its resolution to $\hat{2}$.

EXAMPLE 20.13: Resolutions of the secondary leading-tone seventh chord

Secondary-Function Chords in Dominant Expansions

As the tonic area can be expanded with V or viiº chords and their inversions, so can the dominant area. Write these progressions with the same voice-leading, but replace I prolonged by V with V prolonged by V(7)/V or viiº(7)/V.

The excerpt in Example 20.14, a dominant expansion from Mozart's Horn Rondo in E♭ Major, begins with a strong E♭ major tonic arpeggiation, followed by the dominant. Then in measure 90, with the introduction of ♯$\hat{4}$ (A♮), V7/V chords begin to alternate with V chords; this dominant expansion continues until measure 96. At that point, the dominant harmony becomes V⁷ and is arpeggiated until its eventual resolution to the tonic in measure 101, where the rondo's first theme is restated.

EXAMPLE 20.14: Mozart, Rondo in E♭ Major for Horn and Orchestra (notated in concert pitch), mm. 88-104

One way to expand V with secondary dominants is to think about the prolongation temporarily in the key of the dominant—think of the "tonicization boxes" described earlier. Example 20.15 illustrates how to write V⁶-V⁶₄/V-V in the key of F: think of the familiar progression I⁶-V⁶₄-I in the key of C, changing B♭ to B♮. Similarly, to write V-vii°⁶/V-V⁶ in the key of D (Example 20.16), you could write I-vii°⁶-I⁶ in the key of A: this will remind you to add the G♯ needed for the #$\hat{4}$.

EXAMPLE 20.15: Spelling a V⁶-V⁶₄/V-V dominant expansion 🎧

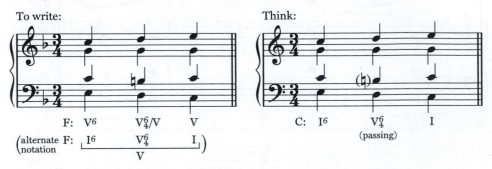

EXAMPLE 20.16: Spelling a V–vii°6/V–V6 dominant expansion 🎧

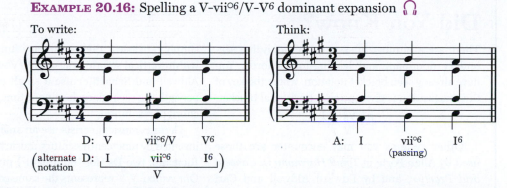

To write:

D: V   vii°6/V   V6

(alternate notation) D: I   vii°6   I6
                                    V

Think:

A: I   vii°6   I6
             (passing)

SUMMARY

Secondary dominant and leading-tone chords to V possess distinctive features that will help you identify them quickly when you prepare a harmonic analysis.

- The first is their location within the phrase: they often appear immediately after the predominant area, followed by the dominant or cadential $^6_4$.
  As we've seen, they may also be found between two dominants as voice-leading chords expanding the dominant area.

- A second clue is the chromatically altered $\sharp\hat{4}$: if you spot this scale degree, check for its resolution to $\hat{5}$.

Try it #3

A. For each secondary-function triad or seventh chord notated below, provide Roman numerals in the key specified. 🎧

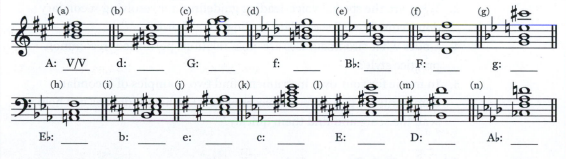

A: V/V   d: ___   G: ___   f: ___   B♭: ___   F: ___   g: ___

(h)   (i)   (j)   (k)   (l)   (m)   (n)

E♭: ___   b: ___   e: ___   c: ___   E: ___   D: ___   A♭: ___

B. Write each progression specified below.

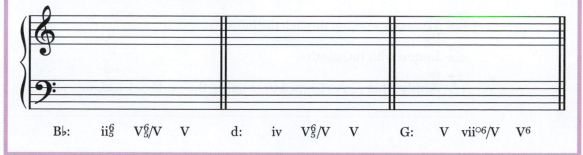

B♭: ii$^6_5$ V$^6_5$/V   V   d: iv   V$^6_5$/V   V   G: V   vii°6/V   V6

Did You Know?

There are a number of systems for analyzing secondary dominant and leading-tone chords. You have already seen bracket notation, where the key of the tonicization is given below a horizontal bracket:

$$\underbrace{\text{ii}_5^6 \quad \text{V}_{4-3}^{6-5} \quad \text{I}}_{\text{V}}$$

Other systems you may encounter are those used by Allen Forte in *Tonal Harmony in Concept and Practice*, and by Edward Aldwell and Carl Schachter in *Harmony and Voice Leading*. Forte simply encloses the secondary-function chord within vertical square brackets: V/V would be [V]. Aldwell and Schachter use a small curved arrow beneath the secondary dominant that points to the chord of resolution, V͜V.

German music theorists use an analytical symbol invented by nineteenth-century music theorist Hugo Riemann, two Ds (for "dominant") interlocked: Ð. Our symbol V/V represents the same concept shown by this "D of D" (dominant of the dominant).

TERMS YOU SHOULD KNOW

applied chord
chromatic voice exchange
cross relation

modulation
secondary dominant
secondary leading-tone chord

temporary tonic
tonicization
tonicized half cadence

QUESTIONS FOR REVIEW

1. Where are secondary dominants used? secondary leading-tone chords?
2. What do you need to remember when spelling secondary dominants? secondary leading-tone chords?
3. What are the special voice-leading guidelines for resolving secondary dominant chords? secondary leading-tone chords?
4. Under what circumstances are cross relations permitted in common-practice style?
5. In music for your own instrument, find two examples of secondary dominants (in two different pieces or keys). What guidelines can help you scan the score and find them quickly?

Know It? Show It!

Focus by working through the tutorials.

Learn with InQuizitive.

Apply what you've learned to complete the workbook assignments..

21

Tonicizing Scale Degrees Other Than V

Overview

In this chapter, we examine secondary dominant and leading-tone chords that tonicize harmonies other than V. We also consider how these chords fit within the basic phrase model and how to interpret them in performance.

Repertoire

Johann Sebastian Bach
  "Es ist gewisslich an der Zeit" ("It Is Certainly the Time," Chorale No. 260)
  Prelude in C Major, from *The Well-Tempered Clavier*, Book I

Ludwig van Beethoven, Piano Sonata in C Minor, Op. 13 (*Pathétique*), mvt. 2

Scott Joplin, "Solace"

Alan Menken and Tim Rice, "A Whole New World," from *Aladdin*

Wolfgang Amadeus Mozart
  Piano Sonata in D Major, K. 284, mvt. 3
  Variations on "Ah, vous dirai-je Maman"

Robert Schumann, "Ich grolle nicht" ("I Bear No Grudge"), from *Dichterliebe* (*The Poet's Love*)

John Philip Sousa, "The Stars and Stripes Forever"

Outline

Secondary-function chords within the basic phrase
- Identifying secondary dominant and leading-tone chords

Secondary-function chords in musical contexts
- Tonicizing harmonies within a phrase
- Providing a temporary harmonic diversion
- Creating forward momentum
- Evading an expected resolution
- Text painting

Spelling secondary dominant and leading-tone chords

Resolving secondary dominant and leading-tone chords
- Irregular and deceptive resolutions

Secondary dominants in sequences

Secondary-Function Chords Within the Basic Phrase

Having learned how to tonicize V in Chapter 20, we now expand that concept to tonicize other scale-degree triads. These new chords serve the same purpose: to intensify the chords to which they resolve.

Listen to measures 5-8 of "The Stars and Stripes Forever," and consider the function of the chromatic tones. Are they embellishing tones, or do they change the chord quality and function?

EXAMPLE 21.1: Sousa, "The Stars and Stripes Forever," mm. 5-8

Several chromatic alterations stand out: the B♮ in measure 5, the E♮ and E♭ in measure 7, and the A♮ and A♭ in measures 7 and 8. The E♮5 in measure 7 is a chromatic neighbor tone, which has no effect on chord quality or function; it simply embellishes the melody. Likewise, you may have heard the B♮4 in the alto of measure 5 as a chromatic passing tone, but this inflection of B♭ to B♮ does change the chord quality: it creates a dominant seventh (G-B♮-D-F), rather than the diatonic G-B♭-D-F, and that usually signals a secondary dominant function. Here the B♮ acts as a temporary leading tone to C (6̂), and the harmony functions as V$\frac{4}{3}$/vi. The A♮3 in measure 7 likewise serves as temporary leading tone to B♭ (5̂); its voice-leading is like a chromatic lower neighbor tone to the repeated B♭3s in the tenor.

The secondary dominants in the Sousa example elaborate the basic progression I-vi-ii-V: the V$\frac{4}{3}$/vi (m. 5) provides a temporary tonicization of vi within the tonic area, and the V$\frac{4}{3}$/V (m. 7) strengthens the half cadence (m. 8) by prolonging the dominant area. That both secondary dominants in this passage appear in second inversion allows a smooth descending bass line and stepwise connections in most voice parts. Stepwise voice-leading is typical of chromatic chords and, in particular, of inverted secondary dominants.

KEY CONCEPT Most triads (other than the tonic) may be tonicized by their own dominant or leading-tone chord.

- In major keys, triads that may be tonicized are ii, iii, IV, V, and vi (iii is less common).

- In minor keys, they are III, iv (or IV), V (or v), VI, and VII (VII is less common).

- Only major or minor triads may be tonicized, because they represent major or minor keys; diminished or augmented triads cannot be tonicized.

Listen to Example 21.2, or sing it with your class, and consider the role of the chromatic tone F♯4 in measure 5.

EXAMPLE 21.2: Bach, "Es ist gewisslich an der Zeit," mm. 5-6

This F♯, again signaling a secondary-function chord, acts as a temporary leading tone to G, the submediant in B♭. Bach expressively embellishes the chord with a 7-6 (G-F♯) suspension. Its function within the basic phrase is to expand the submediant harmony (acting as a tonic substitute) within the tonic area: vi-vii°6/vi-vi. In sum, the tonic area of the phrase moves from I to the prolonged vi and back to I6, before moving to the dominant area and a half cadence.

This short phrase illustrates two important points. First, a tonicization may span more than just two chords: vi-vii°6/vi-vi. Second, the contextual analysis here reveals a long tonic area; this means that the V chord in measure 5 is embellishing, a very different function from the one in measure 6. In performance, you might aim for the cadential arrival on V in measure 6, and consider the first dominant as a less important connector between I and vi.

The most common role of a secondary dominant or leading-tone chord is to highlight an individual harmony within a basic phrase progression, while leaving the overall direction of the phrase unchanged.

Identifying Secondary Dominant and Leading-Tone Chords

If you recognize the sound of dominant-to-tonic motion, it should be easy to locate a secondary dominant or leading-tone chord by ear: it will simply sound like a dominant-function harmony moving to a temporary I or i. In particular, you will hear half-step voice-leading, as the temporary leading tone moves to its temporary tonic.

    KEY CONCEPT One quick way to spot a secondary dominant or lead-ing-tone chord in a score is to scan for chromatically altered pitches. Then con-firm your analysis by checking the chord's quality and resolution.

- A raised third in a minor triad or seventh chord can indicate a temporary leading tone, as can a raised root that transforms a major triad into a dimin-ished one.

- A lowered pitch may signal the lowered seventh of a dominant seventh or diminished seventh chord.

In Example 21.3, part (a) shows the temporary leading tone to each scale-de-gree triad—which can function as the third of a secondary dominant seventh chord (part b), or as the root of a secondary leading-tone chord (part c). Remember that secondary dominant triads (without the seventh) are possible as well, as are secondary leading-tone triads and, less often, half-diminished sevenths.

In major keys, all secondary dominant seventh chords include at least one chromatically altered pitch, usually the raised third. Only one secondary domi-nant triad is already major in its diatonic form: V/IV (C-E-G in C major). Since C-E-G is the tonic in C major, it won't function as a secondary dominant without an added minor seventh (part b). This seventh makes V7/IV the only secondary dominant in major keys with a chromatically lowered pitch; and you need the seventh here, otherwise V/IV-IV (C-E-G to F-A-C in C major) will simply sound like I-IV. As part (c) shows, to spell some diminished seventh chords in major keys, you must include two different accidentals: a sharp or natural (usually on the root), and a flat (usually on the seventh).

EXAMPLE 21.3: Spelling secondary-function chords

C major

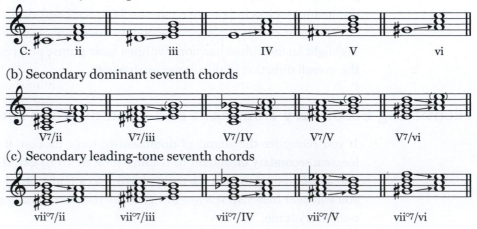

(a) Secondary leading tones

C: ii   iii   IV   V   vi

(b) Secondary dominant seventh chords

V7/ii   V7/iii   V7/IV   V7/V   V7/vi

(c) Secondary leading-tone seventh chords

vii°7/ii   vii°7/iii   vii°7/IV   vii°7/V   vii°7/vi

C minor

(d) Secondary leading tones

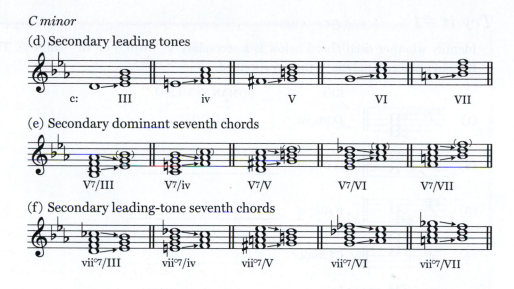

c: III   iv   V   VI   VII

(e) Secondary dominant seventh chords

V7/III   V7/iv   V7/V   V7/VI   V7/VII

(f) Secondary leading-tone seventh chords

vii°7/III   vii°7/iv   vii°7/V   vii°7/VI   vii°7/VII

In minor keys (parts d-f), as in major, diminished triads (ii° and vii°) can't be tonicized. The succession V7/III-III is particularly characteristic of minor-key compositions, as it requires no accidentals and fleetingly tonicizes the relative major. Like V/IV in major keys, the secondary-dominant function of these chords becomes clear only when the minor seventh is added to the triad (part e). In analysis, if there is no seventh, these chord pairs are usually labeled with their diatonic Roman numerals: III-VI (rather than V/VI-VI) and VII-III (rather than V/III-III).

Occasionally you will see a secondary leading-tone chord that is half-diminished; this is less common, used only to tonicize a major-quality triad.

KEY CONCEPT To identify a secondary dominant or leading-tone chord:

1. Look for a chromatically altered pitch, then determine how it changes a chord's quality.

2. If the altered chord is a major triad or dominant seventh, check the following chord. If its root is a perfect fifth below (or a perfect fourth above) the root of the altered chord, you have identified a secondary dominant.

3. If the altered chord is a diminished triad or fully diminished seventh (or, less often, a half-diminished seventh), check the following chord. If its root is a half step above the root of the altered chord, you have identified a secondary leading-tone chord.

4. Sometimes a secondary-function chord (such as V7/III in minor) will not include a chromatically altered pitch. In that case, check the root of the following chord (as in steps 2 and 3) to determine the chord's function.

Try it #1

Identify whether each chord below is a secondary V7 (Mm7) or vii°7 (dim 7). Then give its Roman numeral analysis in the key specified.

		KEY	ROMAN NUMERAL
(1)		D major	vii°7/IV
(2)		G major	
(3)		F major	
(4)		C♯ major	
(5)		C minor	
(6)		F minor	

Secondary-Function Chords in Musical Contexts

Secondary dominant and leading-tone chords may (1) intensify a diatonic harmony, (2) provide a temporary harmonic diversion, (3) create forward momentum in a passage, (4) evade an expected resolution, or (5) contribute to text painting. When you prepare a piece for performance, you may want to identify which role each such chord plays in order to help shape your performance.

Tonicizing Harmonies Within a Phrase

Listen to the excerpt from Beethoven's *Pathétique* Sonata given in Example 21.4. The predominant area in this T-PD-D-T phrase has been expanded by a secondary dominant seventh chord. The A♮ in the melody (m. 6) creates a striking F-A♮-C-E♭ sonority that functions as a secondary dominant to the predominant ii. Because the secondary dominant belongs to the predominant area, the PD label is placed on the second beat of measure 6 rather than on the ii of measure 7.

EXAMPLE 21.4: Beethoven, *Pathétique* Sonata, mvt. 2, mm. 5-8 🎧

Now listen to the Mozart variation shown in Example 21.5. The phrase opens with a tonic expansion, moves to a descending-fifth sequence, alternating seventh chords (in $^6_5$ position) and triads, and closes with PD-D-T and a PAC. The diatonic version of the sequence in root position would be I-IV7-viiº-iii7-vi-ii7-V-I; the iii7 in measure 174 (beat 1), though, has been converted to a V$^6_5$/vi by changing the chord quality to Mm7. This tonicization of a triad within a sequence does not interrupt the sequence's motion, and can in fact intensify its effect.

EXAMPLE 21.5: Mozart, *Variations on "Ah, vous dirai-je Maman,"* Variation VII, mm. 169-176 🎧

Providing a Temporary Harmonic Diversion

Now listen to a second excerpt from "The Stars and Stripes Forever" to hear another use of secondary-function chords. Example 21.6 begins by expanding the tonic in E♭ major with a I⁶-V$^4_3$-I progression, then ends with a HC in measure 12—but not in the primary key of the piece. The cadence tonicizes vi (C minor), though only briefly; the following measures immediately return to E♭ major. We use bracket notation here since several chords fall within the tonicized area (vi).

EXAMPLE 21.6: Sousa, "The Stars and Stripes Forever," mm. 9-12 🎧

The secondary dominant V$^4_3$/vi heard briefly in measure 5, beat 2 (Example 21.1), returns here to add a bit of color and harmonic interest. The B♮ that colored measure 5 appears first as a chromatic passing tone (m. 10), then as a chromatic neighbor tone (m. 11), and finally as the melodic goal of the phrase (m. 12). In this passage, the secondary dominants do not elaborate a basic phrase progression—instead, they temporarily sidetrack the motion from tonic to dominant.

Creating Forward Momentum

Secondary dominants are a familiar feature of Scott Joplin's ragtime piano pieces. In Example 21.7, the basic phrase progression to measure 64 is I-vi7-ii$^6_5$-V7-I (T-PD-D-T).

EXAMPLE 21.7: Joplin, "Solace," mm. 61-65 🎧

This phrase sounds complete, yet the last chord of measure 64 then pushes forward. The shaded F-A-C-E♭ chord is a secondary dominant to IV, in this case in third inversion ($\frac{4}{2}$), resolving in normal fashion to a IV⁶—the temporary leading tone (A4) moves up, and the seventh of the chord (E♭3) down. This chord intensifies the IV⁶ and creates forward motion toward the phrase's eventual authentic cadence in measure 68.

As a performer, you might focus on the intensity of the secondary dominant harmonies found at the end of many four-bar units in this rag. Be sure to follow Joplin's performance indications, lengthening the sonorities that are notated with fermatas, and continuing *a tempo* after each fermata, even when it is not marked. This will propel each basic phrase forward to its cadence, in preparation for the next dominant seventh anacrusis. You may also want to experiment with "voicing out" the tendency tones. Try playing each anacrusis in such a way that you really hear the (temporary) leading tone resolving up and the chordal seventh resolving down.

Try it #2

- Find a secondary dominant in the passage below. Where is it? measure _____, beat _____ What is the Roman numeral? _____
- What are the tendency tones? _____ and _____
- Do they resolve correctly? _____

Joplin, "Solace," mm. 72-73

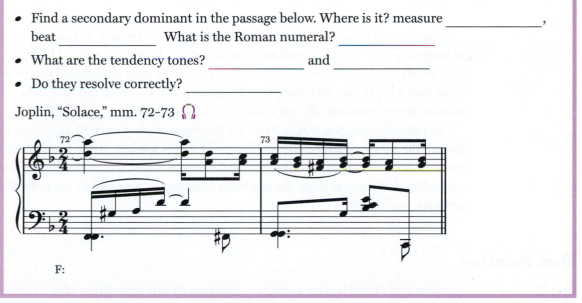

Evading an Expected Resolution

We have already looked at ways of evading or weakening a cadence after a strong V or V⁷: for example, by using a deceptive cadence or resolving to an inverted tonic (or I⁷). Secondary-function chords may also be called on to evade an expected cadence or temporarily redirect a phrase. As an example, listen to a passage from Bach's C Major Prelude (Example 21.8), focusing on measures 30-32.

EXAMPLE 21.8: Bach, Prelude in C Major, mm. 29-35 🎧

Measure 29 initiates a cadential $^6_4$, resolving to V7 (with a 4-3 suspension) in measures 30-31. At this moment, we expect V7 to resolve to I, to bring the prelude to its close. Instead, Bach adds a crucial B♭ that transforms the tonic triad into a V7/IV (m. 32), resolving deceptively and delaying the final close by another three measures, all over a stately tonic pedal point.

In performance, you might focus on the voice-leading aspects that help to thwart the listener's expectations. You could insert a slight delay moving into measure 32—as though this were the final cadence. Once the "deception" of the secondary dominant is clear, the last three measures can unfold to the prelude's ultimate conclusion.

Text Painting

In songs and choral works, secondary-function chords sometimes play a role in text painting, the musical depiction of images found in the words. Example 21.9 shows a deceptive resolution of a secondary dominant in a song from *Aladdin*, sung by the character Jasmine about the "whole new world" she is discovering.

EXAMPLE 21.9: Menken and Rice, "A Whole New World," mm. 30-37

The words "never knew" (m. 31) are highlighted by secondary leading-tone and dominant seventh chords to vi, which arrives on beat 1 of measure 32, making a deceptive cadence that brings out the foreignness of the world Jasmine is now seeing. Another secondary dominant in 32 (on "But when I'm") combines with the rhythmic impetus of the quarter-note triplets to push forward harmonically, emphasizing that she's "way up here," on the highest note she has sung yet in the phrase.

The final text-painting touch in this passage is the setting of "whole new world" in measure 36. The chord on the downbeat is preceded by a V7/V ("in a"); yet the first chord in 36 temporarily evades the expected dominant. We will learn more about this harmonic choice—a ♭VII chord—in Chapter 26. For now, observe how combining the V7/V with the unusual resolution to ♭VII highlights the strangeness of this "whole new world."

Spelling Secondary Dominant and Leading-Tone Chords

Now that you have seen and heard what secondary dominant and leading-tone chords can do, it is time to write some.

KEY CONCEPT Example 21.10 illustrates the steps in spelling a secondary dominant seventh chord.

1. Write the triad it tonicizes. For example, if you want to write a V7/ii in the key of D major, first write the ii chord (E-G-B), leaving a space before it (part a).

2. Imagine the key of the triad you are tonicizing—here, the key of ii, or E minor, with one sharp (F♯) in the key signature (part b).

3. Spell a V7 in that key (part c): V7 in E minor is B-D♯-F♯-A.

To spell a secondary leading-tone chord:

Follow the same procedure, but write vii°7-i in the tonicized key instead (parts d-f). Think of the root a diatonic half step below the tonicized chord.

You can adapt these guidelines for triads, leaving out the seventh, or for the vii⌀7 (presuming that this chord precedes a major triad) by altering the quality of the seventh.

EXAMPLE 21.10: Procedure for writing secondary dominant and leading-tone chords

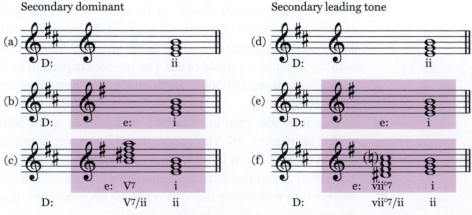

Another Way

Another way to spell secondary dominants quickly is to imagine them as "altered" diatonic chords, following the chart below (in C major). Add whatever accidentals are necessary to create a Mm7 quality. Use this method as a shortcut for spelling only; in analysis, you should write V7/IV, not I7, to capture more accurately how the chord functions.

TO MAKE A...		START WITH...		ALTER QUALITY TO Mm7
V7/IV	→	I7 (C-E-G-B)	→	I7 (C-E-G-B♭)
V7/V	→	ii7 (D-F-A-C)	→	II7 (D-F♯-A-C)
V7/vi	→	iii7 (E-G-B-D)	→	III7 (E-G♯-B-D)
V7/ii	→	vi7 (A-C-E-G)	→	VI7 (A-C♯-E-G)
V7/iii	→	vii⌀7 (B-D-F-A)	→	VII7 (B-D♯-F♯-A)

Try it #3

For each key below, write the tonicized chord in the first measure, then the secondary dominant or leading-tone chord in the second measure. Use whole notes.

	KEY	ROMAN NUMERAL	TONICIZED CHORD	SECONDARY DOMINANT
(1)	B♭ major	V7/IV		
(2)	F♯ minor	vii°7/III		
(3)	A major	V7/ii		
(4)	G major	vii°7/vi		
(5)	E♭ major	V7/vi		
(6)	C minor	V7/V		

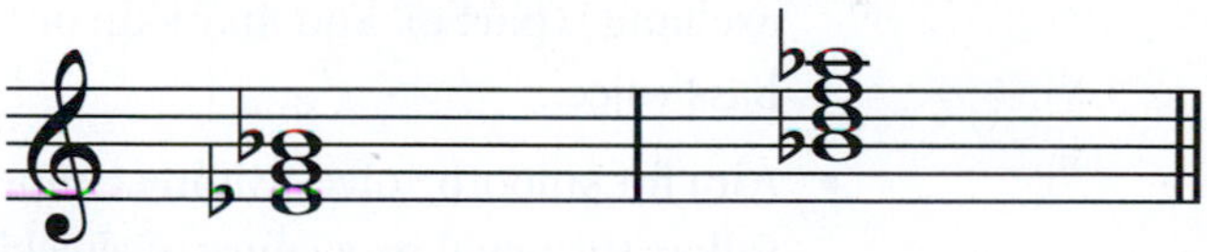

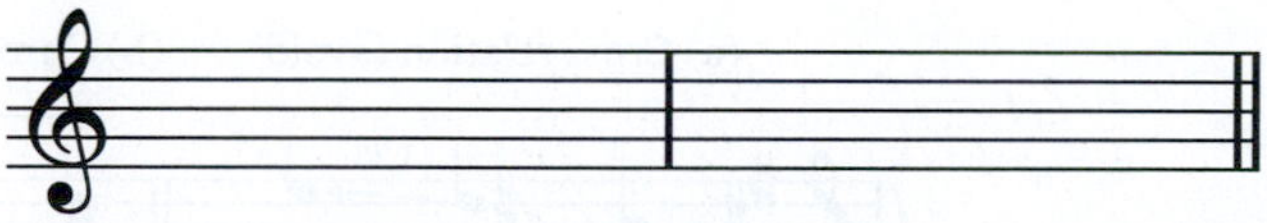

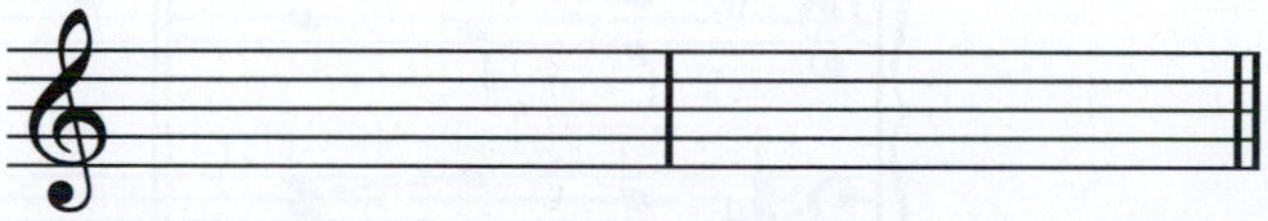

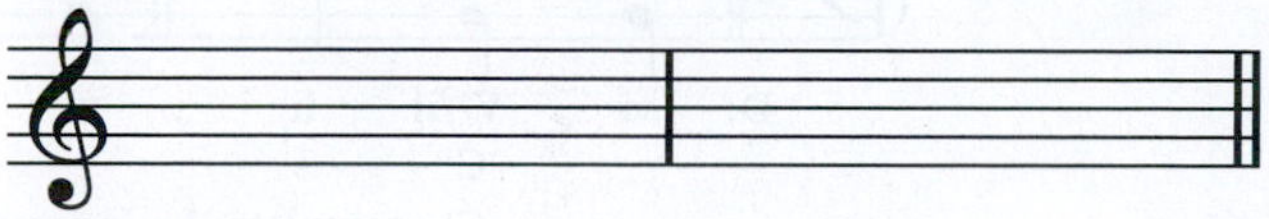

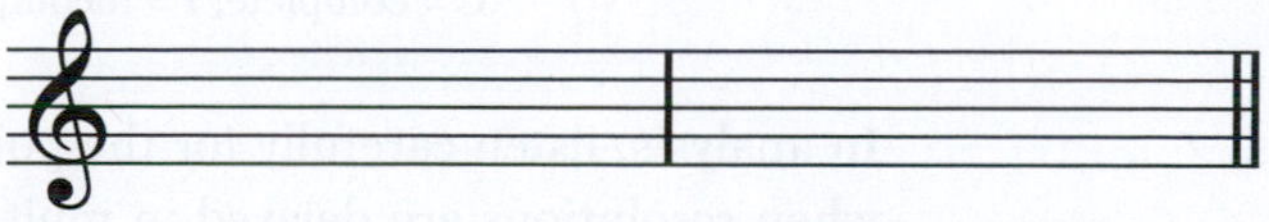

Resolving Secondary Dominant and Leading-Tone Chords

As we have seen, secondary dominant and leading-tone chords normally resolve just like their diatonic counterparts.

⌒ **KEY CONCEPT** To resolve a secondary dominant or leading-tone chord (Example 21.11):

- Move the temporary leading tone up, and the chordal seventh down. (Only when a secondary dominant resolves to a seventh chord may the temporary leading tone resolve down.)

- When a root-position secondary V7 chord resolves to a root-position triad, make one chord complete and one incomplete (leave out the fifth) to avoid parallels.

- Never double the temporary leading tone or the seventh of the chord.

- If the temporary leading tone is preceded by a chord that contains the same scale degree in its unaltered (diatonic) form, either keep the chromatic tone in the same voice (for instance, $\hat{1}$-#$\hat{1}$-$\hat{2}$; part b), or write a chromatic voice exchange (part c). You may skip or leap to the temporary leading tone in the bass voice.

- Aim for smooth voice-leading connections (by step or common tone), and follow the usual procedure of checking for parallel fifths and octaves.

EXAMPLE 21.11: Voice-leading guidelines 🎧

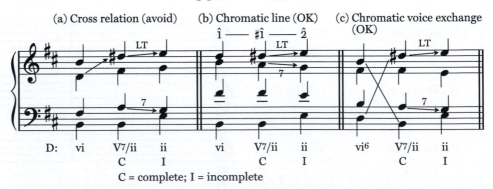

| (a) Cross relation (avoid) | (b) Chromatic line (OK) | (c) Chromatic voice exchange (OK) |

D: vi   V7/ii   ii   vi   V7/ii   ii   vi6   V7/ii   ii
            C   I   C   I   C   I

C = complete; I = incomplete

In analysis, listen carefully for the point of resolution (this is especially helpful when resolutions are delayed in multiple voices by suspensions, passing tones, and retardations), and know what the expected resolution should be, so that you can scan ahead in the score for its arrival.

Try it #4

Prepare and resolve each of the following secondary dominant chords. Resolve all tendency tones correctly, and avoid cross-relations between voices.

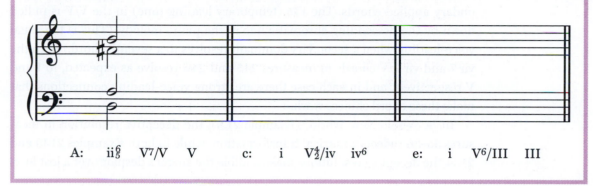

A: ii$^6_5$ V^7/V   V   c: i   V$^4_2$/iv   iv^6 e: i   V^6/III   III

Irregular and Deceptive Resolutions

Although the quality of secondary dominant and leading-tone chords strongly implies a particular resolution, sometimes composers do not resolve these chords exactly as you expect. Instead, they may write an **irregular** or **deceptive resolution**. Such resolutions can add drama and intensity to a phrase.

Listen to the Mozart Variation in Example 21.12, then focus on the passage in measures 244-248. In this passage, the outer voices move conventionally, but the inner voices create some unexpected harmonies.

EXAMPLE 21.12: Mozart, *Variations*, Variation X, mm. 241-248

In measure 245, the expected ii on beat 1 is replaced with V/V (a triad with the correct root but an altered chord quality), and the expected V on beat 2 is replaced by viiº7 (a chord with the same function that shares three common tones with V7, but not the expected root). Both are irregular resolutions of secondary applied chords. The F♯5 (temporary leading tone) in the V/V is pulled down by the descending chromatic line in the piano melody. (This is the usual voice-leading when a secondary dominant resolves to a seventh chord.) Both the viiº7 and viiº7/V chords in measures 245 and 246 resolve as expected, to I and V respectively, and in each case there are strong voice-leading connections that make these chord choices work.

In "A Whole New World" (Example 21.9), the deceptive resolution in measures 35-36 reflects a magical transformation, while in both Examples 21.13 and 21.14 the deceptive resolutions make audible the singer's despair over a lost love.

EXAMPLE 21.13: Schumann, "Ich grolle nicht," mm. 29-32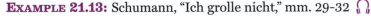

Translation: . . . [you] are miserable. I bear no grudge.

EXAMPLE 21.14: Schumann, "Ich grolle nicht," mm. 10-12

The deceptive resolution in measure 12 of Example 21.14 is especially surprising: here the secondary leading-tone chord A♯-C♯-E-G (m. 11), in C major, implies viiº7/viiº! Since it is not possible to tonicize viiº, this "impossible"

secondary leading-tone chord resolves deceptively to V_5^6, which shares the correct bass note (B) and two other chord members with the expected B triad. Perhaps this deception represents musically how deeply the protagonist feels he has been deceived.

Passages like these are fairly common in highly chromatic voice-leading. To analyze, carefully determine each chord's quality, then compare the actual resolution in the music with the expected one. With that information, you should be able to explain each chord's resolution. Your Roman numerals will show irregular resolutions automatically. For example, if you write V7/IV-ii6, it's clear that the expected IV chord is replaced with a ii6 instead.

Secondary Dominants in Sequences

You might also find secondary-function chords elaborating a sequence, in alternation with triads or as all dominant sevenths in a descending-fifth sequence—creating a **chromatic sequence**. Composers may use a portion of a chromatic sequence to move between functional areas or use a complete sequence to prolong the tonic area. As an example of the former, listen to Example 21.15, a passage in A major.

EXAMPLE 21.15: Mozart, Piano Sonata in D Major, mvt. 3, mm. 8–10 🎧

If this were a diatonic sequence in A, the progression would be ii7-V-I7-IV, but Mozart has changed the ii7 chord to a dominant seventh quality (B-D♯-A, leaving out F♯). This sets up a pattern of alternating secondary dominant sevenths, a chromatic descending-fifth sequence. The descending-fifth sequence leads to the key of D major.

⌒ **KEY CONCEPT** In the most common type of chromatic sequence, the descending-fifth sequence, dominant seventh chords are substituted for all or some of the chords (usually every other chord). The sequence typically features root-position chords, but may also include inversions.

The voice-leading for this type of sequence is the same as for any secondary dominant resolution. In a chain of *all* root-position seventh chords, however, every other chord is incomplete (to avoid parallels). The chordal sevenths resolve down by step as expected, but the leading tones also resolve down—pulled downward by the stepwise chromatic line—to become the seventh of the following chord. (We will learn to write chromatic sequences in Chapter 30.)

Did You Know?

Robert Schumann's song "Ich grolle nicht" (from his song cycle *Dichterliebe*) is based on a poem by Heinrich Heine, from his *Lyrisches Intermezzo* (*Lyric Intermezzo*): a set of poems that provide snapshots of the poet's experiences and emotions. Though the text in this song claims that the speaker "bears no grudge" from his/her "love forever lost," the harmonies—deceptively resolved secondary dominant and leading-tone chords—tell a different story. Other elements of the text, including the image of the lover's dark heart (where no light can penetrate) being devoured by a snake, are set by harmonic sequences (see Chapter 19), and still others are highlighted by chromatic harmonies we will consider in later chapters. Such close links between textual meaning and harmonic choices are typical of Romantic-era art songs, and identifying and interpreting these harmonic nuances is essential to an understanding of the meaning of a song.

TERMS YOU SHOULD KNOW

chromatic sequence	secondary dominant	temporary tonic
cross relation	secondary leading-tone chord	tonicization
irregular resolution		

QUESTIONS FOR REVIEW

1. Which diatonic chords may be tonicized in a major key? in a minor key? What chords (which quality) may not be tonicized?
2. What roles do secondary dominants typically play in a harmonic progression?
3. What are the steps for finding the root and adding the proper accidentals to spell a secondary dominant chord? to spell a secondary leading-tone chord?
4. What tendency tones need to be resolved in a secondary dominant or leading-tone chord? When may the temporary leading tone resolve down?
5. What are two ways that cross relations can be avoided when a secondary dominant is preceded by its diatonic counterpart?
6. How do you identify irregular resolutions of secondary dominant and leading-tone chords in their Roman numeral analysis?
7. What part-writing guidelines are important to remember when secondary dominants appear in sequences of seventh chords?

8. In music for your own instrument, find two examples of secondary dominants other than V/V or V7/V (in two different keys). For each one, examine
   the context—does it fit within one of the common uses of secondary dominants considered in this chapter? How might understanding its role and
   resolution in the phrase influence your performance of the passage?

Know It? Show It!

Focus by working through the tutorials.

Learn with InQuizitive.

Apply what you've learned to complete the workbook assignments..

Chromatic Harmony
and Form

22

Modulation to Closely Related Keys

Outline

Common pivot-chord modulations

- Modulation or tonicization?
- Modulation from a major key to its dominant
- Modulation from a minor key to its relative major
- Closely related keys

Other pivot-chord modulations

- From a minor key to v
- From a major key to ii, iii, IV, and vi
- Writing a pivot-chord modulation

Direct modulations

- Modulations introduced by secondary dominants

Locating modulations

Modulations in musical contexts

- Harmonizing modulating melodies

Overview

This chapter focuses on modulation—the process of changing from one key to another. We learn to modulate by means of pivot chords and to determine which keys are closely related. We will also harmonize a melody that changes keys.

Repertoire

Johann Sebastian Bach
    "Er kommt" ("He comes"), from Cantata No. 140, "Wachet auf"
    "O Haupt voll Blut und Wunden" ("O Head, Full of Blood and Wounds," Chorale No. 74)

Muzio Clementi, Sonatina in C Major, Op. 36, No. 1, mvt. 1

Arcangelo Corelli
    Trio Sonata in A Minor, Op. 4, No. 5, Allemanda
    Sonata in D Minor, Op. 4, No. 8, Preludio

Wolfgang Amadeus Mozart, Piano Sonata in D Major, K. 284, mvt. 3

Franz Schubert, "Nur wer die Sehnsucht kennt (Lied der Mignon)" ("Only One Who Knows Longing [Mignon's Song]")

Clara Schumann, *Drei Romanzen*, Op. 21, No. 1

Andrew Lloyd Webber, "Memory," from *Cats*

Common Pivot-Chord Modulations

Many common-practice forms, such as binary and sonata forms, rely on harmonic changes to create contrast between sections. Indeed, composers show their ingenuity and artistry by how and where they move between key areas. Some analysts view these different harmonic areas as large-scale tonicizations of harmonies within the tonic key; this approach emphasizes the overall harmonic coherence of the work. Other analysts, however, view structurally significant tonicizations as **modulations**, or changes of key, focusing on how chords function within a local new key and how the new key relates to the tonic key. For purposes of this chapter, we will take the latter approach.

Listen to the opening of the third movement of Mozart's Piano Sonata in D Major, while examining the score in Example 22.1. In Chapters 14 and 15, we analyzed the basic phrase model in measures 1-4. Now look at the phrase that follows (mm. 5-8), to see how the cadences in measures 4 and 8 differ.

EXAMPLE 22.1: Mozart, Piano Sonata in D Major, mvt. 3, mm. 1-8 🎧

Both cadences end on an A major triad: the first is a HC in the tonic key (D major); but the second so strongly tonicizes A that it sounds like a PAC in A major, making a modulation to the key of the dominant. The change is so smooth that you may not hear the shift of harmonic focus until the return to D major when measures 1-8 are repeated.

Look carefully at measures 5-6 (Example 22.2). Measure 5 begins with I⁶ in D major, followed by vi⁶; then in measure 6, a G♯ is introduced. This ♯$\hat{4}$ could simply indicate a secondary dominant, V⁷/V, except that the G♯ appears three more times in measures 6 and 7, and the remainder of the phrase functions according to the basic phrase in the key of A major.

EXAMPLE 22.2: Mozart, Piano Sonata in D Major, mvt. 3, mm. 5–8 🎧

When a modulation is composed this smoothly, there are often one or more transitional chords mid-phrase that function diatonically in both keys. The vi⁶ (in D major) on the second half of measure 5 is such a chord: it also functions as ii⁶ in A major, preparing the entrance of the V⁷ in A in measure 6 and the subsequent cadence in that key. In general, when vi⁶ appears outside the context of a sequence or I⁵⁻⁶ motion, as here, it may signal a modulation to the dominant.

> 🎵 **KEY CONCEPT** A chord that has "full membership" in both keys is called a **pivot chord**. Pivot chords often serve a predominant function in one or both keys.

This type of modulation—called a **pivot-chord**, or **common-chord**, **modulation**—is the most common means of moving from one key to another. Analyze a pivot-chord modulation as in the example, by writing the first key and Roman numerals in the normal way, then the second key and Roman numerals on a lower level. Enclose the pivot chord (or chords) in a bracket or box, and indicate the relationship between the primary key and the new one by writing a Roman numeral in parentheses below the new key label.

Modulation or Tonicization?

The decision whether to analyze a passage as a tonicization or modulation is not always clear-cut, and different analysts may hear the passage in different ways. When making this decision, use the guidelines below to inform your choice, and be ready to defend it with concrete musical reasons.

> 🎵 **KEY CONCEPT** A passage that has modulated will feature at least one of the following:
> - a PD-D-T progression in the new key;
> - a firm cadence (usually a PAC or an IAC) in the new key, preceded by a predominant-function harmony and/or followed by music that continues in the new key;
> - an extended progression in the new key (not just dominant-tonic).

Keep in mind that this "establishment of a new key" may only be a temporary emphasis on a harmonic area within the context of the larger harmonic structure. There is some latitude here: what may seem like a modulation on the small scale may be reinterpreted as a tonicization when you consider the entire composition. Occasionally, extended progressions (especially in Romantic-era music) may focus on a temporary tonic without a cadence or clear PD-D-T progression. In such a case, consider how long the progression lasts: does it seem to establish a new key because of its length, even without a cadence? If so, label it a modulation.

Modulation from a Major Key to Its Dominant

The first step in writing a modulating progression is to consider possible pivot chords. The pivot chord in Example 22.2—vi in the primary key = ii in the key of the dominant—is one of the most common means of modulating from a tonic key to its dominant (and may appear in root position instead of first inversion as here). Compare the diatonic chords in D and A major (Figure 22.1) to find other possibilities (these are boxed). You cannot use a chord built on E as the pivot, for example, because this triad has a minor quality in D major (ii) but a major quality A major (V).

FIGURE 22.1: Comparison of chords in D major and A major

D major

Roman numerals:	I	ii	iii	IV	V	vi	vii°
Chords:	D	e	f♯	G	A	b	c♯°

A major

Chords:	D	E	f♯	g♯°	A	b	c♯
Roman numerals:	IV	V	vi	vii°	I	ii	iii

KEY CONCEPT Pivot chords are diatonic in both keys and must have the same quality in both keys.

The pivot vi = ii makes a smooth progression because the triad can serve a predominant function in both keys, and both vi and ii are triads frequently found in major-key progressions. On the other hand, iii = vi is less common since the mediant triad, iii, does not often appear in common-practice progressions. When iii = vi acts as a pivot, it usually appears in a pivot area with several chords. The pivot I = IV is also less effective: it is not easy to convince the ear that the tonic triad is functioning as IV in a new key. For this reason, I^6 is not marked as a pivot chord (IV^6 in the dominant key) in Example 22.2 (m. 5)—you are unlikely to hear this chord functioning as IV^6 in A major. Similarly, the V = I pairing is also rarely found; the V chord tends to sound like V in the tonic key unless it is preceded by other chords in the new key—in which case *they* are the pivot chords.

Though not useful as pivots, chords available only in the second key play an important role in establishing a modulation. Their appearance, and the accidentals that usually accompany them, signal that the key has changed and help confirm the modulation.

When performing a phrase that contains a pivot-chord modulation, you might want to aid in the "deception" of the pivot chord's dual nature by playing or singing it as though nothing unusual has happened. Then once the new key has emerged, aim toward the cadence in the new key, attending to the resolution of the new leading tone with expressive timing, to emphasize the new tonal goal.

Try it #1

Construct a chart of pivot chords for the pair of keys given below, using Figure 22.1 as a model. Draw a box around pivot chords that are diatonic in both keys.

(a) *A♭ major*

Roman numerals:	I	ii	iii	IV	V	vi	vii°
Chords:	A♭	b♭	___	___	___	___	___

(b) *E♭ major*

Chords:	A♭	B♭	___	___	___	___	___
Roman numerals:	IV	V	___	___	___	___	___

Modulation from a Minor Key to Its Relative Major

Listen now to the opening measures of a piano piece by Clara Schumann, shown in Example 22.3. The cadence in measure 4 is a half cadence in A minor, but by measure 8 the piece has modulated to C major (the relative major), which is confirmed by an IAC. To identify the location of the modulation, you need to know what pivot chords would work for modulations between these relative keys.

EXAMPLE 22.3: C. Schumann, *Drei Romanzen*, Op. 21, No. 1, mm. 1-8

HC in A minor

IAC in C major

Compare the chords in common between A minor and C major, given in Figure 22.2.

FIGURE 22.2: Comparison of chords in A minor and C major

A minor:	i	ii°	III	iv	v	V	VI	VII	vii°
Chords:	a	b°	C	d	e	E	F	G	g♯
C major:	vi	vii°	I	ii	iii		IV	V	

As this chart shows, there are several potential pivot chords between relative keys; the most frequently used are i = vi, III = I, iv = ii, and VI = IV. As in modulations from I to V in a major key, pivot chords from minor keys to the relative major are most effective when they fall into the predominant-function area of the phrase (for example, iv = ii).

The dominant-function chords in minor keys, V and vii°, are distinctive because of their altered leading tone—they do not appear as diatonic harmonies in major keys and therefore cannot function as pivot chords. However, the dominant-function chords in the major key (V and vii°) can, since they are diatonic chords in the relative minor (VII and ii°).

Try it #2

Construct a chart of pivot chords for the pair of keys given below, using Figure 22.2 as a model. Draw a box around pivot chords that are diatonic in both keys.

C♯ minor:	i	ii°	III	iv	v	V	VI	VII	vii°
Chords:	c♯	d♯°	___	___	___	___	___	___	___
E major:	vi	vii°	___	___	___	___	___	___	___

Now return to measures 5-8 of the romance (Example 22.4). The first chord of the phrase is i in A minor, the tonic key, followed by a pedal $ii^{\varnothing 4}_{2}$ in measure 6 (decorated by upper voice suspensions) and a return to the tonic. Then on the downbeat of measure 7, instead of the G♯ leading tone of A minor, we hear a G natural in a dominant seventh sonority that signals the shift to the new key, C major. We choose the chord that precedes that dominant harmony as the pivot: i = vi. From measure 6 to the end of the phrase, the harmonies are clearly in C major.

EXAMPLE 22.4: C. Schumann, *Drei Romanzen*, Op. 21, No. 1, mm. 5-8 🎧

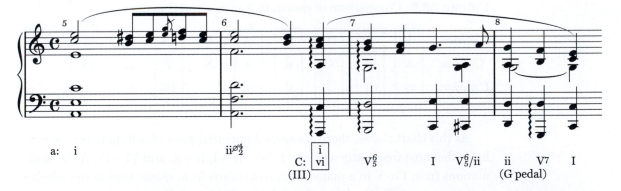

Baroque-era pieces in minor keys sometimes move back and forth freely between the tonic and its relative major, as in Example 22.5. Like the Schumann piece, this passage opens in A minor, the main key of the movement, which is confirmed in measures 1-3. The second half of measure 3 moves toward C major, with a ii^{6}_{5}-V-I progression in C in measures 3-4. The pivot chord ($iv^{6}_{5} = ii^{6}_{5}$), with a predominant function, is diatonic in both keys.

EXAMPLE 22.5: Corelli, Allemanda, from Trio Sonata in A Minor, mm. 1–7 🎧

Measures 4–5 center on C major, but in measure 6, F♯ and G♯ signal a return to A minor. The pivot here is I = III on beat 1 of measure 6. It is not possible to use a more typical predominant pivot, like ii⁶ = iv⁶, on beat 3 because of the need for F♯ in the bass to connect to the leading tone G♯; the chord here is a major IV^6_5 instead. This pivot area will likely be understood as enacting a change of key only retrospectively, once we hear the cadence at the end of the phrase.

Try it #3

The passage below begins and ends in F major, but modulates briefly to D minor in the middle. Analyze with Roman numerals, labeling each pivot chord and cadence.

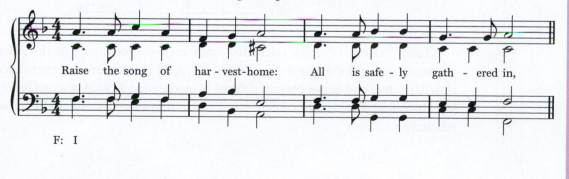

Raise the song of har-vest-home: All is safe-ly gath-ered in,

F: I

Closely Related Keys

The concept of closely related keys can help you determine other modulation possibilities.

KEY CONCEPT The most typical modulations in common-practice tonal music are from the primary key to a **closely related key**, effected by means of a pivot chord. Closely related keys are those whose tonic chords are diatonic in the primary key.

A closely related key to any given major key is represented by the triad on ii, iii, IV, V, or vi. Figure 22.3 gives the closely related keys for D major: E minor (ii), F♯ minor (iii), G major (IV), A major (V), and B minor (vi, the relative minor).

FIGURE 22.3: Closely related keys to D major

D major:	I	ii	iii	IV	V	vi	(vii°)
	D	e	f♯	G	A	b	(c♯°)

Since the chord built on the leading tone is diminished, it cannot serve as a goal of modulation—the tonic must be a major or minor chord. Each key can therefore claim five closely related keys. Practice naming closely related keys from any given tonic, and be aware of the possibilities for pivot-chord modulation when you compose.

A closely related key to any given minor key is represented by the triad on III, iv, v, VI, or VII. The five closely related keys for A minor (Figure 22.4) are C major (III, the relative major), D minor (iv), E minor (v), F major (VI), and G major (VII).

FIGURE 22.4: Closely related keys to A minor

A minor:	i	(ii°)	III	iv	v	VI	VII
	a	(b°)	C	d	e	F	G

Closely related keys are calculated from scale-degree triads in the natural minor scale. The major dominant key, E major, is therefore not considered closely related, and is not normally a goal of modulation from A minor. (Its key signature, four sharps, is too different from zero sharps to be considered a "close" relation.)

Another Way

Since relative major and minor keys share the same set of closely related keys, another way to locate those for a minor key is to consider its relative major: e.g., for A minor, think of C major.

C major:	I	ii	iii	IV	V	vi	(vii°)
	C	d	e	F	G	a	(b°)

If you compare the diagram above with Figure 22.4, you'll see that four of the closely related keys for C major and A minor are the same—D minor, E minor, F major, and G major; the fifth is the relative major or minor key. Key signatures are another help: keys with the same key signature (the relative major or minor) or with a signature that differs by one accidental are closely related.

Try it #4

A. Name the five keys that are closely related to each of the following major keys.

CLOSELY RELATED KEYS

F major   Gm, Am, B♭, C, Dm

E major   _____

A major   _____

G major   _____

B♭ major   _____

B. Name the five keys that are closely related to each of the following minor keys.

CLOSELY RELATED KEYS

E minor   _____

G minor   _____

C♯ minor   _____

F minor   _____

B minor   _____

Other Pivot-Chord Modulations

From a Minor Key to v

In minor keys, the other frequent destination of pivot-chord modulation is the minor dominant (v), a modulation often found in Baroque-period compositions. Listen to the opening of the Corelli prelude given in Example 22.6. The first phrase, beginning in D minor, reaches a Phrygian half cadence on the downbeat of measure 7, followed by a dominant anacrusis to the next phrase. The second phrase also begins in D minor (m. 8), but this one ends with a PAC in A minor. The possible pivot chords are shown in Figure 22.5 below.

EXAMPLE 22.6: Corelli, Preludio, from Sonata in D Minor, mm. 1–14

FIGURE 22.5: Comparison of chords in D minor and A minor

D minor

Roman numerals:	i	ii°	III	iv	v	V	VI	VII	vii°
Chords:	d	e°	F	g	a	A	Bb	C	c#°

A minor

Chords:	d	e	E	F	G	g#°	a		b°	C
Roman numerals:	iv	v	V	VI	VII	vii°	i		ii°	III

As you can see, this pairing of keys yields few workable pivot chords; the most typical is i = iv. In the Corelli sonata example, we have marked i = iv in measure 8, since the B♮ and G♯ of the new key are introduced in measure 9 and remain in effect through the cadence.

From a Major Key to ii, iii, IV, and vi

These pivot modulations are possible, but some are problematic in ways we will see below. Here is a good chance to practice identifying pivot chords.

Try it #5

Construct a chart of pivot chords for the pair of keys given below, using Figure 22.1 as a model. Draw a box around pivot chords that are diatonic in both keys.

(a) *D major*

Roman numerals:	I	ii	iii	IV	V	vi	vii°
Chords:	D	e	f♯	G	A	b	c♯°

E minor

Chords:	D	___	___	___	___	___	___
Roman numerals:	VII	___	___	___	___	___	___

(b) *D major*

Roman numerals:	I	ii	iii	IV	V	vi	vii°
Chords:	D	e	f♯	G	A	b	c♯°

F♯ minor

Chords:	___	___	___	___	___	___	___
Roman numerals:	___	___	___	___	___	___	___

(c) *D major*

Roman numerals:	I	ii	iii	IV	V	vi	vii°
Chords:	D	e	f♯	G	A	b	c♯°

G major

Chords:	___	___	___	___	___	___	___
Roman numerals:	___	___	___	___	___	___	___

(d) *D major*

Roman numerals:	I	ii	iii	IV	V	vi	vii°
Chords:	D	e	f♯	G	A	b	c♯°

B minor

Chords:	___	___	___	___	___	___	___
Roman numerals:	___	___	___	___	___	___	___

Check your answers before reading further.

The pivot choices from a major key to its supertonic are limited: two of the pairings involve the tonic in one of the keys (I = VII and ii = i), one includes the mediant chord (IV = III), and one involves minor v (vi = v). Modulation to ii is often accomplished by tonicizing ii with V7/ii or vii°7/ii, then continuing in the key of ii, or by sequence.

Modulation from a major key to its mediant is not a popular choice of Baroque or Classical composers, possibly because making vii° (C♯-E-G in D major) into V of the mediant (C♯-E♯-G♯) means altering two chord members. The pivot choices are I = VI, iii = i, V = III, and vi = iv; of these, I = VI and vi = iv work best.

The problem with modulating from a major key to its subdominant is that to be a convincing modulation, I of the original key has to stop sounding like the tonic and take on the role of the dominant. But if it starts sounding too convincingly like the dominant of IV, then we lose the sense of tonic as the home key. Modulations to IV in common-practice music are usually brief, or they occur well into a longer composition, so that the sense of home key is already well established. There are several good pivot chords, however, including I = V, ii = vi, IV = I, and vi = iii. The best is ii= vi, which often appears in a pivot area with i = iii or IV = I.

There are many options for modulating from a major key to its relative minor (a relatively common modulation in Classical-era works) because of the large number of shared diatonic triads between these keys: I = III, ii = iv, iii = v, IV = VI, V = VII, vi = i, and vii° = ii°. Again, typical pivot choices are those where both chords have a predominant function, in this case, ii = iv and IV = VI.

When planning a modulation between closely related keys, you may want to make a chart like those above to help you choose a pivot chord.

- The smoothest pivots are chords that occur in the predominant-function area in both keys.

- When you construct a chart, pay careful attention to the two key signatures in determining chord quality; don't try to use a "pivot" that has a different chord quality in the two keys.

- Keep in mind that some closely related keys are more easily reached by a different method, such as an initial tonicization confirmed by continuation in the new key, or by sequence.

Writing a Pivot-Chord Modulation

KEY CONCEPT To create a pivot-chord modulation:

1. Establish the first key, by writing one or more phrases in the initial key or a progression that firmly establishes a sense of the tonic.

2. Examine the possible pivot chords. Compare the diatonic chords in the two keys, and determine which chords can function in both.

3. Write a progression in the first key through the pivot chord(s).

4. Continue from the pivot chord with a normal progression in the new key, remembering to add or subtract accidentals as needed.

5. Write a cadence in the new key.

The music that follows the modulation may continue in the new key or return to the old. Follow normal guidelines for doubling and parallels, resolve leading tones according to the prevailing key at that moment, and don't forget to add the appropriate accidentals and to resolve sevenths and other tendency tones.

Direct Modulations

Not all modulations to closely related keys involve pivot chords. Sometimes a new phrase simply begins in the new key, a process called **phrase modulation**; or a new key may be introduced midphrase by dominant-to-tonic motion in that key. These **direct modulations** are usual in chorale settings, but may also be found in other contexts. Depending on how sudden and unexpected the change of key is, some writers refer to direct modulations as **abrupt modulations**.

Listen, for example, to the first two phrases from the Bach chorale in Example 22.7.

EXAMPLE 22.7: Bach, "O Haupt voll Blut und Wunden," mm. 1-4

F: vi   IV   I⁶ viiº⁶ I   ii⁶₅ V   I d: V⁶   i   i⁶   V⁶₄ — ⁵₃   i

The first phrase cadences in F major (m. 2), the primary key of this setting, with the progression (beginning in m. 1, beat 4) I-ii$^6_5$-V-I. The next phrase starts right out in the new key of D minor, with V⁶-i. If those two chords were immediately followed by chords in F major, we would label them V⁶/vi-vi and consider them a tonicization of vi. Instead, the phrase continues in D minor and cadences in that key, confirming a modulation to D minor. The direct modulation in this chorale is less abrupt than it could be because we have been prepared for D minor by the beginning of the first phrase, whose first two chords could be labeled i-VI in D minor instead of vi-IV in F major. Without this opening D minor triad, the shift to D minor after the fermata might seem more sudden.

Direct modulations are often used in popular music to heighten emotion. These can be considered phrase modulations or abrupt modulations, depending on the effect created. Sometimes, as in Example 22.8, there is connecting material to smooth the entrance of the new key, but not a pivot chord. These modulations are normally not made to closely related keys—this one goes from C major to A♭ major.

EXAMPLE 22.8: Lloyd Webber, "Memory," from *Cats*, mm. 32-37

And a new day ___ will __ be - gin.

C: V7   I   A♭:   I

Modulations Introduced by Secondary Dominants

A secondary-dominant chord can introduce a modulation anywhere within a phrase: write the progression with a secondary dominant as though a tonicization, then continue the progression in the new key. Be sure to include predominant-function chords and a cadence in the new key to confirm the modulation. While this type of modulation is not as seamless as a pivot-chord modulation, it does not have to sound abrupt.

For an example, listen to the first eight measures of Clementi's Sonatina in C Major (Example 22.9).

EXAMPLE 22.9: Clementi, Sonatina in C Major, mvt. 1, mm. 1-8

After establishing the main key of the piece, C major (mm. 1-4), Clementi moves to a new key by what may seem at first to be a tonicization: a secondary leading-tone chord, vii°7/V, resolving to V in measure 7. This resolution is followed, however, by a familiar phrase-model conclusion (T-PD-D-T) in G major (I–ii⁶–V⁶₄–⁵₃–I) without any sense of return to C major. The G major key area then continues to measure 15, the secondary dominant having introduced an ambiguity between keys that helps smooth the transition between them.

Locating Modulations

The procedure for locating modulations is similar to the one followed in Chapters 20 and 21 to find secondary dominants. First, determine the tonic key. Then scan for accidentals to locate a dominant-function chord that resolves to a new, temporary tonic. Remember that dominant-function chords may include both dominant sevenths (Mm7) and leading-tone seventh chords (usually fully diminished). Scan the score for the characteristic $\hat{5}$-$\hat{1}$ bass motion associated with dominant-to-tonic progressions; in many cases where there is a modulation, the dominant-to-tonic motion falls at the end of a phrase, making the secondary dominant easy to spot.

KEY CONCEPT To find a pivot chord, back up from the cadence or the first appearance of chromatic alterations: the pivot will usually be located just before the accidentals are introduced and may be a predominant-function harmony. Keep in mind that there may be more than one chord that makes sense in both keys. In that case, choose one or label the whole pivot area in both keys.

If the modulation is made by a secondary dominant, look for a continuation in the new key, including a PD-D-T progression. If there is only a dominant-to-tonic cadence (without a predominant), check to see whether the next phrase continues in the new key. If so, the cadence may be interpreted as a modulation; if not, it should be labeled with a secondary dominant (a tonicization).

Modulations in Musical Contexts

Listen to the opening of "Er kommt," a tenor solo from Bach's Cantata No. 140. To analyze this modulatory passage, begin by determining the opening and closing keys, then find a possible pivot chord that shifts the tonal center from the first key to the second. As marked in Example 22.10, the passage begins in C minor, with a tonic triad expanded by a neighboring ii°⁴₃ and leading-tone triad above a tonic pedal, and closes with a T-PD-D-T progression in G minor. Where does the key shift?

EXAMPLE 22.10: Bach, "Er kommt," mm. 1-6

Look for specific new accidentals: for a modulation from C minor to G minor, the A♭ of the key signature should shift to A♮, and the C minor leading tone (B♮) will disappear in favor of the new F♯ leading tone of G minor. Find the measure in which these accidentals begin to appear consistently (m. 4)—the pivot chord should come right before, in this case measure 3. Either chord in that measure is a potential pivot: i = iv (beat 1) or III⁶ = VI⁶ (beat 2). Choose one, or include both for a pivot area, then write Roman numerals for measures 3-4 to complete the analysis. If you follow this procedure when analyzing modulatory passages, the choice of pivot chord should be clear.

Harmonizing Modulating Melodies

The principles of pivot-chord and direct modulations may be applied to the harmonization of melodies as well.

KEY CONCEPT To harmonize a melody with an implied change of key, start by making a harmonic plan.

1. Write the scale degrees for the first few pitches of the melody. Harmonize these pitches with chords that clearly establish the primary key.

2. Divide the melody into phrases. A period will require two phrases, while a chorale-style melody will include several short phrases.

3. Examine the melody at the end of each phrase to see what key it suggests. For phrases whose accidentals and/or melodic scale degrees imply a change of key, write the scale degrees for the cadence in the new key, and select chords that make an effective cadence in that key.

4. In the middle of a modulating phrase, pick a spot for the pivot chord or direct modulation before any accidentals appear in the new key, then write the scale degrees for the entire melodic phrase, indicating the change of key.

5. Choose the remaining harmonies to make a good phrase progression. Remember to add all the necessary accidentals for the new key.

If a phrase ending indicates a cadence in a new key, set the cadence with either a tonicization (V7-I in the new key) or a full modulation. Think about how firmly you want the new key to be established, and choose progressions to make the effect you want. If an entire new phrase seems to be in a new key (most common in chorales), you may use a direct modulation—simply think of the melody pitches for the whole new phrase in the new key, and set them in the normal fashion. Phrases with direct modulations often begin with a dominant-tonic anacrusis.

We now apply these principles to a melody by Schubert, "Nur wer die Sehnsucht kennt" (Example 22.11a).

EXAMPLE 22.11: Schubert, "Nur wer die Sehnsucht kennt"

(a) Mm. 7–14 (vocal line)

Nur wer die Sehn-sucht_ kennt, weiß, was_ ich lei - de
nur wer die Sehn - sucht kennt, weiß, was_ ich lei - de!

Translation: Only one who knows longing knows what I suffer.

Begin by singing both phrases. The first begins and ends (in m. 10) in the primary key of E minor, with $\hat{2}$ implying a half cadence at the end of the phrase. Although there are no accidentals to point toward a modulation, measures 13 and 14 end the second phrase with $\hat{1}$-$\hat{7}$-$\hat{6}$-$\hat{7}$-$\hat{2}$-$\hat{1}$ in G major, which can be set with V^{6-5}_{4-3}-I. Therefore, if you begin with a tonic in E minor at the beginning of measure 11, you need to modulate between 11 and 13. There are several ways to do this. Two are shown in part (b).

(b) Mm. 11–14 (vocal line)

nur wer die Sehn - sucht kennt, weiß, was_ ich lei - de!

(1) e: i   iv⁶   V   i   iv / G: ii

(2) e: i   V7/III   III / G: I   ii

Measures 11–12, beginning in E minor, could be set i iv⁶ | V i iv = ii (in G major). Alternatively, i V7/III | III = I (in G major) ii would work (with a suspension in the melody, beat 2 of m. 12, in both harmonizations). Schubert's setting is shown in Example 22.12.

You may be able to think of other possibilities as well. To complete other settings, compose the bass line, using inversions where needed to make a good counterpoint with the melody, then fill in the inner voices as usual. When setting song melodies like this one, give your piano accompaniment a keyboard figuration.

EXAMPLE 22.12: Schubert, "Nur wer die Sehnsucht kennt," mm. 7-15

Did You Know?

Austrian theorist and composer Joseph Riepel, writing in 1775 in the second volume of his *Anfangsgründe der musikalischen Setzkunst* (*Elements of Musical Composition*), described the relationship between closely related keys as being like the relationships between workers on an estate. In the key of C major, for example, C major is the steward (*Meyer*) of the estate, who appears frequently to keep everything in order; G major is the overseer (*Oberknecht*), second in command; A minor is the head maid (*Obermagd*); E minor is the assistant maid (*Untermagd*); F major is a hired day laborer (*Taglöhner*); and D minor is one of the female household workers who run errands (*Unterläufferin*).

TERMS YOU SHOULD KNOW

closely related keys

modulation

- abrupt modulation
- direct modulation
- phrase modulation
- pivot-chord (common-chord) modulation

pivot area

pivot chord

tonicization

QUESTIONS FOR REVIEW

1. What is a modulation?
2. What is the difference between a tonicization and a modulation? What criteria do you use to identify a modulation?
3. What is the most common key to modulate to from a major key? from a minor key?
4. How do you locate the possible pivot chords between two keys?
5. In music for your own instrument, find a modulation from a major key to its dominant. What clues will you look for to locate this modulation?
6. In music for your own instrument, find a modulation from a minor key to its relative major. What clues will you look for to locate this modulation?
7. What are the steps for harmonizing a melody that modulates from one key to another?
8. How would identifying a modulation help you perform a passage?

Know It? Show It!

Focus by working through the tutorials.

Learn with InQuizitive.

Apply what you've learned to complete the workbook assignments.

23

Binary and Ternary Forms

Outline

Binary form
- Phrase design
- Sections
- Tonal structures
- Writing binary-form pieces

Simple ternary form

Binary forms as part of a larger formal scheme
- Composite ternary
- Composite binary

Overview

In this chapter, we consider how the musical elements we have studied contribute to the overall structure of a composition. Specifically, we learn how to recognize two common forms: binary form and ternary form.

Repertoire

Anonymous, Minuet in D Minor, from the *Anna Magdalena Bach Notebook*

Joseph Haydn, String Quartet in D Minor, Op. 76, No. 2, mvt. 3

Arcangelo Corelli, Trio Sonata in A Minor, Op. 4, No. 5, Allemanda

Wolfgang Amadeus Mozart
  Piano Sonata in D Major, K. 284, mvt. 3
  Sonata for Violin and Piano in C Major, K. 6, mvt. 3, Menuetto I
  String Quartet No. 10 in C Major, K. 170, mvt. 2
  Variations on "Ah, vous dirai-je Maman"
  Variations on "Unser dummer Pöbel meint"

Robert Schumann, from *Album for the Young*, Op. 68
  No. 3: "Trällerliedchen" ("Humming Song")
  No. 9: "Volksliedchen" ("Folk Song")

John Philip Sousa, "The Stars and Stripes Forever"

Binary Form

In earlier chapters, we considered extended passages and phrase forms, but we have not yet addressed larger **musical forms**—the overall harmonic and thematic organization of compositions.

KEY CONCEPT One of the most common musical forms, binary form, is comprised of two sections, each of which is usually repeated (or "reprised").
A quick way to identify a binary-form movement is to look for the symbols
‖: :‖ ‖: :‖ (repeat signs) that mark the two sections. Occasionally one or both of the repeats may be written out instead of indicated with repeat signs. Binary form is often associated in Baroque and Classical styles with dances, but can appear in other contexts as well.

Phrase Design

Listen to the theme of a Mozart theme-and-variations movement, while following Example 23.1. We examined the modulation in measures 1-8 in Chapter 22.

EXAMPLE 23.1: Mozart, Piano Sonata in D Major, mvt. 3, mm. 1-17 🎧

Rounded continuous binary

Since Mozart's theme divides into two parts, each of which is repeated, it is a binary form. The two phrases in measures 1-8, the first part, make up a modulating parallel period, **a** (mm. 1-4) and **a′** (mm. 5-8); this first section is designated **A**.

KEY CONCEPT If the first section (**A**) of a binary form ends with a cadence on the tonic of the primary key, the form is called **sectional binary**: this section is tonally complete and could stand on its own. If the first section ends with a cadence not on the tonic of the primary key, the form is called **continuous binary**: the piece must continue to a cadence on the tonic.

As the first section of Mozart's theme ends on the key of the dominant, this binary form is continuous.

Now examine the second half of the theme (mm. 9-17). This section also divides into two four-measure phrases (with an expressive three-beat silence from m. 12 to m. 13 adding a measure). While listening to this piece, you may have noticed that measures 13-17 are similar in motivic and harmonic design to the two phrases in section **A**. Compare these three phrases: measures 14-15 are identical to 1-2, and 16-17 are a transposition of 7-8 into the key of D major. This phrase can therefore be labeled **a″** to signify its own similarity to the first two phrases.

KEY CONCEPT When the initial melody (or the first part of the melody) from the first phrase returns at the end of a binary piece, the form is called **rounded binary**: the return of material from the beginning "rounds out"

the formal plan. The overall design of rounded binary is represented by
‖: A :‖: B A (or A′) :‖. The final section is labeled **A** if the opening material returns unchanged, and **A′** if it is shortened or altered (changed to remain in the tonic key, for example). When you write a prime (′) with a letter designation in your analyses, be sure to indicate what is changed to merit the prime.

The beginning of the second half (mm. 9-12) shares some motivic connections to the other phrases, but it is less stable harmonically and contrasts with what came before. It is labeled with a small **b** to show that it is a contrasting phrase; and because it plays a role in the larger formal design, we label it **B**. (Lowercase letters show form at the phrase level and uppercase the work's overall form.)

Now consider the harmonic aspects of this phrase. The anacrusis emphasizes the pitch A5, which suggests A major. On the other hand, measure 9 features a short descending-fifth sequence, alternating dominant seventh chords and triads, so that it is hard to hear the tonic; measure 10 doesn't establish the key either. The tonal ambiguity here is intentional. This phrase ends in measure 12 with a half cadence in D major, but Mozart interprets measures 11-13 quite differently in the variations that follow. In some cases, the progression seems clearly in A major; in others, D major. This phrase constitutes a "harmonic disturbance" that is typical of the **B** section of binary forms.

KEY CONCEPT The term "thematic design" refers to a piece's melody, figuration, texture, and musical characteristics other than harmony. "Harmonic structure" describes the harmonic plan. Even though the thematic design of rounded binary suggests three sections (A B A′), its harmonic structure—with (usually) its framing repeat signs and a harmonic disturbance at the beginning of the second half—defines a two-part form.

The form of Mozart's theme is diagrammed in Figure 23.1, with the thematic design elements on top and the harmonic structure (Roman numerals) below. The form is rounded continuous binary: rounded because of its design (the last phrase is **a″**), and continuous because of its harmonic structure (the first section does not cadence on the tonic).

FIGURE 23.1: Rounded continuous binary in the Mozart theme

	A			B	A′	
Thematic design	‖: a	a′	:‖:	b "harmonic disturbance"	a″	:‖
Harmonic structure	D: I-V (HC)	I modulates to V (PAC in V)		sequence (HC)	I-I (PAC)	
mm.	1-4	5-8		9-12	13-17	

Example 23.2 shows a short Baroque-style dance movement. A quick glance at the repeat signs (and the fact that it is a dance movement) indicates a binary form. Listen to the piece, and consider the phrase design of each section.

EXAMPLE 23.2: Anonymous, Minuet in D Minor, mm. 1-16 🎧

Simple continuous binary

Unlike the Mozart example, the first eight measures of this minuet (**A**) consist of two contrasting phrases, **a** (mm. 1-4) and **b** (mm. 5-8). The cadence in measure 4 is an authentic cadence in D minor, but by measure 8 the piece has modulated to F major (III), the relative major, confirmed by a PAC. The two phrases form a contrasting modulating period; and because section **A** does not cadence in the tonic key, the form is continuous binary. The last two phrases are also contrasting (no small letters are repeated here): measures 9-12 (**c**) feature a melodic sequence, and 13-16 (**d**) return to the tonic, D minor.

This type of form, where the end of the second half features no thematic return from the beginning of the movement, is called **simple binary**. In the Corelli minuet, this form is represented by the diagram ‖: A :‖: B :‖ (Figure 23.2), or simple continuous binary: simple because thematic elements of the first phrase do not return in the fourth, and continuous because the first section does not cadence in the main tonic key.

FIGURE 23.2: Simple continuous binary form in the minuet

		A			B	
Thematic design	‖:	a	b	:‖:	c	d	:‖
					"harmonic disturbance"		
Harmonic structure	d:	i–i	i modulates to III	(melodic sequence III, i)	V–i	
		(PAC)	(PAC in III)	(HC)	(PAC)	
mm.		1–4	5–8	9–12	13–17	

The simple binary design ‖: A :‖: B :‖ is prevalent in Baroque-era composition, along with ‖: A :‖: A′ :‖, when the melodic motives of the two sections are quite similar. The rounded binary design is the most common in late eighteenth- and nineteenth-century compositions; the material that returns (**A′**) in rounded binary is usually a shortened version of the initial **A**, made from the opening few measures, with a cadence in the tonic key attached.

Try it #1

For each of the following binary forms, circle the appropriate terminology.

1. If the first section ends on a tonicized half cadence, the form is (a) sectional (b) continuous.

2. If the first section ends on the main tonic of the piece, the form is (a) sectional (b) continuous.

3. If melodic materials from the first section return in the last phrase of the second section, the binary is (a) simple (b) rounded.

4. If the second section consists of new melodic material, the binary is (a) simple (b) rounded.

5. The form diagram ‖: A :‖: B :‖ represents (a) simple binary (b) rounded binary.

6. The form diagram ‖: A :‖: B A′ :‖ represents (a) simple binary (b) rounded binary.

7. The form diagram ‖: A :‖: A′ :‖ represents (a) simple binary (b) rounded binary.

Sections

Repeat signs are often the first visual clue that a piece is in binary form. As you may have noticed, this minuet includes first and second endings as well as repeat signs for each section. The first ending in measure 8 smooths the return to D minor as measures 1–8 are repeated, and the second allows for more finality at the cadence.

Because binary form originated in dance movements, individual phrases in many binary-form pieces are four or eight measures long. In binary pieces written for concert performance rather than dancing, there may be some variation in phrase lengths in the second section, often created by phrase extensions or elision. Recall that the second section in the Mozart theme is nine measures long, not the best theme for dancing. Both sections of the minuet, on the other hand, are eight measures long. You could dance to this minuet!

KEY CONCEPT The two sections of a binary form may be the same length, or the second may be somewhat longer than the first. The first section consists of at least one four- or eight-measure phrase; it is often a two-phrase parallel or contrasting period. Other possible lengths for the first section are sixteen or thirty-two measures, but it may be longer, and need not divide evenly into four-measure phrases.

Tonal Structures

For a piece to be called a binary form, an essential requirement is that it move away from the tonic key. The most common modulation goal in major-key pieces is the key of the dominant; in minor-key pieces it is the mediant (relative major) or the minor dominant (in Baroque-era works). In both pieces we have examined, the **A** sections follow the usual modulatory plan: the Mozart theme modulates to the dominant, and the minuet to the relative major. In some brief and uncomplicated binary forms, a tonicization of V (major keys) or III (minor keys) in the first section may substitute for the full modulation, or the first section may remain in the tonic and cadence there, with either a PAC (sectional) or a HC (continuous).

KEY CONCEPT

- In sectional binary forms, the first (A) section stays in the tonic.
  Major keys: ‖: I to I (PAC) :‖   Minor keys: ‖: i to i (PAC) :‖

- In continuous binary forms, the first section typically modulates, or it may end on a half cadence.
  Major keys: ‖: I modulates to V :‖   Minor keys: ‖: i modulates to III :‖
  ‖: I to tonicized V :‖   ‖: i modulates to v :‖
  ‖: I to HC (V) :‖   ‖: i to tonicized III :‖
  ‖: i to HC (V) :‖

The harmonic disturbance, or instability, of the second (**B**) section may be expressed by a sequence or a modulation to another key (usually one of the closely related keys). In the case of sectional binary forms, the second half may begin with a prolongation of the dominant (major-key pieces) or a modulation to the relative major (minor-key pieces). The dramatic instability of the beginning of the **B** section is then followed by a return to the tonic, with a phrase (or at least a strong cadential pattern) reestablishing harmonic stability in the home key.

KEY CONCEPT The organization of the second section of a binary form depends, in part, on the harmonic plan of the first section. Following are some typical harmonic plans for second (**B**) sections in brief binary pieces.

	1st portion *(harmonic disturbance)*	2nd portion *(return of tonic)*		1st portion *(harmonic disturbance)*	2nd portion *(return of tonic)*
Major keys:	‖: sequence	I–I :‖	Minor keys:	‖: tonicized III	i–i :‖
	‖: tonicized V	I–I :‖		‖: tonicized iv	i–i :‖
	‖: tonicized ii	I–I :‖		‖: tonicized v	i–i :‖
	‖: tonicized vi	I–I :‖		‖: sequence	i–i :‖

In binary-form pieces from the Romantic era, the key areas may be more adventurous, including an excursion into a distantly related key in the first section of a continuous binary, or in the harmonic disturbance at the beginning of the **B** section.

In the Baroque era, phrases are less balanced in length than in the Classical period, and sections may be extended by sequences and multiple tonicizations before returning to the tonic key. Corelli's Allemanda (anthology) provides an example. Example 23.3 shows the harmonic disturbance of the beginning of the second section. Every measure ends with a V in some key that resolves to the tonic on the following downbeat (except for one deceptive resolution); some of these tonics serve as pivot chords, leading to new key areas.

EXAMPLE 23.3: Corelli, Allemanda, from Trio Sonata in A Minor, mm. 13-20 🎧

In this simple continuous binary form, section **A** ends inconclusively with a Phrygian cadence (Figure 23.3). All the remaining "cadences" in the movement are elided until the last one, and only the last four measures of the second section (mm. 24-28) are in the tonic key of A minor. Compare the diagram with your anthology score.

FIGURE 23.3: Key areas and binary form in Corelli, Allemanda

Section **A**			Section **A′**						
‖: a → C → a			:‖: C →	e →	G →	d →	C →	sequence →	a :‖
i III i		V	(III	v	VII	iv	III)		i i
(tonic opening)	(Phrygian cadence)		(harmonic instability)						(PAC)
mm. 1 4 7			13	15	17	19	20	22	24

In simple continuous binary movements (either ‖: **A** :‖‖: **B** :‖ or ‖: **A** :‖‖: **A′** :‖), material from the *end* of the first section may return at the end of the second, transposed to the tonic key. In such cases, we say that the two sections are **balanced**. Example 23.4 shows balanced endings to the two reprises in a minuet for violin and piano by Mozart. Listen for the themes in the piano; the violin plays a countermelody. This design can be diagrammed as ‖: **A** (x) :‖‖: **B** (x) :‖, or ‖: **A** (x) :‖‖: **A′** (x) :‖, where x represents the material that returns. In balanced designs, the return of this material can be quite memorable and can engage a substantial passage of music, not just a cadential pattern. (The term "balanced" is not applied to a rounded continuous binary, however, even if there is a return of cadential material.) In Mozart's minuet, the material in measures 5-8 reappears transposed in 13-16, with the piano part nearly identical and the violin part slightly varied.

EXAMPLE 23.4: Mozart, Sonata for Violin and Piano in C Major, Menuetto I, mm. 1-16

Simple continuous binary with balanced sections

SUMMARY

Binary forms are labeled according to their harmonic structure and thematic design. Focus on these areas to determine the appropriate label.

Harmonic structure, first half

- If it ends on the original tonic: sectional.
- If it ends on anything other than tonic: continuous.

Thematic design, second half

- If it contrasts with the first half: simple binary (‖: **A** :‖‖: **B** :‖).
- If the harmonic disturbance develops material from **A**: also simple binary (‖: **A** :‖‖: **A′** :‖).
- If it brings back material from **A** in the final phrase, following the harmonic disturbance: rounded binary (‖: **A** :‖‖: **B A′** :‖).
- If it is continuous and brings back material from the end of **A** transposed to the tonic key: sections are balanced (‖: **A** (x) :‖‖: **B** (x) :‖).

Writing Binary-Form Pieces

You have already learned most of the techniques needed to compose short binary-form pieces: in Chapter 22, you wrote opening sections that modulate, and you are by now familiar with basic phrase progressions, which usually form the final phrase of the second section. We now focus on how to compose the harmonic disturbance for the beginning of the second section.

To help his students learn how to write this part of a short binary-form piece, Austrian theorist and composer Joseph Riepel (writing in 1755) suggested three strategies, and gave them rhyming Italian names to help students remember them. These are not the only possible progressions, but they suit our purposes nicely. All three are followed by a final phrase that begins and ends in the tonic.

1. *Ponte* (bridge): V | V | V$^{8-7}$ | I |

This first progression is called *Ponte* because it spans the measures with a prolonged dominant harmony; it works well when the first section closes in the tonic key (sectional). Since it is not very interesting harmonically, you would need to re-voice the chords or provide melodic interest. In Example 23.5, for instance, the **A** section ends with a PAC in the original tonic key, C major (mm. 175-176); the **B** section then proceeds with a repeated four-measure unit, with a dominant pedal point in the left hand and scalar flourishes in the right to provide melodic interest. In measure 184, the theme returns (making a rounded form) in the tonic key.

EXAMPLE 23.5: Mozart, *Variations on "Ah, vous dirai-je Maman,"* mm. 174-186 🎧

2. *Monte* (mountain): e.g., V7/IV | IV | V7/V | V |

The second progression is called *Monte* because it sounds like a hiker grad-ually climbing a steep incline; it works well with any of the options for ending the first section, and should include an ascending melodic sequence to highlight the climbing effect. At the beginning of the second large section in Example 23.6 (mm. 41-44), there is a two-measure sequence pattern transposed up by step. You can recognize a *Monte* by its two-chord pattern (a triad preceded by its own dominant) and the pattern's sequential repetition—up a step (from IV to V). It may also be transposed to other pitch levels within the key—for example, V/V | V | V/vi | vi, or V | I | V/ii | ii.

EXAMPLE 23.6: Mozart, String Quartet in C Major, mvt. 2, Trio (mm. 33-48) 🎧

3. *Fonte* (fountain): e.g., V7/ii | ii | V7 | I |

The third progression is called *Fonte* because it sounds like water bubbling from one level of a fountain down to another, and it usually includes a melodic sequence to highlight the bubbling-down effect. You can recognize *Fonte* by its two-chord pattern (a triad preceded by its own dominant) and the pattern's sequential repetition—down a step (from ii to I, in major keys only). This progression may appear transposed to other pitch levels, such as V/iv | iv | V/III | III in minor keys. In Example 23.7, Mozart repeats the V/ii to ii progression (within a two-measure sequence, mm. 5-6) before repeating the V to I.

EXAMPLE 23.7: Mozart, *Variations on "Unser dummer Pöbel meint,"* mm. 1-12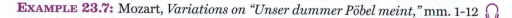

These are by no means the only options for the harmonic disturbance in a binary form. Another possibility is a segment of the descending-fifth sequence—as in measures 9-10 of Example 23.1. In minor-key pieces, the harmonic disturbance may be in the relative major or minor dominant, leading to a modulation back to the tonic with a half cadence on V, or with a cadence in the temporary key followed by a direct modulation to the tonic at the beginning of the next phrase.

Try it #2

For each binary form shown in the examples above, circle the appropriate terms.

In Example 23.5 (see anthology for the complete Variation VII), the binary is
(a) sectional (b) continuous (c) simple (d) rounded.

In Example 23.6, the binary is (a) sectional (b) continuous (c) simple (d) rounded.

In Example 23.7, the binary is (a) sectional (b) continuous (c) simple (d) rounded.

Simple Ternary Form

Another common musical form, comprising three distinct sections, is called **ternary form**. Listen to two pieces from Schumann's *Album for the Young*, "Trällerliedchen" and "Volksliedchen," while following the scores in the anthology. Figures 23.4 and 23.5 show the form of each piece. Brief ternary-form pieces like these are sometimes called **simple ternary**.

In simple ternary form (**A B A** or **A B A'**), the first large section, **A**, usually begins and ends in the tonic, with a conclusive cadence at the end. In both of these pieces, **A** spans measures 1-8, and is a parallel period (**a** = mm. 1-4; **a'** = mm. 5-8) beginning and ending in the tonic key (C major and D minor, respectively). The middle section, **B**, is normally in a contrasting key, usually closely related or the parallel major or minor (more distant keys in Romantic-era ternary forms).

The **B** section (mm. 9-16) in "Trällerliedchen" is a parallel period (**b** = mm. 9-12; **b'** = mm. 13-16) in G major (V), ending with a PAC (harmonically "closed," sectional); while that in "Volksliedchen" is a repeated phrase (**b** = mm. 9-12; **b** = mm. 13-16) in D major (the parallel major). This repeated phrase ends with a HC, leaving the **B** section harmonically "open" (continuous)—though it is firmly in the key of D major throughout and is not unstable or sequential as a **B** section in a rounded binary would be.

FIGURE 23.4: Sectional ternary form in "Trällerliedchen"

	A			**B**			**A**		
‖: a	a'	:‖‖: b	b'	:‖‖: a	a'	:‖
C: I		PAC	G: V		PAC	C: I		PAC	
mm. 1-4	5-8		9-12	13-16		17-20	21-24		

(sectional)

FIGURE 23.5: Continuous ternary form in "Volksliedchen"

	A			**B**			**A**		
‖: a	a'	:‖‖: b	b	:‖‖: a	a'	:‖
d: i		PAC	D: I		HC	d: i		PAC	
mm. 1-4	5-8		9-12	13-16		17-20	21-24		

(continuous)

The **B** section in a ternary piece often contrasts with **A** in at least one way in addition to its change of key—in its motives, texture, or harmonic complexity, for example. In "Volksliedchen" (Example 23.8), the **B** section contrasts sharply in mood, with a change in mode and different melodic motives—but with a chordal left hand part that is similar to the **A** section's. In "Trällerliedchen" (Example

23.9), the melodies in the two hands are reversed in the **B** section, which is otherwise similar in texture to **A**; its primary contrasting feature is the change of key.

EXAMPLE 23.8: Schumann, "Volksliedchen" 🎧

A (mm. 1-2)

B (mm. 9-10)

EXAMPLE 23.9: Schumann, "Trällerliedchen" 🎧

A (mm. 1-2)

B (mm. 9-10)

Individual sections in ternary form may be brief—as little as two phrases—or quite long. The three sections are usually balanced in length, as they are in the Schumann pieces, but they don't have to be. Sections may be repeated (with or without first and second endings or written-out repeats), but often, as here, they are not.

KEY CONCEPT Simple ternary form may be distinguished from rounded binary by observing

- the key and character of the **B** section: in simple ternary form, **B** is usually more stable, in its own contrasting key; the beginning of **B** in binary form is often unstable, sequential, or modulatory.

- the length of the **B** section: **B** is often longer in ternary forms than in rounded binary.

- the repetition pattern: in ternary form, **B** and the return of **A** (or **A′**) are never repeated together as a pair; if any section is repeated, it is repeated by itself.

Figure 23.6 shows the possible harmonic designs of ternary pieces. In the Baroque and Classical styles, the **B** section normally is harmonically stable in one key and will not modulate; in later (and larger) Romantic pieces, it is possible to have more than one key in **B**. When all sections are harmonically closed, the form is called **full sectional ternary**.

FIGURE 23.6: Possibilities for sectional closure in ternary form

A	B	A or A′	When common
harmonically closed (sectional)	harmonically closed (sectional)	harmonically closed (sectional)	Baroque, Classical, and Romantic eras, simple or composite ternary (see below)
harmonically closed (sectional)	harmonically open (continuous)	harmonically closed (sectional)	Romantic era, simple or large ternary (Chapter 33)
harmonically open (continuous)	harmonically open (continuous)	harmonically closed (sectional)	Romantic era, large ternary

Sometimes when the **A** section returns after **B**, unchanged from its original appearance, it is not written out but instead indicated by the words *Da capo al Fine*, written at the end of the **B** section. This marking tells the performer to play from the "head" (*capo*), or beginning of the piece, to the word *Fine* (end) at the end of the **A** section. Another indication, *Dal segno al Fine*, means that an anacrusis or introduction at the beginning of the **A** section should be skipped on the repeat (*segno* means "sign"). These indications were such a common way of saving paper in opera scores that ternary arias (solo songs within operas) are referred to as **da capo arias**, a song form to be covered in more detail in Chapter 28.

Binary Forms as Part of a Larger Formal Scheme

Composite Ternary

Although a binary form can be complete and freestanding, it can also function as part of a larger work. For example, themes for sets of "sectional variations" are often written in rounded binary form (see Chapter 25).

Sometimes two binary forms in contrasting keys are combined to make a large ternary design: an example is a minuet and trio (or scherzo and trio) movement in a sonata, string quartet, or other multimovement work. This design is called "composite ternary": ternary because of the large three-part form (minuet-trio-minuet), and composite because it combines shorter binary forms. In Figures 23.7 and 23.8, the highest-level letters are boxed to distinguish them from the letters on the next level, the **A** and **B** sections of the individual binary forms.

Listen to the Menuetto and Trio from Haydn's String Quartet in D Minor (anthology) for an example. As is typical for a minuet or scherzo, the first large section (A̲) is a complete binary form (in this case, sectional rounded binary) and is followed by a trio (B̲), also in binary form, in a contrasting key or mode—here, a continuous rounded binary in the parallel major key. In this movement, the minuet and trio differ in style as well, with "learned" counterpoint in the minuet contrasting with a rustic country dance in the trio. In performance, the movement concludes with a repetition of the initial minuet, either complete (A̲ again) or without taking the internal repeats. The indication to return to the beginning and repeat A̲ is given at the end of the trio as M.D.C, or "Menuetto da capo."

FIGURE 23.7: Composite ternary in Haydn's Menuetto and Trio

A̲ (Menuetto, D minor) sectional rounded binary				B̲ (Trio, D major) continuous rounded binary			A̲ (Menuetto)
‖: A	:‖‖: B	A′	:‖‖: C	:‖‖: D	C′	:‖	Repeat of minuet ‖
a	b	c	a′*	d	e	d′	
mm. 1–5	5–11	11–22	22–37	38–52	52–64	64–80	

*This **a′** section is unusual, in that it also includes thematic elements from **c**.

Composite Binary

Composite binary forms may be found in marches, ragtime, and other types of pieces. Listen to "The Stars and Stripes Forever" while following the score in your anthology. This work is typical of band marches, with an opening section (March) in the tonic key (E♭), followed by a Trio in a contrasting key (A♭). Follow the diagram below as you listen. As indicated, the March section is a simple continuous binary form and could be played as a complete piece on its own; likewise, the Trio is a rounded sectional binary form and could stand on its own. In marches, the **A**, **B**, **C**, and **D** sections are sometimes called **strains**.

FIGURE 23.8: Composite form in Sousa's march

A̲ (March, E♭ major) simple continuous binary				B̲ (Trio, A♭ major) modified rounded sectional binary					
A		B		C		D		C	
‖: a	b	:‖‖: c	c′	:‖ d	d′	‖: e		d	d′ :‖
I–HC (on vi)	I–V	I–HC	I–I	I–HC	I–I	sequential "dogfight"			
mm. 5–12	13–20	21–28	29–36	37–52	53–68	69–92		93–108	109–124

While Sousa's March is fairly standard in its tonal and thematic design, the lengthy and elaborate Trio presents some features worth noting. First, the "repeat" in the first section (**C**) is written out because of differences in ways the phrases end. Measures 37-40 and 53-56 are identical, but 41-52 are directed toward half cadences in 44 and 51, while 57-68 diverge to tonicize the submediant (F minor) before moving toward the tonic PAC in 68. Second, the Trio's second section (**D**) presents an energetic chromatic and sequential texture that in marches and rags is sometimes called the "dogfight"—a term that aptly characterizes its nature!

The usual formal schemes for marches and rags are similar to composite ternary, except that they have two large sections instead of three—there is no final return of **A** at the end—and within the large sections, the binary forms may be modified. Occasionally, you will find a rag or march in a composite form where one of the embedded smaller forms is ternary rather than binary.

Did You Know?

In the Classical era, the components of binary form were so well established that binary pieces could be composed by throwing dice (or other random procedures) to select the phrase beginnings, cadences, and sequences to "plug in" to the formal model. Composing a variety of different pieces from a few stock segments was called *ars permutoria*—the art of combination and permutation. For example, to make an eight-measure parallel period for section **A** of a binary form, a composer could

- select a two-measure phrase beginning;

- select a standard two-measure inconclusive cadence;

- repeat the two-measure opening;

- choose a standard two-measure conclusive cadence.

For a rounded binary form, the composer could choose a four-measure sequence to begin section **B**, then arrange a four-measure concluding phrase from the components of **A** to make a sixteen-measure piece—all selected by "chance."

TERMS YOU SHOULD KNOW

binary form	composite binary	strain
• balanced	design	structure
• continuous	*Fonte*	ternary form
• rounded	minuet and trio	• composite ternary
• sectional	*Monte*	• full sectional ternary
• simple	*Ponte*	• simple ternary
• simple with balanced sections	scherzo and trio	

QUESTIONS FOR REVIEW

1. What is the basic principle of binary form?
2. What are the most common harmonic structures for the first section (**A**) in a binary form in major keys? in minor keys?
3. What are the most common harmonic structures for the second section (**B**) in a binary form in major keys? in minor keys?
4. Where are you most likely to find a sequence in a binary-form piece? Where are you most likely to find a modulation?
5. What is the difference between simple binary and rounded binary?
6. What distinguishes simple ternary and rounded binary?
7. What is the difference between simple ternary and composite ternary?
8. How are binary forms used in composite ternary pieces?
9. In music for your own instrument, find one piece in simple binary form and one in rounded binary. How can you use the date of composition to help you locate a piece of each type?
10. What larger forms incorporate smaller binary forms within them?

Know It? Show It!

Focus by working through the tutorials.

Learn with InQuizitive.

Apply what you've learned to complete the workbook assignments.

Invention, Fugue, and Baroque Counterpoint

Outline

Baroque melody
- *Fortspinnung*
- Compound melody and step progressions

Invention and fugue: The exposition
- The subject
- The answer and countersubject

Episodes and later expositions

Special features
- Double and triple fugues
- Stretto
- Inversion, augmentation, diminution, and other subject alterations
- Canon
- Vocal fugues

Overview

This chapter focuses on Baroque-era inventions, fugues, and canons. We also consider melodic aspects of Baroque style, including phrase structure, motivic variation, compound melody, and embellished sequences.

Repertoire

Johann Sebastian Bach
  Fugues from *The Well-Tempered Clavier*, Book I:
    C Major, C Minor, D♯ Minor
  Fugue in E♭ Major for Organ (*St. Anne*)
  Invention in C Minor
  Invention in D Minor
  Cello Suite No. 2 in D Minor, Prelude
Wolfgang Amadeus Mozart, Kyrie, from *Requiem*

Baroque Melody

Fortspinnung

Listen to Bach's C Minor Fugue (anthology), and consider its phrase structure. The opening musical idea, or subject, on which the fugue is based is shown in Example 24.1.

EXAMPLE 24.1: Bach, Fugue in C Minor, mm. 1–3 (subject) 🎧

Compared with the binary- and ternary-form compositions we studied in Chapter 23, the music of this fugue shows no obvious breaks or stopping points. Instead it flows on, with the melody "spinning out" motives introduced in the first measures, until the final cadence. This melodic technique, called by its German name, *Fortspinnung*, is found in Baroque preludes, fantasias, and fugues, as well as in choral works and larger instrumental forms. While the opening idea is short—only two measures—the musical line doesn't stop in measure 3 but continues in sixteenth notes as the next voice is added. *Fortspinnung* passages can be quite beautiful; part of their excitement resides in their unpredictable harmonies and their development of motivic material.

⌒ **KEY CONCEPT** *Fortspinnung* passages are characterized by continuous motion, unequal phrase lengths, melodic or harmonic sequences, changes of key, and elided phrases. To analyze such passages, focus on identifying cadential goals and sequence types, but don't expect equal phrase lengths.

Now listen to the beginning of the Prelude from Bach's Cello Suite No. 2 (Example 24.2); listen for harmonic motion and phrase boundaries, and identify any repeated motives.

EXAMPLE 24.2: Bach, Prelude, from Cello Suite No. 2 in D Minor, mm. 1–13 🎧

AC in D minor   Descending-fifth sequence begins.

The opening motive in measure 1—we'll call it x—expresses an ascending eighth-note D minor triad, which returns in measure 13 in a new key. Measure 3 introduces motive y, another ascending arpeggio leading to a dotted-eighth high point, followed by descending sixteenths.

The task of identifying phrases in unaccompanied solo music like this is challenging, in part because you must infer the harmonic structure from the melody. In addition, there are few pitches of longer duration and no rests to identify phrase endings, since the rhythmic structure is mostly continuous sixteenth notes. The moment of "repose" at a cadence may be only a sixteenth note—the end of one phrase is connected to the next through an elision—keeping the motion constant. Sequences also contribute to creating longer phrases.

Still, judging by the location of cadences, we can determine that this passage consists of a four-measure phrase followed by a nine-measure phrase, with the second phrase characterized by a descending-fifth sequence. The sequence pattern, two measures long, features motive y in alternate measures (mm. 5, 7, 9), each time sounding a step lower. The sequence leads to the change of key to the relative major, F (m. 13), eliding with the beginning of the next phrase, with the x motive helping to make the connection.

Compound Melody and Step Progressions

In Baroque melodies, a single-line instrument like the cello may create the effect of several melodic strands or even a four-part harmonic progression.

KEY CONCEPT When two or more musical lines are expressed within a single melody, this technique is called **compound melody.**

The underlying melodic lines in a compound melody may be simple and obvious, as in an arpeggiated accompaniment, or very complex, as in Bach's solo violin and cello suites. Listen to Example 24.3, noting the analytical markings.

EXAMPLE 24.3: Bach, Prelude, from Cello Suite No. 2 in D Minor, mm. 40-48

Most striking at the beginning of the example is the development of motive x, transformed from a perfect fifth (D3-F3-A3) to a diminished twelfth (C♯2-A2-G3). The registral shifts from measures 40-42 set up a clear example of compound melody in 43-44—where the cello's repeated A3 (the dominant) becomes a lower-voice pedal point on the sixteenth-note offbeats, while the upper voice climbs by step from C♯4 to G4.

Another technique for writing compound melody is seen in measures 44-48, where the first pitch of each measure creates a stepwise line—G4, F4, E4, D4, C♯4. This technique, sometimes called a **step progression**, can be marked by stems as in the example. The entire progression prolongs the dominant harmony, as beat 2 of 44-46 touches on a lower-voice A3. If you play the whole passage while singing an A pedal point, the underlying harmonic framework becomes clearly audible. Cellists who can simultaneously convey the dominant prolongation and the different voices of the compound melody will create an exciting approach to the half cadence in measure 48.

Both these types of melodic motion—*Fortspinnung* and compound melody— are essential to fugues, inventions, and other Baroque compositions. After the Baroque era, *Fortspinnung* phrase structure, with its dramatic unpredictability and usefulness in connecting key areas, may be found in sonata forms and in improvisatory pieces such as fantasias.

Invention and Fugue: The Exposition

Baroque fugues and inventions are based on the exploration of an initial melodic idea, called the **subject** (abbreviated S or subj), which establishes the main key and mode, and provides the primary motives for the entire piece. Since part of the joy in listening to a fugue or invention is tracing the path of the subject through various keys and transformations, the subject is presented several times at the beginning to allow listeners to remember it, with each entry introducing one of the parts, or "voices," of the piece. **Inventions** are written in two voices (three-part inventions are usually called **sinfonias**); **fugues** might have three to five voices. The initial section, where the subject is presented in each voice, is called the **exposition**.

The Subject

The subject of an invention or fugue must be immediately recognizable—with a distinctive contour and a memorable rhythmic pattern—and capable of motivic and rhythmic variation. It may be short (a motive implying one or two harmonies) or several measures long, implying an entire basic phrase harmonic progression. The subject is normally unaccompanied in its first appearance.

Examples 24.4 and 24.5 show subjects from an invention and fugue by Bach. They illustrate two common compositional strategies: scalar subjects and subjects that arpeggiate the tonic triad. The simple but elegant subject from the D Minor Invention (Example 24.4) features a D harmonic minor scale with a leap between $\flat\hat{6}$ (B♭) and the leading tone (C♯). This subject introduces the key and mode through the scale and the implied harmonic progression from tonic to dominant (m. 2) and back to tonic (m. 3), and it also displays a distinctive melodic contour with the diminished seventh leap and sixteenth-note rhythmic pattern.

EXAMPLE 24.4: Bach, Invention in D Minor, mm. 1–3 (subject)

The subject from the D♯ Minor Fugue (Example 24.5) begins with a memorable ascending-fifth motive, introducing scale degrees $\hat{1}$ and $\hat{5}$. The first two measures emphasize chord tones from the tonic triad, with $\hat{3}$ on the downbeat of measure 2 followed by motion from $\hat{5}$ back to $\hat{1}$, to establish the initial key and mode.

EXAMPLE 24.5: Bach, Fugue in D♯ Minor, mm. 1–3 (subject)

Bach also employs a striking rhythmic motive here: a quarter note tied across the beat to stepwise descending eighths—in measure 1 (notated with a dot instead of a tie) and, crossing the bar line, from 2 to 3. We'll call this the "cascade" motive; the stepwise descending motion makes the subject easy to recognize when it returns later in the fugue.

Once the initial statement of the subject has been made, the exposition continues with additional statements, one for each voice. In two-part inventions, the second presentation of the subject is usually transposed up or down an octave, as in Example 24.6.

EXAMPLE 24.6: Bach, Invention in D Minor, mm. 1-5 (initial exposition) 🎧

As this example shows, invention subjects often begin with $\hat{1}$ and end on $\hat{3}$, allowing the second part to enter at the interval of a third or sixth. The harmonic implications of the unaccompanied subject become clear as it is set in counterpoint—the upper part in measures 3-4, in combination with the subject, clearly articulates i and V$^6_5$.

🎵 **KEY CONCEPT** The presentation of a melodic idea in one part that is then answered by the same idea in another part is called a **point of imitation**. The initial point of imitation in an invention is an octave apart; in a fugue, the first two points of imitation are a fifth and octave apart.

The Answer and Countersubject

Real and Tonal Answers A fugue exposition normally begins with the entries of the individual voices, one by one. The second entry of a fugue subject, called the **answer** (abbreviated A or ans), is usually transposed up a fifth or down a fourth. In Example 24.7, the subject ends with $\hat{3}$ (E4) on beat 3 of measure 2, and the answer (transposed up a fifth from C4) enters on G4.

EXAMPLE 24.7: Bach, Fugue in C Major, mm. 1-4 🎧

If the subject is transposed exactly, as here, with no changes in the sizes of intervals (though they may change in quality), the second entry is called a **real answer**.

In fugues written for keyboard instruments, each voice is active in a specific part of the keyboard range. For four-voice fugues, use the letters SATB to label each contrapuntal line; for three-voice fugues, use S and B for the highest and lowest parts, and either A or T for the middle, depending on its range. Five-voice fugues may be labeled S1, S2, A, T, B, or some other arrangement. In Example 24.7, for instance, the first two voices of this four-voice fugue enter in the alto and soprano ranges, respectively. While there is no strict guideline for which voice enters first and which second, the parts normally enter in pairs that occupy adjacent spans of the keyboard range: S then A, A then S, B then T, and so on. Another possible strategy in three-voice fugues is to begin in the middle voice, add the voice above, then conclude with voice below (as in Example 24.8).

If the fugue subject emphasizes $\hat{1}$ and $\hat{5}$ at the beginning, the second entry usually answers with $\hat{5}$ and $\hat{1}$, as in Example 24.8. This adjustment, called a **tonal answer**, keeps the beginning of the answer from strongly expressing the dominant key by emphasizing $\hat{5}$ and $\hat{1}$ instead of $\hat{5}$ and $\hat{2}$ (which would result from an exact transposition).

EXAMPLE 24.8: Bach, Fugue in D♯ Minor, mm. 1–10

Other adjustments may also be made in the tonal answer. In Example 24.8, the second interval of the answer (m. 4) is altered: $\hat{5}$–$\hat{6}$ becomes $\hat{1}$–$\hat{3}$ to make a third instead of a step—which preserves the contour of the subject, and allows the tonal answer to begin and end on $\hat{5}$, just as the subject began and ended on $\hat{1}$. These changes make the opening motive (ascending fifth, then step) a contour motive, since its distinctive intervals change in size in the answer. After these initial adjustments, the tonal answer normally continues without alterations, except for accidentals necessary for the dominant key.

SUMMARY

1. A real answer is an exact transposition of the fugue subject up a fifth (or down a fourth).

2. A tonal answer likewise transposes the subject up a fifth, but it modifies the initial intervals and scale degrees of the subject slightly so that it does not express the dominant key too strongly. For example:
   - A leap from $\hat{1}$ to $\hat{5}$ is answered by $\hat{5}$ to $\hat{1}$ (not $\hat{5}$ to $\hat{2}$), and $\hat{5}$ to $\hat{1}$ by $\hat{1}$ to $\hat{5}$.
   - A subject that begins on $\hat{5}$ is answered on $\hat{1}$ (instead of $\hat{2}$).
   - A subject that begins with $\hat{5}$–$\hat{6}$ is answered with $\hat{1}$–$\hat{3}$.

Try it #1

Examine the subject and answer in this excerpt of the C Minor Fugue.

Circle the answer type: real   tonal

If tonal, what intervals and scale degrees are changed? _____

_____

Look back at Example 24.8 to find the third entry of this three-voice fugue, in measure 8. The third entry normally presents the subject on the tonic again, and the exposition ends when all voices have presented the subject or answer. Because the answer may introduce accidentals from the dominant key, a short passage may be needed to prepare for the reappearance of the subject in the tonic. This passage is called a **bridge** if it makes a harmonic adjustment. A rhythmic or metrical adjustment (of only a few beats) to allow the subject to enter in the appropriate part of the measure is called a **link**.

In a four-voice fugue, the fourth entry will usually present the answer immediately following the third-voice subject, to create an exposition design of subject-answer-link-subject-answer. Occasionally, the subject and answer entries may be reversed: in Example 24.9, which follows Example 24.7, the dominant answer precedes the subject as the last two entries (subject-answer-answer-subject). Once each voice has stated the subject or answer, the exposition is concluded.

EXAMPLE 24.9: Bach, Fugue in C Major, mm. 4–7 🎧

The Countersubject In the exposition, the second entry of the subject (the answer) is set with counterpoint.

KEY CONCEPT The counterpoint accompanying the subject or answer is called a **countersubject** (abbreviated CS) if it appears consistently with the subject later in the piece. If not, it is called a **free counterpoint**.

In either case, the counterpoint normally contrasts with the subject in rhythm or contour to keep the two distinct. In Example 24.10, eighth-note arpeggiation in the counterpoint clearly contrasts with the sixteenth-note scalar subject. Later in the invention, a variety of arpeggiated patterns in eighth notes, rather than this exact counterpoint, accompany the invention subject in free counterpoint.

EXAMPLE 24.10: Bach, Invention in D Minor, mm. 1–5 🎧

Invertible Counterpoint The countersubject, if present, is usually written in invertible counterpoint with the subject—that is, either one may appear in an upper voice, with the intervals of the counterpoint working properly in either arrangement. For an example, consider the opening of Bach's Fugue in C Minor (Example 24.11).

EXAMPLE 24.11: Bach, Fugue in C Minor, mm. 1-5 (with intervals for invertible counterpoint) 🎧

The countersubject in measure 3, beginning with the scale descending from C5, is labeled a countersubject (CS1) because it reappears many times in the course of this fugue.

When the third voice enters in the bass (Example 24.12), the countersubject appears in the soprano part, transposed up a third—now above the subject. This fugue is unusual (although not for Bach) in that two countersubjects return consistently throughout: the new counterpoint in measures 7-9 in the alto (CS2) also reappears with the subject and CS1 throughout the fugue. One example of this return is shown in part (b), where the soprano has CS1, the alto the answer, and the bass part CS2. When two parts are set in invertible counterpoint, it is called **double counterpoint**; three voices in invertible counterpoint, as here, are called **triple counterpoint**.

EXAMPLE 24.12: Bach, Fugue in C Minor (triple counterpoint)

(a) Mm. 7-9 🎧

(b) Mm. 15-17 🎧

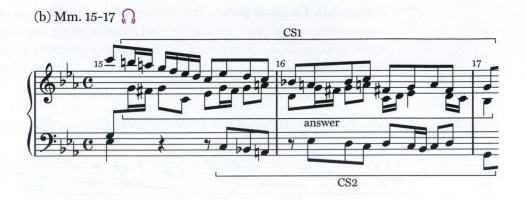

You will see that the intervals labeled in Example 24.11 reveal many thirds and sixths, with embellishing tones between them and a d5 on beat 3 of measure 4 that resolves to a third on the downbeat of 5. When the voices are rearranged, these intervals become inverted (Example 24.12a)—for example, the thirds become sixths and sixths become thirds; the term "invertible counterpoint" comes from the idea that when the voices are rearranged, the intervals between them invert. P4s are avoided (unless they can be interpreted as embellishing tones) because they are harmonic dissonances, and P5s are likewise avoided or treated as dissonances because they become fourths when inverted.

SUMMARY

In invertible counterpoint, the pairs of voices often feature the intervals 3 and 6 between the parts (implying triads) or the successions d5-3 and A4-6 (which imply V7-i). The P4, P5, and dissonances are employed only as embellishing tones.

Episodes and Later Expositions

Following the initial exposition in the main key, a passage called an **episode** leads to the second key area, where the subject is again presented. An episode may include one or more sequence patterns that are usually based on melodic or rhythmic motives from the subject or countersubject. Its harmonic goal is typically the dominant (in major keys) or the relative major (minor keys). As the episode prepares to establish the new key area, several measures of free counterpoint may be added to lead to the cadence. Once a new key has been reached, the subject appears, alone or with its answer, followed by another episode leading to a third key (also closely related), or back to tonic if only two keys, and additional subject entries.

KEY CONCEPT After the initial exposition, many fugues alternate episodes with additional entries of the subject in various keys. Later entries may be called exposition 2, exposition 3, and so forth; some analysts reserve the term "exposition" for the initial presentations of the subject and call these "middle entries."

Example 24.13 gives the first episode of the C Minor Fugue: the sequence begins in measure 9, beat 1, with the bass clef's C4—a measure-length pattern that moves down by step in measure 10, arriving on an E♭ major chord on the downbeat of 11 to prepare for the subject and countersubjects in that key. Measures 11-13 then constitute a middle entry in E♭, or exposition 2.

EXAMPLE 24.13: Bach, Fugue in C Minor, episode, mm. 9-13

Subjects, countersubjects, expositions, episodes, key changes, and cadences may also be represented in a chart, as in Figure 24.1.

FIGURE 24.1: Bach, Fugue in C Minor, mm. 1-16

MM.	1–2	3–4	5–6	7–8	9–10	11–12	13–14	15–16
FUNCTION	exposition	———	(bridge)		episode 1 (modulates to E♭ major)	exposition 2 in E♭ major (III)	episode 2 (modulates to G minor)	exposition 3 in G minor (v)
SOPRANO		tonal answer		CS1	sequence on CS1 and subject	subject	based on CS1 and CS2	CS1
ALTO	subject	CS1		CS2		CS2		subject
BASS				subject		CS1		CS2

Normally the subject and countersubject appear a final time in the tonic key before the end of the fugue, in what are sometimes called the "final entries." As the piece winds down toward the final cadence, the momentum is sometimes slowed by a pedal point, deceptive cadence, or other feature that helps signal the end. Example 24.14 illustrates two of these features: first, a brief eighth-note rest interrupts the entire texture in measure 28—the only such rest in the fugue—and second, a tonic pedal point in 29-31 undergirds the final presentation of the subject in the tonic key.

EXAMPLE 24.14: Bach, Fugue in C Minor, mm. 28-31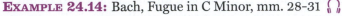

SUMMARY

Inventions and fugues share many design features. Both begin with a subject that is repeated in another voice in transposition, accompanied by a counter-subject or free counterpoint. Both are structured with an exposition, modulating episodes, and middle entries in closely related keys; they end with final entries in the tonic key. There are important differences, however.

Inventions:

- Written in two or three voices (three-voice inventions are called sinfonias).
- Points of imitation are at the octave only.

Fugues:

- Written in three, four, or five voices.
- Points of imitation are at the fifth (the answer) or octave (the subject).
- Answers may be real (exact transposition) or tonal (modified to stay in the tonic key).

Special Features

Double and Triple Fugues

Longer, more elaborate fugues may be based on more than one subject; these are called double (two subjects) and triple (three subjects) fugues. Here, one subject is introduced in an exposition at the beginning and the other subject(s) introduced later, either in separate sections or in combination with the previous subject(s).

KEY CONCEPT

1. A **double fugue** features two subjects (not necessarily appearing at the same time); it should not be confused with double counterpoint, another term for invertible counterpoint in two parts.

2. A **triple fugue** features three subjects (not necessarily appearing at the same time); triple counterpoint is a relatively rare variety of invertible counterpoint in three parts (usually S, CS1, and CS2).

Bach's *St. Anne* Fugue is a five-voice triple fugue for organ, with three subjects introduced in three distinct sections, each with its own character (Example 24.15). The first subject so resembles the hymn tune "St. Anne" (anthology) that the fugue has come to be known by that name. The opening section is set in a stately style, with a half-note beat unit reminiscent of earlier eras. The second section features a lilting compound duple meter (with dotted-half beat unit), and the third a spritely subject that sounds almost dance-like in its $\frac{12}{8}$ meter.

EXAMPLE 24.15: Bach, *St. Anne* Fugue subjects (triple fugue)

(a) Mm. 1–7: subject 1

(b) Mm. 37–41: subject 2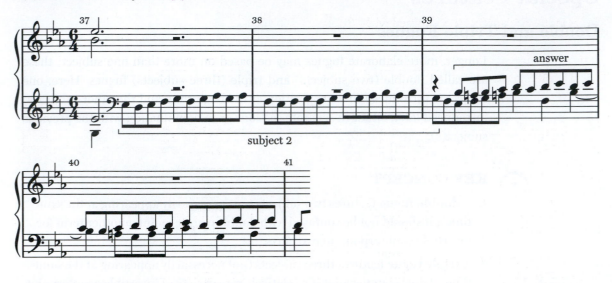

subject 2

answer

(c) Mm. 82–85: subject 3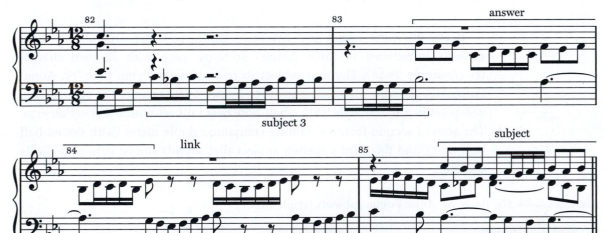

subject 3

link

subject

answer

One thing that makes this fugue so remarkable is that Bach combines modified statements of subject 1 ("St. Anne") with each of the other two subjects as each section drives to its climax. Example 24.16 shows the introduction of the "St. Anne" subject in parts 2 and 3 of the fugue.

EXAMPLE 24.16: Bach, *St. Anne* Fugue

(a) Mm. 59-64: subject 2 combined with "St. Anne" subject 🎧

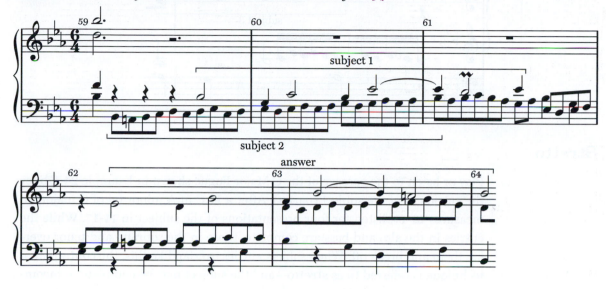

(b) Mm. 91-96: subject 3 combined with "St. Anne" subject 🎧

Stretto

Play or listen to the passage of the C Major Fugue shown in Example 24.17b for the entrances of the subject (part a). After a PAC in A minor (vi of C major) in measures 13-14, listen for four presentations of the subject in 14-15. While the entries in the alto and bass are complete, those in the soprano and tenor overlap them and break off. When subject entries overlap like this, the contrapuntal technique is referred to as **stretto**—and the subject may be complete or incomplete, as here.

EXAMPLE 24.17: Bach, Fugue in C Major

(a) Mm. 1-2 (subject)

(b) Mm. 13-18 (stretto)

Try it #2

In measures 16-18 of Example 24.17, the subject enters in stretto in each of the four voices, beginning with the soprano. Mark the subject entries on the score, and complete the chart below.

MEASURE	BEAT	VOICE PART	STARTING PITCH	COMPLETE OR INCOMPLETE ENTRY?
16	2	soprano	C5	complete

Inversion, Augmentation, Diminution, and Other Subject Alterations

For some additional contrapuntal techniques, we return to the D♯ Minor Fugue, whose subject and answer are given again in Example 24.18. In part (b), the answer appears in stretto in measure 27 in the soprano and alto, accompanied by the cascade motive. Measure 30 introduces another form of the answer in the soprano—in **inversion**, accompanied by inverted and noninverted cascade motives.

EXAMPLE 24.18: Bach, Fugue in D♯ Minor

(a) Mm. 1-6

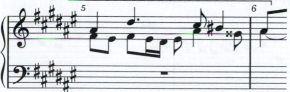

(b) Mm. 27-34

As the fugue continues, Bach also adds **augmentation**—where the duration of each note of the subject is doubled—as shown in Example 24.19. Here, an augmentation of the answer in the bass (beginning in m. 62) is combined in stretto with an ongoing statement of the answer in the alto (which began in m. 61 and moves from treble to bass clef). After the alto answer concludes, the ongoing bass augmentation is set in stretto with an inverted answer (beginning in m. 64) in the soprano. One of the few techniques Bach does *not* employ in this figure is **diminution**, where the subject's durations are halved.

EXAMPLE 24.19: Bach, Fugue in D♯ Minor, mm. 61-67 (subject in augmentation)

Example 24.20 illustrates one last subject alteration in this fugue: at the end of measure 47, the soprano enters with a rhythmic variation of the answer in inversion. This type of variation might at first seem too far removed from the original subject to constitute a subject entry, but because it is prominently placed in the soprano part and returns in measure 77 to accompany the augmented subject, it should be recognized as a subject variant.

EXAMPLE 24.20: Bach, Fugue in D♯ Minor, mm. 47-50 🎧

Try it #3

In Example 24.20 another answer sounds at the same time as the soprano's rhythmically altered answer. This answer enters in m. _____ beat _____, in the (circle one):

soprano   alto   tenor   bass

The answer is (circle any that apply):

inverted   augmented   diminished   complete   incomplete

When studying fugues and other types of Baroque counterpoint, look for the subject or answer to be transformed by transposition, inversion, augmentation, diminution, or rhythmic variation. The subject or answer often becomes more complex or hidden as a fugue progresses, making these entries a challenge to hear but also a musical joy to discover.

Canon

Another contrapuntal technique common in the Baroque era is illustrated in Example 24.21, from the beginning of Bach's C Minor Invention. The long subject (mm. 1-2) is presented unaccompanied in the upper part, then answered at the octave below (mm. 3-4) while the upper part continues with a countersubject. The lower part continues with the countersubject as well, after the answer is completed (mm. 5-6), and in fact completely replicates in measures 3-8 the upper part's measures 1-6, transposed down an octave.

This passage and other large portions of the invention are set in **canon**: a contrapuntal procedure where the second part can be derived from the first by following a set of instructions (in this case, "transpose down an octave and delay by two measures"). This canon not only spans the exposition but also serves as the episode, modulating to prepare the second entrance of the subject.

EXAMPLE 24.21: Bach, Invention in C Minor, mm. 1-8

mm. 3-8 = a canon at the octave with mm. 1-6

(canon continues)

Vocal Fugues

Although inventions and fugues are commonly associated with keyboard instruments such as harpsichord and organ, composers from the Baroque era onward have occasionally adapted their contrapuntal principles to vocal and other instrumental genres as well. In Example 24.22, from Mozart's *Requiem*, the "Kyrie eleison" and "Christe eleison" texts are set as an invertible subject-countersubject pair, doubled by the orchestra. The subject and countersubject are distinctly different: an angular ♩. ♪♩ subject ("Kyrie") contrasts with a countersubject that begins with repeated eighths and continues with a long series of sixteenth notes moving primarily in stepwise motion ("Christe").

EXAMPLE 24.22: Mozart, Kyrie, from *Requiem*, mm. 1-6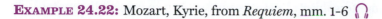

Translation: Lord, have mercy on us. Christ, have mercy on us.

SUMMARY

To analyze an invention or fugue:

1. Examine the subject: What are its key and mode, what harmonies does it imply? What motives does it introduce? Is the answer real or tonal?

2. Examine the countersubject: Does it reappear? Is it in invertible counterpoint with the subject? How does it interact rhythmically, melodically, and contrapuntally with the subject?

3. Label the entries of the subject, answer, and countersubject in the initial exposition.

4. Locate the returns of the subject (or answer) and countersubject throughout the piece. Wherever the subject is present, label and number these expositions.

5. Examine the episodes: Do they include sequences, and if so, what type? Which motives from the subject or countersubject appear? If an episode modulates, how does it accomplish the modulation?

6. What key areas are presented? Where is each established, and how? How do these keys relate to the main key of the piece?

7. Is the subject or answer ever transformed (by inversion, augmentation, diminution, or rhythmic variation)? Are there strettos?

8. How does the composer bring the invention or fugue to a close?

Did You Know?

The *St. Anne* Fugue is the concluding work of Bach's monumental *Clavierübung III*, sometimes called his *Organ Mass*. Bach wrote four different sets of works that he called *Clavierübung*—literally, "keyboard practice." Other keyboard works bearing this title include the French and Italian Suites and the *Goldberg Variations*. *Clavierübung III*, for organ, positions the E♭ Major Prelude and Fugue like bookends, on either end of a large collection of chorale preludes. These preludes are based on chorales whose texts are derived from the Lutheran mass and biblical texts, such as the Ten Commandments and Lord's Prayer. The *St. Anne* Fugue is thought to be infused with Christian symbolism of the Holy Trinity ("three in one"). For one thing, it is written in E♭ major, three flats. For another, three subjects are set in three large sections, where duple beat divisions give way to triple as the fugue progresses: the half-note beat unit of the first section divides into quarter-note threes for part two (in $\frac{6}{4}$), and then further into eighth-note threes for part three (in $\frac{12}{8}$).

TERMS YOU SHOULD KNOW

answer	double fugue	link
• real	episode	middle entries
• tonal	exposition	pedal point
augmentation	*Fortspinnung*	sinfonia
bridge	free counterpoint	step progression
canon	fugue	stretto
compound melody	invention	subject
diminution	inversion	triple counterpoint
double counterpoint	invertible counterpoint	triple fugue

QUESTIONS FOR REVIEW

1. How do *Fortspinnung* melodies differ from antecedent-consequent phrases?
2. What are some differences between expositions in inventions and those in fugues?
3. In what order do fugue voices typically enter?
4. What scale-degree patterns in a fugue subject require a tonal answer?
5. In what portion of a fugue is invertible counterpoint commonly written?
6. What is the tonal function of an episode, and how is this accomplished?
7. How might a fugue slow its motion into the final cadence?
8. What is the difference between double counterpoint and a double fugue? between triple counterpoint and a triple fugue?
9. What distinguishes subject entries in a stretto?
10. What techniques may transform the subject in the middle of a fugue to add interest?
11. In music for your own instrument, find examples of (a) a *Fortspinnung* melody and (b) a compound melody.

Know It? Show It!

Focus by working through the tutorials.

Learn with InQuizitive.

Apply what you've learned to complete the workbook assignments.

25

Variation

Overview

This chapter considers two types of variation forms—Baroque continuous variations and Classical sectional variations—and musical "topics."

Repertoire

Johann Sebastian Bach, Violin Partita No. 2 in D Minor, Chaconne

Ludwig van Beethoven
Piano Sonata in C Minor, Op. 13 (*Pathétique*), mvt. 3
Variations on "God Save the King"

Gustav Holst, Second Suite in F Major for Military Band, mvt. 4 ("Fantasia on the 'Dargason'")

Wolfgang Amadeus Mozart, *Variations on "Ah, vous dirai-je Maman"*

Henry Purcell, "Music for a While"

Outline

Continuous variations
- Formal organization

Sectional variations
- Themes and formal organization
- Variation procedures

Musical topics

Performing variations

Continuous Variations

We encountered individual variations in previous chapters, like those from Mozart's *Variations on "Ah, vous dirai-je Maman,"* that are based on a recognizable theme. Such Classical-style sets are known as **sectional variations** because the theme, as well as each variation, is harmonically closed. Many variation movements in Baroque style follow a different organizational plan: rather than divisions articulated by authentic cadences and double bar lines, these **continuous variations** feature a continuous flow of musical ideas and *Fortspinnung* phrase structure. The repeated element—the basis for the variations—is usually a bass line or a chord progression, rather than a melody with accompaniment.

Listen to Bach's Chaconne and Purcell's "Music for a While," both continuous variations, while following the scores in your anthology. Examples 25.1 and 25.2 reproduce the opening two statements of the theme for each work.

EXAMPLE 25.1: Bach, Chaconne in D Minor, mm. 1-8

EXAMPLE 25.2: Purcell, "Music for a While," mm. 1-7

Continuous variation themes are usually shorter than those of sectional variations, spanning perhaps two to eight measures, and though there may be a cadential harmonic progression at the end of those measures, there is no pause: the repetitions of the theme tend to be elided at the cadence to maintain the continuous structure. The rhythmic flow throughout the variation set is likewise continuous. Where phrases are not connected by elision, a lead-in (or connecting idea) often links one variation with the next.

Some of the names associated with Baroque continuous variations are "passacaglia," "chaconne," and "ground bass." These terms are not always applied consistently because the musical characteristics associated with each term (especially chaconne and passacaglia) varied depending on the time and place of composition.

KEY CONCEPT There are two general types of continuous variation.

- In a **ground bass** or **passacaglia**, the *bass line* is repeated while the upper voices are varied. The variations may reharmonize the bass line and may include phrase lengths that differ from, and overlap with, the statements of the ground bass.

- In a **chaconne**, the *harmonic progression* is repeated and varied. While the bass line may remain unchanged for several successive variations, it is usually altered as the piece progresses—rhythmically, harmonically, or through inversion.

The Bach Chaconne (Example 25.1), then, is based on a chord progression, with the bass line maintained in only some of the variations; in the Purcell song (Example 25.2), the bass line, or ground bass, serves as the foundation throughout. It is helpful to differentiate between these two types of compositional methods—ground bass versus repeated harmonic progression—even if historically the application of labels has varied.

Example 25.3 shows several traditional bass patterns found in Baroque continuous variation sets and the names associated with them; the first two predate the Baroque era. Both Purcell and Bach created famous variation bass lines by taking a traditional ground bass and adding an extension. Purcell's (part c) extends the "lament" tetrachord (so called because of its association in early opera with sadness and death; see Example 25.4), while Bach's (part d) extends a bass used by French Baroque composer André Raison. Some of these bass lines, such as the lament bass (which appears in both diatonic and chromatic forms) and Pachelbel's bass (Chapter 19), continue to be employed in both concert and popular music today.

EXAMPLE 25.3: Traditional bass lines for continuous variations

(a) Romanesca

(b) La Folia

(c) Lament bass from Purcell's "When I am laid in earth"

(d) Bass from Bach's Passacaglia in C Minor

(e) Bass from Pachelbel's *Canon in D*

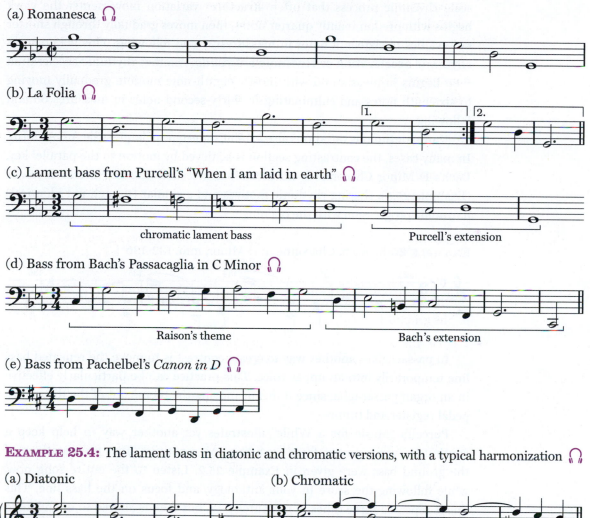

EXAMPLE 25.4: The lament bass in diatonic and chromatic versions, with a typical harmonization

(a) Diatonic   (b) Chromatic

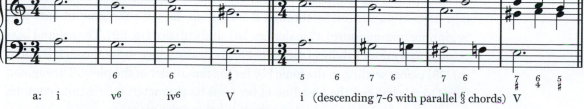

Formal Organization

Chaconnes and passacaglias may include as many as sixty or more short variations. They are often grouped into pairs or sets that are linked by a shared figure or other musical characteristic; for example, the first and second variations might form a pair, as well as the third and fourth, and so on. Paired variations help keep the movement from sounding choppy or heavily segmented.

The first forty measures of the Bach Chaconne (anthology) illustrate a large-scale rhythmic process that often structures variation movements: the work begins with predominantly quarter notes, then moves gradually through shorter note values to sixteenth notes in measures 27 and following. This is known as **rhythmic acceleration** or **rhythmic *crescendo***. Another rhythmic acceleration then begins in measure 56 with mostly eighth-note motion, gradually moving to sixteenth notes and culminating in thirty-second notes in measures 65 and following.

Many continuous variations also exhibit some type of large-scale **A B A′** form. In many cases, the contrasting section is achieved by motion to the parallel key. Bach's D Minor Chaconne is no exception: measures 132-207 are in D major (Example 25.5), sharing rhythmic motives and a similar (though not identical) harmonic progression with the opening.

EXAMPLE 25.5: Bach, Chaconne in D Minor, mm. 132-136

In passacaglias, another way to create contrast is to move the repeated bass line temporarily into an upper voice. This practice can be particularly effective in an organ passacaglia, since it means moving the theme out of the distinctive pedal register and timbre.

Purcell's "Music for a While" illustrates yet another way to help keep a continuous variation set from sounding too repetitive. Two presentations of the ground bass were given in Example 25.2. Listen to the entire song now, while following the score in your anthology, and focus on the bass line. This line is repeated three times in measures 1-12, but then is altered to modulate to new keys. It passes briefly through E minor (m. 15, with the ground bass now beginning mid-measure), G major (m. 18), and C major (m. 22). The ground bass returns to A minor briefly in measure 23, and passes once more through E minor (m. 28) before settling in the tonic key for the remainder of the piece. Throughout these tonal changes, the bass line never loses its characteristic rhythm, contour, or prominence as the organizing principle behind the piece.

Now if you focus on Purcell's vocal melody and large-scale design, you should hear an **A B A′** structure superimposed on the continuous variation. This organization is most clear when the **A** section returns in measure 29: at this point, the text and a substantial part of the melody from the song's opening return, and the ground bass returns to its downbeat metrical position. The beginning of the **B** section (Example 25.6) is more difficult to determine, but it surely includes the modulatory statements of the ground bass and introduction of new text. We can therefore begin the **B** section in measure 10, with statement 4.

EXAMPLE 25.6: Purcell, "Music for a While," mm. 9-15 🎧

This new vocal phrase ("Wond'ring"), beginning on the third beat of ground bass 4, continues right through the beginning of ground bass 5 in measure 13 ("were eas'd"). Ground bass and vocal line are then back in alignment at the cadence in E minor in measure 15. Places where the vocal melody and bass pattern do not align help create a more seamless (and more interesting) piece than complete alignment of the two would provide.

SUMMARY

In continuous variations:

- The repeated element (theme) may be a bass line, a harmonic progression, or both, and is normally quite short: two to eight measures long.

- There are many repetitions of the theme, each elided into the next, often grouped into pairs.

- The variations overall often fall into three large sections (**A B A'**), with the middle section in a contrasting mode or key.

- Each large section usually features a rhythmic acceleration or some other type of intensification to shape the section and build toward the final close.

Sectional Variations

Variation movements in the Classical era, a time when clear phrases and sectional organization were prized, are more often constructed with a sectional design: each variation is clearly articulated from the next by a strong conclusive cadence (usually before a double bar) and sometimes by a striking change in style or texture. Since each variation could be played as a complete stand-alone section, these sets are called **sectional variations** or **theme and variations**, and may vary in length from five to twelve variations or more. This type of movement can also be found in works from the Romantic era and beyond.

Themes and Formal Organization

Sectional variations are based on a melody that serves as a **theme**, the main idea to unify the set. While the length may vary, Classical-era themes are usually sixteen measures or more and show a clear phrase structure.

A theme may comprise a complete formal unit, as does the rounded binary of the Mozart theme in Example 25.7, that makes a complete short piece in itself. Though the theme may be newly composed, many are based on a preexisting melody, like Mozart's—folk songs, patriotic songs, and other familiar melodies work particularly well because listeners can more easily follow the melody's transformation through the variation process.

Mozart's theme is a melody we know as "Twinkle, Twinkle, Little Star" but he knew as a French folk song, "Ah, vous dirai-je Maman." Listen to Example 25.7 to review its phrase structure and formal organization.

EXAMPLE 25.7: Mozart, *Variations on "Ah, vous dirai-je Maman,"* theme, mm. 1-24 🎧

Sectional rounded binary

In this piece, the variations are numbered in the score, a convention typical of sectional variations; otherwise the next step would be to locate the starting point for each new variation. In Mozart's score, most variations follow the rounded binary form of the theme: ‖: **A** :‖‖: **B A** (or **A′**) :‖. Take a close look at the last variation: the first section is eight measures long as before, and the first ending of the second section cadences as expected, but the second ending adds eleven measures. These added measures constitute a coda, helping to bring the entire piece to a close.

Variation Procedures

Now listen to the entire piece. As you listen, think about what has been changed in each variation compared with the theme, and also how the variations work together as a set.

KEY CONCEPT   When you analyze variation movements, keep the following questions in mind.

- Does the variation differ in key, mode, meter, phrase structure, length, or character from the theme?
- Is there a melodic or rhythmic figure or a specific embellishment pattern? If so, what is it?
- Does the variation form a pair with another, or a unit with several others?
- Is chromaticism used? If so, does it embellish a melody line, or does it change the harmonic function?
- Are the harmonies more complex than in the theme or previous variation? Are they simplified?

Try it #1

In the Mozart *Variations*, the key, meter, and form are consistent in almost every variation. Flip through the score to identify one variation that is in minor, and one that has a different meter.

Minor key: Variation number _____   key _____

Meter change: Variation number _____   meter _____

Figural Variation Most of the variations in this piece are **figural**: they feature a specific embellishment pattern or figure throughout. Figural variations are often grouped in pairs. In the Mozart set:

- Variations I and II share sixteenth notes in one hand against quarter notes in the other; this rhythmic relationship reverses hands in the two variations.

- Variations III and IV share triplets in one hand against primarily quarter notes in the other.

- Variations VIII and IX both feature imitative textures and suspensions in the upper voices.

- Rounding out the piece is a return in Variation XII of the sixteenth-note accompanimental pattern heard in Variation II, now adapted for triple meter.

Compare Example 25.8a with measures 9-12 of the theme to see how the melody is embellished in Variation I—with upper and lower neighbors, as marked. A second figure with a leap and a scale appears in measures 28-30 (part b).

EXAMPLE 25.8: Mozart, *Variations on "Ah, vous dirai-je Maman,"* Variation I

(a) Mm. 33-36

(b) Mm. 28-30

Variation V is built on a rhythmic figure—𝄾 ♪ ♩—heard in both the melody and accompaniment (Example 25.9). In other variations, such as VI (Example 25.10), each hand is characterized by a different figure. Some figures embellish and disguise the melody, while others appear in the accompanimental voice, with the melody floating above.

EXAMPLE 25.9: Mozart, *Variations*, Variation V, mm. 121-124

EXAMPLE 25.10: Mozart, *Variations*, Variation VI, mm. 145-148

Chromatic Variation

When you find chromaticism, as you will in several of Mozart's variations, check to see whether it embellishes a melodic line or represents a change in harmony. In Example 25.8a, for instance, the F♯5, D♯5, and C♯5—all chromatic neighbors—decorate the melodic figure.

For chromaticism that changes the harmonic progression, listen to Example 25.11. In measure 68, the C♯3 and B♭4 on beat 2 transform the original C major tonic into a diminished seventh chord that resolves in the next measure. The addition of A♭4 on beat 2 of measure 69 then creates another diminished seventh chord that resolves in measure 70. In both cases, the chromatic pitches are part of secondary leading-tone chords. The C♯4 and A♯3 in measure 69, in contrast, are simply chromatic neighbors.

EXAMPLE 25.11: Mozart, *Variations*, Variation II, mm. 68- 69

In variation sets built on a major-key theme, you may also find chromaticism in passages that include modal mixture (Chapter 26) or a complete change of mode. Listen, for instance, to measures 197-198 of Variation VIII (Example 25.12). Minor-mode variations, like this one, are normally in the parallel rather than the relative minor, to retain the same key center, allowing a good opportunity for expressive chromaticism. Here, the accidentals in the bass line indicate the melodic minor scale; much of the expressive effect comes from the chain of suspensions in the right hand. Elsewhere in minor-mode variations, composers often substitute dramatic chromatic harmonies such as the Neapolitan and augmented-sixth chords—chords we will investigate in Chapter 27.

EXAMPLE 25.12: Mozart, *Variations*, Variation VIII, mm. 193–200

Textural Variation

Textural Variation In most variation sets, one of the elements varied is texture. In a general sense, we might refer to a "thin" texture when there are only a few voices and/or simple rhythmic patterns—as in the theme for the Mozart variations—and a "thick" texture when there are many voices and/or a lot of rhythmic activity. Remember that lines may be doubled in octaves, doubled by other instruments, or sometimes doubled in thirds or sixths; but while this may create a somewhat thicker texture, doubling does not create additional independent lines.

Variations tend to be organized texturally from the simplest to the most complex, but sometimes composers may include a variation with a thin texture or reduced harmonic palette in the middle of a set for contrast. Variation VII (Example 25.13), with the left-hand part thinned out to showcase the scalar patterns in the right hand, is an example; this type is sometimes called a **simplifying variation**.

EXAMPLE 25.13: Mozart, *Variations*, Variation VII, mm. 169–172

Another relatively common textural variation, a **polyphonic** or **contrapuntal variation**, may include imitative entries, as several of the Mozart variations do (Example 25.14), or a change from a harmonically based setting to one with independent voices.

EXAMPLE 25.14: Mozart, *Variations*, Variation VIII, mm. 193-196

Timbral Variation Unlike a set of piano variations, those in the fourth movement of Holst's Second Suite explore a wide range of timbral combinations. Example 25.15 shows the opening theme, played softly by only three performers (E♭ clarinet, alto saxophone, and tenor saxophone). Now listen, following your anthology score, to measures 41-48, where almost the entire band is playing—a contrast in timbre, musical range, dynamic level, and texture. In the rest of the variations, Holst passes the melody to every section of the band in turn, exploring timbre and texture by changing instrumental colors and building up layers. Some later variation sets, like this one from the early twentieth century, combine elements of sectional and continuous variations.

EXAMPLE 25.15: Holst, Second Suite in F Major, mvt. 4, mm. 1-8

SUMMARY

In sectional variations:

- The theme constitutes a complete, harmonically closed little piece, and serves as the basis for the variations.

- A particular variation may employ figural, chromatic, textural, timbral, or other type of variation procedure. Feel free to combine the labels as needed, or come up with your own to describe what you are hearing.

Musical Topics

Some variations are designed to represent a particular style or character—generally called a **musical "topic."** Musical topics were widely used as design elements in Classical and early Romantic instrumental music as a way of evoking a location (pastorale), activity (hunt), emotion (*Sturm und Drang*; storm and stress, or tragic), or musical style (minuet). They engage melodic, harmonic, rhythmic, or textural features to help the listener recognize the "cross reference." When an entire variation is consistent in the topic evoked, it is referred to as a **character variation**.

Several variations from Beethoven's *Variations on "God Save the King"* are of this type. Listen to Example 25.16, an excerpt from Variation VI. Here, the tempo, meter, and rhythmic patterns are all typical of march (or military) style; there are even "trumpet flourishes" in the last measure. The march strongly contrasts with the previous variation in this set, a lyrical, minor-mode serenade (Example 25.17), whose melody is in "singing style"—another musical topic. Although a character variation may feature a repeated melodic or rhythmic figure, it differs from a figural variation in that the figure itself is not the driving impetus; the entire texture represents the "character."

EXAMPLE 25.16: Beethoven, *Variations on "God Save the King,"* Variation VI, mm. 1-6

EXAMPLE 25.17: Beethoven, *Variations on "God Save the King,"* Variation V, mm. 1-3

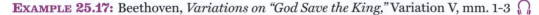

Frequently encountered musical topics are listed below; some allude to a style of piece, while others invoke emotional states, locations, or musical textures. These may come to seem obvious once you are familiar with them; still, their identification can be subjective, depending on how you hear the passage and how the performer interprets it.

Types of pieces:	Other topics:
aria	bravura
cadenza	brilliant style
fantasia	fanfare
French overture	hunt style
hymn	learned counterpoint
invention	pastorale
march	orchestral tutti
minuet	sigh motive
musette	singing style
recitative	*Sturm und Drang*
sarabande	

Beethoven's Variation IV (Example 25.18) displays a **bravura** style—a dashing, theatrical, showy passage requiring great skill and energy.

EXAMPLE 25.18: Beethoven, *Variations*, Variation IV, mm. 58-61 🎧

The passage shown in Example 25.19, from the third movement of Beethoven's *Pathétique* Sonata, reflects **learned** style, a reference to species counterpoint, with its half-note durations and the points of imitation, inversion, diminution, and augmentation characteristic of Baroque fugues. We will learn more about musical topics in later chapters, as we consider examples in which they are invoked.

EXAMPLE 25.19: Beethoven, *Pathétique* Sonata, mvt. 3, mm. 79-86 🎧

Performing Variations

In the centuries before recorded music, variation movements were an ideal format for listeners who might hear a piece of music only one time. They would listen to the initial idea—perhaps a familiar chord progression or tune—then follow the transformation of the idea through a series of variations without having to hear the work several times to perceive its organization. When performing variations, however, you need not "bring out" the theme each time you play it. Instead, shape the music in a way that is appropriate to the style, being aware of the repeated theme but not overemphasizing it.

A first step in preparing a variation set for performance might be to locate each presentation of the theme. In the case of continuous variations, you may want to choose an articulation for the bass line that remains consistent so that the beginning of each repetition is clear without being emphasized. In sectional variations, be careful that you don't "miss the forest for the trees"—that is, that you don't overemphasize the embellishments and lose the theme. It is then the listeners' task to discern the increasingly disguised melody, the repeated bass line, or the varied harmonic progression as the set progresses—if they wish to listen that way.

To further prepare for performance, determine the style or character of individual variations. If there are passages that might represent musical topics, consider how you can make that character clear. Understanding the role of overall form—especially paired or grouped variations, rhythmic acceleration, contrasting sections, and the dramatic shaping of the set—will help you achieve the sweep and grace of a well-designed variation movement in performance.

Did You Know?

Musical "character" was an important element to composers of the eighteenth century, as evidenced by the many treatises and reference works that refer to it. The German word *Charakter* includes various nuances; to get a sense of some of these, think of a "character" in a play, and imagine a collegiate actor playing the part of someone much older or younger. To create the illusion that the actor is older, he may slow his step, use a cane, and hunch forward; to play someone much younger, she might roll her eyes and strike poses while pretending not to care about what is going on. Each portrayal requires characteristic timing, motion, and gestures to make the role believable. Add to this the meaning of "character" as a person's nature, and you have the point of reference for musical topics.

TERMS YOU SHOULD KNOW

chaconne
coda
ground bass
musical topic
passacaglia
rhythmic acceleration (rhythmic *crescendo*)

variation
- character
- chromatic
- contrapuntal
- continuous
- figural
- polyphonic
- sectional
- simplifying
- textural
- timbral

QUESTIONS FOR REVIEW

1. How do continuous variations differ from sectional variations?
2. In what ways may a theme be varied?
3. What are some types of larger structural organization in variation movements?
4. What are musical topics? How might they apply to variations?
5. In what ways can analysis inform a performance of variations?
6. In music for your own instrument, find an example of one of the following: (a) a continuous variation movement, (b) a sectional variation movement, (c) a movement combining sectional and continuous characteristics.

Know It? Show It!

Focus by working through the tutorials.

Learn with InQuizitive.

Apply what you've learned to complete the workbook assignments.

Outline

Harmonic color and text setting

Mixture chords

- The spelling and function of mixture chords
- Tonicizing mixture chords
- Embellishing tones
- Mixture and the cadential $^6_4$ chord
- Intonation and performance
- Mixture in instrumental music

Mixture and modulation

Modal Mixture

Overview

In this chapter, we add harmonic color to pieces by incorporating chords from the parallel minor or major key. These dramatic and unexpected chords are especially effective in music with text, where the color change may highlight important words.

Repertoire

Wolfgang Amadeus Mozart
  Piano Sonata in D Major, K. 284, mvt. 1
  "Voi, che sapete" ("You Who Know"), from *The Marriage of Figaro*

Henry Purcell, "When I am laid in earth," from *Dido and Aeneas*

Franz Schubert
  "Du bist die Ruh" ("You Are Rest")
  "Im Dorfe" ("In the Village"), from *Winterreise (Winter Journey)*
  Moment musical in A♭ Major, Op. 94, No. 6

Robert Schumann, "Ich grolle nicht" ("I Bear No Grudge"), from *Dichterliebe (The Poet's Love)*

Harmonic Color and Text Setting

Begin by listening to excerpts from two contrasting vocal works: Mozart's "Voi, che sapete" and Schumann's "Ich grolle nicht." First read the text translations, given beneath Examples 26.1 and 26.2, and choose one important word or phrase that you would highlight musically if you were the composer. Then listen to see how these composers handle the texts.

EXAMPLE 26.1: Mozart, "Voi, che sapete," mm. 29-36

Translation: I feel an emotion, full of desire, which now is pleasure, now is suffering.

The two phrases of Example 26.1 (mm. 29-32, 33-36) have a parallel structure, but compare measures 31 and 35, and the shift in the vocal line from $\hat{3}$ to $\flat\hat{3}$. This unexpected change of harmonic color makes measure 35 stand out from its surroundings and illuminates its text ("which now is . . . suffering"); the appearance of minor i instead of major I emphasizes the character Cherubino's state of simultaneous pleasure and pain. (The last chord in this measure, an augmented-sixth chord, will be explored in Chapter 27.)

EXAMPLE 26.2: Schumann, "Ich grolle nicht," mm. 1-4

Translation: I bear no grudge, even if my heart breaks.

In Example 26.2, Schumann highlights the word "Herz" with the longest-held pitch of the phrase and a striking A♭, which colors the accompanying supertonic seventh and changes it to a half-diminished sonority, depicting the singer's breaking heart. This shift from from $\hat{6}$ to ♭$\hat{6}$—like Mozart's shift from $\hat{3}$ to ♭$\hat{3}$—is an example of mixture.

Mixture Chords

Modal **mixture**, a "mixing" of parallel major and minor modes, is a technique composers employ to enrich their melodic and harmonic palette with more expressive possibilities.

KEY CONCEPT Mixture is applied most often in major keys, where the modal scale degrees ♭$\hat{3}$, ♭$\hat{6}$, and ♭$\hat{7}$ are borrowed from the parallel natural minor. For this reason, mixture chords are sometimes called "borrowed chords." The most common mixture chords in major keys, aside from the minor tonic (i), are those that include ♭$\hat{6}$: ii°⁶, ii$^{ø\frac{6}{5}}$, iv, ♭VI, and vii°⁷.

To label a mixture chord:

- Adjust the quality of the Roman numeral (uppercase for major or lowercase for minor).
- If necessary, add a ° or ^{ø} to a lowercase Roman numeral for a diminished triad or seventh chord.

- If the root has been lowered, add a ♭ before the Roman numeral (for example, ♭VI for a chord built on ♭6̂).

For consistency, we will refer to the modal scale degrees as ♭3̂, ♭6̂, and ♭7̂ and the common mixture chords created with them as ♭III, ♭VI, and ♭VII, even when they are spelled with naturals (in sharp keys) instead of flats.

Example 26.3a shows triads built on each degree of an E♭ major scale. In part (b), the triads built on an E♭ natural minor scale are labeled as though they were mixture chords in E♭ major.

EXAMPLE 26.3: Roman numeral analysis of mixture chords

(a) Triads built on the E♭ major scale 🎧

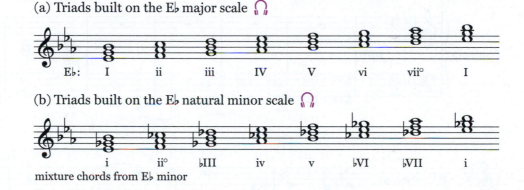

E♭:   I   ii   iii   IV   V   vi   vii°   I

(b) Triads built on the E♭ natural minor scale 🎧

        i   ii°   ♭III   iv   v   ♭VI   ♭VII   i

mixture chords from E♭ minor

Try it #1

For each major key below, identify the key signature of the parallel minor (give the number of sharps or flats), and list the modal scale degrees.

KEY	PARALLEL MINOR SIGNATURE	♭3̂	♭6̂	♭7̂
C major	3 flats			
E major				
B♭ major				
D major				
B major				

Minor keys offer fewer opportunities for these colorful and surprising changes of mode. Both versions of scale degrees 6̂ and 7̂ are routinely employed in harmonic progressions and melodic lines in minor; V and vii°, ostensibly from major, are commonplace, and minor v is used for a modal effect. Occasionally composers may transform the minor iv to IV, the major VI to vi, or the minor i to

I (known as a "Picardy third" when placed at an authentic cadence). But the term "mixture" almost always refers to a major-key passage.

One place where mixture chords are employed in minor is in a chromatic bass line, like the lament bass shown in Example 26.4. Various harmonizations of this bass are possible, but $\hat{7}$ (F♯) is usually set with V⁶ or V$^6_5$, ♭$\hat{7}$ (F) with v or a secondary dominant to IV or iv, and $\hat{6}$ (E) and ♭$\hat{6}$ (E♭) with IV⁶ and iv⁶, respectively.

EXAMPLE 26.4: Purcell, "When I am laid in earth," mm. 10–19

The Spelling and Function of Mixture Chords

Mixture chords have the same harmonic function and follow the same common-practice voice-leading guidelines as the diatonic chords they replace. Most typical in major keys are iv, iv⁶, ii°⁶, and ii°$^6_5$ in the predominant area, and i, ♭VI, iv, vii°7, and their inversions to expand the tonic area. Spell mixture chords as if they appeared in the parallel minor key. For example, to spell iv in C major, imagine iv in C minor: F–A♭–C. To spell ♭VI in F major, imagine VI in F minor: D♭–F–A♭, and so on.

Try it #2

Spell the mixture chords requested in the major keys below. Begin with the key signature, then add accidentals borrowed from the parallel minor key to spell each chord.

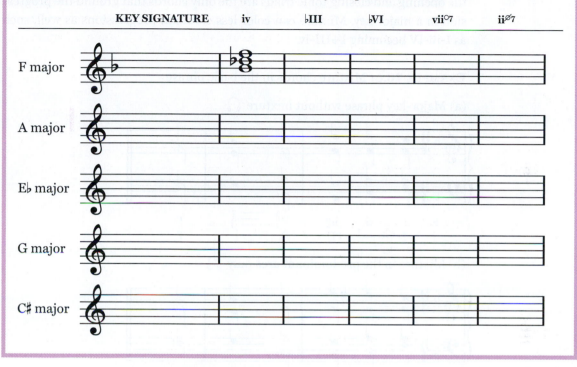

	KEY SIGNATURE	iv	♭III	♭VI	vii°7	ii∅7

When part-writing or composing progressions with mixture chords, follow the same principles for doubling and voice-leading as in the parallel minor:

- double the root in a root-position chord;
- double any stable chord member in a first-inversion chord (often the soprano or bass);
- double the bass in a second-inversion chord; and
- double the third (usually in the bass) of a diminished chord.

"Borrowed" tones may be doubled, and the chords follow the basic phrase model, T-PD-D-T. For example, place iv or ii° in the predominant area, where you would expect IV or ii to precede V. Write ♭VI as a prolongation of the tonic area or for a dramatic deceptive cadence: V-♭VI. Another common progression with ♭VI descends by thirds: I-♭VI-iv. Use ♭VII as a secondary dominant to ♭III, and ♭III as a secondary dominant to ♭VI.

Examples 26.5 and 26.6 demonstrate how a standard basic phrase progression in major may be chromatically enriched by including mixture chords. In part (b) of Example 26.5, a standard T-PD-D-T progression in F major, only the ii$^6_5$ has been altered, to ii$^{ø6}_5$ (as in Example 26.2). Part (c) features mixture in both the predominant and dominant areas, including a cadential $^6_4$ with $\flat\hat{3}$. In (d), the opening and closing tonic triads are the only chords that ground the progression in a major key. Mixture can color less common progressions as well, such as I–iii–IV becoming I–$\flat$III–iv.

EXAMPLE 26.5: Mixture chords in the basic phrase

(a) Major-key phrase without mixture

(b) Mixture in the predominant area only

(c) Mixture in the predominant and dominant areas

(d) Mixture permeating the phrase

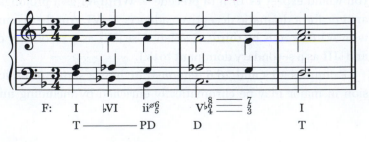

Example 26.6a features two common mixture chords: the diminished vii°7 chord and a deceptive cadence to ♭VI. This alteration of the leading-tone seventh chord (introduced in Chapter 17) softens the dissonance of the diatonic viiø7 and may be used in passages that do not otherwise feature mixture. Listen to the effect of the V7–♭VI cadence in part (a), rendered all the more surprising by the half-step motion in the bass and the major quality. The ♭VI chord always involves two alterations: ♭3̂ and ♭6̂.

Measure 2 of part (b) illustrates one potential voice-leading problem that may arise when a major triad is shifted through mixture to minor: a cross-relation results when a diatonic pitch (D4 in the alto) is altered chromatically in the next chord in a different voice (D♭3 in the bass). The voice-leading will be much smoother if the IV chord on beat 1 is placed in first inversion so that the bass (D) can move chromatically down from 6̂ to ♭6̂ to 5̂. Another alternative, shown in part (c), is to introduce mixture one beat earlier, with a root-position iv.

EXAMPLE 26.6: More progressions with mixture chords

(a) Mixture chords in a tonic expansion and deceptive cadence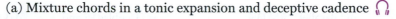

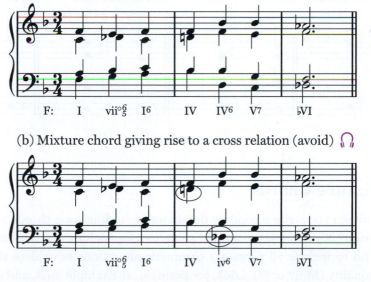

(b) Mixture chord giving rise to a cross relation (avoid)

(c) Mixture chords permeating the phrase, except for tonic triads

⌒ **KEY CONCEPT** Pay careful attention to altered tones that may create melodic augmented seconds in any voice. Where possible, keep the chromatic semitone (half-step motion between two notes with the same letter name) in a single voice to avoid cross relations, especially between the outer voices. As a general rule, in major keys resolve chromatic tones that arise from mixture down, since they are derived from lowered scale degrees: for example, ♭6̂-5̂.

Occasionally you will need to change the standard doubling guidelines for smooth voice-leading or to avoid parallels (see Example 26.7). When writing the progression V–♭VI or ♭VI-V, avoid doubling ♭6̂, since this creates parallel octaves moving 5̂–♭6̂ or 6̂ to ♭5̂ (part a) or a melodic augmented second ♭6̂ to 7̂ (part c). Remember also, when setting a stepwise bass, to move the upper voices in contrary motion to the bass where possible.

EXAMPLE 26.7: Doubling in V–♭VI or ♭VI-V 🎧

Tonicizing Mixture Chords

When you write secondary dominant or leading-tone chords to tonicize a mixture chord, follow the normal guidelines for spelling and resolution, but be careful to include all necessary chromatic alterations to achieve the correct chord quality (Mm7 or °7). Look, for example, at Example 26.8, and compare the two parts. Part (a) gives the singer's opening vocal phrase, a completely diatonic setting with a quiet accompaniment that depicts the peaceful imagery of the text. Part (b), however, turns to a passionate statement of love. In measures 54-55, the expected I-vi⁶ motion of measures 8-9 is transformed into I-♭VI⁶. This progression highlights the word "Augenzelt" (tabernacle of my eyes) and introduces the accidentals G♭ (♭3̂) and C♭ (♭6̂).

EXAMPLE 26.8: Schubert, "Du bist die Ruh"

(a) Mm. 8-11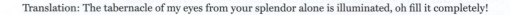

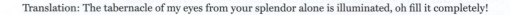

E♭: I   vi⁶   I⁶   V⁷   I

Translation: You are rest, the gentle peace.

(b) Mm. 54-65

E♭: I   ♭VI⁶   V/♭VI ⁴——³   ♭VI ⁹——⁸   V ⁴——³

V⁷/IV   IV   IV⁶   V ⁸⁶₄ ——— ⁷₃   I

Translation: The tabernacle of my eyes from your splendor alone is illuminated, oh fill it completely!

Consider how the harmonic analysis above can help shape a performance of this passage. First, the introduction of C♭ in the vocal line at measure 55 is an unexpected and dramatic moment. One way to interpret it is for the pianist and singer to hesitate here almost imperceptibly between measures 54 and 55, then continue in tempo—perhaps even pushing the tempo forward a bit until the climax of the phrase, lingering on the temporary tonicization of IV, setting the word "erhellt" (illuminated). This is not the end of the phrase, however: a phrase is defined by a cadence, which in this passage does not arrive until 64-65. You may want to lengthen the tension-filled silence in measure 61 slightly, before continuing the phrase in measure 62 with a startling change of mood, dynamic, tessitura, and harmonies. The gentle music concludes with not a hint of the dissonance and chromaticism (suspensions, mixture chords, and secondary dominants) that shaped the first half of the phrase.

Embellishing Tones

Mixture can also serve as an expressive embellishment in melodic lines, without necessarily borrowing whole chords from the parallel key. Sometimes melodic mixture foreshadows mixture chords or modulations occurring later in a work. Listen, for instance, to the passage in Example 26.9, an interlude that falls between verses of "Du bist die Ruh." Up to this point, Schubert's setting has been mostly diatonic, except for the chromatic ♭3 (G♭) in measure 16. In measure 26, he introduces ♭6 (C♭) as a passing tone, then emphasizes this chromatic embellishment by alternating between C♮ and C♭ in the following measures. These two chromatic notes prepare the mixture chords that arrive some twenty measures later—a type of chromatic "foreshadowing" that is a hallmark of Schubert's style.

EXAMPLE 26.9: Schubert, "Du bist die Ruh," mm. 26-30 🎧

Mixture and the Cadential $^6_4$ Chord

Listen now to two final excerpts by Schubert, from "Im Dorfe," shown in Examples 26.10 and 26.11. This song is highly colored by mixture and provides a good summary and review of mixture chords in major-key compositions.

Try it #3

Example 26.10 is partially analyzed with Roman numerals. Where there is a blank below the staff, provide the appropriate Roman numeral for the mixture chord.

EXAMPLE 26.10: Schubert, "Im Dorfe," mm. 31-41 🎧

D: V7   I   6

I   6

V^6_5/V $^4_3$

Translation: Bark me away, you watchdogs, don't let me rest in the hour of slumber. I am finished with all dreams, why should I linger among the sleepers?

In measures 39-40, a cadential $^6_4$ chord is prolonged by neighbor and passing tones. In a parallel passage, measures 44-46 (Example 26.11), the cadential $^6_4$ is colored by mixture. Add an accidental to the figures here to indicate that the sixth above the bass has been lowered: $\text{V}^{6-\flat6-5}_{4-\;4-3}$.

EXAMPLE 26.11: Schubert, "Im Dorfe," mm. 43-47

Intonation and Performance

If you are a singer or play an instrument (such as the violin) that requires careful attention to intonation, you may find that passages with mixture are more difficult to sing or play in tune. If that is the case, try drawing on a sight-singing strategy for intonation.

KEY CONCEPT To sing or play passages that include mixture pitches, use altered (movable-*do*) solfège syllables.

$\hat{3} \rightarrow \flat\hat{3}$: *mi* becomes *me*

$\hat{6} \rightarrow \flat\hat{6}$: *la* becomes *le*

$\hat{7} \rightarrow \flat\hat{7}$: *ti* becomes *te*

In Example 26.10, for instance, the melody of measures *36–38* is *re-me-fa-me-do* ($\hat{2}$-$\flat\hat{3}$-$\hat{4}$-$\flat\hat{3}$-$\hat{1}$); changing the syllable from *mi* to *me* can remind you of the narrow half step that mixture provides here. In contrast, in measure 39, the vocalist sings the diatonic *la*, not *le* ($\hat{6}$, not $\flat\hat{6}$) on "unter," despite the prolonged $\flat\hat{6}$ (B♭) in the piano the measure before. Careful distinction between diatonic and lowered scale degrees is essential for performing passages with mixture. Finally, to appreciate the implications of mixture for the interpretation of the text, you need to find a good translation (not a "singing translation," which may change the meaning slightly) if the song is not in English. Then check the meaning of any words set with chromatic inflection or mixture chords. In "Im Dorfe," the use of $\flat\hat{3}$ for the words "finished" and "dreams" may foreshadow the protagonist's unhappy end.

Mixture in Instrumental Music

In addition to highlighting important text in vocal music, mixture chords can create an analogous effect in instrumental music. Listen to a dramatic passage with pervasive mixture from a Mozart sonata (Example 26.12).

EXAMPLE 26.12: Mozart, Piano Sonata in D Major, mvt. 1, mm. 64–72 🎧

Here, as is typical, the mixture chords are mostly predominant harmonies in a transitional passage leading to V in measure 70. In measure 64, Mozart begins with a diatonic ii⁶, which is colored on beat 2 by B♭ (♭6̂), derived from mixture. The predominant harmony then intensifies to ii°⁶₅, leading to a fully diminished vii°⁴₃ (its quality results from the B♭5 on beat 4) that resolves to a minor tonic (with the introduction of F♮, ♭3̂). The following measures introduce ♭VI, iv, and ♭III as well. (Measure 69 introduces a new harmony that will be the topic of Chapter 27: ♭II⁶.)

Mixture and Modulation

Mixture can color longer spans of music when a piece modulates to the key of a mixture chord. Often composers introduce elements of mixture within the primary key to prepare for such a modulation. Look, for example, at the excerpt from Schubert's *Moment musical* in Example 26.13. After the repeat sign, Schubert introduces the modal scale degrees ♭3̂ (C♭) and ♭6̂ (F♭) in a transitional chromatic section (mm. 17-28) that leads to a new phrase clearly in E major (in m. 29), complete with change of key signature—an enharmonic respelling of ♭VI (F♭ major). Seemingly distant key relations, especially in Romantic-era pieces, may be considered tonicizations of respelled mixture chords—allowing the performer to read the score in a more comfortable key.

EXAMPLE 26.13: Schubert, *Moment musical* in A♭ Major, mm. 9-33

A♭:   I   ♭VI

A♭:   ♭VI = E: I

SUMMARY

Mixture chords expand composers' harmonic possibilities by drawing on pitches and harmonies from the parallel key. These unexpected chords are often used for dramatic effect.

- Mixture is more common in major keys, where $\flat\hat{3}$, $\flat\hat{6}$, or $\flat\hat{7}$ is borrowed from minor.

- Such chords often (but not always) have a predominant function.

- Roman numerals reflect the quality of the mixture chord; for consistency, we write $\flat$III, $\flat$VI, and $\flat$VII even in sharp keys.

- Mixture chords may be tonicized (e.g., V7/$\flat$III) or may be the goal of a modulation.

- Composers often foreshadow such a modulation by introducing the scale degrees of the new key earlier as embellishing tones (e.g., a $\flat\hat{6}$ neighbor to $\hat{5}$ foreshadows a modulation to the key of $\flat$VI).

Did You Know?

Text painting was not new with Classical- and Romantic-era music. Renaissance composers sometimes used melodic patterns and rhythms to represent bird cries or other natural sounds, or they might depict heaven or a word like "ascending" with a rising melodic line.

Certain Baroque composers employed chromaticism to convey pain or death (see, for example, Bach's settings of the Passion chorale "O Haupt voll Blut und Wunden"). Their chromatic alterations typically involved inflections within a melodic line and secondary dominants or diminished seventh chords, rather than mixture chords. Bach also used suspensions and other types of accented dissonance to help portray death.

Another feature of Baroque composition was the use of "nontempered" tunings, in which different keys sounded distinctive; thus the key or mode used by a composer was, on its own, enough to convey an emotion. The types of rhythms and meter selected by the composer were also an important key to the "affect," or mood, of the piece. For example, long-note durations (whole and half notes, indicating a slow tempo) might represent majesty or grandeur; short-note durations (indicating a quick tempo) might represent gaiety. The interplay of text and music is a rich area for exploration as you prepare vocal music for performance.

TERMS YOU SHOULD KNOW

borrowed chord	mixture	parallel key
lament bass	modal scale degree	Picardy third

QUESTIONS FOR REVIEW

1. What does the term "mixture chord" signify? Why are such chords sometimes called "borrowed chords"?
2. What are the most common mixture chords in major keys? Where in the phrase do they typically appear?
3. What are the most common mixture chords in minor keys, and where in the phrase do they typically appear?
4. Explain how to label mixture chords with Roman numerals.
5. What part-writing guidelines apply to mixture chords?
6. What alterations are needed in solfège syllables when singing mixture chords?
7. In a major-key piece for your own instrument, find a passage that includes mixture chords and bring it to class. (Hint: Look in Romantic-era pieces, and hunt for characteristic alterations such as $\flat\hat{3}$ and $\flat\hat{6}$.) Be prepared to analyze with Roman numerals and sing the melodic line on solfège syllables.

Know It? Show It!

Focus by working through the tutorials.

Learn with InQuizitive.

Apply what you've learned to complete the workbook assignments.

The Neapolitan Sixth and Augmented-Sixth Chords

Outline

Chromatic predominant chords

The Neapolitan sixth
- Spelling and voicing
- Voice-leading and resolution
- Intonation and performance
- Tonicizing the Neapolitan

Augmented-sixth chords
- Voice-leading, spelling, and resolution
- Italian, French, and German augmented sixths
- Approaches to augmented-sixth chords
- Aural identification and performance
- Less common spellings and voicings
- Secondary augmented-sixth chords

Overview

This chapter considers two new ways in which chromatic voice-leading can intensify motion toward the dominant. The chords created by this voice-leading—the Neapolitan sixth and several types of augmented-sixth chords—are among the most distinctive in tonal harmony.

Repertoire

Ludwig van Beethoven, Piano Sonata in C♯ Minor, Op. 27, No. 2 (*Moonlight*), mvt. 1

Frédéric Chopin, Prelude in C Minor, Op. 28, No. 20

Fanny Mendelssohn Hensel, "Nachtwanderer" ("Night Wanderer")

Jerome Kern and Oscar Hammerstein II, "Can't Help Lovin' Dat Man," from *Show Boat*

Wolfgang Amadeus Mozart
Dies irae (Day of Wrath), from *Requiem*
Piano Sonata in D Major, K. 284, mvt. 3
String Quartet in D Minor, K. 421, mvt. 3

Franz Schubert
"Der Doppelgänger" ("The Ghostly Double"), from *Schwanengesang* (*Swan Song*)
"Erlkönig" ("The Elf King")

John Philip Sousa, "The Stars and Stripes Forever"

Chromatic Predominant Chords

Among the mixture variants discussed in Chapter 26 was the replacement of $\hat{6}$ with $\flat\hat{6}$ in major keys. This substitution creates a new tendency tone, one with a strong pull to resolve down by half step: $\flat\hat{6}$-$\hat{5}$. In this chapter, we explore two new harmonies that share this $\flat\hat{6}$-$\hat{5}$ voice-leading. They are usually found in minor keys (where $\flat\hat{6}$ is the "normal" sixth scale degree) or in major-key passages that include elements of mixture. These harmonies—the Neapolitan sixth and a family of chords called augmented sixths—characteristically share the same position in the basic phrase: as chromatic predominant chords that intensify motion to V.

The Neapolitan Sixth

Listen to the serene first movement of Beethoven's *Moonlight* Sonata. Follow Example 27.1a as you listen, watching for accidentals that signal chromaticism.

EXAMPLE 27.1: Beethoven, *Moonlight* Sonata, mvt. 1

(a) Mm. 1-5

(b) Mm. 1-5 in block chords

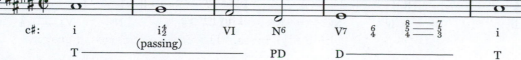

We can easily recognize the accidental on $\hat{7}$ in measure 4, creating the leading tone, but in measure 3 there is an unexpected accidental: D♮, the lowered supertonic. This pitch supports a major-quality triad (D♮-F♯-A), which appears in first inversion—a Neapolitan sixth chord, taking the place of the diatonic iv chord (F♯-A-C♯) or ii°6 chord (F♯-A-D♯).

> **KEY CONCEPT** A **Neapolitan sixth** is a chromatic predominant chord that includes ♭$\hat{2}$, $\hat{4}$, and ♭$\hat{6}$; it appears in minor keys, and in major keys with mixture. The Neapolitan substitutes for ii°6 or ii6 in the basic phrase, and like those chords usually appears in first inversion, though with a major quality: ♭II6.

In analysis, this chromatic harmony may also be labeled N6 in place of a Roman numeral (as in part b). (Another possible name for these chords is Phrygian II, after the distinctive half-step motion ♭$\hat{2}$ to $\hat{1}$ of that mode.) As with other mixture chords, use a flat to designate the lowered second scale degree, even in sharp key (as in the Beethoven example), where the actual accidental is a ♮. (The D♯ in m. 4 is a courtesy accidental, reminding performers that the D♮ has been canceled by the bar line.)

Spelling and Voicing

> **KEY CONCEPT** To spell Neapolitan sixths (Example 27.2):
>
> - find ♭$\hat{2}$, spell a major triad from this root, then place it in first inversion (part a); or
> - spell iv, then raise its fifth a minor second, to ♭$\hat{2}$ (part b). In major keys, remember to begin with the minor iv, from mixture, or alter $\hat{6}$ to ♭$\hat{6}$.
> - Doubling $\hat{4}$ (usually the bass) is the norm in four-part writing.
> - If the chord after the N6 is a cadential $^{6}_{4}$, place ♭$\hat{2}$ or $\hat{4}$ in the highest voice (part c); if ♭$\hat{6}$-$\hat{5}$ is placed above ♭$\hat{2}$-$\hat{1}$, this voicing invariably results in parallel fifths (part d).

EXAMPLE 27.2: Spelling N6

Try it #1

Spell N⁶ chords ($\hat{4}$–$\flat\hat{6}$–$\flat\hat{2}$) in the following keys. Provide the minor or major key signature, then write the chord with appropriate accidentals.

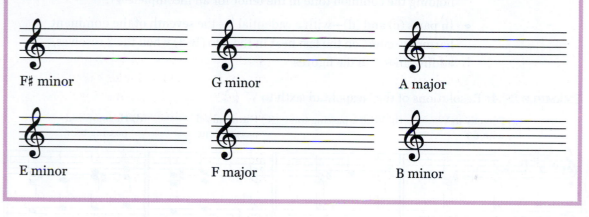

F♯ minor   G minor   A major

E minor   F major   B minor

Voice-Leading and Resolution

The progression in Example 27.1b clearly follows the basic phrase model, T-PD-D-T, with the Neapolitan chord filling a predominant function and moving directly to V. Follow the alto voice of the reduction to see how $\flat\hat{2}$ moves directly to the leading tone in measures 3–4, spanning the interval of a diminished third (D♮–B♯). Although augmented or diminished melodic intervals are generally avoided in common-practice voice-leading, composers permit the diminished third in the context of a N⁶ resolution (see Example 27.3a). Some composers smooth the motion from $\flat\hat{2}$ to $\hat{7}$ by inserting a passing tone to soften the effect: $\flat\hat{2}$–$\hat{1}$–$\hat{7}$ (part b). If the passing tone is harmonized, the prevailing choice is a cadential $^{6}_{4}$ chord (parts c and e) or vii°7/V (parts d and e).

EXAMPLE 27.3: Resolutions of the Neapolitan sixth 🎧

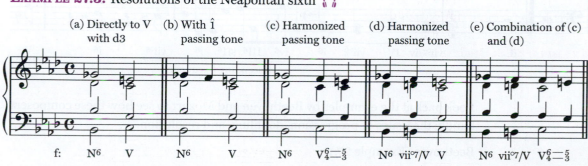

(a) Directly to V with d3   (b) With $\hat{1}$ passing tone   (c) Harmonized passing tone   (d) Harmonized passing tone   (e) Combination of (c) and (d)

f: N⁶   V   N⁶   V   N⁶   V$^{6}_{4}$–$^{5}_{3}$ N⁶   vii°7/V   V   N⁶   vii°7/V   V$^{6}_{4}$–$^{5}_{3}$

It is also possible to resolve the N6 to a V7. The voice-leading (Example 27.4) is quite similar; compare with Example 27.3:

- In parts (a) and (b), G3 in the dominant harmony is replaced with Bb3, holding the common tone in the tenor for an incomplete V7.

- In parts (c) and (d)—with a cadential $\frac{6}{4}$—the seventh of the dominant harmony enters on the last beat in the alto (Bb3) when the $\frac{6}{4}$ resolves, adding an 8-7 to the figures.

EXAMPLE 27.4: Resolutions of the Neapolitan sixth to V7

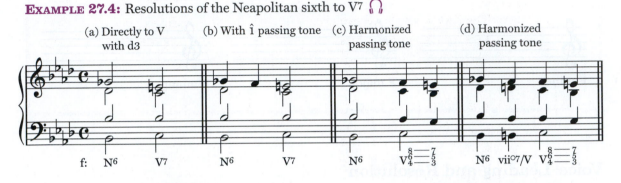

(a) Directly to V   (b) With î passing tone   (c) Harmonized   (d) Harmonized
    with d3   passing tone   passing tone

f: N6   V7   N6   V7   N6   V$\frac{6}{4}$—$\frac{5}{3}$ N6   vii°7/V V$\frac{6}{4}$—$\frac{7}{3}$

Now listen to a minor-key passage from a set of Mozart variations (Example 27.5); the excerpt comes from the harmonically unstable beginning of the second half of this binary form. In measures 129-130, a descending $\frac{6}{3}$ sequence passes from the subdominant to the leading-tone harmony. Instead of a ii°6, Mozart has used a Neapolitan sixth (Eb-G-Bb, labeled bII6 to show its place in the $\frac{6}{3}$ sequence) as a colorful variant.

EXAMPLE 27.5: Mozart, Piano Sonata in D Major, mvt. 3, mm. 127-131

d: vii°7/iv IV vii°$\frac{6}{5}$ i6   iv6 III6 bII6 i6   vii°6   i6   V
                                                                                            (HC)
                                              descending $\frac{6}{3}$ sequence

Look back at the examples by Beethoven and Mozart to see how these composers handle the issues of progression, doubling, and resolution.

Beethoven (Example 27.1):

- In measure 3, the Neapolitan is preceded by a VI (a tonic expansion).
- The third (bass) of the Neapolitan chord ($\hat{4}$) is doubled.
- $b\hat{2}$ moves down to $\hat{7}$ in the dominant harmony.

Mozart (Example 27.5):

- In measure 129, the Neapolitan is preceded by a string of $\frac{6}{3}$ chords.
- $\hat{4}$ is doubled in the left hand in octaves, but there are only three voice-leading strands (this is an octave duplication of the bass note, a sonority doubling).
- $\flat\hat{2}$ moves down to $\hat{1}$ within the sequence and then to $\hat{7}$ on the downbeat of the next measure.

SUMMARY

The N^6 (or $\flat$II^6) typically appears as a predominant near a cadence in minor keys, or in major-key passages with mixture chords. It is preceded by any harmony that would normally lead to a PD harmony, such as

- another PD harmony;
- a tonic harmony, tonic substitute, or tonic expansion; or
- a string of parallel $\frac{6}{3}$ chords.

It resolves

- directly to V or V^7,
- to V or V^7 through a cadential $\frac{6}{4}$, or
- to V through a vii$^{\circ 7}$/V (with or without a cadential $\frac{6}{4}$).

Both tendency tones normally resolve down: $\flat\hat{6}$ to $\hat{5}$ and $\flat\hat{2}$ (usually through a passing tone $\hat{1}$) to $\hat{7}$. Avoid moving from $\flat\hat{2}$ to $\natural\hat{2}$; this is only permitted in an inner voice, not in the soprano.

Some composers will diverge from these guidelines. For an example, listen to the dramatic excerpt from Mozart's *Requiem* shown in Example 27.6, or sing it with your class. The text, taken from the Requiem Mass (Mass for the Dead), depicts a wrathful Judgment Day when, according to Christian texts, sinners will be punished and the world destroyed. Mozart represents the day of wrath with agitated string arpeggiation, full chorus, a minor key, diminished seventh sonorities, and colorful Neapolitan harmonies—with $\flat\hat{2}$ prominently voiced in the soprano line (mm. 37 and 39).

In this passage, Mozart prolongs the predominant area in measures 37–39 by means of parallel $\frac{6}{3}$ chords that extend from one Neapolitan chord to the next. The $\flat\hat{2}$ (E$\flat$) in measure 39 resolves normally, down through a harmonized passing tone $\hat{1}$ to $\hat{7}$ in the dominant harmony, but because of the doubled $\flat\hat{6}$ (B$\flat$) in the choral parts, Mozart must resolve one of them irregularly in order to avoid parallel octaves. His choice is to have the tenor leap up a perfect fifth (on "dis-cus").

The first Neapolitan of this passage (m. 37) shows another unconventional doubling, with ♭2̂ in the soprano and tenor. This results in unusual voice-leading in the soprano, which moves upward by an augmented second (E♭ to F♯). Perhaps Mozart felt that the A2 in measure 37 and the tenor leap to a high F4 in measure 39 would contribute to the text's overall sense of despair and frenzy. In your own writing, conform to the guidelines for doubling and voice-leading unless you have a good reason for doing otherwise.

KEY CONCEPT When writing the N⁶ chord, double 4̂, the bass note, when the chord appears in its characteristic first inversion. Other doublings are found occasionally, but they result in leaps (as in the Mozart example, m. 39) or may cause parallels or other voice-leading issues. If ♭2̂ is doubled, it moves to ♮2̂ in an inner voice only, not in the soprano.

EXAMPLE 27.6: Mozart, Dies irae, from *Requiem*, mm. 34–40

Translation: When the judge comes to adjudicate all things strictly.

Intonation and Performance

When performing passages with Neapolitan sixth chords, keep the following issues in mind. Since ♭$\hat{2}$ lies outside the diatonic major and minor scales, and since the Neapolitan relies on its major quality for its identity, correct tuning should be a primary concern. If you sing the soprano line of the Mozart example with solfège syllables, you will need to inflect three of them: *ti* for $\hat{7}$, *ra* for ♭$\hat{2}$ (*re* lowered a half step), and *mi* for $\hat{3}$.

Try it #2

Write the correct solfège syllables or scale-degree numbers for the soprano line of Example 27.5 in the blanks below.

m. 34	m. 35	m. 36	m. 37	m. 38	m. 39	m. 40
ti *fa* ___	___ ___	___ ___	___ ___	___ ___	___ ___	___ ___
$\hat{7}$ $\hat{4}$						

The soprano's diminished fifth $\hat{7}$–$\hat{4}$ (*ti-fa*) in measure 34 of Example 27.6 can be somewhat difficult to tune, but probably more challenging is the augmented second in measure 37, ♭$\hat{2}$–$\hat{3}$ (*ra-mi*). It is sometimes helpful to exaggerate the altered ♭$\hat{2}$ (*ra*) very low, and think $\hat{3}$ (*mi*) very high. You might even employ a darker tone color for the lowered pitches and brighter for the raised pitches. Such exaggerations hold true especially in ensemble singing and playing, where this line is crucial in tuning the chord qualities.

Tonicizing the Neapolitan

The Neapolitan harmony can be tonicized, either by its own secondary dominant or by an extended progression in the ♭II key area; the secondary dominant is diatonic in minor keys (VI) or available by mixture in major keys (♭VI). Listen to the passage from Schubert's "Erlkönig" given in Example 27.7, and follow the Roman numeral analysis beneath the score.

EXAMPLE 27.7: Schubert, "Erlkönig," mm. 115–123 🎧

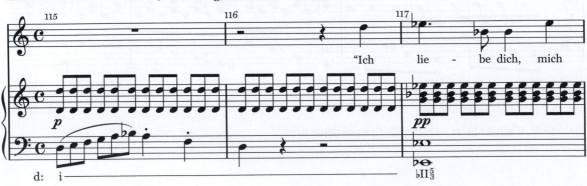

Translation (sung by the Elf King): "I love you, I am tempted by your beautiful form; and if you are not willing, I will use force."

Measures 117-119 tonicize ♭II, with this harmonic area prolonged by the secondary vii°7. This Neapolitan, though, appears in root position—a common occurrence when the Neapolitan is tonicized. Consider how the harmonies in this passage correspond with the meaning of the text. The Elf King is a sinister creature who tries to entice a young boy to his death, while the boy and his father ride on horseback through a dark forest. Schubert's tonicization of the Neapolitan coincides with the otherworldly character and falsely affectionate words of the Elf King, while the return to tonic signals a return to the reality of the situation: if the boy will not go willingly, the Elf King will take him by force.

KEY CONCEPT When you tonicize ♭II:

1. **Think temporarily in the ♭II key area in order to remember the correct accidentals (♭II is usually in root position when tonicized, and ♭$\hat{2}$ may be doubled).**

2. **Double-check that secondary dominant or leading-tone chords have the correct quality (V7 or vii°7).**

3. **Follow the regular guidelines for part-writing and dissonance resolution.**

Augmented-Sixth Chords

Listen to Variation VII from Mozart's sonata, and pay special attention to the cadence in measures 122-123 (Example 27.8).

EXAMPLE 27.8: Mozart, Piano Sonata in D Major, mvt. 3, mm. 122-123 🎧

With the predominant IV⁶ chord on the third beat of measure 122, we expect motion from IV⁶ to V—a typical half cadence. At the last moment, though, Mozart raises $\hat{4}$ to $\sharp\hat{4}$ (G to G♯), resolving in the next measure to $\hat{5}$ (A). This chromatic alteration ($\sharp\hat{4}$-$\hat{5}$) should be familiar from your study of the V7/V and vii°7/V chords. He also lowers $\hat{6}$ to $\flat\hat{6}$ (B♮ to B♭)—a familiar operation from modal mixture—which then moves down by half step to $\hat{5}$.

These chromatic alterations are what define the predominant family of chords called **augmented-sixth chords**, so called because the harmonic interval from $\flat\hat{6}$ up to $\sharp\hat{4}$ is an augmented sixth. The particular chord on beat 4 of the Mozart example—$\flat\hat{6}$, $\sharp\hat{4}$, and $\hat{1}$ (*le*, *fi*, and *do*), resolving to V by half-step motion outward ($\sharp\hat{4}$-$\hat{5}$ in an upper voice and $\flat\hat{6}$-$\hat{5}$ in the bass)—is called an **Italian augmented-sixth chord**, labeled It⁶.

⌒ **KEY CONCEPT** To identify an A6 chord quickly, look for $\flat\hat{6}$-$\hat{5}$ in the bass, then confirm by checking for $\sharp\hat{4}$-$\hat{5}$ in an upper voice.

Try it #3

Identify the characteristic tendency tones of the augmented-sixth sonorities in the following keys.

KEY	$\flat\hat{6}$	$\sharp\hat{4}$	KEY	$\flat\hat{6}$	$\sharp\hat{4}$
A minor	F	D♯	E major	____	____
C♯ minor	____	____	B minor	____	____
F major	____	____	G♯ minor	____	____

In measures 124-127 of the Mozart sonata (Example 27.9), the key has changed from D minor to A minor (the minor dominant). The chord in measure 125 contains $\flat\hat{6}$, $\hat{1}$, and $\sharp\hat{4}$ (F, A, and D$\sharp$) of the Italian augmented sixth plus $\flat\hat{3}$ (C). This sonority is known as the **German augmented-sixth chord**, labeled Gr^6. As expected, D$\sharp$5 resolves up by half step to E5 in measure 126, and F3 moves down by half step to E3. As in this example, the Gr^6 usually resolves to an embellished V$^{6-5}_{4-3}$ rather than directly to V: the left-hand triad (F-A-C) would produce audible parallel fifths if it were to move directly to V (E-G$\sharp$-B). Scale degree $\flat\hat{3}$ (C) serves as a common tone between the two.

EXAMPLE 27.9: Mozart, Piano Sonata in D Major, mvt. 3, mm. 124-127

Sometimes $\hat{2}$ (*re*) is added to the $\flat\hat{6}$, $\hat{1}$, and $\sharp\hat{4}$ of the Italian sixth, making the sonority known as the **French augmented-sixth chord** (Fr^6). Look, for example, at the second chord in measure 6 below.

EXAMPLE 27.10: Chopin, Prelude in C Minor, mm. 5-6

Like the A6 in Example 27.7, this Fr^6 is approached by a descending chromatic bass line, and the chord immediately preceding it is a tonic triad (with chromatic passing tone in the bass). The Fr^6 resolves as expected to V, with F$\sharp$ in the alto moving up to G, A$\flat$ in the bass resolving down to G, and $\hat{2}$ (D) serving as a common tone.

The three types of augmented-sixth chords are summarized in Example 27.11. All three share $\flat\hat{6}$-$\hat{5}$ in the bass and $\sharp\hat{4}$-$\hat{5}$ in an upper voice when they resolve to V. All chords include $\hat{1}$; in addition, the Gr^6 contains $\flat\hat{3}$ (part b) and the Fr^6 $\hat{2}$ (part c).

EXAMPLE 27.11: Augmented-sixth chords 🎧

Occasionally, composers will write all three types in quick succession to intensify motion to the dominant at a cadence—usually in the order Italian, French, German. Example 27.12, though, shows the opposite order: here, the "world tour" of augmented-sixth chords heralds the return of the opening theme (m. 29) in a sectional rounded binary form.

EXAMPLE 27.12: Mozart, String Quartet in D Minor, mvt. 3, mm. 27- 31 🎧

In Classical style, these chords are usually positioned to emphasize the arrival of a particularly significant dominant harmony. Their dramatic sound is more freely employed in Romantic-era compositions, but even then the sound is saved for dramatic points. The A6 sonority is not often heard in pre-Classical-era works or in popular music, though there are some examples. Look at the approach to the cadence in measure 33 of Example 27.13, an excerpt from "Can't Help Lovin' Dat Man." Measure 32 features the now-familiar tendency tones of the Gr6: C♭ (♭$\hat{6}$) in the bass, resolving down to B♭ ($\hat{5}$), and A♮ (♯$\hat{4}$) in the alto. In this freer style, the ♯$\hat{4}$ does not resolve up to $\hat{5}$, but the augmented-sixth sound is still a distinctive intensification of the motion to V. Interestingly, the chord symbol given above the staff is B♭7, an enharmonic respelling of the A6 chord.

EXAMPLE 27.13: Kern and Hammerstein, "Can't Help Lovin' Dat Man," mm. 31–33

Voice-Leading, Spelling, and Resolution

As we have seen, all varieties of augmented-sixth chords share the same pattern of voice-leading to V: #$\hat{4}$ up to $\hat{5}$ in an upper voice, and ♭$\hat{6}$ down to $\hat{5}$ in the bass (see Example 27.10). In addition, these chords include $\hat{1}$, which usually resolves down to the leading tone. Think of the two tendency tones of the A6 as derived from two ideas we have already studied: #$\hat{4}$ up to $\hat{5}$ captures the temporary leading tone of secondary dominants to V, while ♭$\hat{6}$ down to $\hat{5}$ derives from mixture. Because of these two chromatic elements, A6 chords have the strongest tendency of any predominant harmony to move to V; they usually go directly to V (in the case of Gr⁶, to V$^{6-5}_{4-3}$), without intervening chords.

For the bass-line resolution pattern (♭$\hat{6}$ to $\hat{5}$) to work in major keys, $\hat{6}$ must be lowered to ♭$\hat{6}$. Two accidentals are therefore necessary in major keys, as opposed to only one (#$\hat{4}$) in minor keys. One familiar example of an augmented sixth in a major key is the introduction to "The Stars and Stripes Forever." Listen to Example 27.14 to hear how Sousa prepares for the #$\hat{4}$ and ♭$\hat{6}$.

EXAMPLE 27.14: Sousa, "The Stars and Stripes Forever," mm. 1–4

First Sousa expands the tonic area with a vi chord, then introduces an element of mixture by transforming the submediant harmony to ♭VI; this prepares the bass motion of the augmented sixth. In the soprano, he introduces a chromatic ascent that naturally leads through #$\hat{4}$ to $\hat{5}$.

SUMMARY

Like the N⁶, augmented-sixth chords usually appear in minor keys, or in major-key passages with mixture chords.

- All share ♭$\hat{6}$, $\hat{1}$, and ♯$\hat{4}$, and resolve to V.

- All share the same voice-leading pattern: ♯$\hat{4}$ up to $\hat{5}$ in an upper voice, and ♭$\hat{6}$ down to $\hat{5}$ in the bass.

- Consider the ♯$\hat{4}$-$\hat{5}$/♭$\hat{6}$-$\hat{5}$ outer-voice pattern as the scaffold upon which to build any of the three types: Italian, French, or German.

Italian, French, and German Augmented Sixths

KEY CONCEPT To write an A6 progression to V in four voices (Example 27.15):

1. In the resolution chord, place $\hat{5}$ in the bass and an upper voice (the soprano is a characteristic voicing but not required), leaving an empty space before it for the augmented sixth (part a).

2. In the empty space, write the two tendency tones leading to $\hat{5}$: ♭$\hat{6}$-$\hat{5}$ in the bass and ♯$\hat{4}$-$\hat{5}$ in the upper voice (part b). In a major key, add the correct accidental to lower $\hat{6}$ to ♭$\hat{6}$.

3. Add $\hat{1}$ to one of the inner voices (part c).

4. Add a fourth note, following these guidelines (part d):

   - For It⁶, double $\hat{1}$.

   - For Fr⁶, add $\hat{2}$ (an augmented fourth above the bass note).

   - For Gr⁶, add ♭$\hat{3}$ (a perfect fifth above the bass note). In major keys, add an accidental to lower $\hat{3}$ to ♭$\hat{3}$.

EXAMPLE 27.15: Spelling augmented-sixth chords 🎧

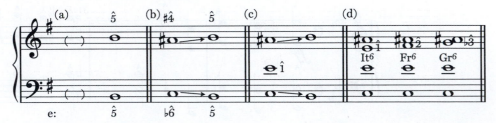

One way to remember the augmented-sixth chord abbreviations is to think of the geography of these countries in relation to the scale degrees added: moving from south to north, you have Italy ($\hat{1}$), France ($\hat{2}$), and Germany (♭$\hat{3}$). Another way is to memorize the figured bass associated with each chord: It⁶, Fr$^{4}_{3}$, and Gr$^{6}_{5}$.

Figures help remind you that the Fr$\frac{4}{3}$, for example, has a third ($\hat{1}$) and a fourth ($\hat{2}$) above the bass, in addition to the augmented sixth, and that the Gr$\frac{6}{5}$ has a perfect fifth. Keep in mind that these numbers represent figured bass, not inversion symbols. Augmented-sixth chords function as voice-leading chords, not as inversions of an "altered chord." Don't attempt to stack the thirds to find a "root."

Try it #4

Spell the specified A6 chords in three or four voices in the keys indicated. Place #$\hat{4}$ in the highest voice and $\flat\hat{6}$ in the lowest. If it helps to write the octave $\hat{5}$ after the augmented sixth, as shown below, do so.

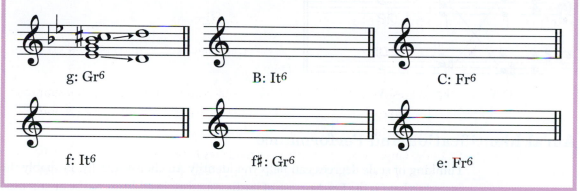

g: Gr^6 B: It^6 C: Fr^6

f: It^6 f#: Gr^6 e: Fr^6

Approaches to Augmented-Sixth Chords

Augmented-sixth chords are generally preceded by harmonies from the tonic or predominant area of the basic phrase, as in Example 27.16. A common approach is one that features $\flat\hat{6}$—either iv^6 or VI—accompanied by the alteration of $\hat{4}$ to #$\hat{4}$. The iv^6-V motion should be familiar from the Phrygian cadence.

EXAMPLE 27.16: Predominant approaches to augmented-sixth chords 🎧

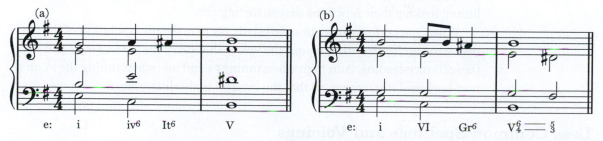

Another elegant way to introduce these pitches is by means of a chromatic voice exchange, where $\hat{6}$ and $\hat{4}$ exchange with $\flat\hat{6}$ and #$\hat{4}$ (Example 27.17a). This voice exchange also works if one of the chromatic elements is present in the first chord through mode mixture (part b) or the use of a secondary dominant (part c).

EXAMPLE 27.17: Predominant approaches with chromatic voice exchange 🎧

E: I⁶   IV   Fr⁶   V

E: I   iv   Fr⁶   V

e: V⁶₅/V   Fr⁶   V

Aural Identification and Performance

Thinking of scale degrees can help you identify A6 chords aurally. Probably the easiest to hear is the Fr⁶, because of its dissonances: in addition to the augmented sixth between ♭$\hat6$ and ♯$\hat4$ and the augmented fourth (or diminished fifth) between $\hat1$ and ♯$\hat4$, you can also listen for the augmented fourth between ♭$\hat6$ and $\hat2$. Another way to identify the Fr⁶ is from the whole step (or minor seventh) between $\hat1$ and $\hat2$.

To distinguish the It⁶ and Gr⁶, listen carefully for ♭$\hat3$ (the perfect fifth above the bass), which indicates the Gr⁶. The Gr⁶ may also be recognized by its similarity in sound to a dominant seventh chord (with which it is enharmonic). Still, although the sound is similar, the characteristic pattern of resolution for the ♯$\hat4$ and ♭$\hat6$ in the augmented sixth is quite different from the dominant seventh resolution, making their functions easy to distinguish.

When you perform an augmented sixth, try to make the resolution of the tendency tones clear by bringing out the voices that carry the ♯$\hat4$-$\hat5$ (*fi-sol*) and ♭$\hat6$-$\hat5$ (*le-sol*) voice-leading. Aim high when tuning ♯$\hat4$ and low when tuning the ♭$\hat6$ on a non-keyboard instrument, so that the interval is absolutely clear.

Less Common Spellings and Voicings

Occasionally you might see an augmented-sixth chord in a less characteristic voicing—with ♭$\hat6$ above ♯$\hat4$, creating a diminished third rather than an augmented sixth. Listen, for example, to the final cadence of Hensel's "Nachtwanderer" (Example 27.18).

EXAMPLE 27.18: Hensel, "Nachtwanderer," mm. 34–39 🎧

Translation: My singing is a cry, a cry only from dreams.

Since the chord in question (in m. 37) appears on "Träumen" (dreams), its dissonant ambiguity may be an element of text painting. The analyst who tries to stack this chord in thirds gets B♮–D♭–F–A♭—not a familiar type of seventh chord, given its diminished third from B♮ to D♭. Instead, recognize the familiar elements of the augmented sixth in this F major context: B♮ is #$\hat{4}$, and D♭ is ♭$\hat{6}$. Since the chord also includes $\hat{1}$ and ♭$\hat{3}$, it is called a **German diminished-third chord** (Gr°3), normally approached by a chromatic voice exchange (as marked in the example). In measure 35, Hensel elegantly prepares all the chromatic elements of the diminished-third chord by introducing D♭ as a chromatic passing tone in the bass, and B♮ and A♭ as the root and seventh of a vii°7/V; she then maintains ♭$\hat{3}$ as an element of mixture on the word "Rufen" (cry) in measure 36.

For voice-leading purposes, composers may sometimes spell the Gr6 in major keys with a doubly augmented fourth above the bass, rather than a perfect fifth (that is, with #$\hat{2}$ instead of ♭$\hat{3}$), as in Example 27.19a. In analysis, it is easier simply to call this chord a Gr6 rather than create a new name and symbol. Another possible chord is ♭$\hat{6}$-$\hat{7}$-$\hat{2}$-#$\hat{4}$—the so-called half-diminished augmented-sixth chord, where $\hat{7}$ substitutes for $\hat{1}$ of a Fr6 (part b). In these and related chords, the augmented sixth usually resolves as expected, and the other voices move by step to members of the next chord.

EXAMPLE 27.19: Other types of augmented-sixth chords 🎧

Secondary Augmented-Sixth Chords

For special effect, composers may apply the voice-leading principles of the augmented sixth to î and the tonic triad, lending the A6 a kind of secondary function. Label this type of chord as though it were a secondary dominant: for example, Gr⁶/i (German sixth of i). Here, the characteristic voice-leading is ♭2̂-î in the bass and 7̂-î in an upper voice. The augmented-sixth interval is now from ♭2̂-7̂ rather than ♭6̂ to #4̂. All varieties of the "secondary" A6 (It, Fr, Gr) include 4̂; the French adds 5̂, and the German adds ♭6̂. Look at Example 27.20, from Schubert's song "Der Doppelgänger," to see how this voice-leading chord operates (m. 41).

EXAMPLE 27.20: Schubert, "Der Doppelgänger," mm. 36–43 🎧

Translation: [I shudder] when I see his face—the moon shows me my own form.

SUMMARY

The Neapolitan ($\flat$II^6) and the family of augmented-sixth chords share a number of important characteristics:

- They typically appear in minor keys, or in major-key passages with mixture.

- They share $\flat\hat{6}$ as an important scale-degree component.

- They are predominant chords that intensify motion to V through chromaticism.

- In addition to $\flat\hat{6}$, N^6 includes $\hat{4}$ (usually in the bass) and $\flat\hat{2}$; $\flat\hat{2}$ resolves down to $\hat{7}$ of the dominant harmony, often via a passing $\hat{1}$.

- In addition to $\flat\hat{6}$ (usually in the bass), all A6 chords feature $\sharp\hat{4}$ and $\hat{1}$; $\flat\hat{6}$ and $\sharp\hat{4}$ resolve by contrary motion to $\hat{5}$.

Did You Know?

The geographical names for augmented-sixth chords first appear in an 1806 treatise by John Callcott called *A Musical Grammar* (London). The chords were named according to Callcott's perception of the national character of the Italians ("elegance"), French ("feebleness"), and Germans ("strength"). Most treatises from that time, however, do not refer to these terms when they describe augmented-sixth sonorities. The origin of "Neapolitan" is likewise unclear; some believe it arose from the use of this sonority by eighteenth-century opera composers centered in Naples, but the chord appears in earlier works as well, including some by non-Italian composers.

TERMS YOU SHOULD KNOW

augmented-sixth chord (A6)   Fr^6 It^6

diminished-third chord   Gr^6 Neapolitan sixth (N^6)

QUESTIONS FOR REVIEW

1. Why are the Neapolitan and augmented-sixth chords often found in minor-key pieces or major-key pieces that employ mixture?
2. Where are Neapolitan chords typically found in a phrase? What is their function?
3. In what voicing of N^6 are parallel fifths a possibility, and how do you avoid them?
4. What chords may precede a N^6? What chords usually follow it?
5. Under what conditions might Neapolitan chords appear in root position? What is doubled if the N^6 is in root position?

6. Where are augmented-sixth chords usually found in a phrase? What is their function?

7. Which elements of the augmented-sixth chords are shared with secondary-dominant-function chords to V? In major keys, which elements are shared with mixture chords?

8. Which A6 may lead to parallel fifths, and how are they avoided?

9. What chords may precede an A6? What chords usually follow it?

10. In music for your own instrument, find one N^6 and at least two different types of A6 chords (solo-line instrumentalists will need to examine both melody and accompaniment). How does the chord color the passage in question? How might you play the passage to bring out this unusual chord color?

Know It? Show It!

Focus by working through the tutorials.

Learn with InQuizitive.

Apply what you've learned to complete the workbook assignments.

28

Vocal Forms

Overview

We now consider chromatic harmonies as employed in art song, opera, and oratorio. We examine standard formal designs for solo vocal works, and see how composers use harmony and motivic development to realize their interpretation of the text.

Repertoire

Johann Sebastian Bach, "Schafe können sicher weiden" ("Sheep may safely graze"), from Cantata No. 208

Gabriel Fauré, "Après un rêve" ("After a Dream")

George Frideric Handel, "Thy rebuke hath broken his heart," from *Messiah*

Wolfgang Amadeus Mozart
"Quanto duolmi, Susanna" ("How I grieve, Susanna," recitative) and "Voi, che sapete" ("You who know," aria), from *The Marriage of Figaro*

Franz Schubert
"Erlkönig" ("The Elf King")
"Morgengruss" ("Morning Greeting"), from *Die schöne Müllerin* (*The Fair Maid of the Mill*)

Clara Schumann, "Liebst du um Schönheit" ("If You Love for Beauty")

Robert Schumann, "Im wunderschönen Monat Mai" ("In the Lovely Month of May"), from *Dichterliebe* (*The Poet's Love*)

Outline

Three-part vocal forms
- Aria da capo
- Other ternary arias
- Recitatives

Text and song structure
- Strophic form
- Text painting
- Analysis and interpretation

Other vocal forms
- Modified strophic form
- Through-composed form
- French mélodie

Three-Part Vocal Forms

Aria da capo

Most songs divide clearly into sections, usually (though not always) corresponding with the division of the text into verses, or strophes. One common design divides a song into three parts, marked by changes in accompanimental pattern, key, and/or contrasting melody. **Three-part** (or **ternary**) vocal forms are typically arranged **A B A′** or **A A B**. In Baroque arias, ternary design usually takes the form of a da capo aria.

KEY CONCEPT An **aria** is an art song situated within an opera, oratorio, or cantata. In a Baroque **da capo aria**, an **A B A** design, the final **A** section is not written out again. Rather (as mentioned in Chapter 23), performers are instructed to return "da capo" (to the beginning) or "dal segno" (to the sign) and repeat the first section until they come to a fermata marking the end. The repeat of the **A** section may be abbreviated to include only the opening instrumental introduction or only a portion of the **A** section.

Listen to the opening of an aria from a cantata by Bach (Example 28.1). Da capo arias like this one usually feature a solo instrument (or instruments) in the introduction and in interludes between the singer's phrases. The solo instrument often has its own thematic material, referred to as the **ritornello**, which may foreshadow the vocal line or play in counterpoint with it. The **B** section is usually in a contrasting key (the dominant or a closely related key) or may modulate through several keys.

Part (a) of the example gives the B♭ major ritornello, played by two flutes or recorders, and the opening vocal phrase, accompanied by continuo (here, an unfigured bass to be performed by cello and keyboard). As you can see from the anthology score, this section ends with a PAC in measure 21. Then the **B** section, in G minor, tonicizes C minor for two phrases before returning to G minor; the section ends with a modulation to F (part b) to prepare for the return of the opening B♭ major section. Note the *Da Capo* marking below the staff in the last measure, telling the performers to return to the "head" (beginning) and play to the fermata (or *Fine*) at the end of the repeated **A** section. The score in your anthology is a modern arrangement that instead uses a *Dal Segno* sign, meaning return to the sign (m. 6) and play to the *Fine* (m. 21).

EXAMPLE 28.1: Bach, "Schafe können sicher weiden"

(a) Mm. 1–8, opening ritornello 🎧

Translation: Sheep may safely graze, where a good shepherd keeps watch.

(b) Mm. 37-41, end of **B** section and return to **A**

Translation: [One can] feel peace and tranquility, and that which makes countries fortunate.

Other Ternary Arias

We turn now to an example of ternary form in a vocal work from the Classical era: Mozart's "Voi, che sapete" (anthology). Listen to the whole aria to determine the measure numbers in each formal unit (the **A** section should be familiar from previous chapters).

Try it #1

Write the measure numbers spanned for each section of "Voi, che sapete."

	Introduction	**A**	**B**	**A'**
Measures:	_____	_____	_____	_____

As is the case here, the three parts of a ternary form may not be equal in length, and section **B** typically explores a contrasting tonal area or may be tonally unstable. In Mozart's aria, the **A** section is a tonally stable three-phrase period in B♭ major. **B**, longer and less stable, moves first to F major (m. 21) and then is modally inflected to F minor (m. 35) as a means to tonicize A♭ major (m. 37) before passing through C minor to cadence in G minor (mm. 51-52). This section ends with an ascending sequential passage (Example 28.2) that leads to the tonic B♭ and the **A′** section in measure 62.

EXAMPLE 28.2: Mozart, "Voi, che sapete," mm. 52-63, end of **B** section 🎧

Translation: I sigh and moan without wanting to, throb and tremble without knowing why, I find no peace night or day, yet I enjoy languishing this way.

While Lorenzo da Ponte's words for the character Cherubino consist of rhyming couplets (aabbccdd, etc.) and no return of the opening text, Mozart made the decision to repeat the opening "Voi, che sapete" to create a rounded form. The first two lines of text are set in the **A** and **A′** sections, with the remaining twelve lines forming the **B** section. These first two lines are addressed to the other characters ("You who know what love is, ladies . . ."), while the remaining lines are a first-person description of Cherubino's tremulous feelings ("I sigh," "throb," "tremble," etc.). These agitated lines set the context for the modulatory **B** section and its sequential ending, which climbs ever higher as his excitement grows. **Text painting** is abundant here with the rising line, sixteenth-note rapid-fire text, short subphrases to suggest breathlessness, and the poignant D♭ on "languir" (languishing) over a diminished seventh chord. In sum, three-part vocal forms vary quite a bit in terms of the dimensions, variation, tonal stability, and degree of contrast between sections—much of this hinges on the historical era, the text, and, of course, the composer's interpretation.

Recitatives

Cherubino's aria in *The Marriage of Figaro* is preceded by a recitative sung by a trio of characters (the Countess, Susanna, and Cherubino) as a conversation.

KEY CONCEPT A recitative is a relatively short vocal movement, normally paired with an aria, written in a style intended to simulate speech. Recitatives feature a quick declamation of text over sustained chords, and often modulate—sometimes rapidly and repeatedly—to underscore the drama of the text or to provide a transition to the key of the aria. They are often **syllabic** (one note per syllable)—unlike arias, which are often **melismatic** (several notes per syllable).

Recitatives serve to advance the story in operas, oratorios, and cantatas. Example 28.3 shows an excerpt of the Mozart recitative, in which Susanna asks Cherubino to sing the song he has written. Beginning in C major, it modulates to B♭ major, the key of "Voi, che sapete." Recitatives of this type are sung with considerable rhythmic freedom, in imitation of speech (*parlando* style), and rhythms notated here only approximate what you would hear in a performance. This type of recitative, accompanied by sustained chords on a continuo instrument (like harpsichord), is known as ***recitativo secco*** (dry recitative). In contrast, ***recitativo accompagnato*** (accompanied recitative) employs, as the name implies, a fully notated orchestral accompaniment, and is performed more closely to the notated rhythms.

EXAMPLE 28.3: Mozart, "Quanto duolmi, Susanna," mm. 23-29 🎧

Translation: (Susanna) Look, he has two blushing embers on his face. (Countess) Take my guitar and accompany him. (Cherubino) I am trembling, but if Madame wishes. (Susanna) She wishes, yes she wishes—no more talk.

Baroque-era recitatives tend to be highly expressive and tonally less stable than the Mozart recitative. Look, for example, at a passage from "Thy rebuke hath broken his heart," a tenor recitative from Handel's *Messiah*. Within the recitative's short eighteen measures are numerous brief tonicizations (see Example 28.4). In analyzing the shifting tonality, the best strategy may be to listen for cadential formulas, such as $V7$-i and $V_4^{6-5}_3$, which clearly articulate the tonal arrivals in measures 8-10 and 13, then work backward from those points. Expect sudden direct modulations, without pivot chords. Some abrupt key juxtapositions may be prepared by the same series of harmonies previously heard in another key: for example, the distinctive progression of measures 11-13 in D minor reappears in 16-18 in B minor.

EXAMPLE 28.4: Handel, "Thy rebuke hath broken his heart," mm. 8-18

Try it #2

Provide a Roman numeral analysis for measures 4–7 of the Handel recitative. 🎧

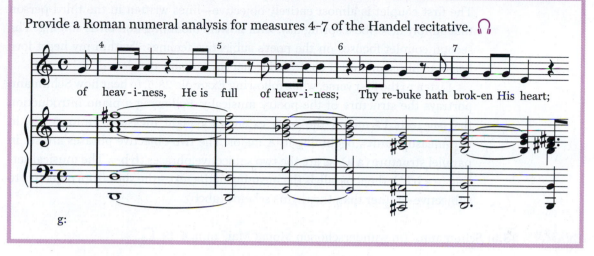

of heav-i-ness, He is full of heav-i-ness; Thy re-buke hath brok-en His heart;

g:

Text and Song Structure

To explore how the form and meaning of a text interact with musical structure, we turn now to the German **Lied** (plural **Lieder**), a type of art song that flourished in Germanic countries in the late eighteenth to early twentieth centuries. **Art songs** are settings of mostly poetic texts for voice and piano, intended for performance in recitals. An analysis of any art song requires us to study the words as well.

Consider the poem "Im wunderschönen Monat Mai," by nineteenth-century German poet Heinrich Heine, set to music by Robert Schumann.

Im wunderschönen Monat Mai,	a	In the lovely month of May,
Als alle Knospen sprangen,	b	When all the buds were bursting,
Da ist in meinem Herzen	c	Then within my heart
Die Liebe aufgegangen.	b	Love began to blossom.
Im wunderschönen Monat Mai,	a	In the lovely month of May,
Als alle Vögel sangen,	b	When all the birds were singing,
Da hab' ich ihr gestanden	d	Then I confessed to her
Mein Sehnen und Verlangen.	b	My longing and desire.

Begin by thinking about the poem's imagery, story, and structure, apart from its musical setting. Often the pattern of words, lines, and rhymes will suggest a particular type of musical design that may or may not be borne out in the composer's realization.

Heine's text consists of two four-line **strophes**, sometimes called "stanzas" or "verses." The letters indicate the rhyme scheme: rhyming German words at the end of each line take the same lowercase letter. The first two lines of each strophe show a parallel structure: both begin with the same six words. This structure suggests that the composer might set these parallel lines with parallel music.

Further, each group of four lines pairs into two couplets (of two lines each). The first couplet is almost entirely objective—lines written in the third person that simply describe a spring day, with flowers blooming and birds singing. The second couplet focuses on the poet's subjective feelings: "within my heart love began to blossom" and "I confessed to her my longing and desire."

Listen to the first verse, while following Example 28.5, to hear how Schumann portrays the structure of the poetry musically. Following a piano introduction that suggests F♯ minor, the verse extends for eight measures (mm. 5–12), in two-measure units, beginning in A major. The two objective phrases are set in parallel structure (**a a**), as are the two subjective phrases (**b b′**). The musical setting (**a a b b′**), then, parallels the meaning of the text—the shift from objective to subjective—rather than the rhyme scheme (abcb).

EXAMPLE 28.5: Schumann, "Im wunderschönen Monat Mai," mm. 4–12

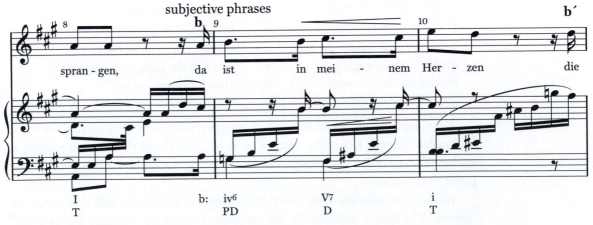

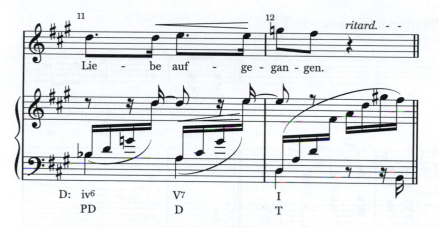

Translation: In the lovely month of May, when all the buds were bursting, then within my heart love began to blossom.

Each two-measure grouping in measures 5-12 expresses only the PD-D-T portion of the phrase: the objective lines in A major (ii⁶-V⁷-I) and the subjective lines in different transpositions, tonicizing B minor and D major (iv⁶-V⁷-i or I). The objective couplet of each strophe also contrasts with the subjective by its lower range, stable major key, and stepwise approach to the tonic: $\hat{6}$-$\hat{7}$-$\hat{1}$ over a V⁷-I harmony. The shift to first person narrative in the subjective text is marked by upward transpositions, a higher vocal range, an ascending melody, and vocal skips to downbeat appoggiaturas (incomplete neighbors, mm. 10 and 12)—all expressive means to depict the longing of the protagonist.

Strophic Form

As you can see in the anthology score, the second verse of Schumann's Lied (mm. 16-23) is set to exactly the same music.

KEY CONCEPT Songs in which more than one strophe (or verse) of text is sung to the same music are called **strophic**, a term derived from the strophes of poetry. Hymns and carols, folk songs, and popular songs are often strophic.

Because strophic settings feature the same music for several verses, they may appear printed with the strophes of text aligned under a single melodic line, as in Example 28.6, with repeat or "da capo" signs indicating a return to the beginning; or each verse may be written out separately, as in Schumann's song. Verses may also be preceded or followed by instrumental introductions or postludes, as in both examples.

EXAMPLE 28.6: Schubert, "Morgengruss," mm. 1-10

(See anthology for translation.)

SUMMARY

Poetry set to music is generally analyzed with respect to

- strophes — the division of the poem into verses;

- couplets — paired lines within the poem;

- rhyme scheme — the pattern of rhymes at the end of each line;

- parallel text — repeated words, or a similar change in narrative voice, in two or more strophes;

- objective or subjective stance—third person narrative vs. personal reflection.

Try it #3

Provide a rhyme-scheme analysis for the poem below, set to music by Clara Schumann, by writing alphabet letters at the end of each line of German text. Does this lyric feature a shift from an objective to subjective stance? Are there parallelisms in the text that might suggest a particular musical design? Listen to the song while following the anthology score.

Friedrich Rückert, "Liebst du um Schönheit"

Liebst du um Schönheit, o nicht mich liebe!	____	If you love for beauty, oh do not love me!
Liebe die Sonne, sie trägt ein goldnes Haar!	____	Love the sun; she has golden hair!
Liebst du um Jugend, o nicht mich liebe!	____	If you love for youthfulness, oh do not love me!
Liebe den Frühling, der jung ist jedes Jahr!	____	Love the springtime; it is young every year!
Liebst du um Schätze, o nicht mich liebe!	____	If you love for wealth, oh do not love me!
Liebe die Meerfrau, sie hat viel Perlen klar!	____	Love the mermaid; she has many fair pearls!
Liebst du um Liebe, o ja—mich liebe!	____	If you love for love itself, oh yes, love me!
Liebe mich immer, dich lieb ich immerdar!	____	Love me always, and I will love you forever!

Text Painting

Heine's poem "Im wunderschönen Monat Mai" seems to express the joys of spring and first love, which might best be represented by an exuberant major-key setting. Yet Schumann's song instead seems uneasy and restless: his choice of harmonies suggests that all is not well—perhaps the poet's love is not returned. This uneasiness begins with the piano introduction (Example 28.7), which implies F♯ minor ambiguously through a series of Phrygian resolutions (iv6-V7), without ever expressing a complete phrase or tonic harmony; the leading tone (E♯) is left dangling in the piano's melodic line (mm. 2 and 4), and even the iv6 is clouded with a dissonant incomplete neighbor, A♯3. Further obscuring the harmony is the initial C♯5, part of a dissonant 7-6 suspension, that emerges in measures 4-5 as the first pitch of the vocal line. Only with the entrance of the voice does the C♯5 finally lead unambiguously into A major.

EXAMPLE 28.7: Schumann, "Im wunderschönen Monat Mai," mm. 1-6 🎧

The conflict between the F# minor introduction and the A major start of the verse raises questions regarding the main key of the song. The tonality continues to be unstable throughout; not even the postlude brings resolution—the song ends on an unstable V7 chord in F# minor. This unstable harmonic setting could foreshadow the state of this lover's relationship as the songs continue; as such, the setting is an example of text painting.

KEY CONCEPT Text painting is a means of depicting images or ideas from a text through music. Piano accompaniments may sound like the rustling of trees, the babbling of a brook, the thunder of horse hooves, or the cooing of a dove. Text painting in vocal lines may include rising passages or upward leaps to depict joy or heaven, and dissonances, downward leaps, or descending semitones to depict sadness or the grave.

You may come across similar effects in Romantic-era instrumental compositions without text, particularly when these works are based on a "program"—a story line, characters, or a specific setting—as is the case for piano character pieces or symphonic tone poems. Typical subjects in Romantic poetry are nature, wandering, hunting, unattainable or lost love, and death—all well suited to musical depiction through text painting. Sometimes several poems are linked by a narrative, characters, and certain imagery.

KEY CONCEPT A **song cycle** is a group of songs, generally performed as a unit, set either to a single poet's cycle or to poems that the composer has grouped to create a cycle. The songs are often ordered to tell a story and may be connected by key relationships or recurring motives.

"Im wunderschönen Monat Mai" is the first song of Schumann's cycle *Dichterliebe* (*The Poet's Love*). He wrote several other cycles, including two simply entitled *Liederkreis* (*Song Cycle*) and one specifically from a woman's point of view, *Frauenliebe und -leben* (*A Woman's Love and Life*). Among other famous song cycles are two by Schubert, *Die schöne Müllerin* (*The Fair Maid of the Mill*) and *Winterreise* (*Winter Journey*).

Analysis and Interpretation

In a performance of Schumann's song, pianist and singer alike might bring out its musical ambiguities, as preparation for the story of love and loss to come. For example, the pianist could hesitate on the opening C♯5 (Example 28.7), whose role is unclear, before adding the supporting harmony that explains its dissonant function. The perpetual arpeggiated texture of the piano part—perhaps representing a breeze blowing on the flower blossoms—might be played with the rhythmic freedom of nature, especially where the voice is not present. Also important for the pianist is the close of the song, with its unresolved dominant seventh harmony and incomplete iv⁶-V⁷ motion (Example 28.8).

EXAMPLE 28.8: Schumann, "Im wunderschönen Monat Mai," mm. 22-26

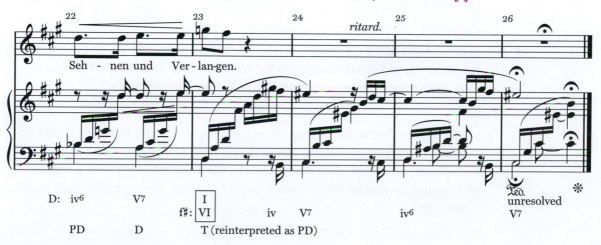

Translation: Longing and desire.

Here Schumann notates a ritard in measure 24 and a fermata both on the downbeat of measure 26 and on the final chord—leaving the most active pitches of this chord exposed in the upper voices: the leading tone in the soprano (E♯5) and the unresolved chordal seventh (B4). The next song will immediately return to A major.

When the singer enters with the first line, he may want to linger on the beautiful C♯ dissonance, which highlights the descriptive word "wunderschönen" (lovely), before proceeding. The objective lines might be sung with a vocal tone that supports the joy in the spring day; with the subjective lines, the singer could change to a tone that expresses love, longing, and uncertainty of what is to come. As he climbs to the higher register, he may also want to *crescendo* and emphasize the accented dissonances, especially on "Verlangen" (desire). The singer's face and body should likewise maintain the sense of longing throughout the postlude, as the piano reinforces the mood of the text so effectively.

Other Vocal Forms

Modified Strophic Form

Sometimes you will encounter songs where the music seems strophic, but each verse is somehow varied. Listen, for example, to Clara Schumann's "Liebst du um Schönheit" while following the anthology score. Friedrich Rückert's poem, given in *Try it #1*, is structured in a way that suggests a strophic setting, as each strophe begins the same: "Liebst du um . . ." Also, as you may have discovered, each couplet displays the same rhyme scheme, ab. Yet there is a difference in the last verse: the singer turns the negative first line to an affirmative one, "o ja—mich liebe!" (oh yes, love me!), suggesting a different compositional treatment.

KEY CONCEPT In modified strophic form, each verse of a song may begin the same way but end differently, or the song may vary the verses through harmonic or melodic changes, interpolated music, or other means.

Schumann begins her setting of each stanza identically, but adds subtle differences in each continuation. The first and third stanzas are quite similar; the second and fourth end differently, and the fourth is extended with a repetition of text and its crucial "oh ja—mich liebe!" to mark the climactic shift to the affirmative.

Through-Composed Form

In a sense, the "opposite" of a strophic song is a through-composed one: here, rather than repeating the melody from stanza to stanza, the music for each stanza (or each line) is different.

KEY CONCEPT A through-composed song is one in which the composition develops continuously—in new, though perhaps motivically related, ways—as the song unfolds. While a through-composed song may include patterns of repetition, these patterns will not fall into typical musical forms, such as **A A′**, **A B A, A A B, or A A B A**.

Schubert's "Erlkönig" is a dramatic example of a through-composed song, united from verse to verse by a piano motive that appears as introduction, interlude, and accompaniment to some verses. You have listened to excerpts in recent chapters, but now consider the song as a whole, to see how its text, harmony, and motivic structure work together to create a powerful musical drama. Read through Goethe's poem and translation in your anthology; in your score, mark the beginning and end of each strophe, as well as who is speaking—the narrator, the father, the son, or the Elf King. Observe any motives or accompanimental patterns that are associated with particular characters.

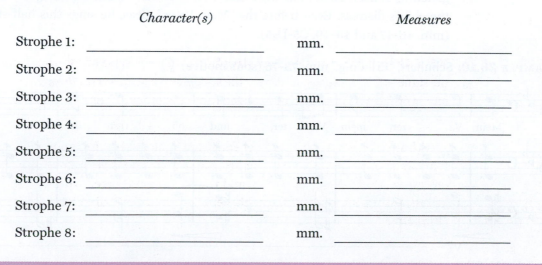

Try it #4

Listen to "Erlkönig" in its entirety.

1. Each strophe has the same rhyme scheme. Circle the alphabet letters that best capture this design: abab   abcb   aabb   abca

2. For each of the eight strophes, write the name of the character(s) speaking, and the corresponding measure numbers.

	Character(s)		Measures
Strophe 1:	_____	mm.	_____
Strophe 2:	_____	mm.	_____
Strophe 3:	_____	mm.	_____
Strophe 4:	_____	mm.	_____
Strophe 5:	_____	mm.	_____
Strophe 6:	_____	mm.	_____
Strophe 7:	_____	mm.	_____
Strophe 8:	_____	mm.	_____

Although it is through-composed, "Erlkönig" includes a number of compositional features—particularly recurring motives—that help tie the work into a unified whole. One of the most striking motives appears in the piano left hand (Example 28.9). This triplet motive (mm. 2-3, 4-5), which accompanies the narrator, is heard in G minor at the beginning and end of the song, and in other keys elsewhere. Meanwhile the triplet octaves in the right hand evoke the thundering of horse hooves through the night as the boy and his father ride through the forest (for convenience of reading, the triplet eighths are notated ♪.).

EXAMPLE 28.9: Schubert, "Erlkönig," mm. 1-5 (riding motive)

The motive most associated with the son is the half-step neighbor tone, shown in Example 28.10. This motive is often sung to the text "Mein Vater, mein Vater" (My father), and each time the boy sings this plaintive plea, it appears higher in his range: compare measures 72-74 (D5-E♭5-D5) with 97-99 (E5-F5-E5) and 123-125 (F5-G♭5-F5). Further, it is sung as dissonant 7-6 motion above an arpeggiated V_5^6 of the local key (adding a minor ninth to the V7 harmony), emphasizing the child's distress. Even before the "Mein Vater" pleas, he sings this half-step (mm. 46-47 and 48-49, C5-D♭5).

EXAMPLE 28.10: Schubert, "Erlkönig," mm. 73-76 (son's motive)

Translation: My father, my father, don't you hear?

The father's reassurances to his son often feature perfect intervals of the fourth or fifth to the text "Mein Sohn" (My son)—in staunch denial of any danger—and his vocal range lies consistently lower. Example 28.11 shows the father's first rising P4 motive, which also climbs higher and higher as the song progresses, from measures 36-37 (D4-G4) to 80-81 (F#4-B4) and 105-106 (G#4-C#5).

EXAMPLE 28.11: Schubert, "Erlkönig," mm. 37-40 (father's motive)

Translation: My son, why do you hide your face, so afraid?

Both of these motives appear also in the music of the narrator and—more chillingly—the Elf King. This evil forest spirit attempts to coax the boy rather than frighten him, therefore his music is almost always in a major key. In measures 69-70, the Elf King appropriates the rising P4 from the father and sings it to the text "meine Mutter" (my mother). In 116-117, in his final appeal before snatching the boy away, the Elf King uses both the son's neighbor-tone motive and the father's perfect fourth, now descending as well as rising, as he sings "Ich liebe dich" (I love you). Example 28.12 gives this climactic moment, tonicizing the Neapolitan of the local D minor tonic.

EXAMPLE 28.12: Schubert, "Erlkönig," mm. 115-119 (son and father motives sung by the Elf King)

Translation: I love you, I am tempted by your beautiful form.

Sometimes composers embed motives in their works at different hierarchical levels. That is, a motive that originally appears within a single measure may be drawn out to span many measures, in a new rhythmic and tonal context—a practice called **motivic parallelism**. One example is the left-hand G minor "riding" motive from the song's introduction (mm. 2-3). This motive is characterized by two parts. The first is a rising scale with half-step neighbor tone at the top, perhaps the source of the son's half-step motive: G-A-B♭-C-D-E♭-D. The second part is a descending minor triad: D-B♭-G. As Example 28.13 shows, the narrator's final speech is a large-scale replication of the G minor scale—with the neighbor E♭-D as a grace note on "Armen"—accompanied by the original version simultaneously in the piano. This subphrase ends by poignantly combining the P4 and neighbor-tone motives to "ächzende Kind" (moaning child).

EXAMPLE 28.13: Schubert, "Erlkönig," mm. 135-141 🎧

Translation: [The father] rides quickly, he holds in his arms the moaning child.

While the motivic recurrences provide unifying elements in this long and complex song, the pattern of tonicized keys likewise plays a unifying role. In a striking motivic parallelism, the large-scale succession of keys also "spells out" most of the riding motive: G minor (beginning in m. 1), B♭ major (m. 58), C major (m. 87), D minor (m. 112), E♭ (briefly tonicized as a Neapolitan, m. 117), D minor (m. 123), tonicized V/B♭ (m. 124), G minor (m. 131).

French Mélodie

Romantic-era songs in the French tradition are called **mélodie**, and principal composers include Charles Gounod, Jules Massenet, Henri Duparc, and Gabriel Fauré (and, somewhat later, Claude Debussy and Maurice Ravel). French mélodie typically fall into two- or three-part forms, which tend to be more concise than German Lieder, with a harmonic palette that is enriched in different ways. Before we turn to the harmonic analysis of Fauré's "Après un rêve" ("After a Dream"), first read the poem by Romain Bussine.

Dans un sommeil que charmait ton image	In a sleep that your image charmed,
Je rêvais le bonheur, ardent mirage,	I dreamed of happiness, ardent mirage,
Tes yeux étaient plus doux, ta voix pure et sonore,	Your eyes were softer, your voice pure and sonorous,
Tu rayonnais comme un ciel éclairé par l'aurore;	You shone like a sky lit by the dawn;
Tu m'appelais et je quittais la terre	You called me and I left the earth
Pour m'enfuir avec toi vers la lumière,	To run away with you toward the light,
Les cieux pour nous entr'ouvraient leurs nues,	The skies parted their clouds for us,
Splendeurs inconnues, lueurs divines entrevues,	Splendors unknown, divine light glimpsed,
Hélas! Hélas! triste réveil des songes	Alas! Alas! sad awakening from the dreams,
Je t'appelle, ô nuit, rends moi tes mensonges,	I call you, O night, give me back your lies,
Reviens, reviens radieuse,	Return, return radiant,
Reviens, ô nuit mystérieuse!	Return, O mysterious night!

Each strophe has an aabb rhyme scheme, with the two couplets in the last strophe set apart from the rest of the poem by their repeated words: "Hélas! Hélas!" and "Reviens, reviens." There is also a shift from dreaming to wakefulness: the first two verses speak of rapturous love taking place in a dream, but the last describes a sad awakening and a plea to return to pleasant dreams. This poetic structure suggests an **A A B** song form, which Fauré indeed follows in his setting (anthology).

Look at the opening of the mélodie, in Example 28.14. The dreamlike mood is established at the beginning by the *pianissimo* dynamic level, placid reiterated chords, and languid descending triplets in the vocal line. The harmonies, even in the first measures, already differ from the earlier Germanic music we have encountered by the absence of a leading tone in minor: for example, the minor dominant of measure 2 and subtonic ninth chord (a product of 9-8 motion above the stationary bass) in measure 4. The leading tone does not appear until the half cadence in measures 7-8 (not shown). Similar alterations of diatonic harmonies, idiomatic of late-Romantic French style, color the entire song, which rarely strays from its C minor tonality—only briefly tonicizing the relative major.

EXAMPLE 28.14: Fauré, "Après un rêve," mm. 1-4

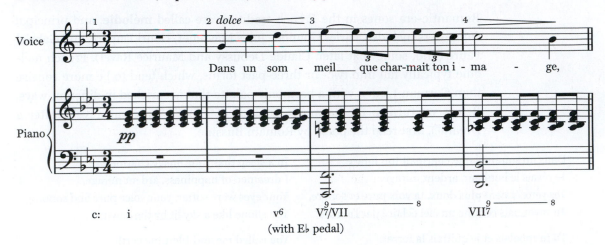

Formally, the mélodie begins as though strophic, with measures 17-26 (verse 2) nearly identical to 2-11 (verse 1). But verse 2 builds to the word "entrevues" and elides directly into a contrasting, dramatic verse 3 that makes this a ternary form: **A A′ B**.

When you prepare a song for performance, consider well the structure and meaning of the text, as well as whether it fits one of the forms discussed in this chapter. In strophic settings, think about how to create a sense of the story's development despite the literal repetition of music—perhaps by inflecting particular words, selecting contrasting dynamic levels, or making subtle changes in tempo. In ternary songs, the same strategy applies for the repeated **A** sections, while the **B** sections need to be set apart through interpretive choices—changes in color, articulation, or tempo, for example. In Baroque da capo arias, performers often ornament the return of **A** to create variety and a graceful close to the work.

In any song form, think about the distinction between a phrase of text and a phrase of music. Look for the cadence to determine musical phrase endings, and examine the harmonic (as well as poetic) structure to determine points of arrival, where to take a breath, and where not to breathe if possible. Think about the effect of unexpected harmonies or mixture chords and how these relate to crucial words. Above all, the singer and accompanist should study the text and music together to make collaborative decisions in service of the poetry and song.

Did You Know?

Oratorios, like operas, are extended works for vocal soloists and chorus accompanied by orchestra. They are intended for concert performance and usually recount religious or historical stories (as does Handel's *Messiah*). Cantatas are similar—especially in their mature form in eighteenth-century Germany—in that they also feature soloists, choir, and small orchestra, but they were originally composed as religious service music with texts appropriate to their position in the church year. The sacred cantatas of J. S. Bach incorporate chorale settings, other choral movements, recitatives, and arias with religious texts. The performance of sacred cantatas in church settings allowed people who would not normally have an opportunity to hear opera or oratorios to enjoy the latest art-music styles. Bach wrote secular cantatas as well, including Cantata No. 208, which features pagan gods Diana, Endymion, Pan, and Pales, and depicts pastoral images of sheep and shepherds and the joys of the hunt.

TERMS YOU SHOULD KNOW

aria
- da capo aria

art song

cantata

couplet

libretto

Lied

mélodie

objective-subjective stance

oratorio

recitative
- accompagnato
- secco

ritornello

song cycle

song forms
- strophic
- modified strophic
- ternary (three part)
- through-composed

strophe (or verse or stanza)

text painting

textual analysis

text setting
- melismatic
- syllabic

QUESTIONS FOR REVIEW

1. What formal designs are commonly found in song settings?
2. How do da capo arias differ from other arias? from other ternary forms?
3. What strategies might an analyst use to interpret rapidly shifting keys in recitatives?
4. How might an analysis of the text help determine the form of a song? How might it influence analysis of the music? How might analysis influence performance choices?
5. How might a composer create unity or continuity in a through-composed song?
6. What differences in harmonic choices are found in French mélodie in comparison with German Lieder?

7. In music for your own instrument, find a piece that uses text painting. (Instrumentalists: Examine pieces with titles that imply a story line or other programmatic element; consider ensemble works as well.) What types of motives represent the ideas in the text or program? How might you perform those motives to express the meaning of the text or program?

Know It? Show It!

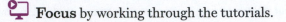 **Focus** by working through the tutorials.

Learn with InQuizitive.

Apply what you've learned to complete the workbook assignments.

29

Popular Music

Overview

In this chapter, we examine the harmonic features and formal organization of songs at the foundation of modern popular music: Broadway show tunes, Tin Pan Alley songs, jazz standards, folk music, parlor ballads, and the blues. We then consider innovations in more recent styles.

Repertoire

"The Ash Grove"

Count Basie, "Splanky"

George Gershwin and Ira Gershwin, "I Got Rhythm," from *Girl Crazy*

Brian Holland, Lamont Dozier, and Edward Holland Jr., "Baby Love"

Carole King, "You've Got a Friend"

Jerry Leiber and Mike Stoller, "Hound Dog"

John Lennon and Paul McCartney, "Eleanor Rigby," from *Revolver*

Freddy Mercury, "Crazy Little Thing Called Love"

James Myers and Max Freedman, "Rock Around the Clock"

Katy Perry, Lukasz Gottwald, Max Martin, Bonnie McKee, and Henry Walter, "Roar"

Vicki Sue Robinson, "Turn the Beat Around"

Tiësto (Wayne Anthony Hector, Carl Falk, Rami Yacoub, Tijs Verwest, and Michael Zitron), "Red Lights"

Brian Wilson and Mike Love, "Help Me, Rhonda"

Outline

Popular song
- Quaternary and verse-refrain forms
- Harmonic practices
- Suspensions and rhythmic displacement
- Altered fifths and tritone substitutions

The twelve-bar blues
- Pentatonic and blues "scales"
- Blues harmonic progressions and phrase structure

Post-1950 popular song
- New elements of form
- Harmony and melody

Popular Song

The popular song literature is expansive—from folk songs and parlor ballads of the late nineteenth century to Tin Pan Alley, Broadway show tunes, and the blues in the early twentieth, to ongoing adaptations of these tunes as "standards" by jazz musicians, to what we hear today. Rock and roll emerged mid-century to become a worldwide phenomenon, followed by progressive rock, punk, metal, hip-hop, rap, emo, indie, and myriad other genres. These newer styles draw on compositional elements of earlier twentieth-century popular songs, but also introduce new harmonic practices and musical forms, and they incorporate production techniques made available by the explosion of new technologies after 1945. While these repertoires share many characteristics with common-practice tonal music, there are also significant differences in the ways that scales and melody, rhythm and meter, harmony, and form are treated.

Quaternary and Verse-Refrain Forms

Listen to "The Ash Grove," a traditional Welsh folk song (anthology). The song begins with a repeated phrase (**a a**) that ends with an authentic cadence in measures 7-8 (Example 29.1a) and 15-16. In the following, contrasting phrase (**b**), shown in part (b), the contour is different, and it features a melodic sequence leading to a tonicized HC in measure 24. The opening melody then returns with the upbeat to measure 25, rounding out a four-part **a a b a** formal design.

EXAMPLE 29.1: "The Ash Grove"

(a) Mm. 1-8

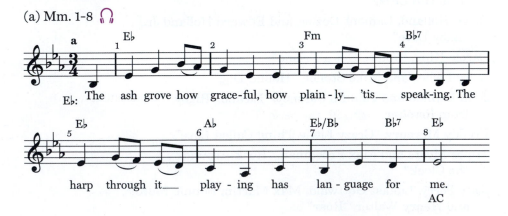

(b) Mm. 17-24 🎧

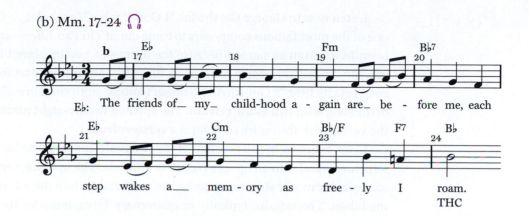

A song with four phrases like this one is in **quaternary form**. Each phrase is typically four or eight measures long; if eight measures, the form may be referred to as **thirty-two-bar form**. The first two phrases often begin the same—they may be identical (**a a**) or may differ at the cadence (**a a′**)—and are followed by a contrasting section and a return to the opening material.

> ⌣ **KEY CONCEPT** In quaternary (**a a b a**) song form, the contrasting section (**b**) is known as the **bridge**. The bridge may temporarily tonicize another key, and may end harmonically open (on a HC or with no cadence) to prepare the return of the **a** section.

Quaternary songs may also be written with other phrase designs, most often **a b a c**, with a contrasting period instead of a parallel one, and no bridge. Other possibilities are **a b c b** (or **b′**) and **a b c a** (or **a′**), where **c** is the bridge.

Try it #1

Write in the phrases (measure numbers and letters) for measures 1-32 of "The Ash Grove" on the graph below. Identify any period structures.

Measures: 1-8   _____   _____   _____

Phrase letters: **a**   _____   _____   _____

Period structures? _____

Listen now to George Gershwin's "I Got Rhythm" (anthology). Gershwin was one of the most famous composers to come out of Tin Pan Alley—an area of midtown Manhattan so named because the dozens of pianos played in publishers' offices sounded like people banging on tin cans. The familiar part from which the song gets its title, "I Got Rhythm," doesn't appear until measure 29: this portion of the song is known as the **refrain**. The opening twenty-eight measures make up the **verse**, with the entire song form a **verse-refrain**.

Many songs from the first half of the twentieth century employ this two-part structure, similar to an opera's recitative and aria. The opening verse sets up the story; its harmonic structure may be less predictable than the refrain, and it may modulate. The refrain, typically in quaternary form, includes the song's **hook** (usually the title idea, the most memorable part of the song), and it may be performed on its own, without the verse. In some songs, the verse is repeated two or more times, with the same music but different texts. The refrain, though, normally returns with the same music and text.

SUMMARY

The design of a verse-refrain song generally follows this model:

verse: like a recitative, may modulate
refrain: like an aria, but **a a b a**

Harmonic Practices

The formal elements of early twentieth-century popular songs are not the only aspect that distinguishes them from their art-song predecessors: an expanded harmonic palette is another. For an example, listen again to measures 3-10 of Gershwin's verse (Example 29.2).

EXAMPLE 29.2: Gershwin, "I Got Rhythm," mm. 3-10 🎧

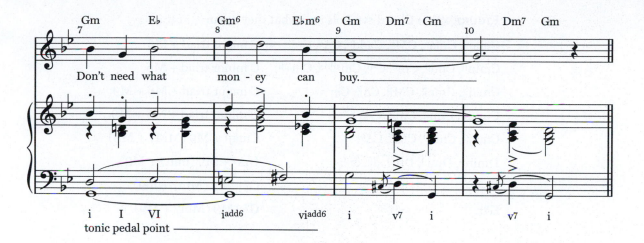

The first three measures express a common phrase opening, with a neighboring $^6_4$ chord prolonging the tonic harmony i$^5_3$–$^6_4$–$^5_3$, yet the tonic harmony of measure 5 is "clouded" by an additional pitch, E♮3, a major sixth above the bass note. Pitches added to triads or seventh chords are sometimes called **extensions** (or "tensions" by jazz musicians). The sonority here is an **added-sixth chord** (its chord symbol could be Gm^add6 or Gm^+6, as well as Gm^6). Don't confuse the numeral 6 with an inversion symbol—it would be a strange chord indeed if stacked in thirds above the E♮ "root," and it would not correctly identify the chord's tonic function. The next chord (m. 6) consists of E♭–G–B♭–D♭–F: a **ninth chord**, an E♭ dominant seventh chord plus a major ninth (F) above the root.

KEY CONCEPT In popular styles, major or minor sevenths may be added to chords on almost any degree of the diatonic scale without changing the root, inversion, or function of the chord in the phrase. Any triad or seventh chord may be extended—the added sixth and the ninth are the two most common extensions. No matter what the quality of the underlying harmony, the added sixth is generally a major sixth, and the added ninth is usually a major ninth—except in the case of dominant seventh chords, where the ninth may be minor.

Analyze an added-sixth chord with its regular Roman numeral plus the label ^add6 or ^+6. For ninth chords, either use Roman numerals with figured-bass symbols (e.g., V$^9_7$) or chord symbols (E^9). In Example 29.2, measure 6, the chord symbol shows only the seventh, not the added ninth; think of the score as a transcription of an improvised performance, where ninths or sixths are added by the performer at will—chord symbols and score won't always match precisely. Finally, to identify chords with extensions, consider the bass line and progression: the bass line should make a logical harmonic progression that would be distorted if analyzed with "inversions" that incorporate the added notes. Chord symbols for these types of progressions are not standardized; Figure 29.1 lists some of the different ways they may appear.

FIGURE 29.1: Chord symbols and what they mean

Cmaj^6, Cma^6, CM^6, Cadd^6, CΔ^6, C^6:	C major triad + M6
Cmin^6, Cmi^6, Cm^6, C^{-6}, Cm^{add6}, Cm^{+6}:	C minor triad + M6
Cmaj$^9_6$, Cma$^9_6$, CM$^9_6$, CΔ^9_6, C$^9_6$:	C major triad + M6 + M9
Cmin$^9_6$, Cmi$^9_6$, Cm$^9_6$, C$^{-9}_6$, c$^9_6$:	C minor triad + M6 + M9
Cmaj^9, Cma^9, CM^9, CΔ^9:	Cmaj7 + M9 (MM7 + M9)
Dmin^9, Dmi^9, Dm^9, d^9, d^{-9}:	Dm7 + M9 (mm7 + M9)
G7($\flat$9):	G7 + m9 (Mm7 + m9)
G9:	G7 + M9 (Mm7 + M9)

Try it #2

Locate a ninth chord and an added-sixth chord (these are not indicated in the chord symbols) in the passage below. Below the staff, circle the measure and beat where you find them.

Gershwin, "I Got Rhythm," mm. 15-18 🎧

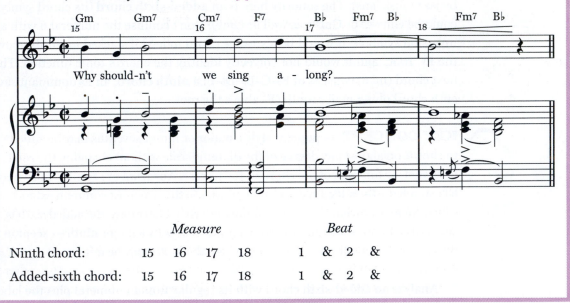

			Measure				Beat			
Ninth chord:		15	16	17	18		1	&	2	&
Added-sixth chord:		15	16	17	18		1	&	2	&

Mixture chords appear often in popular songs, as in art songs, but some show tunes include types of mixture not common in the nineteenth century. In "I Got Rhythm," $\flat\hat{5}$ (D$\flat$) is prominently featured at the end of the first vocal subphrase (Example 29.2, m. 6), coloring "sigh" and creating the minor seventh of the VI$^9_7$. Listen now to Example 29.3; consider whether each accidental is the product of modal mixture and what its effect is on the harmony.

EXAMPLE 29.3: Gershwin, "I Got Rhythm," mm. 37-44

Mixture notes are circled in measures 39, 42, and 44: the G♭ in 42 creates a minor subdominant, and the A♭ in 44 is a brief chordal embellishment (♭$\hat{7}$) that initiates the lead-in to the bridge. The E♮ in measure 39 is ♯$\hat{4}$; with the D♭ it creates a diminished seventh chord built on E. In common-practice style, diminished seventh chords on scale degrees other than $\hat{7}$ usually function as secondary diminished sevenths. We might expect a vii°7/V, where the E♮ resolves up to F and the D♭ down to C, but the chord does not resolve this way, and should therefore be considered a voice-leading chord (CT°7) without a Roman numeral.

KEY CONCEPT In popular styles, fully diminished and half-diminished seventh sonorities may appear on any scale degree, and need not function as secondary diminished seventh chords.

Suspensions and Rhythmic Displacement

While suspensions that conform to common-practice voice-leading may be found in popular styles (for example, the 4-3 suspensions, B♭ to A, in mm. 40 and 43 of Example 29.3), we also sometimes find "4-3 suspensions" with no resolution: an added fourth above the bass displaces the third but never resolves. Such harmonies are called **sus chords** and labeled sus or sus4.

In addition, pitches may be "held over" like suspensions from one chord to the next, or "arrive early" before the rest of a harmony. Look at the first harmony of measure 39 in Example 29.3: the chord symbol implies a B♭ root, yet no B♭ is notated; instead, the C5 from the previous chord is held over across the bar, displacing the B♭, which returns at the end of the measure. Jazz soloists intuit these "missing" pitches; they know the notes will be supplied by bass or piano in the rhythm section (bass, drums, piano). Analyze chords with rhythmic displacement as though the chord tone were present, rather than including the displaced pitch (in m. 39, I^add6). Alternatively, you may hear the C as creating a ninth chord above the missing pitch—this implies an analysis of I$^9_7$. You may also find in some textbooks or lead sheets indications for eleventh or thirteenth chords. To interpret these chord symbols, simply add the specified interval (4 for an eleventh chord or 6 for a thirteenth chord) above the bass.

Altered Fifths and Tritone Substitutions

Listen now to a final excerpt from "I Got Rhythm," this one from the bridge (Example 29.4), focusing on the chromatic voice-leading in the lower notes of the right hand and the chord quality.

EXAMPLE 29.4: Gershwin, "I Got Rhythm," mm. 45-52

The bridge begins with a D7 and articulates a descending-fifth pattern: D7-G(7)-C7-F7 (marked by arrows). In measure 45, the right hand's lower voices begin a chromatic ascent in parallel thirds, prolonging a ninth chord at the end of 46. In measure 47, the parallel thirds reach their high point and begin to *descend* chromatically. Gershwin's voice-leading results in two chords with altered fifths: the Dm7 chord of measure 46 has its fifth lowered by a half step (shown as Dm7-5), and the last sonority of 47 has its fifth raised by a half step (Daug5). Triads and seventh chords with altered fifths are a familiar harmonic feature of popular song, and may also be found in common-practice music of the nineteenth century.

KEY CONCEPT Triads or seventh chords may be colored and intensified by lowering or raising the fifth of the chord by a half step, resulting in an augmented or diminished interval between the root and fifth.

When analyzing harmonies with altered fifths, add traditional symbols (°7 or ø7) to Roman numerals for those that create diminished or half-diminished seventh sonorities. Major triads or dominant sevenths with raised fifths are labeled with Roman numeral plus +5 or #5, and lowered fifths with -5 or b5 (alternatively, you may see "aug5" or "dim5" attached to chord symbols). They often function as secondary dominants (e.g., V7b5/IV).

Try it #3

Find two additional triads or seventh chords with altered fifths in measures 49-52 of Example 29.4. What are their chord qualities? What Roman numeral would you assign each harmony, assuming a Bb tonic key?

	Measure	Quality	Roman numeral
(a)	_____	_____	_____
(b)	_____	_____	_____

In jazz performance, you will hear many types of chord alterations and substitutions; one example is the **tritone substitution** (or tritone sub), which replaces a V7 with a dominant-seventh-quality chord a tritone away (see Example 29.5a). The substitution is essentially a Neapolitan (♭II) with a minor seventh, but in jazz practice it is sometimes indicated by V7/♭V. The tritone sub "works" because the essential ingredients of the original V7—the leading tone and seventh (B and F in the example)—are present in the tritone sub, though the leading tone may be enharmonically respelled as ♭1̂ (here, C♭). It is also common to add a "sharp eleventh" (a ♯4 or ♭5 above the root of the V7/♭V) to the tritone sub, because that note (here, G) is the root of the original V7 it substitutes for (part b). The tritone sub may resolve the tritone as in the original V7—here, with C♭ to C♮ and F to E (part c)—which creates a double leading-tone effect (C♭–C♮ and D♭–C) similar to the resolution of augmented-sixth chords. Alternatively, it may resolve to ♭V (part d) to add harmonic interest (and any of these chords can add sevenths, ninths, or other extensions).

EXAMPLE 29.5: Tritone substitutions

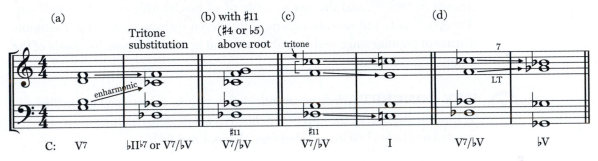

The Twelve-Bar Blues

Another early twentieth-century song style that has influenced subsequent popular music is a genre known as the **blues**. While this style originated in the Mississippi Delta among African American musicians, it spread worldwide; it was an essential influence on rock and roll in the 1950s, and continues to be a significant element of popular-song styles today. Blues songs normally feature a minor-sounding vocal melody, accompanied by chords in the parallel major key.

Pentatonic and Blues "Scales"

Listen to the beginning of Count Basie's "Splanky" while following Example 29.6, a transcription of the melody and chords.

EXAMPLE 29.6: Basie, "Splanky," mm. 1-12 (includes an introduction) 🎧

This melody has C as its tonic—evident from both the shape of the tune and the chord progression in C major—but it also includes ♭3̂, lending it a minor quality, as well as ♯4̂ or ♭5̂ (the spelling is based on the direction the line is moving).

Example 29.7a shows the notes in "Splanky" written as a scale—the so-called **blues scale**—plus ♭7̂, a note not played in this melody but heard as part of the C7 accompanying chord. Part (b) gives the C minor pentatonic (1̂-♭3̂-4̂-5̂-♭7̂, or *do-me-fa-sol-te*) on which this scale is based: ♯4̂ and/or ♭5̂ is added to the minor pentatonic to make the blues scale.

EXAMPLE 29.7: Blues and minor pentatonic scales

(a) Blues scale on C 🎧

(b) C minor pentatonic 🎧

The blues scale is not a scale proper, but rather a collection of notes from which selections are made when improvising a melody. The ♭3̂, ♭7̂, and ♯4̂ or ♭5̂ are sometimes called **blue notes** because they lend a hint of sadness to the melodic line that contrasts with the major-key accompaniment. When sung, and in instrumental performances where the player can vary the intonation, the blue notes on ♭3̂ and ♭7̂ may vary from 3̂ or 7̂ played a little flat to ♭3̂ or ♭7̂ played a little flat; the ♯4̂ or ♭5̂ may sound anywhere between 4̂ and 5̂.

KEY CONCEPT In the blues style, the distinction between major and minor is blurred by contrasting $\flat\hat{3}$ and $\flat\hat{7}$ in the melody (sounds minor) with $\hat{3}$ and $\hat{7}$ in the accompanying chords (sounds major). Scale degrees $\sharp\hat{4}$ and $\flat\hat{5}$ may also appear in the melody to make a series of half steps between $\hat{4}$ and $\hat{5}$: $\hat{4}$-$\sharp\hat{4}$-$\hat{5}$ or $\hat{5}$-$\flat\hat{5}$-$\hat{4}$.

Blues Harmonic Progressions and Phrase Structure

One of the most recognizable aspects of blues compositions is a repeated harmonic progression in the accompaniment known as the **twelve-bar blues**. The basic progression (Figure 29.2) consists of three subphrases, each four measures long: (1) four measures of tonic harmony, followed by (2) two measures of IV and two of I, then (3) V-IV-I-I. Minor sevenths may be added to any of these chords to make a dominant seventh quality, as in "Splanky" (Example 29.6). The last measure may end on the tonic or serve as a "turnaround," a V7 leading back to the beginning and a repeat of the progression. These harmonies, as well as other harmonic progressions in jazz or popular styles, are often referred to as **changes**, short for "chord changes."

FIGURE 29.2: Twelve-bar blues progression

```
(1)   I⁽⁷⁾  |        |        |        |
(2)   IV⁽⁷⁾ |        | I⁽⁷⁾   |        |
(3)   V⁽⁷⁾  | IV⁽⁷⁾  | I⁽⁷⁾   | I (V⁽⁷⁾):‖
                                 ↑
                        (optional turnaround)
```

In blues-style songs, the phrases of the vocal part usually conform to those of the harmonic progression, with one subphrase every four measures and the only conclusive close when the tonic returns in measures 11-12. The texts may describe hard times, lost love, or other sorrows, expressed in simple colloquial language that may take on added meaning through metaphor. The first two subphrases (mm. 1-4 and 5-8) normally present a "problem," with the third offering a consequence of that problem, as in "Hound Dog" as sung by Willie Mae "Big Mama" Thornton. In Big Mama's performance, it is clear that this "hound dog" is two-legged rather than four-legged.

> You ain't nothin' but a hound dog,
> Been snoopin' round my door.
> You ain't nothin' but a hound dog,
> Been snoopin' round my door.
> You can wag your tail,
> But I ain't gonna feed you no more.

In Elvis Presley's version, however, the lyrics are changed to make the meaning ambiguous (see the "Did You Know?" box for more details). This example and others in this chapter are available online; listen to them while reading the discussions.

In a performance of "Hound Dog," "Splanky," or any other blues tune, two or more presentations of the melody (with text, if sung) and harmonies are followed by additional repetitions of the harmonic progression with improvised instrumental solos over it. After these improvisations, the original melody returns. In jazz settings, the clearly recognizable melody—whether sung or instrumental—is called the **head**. This practice of playing solos in the middle of a performance, showcasing members of the ensemble, is a common feature in jazz and post-1950s popular music as well (where the solo instrument is usually lead guitar), whether the music is based on the blues progression, a quaternary song form, or some other form.

The twelve-bar blues progression, adopted by rock musicians in the 1950s, appears in songs of various styles after that time—one such song is "Rock Around the Clock" (Example 29.8).

EXAMPLE 29.8: Myers and Freedman, "Rock Around the Clock"

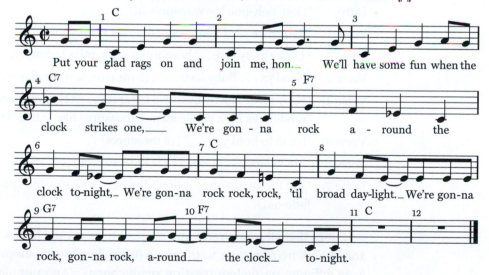

Try it #4

Play through the progression in Example 29.8 in block chords while singing the melody.

(a) Does this blues progression include a turnaround?   yes   no

(b) Blue notes appear in mm. _____, _____, _____, and _____.

Listen to various performances online to hear where singers place blue notes and where there are turnarounds.

Post-1950 Popular Song

New Elements of Form

After 1950, the terminology for labeling sections of songs shifted. **Verse** came to designate a musical section that might appear in a song multiple times with the same music but different words. A verse may be based on quaternary or twelve-bar blues design, or may follow some other formal plan. It normally carries the story line for the song. **Chorus** refers to a section of music that is repeated, each time with the same (or a similar) text. The chorus often includes the song's hook (the most memorable part).

Many popular songs from the 1950s and 1960s are made of only these two elements. A song with only verses is in **simple verse form** (a comparable art song would be called strophic). Examples include Elvis Presley's "Heartbreak Hotel" (six repetitions of the verse; the fifth is instrumental), Bob Dylan's "Blowin' in the Wind," and "Baby Love" by the Supremes (Figure 29.3). The hook for this song, "Baby love," appears in various places in the verse.

FIGURE 29.3: Simple verse form in "Baby Love"

Intro: "Ooh, ooh-hoo" (4 measures in)

Verse 1: "Baby love . . . I need you, oh how I need you . . ." (12 measures)

Verse 2: "'Cause baby love . . . been missing ya, miss kissing ya . . ." (12 measures)

Verse 3: "Need ya . . . Baby love . . ." (12 measures; 4 vocal + 8 instrumental)

Verse 4: "Baby love . . . why must we separate . . ." (12 measures)
          (modulates up a whole step; 2 measures like intro, "Ooh, ooh")

Verse 5: "Need to hold you . . ." (12 measures)

Verse 6: "Me my love . . . I need ya." (12 measures)

Verse 7: "Till it's hurtin' me . . . don't throw our love away." (partial verse with fade-out)

Songs that alternate verse and chorus are in **verse-chorus form**: both verse and chorus may be sung to the same or similar music (**simple verse-chorus**), or to different music (**contrasting verse-chorus**). An example of simple verse-chorus is Little Richard's "Tutti Frutti"—both verses ("Got a girl named . . .") and the chorus ("Tutti-frutti, oh Rudy") are sung to the same music. Chuck Berry's "Rock and Roll Music," Deep Purple's "Smoke on the Water," and the Beach Boys' "Help Me, Rhonda," whose form is outlined below, are contrasting verse-chorus.

FIGURE 29.4: Contrasting verse-chorus form in "Help Me, Rhonda"

Verse 1: "Since she put me down . . ." (16 measures)

Chorus: "Help me, Rhonda . . ." (16 measures)

Verse 2: "She was gonna be my wife . . ." (16 measures)

Chorus: "Help me, Rhonda . . ." (16 measures)

Verse 3: Instrumental (16 measures)

Chorus: "Help me, Rhonda" (6 measures + 2 instrumentals to fade)

In post-1950 popular music, **refrain** refers to a line or pair of lines that normally appear at the end of each verse with the same music and words. A familiar example is the line "All the lonely people . . ." that ends each verse of the Beatles song "Eleanor Rigby." The refrain differs from a chorus in that it is not a full-length independent section but rather a repeated line that completes the verse. Occasionally a refrain will appear on its own without being a part of the verse, but it remains only one or two lines long—shorter than a chorus normally would be.

SUMMARY

- Verse: the same music reappears later in the song with different text(s).
- Chorus: the same music reappears later in the song with the same text.
- Refrain: one- or two-line text at the end of the verse that reappears with the same music.
- Simple verse form: a song with only verses (no chorus or other sections).
- Verse-chorus: a song that alternates verses and choruses.
- Simple verse-chorus: both verse and chorus are sung to the same music.
- Contrasting verse-chorus: verse and chorus have different music.

In "Rock Around the Clock," the music shown in Example 29.8 serves as the main harmonic-melodic material for the entire song. The music to measures 1-4 reappears with different words in other verses ("When the clock strikes two, three and four, if the band slows down we'll yell for more"), but the words and music of 4-10 are consistently the same throughout the song (a refrain). This entire example is based on the twelve-bar blues progression, and the thought expressed in the text is not concluded until the end of the harmonic progression. Both "Rock Around the Clock" and "Eleanor Rigby" are in simple verse form.

"Rock Around the Clock" begins, as do many popular songs, with an eight-measure introduction (intro), to the words "One, two, three o'clock, four o'clock, rock . . ." An introduction is usually instrumental, but may also include text, as does this one, or a repeated syllable like "Oh" or "Ooh" (as in "Baby Love"). It may be based on music later associated with the verse or chorus, or on a chord progression or a **riff** (a repeated instrumental motive); sometimes the intro fades in, or instruments may join in to build up the sound for the entry of the main part of the song. In this song, an instrumental accompaniment entering after the introduction establishes the "groove."

KEY CONCEPT The underlying rhythmic "feel" of a performance, created by a recurring pattern of pitch and rhythmic elements (performed by the rhythm section; in rock—drums, electric or double bass, guitar, and keyboards), is called its **groove**. The groove encourages listeners to engage with the music by dancing, tapping their feet, or bobbing their heads, and helps establish the style or genre to which the piece belongs.

Many songs also end with music known as an "outro," or coda, often instrumental. The outro may fade out, or it may repeat the hook. For example, the last verse in "Baby Love" serves as an outro—it is incomplete, repeats the hook, and fades out—while "Help Me, Rhonda" has an instrumental outro that fades out. The length of the intro and outro (their proportion relative to the rest of the song) and their content can be a marker of a particular group's or musician's style. The term "coda" is more likely to be used if it follows the last substantial cadence of the song, as in common-practice music.

An instrumental section in the middle of a song from the 1960s until the 1990s is referred to as an **instrumental break** (if several instruments are featured) or a **solo break** (one instrument); the term "break" is used somewhat differently in later popular songs. Instrumental breaks may be based on the melody and chord progression of the verse and/or chorus (as in "Rock Around the Clock" as performed by Bill Haley and the Comets) or may include improvisation over a harmonic progression only. In hip-hop or rap songs, a "rap break"—a passage with a rhythmic spoken solo, usually accompanied by background instruments—may substitute for the verse (or chorus). Some songs include an **instrumental interlude**, a passage with new music that serves as a transition between or change of pace from other sections. A short instrumental link may be used to connect two musical sections.

KEY CONCEPT Beginning in the mid-1960s, **bridge** came to refer to a section of music with text that contrasts with the verse and/or chorus. The bridge in songs up to the 1990s usually appears only once, and serves to heighten anticipation of the return of the verse or chorus.

For an example, consider "You've Got a Friend," a Grammy-winning song written by Carole King in 1971, and popularized by James Taylor. (Listen to either performance online.)

FIGURE 29.5: Form in "You've Got a Friend"

Intro

A Verse 1: "When you're down and troubled . . ."

Chorus: "You just call . . . "

A′	Verse 2:	"If the sky above you . . ."
	Chorus:	"You just call . . ."
B	Bridge:	"Now ain't it good to know . . ."
A″	Chorus:	"You just call . . ."
Outro		

The verse and chorus in this song appear together, forming a larger section **A**; with the bridge as section **B**, this makes what is called a composite (or compound) **A A′ B A″** design, replicating the phrase design of the quaternary song form at a higher level. In these designs, the **B** section is usually not as long as the **A** sections, and in the final return of **A** (as **A″**) the chorus may appear alone and may be repeated, instead of the verse-chorus pairing of previous **A** sections.

KEY CONCEPT Small sections of a popular song that always appear together can be considered to form a larger formal section at a higher hierarchical level, making a composite (or compound) **A A′ B A″** or **A B A′**. A sections consisting of a verse and chorus and **B** representing the bridge are common, but other designs are possible as well.

In songs where the verse and chorus are strongly contrasting, or where the verse ends without harmonic closure, there may be a **prechorus**: a short passage of music with text that comes between the verse and the chorus. "City of Blinding Lights" by U2 illustrates this element. The song opens with two verses ("The more you see the less you know . . ." and "Neon heart dayglo eyes . . ."), followed by a prechorus ("And I miss you when you are not around . . .") and then the chorus ("Oh . . . Oh you look so beautiful tonight . . ."). Following the chorus there may be a **postchorus**, a short passage of music preparing for the return of the verse. The prechorus and postchorus are most often encountered in post-millennial popular music, where many small sections may combine to form larger ones.

SUMMARY

- Bridge: music with text that contrasts with the verse and chorus, usually appearing once in the song to prepare a final return of the chorus or verse.
- Prechorus: short passage of music between the verse and the chorus.
- Postchorus: short passage of music between the chorus and the verse.
- Instrumental break: a section in the middle of a song (usually based on one of its harmonic progressions) played only by instruments.
- Instrumental interlude: a passage with new music connecting other sections of a song.

Katy Perry's chart-topping song from 2013 "Roar" provides an example of most of these formal elements—intro, verse, chorus, prechorus, postchorus, and bridge (see Figure 29.6). Here, the repeated text plays a role in distinguishing the sections: the prechorus has the same text each time it returns, which differentiates it from the verse; and the postchorus also features the same text each time, distinguishing it from the chorus.

FIGURE 29.6: Form in "Roar"

Intro			(2 measures; 4 mm. in video version)
A	Verse 1:	"I used to bite my tongue . . ."	(4 measures)
	Verse 2:	"I guess that I forgot . . ."	(4 measures)
	Prechorus:	"You held me down . . ."	(4 + 4, for 8 measures *)
	Chorus:	"I got the eye . . . [refrain]"	(8 measures *)
	Postchorus:	"Oh oh oh . . . [refrain]"	(5 measures *)
A'	Verse 3:	"Now I'm floating . . ."	(4 measures)
	Prechorus:	"You held me down . . ."	(4 + 4, for 8 measures *)
	Chorus:	"I got the eye . . . [refrain]"	(8 measures *)
	Postchorus:	"Oh oh oh . . . [refrain]"	(5 measures *)
B	Bridge:	(instrumental, then) "Roar-oar . . ."	(3 + 4, for 7 measures)
A″	Chorus:	"I got the eye . . .[refrain]"	(8 measures)
	Postchorus:	"Oh oh oh . . . [refrain]"	(9 measures; extension!)

*ambiguous phrase boundary

These extra sections in post-millennial songs contribute to a feeling of shifting levels of intensity and energy: in this track, the prechorus between the verse and chorus builds anticipation of the chorus; likewise, though at the same volume as the chorus, the repeated "Oh oh oh" of the postchorus releases some of the intensity. Both the chorus and prechorus end with the refrain line "You're gonna hear me roar!," the hook of the song.

While almost the entire song is set over repeating four-measure patterns, the vocal line sometimes enters after the downbeat (as in the verses) but other times enters with an anacrusis to the downbeat (as in the prechorus and chorus). The shifting of the entry relative to the strong downbeat of each measure corresponds to the assertiveness of the text, with the longest anacrusis on "I got the eye . . ." (chorus). Since phrase and section lengths in popular songs tend to be regular, any irregularities or ambiguities like these draw our attention and may signal significant locations in the form.

The bridge, substantially different from the rest of the song, provides a **build** (an increase in intensity in anticipation of the chorus), with the instruments cutting out to signal the **drop** (the return of the drums and full texture in the final chorus). As the chart shows, the smaller sections combine to create a composite form: another **A A′ B A″**. In older sectional forms, we would expect the lengths of the **A** sections to be the same or, as in rounded binary, **A′** to be about half the length of **A**; in songs like this one, however, the large sections tend to become progressively shorter. Also, the **A′** and **A″** sections add layers of musical texture (vocal overdubbing and enriched instrumental parts) each time the chorus and postchorus return.

Since recent popular music typically appears first in a recorded format, for some songs discussed here we have determined the duration of various sections by listening to the recording and counting measures. Scores may be available, but they are often fraught with errors created in the transcription process or may be targeted to a particular audience (such as "easy piano"). Recent pieces, in particular, also depend on specific production and recording techniques to produce their trademark sounds, and many timbral, textural, and temporal effects cannot be represented accurately in standard notation. Researchers can, however, study the **waveform** of a song using sound-processing software (such as the free Audacity program), as shown in Figure 29.7: the waveform for Tiësto's "Red Lights."

FIGURE 29.7: Waveform graph (made using Audacity) for Tiësto, "Red Lights"

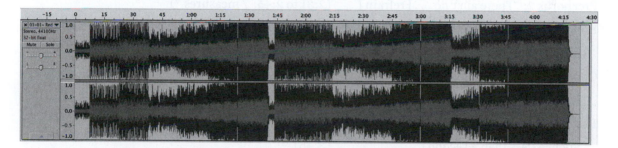

When a song is loaded into a program like this one, there are several advantages for the analyst:

- it is possible to listen to the song with a counter that tracks where events enter (even down to the millisecond, if desired) and replay from any point;

- the display shows the waveform for both tracks of a stereo song like this one, and allows each to be heard separately from the other;

- and often the waveform clearly illustrates where there are section divisions.

Listen to this song as you follow the timings in Figure 29.8 below (the measures were determined by conducting along and counting). The refrain "We're gonna run them red lights" appears at the end of each prechorus and instrumental chorus, providing a sense of closure to those sections. Refer also to the waveform image above to locate each section.

FIGURE 29.8: Form in "Red Lights"

Intro	(0:00 to 0:08; 4 measures)
Verse 1: "Blacked out . . ."	(0:08 to 0:23; 8 measures)
Verse 2: "So let's break . . ."	(0:23 to 0:40; 8 measures)
Prechorus 1: "Nobody else . . . [refrain]"	(0:40 to 0:55; 8 measures)
Prechorus 2: "There ain't no . . . [refrain]"	(0:55 to 1:09; 7 measures *)
Build to chorus (instrumental) (refrain)	(1:09 to 1:24; 8 measures)
Silence (less than a second)	(1:24)
Chorus: instrumental, ending with refrain	(1:25 to 1:40; 8 measures, 4 + 4)
Instrumental interlude (like intro)	(1:40 to 1:44; 2 measures)
Verse 3: "White lights . . ."	(1:44 to 1:58; 8 measures)
Verse 4: "We can't back . . ."	(1:58 to 2:15; 9 measures)
Prechorus 1: "Nobody else . . . [refrain]"	(2:15 to 2:31; 8 measures *)
Prechorus 2: "There ain't no . . . [refrain]"	(2:31 to 2:45; 7 measures *)
Build to chorus (instrumental) (refrain)	(2:45 to 3:00; 8 measures)
Silence (less than a second)	(3:00)
Chorus varied, with refrain	(3:00 to 3:16; 8 measures)
Instrumental interlude (different one)	(3:16 to 3:31; 8 measures)
Build to chorus (instrumental; new)	(3:31 to 3:46; 8 measures)
Silence (less than a second)	(3:46)
Chorus, with refrain	(3:46 to 4:18; 16 measures, 4 + 4 + 4 + 4)
(Echo on fade-out)	*ambiguous phrase boundary

One element of the song that is obvious on the waveform graph is the brief silence that precedes the entrance of the chorus, which looks like a white vertical line drawn through the shading; this represents the end of the build and signals the coming of the drop (the return of the drums and full texture in the chorus).

Harmony and Melody

Many popular songs written after 1950 continue to follow the harmonic conventions of earlier tonal music—the basic phrase progression and principles of voice-leading—though they may include chord extensions, mode mixture, sus chords, added sixths, secondary dominants, and other chromatic harmonies. In some songs, common-practice voice-leading has been replaced by chord connections that are easier to make on a guitar fretboard. With electric guitars, new types of chord voicing and doubling came into use—including **power chords**, with only root and fifth (no third, which leaves its quality ambiguous). When combined with amplification and distortion and played in the middle register of the guitar, power chords generate overtones that increase the volume and richness of the sound. They are usually connected by shifting the hand in a parallel motion, rather than by traditional voice-leading.

For songs clearly in a major or minor key that follow basic phrase progressions, we can provide a Roman numeral and contextual analysis (T-PD-D-T), even though the voice-leading may not follow earlier practice. Songs based on the twelve-bar blues progression can be labeled with either chord symbols or Roman numerals, though a contextual analysis will not conform to the basic phrase design because of the V-IV-I progression in the last four bars and the underlying pentatonic framework. And while some songs include common-practice cadence types—PAC, IAC, and HC—others may feature melodic units with no standard harmonic or melodic cadence. For an example, look at the opening of the verse of "Eleanor Rigby" (Example 29.9); the five measures that follow this example have the same melody and harmonies.

EXAMPLE 29.9: Lennon and McCartney, "Eleanor Rigby," mm. 9-13

These five-measure groupings constitute a melodic thought, but neither the melody nor harmonies follow a traditional progression—the chords are Em to C (is this e: i-VI?). The introduction to the song starts with a C major triad, but then moves to Em and back again (is this C: I-iii?). The refrain ("All the lonely people") is also based on Em and C, and the song ends on an E minor triad, with the melody on the third (G) of the chord. In deviating from a common-practice progression, the harmonies reflect the loneliness and the repetitive life of the characters described in the lyrics. When analyzing popular songs, such as this one, don't be surprised to find progressions that are not based on the basic-phrase progressions—instead consider what chords are being used, how they are connected, and what their possible relation might be to the lyrics.

Other options explored in post-1950 popular styles include progressions derived from the major and minor pentatonic scales and modal scales. The minor pentatonic can generate root progressions that include the triads I (or i), ♭III, IV, V, or ♭VII in various combinations, as in Example 29.10.

EXAMPLE 29.10: Examples of progressions from the minor pentatonic

(a) Robinson, "Turn the Beat Around" (chorus)

(b) Mercury (Queen), "Crazy Little Thing Called Love" (repeated figure throughout song)

	D		D		G		C	G	
D:	I		I		IV		♭VII	IV	

(c) "Crazy Little Thing Called Love" (refrain)

	B♭		C		D	
D:	♭VI		♭VII		I	

The progression in Example 29.10c is sometimes referred to as the Aeolian cadence—whether in a major or minor context—as it is associated with folk-music chord progressions in that mode. The final two chords of part (c), ♭VII (subtonic) to I, are also associated with folk music based on the Mixolydian mode. The subtonic in these cases can be considered a dominant substitute, leading to the cadential tonic.

Other progressions, such as I–♭VII–♭VI–V, follow a bass line familiar from Handel's G Major Chaconne—a descending minor tetrachord—but the chords may now be connected with parallel motion that was not typical of the earlier style. While these chords may be identified with Roman numerals, the progressions may have little or no resemblance to common-practice voice-leading—instead, the Roman numerals simply represent the motion between roots. Chord symbols may be used instead, especially if there is no clear sense of which chord is the tonic.

Sometimes a section (or even an entire song) may be based on the alternation of two chords, as in the introduction to Jim Croce's "Bad, Bad Leroy Brown"; theorist Phillip Tagg refers to this alternation as a **shuttle**. Three or more chords repeated in the same sequence and harmonic rhythm constitute a **loop** (a term that can apply both to a repeated chord progression without any cadence, and to "tape" loops, a segment of electronic music that repeats). Listen again to "Roar" while following Figure 29.9, which lists the chords of the harmonic loop and duration of each. This progression, which is repeated throughout the song except for the bridge, is harmonically ambiguous as to function, though it is certainly possible to identify a tonic and provide Roman numerals for the chords. It has an added feature of including two IV-I progressions, if the Cm-Gm is considered iv-i in G minor; in any case, those chords lend a strong minor presence in the middle of the loop.

FIGURE 29.9: "Roar" harmonic loop

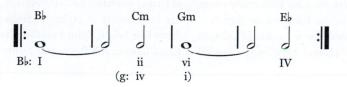

"Red Lights" features both harmonic loops and "tape" loops—repeated segments made from synthesized sounds—that are four measures long (throughout most of the song; see Figure 29.10).

FIGURE 29.10: "Red Lights" harmonic loop

Guitar chords in score:	Gm⁷	Eb⁶₉	Bb	Dm/A
Bb:	vi⁷	V	I	iii
Over the bass line:	G	Eb	Bb	A
Before vocals, sounds like g:	i⁷	VII	III	v

Though the vocals express Bb major, the accompaniment at the beginning sounds more like G minor (i7-VII-III-v)—a contradiction that is fairly common in popular styles, sometimes referred to as the "melodic-harmonic divorce."

The chord progressions explored in the rock era (post-1950) are rich and varied—to study them in the same detail as we have the progressions of Baroque, Classical, and Romantic music would require as many pages as have been devoted to those styles. For now, listen with an open mind—don't expect the progressions to follow earlier norms. When you encounter a progression you like, analyze it: What are the chords? How do they connect? How are they used in this song? And how do they relate to the meaning of the song's lyrics or to its style?

Did You Know?

The 1956 remake of "Hound Dog" by Elvis Presley is the best-known version of the song; it ranked as #19 on *Rolling Stone*'s list of "500 Greatest Songs of All Time" and is heard in several movie soundtracks, including *Forrest Gump, Lilo & Stitch*, and *Indiana Jones and the Kingdom of the Crystal Skull*. The original version, written by Jerry Leiber and Mike Stoller, was recorded in 1952 by Willie Mae "Big Mama" Thornton, and the following year held the #1 spot on the Billboard Rhythm and Blues charts for seven weeks. Like many songs achieving popularity on the R&B charts (which at that time were intended for a primarily African American audience), "Hound Dog" was released in cover versions almost immediately by various country singers. A version with the revised lyrics used by Presley—"snoopin' round my door" was replaced with "cryin' all the time," and "You can wag your tail, but I ain't gonna feed you no more" was replaced by "You ain't never caught a rabbit, and you ain't no friend of mine"—by Freddie Bell and the Bellboys, was intended to appeal to a broader radio audience by removing the sexual innuendo typical of blues songs. "Hound Dog" (with both sets of lyrics) has since been covered by artists performing in a variety of styles, including Jimi Hendrix, Jerry Lee Lewis, John Lennon, the Rolling Stones, Eric Clapton, Jeff Beck, and James Taylor.

TERMS YOU SHOULD KNOW

added-sixth chord	head	quaternary song form
altered fifth	hook	rap break
Aeolian cadence	instrumental break	refrain
blue notes	instrumental interlude	riff
blues scale	intro	shuttle
bridge	link	simple verse form
break	loop	thirty-two-bar song chorus
build	ninth chord	tritone substitution (sub)
changes	outro	twelve-bar blues
chorus	prechorus	verse
drop	postchorus	verse-chorus form
extensions	power chords	verse-refrain form
groove		

QUESTIONS FOR REVIEW

1. What are some phrase designs found in early twentieth-century popular songs?
2. What added notes might you find in the chords used to harmonize early twentieth-century popular songs?
3. Which scale degrees may be altered to create blue notes?
4. When jazz combos play a jazz standard, how do solos alternate with ensemble playing, and improvised music with notated music?

5. What changes have taken place in the use of the terms "verse," "refrain," and "chorus"?

6. What other formal designs are found in post-1950 song settings?

7. What new sections have been added in post-millennial popular music? How do they combine to create larger formal sections?

8. Find a piece with added notes in chords, altered fifths, or blue-note alterations. (Hint: Look in music by jazz composers or those who have been influenced by jazz.)

Know It? Show It!

Focus by working through the tutorials.

Learn with InQuizitive.

Apply what you've learned to complete the workbook assignments.

30

Chromatic Harmony and Voice-Leading

Outline

Chromatic elaboration of diatonic frameworks

- Chromatic sequence patterns
- Descending chromatic bass lines
- Chromatic voice exchanges and wedge progressions
- Common-tone diminished seventh and augmented-sixth chords
- The raised chordal fifth

Chromatic mediant relations

Overview

In this chapter, we consider harmonies and voice-leading characteristic of Romantic-era chromaticism, and learn how to write chromatic progressions by embellishing familiar diatonic ones.

Repertoire

Brahms, Intermezzo in A Major, Op. 118, No. 2

Gabriel Fauré, "Après un rêve" ("After a Dream")

George Frideric Handel, Chaconne in G Major

Fanny Mendelssohn Hensel, "Neue Liebe, neues Leben" ("New Love, New Life")

Jerome Kern and Otto Harbach, "Smoke Gets in Your Eyes," from *Roberta*

Wolfgang Amadeus Mozart, String Quartet in D Minor, K. 421, mvt. 3

Franz Schubert

"Am Meer" ("By the Sea"), from *Schwanengesang* (*Swan Song*)

"Der Wegweiser" ("The Sign Post"), from *Winterreise* (*Winter Journey*)

Robert Schumann, "Ich grolle nicht" ("I Bear No Grudge"), from *Dichterliebe* (*The Poet's Love*)

Hugo Wolf, "In dem Schatten meiner Locken" ("In the Shadow of My Tresses"), from *Spanisches Liederbuch* (*Spanish Songbook*)

Chromatic Elaboration of Diatonic Frameworks

Chromatic Sequence Patterns

As we have seen, the most ubiquitous sequences in tonal music are descending-fifth sequences, which provide a fertile source for chromaticism. For one example, listen to the Menuetto of the Mozart String Quartet in D Minor, and focus on measures 22-29, the end of the **B** section (the harmonic disturbance) of this binary form (Example 30.1a).

EXAMPLE 30.1: Chromatic and diatonic descending-fifth sequences

(a) Mozart, String Quartet in D Minor, mvt. 3, mm. 22-29

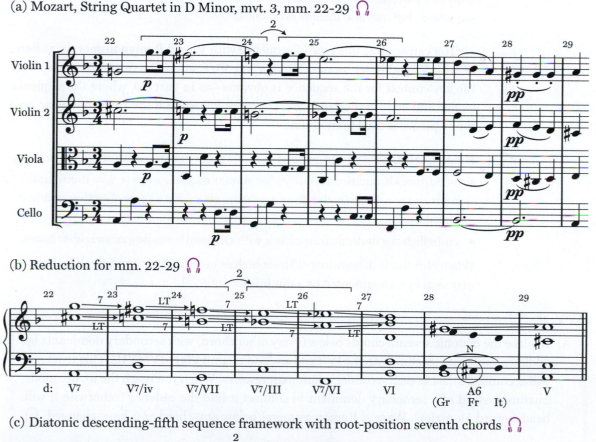

(b) Reduction for mm. 22-29

(c) Diatonic descending-fifth sequence framework with root-position seventh chords

The bass line (cello part) reveals the harmonic foundation of the passage. In this descending-fifth sequence, each triad's quality has been altered to make a

dominant seventh chord—the V7 of the chord that comes next. Part (b) shows a reduction of this chromatic sequence, while part (c) gives a diatonic version for comparison. The voice-leading in (c) is typical of this kind of sequence in that the chordal sevenths all resolve down by step as expected; in the chromatic version (part b), all leading tones except the last one also resolve down—pulled downward in a stepwise descending chromatic line.

KEY CONCEPT The most common type of **chromatic sequence** is a descending-fifth sequence in which dominant seventh chords are substituted for all or some of the chords in the diatonic pattern (usually every other chord). The sequence patterns usually feature root-position seventh chords (like diatonic sequences) but may also include inversions.

You can analyze this type of sequence with V7 and Roman numerals, as here, or with V7 and letter names (V7/G, V7/C, V7/F, etc.). The former is preferred if the key context for the sequence is obvious—as in part (a), where the sequence begins and ends in the same key. The latter is helpful if the key is not clear, or if the sequence is used to modulate.

KEY CONCEPT To transform diatonic sequences into chromatic sequences,

- substitute chromatic harmonies for similar diatonic ones (e.g., a dominant seventh for a diatonic chord, or a mixture chord for a same-function diatonic chord); or

- embellish the diatonic framework with chromatic passing or neighbor tones.

When chromatic descending-fifth sequences include inversions, the bass line may skip by an augmented or a diminished interval.

Try it #1

A. Replace the diatonic seventh chords below (every other chord) with secondary dominants by adding accidentals, starting with the IV7: add an A♭ to make it V7/E♭ (V7/♭VII). This sequence will accumulate flats as each secondary dominant resolves. When you reach the ii7, use mode mixture instead of a secondary dominant to connect it into the cadence (otherwise it will head toward F♭ major). Write a Roman numeral below any chord you have changed.

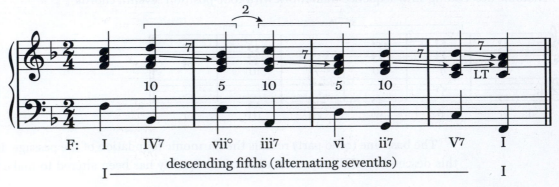

B. Replace the diatonic seventh chords with secondary dominants, starting with the vii⌀⁶₅: alter it to make it V⁶₅/A . This sequence will acquire sharps in the bass line to create leading tones. Change the qualities of the iii and ii chords to create a chromatically descending soprano line. Watch out for needed accidentals to make the correct qualities. Provide a Roman numeral below any chord you have changed.

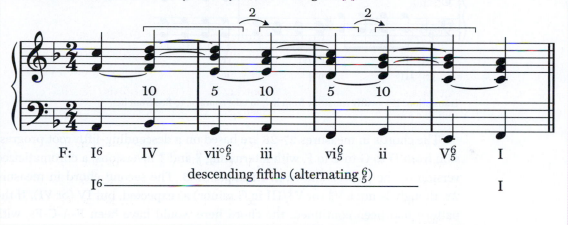

Descending Chromatic Bass Lines

Listen to the excerpt from "Neue Liebe, neues Leben" shown in Example 30.2. After a repetition of the opening parallel period (mm. 1-8) in measures 17-24, and a two-measure extension that cadences in B♭, the character of the song begins to change—with a new vocal line and accompanimental texture, and a chromatic descent in the bass line. Undoubtedly, this change is sparked by the unrest of the text, which speaks of quickly fleeing away. Because of the sequence with secondary dominants and the lack of a cadence to confirm the key, the key in this passage could be read as B♭ major (the key of the previous phrase) or G minor (the key of the following phrase); both analyses have been provided.

EXAMPLE 30.2: Hensel, "Neue Liebe, neues Leben," mm. 26-30

man - nen, ___ ihr ent - flie - hen,

Bb: I⁶   vii°⁴₃/vi   vi⁶
g: III⁶   vii°⁴₃   i⁶

Translation: If I swiftly run away from her, to take courage, to flee from her.

The chords in measures 27-28 are based on a descending-fifth root progression from D to G to C to F, with alternating ⁶₅ and ⁴₂ inversions, a chromaticized version of the pattern shown in Example 30.3. The second chord in measure 28, though, is not a V⁴₂ (or V⁴₂/III in G minor) as expected, but IV (or VI). If the pattern had been continued, the chord here would have been F-A-C-Eb, with the Eb in the bass, which would have resolved normally to the chord in measure 29. Instead, Hensel holds two common tones, Bb3 and G4, and moves the other two voices by step—E3 to Eb3, and C5 to Bb4—breaking the sequence. The key of G minor is not confirmed until measures 33-34 (with an IAC). Perhaps Hensel chose to reflect the indecisiveness expressed by the text in this harmonic progression.

EXAMPLE 30.3: Diatonic descending-fifth sequence with seventh chords alternating and inversions 🎧

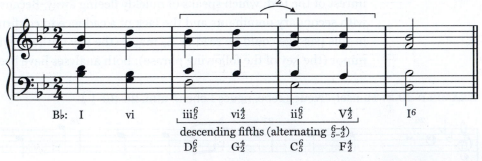

Bb: I   vi   iii⁶₅   vi⁴₂   ii⁶₅   V⁴₂   I⁶
                descending fifths (alternating ⁶₅₋⁴₂)
                            D⁶₅   G⁴₂   C⁶₅   F⁴₂

For another type of chromatic sequence based on a stepwise descending bass line, consider Example 30.4, from the Handel Chaconne. Compare the opening of Variation 9 in part (a) with the opening of Variation 16 in part (b). Both variations begin with a 5-6 intervallic gesture in the left hand, setting up an expressive chain of 7-6 suspensions in the bass and tenor voices. In part (b), the stepwise bass line of part (a) has been elaborated to create a chromatic descent from 1̂ to 5̂.

EXAMPLE 30.4: Handel, Chaconne in G Major

(a) Variation 9, mm. 73–76

(b) Variation 16, mm. 129–132

An attempt to apply Roman numerals to measures 130–132 would be an exercise in futility; the passage is strongly linear, and is not based on a root progression. If these simultaneities are stacked in thirds to spell diminished seventh chords followed by triads, the chordal sevenths of the diminished seventh chords do resolve downward, following the 7–6 linear pattern of previous variations. However, the roots F♯3 and E3 on the downbeats of measures 130 and 131 move downward as part of the chromatically embellished bass line that created them in the first place. These voice-leading chords are best analyzed as a chromaticized 7-6 sequence. Similarly, the C♯-E-G sonority in measure 131, beat 2, is a diminished triad produced by chromatic embellishment; although it could be given a Roman numeral (a vii°⁶/V that resolves irregularly), this "chord" is best labeled simply by identifying the C♯s as chromatic passing tones.

SUMMARY

- Any sequence that features stepwise voice-leading is a candidate for chromatic embellishment.

- The embellishment can be as simple as filling in whole steps chromatically in one voice (usually the bass), or it may involve elaborate chromaticism in several voices.

- In descending-fifth sequences, some or all of the seventh chords may be replaced with chromatic secondary-dominant-function chords in root position or inversions.

Try it #2

A. Insert notes with accidentals in the bass line, beginning with E3, to make it descend chromatically (change the bass-line quarter notes to eighth notes). 🎧

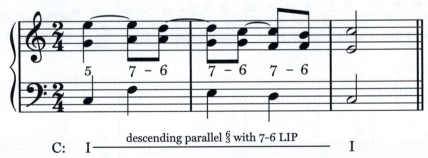

B. Insert notes with accidentals in the bass line to make it ascend chromatically (changing the bass-line quarter notes to eighth notes). 🎧

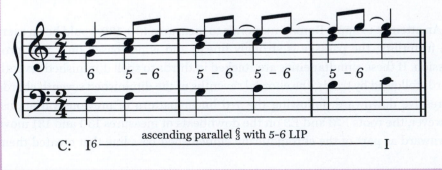

Chromatic Voice Exchanges and Wedge Progressions

Example 30.5 shows a chromatic progression written in the style of a march introduction. In this progression, the inner voices (D4 and F4) stay the same throughout, while the outer voices move in contrary motion from G2 (bass) and B4 (soprano) to B2 and G4 and back again—making a voice exchange, filled in with half steps. As is usual with a voice exchange, the chord with the interval that is exchanged, in this case V7, is prolonged; the "chords" in between are not strong functional harmonies but rather by-products of voice-leading. Progressions like this—where two voices move chromatically in contrary motion—are called **chromatic wedge progressions**.

EXAMPLE 30.5: Chromatic introduction 🎧

C: V7

Example 30.6 demonstrates a number of ways that voice exchanges may be filled in chromatically. Previous chapters considered voice exchanges filled in with a diatonic passing chord—usually a second-inversion triad or seventh chord, as in part (a). In Romantic-era pieces, a relatively simple elaboration can be made by filling in the half steps between the notes that are exchanged, as in part (b). Part (c) shows a chromatic voice exchange between ii^7 and V$^6_5$/V, where $\hat{2}$ and $\hat{4}$ in the ii^7 chord change places with $\hat{2}$ and $\sharp\hat{4}$ in the V$^6_5$/V. Here, the soprano descends by a m3, while the bass ascends a M3. To chromaticize this voice exchange requires a repeated pitch (or a longer note value) in the upper voice to match the duration of the lower (part d). Either of these elaborated progressions may be reversed to return chromatically to the beginning point, as in the march introduction of Example 30.5.

EXAMPLE 30.6: Voice exchanges and their chromatic elaborations

(a)   (b)

D: I   V$^6_4$ I^6 D: I   V$^6_4$ I^6
T   T

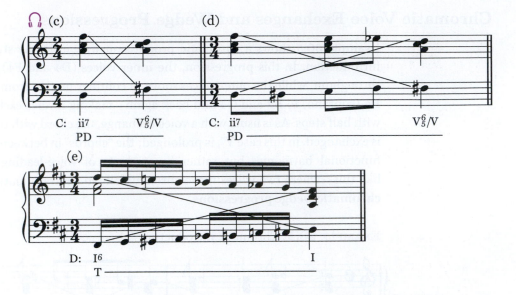

There are many possible variants of the chromatically filled voice exchange: as one example, the frameworks here can be inverted to begin with outer voices spanning a sixth rather than a third (part e). While it is sometimes possible to analyze the chords between the "ends" of the voice exchange with Roman numerals, these labels do not make sense functionally; rather, these chromatic successions serve to prolong the chords at either end.

Now listen to Example 30.7a, from Schubert's "Der Wegweiser," for an extended chromatic wedge (or omnibus) progression. In measures 68-75, two voices move in contrary motion by half step. The upper voice spans G4 (supplied by the vocal anacrusis to m. 69 and continuing in the piano part) down to B♭3 (beat 2 of m. 75), while the bass line spans B♮1 to G2—a chromatic voice exchange. Part (b) clarifies how each voice progresses chromatically, with the held root of the G chord filling in an inner voice.

EXAMPLE 30.7: Schubert, "Der Wegweiser"

(a) Mm. 68-77

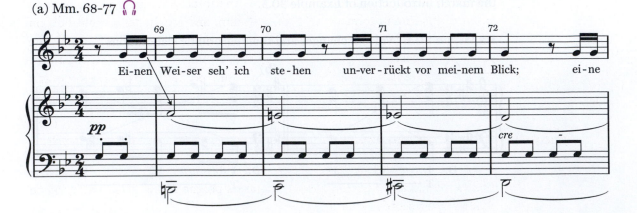

Translation: One sign I see standing, unmoving before my gaze; one street must I go down, from which no one has come back.

(b) Reduction of mm. 68-75 🎧

Again, an analysis of these sonorities with Roman numerals does not make sense: you would end up with a series of secondary dominants and augmented-sixth chords (even a diminished third chord!), with their implied resolutions unfulfilled. Better simply to label the chord that is prolonged, and not worry about the simultaneities in between.

Listen to the excerpt again to hear how Schubert interprets the words "unverrückt" (unmoving) and "keiner" (no one) musically. The phrase begins with the vocal line literally unmoving, a repeated G4 unremitting above the accompaniment's chromatic lines. These repeated notes might be sung with a fairly uninflected "straight" interpretation to portray the unmoving street sign. The high point of the line in terms of register, duration, and emotional content falls on "keiner," and Schubert's use of the lowered $\hat{2}$ and Neapolitan harmony on the last syllable works to create a sense that this is a road from which no one returns. Singer and pianist alike can intensify this foreboding through tone color and timing decisions.

Common-Tone Diminished Seventh and Augmented-Sixth Chords

Turn now to two contrasting songs to learn additional ways to embellish harmonies chromatically. Listen first to Schumann's poignant "Ich grolle nicht," while following the score in your anthology.

EXAMPLE 30.8: Schumann, "Ich grolle nicht," mm. 16-19

Translation: That I have known for a long time.

The harmonic analysis of the passage in Example 30.8 is fairly straightforward except for two chords—the IV⁶ in measure 17 (because it is unexpected after V7) and the diminished seventh chord on the downbeat of measure 18 (because it does not resolve as a secondary diminished seventh). Both sonorities result from passing motion against the reiterated common tone G4 in the uppermost voice of the piano and vocal line. The diminished seventh is called a **common-tone diminished seventh chord** (abbreviated CT°7), or **embellishing diminished seventh chord**, because it carries the fully diminished quality, but does not function as a diatonic or secondary diminished seventh chord. These types of embellishing chords function in the same way as passing or neighboring $^6_4$, $^4_2$, or other voice-leading chords, but with additional chromaticism.

Look now at another diminished seventh chord, from "Smoke Gets in Your Eyes" (Example 30.9). Listen to the passage, concentrating on the diminished seventh chord in measure 23, beat 3 (D♯-F♯-A-B♯ [C♮]). As in the Schumann example, the diminished seventh here embellishes the dominant harmony, and the common tone of the CT°7 is in the uppermost voice.

EXAMPLE 30.9: Kern and Harbach, "Smoke Gets in Your Eyes," mm. 21-24

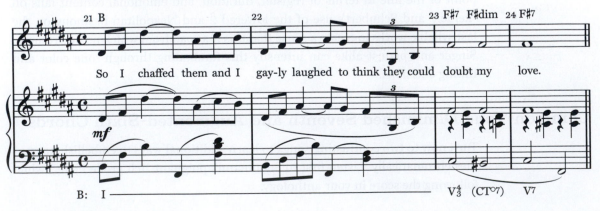

KEY CONCEPT Common-tone diminished seventh chords are collections of chromatic and diatonic neighbor or passing tones that happen to make a fully diminished seventh sonority. They always share one pitch with the chord that precedes or follows them. They do not resolve as dominant-function chords, but have an embellishing role in the progression.

To write a common-tone diminished seventh chord (Example 30.10):

1. Find a position for the chord between two harmonies that share one or more common tones (it may be the same harmony, possibly with a change of voicing).

2. Write the first and third chords, leaving a space in the middle.

3. Choose a common tone to share with the first or third harmony (usually the soprano or bass note); build a diminished seventh chord with that common tone as one element and stepwise motion in the other voices.

4. Remember that CT°7 chords have an embellishing function. In part (a), the bass line features a chromatic neighbor tone, in part (b) a chromatic passing tone, and in part (c) a pedal.

5. Because the $\frac{4}{2}$ inversion is typical for CT°7 chords, you may keep the common tone in the bass and build a °7 chord in $\frac{4}{2}$ position by raising the fourth and second above the bass (part c).

EXAMPLE 30.10: Common-tone diminished sevenths

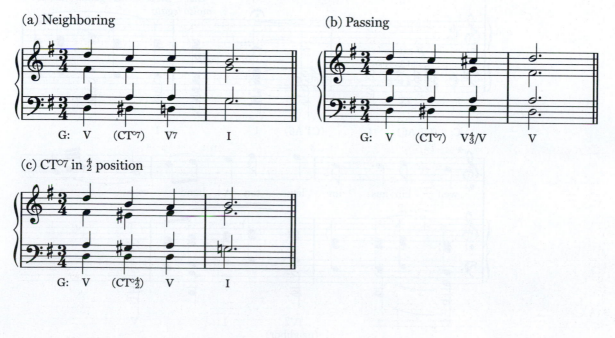

(a) Neighboring

G: V   (CT°7)   V7   I

(b) Passing

G: V   (CT°7)   V$\frac{4}{3}$/V   V

(c) CT°7 in $\frac{4}{2}$ position

G: V   (CT°$\frac{4}{2}$)   V   I

Try it #3

Write a CT°7 that departs from and returns to the given chord, first using model (a) in Example 30.10 (neighboring motion in the bass), then model (c) (common tone in the bass).

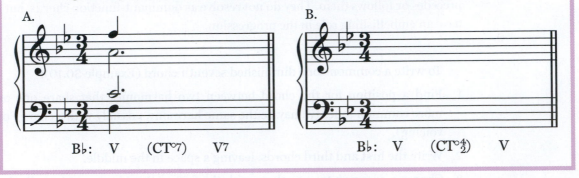

It is also possible to find similar collections of chromatic neighbors that make a so-called **common-tone augmented sixth** (CT A6). This chord usually prolongs the tonic harmony, as in Example 30.11; both pitches of its distinctive augmented sixth still resolve outward to $\hat{5}$—though in this context, to the fifth of the tonic harmony. Here, the $\flat\hat{3}$ of the CT A6 is spelled $\sharp\hat{2}$ (D♯ rather than E♭). A French version is also possible, with $\hat{2}$ instead of $\flat\hat{3}$.

EXAMPLE 30.11: Schubert, "Am Meer," mm. 1-6

Translation: The sea sparkled in the distance in the last light of the evening.

⌣ **KEY CONCEPT** To write a progression with a common-tone augmented-sixth chord:

1. Write the root-position tonic chord as the first and third chords of the progression. In both tonic chords, double the fifth instead of the root (see Example 30.12; the CT A6 may also appear without a tonic chord preceding it).

2. For the CT A6, write a note a half step below the upper $\hat{5}$ to make $\sharp\hat{4}$, and a note a half step above the lower $\hat{5}$ to make $\flat\hat{6}$; these should resolve to the doubled fifth in the third chord.

3. Fill in the remaining pitches of the A6 chord. The common tone ($\hat{1}$) is usually maintained in the bass. The missing element is $\flat\hat{3}$ for a Gr6 (the most frequently used CT A6). Because it lies a chromatic half step below the third ($\hat{3}$) of the tonic chord, $\flat\hat{3}$ is sometimes spelled $\sharp\hat{2}$, as a chromatic neighbor tone. In minor keys, the $\flat\hat{3}$ and $\flat\hat{6}$ are already in the key signature; the only note with an accidental will be $\sharp\hat{4}$.

EXAMPLE 30.12: Common-tone Gr6

G: V6   I   (CT A6)   I

Try it #4

Write three chords in each measure below. The first and third should be the tonic chord in the given key: for the second chord, write a CT A6.

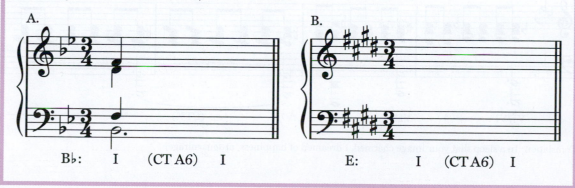

A.   B.

Bb: I   (CT A6)   I   E: I   (CT A6)   I

The Raised Chordal Fifth

Another common chromatic alteration of a diatonic harmony—one you have already seen in a popular-music context—is the inflection of a chordal fifth up a half step to create an augmented triad. This occurs frequently in the dominant or dominant seventh harmony, but may also appear in the tonic triad (sometimes as a variant of 5-6 motion to 5-#5-6), or it may chromatically embellish other diatonic harmonies. One way to analyze these chords is by identifying the embellishing tones that create the augmented triad; alternatively, analyze them with Roman numerals and figures such as I#5, V#5 or V#$\frac{7}{5}$.

Example 30.13 shows both a secondary dominant (m. 5) and a diatonic triad with raised chordal fifth (m. 6). The excerpt ends with a dominant seventh expanded by a CTø7 (less typical than the fully diminished CT°7).

EXAMPLE 30.13: Fauré, "Après un rêve," mm. 1-8

Translation: In a sleep that your image charmed, I dreamed of happiness, ardent mirage.

Chromatic Mediant Relations

Before the Romantic era, the most common modulation in a major key was to the dominant. With the increasing exploration of chromaticism in the nineteenth century, however, motion to third-related keys became much more common.

KEY CONCEPT A **chromatic mediant** is a nondiatonic triad whose root is a major or minor third above or below the tonic. Many chromatic mediants share a common tone with the tonic triad; for example, B♭ major (B♭-D-F) and D major (D-F♯-A) share D. The term encompasses triads built both a third above (mediant) and a third below (submediant) the tonic. While chromatic mediants can appear as individual harmonies within a progression, they are most often employed as key areas.

The first two phrases of Wolf's "In dem Schatten meiner Locken" (Example 30.14) provide an example of chromatic mediant relations. The first phrase begins with an expansion of the tonic area by IV, with chromatic embellishments (and an inflection of IV to iv through mixture); it ends with a tonicization of V (m. 4). The second phrase begins with a D major triad (m. 5), a major-quality chromatic mediant (III), by direct modulation. Another direct modulation, to G♭ major (♭VI, another chromatic mediant key and also a tonicized mixture chord) in measure 9, ends phrase 2 in the lowered submediant key.

EXAMPLE 30.14: Wolf, "In dem Schatten meiner Locken," mm. 1–10

Translation: In the shadow of my tresses my beloved has fallen asleep. Shall I wake him up now? Ah, no!

This sequence of keys—B♭ to D to G♭, and eventually back to B♭—spans a cycle of major thirds. Tonicizations that span the entire octave by some equal interval are called **symmetrical divisions of the octave**. Most typical of the Romantic era are symmetrical designs that divide the octave by major third, as here, or by minor third. It takes three modulations to bring a major-third cycle back to the tonic (as in the Wolf song, B♭–D–G♭–B♭) and four modulations to bring a minor-third cycle back to the tonic (e.g., C–E♭–G♭–A–C).

Chromatic mediants, while not common as individual chords, frequently serve as key areas in Romantic-era pieces. When analyzing such chords, first check to see whether the alterations in chord quality and resolution may be attributed to a temporary tonicization or secondary-dominant function. In the Wolf song, the second phrase begins as a sequential repetition of the first (transposed up a major third), though it ends with a phrase extension (making it a six-measure phrase) and a cadence in G♭ major. The G♭s in measures 1-2 and the F♯s in measures 5-8 prepare the listener for this abrupt shift in key.

KEY CONCEPT When analyzing chords that have been chromatically altered:

- Use uppercase Roman numerals for major and augmented chords and lower-case for minor and diminished chords.

- Include ⁺ or ° for augmented and diminished chords.

- Check whether seventh chords need ⌀ or ° designations.

- Place an accidental before the Roman numeral only if the root has been altered from the diatonic scale degree.

Remember: With Roman numerals or scale-degree numbers, use ♭ for lowered and ♯ for raised regardless of the key signature. For example, the lowered-sub-mediant root in A major is spelled with a natural sign, F♮, but the chord is still designated ♭VI.

The table below illustrates how to locate the chromatic mediant keys relative to B♭ major. Start by finding the diatonic mediant and submediant harmonies; changing the quality from minor to major yields two of the chromatic mediant keys (III and VI). Next, find the mixture mediant (♭III) and submediant (♭VI), which are also chromatic mediant keys; changing the quality of those yields the remaining two chromatic mediant keys (♭iii and ♭vi, though rarely used).

Chord	Root of chord	Relationship of root to tonic	Diatonic	Mixture chromatic mediants	Chromatic mediants
Mediant in B♭ major	D (3̂)	M3 above	D-F-A (iii)		D-F♯-A (III)
	D♭ (♭3̂)	m3 above		D♭-F-A♭ (♭III)	D♭-F♭-A♭ (♭iii) (rare)
Submediant in B♭ major	G (6̂)	m3 below	G-B♭-D (vi)		G-B-D (VI)
	G♭ (♭6̂)	M3 below		G♭-B♭-D♭ (♭VI)	G♭-B♭♭-D♭ (♭vi) (rare)

Try it #5

Complete the table of chromatic mediants below, for E major.

Chord	Root of chord	Relationship of root to tonic	Diatonic	Mixture chromatic mediants	Chromatic mediants
Mediant in E major	G♯ (3̂)	M3 above	G♯–B–D♯ (iii)		
	G (♭3̂)	m3 above			
Submediant in E major		m3 below			
		M3 below			

Three brief snapshots from Brahms's Intermezzo in A Major demonstrate how Brahms prepares the listener for the chromatic-mediant relation he will be exploring. The piece begins in A major (Example 30.15a), with a phrase that ends in a half cadence preceded by a cadential $^6_4$; the melody is then repeated and varied in the first large section. In contrast, a second large section begins with the music shown in part (b), in F♯ minor (vi), the relative minor of A major. The excerpt in part (c), which follows shortly after the F♯ minor passage, is in F♯ major (VI), a chromatic mediant. The modulations in each case are direct—a new section of the piece simply begins in the new key—but Brahms reaches this relatively distant key by first "traveling" through a closely related key, then by modal coloration.

EXAMPLE 30.15: Brahms, Intermezzo in A Major

(a) Mm. 1-4

(b) Mm. 49-52

f♯:
(vi)

(c) Mm. 57-61

F♯:
(VI)

You have now learned all the common diatonic and chromatic triads and seventh chords employed in common-practice tonal music. These chords, and the relationships between them, are summarized in Example 30.16—a master table of diatonic and chromatic chords. The table illustrates the chords related to C major / C minor, but the same relationships hold in all other keys. The diatonic triads for C major and C minor are given in part (a), marked by a curly brace. The diatonic sevenths are given in (b), above and below the central rows. Their respective secondary dominants are shown in (c), and the chromatic mediants and other related chords in (d). Everything above the dotted line applies to major keys, everything below to minor keys as though through mixture with C major (e.g., ♭VI).

EXAMPLE 30.16: Diatonic and chromatic chords related to C major and C minor

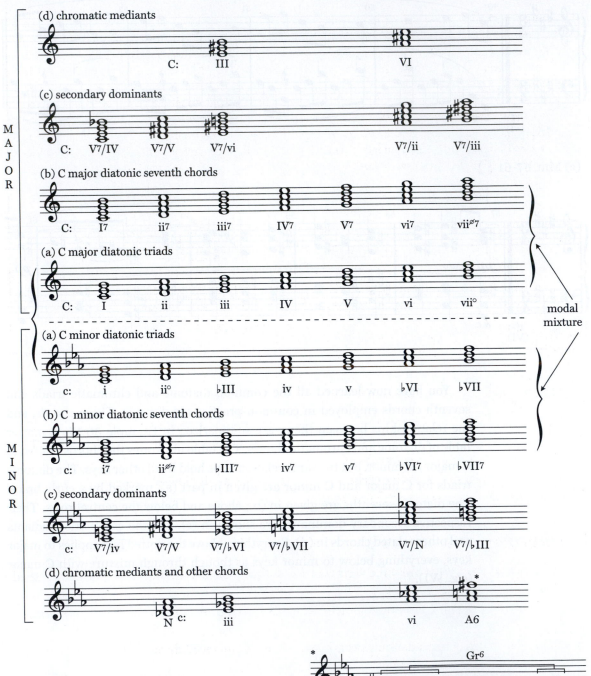

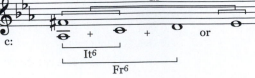

Did You Know?

You may be thinking that the omnibus progression from Schubert's "Der Wegweiser" (Example 30.7) is a Romantic-era innovation because of its extreme chromaticism. Yet theorist Paula Telesco has found that the omnibus and other chromatic wedge progressions originated in harmonizations of the lament bass—a chromatic descent in the bass line from $\hat{1}$ to $\hat{5}$ in minor found in Baroque continuous variations (including Handel's Chaconne in G Major, Example 30.5a, and Purcell's "Dido's Lament"), but also appears in later compositions, such as the Mozart sonata excerpt below.

In Mozart's chromatically filled wedge (mm. 122-123: D3-A2 in the left hand and F5-A5 in the right hand), the inner voices form chords that make a logical, functional harmonic progression from tonic to dominant. Schubert takes this one step further: his inner voices are static, and create a harmonic progression that does not make functional sense when analyzed with Roman numerals.

Mozart, Piano Sonata in D Major, K. 284, mvt. 3, mm. 121-123

TERMS YOU SHOULD KNOW

chromatic mediant

chromatic sequence

chromatic submediant

chromatic voice exchange

chromatic wedge progression

common-tone augmented-sixth chord (CT A6)

common-tone diminished seventh chord (CT °7)

omnibus progression

symmetrical divisions of the octave

QUESTIONS FOR REVIEW

1. What are some ways that diatonic sequence frameworks may be embellished chromatically?
2. What are some standard harmonizations for a descending chromatic bass line?
3. Which diatonic progressions may be enhanced through chromatic voice exchanges?
4. What is the function of common-tone diminished seventh and augmented-sixth chords?
5. What keys are related by chromatic mediant to E♭ major?

6. In music for your own instrument, find examples of (a) a chromatic sequence, (b) a chromatic voice exchange, and (c) a chromatic mediant key area. (Hint: Think first about the time period when each technique was widespread.)

7. How might the function of chromatic elements affect the way they should be interpreted in performance?

Know It? Show It!

Focus by working through the tutorials.

Learn with InQuizitive.

Apply what you've learned to complete the workbook assignments.

31

Chromatic Modulation

Overview

This chapter introduces new modulation techniques that are characteristic of the Romantic era, along with linear harmonic practices of late-Romantic chromaticism.

Repertoire

Ludwig van Beethoven
>Piano Sonata in C Minor, Op. 13 (*Pathétique*), mvts. 1 and 2
>Piano Sonata in C Major, Op. 53 (*Waldstein*), mvt. 1

Frédéric Chopin
>Prelude in C Minor, Op. 28, No. 20
>Prelude in E Minor, Op. 28, No. 4

Jerome Kern and Otto Harbach, "Smoke Gets in Your Eyes," from *Roberta*

Wolfgang Amadeus Mozart, String Quartet in D Minor, K. 421, mvt. 1

Schubert, Waltz in A♭ Major, Op. 9, No. 2

Richard Wagner, Prelude to *Tristan und Isolde*

Outline

Chromatic modulation employing common tones
- By common tone
- By common dyad and chromatic inflection
- Through mixture
- Enharmonic modulation with augmented-sixth chords
- Enharmonic modulation with diminished seventh chords

Chromatic modulation with sequences
- By descending-fifth sequence
- Other chromatic sequences

Linear chromaticism
- Chromaticism and voice-leading chords
- Intentional harmonic ambiguity
- Analyzing and performing chromatic passages

Chromatic Modulation Employing Common Tones

In the Romantic era, as we saw in Chapter 30, composers began to explore distant key relationships. For example, from C major, instead of modulating to the closely related keys of G major (V), A minor (vi), F major (IV), or D minor (ii), they might modulate to A♭ major (♭VI), A major (VI), E♭ major (♭III), E major (III), or D♭ major (Neapolitan ♭II), or even to such keys as C♯ minor (♯i), F♯ major (♯IV), or B♭ major (♭VII). With distant keys like these, fewer pivot or common chord choices are available. A direct modulation may be effected by means of a secondary dominant or simply by starting a phrase in the new key, but the change may sound quite abrupt if it occurs without preparation or transition. Composers have devised a wide range of methods to facilitate smoother modulations.

KEY CONCEPT There are two main strategies for writing a seamless transition between two closely or distantly related keys, especially in Romantic-era music:

- modulation with one or more common tones, and
- modulation by chromatic sequence.

Along with these strategies, other techniques—such as chromatic inflection, mixture, and enharmonic reinterpretation—may be necessary to transform a chord in the first key to function well within the second key.

By Common Tone

Composers in the Romantic era continued to use pivot- (or common-) chord modulation between closely related keys. For pairs of keys that did not share an entire diatonic triad but had chords with one, two, or three pitches in common, the common tones were held and the other pitches shifted up or down, usually by half step. This type of modulation is called a **common-tone** (or pivot-tone) **modulation** if only a single pitch is held between the two keys, and **common-dyad** (pivot-dyad) **modulation** if two pitches are held.

A single shared pitch is enough to make a smooth modulation to either a closely related or a more distant key. Listen to the short passage from the second movement of Beethoven's *Pathétique* Sonata shown in Example 31.1. Here, the C4 from the cadence in A♭ major in measure 16 becomes an anacrusis for the melody in measure 17, accompanied by a repeated C in the left hand. This isolation of a single pitch smooths the transition to F minor (vi in A♭), tonicized in 18-19. In this case, the keys A♭ major and F minor are closely related, but the example shows very clearly how the common tone modulation normally works: the common tone, typically a member of the initial tonic triad, is isolated after a cadence in the first key and sustained or repeated to make the connection to the new tonic.

EXAMPLE 31.1: Beethoven, *Pathétique* Sonata, mvt. 2, mm. 15-19 🎧

A♭: ii   V7   I   C = common tone   f: V6   I   V4/3   i6
                                                     (vi)

Now look at the excerpt from "Smoke Gets in Your Eyes" shown in Example 31.2. The first verse of the song cadences in measures 19-20 in E♭ major; the key for the following phrase is B major, an enharmonic spelling of the chromatic submediant ♭VI, C♭ major. The connection to this distant key is made by the melody pitch E♭4 of measures 19-20, which seamlessly becomes D♯4 in the following measure. To foreshadow this modulation, Kern introduces the pitch class B (the new tonic) as a prominent embellishing tone in measure 16.

EXAMPLE 31.2: Kern and Harbach, "Smoke Gets in Your Eyes," mm. 16-24 🎧 (mm. 18-24 recorded)

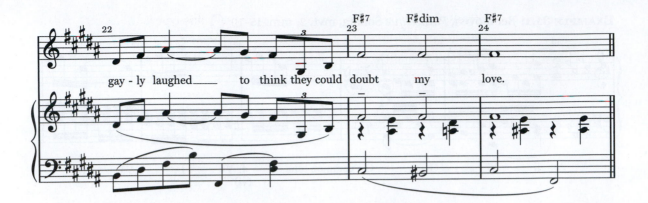

gay - ly laughed____ to think they could doubt my love.

SUMMARY

To connect the key of one section with a mixture-related or distant key in the next section, Romantic-era composers and beyond might end a phrase on the tonic chord of the first key, then let one chord member connect into the tonic chord of the following new key. Using a member of the tonic triad in a major key as a common tone, it is possible to modulate to the following:

MEMBER OF TONIC TRIAD	CLOSELY RELATED KEYS	MIXTURE-RELATED KEYS (DISTANT)	OTHER DISTANT KEYS
root (1̂)	vi, IV	i, iv, ♭VI (or ♯V)	
third (3̂)	iii, vi		III, ♯i or ♭ii, VI
fifth (5̂)	V, iii	v, ♭III, i	

By Common Dyad and Chromatic Inflection

Sometimes the common element between two keys is a dyad instead of one pitch. Unlike the examples above, this type of connection usually occurs within a phrase—where two elements of a chord in the initial key form the basis of a different chord in the second key. The other members of the initial chord are then chromatically inflected (moved up or down by half step) to form the new chord. This technique works best when the chromatically inflected chord is a dominant seventh chord, secondary leading-tone chord, augmented-sixth chord, or some other type of harmony that has an expected resolution. The chromatic inflection heightens the forward momentum as it leads to the expected resolution in the new key.

For an example, listen to measures 18-30 of Beethoven's *Waldstein* Sonata while following the score in your anthology. This passage is part of a transition from the first key area, C major, to the second, E major—a chromatic mediant, quite a distant tonal area from C major. In measures 20-23 (Example 31.3), the harmony changes from C major to V of E major. The A minor first-inversion chord in 20-21 (C-E-A) moves in 22 to C-E-A♯, an Italian sixth in the key of E major, which then resolves normally to the B-D♯-F♯ chord in 23. Because the modulation is activated by the shift of one pitch by a half step, this type is sometimes called modulation by **chromatic inflection**, though it also involves a common dyad. The chromatic motion here does not sound abrupt; rather, it seems an intensification of the drama already unfolding. And the blurring of the key by the sequence in measures 14-21 helps make this striking modulation seamless.

EXAMPLE 31.3: Beethoven, *Waldstein* Sonata, mvt. 1, mm. 20-23

Through Mixture

Sometimes it is easier to modulate to a distantly related key by shifting first to the parallel major or minor key through mode mixture. This modulatory procedure depends on an intermediary chord that is a mixture chord in one of the keys and diatonic in the other.

KEY CONCEPT When a mixture chord acts as a pivot between two distantly related keys, one of the two keys will be closely related to the key of the mixture chord. Modulations that include a chromatic pivot chord—typically a mixture chord such as i, ♭III, or ♭VI, or possibly a secondary dominant or leading-tone chord—are sometimes called **altered common-chord**, or **altered pivot-chord, modulations**.

The second movement of the *Pathétique* Sonata modulates from A♭ major to E major—the key of the mixture chord ♭VI (an enharmonically respelled ♯V)—but not with ♭VI as a pivot. Listen to the excerpt in Example 31.4, which begins in A♭ minor, a direct shift to the parallel minor from the A♭ major that preceded it. Measure 41 starts to repeat the motive from 37-40 when something unusual happens—look at all the sharps in measure 42! The chord on the downbeat of 42 is A-B-D♯-F♯, or V$_2^4$ in E major, resolving to a first-inversion E major chord on beat 2 and leading to a cadence in measures 43-44 in E major. The move first to the parallel minor (A♭ minor) through mixture allowed for the common-dyad (enharmonically respelled: C♭-E♭ = B-D♯) modulation. One of the remaining pitches of the V$^4_2$ is approached through chromatic inflection (A♭-A♮ in the bass), while the other is approached by whole step (A♭-G♭, with G♭ spelled as F♯) through a dramatic minor-seventh leap in the upper voice.

EXAMPLE 31.4: Beethoven, *Pathétique* Sonata, mvt. 2, mm. 39-44

Enharmonic Modulation with Augmented-Sixth Chords

As is evident in the previous example, how a composer spells a chord has implications for how we expect it to resolve. There are several types of chords used in chromatic modulations where the entire chord is held in common, but the chord is enharmonically respelled to reflect a different expected resolution. For example, the Gr⁶ is especially valuable in modulations: it sounds exactly like a dominant seventh chord, which can be resolved two or more ways depending on how it is spelled.

Look back at Example 31.3. If you weren't looking at the spelling of the chord in measure 22 but only listening to the passage, you might expect the chord to resolve as V7/IV in C, as though spelled C-E-(G)-B♭ (a dominant seventh chord in C). But Beethoven's spelling, C-E-A♯ (an augmented-sixth chord), and the voice-leading of the chord's resolution move this passage toward the new tonal area of E major.

Now look at Example 31.5a, an excerpt from Mozart's String Quartet in D Minor. The key in measure 42 is E♭ major, the Neapolitan of D minor. This passage is heavily colored by mixture chords, including the minor subdominant and tonic, as shown in the reduction in part (b). We would expect the V7/V in E♭ major (m. 45) to resolve to a B♭ dominant harmony, yet it resolves instead to a cadential V$^{6-5}_{4-3}$ in A minor.

EXAMPLE 31.5: Mozart, String Quartet in D Minor, mvt. 1

(a) Mm. 42–46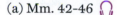

(b) Reduction of mm. 42–46

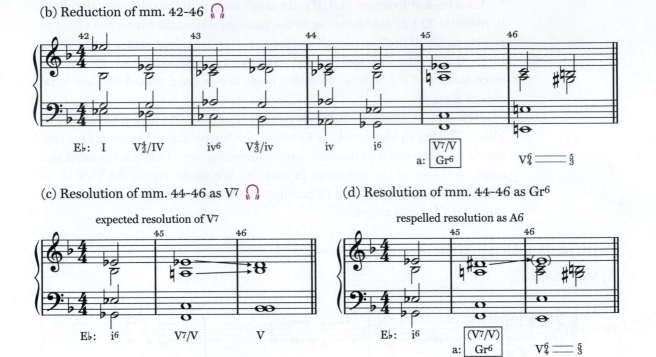

(c) Resolution of mm. 44–46 as V7

(d) Resolution of mm. 44–46 as Gr6

Although this resolution sounds a bit surprising, it makes sense in retrospect. Part (c) shows the chords from measures 44–46 with the resolution we expect, while part (d) gives the measure 45 chord respelled as an augmented sixth—with D♯ instead of E♭. The modulation to A minor is confirmed when the passage continues in that key through measure 53.

In this type of modulation, called an **enharmonic modulation**, the entire contents of a chord are held in common between the first key and the second, with the chord respelled (or resolved as though respelled) in the second key. Because the harmonies resolve in ways that require reinterpretation (whether the resolutions are respelled or not), such progressions can also be called modulation through **enharmonic reinterpretation**.

KEY CONCEPT Use enharmonic reinterpretation between Gr6 chords and dominant sevenths to modulate to a new key a half step higher or lower than the original (Example 31.6).

- Up by half step: reinterpret a Gr6 as a V7; the ♯$\hat{4}$ is respelled as the seventh of a V7, and the V7 then resolves to the tonic (part a).

- Down by half step: reinterpret a V7 as a Gr6; the seventh of the V7 is respelled as ♯$\hat{4}$ of a Gr6, and the Gr6 resolves to V in the new key (part b).

- Additional keys may be reached by interpreting the V^7 as a secondary dominant, rather than a diatonic chord in one of the keys (as in Example 31.5, for keys a tritone apart).

When you write enharmonic modulations, pay careful attention to accidentals in the new key. Play these examples to hear how the harmonic "deception" sets up the new tonic.

EXAMPLE 31.6: Enharmonic modulation with V^7 and Gr^6

(a) Enharmonic modulation up by half step 🎧

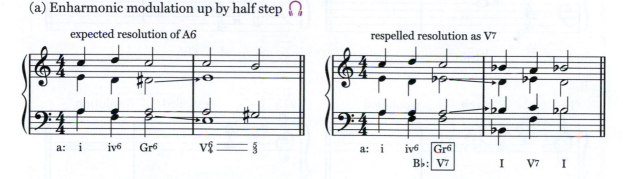

(b) Enharmonic modulation down by half step 🎧

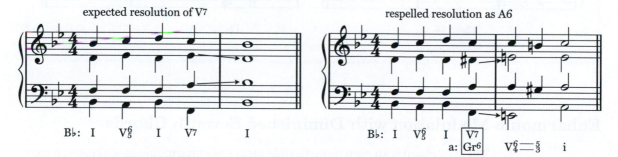

Try it #1

Write the requested V7 or Gr⁶ chord in each progression, and resolve it normally. Then respell the chord as requested in the given key, and resolve it normally. Use primarily whole notes. Avoid parallel fifths in resolving the Gr⁶ by writing a V$_{4-3}^{6-5}$ in half notes.

A.

(1)   given   resolution   (2)   respelled   resolution

d: V7   _____   c♯:   Gr⁶   _____

B.

(1)   given   resolution   (2)   respelled   resolution

f: Gr⁶   _____   f♯:   V7   _____

Enharmonic Modulation with Diminished Seventh Chords

The vii°7 chord is an even more flexible means of enharmonic modulation: it may potentially resolve in four different ways (to either a major or minor "temporary tonic"), depending on how it is spelled. Because it is constructed of all minor thirds, any of its four pitches may serve as the root. For example, a B diminished seventh, if spelled with B as the root (Example 31.7a, part 1), can resolve to either C major or C minor; if spelled with D as the root (part 2), it resolves to either E♭ major or E♭ minor, and so on. Parts (b) and (c) show the other possible vii°7 sonorities; all possible °7 chords are represented in the example. In addition, in music of the Romantic era you may see a voice-leading shift from one vii°7 up or down a half step to a second vii°7 before the chord resolves to a new key.

EXAMPLE 31.7: Diminished seventh chords and their possible resolutions

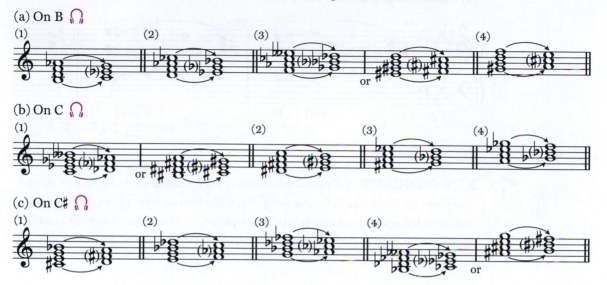

(a) On B

(1)   (2)   (3)   (4)

or

(b) On C

(1)   (2)   (3)   (4)

or

(c) On C♯

(1)   (2)   (3)   (4)

or

The diminished seventh chord can also serve as a secondary leading-tone chord to modulate to any major or minor key. For an example of such an enharmonic modulation, look at Example 31.8a, a passage beginning in G minor. In measure 134, an F♯-A-C-E♭ diminished seventh chord resolves to G-B♭-D after a voice exchange involving C and E♭ in the highest and lowest parts. The motive is repeated in measure 135, but the F♯-A-C-E♭ is respelled D♯-F♯-A-C on the third beat, and now resolves to a cadential $\frac{6}{4}$ in the key of E minor—the chromatic submediant of G minor. Play through the reduction in part (b) several times to hear the effect of the different resolutions of the vii°7 chord.

EXAMPLE 31.8: Beethoven, *Pathétique* Sonata, mvt. 1

(a) Mm. 133–136

g:

F♯-A-C-E♭ = D♯-F♯-A-C

(b) Reduction of mm. 134-136

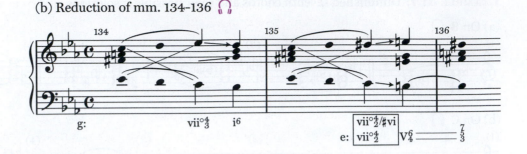

KEY CONCEPT A diminished seventh chord used as an enharmonic pivot chord can be spelled as it functions in either the first or second key. It may also appear twice, spelled once each way (Example 31.8). The enharmonically respelled chord can be used to modulate to ♭III or ♭iii, ♭V (♯IV) or ♭v (♯iv), and VI or vi.

Sometimes modulations involve a combination of techniques. Listen to the modulation in measures 49-50 of Example 31.9, the transition from E major (F♭ major) back to A♭ major.

EXAMPLE 31.9: Beethoven, *Pathétique* Sonata, mvt. 2, mm. 47-51

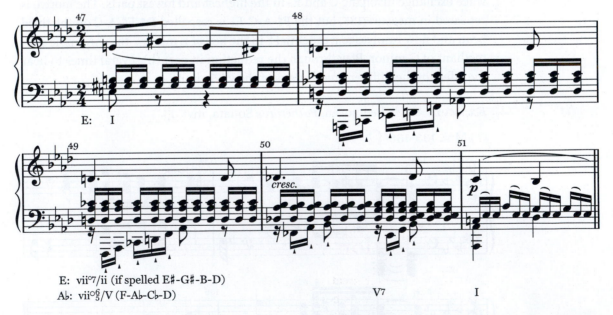

The chord in measure 47, an E major triad, is followed by a diminished seventh chord (D-F-A♭-C♭) in 48-49. This chord might be heard as vii°7/ii in the old key of E major or as vii°⁶₅/V in the new key of A♭. The chord that begins measure

50, a half-diminished seventh (B♭-D♭-F♭-A♭), is approached from the D-F-A♭-C♭ chord by holding the common tone, A♭, and moving the other voices down by half step. This B♭ half-diminished chord typically functions as vii°7 in C♭ major, but it does not resolve that way here; instead, the B♭ and D♭ are held as a common dyad, and F♭ and A♭ both move down a half step, forming an E♭-G-B♭-D♭ chord (V7 of A♭ major) on beat 2.

As should be clear, the Romantic era brought many ways to modulate, especially between distant keys. When you come across a modulation in music you are analyzing or performing, listen carefully to the passage, then examine the evidence with the techniques you have learned. With patience, you should be able to solve the puzzle.

Try it #2

Resolve the given diminished seventh chord in (1) to i or I, as shown. Then invert the chord and respell it enharmonically in (2)-(4) so that each note in turn of the original chord is the root. Resolve each chord to its tonic (i or I). In the blanks, write the key of the tonic to which each respelled chord resolves.

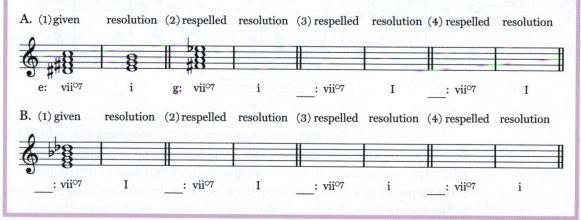

A. (1) given   resolution   (2) respelled   resolution   (3) respelled   resolution   (4) respelled   resolution

e: vii°7   i   g: vii°7   i   ___ : vii°7   I   ___ : vii°7   I

B. (1) given   resolution   (2) respelled   resolution   (3) respelled   resolution   (4) respelled   resolution

___ : vii°7   I   ___ : vii°7   I   ___ : vii°7   i   ___ : vii°7   i

Chromatic Modulation with Sequences

Another method for creating a smooth modulation to either close or distantly related keys is by sequence. For an example, listen to the Schubert waltz shown in Example 31.10; the melody often has accented dissonances on the downbeat that resolve on beat 2.

EXAMPLE 31.10: Schubert, Waltz in A♭ Major 🎧

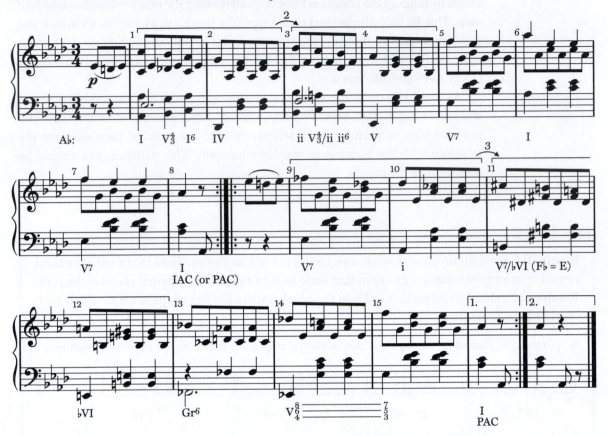

This little waltz features two sequences: one in measures 1–4, where the two-measure pattern is transposed up a whole step; and a second one in 9–12, where the two-measure pattern is transposed down by a major third (enharmonically respelled as a diminished fourth) to tonicize the mixture chord ♭VI—part of the harmonic disturbance of the simple sectional binary form. (F♭ major is respelled as E major to avoid excessive accidentals.) Though ♭VI is only tonicized here, this method can be used in longer pieces to prepare a distant modulation—all that is needed is a confirmation of the new key area. Notice how Schubert foreshadows the F♭ major key area by introducing F♭5 as a dissonance on the downbeat in measure 9 and C♭5 in measure 10. He smoothly returns to the tonic key by respelling the common tones between the ♭VI in measure 12 (E–G♯–B) and the Gr⁶ in 13 (F♭–A♭–C♭).

By Descending-Fifth Sequence

While any type of sequence may be used to modulate, descending-fifth sequences with secondary dominants work particularly well. A dominant seventh chord at any point in a descending-fifth sequence may resolve to a triad that can be established as a new key by a cadence, a continuation in the new key, or both. Beethoven's *Waldstein* Sonata provides an example; the initial pattern for this sequence is shown in Example 31.11.

EXAMPLE 31.11: Beethoven, *Waldstein* Sonata, mvt. 1, mm. 112–116 🎧

The four-measure sequence pattern begins with an arpeggiated C major triad and ends (in m. 115) with a C dominant seventh chord (with an added flatted ninth, D♭). This C♭$^9_7$ is a secondary dominant that resolves down by fifth as expected, to an F major triad in measure 116, then the entire four-measure pattern is repeated in 116–119, transposed to F major (with a very slight alteration in the arpeggiation in m. 118). The third and final statement of the sequential pattern—again transposed down a fifth, to B♭—begins in measure 120 and ends in 124–125 with the resolution of the B♭ dominant harmony to E♭ minor, a chromatic mediant not closely related to C major. E♭ minor is tonicized for only two measures (124–125) before moving on.

Other Chromatic Sequences

Now listen to the opening of the sonata to hear how a sequence can be transposed to a distantly related key without sounding jarring. The opening four measures (Example 31.12) are transposed down a whole step in measures 5–8, creating a "distantly related" phrase in B♭ major. This type of modulation by sequential transposition is like a direct modulation, yet the repetition of the melodic pattern makes the effect seem less abrupt. Such modulations often function as tonicizations when considered in the larger musical context. In this case, the B♭ might be heard as a passing tonicization in a C major context with mode mixture.

EXAMPLE 31.12: Beethoven, *Waldstein* Sonata, mvt. 1, mm. 1-8 🎧

Linear Chromaticism

Chromaticism and Voice-Leading Chords

Many types of passing and neighboring chords may be created by combining embellishing tones into **voice-leading chords** (VL) that expand a functional harmony, a type of **linear chromaticism**. Since there are too many possible chords of this type for each one to have a specific name, we refer to them as a category by this term (VL), but you may also see them called linear chords, apparent chords, or embellishing chords. There are times when it makes sense simply to label the individual embellishments, instead of considering the "chord" they make—particularly if their duration is less than the prevailing harmonic rhythm, or if they are metrically unaccented. A contextual analysis will clarify the musical contexts for these sonorities.

For an example, look at the passage from a Chopin prelude in Example 31.13. The chords on beats 1, 2, and 4 in measure 5 are i$^{5-6}$ and v^6 (or alternatively, i-VI^6-v^6). As for the third chord, we can best explain it by considering the relationship of each of its pitches to those of the chords on either side. The bass is an octave-doubled chromatic passing tone. The soprano and tenor parts are shared with the chord that follows, and the alto skips from A♭ (a pitch in the previous chord) to F♯, making a kind of double neighbor around the G to which it resolves on beat 4. Each individual voice makes sense in the context, but if we stack this simultaneity in thirds, we get B-D-F♯-A♭, a very bizarre seventh chord. Another interpretation of the chord is to hear the embellished motion from A♭ to G in the alto as a 7-6 suspension with a chromatic change of bass.

EXAMPLE 31.13: Chopin, Prelude in C Minor, mm. 5-6 🎧

The first chord in measure 6 is also linear in origin, and can be interpreted as a tonic chord with a passing tone in the bass. Harmonic analysis with Roman numerals in these cases may not provide much useful information beyond what is gleaned from analyzing the embellishments. If you like, write "linear" (or VL) in the analysis, then label the embellishments in the score.

Some Romantic composers took the voice-leading idea even further, writing pieces where long spans of music consist of linear chords held together by their smooth, chromatic voice-leading without much, if any, sense of progression or root motion. For a famous example, listen to Chopin's Prelude in E Minor, whose opening phrase is given in Example 31.14. Only at the beginning and end of the phrase are there clearly functional harmonic progressions.

EXAMPLE 31.14: Chopin, Prelude in E Minor, mm. 1-12 🎧

Try it #3

Write the chords in measures 1-4 of Example 31.14 on the staff below, and determine their quality and inversion. Include pitches from the right-hand melody only where they seem to fit in the chord; the others should be considered embellishing tones. What chord qualities can you identify? Do any resolve correctly?

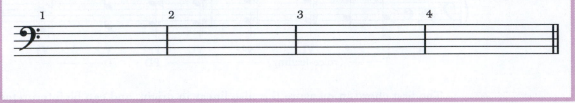

While providing a Roman numeral analysis is good practice for identifying chord types, such an analysis does not explain much about this passage other than the general qualities of the sounds. Concentrate rather on the linear motion. The melody in the right hand prolongs a B4 with a neighboring C5 in measures 1-4, then descends via a passing-tone Bb4 to prolong A4 in measures 5-8 with a neighboring B4. A skip from A4 in measure 8 to F♯4 in measure 10 is embellished in 8-9 and reiterated in 10-11. The basic strategy for both the melody and accompanying harmonies seems to be a gradual descent from the i chord at the beginning to the V7 in measure 12. While the descent in the melody is primarily diatonic, though, the descent in the left hand is primarily chromatic, with voices taking turns moving chromatically downward.

We have tried to draw a balance between discussing "strength of progression" (that is, passages with strong root-based chord progressions) and "strength of line" (passages with less strong root movement, but smooth linear connections between chords). The chord patterns in the Chopin prelude do not make much sense from a root-progression standpoint, yet the strength of line—in particular, voice-leading based on chromatic half steps—makes this phrase work musically.

Intentional Harmonic Ambiguity

Harmonic ambiguity like that found in the Chopin prelude is often used in songs to express multiple meanings of the text, and is an important element in Romantic-era opera. Perhaps the most famous intentionally ambiguous passage in Romantic music is the opening of the Prelude to Richard Wagner's opera *Tristan und Isolde* (Example 31.15). Examine this passage for clues regarding key areas.

EXAMPLE 31.15: Wagner, Prelude to *Tristan und Isolde*, mm. 1–17

Measures 1–3 and 4–7 form a sequence, with the entire texture transposed up a minor third except for the anacrusis (perhaps to make the first two pitches in mm. 4–5 match the B-G♯ in m. 3). Since the Prelude begins with A3 and measure 3 ends with an E dominant seventh chord, the opening could imply A minor. Yet this opening is quite ambiguous—by measure 7, no key has been established as a point of departure.

The third presentation of the sequence pattern, in measures 8–11, is not an exact transposition. It begins with the anacrusis transposed up a minor third from the previous pattern, again matching pitch classes in the last chord of measure 7. But the next portion is expanded, with notes added as it strives forward and upward. Measures 12–15 then simply reiterate 10–11 in a truncated form. In 16–17, the first standard cadence, an E dominant seventh resolves deceptively to an F major triad. Does that mean the piece is in A minor? Clearly the ambiguity of harmony and key is a musical depiction of unfulfilled desire or longing, and it prepares the listener beautifully for the drama between two lovers that follows.

Analyzing and Performing Chromatic Passages

When you find chromaticism in a piece you are analyzing or performing, think about whether it represents a surface embellishment, a change of chord quality, or a change in chord function.

- Can the chromatic pitches be attributed to embellishing (e.g., passing or neighbor) tones? These are basically surface events and may not imply a harmonic function or need resolution, but they may foreshadow additional chromaticism later in the piece or may create chromatic VL chords.

- Do the chromatic pitches change the quality of the chords, indicating mixture or other identifiable chords such as Neapolitan or augmented-sixth chords? These can serve as substitutes for diatonic chords within the basic phrase, adding color and drama to the progression.

- Do the chromatic pitches create secondary dominant or leading-tone chords? Do they create chromatic descending-fifth sequences? These may change the direction of the phrase by tonicization or modulation.

Substituting a chromatic chord for a diatonic one can intensify the sense of forward motion or signal a change of mood, which performers might highlight through a change of tone color. It is vitally important to the character of the music and its sense of direction that chromatic alterations be performed in tune.

Passages that are in their very essence chromatic and linear can present quite a challenge to the analyst and performer both. In studying such a passage, determine the harmonic points of arrival and shape your performance toward them. Establish which embellishments affect the underlying harmonic progression and which are ornamental. Identify the quality of each sonority, and determine whether dominant-function seventh chords or A6 chords resolve as expected, resolve deceptively, tonicize scale degrees, or initiate new keys. Locate sequences and transitory or modulatory passages. All this information will help you identify a hierarchy of musical function.

Finally, when analyzing pieces that include chromatic voice-leading, don't forget to listen. In pieces like the Chopin prelude, there are some progressions that sound (and are) functional—label those first, then listen attentively to the rest. Careful analysis of some chromatic musical surfaces may reveal a relatively simple underlying diatonic progression, which you can convey through performance; other passages may rely almost entirely on harmonic ambiguity. It is your job as musical interpreter to determine which view to present.

Did You Know?

The opera *Tristan und Isolde* was composed in 1865-69 by Richard Wagner, but the story of Tristan and Isolde dates back to the Middle Ages and Renaissance, when it was a well-known and often-retold romance. For his setting, Wagner relied on Gottfried von Strassburg's poetic retelling of the story, with the traditional characters placed in a courtly setting. For other operas—including the *Ring of the Nibelung* cycle and *Parsifal*—Wagner based his librettos on tales set in poetry by medieval Germanic poets. The rediscovery of these early poems was influential on the German Romantic movement.

The story of *Tristan und Isolde* is one of intense love and passion, but each time there is an opportunity for the lovers to be together, they are separated. To represent the theme of unfulfilled love, Wagner composed progressions that repeatedly lead toward a cadence that is evaded at the last moment, with the dissonant intervals instead moving linearly to form another dissonant chord. It becomes clear in the course of the opera that Tristan and Isolde will only be permanently united in death; during the "Liebestod" (the "love-death"), a final aria that Isolde sings over the body of Tristan just before dying of grief herself, the series of dissonances set in motion at the very beginning of the Prelude (Example 31.15) finally finds resolution.

TERMS YOU SHOULD KNOW

chromatic inflection
chromatic modulation
- altered common-chord
- altered pivot-chord
- common-dyad
- common-tone
- enharmonic
- pivot-dyad

enharmonic reinterpretation
intentional harmonic ambiguity
linear chromaticism
voice-leading chord (VL)

QUESTIONS FOR REVIEW

1. How may the principle of diatonic pivot-chord modulations be expanded to modulate to distant keys?
2. How can mixture smooth a modulation to a distant key?
3. How may a chromatic descending-fifth sequence be used to modulate?
4. Chords of what quality are suitable for enharmonic reinterpretation?
5. List as many ways to modulate from C major to A♭ major as you can.
6. In music for your own instrument, find a Romantic-era piece with one of the following: (a) common-tone or -dyad modulation, (b) a modulation with an altered pivot chord, (c) a modulation with enharmonic reinterpretation. If this proves difficult for your instrument, check the piano repertoire.
7. How does the function of chromatic elements affect the way they should be interpreted in performance?

Know It? Show It!

Focus by working through the tutorials.

Learn with InQuizitive.

Apply what you've learned to complete the workbook assignments.

32

Sonata, Sonatina, and Concerto

Overview

The focus of this chapter is sonata form. We consider the roles of melody and harmony in shaping a sonata-form movement, and observe how sonata form changed from the Classical to the Romantic era. We also examine two related forms: sonatina and concerto.

Repertoire

Ludwig van Beethoven, Piano Sonata in C Major, Op. 53 (*Waldstein*), mvt. 1

Muzio Clementi, Sonatina in C Major, Op. 36, No. 1, mvt. 1

Joseph Haydn, Concerto for Corno di caccia in D Major, mvt. 1

Wolfgang Amadeus Mozart, Piano Sonata in G Major, K. 283, mvt. 1

Outline

Sonatas and sonata form

Classical sonata form
- The first large section: Exposition
- The second large section: Development and recapitulation

Sonata form in the Romantic era
- Increasing length and complexity
- Key areas and the organization of the exposition
- The development section
- The recapitulation and coda

Related forms
- Sonatina
- Concerto form

Performing and listening to sonata-form movements

Sonatas and Sonata Form

The term **sonata** technically refers to a composition for instruments, yet its meaning has changed over time. In the Classical and Romantic eras, a sonata is a multimovement composition for piano, or piano and solo instrument, usually in three or four movements. The first is almost always in **sonata form**, sometimes called **sonata-allegro form** after the standard tempo marking for such movements; the second is usually slow; and the last movement (third or fourth) may be in rondo, sonata, or sonata-rondo form. Though first movements of symphonies, string quartets, and other chamber pieces may also be cast in a sonata form, in this chapter we will focus on the sonata-form movement for piano.

There are several Baroque compositions called "sonata" in the anthology—these include works consisting of a prelude followed by a series of movements (often binary forms) for a small group of instruments, such as the Corelli Sonata in D Minor and Trio Sonata in A Minor. In form and style, though, they are quite different from what came to be known in the Classical era as sonata form.

Classical Sonata Form

Listen to the entire first movement (*Allegro*) of Mozart's three-movement Sonata in G Major, while following the score in your anthology. Think about the overall formal organization, and listen for cadences, which often mark the end of formal divisions; indicate in the score where you hear sections beginning or ending. Label any material that reappears later in the movement, and write the measure numbers of where you first heard these themes or motives. As you read this chapter, keep your score and recording at hand to see and hear each new element under discussion.

While you were listening, you may have noticed some musical clues to the movement's formal boundaries. One obvious clue is the repeat signs—at measure 53 to indicate a repeat of measures 1-53, and at the end to indicate a repeat of 54-120. The movement seems to resemble a large-scale continuous rounded binary form.

The First Large Section: Exposition

The first section in a sonata-form movement (here, mm. 1-53) is called the exposition.

KEY CONCEPT In the exposition, themes and motives for the entire movement are "exposed" for the first time. Its structure is in three parts: (1) opening material in the tonic key; (2) a modulatory passage that leads to a second key; and (3) new material in the second key, leading to a strong cadence ("expositional closure") in that key.

This exposition's first phrase (Example 32.1) is a sentence (2+2+6) that establishes the key of G major; with its triple meter and Alberti bass, it may be invoking a minuet musical topic. The second half of the phrase (mm. 5-10) is extended beyond the expected cadence in measure 8, with scalar flourishes in the right hand that lead to a PAC in measure 10. This second half is then repeated with slight variations, bringing the opening idea to its conclusion in measure 16.

EXAMPLE 32.1: Mozart, Piano Sonata in G Major, mvt. 1, mm. 1-16 🎧

First theme group (FTG)

In sonata form, this opening musical idea in the tonic is often called the **first theme** (**FT**), or **primary theme** (**P** or **PT**). We prefer **first theme group** (**FTG**), which indicates that the section may consist of more than one thematic idea (as it does here), but expresses the tonic key throughout. Another possible term, "first tonal area" (FTA) focuses on the harmonic scheme.

The next significant cadence comes in measure 22 (Example 32.2). This cadence could be interpreted as a HC preceded by a secondary dominant (a tonicized half cadence), but the music continues in the new key of D major, as evidenced by the consistent presence of C♯ in the following measures and by cadences in D through measure 53. Measures 16-22 therefore have a transitional and modulatory function.

EXAMPLE 32.2: Mozart sonata, mm. 16-22

Transition (TR)

G:

cadence in V   (medial caesura)

> **KEY CONCEPT** Transitions (TR) lead from the first theme group to a cadence that prepares a second key area. They are usually sequential and modulatory, and may express an increase in momentum and volume as they lead to the second key area. The end of the transition may be marked by an abrupt silence, called a **medial caesura** (MC—"caesura" means "pause"), sometimes preceded by a dramatic chord or octave leap. If there is a medial caesura, it divides the exposition into two parts; if there is none, the section can be called a "continuous exposition."

Transitions that incorporate motives from the first theme are called **dependent transitions**, while those that introduce new material are **independent transitions**. Mozart's transition is independent and consists of two short melodic sequences—measures 16-19 and 19-21—with a modulation at the end of the second and a medial caesura in measure 22.

With a dependent transition, it may be difficult to decide where the first theme group ends and the transition begins—after all, they use the same thematic material. Listen for tonal function: if the passage sounds like it is leaving the tonic key, it is transitional. Independent transitions can be identified by the change in melodic material and by sequential activity, even when the modulation is delayed until the very end.

Measures 23-53, in the key of D major, constitute the second tonal area, or second theme group. (Other possible terms include "secondary theme" (S) or "subordinate theme.")

KEY CONCEPT The **second theme group** (STG) typically divides into a number of themes that may seem unrelated, except for the fact that they are in a single key: usually the dominant or, in minor keys, the relative major. Once an authentic cadence in the secondary key is reached, the tonal goal of the STG is complete, although closing material (or a closing theme) may follow.

The first and second theme groups *always* contrast in key, and may present themes with contrasting moods. In some early sonata-form movements, particularly those of Haydn, the first and second themes are quite similar, differing primarily in their keys; sonatas like this are called "monothematic."

SUMMARY

The first large section of a major-key sonata form (the exposition) usually has two main parts, defined primarily by their key relationship:

- The first theme group expresses the tonic and the second theme group (most often) the dominant.

- The first theme group is usually shorter than the second, and the second may be divided into several thematic units.

- The transition section modulates between the two groups and may end with a medial caesura.

Mozart's second theme group is a good illustration of how several short thematic ideas—some stable melodies, others more transitional in nature—can work together in a single unified key area. Measures 23-31 present a syncopated lyrical melody that is clearly in D major. The first phrase of this theme, 23-26 (Example 32.3), ends with a half cadence; then the phrase is repeated and varied in 27-30, also ending with a HC.

EXAMPLE 32.3: Mozart sonata, mm. 23-26 🎧

Second theme group (STG)

Measures 31-34 (Example 32.4) exhibit a transitional character because of the repeated motive and secondary leading-tone chords, but they do not modulate. A second melodic idea follows, still in D major (35-38); and 38-43 are a varied repetition of 33-38. With the substantial PAC in D in measure 43 (repeated from m. 38), the STG's tonal motion is complete.

EXAMPLE 32.4: Mozart sonata, mm. 31-38 🎧

Second theme group (continued)

Measures 43-44, based on a motive from the transition (mm. 16-18), then connect to a final theme in 45-51 (Example 32.5). Some analysts consider a new idea at the end of the exposition, following a PAC in the second key, a **closing theme (CT)**; others call it another subsection within the STG. We will refer to it as a CT, understanding it as part of the STG.

EXAMPLE 32.5: Mozart sonata, mm. 45-51 🎧

Closing theme (CT)

In sonata-form movements of the late Romantic era, the closing theme may appear in a third key area, and may include more than one distinct melody. In that case, it may be called the "third theme group," "closing theme group," or simply "closing group." In this movement, the theme in measures 45-47 and 48-51 is reminiscent of the syncopated melody of 23-31, making a connection back to the beginning of the D major key area (compare Examples 32.3 and 32.5).

Finally, measures 51-53 form a codetta that extends and repeats the cadence in D major.

EXAMPLE 32.6: Mozart sonata, mm. 51-53 🎧

Codetta

Although this exposition is similar to a continuous binary-form first section in its key areas, it is much longer and includes transitional passages and a codetta. In addition, it features harmonically stable areas in each key.

KEY CONCEPT Classical-era sonata-form expositions are usually repeated, and generally consist of the following sections:

First theme group	*Transition*	*Second theme group (optional codetta)*
Major key: I	Modulates to V	V (may include a closing theme, still in V)
Minor key: i	Modulates to III (or v)	III (or v) (may include a closing theme in the same key)

The Second Large Section: Development and Recapitulation

When you analyze the second large section of a sonata form, it's helpful to begin by identifying the return of the opening material. Listen again to the Mozart movement while following the score. Listen in particular for the return of the first and second theme groups (including the closing theme) in the second section; this return of earlier material is another similarity between sonata form and rounded binary form, but the way the two forms treat the returning material differs.

Recapitulation: Return of the Opening Material The return of the exposition in the second large section is called the recapitulation (meaning "return to the head," or beginning). When the exposition's music returns, however (compare measures 1-53 with 71-120), some changes are customary.

> 🎧 **KEY CONCEPT** The **recapitulation** traditionally presents *all* of the exposition materials in the tonic key. The first theme group, already in the tonic in the exposition, can usually be restated in the recapitulation with little alteration. The second theme group, and closing theme if present, are usually transposed to the tonic. Since the transition no longer needs to modulate, it is altered to stay in the tonic.

Example 32.7 shows the return of the FTG in Mozart's sonata. Compare this passage with the FTG in the exposition (mm. 1-16).

EXAMPLE 32.7: Mozart sonata, mm. 72-83 🎧

Recapitulation

The first four measures of the first theme group return unchanged in the recapitulation, but the second half (4-10 in the exposition) has been replaced with a variant; this passage, based on the opening material, tonicizes A minor (ii) by means of its secondary dominant (represented by the G♯s).

The transition from the first to the second theme group, which modulates in the exposition, is usually modified in the recapitulation to stay in the original key. In this case, however, the transition passages are identical (compare mm. 16-22 with 83-89). Recall that in the exposition, the end of the transition could have been analyzed as a HC with V tonicized, except that the movement continued in the key of D. Here, the cadence *is* treated as a THC—there is no modulation—and the movement continues in the tonic key, G. Perhaps, in retrospect, the changes to the second phrase of the first theme (mm. 75-83) were intended to balance the reappearance of the transition exactly as before.

Since the second theme group and codetta (if any) are usually transposed from the key of the dominant (in the exposition) to the original tonic for the recapitulation, we would expect measures 90-120, corresponding to 23-53, to appear in G major—and they do. We also make note of the return of the substantial PAC that confirmed the second key in the exposition (mm. 42-43); this cadence in the recapitulation (109-110), now in G, confirms the triumph of the original tonic.

Try it #1

Compare the components of the second theme in the recapitulation with those in the exposition. What has been transposed up? What has been transposed down? Has anything been changed other than by transposition?

Development: Harmonic Instability   In a rounded binary form, we would expect the beginning of the second large section to display harmonic instability through a modulation or through sequences that touch on different keys; the same is true for Classical-era sonata-form movements.

KEY CONCEPT   The beginning of the second large section in a sonata-form movement is called the **development**, because in sonatas by Beethoven and later Romantic-era composers it was devoted to the development and exploration of motives and themes from the exposition. Developments are marked by harmonic instability and sequential motion, and end on the dominant to prepare the recapitulation's tonic return.

A close examination of measures 54-62 (Example 32.8) reveals few connections to the motives of the exposition. Instead, the dominant (D major) is prolonged through its own dominant, A major (hence the C♯s). Mozart's "development," typical for sonata-form movements of the early Classical era, is in essence an expanded version of the same type of harmonic instability and sequential material that would be found in a rounded binary form.

EXAMPLE 32.8: Mozart sonata, mm. 54-62

Development (excerpt)

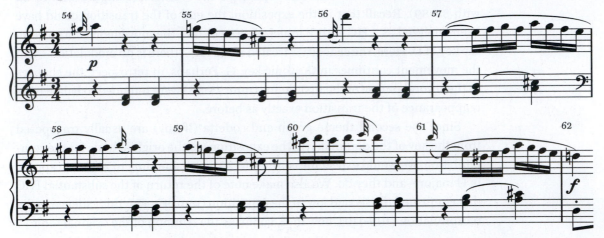

The Retransition   At the conclusion of the development section, a few measures perform a special task: preparing for the recapitulation. This part of the development, the **retransition**, sets up the return of the first theme harmonically—by establishing and often prolonging the V7 chord of the tonic key. The retransition also sets the mood for the first theme's return. In some sonata-form movements, it builds tension, making the listener anticipate the first theme's triumphant return; in others, it sets up the first theme's return almost as a surprise. Other dramatic roles for the retransition are possible, but its harmonic function is consistent: to establish the dominant seventh chord of the tonic key.

In Mozart's sonata, the retransition features a long dominant pedal, extending from measure 62 to 68 (Example 32.9). This rearticulated pedal point, with a melodic sequence above it, builds tension but does not immediately connect to the return of the first theme. Instead, Mozart inserts two ascending pentachords (68-70), each ending with a brief rest, as if to say, "Not yet, not yet." Finally, in 70-71, a descending scalar pattern brings back the first theme.

EXAMPLE 32.9: Mozart sonata, mm. 62-73

Retransition

Listen to this retransition in several different performances: in some, the pianist will slow measures 68 and 69 noticeably, perhaps extending the rests, to heighten the anticipation; in others, he or she maintains a consistent tempo throughout.

SUMMARY

The second large section of Classical-era sonata-form movements includes the development and recapitulation sections; it is usually repeated, and may end with a coda.

Development sections may explore thematic material from the exposition or may simply represent an area of harmonic instability. In early sonata forms, the development section is usually brief compared with the exposition and recapitulation.

Overall, typical Classical-era sonata forms consist of the following sections:

‖: *Exposition*			:‖: *Development*	*Recapitulation*				:‖
FTG TR	STG (CT)		DEV	ReTR	FTG TR	STG	(codetta)*	
(MC)								
I	V			V of	I	I		
i	III			tonic key	i	i		
							*optional	

Sonata Form in the Romantic Era

Increasing Length and Complexity

The rise of the Romantic style brought new developments to sonata form. We will look at some of these changes as they appear in the first movement of Beethoven's *Waldstein* Sonata. Listen to the entire movement while following the score in your anthology. While listening, mark any formal elements you notice—themes, transitions, phrases, cadences, key areas, and so on—and try to identify the main parts of the form. Some Romantic sonata forms also add a slow introduction and lengthy coda—listen also for these possibilities.

Some differences between the Mozart and Beethoven movements that are immediately apparent are the length—302 measures for Beethoven, 120 for Mozart—and the later sonata's chromatic and exuberant Romantic character. Mode mixture, embellishing and harmonically functional chromaticism, and sequences associated with Romantic-era harmony are all present in the *Waldstein* Sonata.

Scan through the score to find the repeat signs marking the end of the exposition (with a first and second ending, mm. 86 and 87). After you have identified the first theme as beginning in measure 1 (there is no slow introduction), mark the beginning of the recapitulation (m. 156). As this movement illustrates, in the Romantic era the development grew to balance the exposition in length and complexity, overlaying a ternary element—exposition (**A**), development (**B**), recapitulation (**A′**)—on the formerly binary-based organization.

Key Areas and the Organization of the Exposition

As you focus on the exposition, consider these questions: Are the themes and transitions located where you would expect, based on the Mozart sonata model? Are the key areas what you would expect?

The first idea of the first theme group is four measures long (as in the Mozart sonata), ending on a tonicized V^6 chord (see Example 32.10). In a Classical sonata, the first phrase probably would have been followed by a phrase of similar length that ended with a conclusive cadence, making a period structure to firmly establish the tonic key. Here, however, the initial idea is abruptly transposed down a whole step to B♭ major (♭VII). This dramatic shift in harmony brings in elements of mode mixture, E♭ and B♭, which remain present through the C minor HC in measures 11–13. Measures 1–4, 5–8, and the elaboration in 9–13 display elements of a sentence structure, but with Romantic-era modification and Beethovenian innovation: the harmony of the second subphrase is ♭VII rather than the more usual V, and the length of the third subphrase is an asymmetrical five measures. There is no strong cadence in C major in the first theme group; the movement's first PAC in C major appears only at the end of the exposition, measures 85–86, in a transitional passage that prepares for the exposition's repeat.

EXAMPLE 32.10: Beethoven, *Waldstein* Sonata, mvt. 1, mm. 1–13 🎧

First theme group

On first listening, measures 14–17 (Example 32.11) sound like a rhythmic variation of 1–4, but in 18 the passage begins to veer in a new harmonic direction—to D minor (ii)—and then, with a chromatic inflection in 22, moves decisively away from C major toward the second key. (Two layers of Roman numerals show two possible harmonic readings of this passage.) Measure 14 is the beginning of the transition—a "dependent transition" because it sounds so much like a variant of the opening phrase.

EXAMPLE 32.11: *Waldstein* Sonata, mm. 14–23 🎧

Dependent transition (first part)

Measures 23–30 continue the transition section with a prolonged B major (and B dominant seventh) chord expanded by an E minor $^6_4$, which implies a move to E minor (iii in C major). This dissipates into a B major arpeggiation in 29–30, then, with a dramatic change of character, connects to an ascending scale fragment in 31–34, which leads to E major (not minor) on the downbeat of measure 35.

The E major theme that begins in measure 35 initiates the second theme group (Example 32.12), identified by its harmonic stability, regular phrase lengths, and chorale-style voicing—a hymn musical topic, which is associated in Beethoven's music with the heroic. The key of E major is related by chromatic mediant, rather than the expected G major (dominant) of the Classical-era movement, and is confirmed by a cadence in measure 42. This type of harmonic innovation is a hallmark of Romantic sonatas. The eight-measure second theme is then followed immediately by a variation (mm. 43–50), with the chorale decorated by a triplet melody in the highest part.

EXAMPLE 32.12: *Waldstein* Sonata, mm. 35-42

Second theme group (2a)

The rest of the exposition may be divided into a number of distinct subsections, all part of the second theme group. In larger sonata forms like this one, it is sometimes helpful to label the subsections of the second theme group with letters: 2a, 2b, 2c, and so on. If we call the chorale melody (mm. 35-42) and its embellished restatement (43-50) 2a, then measures 50 and following, where a syncopated rhythmic idea joins the triplets, could be labeled 2b.

Measures 50-57 provide transitional material that prolongs I in E major. The triplets then accelerate to sixteenth notes, and the introduction of a D6 in the upper voice (m. 60, Example 32.13) turns the tonic function into V_5^6/IV, which then resolves to IV (A-C♯-E) in 62-63. A V_5^6/V in 64-65 introduces a new arpeggiating motive in 66, when the progression reaches a climactic cadential $_4^6$ chord, increasing in tension as the $_4^6$ resolves to a V_7^9 (in m. 70). This harmony is prolonged for four drawn-out measures, delaying its resolution, before the most dramatic point of arrival of the entire exposition in measure 74—an authentic cadence in E major.

EXAMPLE 32.13: *Waldstein* Sonata, mm. 59-74

Second theme group (continuation of 2b)

E: I⁶ ————————————————————————— V_5^6/IV ———————

E: V_5^6/IV ———————— IV ————————

IV ———————————————— V_5^6/V ————————

V_5^6/V ———————————————— V_4^6 ————————

V_4^6 ————————

V_7^9 ————————

V_7^9 ———————————————— I ————————

The cadence initiates a new subsection in measure 74, which we could call 2c. This passage could also be labeled the closing theme (still part of the E major second key area) or codetta, since it follows harmonic closure in E major and since it serves a dual role—as preparation for the repetition of the exposition and for the sequence that connects to the development section.

Try it #2

There are many motivic links between themes in this movement. Where, for example, have you heard the upper part of measures 74-76 before? What is the origin of the left-hand material here?

Mm. 74-76, right hand, are similar to mm. _____ .

Mm. 74-77, left hand, are drawn from mm. _____ .

The Development Section

In a typical Classical-era sonata-form movement, the development section is easy to locate: it begins after the repeat markings, usually following the exposition's definitive final cadence. For this Romantic-era sonata, the situation is much less clear-cut. Listen again to the movement through measure 90 to identify the beginning of the development; the sequence in 80-89 may make locating it difficult. This sequence, the first time through, modulates from E minor back to C major for the repeat of the exposition; yet the second time through, the same music keeps spinning on past C to cadence in measure 90 (on F major), with a motion so smooth that the modulation is hardly noticeable.

To consider this question more broadly, think about the developmental aspects of the exposition: what are measures 14-22 if not a "development" of the primary theme? The "variation" of the second theme in 43-50 is developmental in nature as well. One of Beethoven's innovations in writing sonata-form movements was the incorporation of the principle of development into *all* aspects of the movement, and other Romantic composers to a greater or lesser extent followed his lead. Here, the development section is measures 90-156.

Try it #3

Which of the materials in the exposition does Beethoven explore in the development section? Identify three elements from the exposition and where they are developed (give measure numbers).

	Element	*Measures*	*Where developed*
(a)	_____	_____	_____
(b)	_____	_____	_____
(c)	_____	_____	_____

Now locate the harmonic goal of the development: the retransition, which normally prolongs a V^7 of the primary key (here G^7), preparing for the key's return in the recapitulation. The first G^7 comes in measure 136, but the texture and rhythm of this passage connect it to the sequential passage that came before. A better location for the retransition is measure 142, where both texture and rhythm change and a new section clearly begins. This retransition is quite long and dramatic, beginning with the introduction of a rumbling motive and G pedal point in the bass. The development process continues through the retransition, with the sixteenth-note motive that originated from measure 3.

With the retransition (and therefore the end of the development) located, return now to consider how the development itself is structured. Of the many motives developed in measures 90–156, we will focus on two especially prominent ones, shown in Example 32.14a: the skip up a third with a stepwise return (skip motive), and the descending five-note scale (scale motive). The derivation of these motives from the first theme should be obvious; the variants and repetitions in measures 97 and following are given in part (b). Think about their role in the retransition: the "rumble" in the left hand in measure 142 might be considered a combination of the skip and scale motives. The ascending fragments in the right hand in 146–156 also feature rhythms that are reminiscent of the skip motive's sixteenths without the opening dotted quarter, with its contour inverted; other fragments seem related to the scale motive, again ascending instead of descending.

EXAMPLE 32.14: *Waldstein* Sonata

(a) The two motives from mm. 92–93

skip motive   scale motive

(b) The motives in context, mm. 97–99

Most of the harmonic activity of the development is built on descending-fifth sequences, and a glance at the accidentals indicates that the mode mixture of the exposition is featured here as well. Some of the tonal areas briefly tonicized include G minor (v in C major; mm. 96-99), C minor (i; 100-103), and F minor (iv; 104)—a pattern of descending fifths. Then beginning in 112, Beethoven initiates another extended descending-fifth sequence, including tonicizations of C major (I; 112-113), F major (IV; 116-117), B♭ major (♭VII; 120-121), E♭ minor (♭iii; 124-125), and B minor (vii; 128-129). While these tonicizations are brief, each may be identified by the presence of at least a dominant seventh chord and its resolution to the temporary tonic. Some of these sequences include a chain of secondary dominants, a particularly common type of chromatic sequence.

The Recapitulation and Coda

In the recapitulation, beginning in measure 156, we expect each of the main parts of the exposition to return in order, all in the tonic key. The first theme does return essentially unchanged, as measures 156-168, with one unusual and striking difference: the arpeggiated C minor triad (m. 167, Example 32.15) is followed by a deceptive move to A♭, instead of the expected G. Another arpeggiation in measure 169 spans a D♭ major chord, then ends on B♭. In such ways, measures 167-173 explore more deeply the modal mixture only hinted at in the exposition.

EXAMPLE 32.15: *Waldstein* Sonata, mm. 166-176

Try it #4

Write a Roman numeral analysis for measures 167-174 in Example 32.15. For measures with only one note, assume it is the root of a triad.

After three measures (171-173) of new material, 14-21 return as 174-181; 22 is expanded and altered as 182-183; and 23-34 reappear as 184-195. Since the transition section in a recapitulation no longer needs to serve a modulatory function, it is usually altered, often extended, so that its sequential motion will return to the tonic key. Here, however, the chorale theme (2a, originally mm. 35-50) extends from 196 to 211 in A major, a chromatic submediant, and the transition that precedes it in 184-195 is altered to move toward A major instead of staying in C major.

In measure 200, the mode shifts to A minor, in part to bring back the expected key of C major for the triplet variation (204-211), followed by the return of 50-74, now in C (211-235). The closing theme, or codetta, starts off in measure 235 in C major, incorporating elements of mixture even more, as evidenced by all the flats. Measures 241-249 present the sequence that connected the exposition and the development. Compare 245-249 with 86 (second ending)-90: both statements suggest motion toward F major by transforming the C major tonic to a C7: V7/IV. The second time, however, the passage is colored through mixture to F minor, and the V7 resolves deceptively, to ♭VI (D♭ major, m. 249), to begin the coda. Though surprising and quite far afield from C major, this D♭ arrival has been prepared by the ♭II (Neapolitan) in the recapitulation (m. 169), and also briefly in the development (m. 134).

There are now almost three pages of music left, revealing a coda that is longer than some entire sonata-form movements. Uncharacteristically, there was no PAC in C major to initiate the coda. Further, the second theme has yet to reappear in the tonic key. This coda has the character and structure of another development section—it is a Beethovenian innovation, the "developmental coda." Measures 249-277 precede another retransition in 278-283 that ends on a strong and convincing V7 in the key of C major (Example 32.16). The resolution of the V7 in 284 forms a PAC that is elided with the "missing" second theme in C major. At the cadence in 295, all the tasks of the recapitulation are completed. A brief codetta based on the main theme finally brings the movement to an end.

EXAMPLE 32.16: *Waldstein* Sonata, mm. 281-292

Continuation of coda: Return of second theme (2a) in I

SUMMARY

In Romantic-era sonata forms:

- The exposition usually includes several distinct contrasting themes.
- The second key area is typically the dominant (major key) or relative major (minor key), but sometimes a more distant key.
- In late Romantic movements, a third key is sometimes introduced in the closing theme.
- The exposition in Romantic (and some Classical) movements may be preceded by an introduction, possibly in a contrasting tempo and/or key area.
- The exposition may or may not be repeated.
- The development and recapitulation are sometimes paired as a section and repeated, as in Classical sonatas, but often constitute separate sections that are near-equal in length.
- Typical development sections explore thematic material or motives from the exposition and may feature sequences, modulation to distant keys, harmonic instability, or even a new theme.
- The retransition normally follows the pattern of Classical sonatas by prolonging V7.
- The movement may end with a substantial coda, which includes additional development of the themes.

Related Forms

Sonatina

A **sonatina** is simply what it sounds like—a little sonata. Sonatinas are associated with Classical-era composers, but these "little sonatas" were written in the Romantic era as well, usually composed for children or beginning players.

The first movement is usually in an abbreviated sonata form, with compact first and second themes; the Clementi sonatina we have looked at before is a good illustration (Example 32.17). The first theme is a parallel period (mm. 1-8), with the second phrase modulating to the dominant (V); there is no transition—as we saw earlier, the second theme (8-15) is elided with the end of the first, and divides into 2+2+4 (a sentence).

EXAMPLE 32.17: Clementi, Sonatina, mvt. 1, mm. 1-15 🎧

First theme (modulating parallel period to V)

Second theme in V (elided, no transition)

Sonatinas may have a very short development section (about the same scope as the **B** section, or harmonic disturbance, in a rounded binary) or none at all. In this sonatina (see Example 32.18), the very brief development is measures 16-23; it begins by focusing on the first theme, touching on C minor, while the retransition (m. 20) features a G pedal point and octaves reminiscent of the second theme.

EXAMPLE 32.18: Clementi sonatina, mm. 16–23 🎧

The entire recapitulation is in the tonic key, C major, with the first phrase transposed down an octave and the second phrase a melodic inversion that stays in C major rather than modulating (Example 32.19).

EXAMPLE 32.19: Clementi sonatina, mm. 24–31 🎧

This entire movement is about the size of a rounded binary form, but the arrangement of the themes, the placement of the modulations, the retransition, and the return of the **A** section in the tonic key follow the sonata-form model. The development (including the retransition) is the length we would expect of a **B** section in a thirty-two-measure rounded binary, and the whole piece is only slightly longer than that, thirty-eight measures.

SUMMARY

> Sonatina form is distinguished from rounded binary by the presence of themes, transitions, development, and other elements of sonata form—only on a reduced scale.

Concerto Form

Concertos—compositions for a solo instrument and orchestra—often consist of three movements, arranged fast-slow-fast, that follow a formal pattern similar to the three-movement sonata. Concerto first movements are similar in many ways to sonata form, but alternate sections featuring the orchestra and the soloist.

KEY CONCEPT In early Classical concertos, the first movement is often written with a "double exposition." That is, the orchestra begins the movement by playing both the first and/or second theme group in the tonic key without the soloist. Then the soloist enters and the ensemble plays material from the exposition a second time, this time accompanying the solo instrument and modulating to the dominant or relative-major key.

Double exposition

Orchestra			*Soloist* (with orchestra)		
FTG	TR	STG	FTG	TR	STG
I (i)	(no mod.)	I (i)	I (i)	(mod.)	V (III)

Example 32.20 shows the first theme in the orchestra in Haydn's Concerto for Corno di caccia in D Major and the later entrance of the soloist with the same theme. (The solo horn in D sounds a step higher than notated.) The double-exposition format is not normally maintained in the recapitulation, however, where the orchestra and soloist share thematic material more equally. In later Romantic concertos, the double exposition was less favored; indeed, some concertos begin with the solo performer. When analyzing a concerto, listen for the themes and key areas—as you would for a sonata—but be prepared for variability in its formal design.

EXAMPLE 32.20: Haydn, Concerto for Corno di caccia in D Major, mvt. 1

(a) Mm. 1-4, beginning of first theme in the orchestra 🎧

(b) Mm. 28-34, entrance of horn soloist (in m. 31) 🎧

Concertos are showcases for virtuosic performers, and nowhere are their talents more evident than in the **cadenza**, a solo passage filled with rapid passage-work and other technical challenges. It is generally positioned between the end of the recapitulation and the beginning of the coda, and is prepared harmonically by a cadential $^6_4$ chord played by the orchestra, which the soloist expands. The cadenza's end is signaled in the solo instrument by a prominent scale degree $\hat{2}$ (often with a trill or other ornamentation) over a dominant-function harmony, which resolves to the tonic with the beginning of the coda (and the re-entrance of the orchestra).

In Classical concertos, the location of the cadenza was indicated by a fermata and the word "cadenza" in the relevant language. It was expected that soloists would improvise this passage (or prepare it in advance) to showcase both their technical and compositional skills. In later concertos, cadenzas were more often composed. Today, most concerto editions include a cadenza written out by the composer, a different composer, a reputable soloist, or the score's editor.

Performing and Listening to Sonata-Form Movements

Here are some questions you might ask as you prepare or listen to a movement in sonata form.

In the exposition:

- Which passages exhibit a stable key area?
- Where are there clear phrases?

- What is the character of each theme—is it assertive, placid, humorous, energetic, lyrical? What musical clues help you decide?

- Which passages are transitional? How does the piece modulate from the primary key to the next key?

- What is the intended effect of a transition—do the harmonies and melodic patterns indicate increasing tension that is released with the arrival of the new key, or is the section designed to flow to the new key area without the listener even noticing?

In the development section:

- Are there motives that should be brought out by the performer?

- Is the affect mysterious, agitated, seemingly aimless, joyous, or something else?

- Which keys are visited, and where?

- At what point do the harmonies begin to turn toward the home key by re-establishing the dominant?

- Is the retransition intended to build tension, to be released as the first theme reappears? Or does the return come as a surprise?

And in the recapitulation:

- When the music from the exposition returns, what has changed?

- Are there coda and codetta passages?

- Do the closing sections bring the piece to a gentle end, or do they end with a flourish?

Finally, consider the date of composition. Classical-era pieces need to be played cleanly, with lightness, precision, and grace. In the Romantic era, on the other hand, the overt expression of emotion was valued and encouraged. Think also about the drama that unfolds in the sonata you are playing. If you are a listener, ask what the performer is trying to convey. Music is about so much more than simply "music"—it expresses the emotion and flow of life. A musician who only plays the correct notes is like an actor who reads a text accurately but without feeling. If you are the performer, relish the dramatic aspects of this extended form, and your audience will too.

Did You Know?

Beethoven's *Waldstein* Sonata gets its name from the dedicatee, Count Ferdinand Ernst Gabriel von Waldstein, a German count and patron of the arts. Count Waldstein recognized the young composer's huge talent and in 1787 accompanied Beethoven on a visit from Bonn to Vienna, the city he would make his home (five years later) and where he would achieve his fame. Waldstein also arranged for Beethoven to meet Mozart on that first visit, and later recommended him to Joseph Haydn.

Though Waldstein is primarily known today as an early admirer, patron, and personal friend of Beethoven, he led an extraordinary life as a diplomat. He expended much of his fortune raising an army in an attempt to defeat Napoleon in the Napoleonic Wars, then traveled to London in 1796 and joined the British army, before finally returning to Vienna and his estates in 1809. After depleting his wealth in unwise expenditures, he died in poverty in 1823.

TERMS YOU SHOULD KNOW

cadenza	exposition	secondary theme (S or ST)
closing theme	• double exposition	second theme group (STG)
coda	first theme group (FTG)	sonata
• developmental coda	medial caesura	sonata (sonata-allegro) form
codetta	primary theme (P or PT)	sonatina
concerto	recapitulation	transition (TR)
development	retransition	• dependent transition
		• independent transition

QUESTIONS FOR REVIEW

1. What key areas are expected in the exposition of a sonata-form movement in a major key? in a minor key?
2. What characteristics distinguish the first theme group from the second theme group?
3. What are the characteristics of a codetta? Where are you likely to find one?
4. What are some common elements of a development? How do you identify where a development section starts? How do you locate the retransition?
5. How is the material from the exposition changed when it reappears in the recapitulation? Where are changes expected? Why?
6. How is Classical-era sonata form like a continuous rounded binary form? How are the two forms different?
7. What are some differences between Romantic and Classical sonata form?
8. How do you identify themes? transitional passages? In performance, how might you differentiate between themes and transitional passages?
9. How might knowing that a piece is in sonata form save you time in preparing and memorizing the music? Which sections might you compare as you prepare the work for performance?

10. How does a sonata differ from a sonatina?

11. In music for your own instrument, or for symphony orchestra or string quartet, find a sonata-form movement. How does the movement correspond to the description presented here?

Know It? Show It!

Focus by working through the tutorials.

Learn with InQuizitive.

Apply what you've learned to complete the workbook assignments.

Rondo, Sonata-Rondo, and Large Ternary

Outline

Five-part rondo
- Refrain (**A** section)
- Episode (contrasting section)
- Transition and retransition
- Coda

Seven-part rondo and sonata-rondo

Large ternary form

Overview

This chapter considers three formal designs that employ contrasting large sections: rondo, sonata-rondo, and large ternary.

Repertoire

Ludwig van Beethoven, Piano Sonata in C Minor, Op. 13 (*Pathétique*), mvt. 2

Clara Schumann, *Drei Romanzen* (*Three Romances*), Op. 21, No. 1

Five-Part Rondo

Begin by listening to a five-part rondo: the lyrical second movement of Beethoven's *Pathétique* Sonata, played on a fortepiano (a predecessor of the modern piano and the instrument for which this piece was composed). In a rondo, the music from the beginning of the movement, called a **refrain** or **ritornello**, returns several times, with contrasting sections called **episodes** in between.

Refrain (A Section)

The first sixteen measures are based on an eight-measure-long musical idea. Find each cadence in measures 1-8 (Example 33.1), then use this information to determine the phrase organization of the entire sixteen-measure **A** section.

EXAMPLE 33.1: Beethoven, *Pathétique* Sonata, mvt. 2, mm. 1-8

Refrain

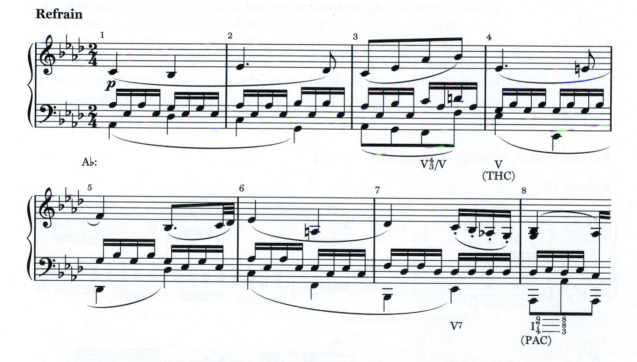

The **A** section, or **refrain**, is divided into two periods—measures 1-8 and 9-16—each of which is made up of two contrasting phrases; the first phrase ends with a tonicized HC (m. 4), the second with a PAC (m. 8). Measures 9-16 are a varied repetition of 1-8. Now listen to the entire movement, and mark the returns of the **A** material in your score. We can show this initial analytical information in a form chart, leaving spaces ("not **A**") for the contrasting passages:

A	(not **A**)	**A′**	(not **A**)	**A″**	Coda
mm. 1-16	17-28	29-36	37-50	51-66	67-73
A♭		A♭		A♭	A♭

The first time **A** is restated, beginning in measure 29, the section is varied only by being shortened to eight measures, an exact repetition of 1-8; we label measures 29-36 **A′**. The final return of the refrain, beginning in measure 51, is the same length as the initial **A**, with yet other variations: **A″**.

Episode (Contrasting Section)

A rondo's refrain is usually harmonically closed—it ends with a conclusive cadence—and it returns each time in the tonic key, as in this Beethoven movement. Its phrase structure is typically balanced and symmetrical. In contrast, the first episode, **B** (shown in Example 33.2), does not exhibit four-measure phrase lengths or regular hypermeter, and is also harmonically unstable: the section begins by touching on F minor (vi of A♭), then drifts to E♭ major (V of A♭, m. 23). In addition, the leaping melody of **B** contrasts with the lyrical **A** melody. As we saw in Chapter 31, a common tone modulation smooths the connection between the harmonically closed initial refrain in measure 16 and the beginning of **B** in 17. The cadence at the end of **B** then elides with the beginning of **A′** (mm. 28-29).

EXAMPLE 33.2: *Pathétique* Sonata, mm. 16-23 🎧

Episode (B)

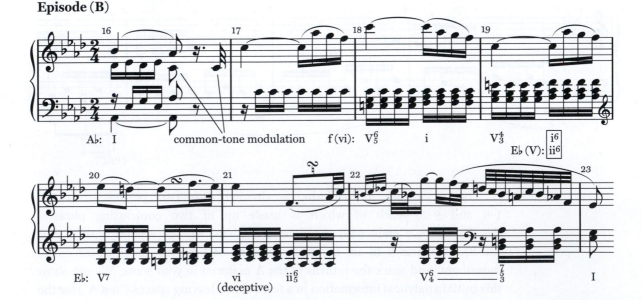

The next episode, **C**, is chromatic and dramatic, as represented by the first few measures in Example 33.3. As we discovered in Chapter 31 (Example 31.3), the initial key of A♭ minor (related by mode mixture to the preceding refrain) is followed by a modulation to E major (the enharmonically respelled chromatic submediant, F♭ major). This **C** section introduces triplet sixteenth notes that will reappear in the **A″** section, with which it elides measure 51.

EXAMPLE 33.3: *Pathétique* Sonata, mm. 36–38

Episode (C)

We can now complete the form chart of this five-part rondo, adding the keys for each section (arrows are used to indicate areas of tonal instability).

A	B	A′	C	A″	Coda
mm. 1–16	17–28	29–36	37–50	51–66	67–73
A♭	f → E♭ →	A♭	a♭ → E →	A♭	A♭

As in this movement, episodes are generally in contrasting keys and tend to fall into irregular phrases with irregular hypermeter. They may include modulations, and they may elide with the refrain that follows without achieving harmonic closure.

Transition and Retransition

The end of an episode will often provide cues that the refrain is about to return. For example, both episodes in the Beethoven movement end with a modulation back to the **A** section's key, A♭. In addition, the **B** section also ends with a short dominant pedal (mm. 27–28, Example 33.4), while the **C** section closes with an acceleration of the harmonic rhythm (Example 33.5).

EXAMPLE 33.4: *Pathétique* Sonata, mm. 23–29 🎧

EXAMPLE 33.5: *Pathétique* Sonata, mm. 47–51 🎧

KEY CONCEPT The end of an episode, where the music begins to turn back toward the A section's return, is called a **retransition**. Like retransitions at the end of a sonata-form development, rondo retransitions usually prolong the dominant harmony in preparation for the return of the refrain's tonic key. In longer rondo movements, refrains in turn may be linked to episodes by transitions, modulatory passages that move toward the key of the new section.

Both transitions and retransitions in rondos usually consist of repetitions of short motives (possibly transposed) and irregular hypermeters, rather than balanced four- or eight-measure phrases. Unlike sonata form, where transitions and retransitions are expected in certain locations, they are not obligatory in a rondo; they may be absent in earlier (Baroque) or shorter rondos, but normally are present in extended rondo forms.

Coda

At the conclusion of Beethoven's rondo (Example 33.6), the **A″** section's final PAC (m. 66) elides with the beginning of the final section—a coda. The remaining music has the character of a cadential extension, with repeated dominant-tonic chord successions. This coda fulfills multiple functions: it reminds listeners of the motives of the piece, "closes out" each of the registers (in mm. 66-68 and 68-70), and slows down the action by shortening the length of melodic ideas (mm. 70-73) until all that remains is a repeated chord to end the movement.

EXAMPLE 33.6: *Pathétique* Sonata, mm. 64-73

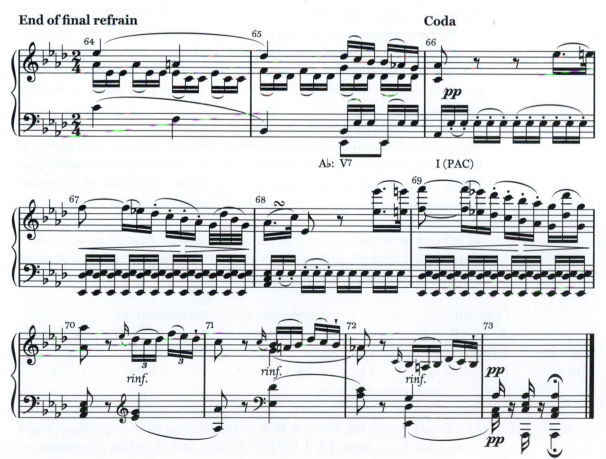

SUMMARY

Rondo form is characterized by a repeated section (a **refrain** or **ritornello**) alternating with sections (episodes) that contrast in key, mode, texture, phrase rhythm, harmonic complexity, thematic content, and/or style. Although other designs are possible, the most common is the five-part rondo diagrammed below: **A B A C A** (plus optional coda). Romantic-era rondos may explore more distant key areas in the episodes.

Refrain	Episode	Refrain	Episode	Refrain	
A	**B**	**A**	**C**	**A**	(optional coda)
I-I	V* →	I-I	i* →	I-I	
i-i	III or v* →	i-i	I* →	i-i	

*or other contrasting key

Seven-Part Rondo and Sonata-Rondo

There in one way in which the Beethoven movement is not typical of rondo form: it is the slow movement of the sonata. Most rondos are "fast and last": they are in an allegro tempo (or faster, such as presto), and serve as the final movement of a sonata, symphony, or string quartet. Sometimes these final movements are extended to seven sections, falling into either a **seven-part rondo** or **sonata-rondo** design.

Typical designs for a seven-part rondo and a sonata-rondo are given below, with possible locations for transitions and retransitions indicated with arrows. If the sections fall into an **A B A C A B′** (or **D**) **A** plan, the movement is a seven-part rondo. Its transitions or retransitions may be longer than those of a five-part rondo, and its episodes may be self-contained formal units that are harmonically closed.

When a seven-part rondo includes a developmental center section that is harmonically unstable and much longer than the other sections, creating an overall tripartite design, it is called a **sonata-rondo**.

	[Exposition			Development		Recapitulation]			
	A	**B**	**A**	**C**		**A**	**B′** (or **D**)	**A**	**Coda**
Major key:	I-I	V* →	I-I	i* →	dev →	I-I	I (or i)	I	
Minor key:	i-i	III or v* →	i-i	I* →	dev →	i-i	i (or I)	i	

*or other contrasting key

In a sonata-rondo, the initial **A B A** (corresponding to an exposition) might express the tonal areas I-V-I (or i-III-i), with the **C** section (development) providing large-scale contrast through its key area(s) and developmental character, and the final **A B′ A** (recapitulation) returning with all three sections in the tonic key. The sonata-rondo differs from sonata form in that the "exposition" ends with a return of the **A** section (refrain) in the tonic key, instead of staying in the second key area and adding a closing theme; the extra **A** section likewise returns at the end of the "recapitulation." The entire movement usually ends with a coda.

SUMMARY

When a seven-part rondo includes one or more of the following characteristics, it may be called a **sonata-rondo**:

- a developmental, harmonically unstable **C** section that is much longer than the other sections;

- extended transitions and retransitions between the refrain and contrasting sections;

- a return of the first three sections (**A B A**) in the tonic key.

Large Ternary Form

As its name implies, the **large ternary form** is an extended movement with three large sections, usually **A B A′**; the form is typical of Romantic style, but may be found in Classical works as well. As in simple and composite ternary (and rondo), the **A** sections are normally harmonically closed—beginning and ending in the tonic key—and the **B** section modulatory and unstable; in Romantic works, **B** may explore several different keys. The sections may be connected by a transition and a retransition, though (as in rondo forms) the latter is more common, and the movement usually ends with a coda. This formal plan is used for second movements of multimovement works as well as free-standing pieces, such as those labeled "Intermezzo," "Nocturne," or "Romance." The difference between this form and simple ternary is primarily one of size and scope.

As an example, listen to Clara Schumann's Romanze while following the score in your anthology. The three large sections of this ternary form are easy to identify because the end of the first and second sections are marked by double bar lines and a change of key signature, and also because of the striking contrast in style, tempo, and texture of the **B** section. We can represent the three main sections in the chart below; a cadence in measure 105 marks the beginning of the coda.

A	B	A′	Coda
mm. 1-26	27-72	73-105	105-112

Now consider more closely the music of the **A** section, beginning with the first eight measures (Example 33.7).

EXAMPLE 33.7: Schumann, Romanze, mm. 1-8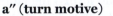

These two phrases form a parallel modulating period (**a a′**), ending with a IAC in C major (III), the relative major of A minor (i). In listening to the large ternary's **A** section, you probably noticed that these two phrases return at the end of the **A** section as measures 19-26, shown in Example 33.8. These are clearly a transformation of the previous phrases. Yet they are varied (**a″ a‴**) in numerous small ways and one big one: the second phrase is altered to remain in A minor. This change makes the large **A** section harmonically closed in the main key of the piece.

EXAMPLE 33.8: Schumann, Romanze, mm. 19-26

a″ (turn motive)

Compare the four **a** phrases in the examples above: they are similar enough to be readily recognized as the same musical idea, but it is as if each repetition is a variation of one of the previous statements—either the initial statement or one of the other variants. This concept is referred to as "developing variation," a technique often associated with the music of Brahms, a close friend of both Clara and Robert Schumann.

KEY CONCEPT The term **developing variation** is applied to pieces where musical ideas, instead of being repeated exactly, undergo continuous mutation or development: later variations may build on previous variants, rather than being directly traceable to the initial idea.

You may also have noticed that measures 9-18 (Example 33.9) contrast with the period structures framing them: the phrase structure is less regular and the key area(s) less clear-cut, though D minor (iv) is tonicized (see mm. 11-12 and 16-17). Still, there are motivic links between this passage and the beginning of **A**: the "turn" motive E-D♯-E-G-F-E from measure 1 returns in 11 and 15, transposed down a fifth (to A-G♯-A-C-B♭-A) within the D minor context, and again in 17, transposed down an octave from measure 1 as a part of the return to the key of A minor. Within the **A** section, there is a smaller ternary design, but it does not have the clear-cut sectional character of small forms in composite ternary movements.

EXAMPLE 33.9: Schumann, Romanze, mm. 9-19

The **B** section of this large ternary piece (mm. 27-72) contrasts with **A** in obvious ways: tempo (*Sehr innig bewegt*, with very heartfelt motion), triplets making an implied $\frac{12}{8}$ meter, and a change of key to F major (VI)—though this section is modulatory, sequential in places, and harmonically unstable. There is one strong connection between the large sections, however (Example 33.10): the melody in the right hand begins with a neighbor motive similar to the turn motive of measure 1, which reappears transformed in various ways throughout the **B** section.

EXAMPLE 33.10: Schumann, Romanze, mm. 27-28

The turbulence of the **B** section reaches its peak in measures 56-59 (Example 33.11), where three measures of linear chromaticism prepare the cadence. Here, the bass line (moving into the tenor line in m. 57) ascends by step and half step a full octave from A2 to A3, while the soprano simultaneously descends chromatically from E♭5 (moving into the alto in m. 58) to F4. The contrary motion ends in measure 59, where mixture chords color the approach to a PAC, a rare event for the **B** section. Finally, in measure 64, an E pedal point emerges to prepare the key of A minor and the **A′** section. To foreshadow the thematic material of **A′**, the turn motive appears in 70 and 72.

EXAMPLE 33.11: Schumann, Romanze, mm. 54-65

ii⌀7   V7   I (PAC)

return to **A'**

dominant pedal (in A minor)

A comparison of the initial **A** section (1-26) and **A'** (mm. 73-105) reveals that the first eighteen measures return unaltered in **A'**. Beginning in measure 91, however, the final parallel period is extended and builds via syncopated rhythms and increasing tempo to a climax in measure 101 (Example 33.12). After the cadence in 104-105, a coda—over a tonic pedal—brings back the triplet texture from **B** one last time.

EXAMPLE 33.12: Schumann, Romanze, mm. 95-112 🎧

This piece exemplifies many of the features associated with large ternary: the first and last sections employ the same musical materials, but the middle section (**B**) contrasts in key and texture, is unstable and developmental, and ends with an extended retransition preparing the return of the **A** section.

Try it #1

Listen to the second movement of Mozart's C Major Piano Sonata, K. 545 (anthology).

A. Circle the correct form.

rounded binary   large ternary   five-part rondo   sonata-rondo

B. Complete the form chart below

Section:	A					
Measures:	1–16					
Key:	G					

SUMMARY

All ternary forms feature three main sections, where the middle section is in a contrasting key or mode.

	Overall length and complexity	Harmonic closure	Distinguishing features	Where used
Simple ternary (full sectional)	short, simple	Each section is harmonically closed in the key of that section.	Short, straightforward pieces, with the **B** section contrasting in texture and in a different key.	in short and simple movements; Baroque era; pieces for children
Composite ternary	medium	Each section is typically harmonically closed in the key of that section; occasionally **B** section is harmonically open.	The large sections contain a complete smaller binary or ternary form; **B** is harmonically simpler and has a thinner texture.	in the minuet or scherzo and trio movement of the Classical and early Romantic periods
Large ternary	long, complex	**B** section is usually harmonically open; **A** section is usually harmonically closed in the main key.	**B** section is contrasting and developmental; includes transition/retransition; large sections may contain smaller, less clearly delineated formal sections.	in the second movement of sonatas; free-standing pieces in Romantic style

Did You Know?

Clara Wieck Schumann (1819–1896) was born into a musical family. Her father, Friedrich Wieck, was a well-known piano pedagogue who was a proponent of performing music from memory (not standard practice at the time). He devoted his life to promoting Clara's flourishing career as a concert pianist, while continuing to teach other students—among them the composer and pianist Robert Schumann, who was also a boarder in the Wieck home. The romance between Clara and Robert seemed doomed from the start, though, since Friedrich disapproved of their relationship and contrived to keep them apart. In the end, the couple had to go to court to sue for the right to marry. The year of their marriage, 1840, is often called Robert's "song year," and his many love songs are thought to have been inspired by her. The two were musical soul mates: Robert encouraged Clara's composing and performing, and she was a strong proponent of her husband's music. Their marriage was challenged by the death of several children and Robert's physical and mental illnesses, which eventually led to a suicide attempt and confinement in an asylum. After his death, Clara supported herself and her children by concertizing and teaching at the music conservatory in Frankfurt, where she effectively promoted memorization, improvisation, and innovative concert programming.

TERMS YOU SHOULD KNOW

coda	refrain	rondo	transition
episode	retransition	• five-part rondo	
large ternary	ritornello	• seven-part rondo	
		• sonata-rondo	

QUESTIONS FOR REVIEW

1. In a rondo, how do the episodes contrast with the refrain?
2. What are the differences between a seven-part and a five-part rondo? between a seven-part rondo and a sonata-rondo?
3. What characteristics are common to sonata form and large ternary form? to sonata form and sonata-rondo form?
4. What characteristics distinguish the following types of ternary forms: simple ternary, composite ternary, large ternary?
5. In music for your own instrument, find an example of a rondo, a sonata-rondo, or a large ternary form. Make a form chart that gives measure numbers and keys for each section.

Know It? Show It!

Focus by working through the tutorials.

Learn with InQuizitive.

Apply what you've learned to complete the workbook assignments.

The Twentieth Century and Beyond

34

Modes, Scales, and Sets

Listening to twentieth-century compositions

Pitch-class collections and scales revisited
- Analyzing mode and scale types
- Composing with diatonic modes
- Sets and subsets

Other scale types and their subsets
- Pentatonic scales
- Whole-tone scales
- Octatonic scales
- Hexatonic scales

Overview

This chapter focuses on scales and pitch-class collections other than major and minor, and introduces the terminology musicians have developed to discuss the motives, chords, and compositional techniques heard in music after 1900.

Repertoire

Béla Bartók
  "Five-Tone Scale," from *Mikrokosmos* (No. 78)
  "Song of the Harvest," for two violins

Claude Debussy
  "Fantoches" ("Puppets"), from *Fêtes Galantes* (*Gallant Festivities*)
  "Mandoline"
  "Voiles" ("Sails"), from *Preludes*, Book I

Maurice Ravel
  "Aoua!" from *Chansons madécasses* (*Songs of Madegascar*)
  Pavane pour une infant défunte (*Pavane for a Dead Princess*)

Igor Stravinsky
  "Lento," from *For the Five Fingers*
  From *Trois mouvements de "Petrouchka"* (*Three Movements from "Petrouchka"*): "Chez Petrouchka" ("Petrouchka's Room") and "Danse Russe" ("Russian Dance")

Anton Webern, String Quartet, Op. 5, mvt. 3

Listening to Twentieth-Century Compositions

Although the works of the five prominent composers of the early twentieth century we consider here—Béla Bartók, Claude Debussy, Maurice Ravel, Igor Stravinsky, and Anton Webern—sound very different, these composers employ some of the same compositional techniques. Here and in the following chapters, we leave functional tonality behind as we learn new ways composers organize musical ideas.

Listen to two works for strings, Bartók's "Song of the Harvest" and the third movement of Webern's String Quartet, Op. 5—first without the music, then following your anthology scores. As you listen, consider the following:

- Can you hum a tonic at any point in the piece?
- Can you identify phrases or distinct sections? changes in motive, texture, or mood?
- Can you hear familiar compositional techniques (transposition, imitation, inversion)?
- What musical features contribute to your emotional reaction to the piece?

Mark on your score any of these aspects you notice.

When you analyze music of the twentieth or twenty-first century, don't make the mistake of working solely from the score. Always take time to listen, preferably several times through, then use your musical intuition to make basic observations about form, phrase, texture, imitation, variation, contrast, and other elements. Such observations will inform your more detailed analysis and give you a deeper appreciation for the music.

Pitch-Class Collections and Scales Revisited

Many stylistic features make these Bartók and Webern pieces sound different from each other. Webern's quartet features shorter motives and fuller instrumentation than Bartók's duo; it also covers a wider range and calls for numerous string effects—for example, *pizzicato* (plucking rather than bowing the strings) and *col legno* (playing with the wood, rather than the hair, of the bow). Bartók, on the other hand, writes longer melodic lines and easily perceived patterns of imitation between the two violin parts. He incorporates tempo and meter changes, as well as the transposed repetition of melodies, to distinguish between musical sections. The collections of pitch classes (abbreviated pcs) that these composers choose also give the works their distinct sounds.

Remember from Chapter 1 that a pitch class represents all the pitches that sound exactly one or more octaves apart—for example, C4, C6, C3, B♯2, and D♭♭5.

The term invokes both enharmonic equivalence (C and B♯) and octave equivalence (C4 and C6).

KEY CONCEPT The word "collection" refers to a group of pitch classes that serves as a source of musical materials for a work or a section of a work. Examine the pitch-class materials of a piece by "collecting" them and writing them in ascending order, without repetitions.

The pc collections of Examples 34.1 and 34.2 are given below each example. As you listen, determine how these collections differ, and whether there is one pitch class that seems more important than the others.

EXAMPLE 34.1: Webern, String Quartet, mvt. 3, mm. 6-7

pitch-class collection: C♯ D E♭ E♮ F F♯ G G♯ A B♭ B♮ C♮ (C♯)

EXAMPLE 34.2: Bartók, "Song of the Harvest," mm. 30-33

pitch-class collection: E♭ F G♭ A♭ B♭ C♭ D♭ (E♭)

You were probably unable to identify a prominent pc in the Webern movement, since this composition features all twelve—a complete chromatic collection—without strongly emphasizing any one pc.

KEY CONCEPT Music that does not establish a tonic or tonal hierarchy is called **nontonal**, or **post-tonal** to signal its chronological position after the era of tonal music.

Nontonal music differs from tonal music in important ways. Recall that tonal music is characterized by

- melodies composed in major and minor keys, whose scale-degree functions gravitate toward the tonic (for example, $\hat{7}$ resolves to $\hat{1}$);

- harmonies that relate to each other in predictable functional progressions leading toward a tonic harmony;

- identifiable embellishing tones (dissonant suspensions, neighbor or passing tones) that decorate a harmonic framework and resolve, or imply a resolution.

Nontonal compositions may show *some* tonal characteristics—scalar passages, chords built of thirds, bass lines that move by fourths and fifths—but without all three aspects of tonality, the works are not truly tonal.

Unlike the Webern movement, Bartók's work does include a pitch that receives more emphasis: E♭4 (the first and last pitch of Example 34.2) provides a strong starting and ending point for the excerpt. This E♭ serves a similar function to the tonic in a tonal piece, even though "Song of the Harvest" is not built on functional harmonies. The other pitches of the phrase expand outward from the E♭4 and converge back to form a type of cadence. Although the context is different, we will continue to use the terms "phrase" and "cadence" when they seem musically appropriate, even in nontonal compositions.

KEY CONCEPT A pitch or pc that appears pervasively in a work (or section) and establishes a sense of hierarchy that's not dependent on conventions of common-practice tonality is called a **center**, and music that features it is **centric** music. Traditional tonal music falls within the centric category, as does modal music.

Nontonal music may be centric or noncentric.

- If noncentric, like the Webern quartet, the pervasive chromaticism, symmetrical interval patterns, and/or absence of familiar scale segments make it difficult to identify a "tonic" pitch class or hierarchy. This type of music is sometimes called **atonal**.

- If centric, like the Bartok duo, you can still sense a hierarchy that is different in kind from that of common-practice tonality. It may draw on one of the diatonic modes (Chapter 5) or another type of scale. When a work has a pc center, list its collection as you would write a scale, starting and ending with the pc center.

Even in fully chromatic nontonal works, some pitch classes may be temporarily more prominent than others because of repetition, register, duration, or other means. For example, the first measure of Example 34.1 shows a repeated cello C♯2, which begins and ends the movement, and functions as an ostinato (a rhythmic or melodic motive that is repeated successively, to tie a passage together). This C♯ helps provide cohesiveness to the movement, but it is emphasized only through repetition; there is no sense of hierarchy between C♯ and the other pcs. Such pitches or pcs are called **focal pitches** or **pcs**—they differ from centers in that they are localized and create no sense of directed motion toward a more stable point of closure.

Analyzing Mode and Scale Types

Listen for pitch centers, ostinati, and mode types in Example 34.3, two passages from the opening of Stravinsky's ballet *Petrouchka*, transcribed by the composer for piano.

EXAMPLE 34.3: Stravinsky, "Danse Russe"

(a) Mm. 1-4

pc collection: G A B C D E F G (G Mixolydian)

(b) Mm. 9-12

pc collection: A B C D E F♯ G A (A Dorian)

In part (a), the left hand plays a reiterated G7 ostinato, while the right hand presents an exuberant melody doubled by parallel triads (to which we will return). This parallelism works against a sense of functional harmony, and our ears are drawn to G3—the lowest repeated note—as a possible tonal center. (The dominant-seventh ostinato never resolves to a C tonic.) The pc collection is comprised of the piano's white notes above G: G A B C D E F G—a G Mixolydian collection.

Part (b) introduces a new left-hand ostinato, this time above A3. Here the reiterated bass note provides a pc center such that the right-hand melody sounds like it begins on $\hat{5}$. With the F♯ introduced in measure 9, the collection is A B C D E F♯ G A—A Dorian.

KEY CONCEPT

1. When analyzing modal music written post-1900, first identify the collection of pitch classes in the passage by listing them in ascending order, without repetitions.

2. Listen to determine whether you hear a stable center. If you do, then rewrite your list in ascending order beginning with the centric pc.

Composing with Diatonic Modes

As we learned in Chapter 5, the diatonic modes are all rotations of one pc collection: the same one as C major. After around 1900, composers discovered new possibilities for these modes. Unlike their predecessors, modern composers might transpose modal materials to begin on any pitch class; the Dorian mode, for instance, need not begin and end on D (the A Dorian of Example 34.3b is a good example). Further, even if the mode does not emerge in a clear melodic statement, its pc collection may pervade the entire texture.

Contemporary composers are more likely to draw on all possible modal rotations of the diatonic scale, including the **Locrian mode** (the B-to-B rotation of the C major scale), which was avoided in the Renaissance because of its prominent tritone. Some composers create mixed modes by combining a distinctive portion of one with another: for example, the **Lydian-Mixolydian mode** (C D E F♯ G A B♭ C) is derived from the lower pentachord of the Lydian mode and the upper tetrachord of the Mixolydian. Jazz musicians also call this mode the "Lydian-dominant," or "overtone scale."

KEY CONCEPT When you analyze modal passages, use your ear to decide whether the third scale degree suggests a major or minor quality.

Modes with $\hat{3}$:

- Ionian   —identical to major
- Mixolydian   —like major, but with $\flat\hat{7}$
- Lydian   —like major, but with $\sharp\hat{4}$
- Lydian-Mixolydian —like major, but with $\sharp\hat{4}$ and $\flat\hat{7}$

Modes with $\flat\hat{3}$:

- Aeolian   —identical to natural minor
- Dorian   —like natural minor, but with $\sharp\hat{6}$
- Phrygian   —like natural minor, but with $\flat\hat{2}$
- Locrian   —like natural minor, but with $\flat\hat{2}$ and $\flat\hat{5}$

Try it #1

Write each of the following modes, starting with the given pc center, on the staves provided.

MODE	PC CENTER	
Mixolydian	F	(treble clef staff with notes written)
Dorian	C♯	(bass clef staff)
Lydian	B♭	(treble clef staff)
Aeolian	F♯	(bass clef staff)
Phrygian	G	(treble clef staff)
Locrian	E	(bass clef staff)
Ionian	A♭	(treble clef staff)
Lydian-Mixolydian	A	(bass clef staff)

Polymodality and Stratified Textures In both Stravinsky passages of Example 34.3, the music moves in two distinct layers or strata: a top-voice melody with accompanying chords in the right hand, and a left-hand ostinato. This layering is a hallmark of Stravinsky's style, in his orchestral and chamber as well as piano works (as you will hear if you listen to the orchestral version of *Petrouchka*).

KEY CONCEPT The layering of distinct musical materials—which may differ in orchestration, texture, rhythmic characteristics, and pc collections—is called **stratification**. When one layer expresses one mode and another layer expresses a second mode, this technique is called **bimodality** or, if more than two modes, **polymodality**. (If two keys are expressed together, the technique is **bitonality**, and more than two keys, **polytonality**.)

One of the most often-cited instances of bimodality, also from *Petrouchka*, is shown in Example 34.4, where the upper stratum arpeggiates a C major triad and the lower one an F♯ major triad (white keys against black). Yet in this case, the identical rhythms of the two voices cause the strata to merge into a single sonority. The sonority's link to this ballet is so strong that it has come to be called the "Petrouchka chord."

EXAMPLE 34.4: Stravinsky, "Chez Petrouchka," mm. 9–11

Petrouchka chord: C C♯ E F♯ G A♯

For an example of stratified polymodality, listen to an excerpt from a work by Ravel (Example 34.5). Like Bartok's "Song of the Harvest," this composition shows different key signatures in different parts: six sharps in the voice and piano right hand, but no sharps or flats in the remaining parts. Each layer has its own distinctive rhythm and intervallic structure—for example, the cello moves in quarter notes and open fourths and fifths, while the flute plays dotted notes and half steps—which helps to separate them. The "parallel fifths" in the cello and piano are quite characteristic of this style; the cello's fifths (G–D and D–A) are related to the piano's (F♯–C♯ and D♯–A♯) by semitone, creating colorful dissonances between the strata.

EXAMPLE 34.5: Ravel, "Aoua!," mm. 8–12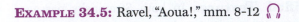

Translation: In the times of our fathers, white men descended to this island; they said to them: "Here is some land."

Try it #2

Listen again to Example 34.5, then answer the following questions.

(a) What are the pitch classes of the vocal line? What is its pc center?

_____

(b) What pc is missing that would make this a seven-note diatonic scale?

_____

(c) The vocal line sounds Aeolian in measures 8-10. What Aeolian scale degree is altered in the vocal line in measure 11, and what mode does this alteration evoke?

_____

(d) For each instrumental layer, specify the types of intervals featured and the pitch classes.

Instrument	Intervals featured	Pc list
flute	m2	C♯ D D♯ E F
cello	_____	_____
piano RH	_____	_____
piano LH	_____	_____

Characteristic Voice-Leading and Sonorities As composers began to explore new ways of using diatonic scales and modes, new voice-leading practices arose, as did new sonorities and new ways of treating familiar ones. In common-practice styles, as we know, parallel fifths were prohibited and chordal sevenths and ninths were considered dissonances in need of resolution. As Example 34.6 shows, this thinking changed radically around 1900 and after. Here, the left hand is doubled throughout at the fifth. This kind of doubling is carried one step further in a technique called **planing**: beginning in the second half of measure 26, both hands move in parallel motion with all voicing and spacing identical, doubling the accented melody line with parallel dominant ninth chords—E9, D9, C9, D9, E9—before concluding the phrase on a D7 chord (V7 of the tonic, G).

EXAMPLE 34.6: Ravel, _Pavane pour une infant défunte_, mm. 25-27 🎧

"parallel fifths" (LH)   planing of dominant ninth chords   V7

Example 34.7 illustrates planing in a Debussy song, where parallel major triads in second inversion are broken up rhythmically into fluttering sixteenth notes above the left-hand melody. Accidentals here and in the Ravel example keep the quality of the chords consistent as they move in parallel motion, but planing can also be written diatonically, as we saw in Example 34.3.

EXAMPLE 34.7: Debussy, "Fantoches"

(a) Mm. 1–3

(b) Planing of parallel major triads in $^6_4$ position

For another characteristic sonority of nontonal centric music, listen to Example 34.8, from Stravinsky's *For the Five Fingers*. While the key signature suggests D minor (or F major) and the pc center is clearly D, the pc collection is no scale or mode that we know of: D E F F♯ G A. This collection does, however, correspond to the combined lower pentachords of the D Ionian (D E F♯ G A) and Aeolian (D E F G A) modes—one mode in each hand. (Stravinsky's emphasis on pentachords surely relates to the *Five Fingers* of the title.) Because this sonority (marked in m. 2) sounds like a triad with both a major and a minor third above the root, it is sometimes called a split-third chord, or a major-minor tetrachord.

EXAMPLE 34.8: Stravinsky, "Lento," mm. 1–4

right hand: D E F♯ G A (Ionian pentachord)
left hand: D (E) F♮ (G) A (Aeolian pentachord)

Sonorities in this style may also be enriched by stacking thirds above seventh chords to create ninths, elevenths, or thirteenths, or by added-sixth chords (Chapter 29). Some composers abandon thirds altogether and instead create chords from stacked fourths or fifths (called **quartal** or **quintal** harmonies). Example 34.9 shows a quintal chord in the piano introduction to Debussy's song "Mandoline," where the open fifths, together with the arpeggiation in two octaves, simulate the strumming of a mandolin.

EXAMPLE 34.9: Debussy, "Mandoline," mm. 1–3 🎧

quintal harmonies

We will learn other ways to name and classify all these chords in Chapter 35.

SUMMARY

When you analyze modal compositions of the twentieth or twenty-first century,

- listen for a pc center, then list all the pcs in ascending order (beginning with that center) to determine the mode;

- if there are "extra" pitches that cannot be explained as embellishing tones, consider a bitonal or bimodal analysis, especially if the texture is stratified;

- watch for voice-leading that mimics common-practice style (e.g., cadences and root motion by fifth), as well as voice-leading that departs from it (planing);

- identify sonorities that impart a distinctive flavor to the composition (e.g., ninth chords, split-third chords, and quartal or quintal harmonies).

Sets and Subsets

One system that musicians have developed to describe the collections and sonorities of music after 1900 is called **set theory**. We will introduce some of its terms here and develop them further in Chapter 35.

KEY CONCEPT The term **set** refers to a group of pitches (pset) or pitch classes (pcset). The pitches or pcs in a set are called its **elements**; list elements of a set only once. A small group of some of a set's elements is called a **subset**. Subsets of different size, or **cardinality**, take different names:

two elements—interval or dyad   six elements—hexachord

three elements—trichord   seven elements—heptachord or heptad

four elements—tetrachord   eight elements—octachord or octad

five elements—pentachord   nine elements—nonachord or nonad

To capture the structure of sets and subsets in a concise way and to reveal their relationships more clearly, we translate pitch classes to numbers, with enharmonic pcs receiving the same number—a technique called **integer notation**. Most theorists adopt C as the reference pitch class: C = 0, C♯ or D♭ = 1, D = 2, D♯ or E♭ = 3, and so on. To avoid confusing 1 and 0 with the two-digit numbers 10 and 11, substitute the letters t for ten and e for eleven.

KEY CONCEPT Since there are twelve pitch classes, it can be helpful to visualize them around a clock face, with 0 (C) at the top and (F♯/G♭) at the bottom.

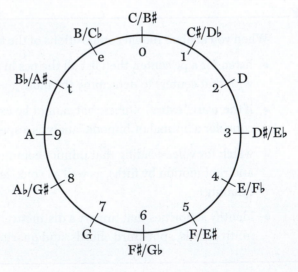

To facilitate your musical analyses, memorize the number that goes with each pitch class, and practice until this notation becomes second nature. Remember that integer notation applies to pitch *classes*; there is no distinction between octave-related pitches. In pcsets, there is also no distinction in order, although it is customary to write the pcs in ascending order. Write the numbers between curly braces, which indicate that order is not important.

When two sets combine to form a complete chromatic collection (all the numbers from 0 to 11), they are said to form an **aggregate**.

Try it #3

Write each sonority below in integer notation, maintaining the ordering of the original. In the third column, rewrite the integers in ascending order with curly braces.

SONORITY	INTEGER NOTATION	ASCENDING ORDER
Dominant seventh chord on A	9147	{1479}
Half-diminished seventh chord on D		
Do-re-mi-fa-sol on E		
Augmented triad on F♯		
Diminished seventh chord on C♯		
Major seventh chord on A♭		
Dorian mode on D		

Other Scale Types and Their Subsets

Pentatonic Scales

Play through measures 1-8 of Bartók's "Five-Tone Scale" (Example 34.10). In this excerpt, we select E as the apparent pc center, since the passage ends on an octave doubling, E3 and E4, and the melody begins with a characteristic skip up a fourth to E5.

EXAMPLE 34.10: Bartók, "Five-Tone Scale," mm. 1–8 🎧

pc collection: E G A B D

As the title implies, the passage contains only five distinct pitch classes: E G A B D. This collection is a minor pentatonic scale, 1̂-♭3̂-4̂-5̂-♭7̂ (*do-me-fa-sol-te*; see Chapter 5), a rotation of the major pentatonic scale, 1̂-2̂-3̂-5̂-6̂ (*do-re-mi-sol-la*); that is, E G A B D can be rotated to G A B D E. You can think of both scales as representing the pentatonic collection, and they are sometimes written as scales, with the first pitch class repeated (in parentheses) at the end: E G A B D (E).

SUMMARY

The pentatonic collection is a subset of the diatonic collection:

- The major pentatonic scales C D E G A, F G A C D, and G A B D E are all subsets of the major scale C D E F G A B.

- The minor pentatonic scale E G A B D is also a subset of C D E F G A B, and consists of the same pcset as G A B D E (in rotation). All major pentatonic scales can be similarly rotated.

- The pentatonic collection may also be represented in integer notation as {02479}.

One easy way to remember the interval pattern that makes up the pentatonic collection is to think of the black keys on the piano: C♯ D♯ F♯ G♯ A♯ (C♯). These pitch classes are a subset of the C♯ major scale, missing E♯ and B♯. The black-key pentatonic collection combined with the white-key diatonic collection (C to C) are considered **literal complements**, because they share no common elements and combine to make a complete chromatic collection, or aggregate.

Because of the pentatonic scale's lack of tendency tones, you may find it difficult to decide which pitch class is functioning as the center in a pentatonic passage. It often doesn't matter, since any of the pcs in the set can be made to sound stable by the musical context.

Now look at Example 34.11, the next section of Bartók's piece; a pc list reveals another pentatonic collection, A B D E F♯. If you compare the collection from Example 34.10 (E G A B D) with this one, you can see and hear that the two share a four-note subset, A B D E (sometimes called the "I Got Rhythm" tetrachord, after the first four notes in Gershwin's famous song). The change from G in the opening section to F♯ in the second creates an effective contrast, while maintaining the pentatonicism that characterizes the work. In the final section, Bartók returns to the opening collection to end the piece.

EXAMPLE 34.11: Bartók, "Five-Tone Scale," mm. 9-19 🎧

pc collection: A B D E F♯

Whole-Tone Scales

Whole-tone scales are made up of six distinct pitch classes that, when listed in scale order, are a whole step apart. The pcs in measures 33–37 of Example 34.12, from Debussy's prelude "Voiles," make such a scale—beginning with B♭, which is emphasized by its constant presence as a pedal tone.

EXAMPLE 34.12: Debussy, "Voiles," mm. 33–40 🎧

pc collection: B♭ C D E F♯ A♭ (B♭)

Using integer notation, we can identify the collection B♭ C D E F♯ A♭ as {t 0 2 4 6 8}. Such notation makes the whole steps between the pcs readily apparent (even when the spelling may obscure them—for example, F♯ and A♭): each integer increases by 2. Integer notation thus gives us a handy way to identify whole-tone collections.

KEY CONCEPT There are only two possible whole-tone (WT) collections: WT0 {0 2 4 6 8 t} and WT1 {1 3 5 7 9 e}; they are literal complements of each other, sometimes referred to as the "even" and "odd" whole-tone collections. Whole-tone collections may be written as a scale, starting with any of their pitch classes.

In major and minor scales, diatonic modes, and pentatonic scales, there are at least two types of intervals between adjacent scale members: half steps, whole steps, or minor thirds. In a whole-tone scale, however, there are only whole steps (or their enharmonic equivalents)—it is not possible to discern any aural landmarks from the scale itself. The whole tone scale is a **symmetrical scale**: the intervals between scale members read the same forward and backward (M2 M2 M2 M2 M2).

A close examination of Example 34.12 reveals that within the whole-tone texture of measures 33-37 there are several strata. There is, for example, the pedal point B♭1. There are also triads in the left-hand part that connect by planing; the lowest note of each chord is doubled at the octave and in the right-hand octaves above. If you write out those triads as stacks of pc integers, as in the diagram below, you can quickly determine their qualities—all are augmented triads {0, 4, 8} or {2, 6, t}, two subsets of the "even" whole-tone collection—and you can see how they connect. Play these chords (leaving out the octave doublings) to hear how the passage works.

FIGURE 34.1: Parallel voice-leading in Debussy's "Voiles"

M. 33	M. 34	M. 35	M. 36	M. 37
4 6 8	t	0 t 8	6 4 6 4	4
0 2 4	6	8 6 4	2 0 2 0	0
8 t 0	2	4 2 0	t 8 t 8	8

A sixteenth-note ostinato—D5 E5 D6 E5—in the upper voice, based on the dyad {2 4}, repeats throughout this passage, helping to stratify three layers clearly in the texture both rhythmically and registrally: bass pedal point, sixteenth-note treble ostinato, and planed augmented triads moving in eighth, quarter, and sixteenth notes.

Octatonic Scales

A pitch-class list from the beginning of Bartók's "Song of the Harvest" (Example 34.13) yields the collection D♯ E♯ F♯ G♯ A B C D, with A D C B in the first violin and G♯ F♯ E♯ D♯ in the second. The pc content in integer notation, beginning with 0, is {0 2 3 5 6 8 9 e}, revealing a clear pattern of alternating whole and half steps. This type of symmetrical scale, called an octatonic scale, is remarkable for its versatility. Among its subsets are the following sonorities: major, minor, and diminished triads; split-third chords; and Mm7, mm7, vii°7, and vii⌀7 chords.

EXAMPLE 34.13: Bartók, "Song of the Harvest," mm. 1-5 🎧

pc collection: D♯ E♯ F♯ G♯ A B C D

KEY CONCEPT The **octatonic scale** consists of eight pcs that alternate whole and half steps. There are three possible octatonic collections, beginning on pc 0, 1, or 2: {0 1 3 4 6 7 9 t}, {1 2 4 5 7 8 t e}, and {2 3 5 6 8 9 e 0}. (If you begin an octatonic scale on any other pc, it simply duplicates the pcs of one of these collections.) The scales are referred to by their first half step: OCT 01, OCT 12, and OCT 23.

These three collections can be arranged into scales beginning with any pc and with either a half or whole step. Depending on the musical context, any pc of the collection can serve as its focal pitch.

Try it #4

Spell each of the following scales, starting with the given pitch class. Then rewrite each answer in integer notation.

SCALE TYPE	STARTING PC	LETTER NAMES	INTEGER NOTATION
octatonic 01	F♯	F♯ G A B♭ C D♭ E♭ E♮ (F♯)	6 7 9 t 0 1 3 4 (6)
whole tone	E♭		
minor pentatonic	D		
octatonic 23	E♭		
major pentatonic	B		
whole tone	B♭		

Compare the focal pitches and mode in Examples 34.13 and 34.14. The first example is somewhat ambiguous, since either the first violin's initial pitch (A4) or the second violin's repeated lowest pitch (D♯4) could be interpreted as the focal pc. In either case, Example 34.13's pc collection is OCT 23: {2 3 5 6 8 9 e 0}.

EXAMPLE 34.14: Bartók, "Song of the Harvest," mm. 6–15 (anthology)

pc collection: C♯ D E F G G♯ A♯ B   1 2 4 5 7 8 t e

The collection in Example 34.14 is {1 2 4 5 7 8 t e} (OCT 12). While both passages are octatonic, they are not the same set. Neither are they complementary sets (like the two whole-tone collections), since they have four pcs in common: {2 5 8 e}. This common subset is a familiar chord type—the diminished seventh chord B–D–F–A♭. Each octatonic collection shares one diminished seventh subset with each of the other two collections. Further, any two different diminished seventh chords may be combined to make an octatonic collection: for example, {0 3 6 9} plus {2 5 8 e} equals {2 3 5 6 8 9 e 0}. The literal complement of that collection will always be the third diminished seventh chord (in this case, {1 4 7 t}). In fact, octatonic scales are saturated with diminished seventh chords—you can build one on every degree of the scale. For this reason, jazz musicians call the octatonic the **diminished scale**.

Hexatonic Scales

This scale is similar to the octatonic in that it is symmetrical, created by alternating two intervals.

KEY CONCEPT The **hexatonic scale** consists of six pitch classes that alternate a half step and minor third. There are four possible hexatonic collections, beginning with pcs 01, 12, 23, and 34.

HEX 01	{0 1 4 5 8 9}	C C♯ E F G♯ A
HEX 12	{1 2 5 6 9 t}	C♯ D F F♯ A A♯
HEX 23	{2 3 6 7 t e}	D D♯ F♯ G A♯ B
HEX 34	{3 4 7 8 e 0}	D♯ E G G♯ B C

Like the octatonic, the hexatonic collection contains a number of subsets that contribute to its characteristic sound: each can be constructed of two augmented triads a half step apart—for example, in HEX 01, C E G♯ and D♭ F A. Each collection also includes three major and minor triads a major third apart—in HEX 01 C♯ major/minor, F major/minor, and A major/minor—which implies split-third chords on each of these pcs as well.

Try it #5

In the examples below, spell each triad or seventh chord with integer notation. Then combine them into an octatonic or hexatonic scale (also in integers).

1. Diminished seventh on C: _____

   Diminished seventh on G: _____

   Combine to form which octatonic scale? _____

2. Augmented triad on C♯: _____

   Augmented triad on D: _____

   Combine to form which hexatonic scale? _____

3. Diminished seventh on D♭: _____

   Diminished seventh on E♭: _____

   Combine to form which octatonic scale? _____

How are the two octatonic scales related? _____

Did You Know?

The title character in Stravinsky's *Petrouchka* has his origins in commedia dell'arte, a type of improvised comic theater that originated in Italy in the early fifteenth century. The most famous of the stock commedia characters are the *zanni* (origin of the word "zany")—the comic male servants Arlecchino (also known as Harlequin), Pierrot, Pulcinella (Petrushka in Russian), and Pagliacci, and female servant Columbina, Arlecchino's love interest. Other character types include the *innamorati* (young lovers) and the *vecchi* (old men)—the pompous doctor (Il Dottore), befuddled lawyer, and rich but miserly merchant (Pantelone)—who are jealous guardians or aged spouses of younger women, and attempt to thwart the young lovers. These characters were all identified by their costumes, and all male actors except those portraying the lovers wore leather masks with exaggerated features. Because masks obscured the actors' faces, their characters were created through their physical moves and speech patterns, including humorous regional accents.

Even those not familiar with theater history likely recognize the character types and scenarios described above, as commedia dell'arte's influence is felt in many later works for the theater. For example, Shakespeare's plays feature character types derived from the commedia; and Mozart's operas include comic servants like Figaro and Susanna, based on the *zanni*, and older male characters that resonate with the *vecchi*. Leoncavallo's tragic melodrama *Pagliacci* depicts a commedia dell'arte company in which the performers find their life situations reflecting events they depict onstage; commedia character types also appear in *opera buffa* of Rossini, Verdi, and Puccini. In addition to *Petrouchka*, such twentieth-century works as Arnold Schoenberg's *Pierrot lunaire* and Debussy's "Fantoches" also reference commedia characters. In short, this type of theater is a historical foundation for many forms of popular entertainment, ranging from situation comedy to circus acts, as well as familiar terms like "slapstick comedy."

TERMS YOU SHOULD KNOW

aggregate	integer notation	polytonal
atonal	literal complement	post-tonal
bimodal	Locrian mode	pset
bitonal	Lydian-Mixolydian mode	pcset
cardinality	major-minor tetrachord	set
center	nontonal	• subset
centric	octatonic	split-third chord
collection	ostinato	stratification
diminished scale	pentatonic	whole-tone scale
element	planing	
focal pitch	polymodal	

QUESTIONS FOR REVIEW

1. Trichords include three elements, tetrachords include four. What word best describes a set with five elements? with six? with seven? with eight?

2. Name the diatonic modes. Explain how to use your knowledge of major and minor key signatures to spell each mode.

3. What is the purpose of integer notation?

4. What is the difference in the pattern of adjacent intervals between the Ionian mode and the whole-tone scale? How does this difference impact your ability to hear a tonic pitch class?

5. Name two symmetrical scales, and describe how they are constructed.

6. In music for your own instrument, find a passage by Debussy, Ravel, Stravinsky, Bartók, or other early twentieth-century composer in any diatonic mode or symmetrical scale, and identify the mode or scale. (Consult with your teacher, if necessary.)

7. How can analysis of modes or scales help you to learn, interpret, and/or memorize a work you are performing?

Know It? Show It!

Focus by working through the tutorials.

Learn with InQuizitive.

Apply what you've learned to complete the workbook assignments.

35

Rhythm, Meter, and Form in Music after 1900

Outline

Rhythm and meter

- Asymmetrical meter
- Perceived and notated meter
- Changing meter and polymeter
- Ametric music
- Additive rhythm

Form after the common-practice era

- Scale analysis and formal design
- Form and register
- Substitutes for tonal function
- Canon and imitation
- The Fibonacci series

Overview

Here, we review types of rhythmic and metrical frameworks explored by composers of the first half of the twentieth century, and consider how elements of pitch and time combine to create musical form in the absence of functional tonality.

Repertoire

Béla Bartók
- *Bagatelle*, Op. 6, No. 2
- From *Mikrokosmos*: "Bulgarian Rhythm" (No. 115), "Six Dances in Bulgarian Rhythm" (No. 148), "Syncopation" (No. 133)
- "Song of the Harvest," for two violins

Olivier Messiaen, "Danse de la fureur" ("Dance of Fury"), from *Quartet for the End of Time*

Igor Stravinsky
- "Bransle Gay," from *Agon*
- *Les noces* (*The Wedding*), Tableau II

Edgard Varèse, *Density 21.5*

Anton Webern
- "Dies ist ein Lied für dich allein" ("This Is a Song for You Alone"), from *Fünf Lieder aus "Der siebente Ring"* (*Five Songs from "The Seventh Ring"*)
- *Variations for Piano*, Op. 27, mvt. 2

Rhythm and Meter

In common-practice style, rhythmic patterns and notated meter reinforce each other—with a few notable exceptions, such as syncopations and hemiola, which contrast with the regular beat to achieve their intended effect. Meter and hypermeter operate hierarchically to reinforce the measurement of time into regular units. In the twentieth century, however, some pieces of music explore new ways of organizing durations.

Asymmetrical Meter

In music we have studied previously, one of the notable features was a constant, even pulse, with groupings of beats into two, three, or four per measure (forming duple, triple, or quadruple meters); divisions of the beat into two or three parts (simple or compound meters); and further subdivisions into twos. Other than occasional changes of meter or tempo, the intervals of time between beats were consistently the same length.

KEY CONCEPT Beats that are spaced evenly are **isochronous** (*iso* means "same," and *chronos* means "time"). Meters with isochronous beats, such as the simple and compound meters we have studied, are called **symmetrical meters**.

Asymmetrical meters have non-isochronous beats. Some beats may have two equally spaced divisions and others three equally spaced divisions (examples are $\frac{5}{8}$ and $\frac{7}{8}$).

In sum:

- simple or compound meters—isochronous beats, isochronous divisions;
- swing, in jazz—isochronous beats, non-isochronous divisions;
- asymmetrical meters—non-isochronous beats, isochronous divisions.

Listen to the opening of Bartók's "Bulgarian Rhythm" (Example 35.1). Conduct the meter in two beats per measure as you listen, to experience how unequal beat units feel. The meter signature is $\frac{5}{8}$, but the primary beat unit is not the eighth note. Each measure divides into two unequal "halves": the first half contains three eighths, the second half only two. As the left-hand part shows, the beat unit is non-isochronous: it shifts between a dotted-quarter and quarter note. Later in the same piece, part (b), the division reverses: $\frac{5}{8}$ is grouped into two eighths, then three.

EXAMPLE 35.1: Bartók, "Bulgarian Rhythm"

(a) Mm. 1–4

(b) Mm. 9–12

The five eighths of $\frac{5}{8}$ may be grouped as 3 + 2 or 2 + 3 (♩. ♩ or ♩ ♩.), 2 + 2 + 1 (♩ ♩ ♪), or some other combination. The meter $\frac{5}{4}$ works the same way (for example, ♩ ♩. or ♩ ♩ ♩). Like compound meters, asymmetrical meters are usually conducted at the beat level or, if the tempo is slow, at the beat-division level. Other common asymmetrical meter signatures are $\frac{7}{4}$ and $\frac{7}{8}$, which may divide 2 + 2 + 3, 3 + 2 + 2, 2 + 2 + 2 + 1, and so on. Less common signatures include $\frac{11}{8}$, $\frac{13}{8}$, $\frac{5}{16}$, and $\frac{7}{16}$.

Sometimes, when the same groupings run through several measures, the composer will indicate the divisions in the meter signature, as in Example 35.2. Listen to or play these measures at the keyboard to hear how the upper numbers indicate the divisions within the measure. The $\frac{4+2+3}{8}$ signature could have been notated in $\frac{9}{8}$ (the sum of 4 + 2 + 3), but that would not have shown the non-isochronous beats, which differ from the expected 3 + 3 + 3 beat divisions.

EXAMPLE 35.2: Bartók, "Six Dances in Bulgarian Rhythm," mm. 1–2

When performing asymmetrical meters, you might want to place a slight stress at the beginning of groups. You may need to practice counting with an accent on 1 (**1**-2-3, **1**-2 or **1**-2, **1**-2, **1**-2-3) until the patterns are familiar and you can feel the proper accentuation. Be sure not to hold the last note in the measure too long, making $\frac{5}{8}$ sound like $\frac{6}{8}$, or $\frac{7}{8}$ like $\frac{4}{4}$.

Meters that are usually considered symmetrical may be divided asymmetrically; for example, the beat divisions in $\frac{8}{8}$ may be grouped as 3 + 3 + 2. Example

35.3 shows several measures of another Bartók piece from *Mikrokosmos*. This passage alternates $\frac{5}{4}$, an asymmetrical meter, with $\frac{4}{4}$, usually a symmetrical one. In this example, however, the $\frac{4}{4}$ meter is treated like the $\frac{5}{4}$, with asymmetrical groupings. Other meters, such as $\frac{3}{2}$, $\frac{9}{8}$, and $\frac{12}{8}$, may also be treated asymmetrically.

EXAMPLE 35.3: Bartók, "Syncopation," mm. 1–3 🎧

Try it #1

Listen to or play Example 35.3 at the piano, then continue to mark the groupings of eighth notes below the score in measures 1 and 2, as shown.

Perceived and Notated Meter

In common-practice compositions, the notated and perceived meter are usually one and the same (with brief exceptions). In twentieth-century music, on the other hand, the notated and perceived meter may not correspond at all. Listen to the second movement of Webern's *Variations for Piano* without the score, and conduct along with the music, choosing a meter that seems appropriate to you (by ear). Now look at measures 1–4, in Example 35.4. Although this movement is notated in $\frac{2}{4}$, beginning with an anacrusis, most listeners would not conduct it that way if they had not seen the notation. What they tend to hear is a series of evenly spaced beats, with downbeats on the second note of each group of two (the G♯3 of the anacrusis, the second A4 of m. 1, the F5 of m. 2, and so on). Some listeners group these stronger pulses into measures of $\frac{3}{8}$; others may choose $\frac{6}{8}$ or another meter—but rarely $\frac{2}{4}$.

EXAMPLE 35.4: Webern, *Variations for Piano*, mvt. 2, mm. 1–4 🎧

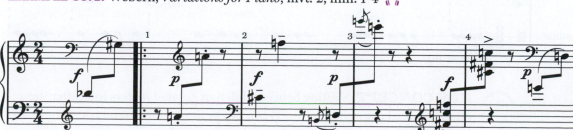

In some cases, pieces carefully notated in traditional ways may not convey a meter of any sort, while other pieces not notated in a traditional meter may convey a regular perceptible beat or meter created by the rhythmic patterns. With twentieth-century scores, what you see is not always what you hear. While the performer must attend to the music as notated, the primary metrical framework of the piece is the one perceived by the listener.

Changing Meter and Polymeter

Listen twice to an excerpt from Stravinsky's "Bransle Gay"—from *Agon*, a ballet based on old dance patterns—without looking at Example 35.5: the first time, conduct along with the castanet; the second time, with the wind parts (flutes and bassoons). Consider any difficulties you experience in choosing a meter, and in reconciling the castinet's meter with the other parts.

Now look at the passage in Example 35.5. Stravinsky notates the castanet rhythm of the first measure in $\frac{3}{8}$. Then, beginning in measure 2, he notates measures of $\frac{7}{16}$ and $\frac{5}{16}$ to match the rhythmic patterns of the wind parts. The castanet part, however, persists in its rhythmic ostinato in $\frac{3}{8}$, which continues to sound throughout the passage.

EXAMPLE 35.5: Stravinsky, "Bransle Gay," mm. 1-6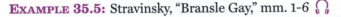

KEY CONCEPT Shifting between different notated meters (one after the other) is called **changing meter**. When two or more different metric streams are heard simultaneously, this technique is known as **polymeter**.

Example 35.5 illustrates both changing meter in the wind parts and polymeter in the relation between the castanet and the winds. Listeners can hear changing meters if the rhythms clearly articulate the metrical organization (as in Example 35.3). On the other hand, the changes may simply be a notational feature for the convenience of the players and conductor, and may be difficult for listeners to perceive. Other terms for changing meter include "mixed meter," "variable meter," and "multimeter."

Polymetrical passages are easiest to identify when the music is notated in two or more meters, but they may be perceived even when notated in one meter throughout all the parts. Look, for instance, at Example 35.6, from Stravinsky's *Les noces*. All parts are notated in $\frac{2}{4}$, and the singer's lines accompanied by pianos 1 and 3 clearly articulate this meter; but the strongly accented ostinato in pianos 2 and 4 and percussion sound on every third beat, like downbeats in $\frac{3}{4}$. We can hear this type of polymeter clearly when the metrical accents in different lines of a piece are not aligned.

EXAMPLE 35.6: Stravinsky, *Les noces*, Tableau II, mm. 54–59

Translation: And to whom do you belong now, beautiful round curls? To the girl with red cheeks, with a name like [Natasia].

Figure 35.1 summarizes four different types of polymeter. In Example 35.7, from Bartók's "Song of the Harvest," the possibilities of Figure 35.1a and b are combined. In measures 11-12, one part is notated in ¾ followed by ²⁄₄, while the other part has the reverse. If you attend to the melody of violin 1, you hear violin 2 enter in canon a fifth below two beats later; the ¾ meter is offset by two beats. Bartók helps listeners perceive this polymeter by placing accents on the downbeats of many measures; these should be carefully articulated when performing the piece.

FIGURE 35.1: Four types of polymeter

(a) Same beat unit but different measure lengths   (c) Same beat unit but different beat divisions

(b) Same beat unit but nonaligned measures   (d) Same beat division but different beat unit

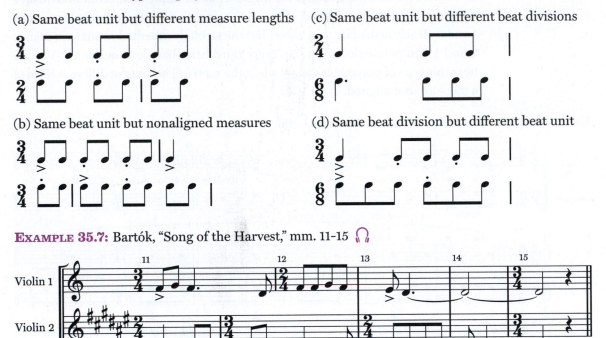

EXAMPLE 35.7: Bartók, "Song of the Harvest," mm. 11-15

In Figure 35.1c, the beat divides in twos (simple meter) in one line and divides in threes (compound meter) in the other, with the same beat duration for the ♩. in ⁶⁄₈ as for the ♩ in ²⁄₄. In part (d), the polymetric structure results in a different number of beats: ¾ is placed against ⁶⁄₈, with the eighths the same duration in each meter. There are six eighth notes in each measure, but the groupings and accent patterns differ (2 + 2 + 2 vs. 3 + 3). In contrast, the eighths in part (c) have different durations.

Ametric Music

Listen now to Varèse's *Density 21.5* without the score, and conduct along. Again, consider what musical cues help you determine which meter to conduct. Then look at your anthology score to see that the work is notated in a regular 𝄴 meter.

Although the piece sounds as if it is played with a lot of rubato, or flexibility in the tempo, the performer is given the following instructions: "Always [play] strictly in time—follow metronomic indications."

To determine how the rhythms in this piece avoid articulating a clear, consistent meter, mark the excerpt in Example 35.8 with the location of each beat, then listen and conduct it again in a quadruple meter while following the score. Circle the places where the beginning of a rhythmic idea lines up with a notated beat.

EXAMPLE 35.8: Varèse, *Density 21.5*, mm. 1-7

Many rhythmic ideas in this excerpt begin on an offbeat after a tied note, which obscures the sense of meter. At the beginning, most of these ties cross the bar line, making the downbeat hard to perceive. Yet several prominent rhythms *do* line up with beats; for example, the initial motive (F4-E4-F♯4) and its repetition in measure 3 fall on notated beats. They do not reinforce a sense of meter, however, since the repetition starts on beat 4 rather than beat 1. Another way Varèse clouds a strong sense of meter is by liberally mixing in eighth- and quarter-note triplets, thus making it hard to discern whether the meter is simple or compound.

KEY CONCEPT In some twentieth-century music notated in the traditional manner, rhythmic patterns may conflict with the notated meter and resist alignment into regular beat and accent patterns. If there is no meter perceived, the music is said to be **ametric**. Ametric music may also be scored in nontraditional ways, such as graphic notation (Chapter 39).

While common-practice composers tend to limit the number of different rhythmic patterns in a piece, we see no such limitation in Varèse's flute solo. If there were a strong sense of beat in an accompaniment or other instrumental part, or if the solo flute had established a clear, regular pulse at the outset, the numerous tied notes would sound syncopated against it. But because there is no regular pulse in this music—or perhaps because there are too many implied meters not corresponding to a consistent beat unit, each lasting only a brief time—the effect is ametric.

Additive Rhythm

One way to write music that sounds ametric is by using **additive rhythm**. That is, instead of conceiving of rhythm in terms of a beat unit with divisions and subdivisions, you begin with a small unit (often a sixteenth note or smaller) and add these small durations together to create larger, ametric patterns. This type of rhythm is usually notated without a meter.

One composer who is well known for his additive rhythms is Olivier Messiaen. Look at the rhythm in Example 35.9, from his *Quartet for the End of Time*. Most obvious are the absence of a meter signature and the irregular durations of the melody notes (doubled in octaves). Among the elements that help Messiaen to achieve this rhythmic structure are ties and what the composer calls "dots of addition." These dots are not balanced by another note to fill out a beat unit as they would be in a simple meter (e.g., dotted quarter plus eighth). Instead, they simply lengthen the note to which they are attached, creating an unpredictable and somewhat jagged rhythm. For example, in measure 27, the durations—♪., ♩ ♪, ♩, ♩ ♪, and ♪.—keep the rhythm from falling into metric regularity. Tap the rhythm of this passage, or chant it on a neutral syllable like "tah." When you first read it through, you may need to count slowly in sixteenth notes: in measure 27, 1-2-3, 1-2-3-4-5, 1-2-3-4-5-6-7-8, and so on. After it becomes familiar, you should be able to feel the durations in larger note values.

EXAMPLE 35.9: Messiaen, "Danse de la fureur," mm. 27–28 🎧

Another interesting rhythmic technique is at work in this excerpt as well. Consider each measure a one-bar unit. Compare the first *duration* of the measure with the last, then the second with the next-to-last, until you reach a single duration that stands at the center. Each measure is a **palindrome**—the same going backward and forward. For example, if you count each duration in six-teenths (♩ = 4, ♩ ♪ = 5), the pattern in measure 27 is 3-5-8-5-3, and in measure 28 is 4-3-7-3-4; the length of the note in the center is the sum of the length of the other two notes. Rhythms like these are another example of Messiaen's delight in the "charm of impossibilities"—it is impossible to run a palindrome in reverse order, since the result is the same as the original.

Try it #2

For each excerpt below, identify the type of rhythmic or metric device used.

Stravinsky, *Three Movements from "Petrouchka,"* mvt. 2, mm. 70-72

(a) Device used: _____

Charles Ives, "The Cage," m. 1

(b) Device used: _____

Holst, Second Suite in F (reduction), mvt. 4, mm. 57-62

(c) Device used: _____

Form after the Common-Practice Era

After the common-practice era and in the absence of functional tonality, such pitch materials as sets, set classes, and rows (to be considered in the following three chapters) as well as collections (Chapter 34) may take the place of triads, keys, and modulation to help define formal sections. Because these pitch materials do not create as strong a sense of closure, musical elements that play supporting roles in defining form in tonal pieces—contrasts in range, register, timbre, tempo, dynamics, motives, articulation, and duration—can play stronger ones in creating new formal sections. These elements are even more salient when combined with changes in pitch materials. Older compositional methods like canon and imitation continue to be employed, and new structural elements, such as symmetry, also help to articulate form.

We will examine formal processes on several levels, from phrases and sections to the overall structure of a work. While most common-practice works show a hierarchical formal organization, not all music after 1900 does. Each piece you study will need to be approached on its own terms.

Scale Analysis and Formal Design

For an example where both pitch and nonpitch elements contribute to musical form, listen once again to "Song of the Harvest" while following the score in your anthology; measures 1-15 are also given in Example 35.10. Listen for changes indicating formal divisions; make a note when you hear motivic, rhythmic, dynamic, tempo, registral, and other changes that distinguish one section from the next.

We examined measures 1-5 in Chapter 34 (Example 34.13), and noted that the pitch collection was octatonic: OCT 23 {2 3 5 6 8 9 e 0}. Another aspect that contributes to the perception of these measures as a single phrase is the *poco ritard* followed by rests in both violin parts in measure 5.

EXAMPLE 35.10: Bartók, "Song of the Harvest," mm. 1-15 🎧

Try it #3

On the score in your anthology, divide "Song of the Harvest" into sections. Identify one or more focal pcs in each section, and write the pcs in scale order (beginning with the focal pc) beneath the staff. Then fill in the chart below.

SECTION	A	B	A′	B′	Coda
MEASURES	1–5	6–15			
SCALE TYPE	OCT 23	OCT 12			
FOCAL PCS	A/D♯				

One thing that makes this short piece so interesting is that although its motivic and rhythmic structure divides into a clear **A B A′ B′** form plus coda, the changes in scale type and focal pcs do not coincide with this form. The pc structure instead is rounded, with OCT 23 in the beginning and ending sections (excluding the coda) and the contrasting OCT 12 in the middle two sections. The focal pcs in each section are tritone-related between the two violins, but the **B′** section brings back the initial pair {D♯ A} as a kind of tonal closure, though respelled enharmonically and reversed between the two instruments. As another reversal, in the first two sections violin 1 is the leader while violin 2 follows in imitation, but thereafter violin 2 becomes the leader and violin 1 follows, until the coda.

As for the motivic structure, the two **B** sections are simply transpositions of each other, up a half step, but the relationship between **A** and **A′** is more complex. **A′** not only swaps the melodic lines between violins 1 and 2, it also inverts each of these lines. The opening violin melody begins with an upward leap of a P4, followed by a descending whole-step, half-step, whole-step sequence. Violin 2 in measure 16 does the opposite: it makes a downward leap of a P4, followed by an ascending whole step, half step, and whole step. The other part is inverted as well.

Finally, consider the pitch structure of the coda, the only non-octatonic measures of the duet. Although we have focused on octatonicism in this piece, the individual melodies for each instrument are tetrachords shared by the diatonic and octatonic collections. In the opening measures, for example, violin 1 plays the diatonic tetrachord A B C D (as from A Aeolian), while violin 2 has the diatonic tetrachord D♯ E♯ F♯ G♯ (D♯ Aeolian). Only when the tetrachords are combined do we hear the full octatonic collection. The coda takes one tetrachord from each octatonic collection—E♭ F G♭ A♭ from the OCT 23 collection, and A♭ B♭ C♭ D♭ from the OCT 12 collection. Together they make the E♭ Aeolian collection.

In performance, knowing that the octatonic collections will change from section to section may help the violinists prepare for key signature changes and avoid playing incorrect accidentals. Assuming that they practice their parts alone first, they will probably be surprised to hear how the two parts sound together. In particular, they may find it difficult to tune the focal pitches, which are a tritone apart. Hearing the underlying octatonic scale in advance (perhaps playing or singing the full scale in preparation for the duo rehearsal), and learning to expect its characteristic diminished sonorities, should help them stay in tune.

SUMMARY

When you analyze modal compositions of the twentieth or twenty-first century, you may find that

- the entire composition expresses a single mode;
- the composer articulates new formal sections by changing the pc center and/or mode;
- the composer presents two modes (bimodality) or more than two modes (polymodality) simultaneously in different musical layers, or strata (stratification).

Form and Register

Composers may also make formal divisions by means of changes in register. As an example, listen to Bartók's *Bagatelle*, Op. 6, No. 2, while following the score in your anthology. Mark in the score where you hear sectional divisions, and consider why you hear a division there.

This piece begins with an ostinato A♭4-B♭4 in the right hand (Example 35.11). The left hand moves outward by half steps from the pitches of the ostinato, making a wedge shape. Most listeners hear this first section as ending on the downbeat of measure 7—because of the resolution of the A♭4-B♭4 dyad outward to G4-B4, the expansion of the left-hand wedge downward to C4, then B3 (joining the chord in the right hand), the slowing of the tempo, and the softer volume. A change of motive, dynamic level, and tempo in measure 7 confirms the perception of a section ending here. Call measures 1-7 section **A**.

EXAMPLE 35.11: Bartók, *Bagatelle*, mm. 1-7 🎧

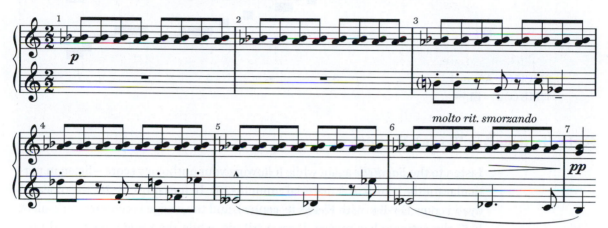

Perhaps the wedge and the relationship between the hands was easier to hear than to see; the traditional notation on two staves disguises the hands' overlapping range and half-step voice-leading. It is sometimes helpful when analyzing pieces in traditional notation to transcribe the work into a graph, to see how range and texture work together to shape musical form.

One example is a **pitch-time graph**. This is easy to construct, either by using the piano-roll notation on a MIDI sequencing program or by hand on graph paper. On a piece of graph paper, plot pitches on the y-axis (vertically, to show the pitch range from high to low) and the passage of time horizontally on the x-axis. Figure 35.2 shows an analytical graph of measures 1-7 of the *Bagatelle*. Each square on the vertical axis represents one pitch of the chromatic scale; each square on the horizontal axis represents one eighth note duration (the smallest duration in this passage). The shading signifies the "voices": the right-hand ostinato is lighter, while the pitches of the left-hand wedge are darker. The **pitch symmetry** around the silent A4 (the note in between the A♭4 and B♭4 of the ostinato) and the interaction of the hand parts are clearly visible in the graph.

⌢ **KEY CONCEPT** Symmetry plays a recurring role in music after 1900, and we have seen two types in this chapter. The Bartók *Bagatelle* (Figure 35.2) shows pitch-space symmetry, with pitches sounding above and below a central axis. The Messiaen quartet (Example 35.9) illustrates temporal symmetry, where durations are placed symmetrically before and after a central time point (as a palindrome). These types of symmetry may be combined.

FIGURE 35.2: Pitch-time graph of Bartók, *Bagatelle*, mm. 1-7 🎧

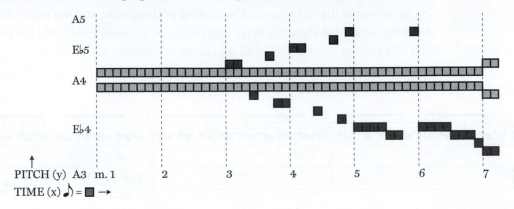

Substitutes for Tonal Function

Listen to the *Bagatelle* again while following your anthology score—listen in particular for the return of **A** material (mm. 18-23). In measures 18-20, the repeated dyad is now D4-E4 (with E♭4 as its center), and the wedge is centered on a silent E♭5: the ostinato has moved down a tritone, while the wedge has moved up a tritone. Call measures 18-23 **A′** to show their relation to the opening section.

In measures 24-30, **A** returns as the center of the symmetries, but now in three octaves. The wedge appears in the left hand, symmetrical around A3, and we hear the A♭-B♭ dyad with A5 as its center. The center of these two symmetries is A4. Because of the octave duplications, this is a pitch-class center. Label measures 24-30 **A″**; they feature a return of the original pc center, but the range has expanded outward a tritone from the E♭4/E♭5 of the previous section. The overall form of this *Bagatelle*, then, is **A B A′ A″**—though in some ways it also resembles a ternary form: the first section (mm. 1-7) and the last (18-30) are similar in material, while the middle section (mm. 7-18) is contrasting, with 15-18 serving as a retransition to **A′**.

In some nontonal music, composers treat the tritone in a way analogous to the tonic-dominant perfect fifth of tonal pieces. In the *Bagatelle*, the motion from A4 as a center of symmetry to pitch-class E♭ and back to pitch-class A can be thought of as replacing the traditional motion of tonic-dominant-tonic. This use of the tritone is called a **tritone axis** (as the traditional motion is called the "tonic-dominant axis"). In Bartók's music, a primary tritone axis may be supplemented by a secondary axis. For an A-E♭ primary axis, the secondary axis would be C-F♯, dividing the octave into four equal parts by minor thirds: C-A-F♯-E♭ (D♯). The relationships between this type of axis and other materials in his music, such as the octatonic collection, should be readily apparent. For good examples of a tritone axis in a larger work, see Bartók's *Music for Strings, Percussion, and Celesta* or *Sonata for Two Pianos and Percussion*. Music analyst Erno Lendvai has written extensively on these two pieces and developed an entire system of analysis for Bartók's "axis tonality."

Canon and Imitation

Many twentieth-century and contemporary composers draw on a pre-1900 technique in their writing: canon and imitative counterpoint. Webern, for example, is well known for his canonic procedures, and we have looked at several pieces by Bartók with imitative entrances between the voices—yet the two composers' works sound quite distinct. We look briefly at two examples that show the composers' differences.

Webern's canonic writing is often fragmentary and can be concealed among other voices. Listen, for example, to the closing of a song where the piano right hand (beginning G–G♭–F) is followed in canon by the voice on beat 3. The canon varies the rhythm between voices, but the pitches are exact. The final four notes of the voice are then echoed again by the piano in the postlude, with some additional embellishing pitches. In other Webern works, the canons are longer but may be concealed by factors such as register and orchestration—divided into small fragments split between instruments or between the two hands of the piano.

EXAMPLE 35.12: Webern, "Dies ist ein Lied für dich allein," mm. 9-12 🎧

Bartók's canonic and imitative writing tends to be easier to recognize by ear, as the melodies are longer and the repetitions are exact or transposed. See, for instance, the passage in Example 35.13, where the canon extends without alteration for seven measures. In the composer's *Music for Strings, Percussion, and Celesta*, the opening points of imitation create a formal design analogous to a tonal fugue exposition that extends over twenty-one measures.

EXAMPLE 35.13: Bartók, "Bulgarian Rhythm," mm. 18-24 🎧

The Fibonacci Series

The **Fibonacci series** is an infinite series of numbers (0 1 1 2 3 5 8 13 21 34 55 89, etc.) in which each new member of the series is the sum of the previous two. Pairs of adjacent Fibonacci numbers converge (as the infinite series continues) toward a proportion that has been associated with balance in artworks since Greek antiquity, known as the **golden section** or **mean**. This proportion, about 62 percent (.618) of the total length of a piece or section, has been shown to be significant in architecture and painting, and in music of previous centuries. For example, in many Classical sonatas, the recapitulation begins about 62 percent of the way through the movement. The golden section is also present in nature, as can be seen by taking measurements within the spirals of a pinecone or conch shell. This proportion has intrigued composers for generations.

Analysts have drawn on the series to locate significant events in several Bartók pieces. For example, in the first movement of *Music for Strings, Percussion, and Celeste*, the fugue begins in measure 1 (with an anacrusis), the second voice enters in measure 5, and the fourth voice in 13. The end of the exposition is in 21, the timpani enters in 34, and the climax occurs right after 55. These measure numbers—1, 5, 13, 21, 34, and 55—come directly from the series. Bartók was also fond of using asymmetrical meters with Fibonacci numbers as the upper value, such as $\frac{5}{8}$, $\frac{8}{8}$, and $\frac{13}{8}$. The Fibonacci series may determine the choice of meter, patterns of durations, length of phrases or sections, or the placement of climactic moments in a piece.

Did You Know?

The Fibonacci series gained some prominence in popular culture when it played a role as a crucial clue (to unlock a safe) in Dan Brown's novel *The Da Vinci Code*, and subsequent movie starring Tom Hanks. Indeed, Leonardo da Vinci's paintings are known for their placement of people and objects according to the golden mean. Among the paintings often cited are *The Annunciation, The Last Supper,* and *Vitruvian Man.* Twentieth-century composers whose music lends itself to analysis by the golden section include Debussy, Erik Satie, and Witold Lutosławski. In fact, there is an entire book devoted to this topic—*Debussy in Proportion,* by Roy Howat.

TERMS YOU SHOULD KNOW

additive rhythm	golden section (mean)	pitch-time graph
ametric	isochronous	pitch symmetry
asymmetrical meter	non-isochronous	polymeter
changing meter	ostinato	symmetrical meter
Fibonacci series	palindrome	tritone axis

QUESTIONS FOR REVIEW

1. How do rhythmic patterns reinforce the perception of a meter? What is the role of metric accent in the perception of a meter?
2. Is it possible to have changing meter and polymeter at the same time?
3. How are asymmetrical meters similar to traditional compound meters? How are they different?
4. How do durations, rhythm, and notated meter interact to make a piece that sounds ametric?
5. How would you recognize a passage that features additive rhythms? With which composer is this technique associated?
6. How have composers adapted common-practice forms after 1900? What are some substitutes for the relationship of tonic and dominant in nontonal works?
7. What are some elements that help establish sections in nontonal works? What features may create closure without functional harmony?
8. In music for your own instrument, find one nontonal piece that has clearly audible formal divisions.
9. In music for your own instrument, find one piece with changing meter, one with an asymmetrical meter, and one with polymeter. How can the date of composition help you locate a piece of each type?

(Ask your teacher for help with questions 8 and 9 if necessary.)

Know It? Show It!

Focus by working through the tutorials.

Learn with InQuizitive.

Apply what you've learned to complete the workbook assignments.

36

Music Analysis with Sets

Overview

In this chapter, we focus on two works—a piano piece by Bartók and a song by Berg—in order to learn how to identify pitch and pitch-class sets, and how to transpose and invert them.

Repertoire

Béla Bartók, "Bulgarian Rhythm," from *Mikrokosmos* (No. 115)

Alban Berg, "Sahst du nach dem Gewitterregen" ("Did You See the Forest after the Rainstorm?"), from *Altenberg-Lieder* (*Five Orchestral Songs*), Op. 4, No. 2

Outline

Relationships between sets

- Listing the elements of a pitch-class set

Pitch and pitch-class intervals

- Pcset transposition and mod12 arithmetic
- Interval classes and the interval-class vector

The inversion of pitch sets and pitch-class sets

- The inversion of pitch sets
- The inversion of pitch-class sets
- Identifying transposition and inversion

Relationships Between Sets

In Chapters 34 and 35, we looked at pieces from the first half of the twentieth century in which pitch centricity, as well as motion between different modes or scales, helped to articulate form. Now we turn to compositions where pitch centricity is less strong (if present at all) and where composers use most or all tones of the chromatic collection without a strong underlying diatonic foundation. In the absence of keys and modes, triads, and other familiar sonorities, new harmonic idioms emerged that brought with them new compositional freedoms and constraints.

KEY CONCEPT When we consider relationships between sets of pitches in a particular octave, we are analyzing **pitch sets** (**psets**); when we look at more abstract properties of pitch classes in a set, without consideration of octave placement, we are analyzing **pitch-class sets** (**pcsets**).

Listen to the opening of the Berg song shown in Example 36.1, focusing on the circled pitches. When analyzing a composition like this—without triads and without centricity—we lose the ability to label with keys, Roman numerals, or scale types. We must rely on new systems, some of which are described below, to make sense of the musical elements. In a context where chromaticism is so pervasive, it is sometimes helpful simply to list all the pcs in a section, melody, or chord so that you can compare it with other similar moments. We will compare the circled sonorities as pcsets using the pc integers introduced in Chapter 34.

EXAMPLE 36.1: Berg, "Sahst du nach dem Gewitterregen," mm. 1-5

pcsets: {1 4 5 8}   {e 2 3 6}

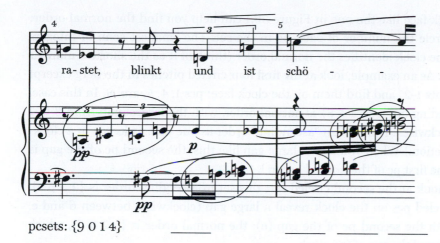

pcsets: {9 0 1 4}

Translation: Did you see, after the summer rain, the forest? All is quiet, sparkling, and more beautiful . . .

Listing the Elements of a Pitch-Class Set

Play the circled pitches in Example 36.1 at a keyboard; you will find that they sound somewhat similar, although you may not know how to describe their relationships. The circled tetrachords (four-note sets) stand out here because they feature repeated major thirds. (There are certainly many other interesting motivic relationships and pcsets in this passage, but we will start with these.)

In order to compare these tetrachords more easily, we will first write out the pitch classes of each one in a uniform order. This step is analogous to identifying triad types, where we removed octave doublings and pitch duplications to write the triad in its simplest form: root-third-fifth. Reordering pcs into a particular order serves a similar function: to make the pcset easier to recognize and compare with others. (Chapter 37 will explain how pcsets are named.)

KEY CONCEPT The elements of a pitch-class set are listed as integers in a compact ascending order called **normal order**. To find normal order,

- arrange the elements in ascending order with the smallest possible gaps between adjacent pcs, and

- the smallest span from the first to last pc.

- Write the pcs of the normal order in curly braces, e.g., {5 6 8 t}.

A clock face like the one in Figure 36.1 can help you find the normal order: simply circle the number of each pc in the set. The smallest span of integers around the clock identifies the normal order (think of it as the shortest number of hours). As an example, look at the first four circled pitches in the Berg excerpt (m. 3, beats 1-2) and find them on the clock face: pcs 1, 4, 5, and 8. In this case, the ascending order {1 4 5 8} is normal order, with the largest gap from 8 to 1 going clockwise. (Think of an "ascending" order as one that proceeds in a clockwise direction.) When you spot a large gap like this, the second pc of the gap is usually the first pc of the normal order.

Now look at the second circled set; this set in ascending order is {2 3 6 e}. These circled pcs on the clock reveal a large gap (clockwise) between 6 and e. Begin with the second pc of the gap (e): the normal order is {e 2 3 6}, which wraps around the top of the clock.

FIGURE 36.1: Clock-face diagram with Berg sets marked

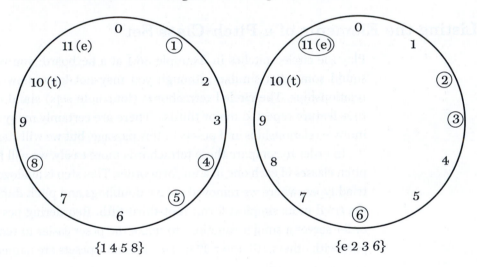

{1 4 5 8}   {e 2 3 6}

🎵 KEY CONCEPT

- Use curly braces, { }, to show sets in normal order. The pcs in normal order (despite its name) are not ordered sets, because they have been rearranged (ascending order, etc.); their order does not match the order of the pcs in the music.

- Use angle brackets, < >, to show ordered sets. In ordered sets, the order within the brackets matches the order of the elements (pcs, intervals, etc.) in the music.

Try it #1

A. In Example 36.1, write the normal order for the remaining circled sets (in mm. 4–5) in the blanks below the example.

B. For each set below, write out the pcs in normal order.

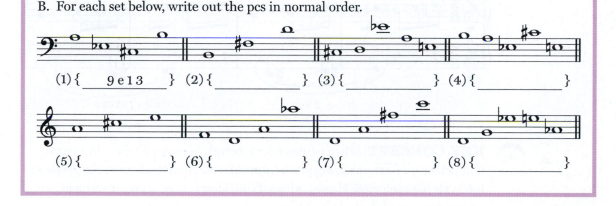

(1) { ___9 e 1 3___ } (2) { _____ } (3) { _____ } (4) { _____ }

(5) { _____ } (6) { _____ } (7) { _____ } (8) { _____ }

One question that might remain about Example 36.1 is how these particular pcsets were selected for circling. This basic first step, choosing groups of pitches to analyze, is called **segmentation**. Thoughtful and musical segmentation is crucial for the success of your analysis. Look for groups of pitches clearly defined as units: these units might be complete melodies or chords, motives slurred together or isolated by rests, or a melody note plus its chordal accompaniment. Another analytical strategy is to look at a melody's component parts—by dividing up a long melody to look at the trichords embedded within it, for example. The sets circled in the Berg example were chosen because of their prominent melodic or harmonic thirds, but they were also segmented by musical features such as register, slurring, and rests—for example, the slurred left-hand melody of measure 3 with the vocal pitch it accompanies, and the right-hand melody of measure 4 (isolated by rests on either side). While your segmentation will normally focus on pitches that are adjacent, you can also group nonadjacent pitches if some feature such as similar register, timbre, or articulation groups them aurally. When in doubt, trust your ears!

Pitch and Pitch-Class Intervals

One way to compare sets in a piece of music is to examine the intervals between pitches or pcs within each set, and then compare the results. Listen to the Bartók passage in Example 36.2, or play it at the piano. The circles in the example correspond with a prominent motive in this work, and a particular succession of pitch intervals.

EXAMPLE 36.2: Bartók, "Bulgarian Rhythm," mm. 5-8

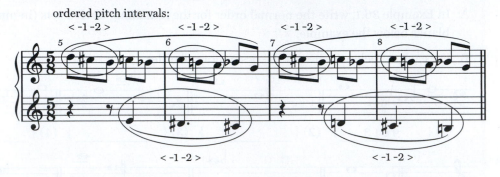

> **KEY CONCEPT** When we consider intervals between pitches (in a particular octave), we are analyzing **pitch intervals**; when we look more abstractly at intervals between pitch classes, without consideration of octave placement, we are analyzing **pc intervals** (or **pcis**).

To measure pitch intervals, simply count semitones; for example, the pitch interval from D5 to C♯5 (the beginning of Example 36.2) is 1, but the pitch interval from D4 to C♯5 is 11. Compound intervals have pitch-interval numbers greater than 12; D3 to C♯5 is pitch interval 23.

When order is important to your analysis, pitch intervals are written with a plus or minus sign to show their order and direction: D4 up to F♯5 is +16, F♯5 down to D4 is -16. This distance is called an **ordered pitch interval**. Write ordered pitch intervals between angle brackets (< >) to show that the order of the intervals matches the order they appear in the music. If two pitches occur simultaneously, or if you don't care to specify an order or direction (up or down), the distance is an **unordered pitch interval**. For example, if D4-F♯5 were set in a chord, where direction didn't matter, you would label the unordered pitch interval 16.

There are only twelve possible pitch-class intervals, each represented by a single integer: for example, a m7 and an A6 are both pci 10, and a d5 and A4 are both pci 6. To speed your analyses, memorize the pci integers in the chart below.

INTERVAL	PCI INTEGER	INTERVAL	PCI INTEGER
unison	0	tritone	6
m2	1	P5	7
M2	2	m6	8
m3	3	M6	9
M3	4	m7	10 (t)
P4	5	M7	11 (e)

SUMMARY

- Ordered pitch intervals, written between angle brackets, represent both direction (plus or minus sign) and size (integer) measured in semitones.

- Pitch intervals accurately represent compound intervals with numbers greater than 12; pitch-class intervals do not, because of octave equivalence.

Pcset Transposition and mod12 Arithmetic

One of the reasons we represent pcsets and intervals with integers is that it allows us to write and recognize musical operations like transposition quickly, using addition and subtraction.

KEY CONCEPT When pcsets are represented in integer notation, you can transpose them by adding one of the pitch-class intervals shown above to each pc of the set. For example:

- To transpose {3 5 7} by a minor third (pci 3), add 3 to each element. You will get {6 8 t}; that is, {E♭ F G} becomes {G♭ A♭ B♭}.

- We can then say that {6 8 t} is T_3 of {3 5 7}; T_3 means transposed by pci 3.

Example 36.3 reproduces two of the sets circled in the Berg song, to show how they are related. Here, the left-hand pcs that end measure 4 are transposed by T_2 to become the first pcs of the following measure.

EXAMPLE 36.3: Berg, "Sahst du nach dem Gewitterregen," mm. 4–5 (left hand) 🎧

{5 8 9 0} T_2 →   {7 t e 2}

Sometimes it is helpful to refer to the clock face when transposing. For example, if you wanted to transpose {e 1 2} by T_2, imagine the clock face (Figure 36.2).

FIGURE 36.2: Clock-face diagram illustrating transposition

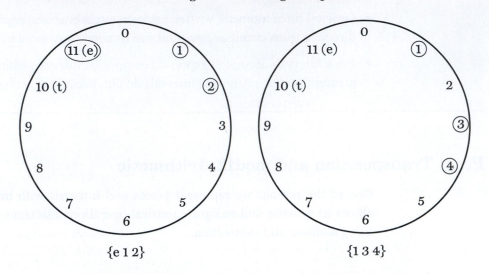

$$\{e\ 1\ 2\}\qquad\qquad\{1\ 3\ 4\}$$

Think of the original set circled on a transparent overlay, fastened in the middle so that it can spin around. Then spin the overlay clockwise the number of "clicks" (semitones) you want to transpose. To transpose $\{e\ 1\ 2\}$ by T_2, circle these pcs and rotate the overlay two positions to the right. Now the circle that was around e is over 1. The other circles will be over 3 and 4, yielding $\{1\ 3\ 4\}$.

You can get the same result with **mod12** arithmetic, which converts a number greater than 11 to an integer between 0 and 11. We already rely on this system when reading twenty-four-hour clocks: when we see a time like 16:00, we convert it to 4:00 p.m.

KEY CONCEPT To convert a large integer to a pc number between 0 and 11, divide the number by 12 and take the remainder. Shortcut: For integers between 12 and 23, simply subtract 12.

Let's return to the trichord $\{e\ 1\ 2\}$ and transpose again by T_2. If you add 2 to each element of $\{e\ 1\ 2\}$ by "regular" arithmetic, you get $\{13\ 3\ 4\}$. Using mod12 arithmetic, however, produces $\{1\ 3\ 4\}$—13 converts to 1 mod12 (shortcut: 13 - 12 = 1). For another example, transpose the same set by T_7, as shown below.

Transposition by 7: $\{\ 11\quad 1\quad 2\ \}$
$$\underline{+\ 7\quad 7\quad 7\ \ }$$
$\{18\quad 8\quad 9\ \}$, which converts (mod12) to $\{6\ 8\ 9\}$.

🎧 **KEY CONCEPT** Use mod12 arithmetic to find the pci between two pitch classes, a and b: subtract (b - a) mod12. If b is a smaller integer than a, add 12 to it and then subtract. When you subtract pcs in this order, the result is an **ordered pitch-class interval**.

Examples:

- The ordered pci between 2 and 7 is (7 - 2), or 5.
- The ordered pci between 7 and 3 is (3 - 7) = (15 - 7), or 8.

To practice subtraction mod12, let's return to Bartók's "Bulgarian Rhythm" (Example 36.4) to find the ordered pcis for the circled trichords. Each one has the same ordered sequence of pcis: < e t >. For example, given the right-hand pcs in measure 5, < 2 1 e >, subtracting the first two pcs makes 1 - 2 (13 - 2) = 11 (e); for the second two pcs, 11 - 1 = 10 (t). The other trichords produce the same ordered pcis.

EXAMPLE 36.4: Bartók, "Bulgarian Rhythm," mm. 5-8 🎧

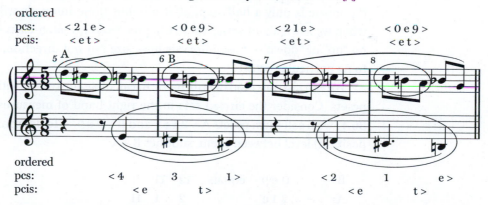

To show how order affects pcis, contrast the pci from D to C♯ with the opposite order—from C♯ to D. Here, we would subtract 2 - 1, for an ordered pci of 1. To summarize, the ordered pci from D to C♯ is 11 and from C♯ to D is 1. These intervals, 11 and 1, are in a complementary relationship—together they span the entire octave (twelve half steps).

🎧 **KEY CONCEPT** The ordered pcis (a - b) and (b - a) always sum to 12. Pcis in this relationship are called **inverses**, or **complementary intervals**. Inverses appear directly across the clock face from each other (3 and 9, 2 and 10, and so on). To compute ordered pcis on a clock face, count the number of moves around the clock from the first integer to the second in a clockwise direction (Figure 36.3).

FIGURE 36.3: Clock-face diagram illustrating ordered pcis (clockwise order)

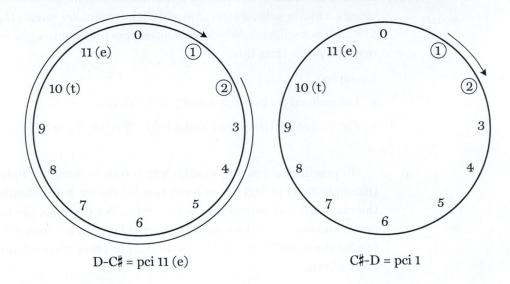

D–C♯ = pci 11 (e)   C♯–D = pci 1

Ordered pcis are sometimes musically counterintuitive—D to C♯ (pci 11) in the music is only a half step, after all—but these intervals will be quite useful when we learn about serialism in Chapter 38. With pitch-class intervals, there is no "up" or "down"—these intervals have size but not direction, since pcs belong to no particular octave.

We can also use mod12 arithmetic to calculate the transposition level between pcsets. Consider the circled sets in the right hand of measures 5-6 of Example 36.4; we'll call them pcsets A < 2 1 e > and B < 0 e 9 >. To determine the T_n (transposition) level between them, subtract B - A:

B:		0 e 9	equals	12	11	21
A:	-	2 1 e		2	1	11
				10	10	10 = T_{10}

SUMMARY

- To transpose a pcset by a particular pc interval (T_n), add that pci integer, n, to each element of the set (mod12).

- To calculate T_n between two pcsets, A and B, subtract the integers of the first set from the second (mod12): B - A.

Try it #2

Translate each trichord on the left into integer notation, then transpose it by the designated pc interval.

TRICHORD	INTEGER NOTATION	TRANSPOSE BY	TRANSPOSED SET
{D F A}	{2 5 9}	T_3	{5 8 0}
{B C C♯}		T_1	
{C♯ D F♯}		T_2	
{E F♯ A♯}		T_5	
{C E G♯}		T_7	
{G♭ A♭ B♭}		T_4	
{C D F}		T_6	

Another Way

You can transpose pcsets without resorting to clock faces, arithmetic, or integer numbers simply by working at the keyboard or other instrument. To transpose pcset {2 4 8} by a tritone, or pci 6: (1) play the set in any pitch realization—for example, {D4 E4 G♯4}; (2) listen for the succession of intervals (up a M2, up a M3); (3) find the first note of the transposed set, a tritone away (A♭); then (4) play the same succession of intervals beginning on that pitch: {A♭ B♭ D}. The same transposition in mod12 arithmetic is: {2 4 8} + 6 = {8 t 2}.

Some advantages of integer notation and arithmetic are precision, speed, the elimination of enharmonic spelling problems and octave placement questions, and the ability to do transpositions quickly in your head. Some advantages of the keyboard realization are the connection with your ear (which can detect mistakes) and the kinesthetic reinforcement of the process in your fingers. Try all of these methods, and tailor an approach that works best for you.

Interval Classes and the Interval-Class Vector

To determine why some pcsets sound similar to each other and others sound different, you can make a list of all the intervals in one pcset and compare it with a list of intervals in another set. The list will also give you a rough idea of the sound of each pcset, since a set with several minor seconds, for example, will sound different from one with several perfect fourths. To make the lists general enough to apply to any musical realization of the set—with any possible contour, order, and octave placement of its pcs—we use unordered pitch-class intervals.

KEY CONCEPT Find **unordered pitch-class intervals** by subtracting both (b - a) and (a - b) mod12 and taking the smaller of the two differences. For the dyads F♯–D and D–F♯, calculate both intervals: (2 - 6) = (14 - 6) = 8 and (6 - 2) = 4. The lower number, 4, is the unordered pci between pcs 6 and 2.

On a clock face, think of an unordered pci as the shortest route between the two pcs, where direction doesn't matter (clockwise or counterclockwise). In Figure 36.4, we have circled the pc integers 2 and 6. Now move the shortest distance (not always clockwise) between them and count the number of moves. The distance from pc 2 to pc 6 is four moves clockwise, but eight moves counterclockwise. The unordered pci is therefore 4, the shortest distance.

FIGURE 36.4: Clock-face diagram illustrating unordered pcis

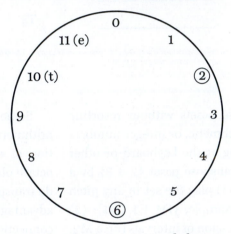

unordered pci 4, or interval class 4

KEY CONCEPT Another name for an unordered pci is an **interval class (ic)**. Each interval class represents one ordered pc interval and its inverse. There are six interval classes, each one grouping together intervals that are similar in sound.

INTERVAL CLASS	PCIS	SOME TONAL INTERVAL NAMES
ic 1	1, e	m2, M7, d8
ic 2	2, t	M2, m7, A6
ic 3	3, 9	m3, M6, A2
ic 4	4, 8	M3, m6, d4
ic 5	5, 7	P4, P5
ic 6	6	A4, d5

To memorize ic numbers, remember that a pci and its inverse always sum to 12 (so ic 3 consists of pci 3 and 9). Interval class 6 is its own inverse. Even pc 0 fits this guideline, since pc 0 is equivalent to 12 mod12.

An **interval-class vector** (or **ic vector**) is a concise list of all possible interval classes in a pcset. We can use them to compare sets and get an idea of their sound. Let's begin with the opening trichord of the Bartók passage in Example 36.4—{e 1 2}, in normal order. First, calculate the interval class between each pair of pcs in the trichord:

- ic 2 between e and 1,
- ic 1 between 1 and 2, and
- ic 3 between e and 2.

All together, the trichord has one each of ic 1, 2, and 3, but no ic 4, 5, or 6. To summarize the analysis, represent each interval class, 1 to 6, with a box, and write in each box the number of times you found that particular ic.

$$1 \quad 2 \quad 3 \quad 4 \quad 5 \quad 6 = \text{interval classes}$$

1	1	1	0	0	0

This tally is the ic vector, which we write within square brackets without commas or spaces: [111000]. The ic vector shows at a glance that pcs in this trichord can be paired to make one half step, one whole step, and one minor third (or compounds or inverses of these)—but no other intervals.

Now calculate the ic vector for a larger pcset: {0 1 2 4 8}. First, find the interval class from every pc to every other pc. You could realize the set as pitches at the keyboard or on staff paper, then make a hand tally of the interval classes you find. A quicker method involves subtraction and a triangular chart of ordered pc intervals, as shown below.

0 1 2 4 8
     1 2 4 8   (subtract 0 from each pc after the first: 1 - 0, 2 - 0, 4 - 0, 8 - 0)
       1 3 7   (subtract 1 from each pc after the second: 2 - 1, 4 - 1, 8 - 1)
         2 6   (subtract 2 from each pc after the third: 4 - 2, 8 - 2)
           4   (subtract 4 from the remaining pc: 8 - 4)

Next, convert each pci above 6 into an interval class (for example, 8 becomes 4), and count how many of each interval class appear in the triangle. Write the count in the appropriate box, as shown.

1 2 4 4

2	2	1	3	1	1

  1 3 5
    2 6
      4

The result is two ic 1s, two ic 2s, one ic 3, three ic 4s, one ic 5, and one ic 6. The ic vector is [221311]. Larger sets, of course, have more ics. The number of possible ics is $\frac{n^2 - n}{2}$, where n is the number of pcs in the set.

Try it #3

Calculate the ic vector for the following pcsets.

A. (1) {1 4 8}   [001110]

(2) {1 3 4 7}   _____

(3) {0 2 4 6 9}   _____

(4) {0 1 3 5 7 8}   _____

B. Which set has the fewest tritones?   _____

C. Which set has the most P4s or P5s?   _____

SUMMARY

Measure the intervals between pitches and pitch classes in the following ways.

1. Pitches: Count the semitones between pitches; show direction with + or -.
   - Ordered pitch interval: B♭3 to C5 = +14
                              C5 to B♭3 = -14
   - Unordered pitch interval: B♭3 and C5 = 14

2. Pitch classes: For two pitch classes, a and b, subtract (b − a) mod12; if order is unimportant, subtract both (a − b) and (b − a) and take the lower number.
   - Ordered pci: B♭ to C (t to 0) = 2
                   C to B♭ (0 to t) = t
   - Unordered pci (also called interval class): B♭ to C or C to B♭ = 2
   - Pcis 2 and t are complements; they sum to 12.

The Inversion of Pitch Sets and Pitch-Class Sets

Passages of music saturated with repetitions of the same type of sets create a different effect from passages that feature diverse or contrasting sets. One task in music analysis is to point out similarities and differences between sets and relate these to observations about form, motives, text, or other musical features. What features make sets "the same"? Some early theories of nontonal music considered any two sets that shared the same ic vector to be equivalent. For example, the triads {C E G}, {A C♯ E}, and {G B♭ D} would be equivalent because their pcs span the same three interval classes: one ic 3, one ic 4, and one ic 5 (pci 7 becomes 5), for an ic vector of [001110]. As you will see, two sets sharing the same ic vector are usually related by transposition (as are {C E G} and {A C♯ E}) or by inversion (as are {C E G} and {C E♭ G}), and it is this relationship that defines set equivalence.

> **KEY CONCEPT** Equivalent sets are related by either transposition or inversion.

The Inversion of Pitch Sets

Listen to the opening of "Bulgarian Rhythm" (Example 36.5), focusing on the circled pentachords A and B to see the inversion of pitch and pitch-class intervals in a musical context.

EXAMPLE 36.5: Bartók, "Bulgarian Rhythm," mm. 1-2 (pentachords A and B)

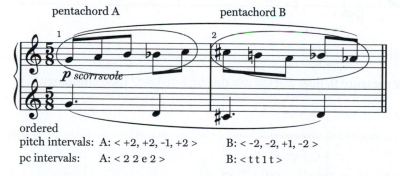

ordered
pitch intervals: A: < +2, +2, -1, +2 >   B: < -2, -2, +1, -2 >
pc intervals: A: < 2 2 e 2 >   B: < t t 1 t >

Pentachords A and B are pitch inversions of each other because they share the same ordered sequence of pitch intervals, but with the directions (+ and -) reversed.

> **KEY CONCEPT** To write or play the inversion of an ordered pitch set:
>
> 1. Analyze its ordered pitch intervals.
>
> 2. Choose a beginning pitch for your inverted set.
>
> 3. Write or play the remaining pitches from the ordered pitch-interval sequence, but with the direction of each sign reversed.

As mentioned above, major and minor triads—{C E G} and {C E♭ G}—are related by inversion. To see why, look at the ordered pitch intervals in Example 36.6: if you reverse the direction of the major triad's pitch intervals, a minor triad results.

EXAMPLE 36.6: Triads inverted around G by pitch intervals

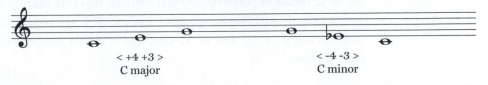

< +4 +3 >   < -4 -3 >
C major   C minor

Try it #4

Sing or play the motive below, and analyze the ordered pitch intervals. Then write or play an inverted set for this motive, beginning on E4, in the empty measure.

Bartók, "Bulgarian Rhythm," m. 9

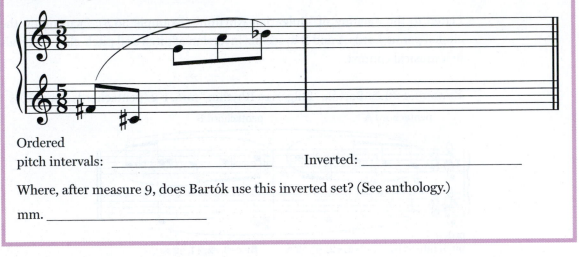

Ordered
pitch intervals: _____   Inverted: _____

Where, after measure 9, does Bartók use this inverted set? (See anthology.)

mm. _____

The Inversion of Pitch-Class Sets

Look back at Example 36.5 to see the pc interval successions for pentachords A and B (written below the pitch-interval analysis). The diagram below shows the two pentachords written in integer notation and their pc intervals. Each ordered pci is determined by subtracting (b - a) mod12.

	pentachord A	pentachord B
pcs:	< 7 9 e t 0 >	< 1 e 9 t 8 >
pcis:	< 2 2 e 2 >	< t t 1 t >

Compare the two patterns of pc intervals to see how inversions work in a pitch-class context: each pc interval in pentachord A is replaced by its inverse in B: pci e becomes 1, and pci 2 becomes t. (Remember: An ordered pci and its inverse always sum to 12.)

You can write the inversion of a given pcset, however, without first calculating the pcis.

KEY CONCEPT To find the inversion of a pcset, replace each pc with its inverse. Inverses appear opposite each other on the clock face (except for 0 and 6, which are their own inverses). To find the transposed inversion of a pcset, always *invert* first, then transpose.

FIGURE 36.5: Clock-face diagram (pcset inversion)

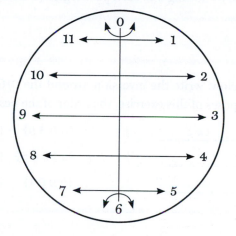

The clock above represents inversion "around the 0/6 axis" because the axis of inversion—the vertical line down the middle—is from 0 to 6. (Other axes are possible.) To see, for example, how Bartók's pentachord A (7 9 e t 0) is transformed into pentachord B, first circle the pcs of A, then draw an arrow from each pc to its opposite number on the clock, and draw a box around that number (Figure 36.6; 0 stays 0). That yields unordered pcset {5 3 2 1 0}. In order to arrive at pentachord B, we would then transpose this set by eight semitones (by spinning a transparency eight clicks clockwise or four counterclockwise) to get {8 9 t e 1}.

FIGURE 36.6: Pcset inversion and transposition

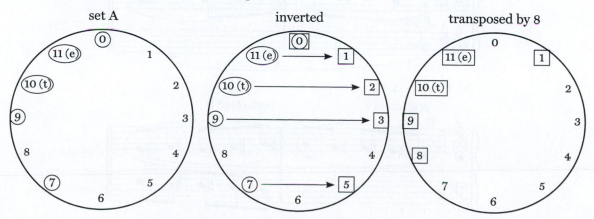

Another Way

If you prefer arithmetic to clocks:

1. Place pentachord A in normal order: {7 9 t e 0}.

2. Invert by replacing each pc with its inverse. You can invert and place pcs in ascending order in a single step, by using the "rainbow method":

$$7\ 9\ t\ e\ 0 \qquad 0\ 1\ 2\ 3\ 5$$

3. Now transpose by adding 8 to each pc integer: {0 1 2 3 5} becomes {8 9 t e 1}.

Try it #5

For each pcset below, write the inversion around the 0/6 axis by substituting for each pc its inverse. (For purposes of this exercise, the order of the pcs is not important.)

{e 1 4}   { ____1 e 8____ }   {3 6 8 9}   { _____ }

{9 t 2 3} { _____ }   {e 1 2 3 5} { _____ }

{e 2 5}   { _____ }   {6 9 0 1}   { _____ }

Identifying Transposition and Inversion

Additional pentachords from "Bulgarian Rhythm" are shown in Example 36.7; all are transpositions and/or inversions of each other.

EXAMPLE 36.7: Bartók, "Bulgarian Rhythm"

(a) Mm. 1-2

pentachord A   pentachord B

(b) Mm. 17-18

pentachord C   pentachord D

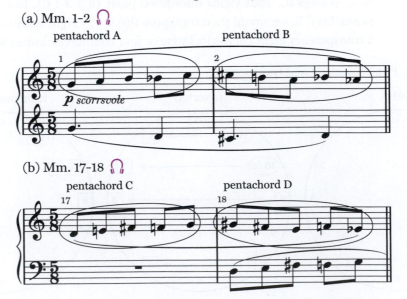

Pentachords A and C are related by transposition. To determine the interval of transposition:

- place the pentachords in normal order and line them up, one beneath the other;
- subtract the integers of one set from the other (mod12).

If you subtract pentachord C from A, you will get a consistent number, 5: A is thus T_5 of C. If you look back at Example 36.7, you will see that A is written a P4 (T_5) above C.

$$
\begin{array}{l}
A \ \{7 \ \ 9 \ \ t \ \ e \ \ 0\} \\
-C \ \{2 \ \ 4 \ \ 5 \ \ 6 \ \ 7\} \\
\hline
\phantom{-C \{}5 \ \ 5 \ \ 5 \ \ 5 \ \ 5 \ \rightarrow \ A = T_5 C
\end{array}
$$

Recall that we are working with ordered pc intervals; therefore the order in which you subtract the pcsets matters. A minus C reveals a T_5 relationship, but C minus A yields the complement, T_7:

$$
\begin{array}{l}
C \ \{2 \ \ 4 \ \ 5 \ \ 6 \ \ 7\} \\
-A \ \{7 \ \ 9 \ \ t \ \ e \ \ 0\} \\
\hline
\phantom{-A \{}7 \ \ 7 \ \ 7 \ \ 7 \ \ 7 \ \rightarrow \ C = T_7 A
\end{array}
$$

KEY CONCEPT To calculate the distance between transpositionally related sets, you subtract pcs. To calculate the relationship between inversionally related sets, you add pcs.

Now look at pentachords C and D of Example 36.7, which are inversionally related (as are A and B). To determine the relationship between these pcsets:

- list the pcs in normal order: C is {2 4 5 6 7}, and D is {3 4 5 6 8};
- reverse the order of one of them—D, for example, becomes {8 6 5 4 3}; and
- add the pcs of each set (mod12).

Each pair of pcs will sum to the same number.

$$
\begin{array}{l}
C \ \{2 \ \ 4 \ \ 5 \ \ 6 \ \ 7\} \\
+D \ \{8 \ \ 6 \ \ 5 \ \ 4 \ \ 3\} \\
\hline
\phantom{+D \{}t \ \ t \ \ t \ \ t \ \ t \ \rightarrow \ C = T_t I \ D \text{ and } D = T_t I \ C
\end{array}
$$

We call 10 the **index number** between the two inversionally related sets, and represent their relationship as above: $C = T_t I \ D$, and also $D = T_t I \ C$ (where I stands for "inversion" and the subscript t stands for the index number 10). For inversion, the order in which you list the sets doesn't matter, because the addition works out the same either way.

Try it #6

Look back at Example 36.7, and write the pcs for pentachords B and C in ascending order. Use the space provided to calculate their inversional relationships. (Hint: Reverse the order of one set and add.)

(a) Pentachord B: _____

(b) Pentachord C: _____

(c) What is the index number? _____

(d) Fill in the blank: C = T _____ I B.

Another Way

Here is a quick way to produce T_nI-related sets. Given pentachord A {7 9 t e 0}, find T_4I. Because two T_nI-related sets will sum to a consistent index number—in this case, 4—you can simply subtract each pc from 4:

$$
\begin{array}{r}
4\ \ 4\ \ 4\ \ 4\ \ 4 \\
-\ 7\ \ 9\ \ t\ \ e\ \ 0 \\
\hline
9\ \ 7\ \ 6\ \ 5\ \ 4
\end{array}
\quad \text{(ascending order } \{4\ 5\ 6\ 7\ 9\})
$$

To check your work, add the pcs of the original set to the new T_4I version. They will consistently sum to 4.

$$
\begin{array}{rl}
\text{pentachord A:} & 7\ \ 9\ \ t\ \ e\ \ 0 \\
T_4I \text{ of A:} & +\ 9\ \ 7\ \ 6\ \ 5\ \ 4 \\
\hline
& 4\ \ 4\ \ 4\ \ 4\ \ 4
\end{array}
$$

In the Berg song, there is a particularly interesting example of pcset inversion in the vocal line of measures 3-5 (Example 36.8). Beginning on the second quarter note of "Wald," the singer's melody zigzags up and down, dividing into a chromatic compound melody where the upper line < F♯ G A♭ A > ascends and the lower line < E♯ E♮ E♭ D > descends. This type of melody is called a **wedge**.

EXAMPLE 36.8: Berg, "Sahst du nach dem Gewitterregen," mm. 3-4 (voice) 🎧

The pcsets of the upper and lower lines of the compound melody—{6 7 8 9} and {2 3 4 5} —are related by both transposition and inversion. If considered transpositionally, {6 7 8 9} is T_4 of {2 3 4 5}. But Berg has voiced the pcsets to show their inversional relationship, as pitches inverted around F/F#. The pcs of these sets sum to an index number of 11 (e):

$$\begin{array}{r} \{6 \ \ 7 \ \ 8 \ \ 9\} \\ + \{5 \ \ 4 \ \ 3 \ \ 2\} \\ \hline e \ \ e \ \ e \ \ e \end{array} \rightarrow \quad \text{the pcsets are } T_eI \text{ related.}$$

This relationship, and all inversional pcset relationships, can be shown on the clock face by moving the axis of inversion from 0/6 (Figure 36.7). For the Berg sets, the axis will extend between pcs e/0 and 6/5 (the F/F# of Berg's melody). This visual aid has the advantage of lining up, on either side of the axis, the pcs that sum to eleven (e and 0, t and 1, 9 and 2, and so on).

FIGURE 36.7: Clock-face diagram showing axis of inversion for T_eI

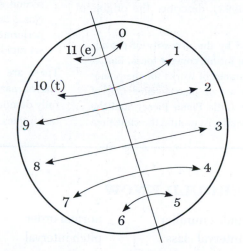

In the two works we have examined in this chapter, it is fairly easy to see and hear that some of their sets are related by transposition or inversion because of the way they are set musically: the composers used specific pitches, contours, and rhythms to make the relationships stand out. As we will see in Chapter 37, however, composers may place pcs from a pcset into any octave, without disturbing the transpositional or inversional relationship between pcsets; this means that the musical contour and effect may differ greatly between equivalent sets. One quality we *can* hear in transpositionally or inversionally related pcsets is their interval classes (as summarized in the ic vector)—a feature analogous to our recognition of chord quality in tonal music.

In analysis, after selecting pcsets for segmentation, we temporarily ignore all musical features except the pcs in order to find their most simplified version. This allows us to explore aspects of similarity or difference that may be obscured by the composer's musical choices (contour, register, timbre, rhythm, and so on). Remember that pcset analysis begins and ends with those compositional features—at the beginning to determine segmentation, and at the end to explore how the pcsets interact with other features. As with other musical structures identified in previous chapters, you may or may not wish to bring out pcset relationships consciously when playing a piece; but knowing about them helps you understand why and how the music sounds the way it does, and what factors make the piece cohesive.

Did You Know?

Bartók's *Mikrokosmos* is a six-volume collection of piano pieces of progressive difficulty, ranging from simple compositions for children to masterful mature compositions. Biographer Halsey Stevens, in *The Life and Music of Béla Bartók* (Oxford University Press, 1993), describes the origins of this massive work:

> In 1926, spurred by the necessity of providing new material for his concert tours, Bartók wrote a large number of works for the piano: the Sonata, the set of pieces called Out of Doors, the Nine Little Piano Pieces, and the (first) Piano Concerto. At around the same time

he began work on a collection of piano pieces, eventually called *Mikrokosmos*, designed to introduce young pianists to the technique and musical problems of contemporary writing. The first two volumes are dedicated to Bartók's second son, Péter; the later ones—especially Nos. 5 and 6—make severe demands upon the performer, and Péter Bartók has said that the set rapidly outgrew his performing abilities.

These are wonderful study pieces for the music analyst, as well as for the pianist, since they beautifully demonstrate many of Bartók's compositional techniques.

TERMS YOU SHOULD KNOW

index number
interval class
interval-class vector
inversion
mod12

normal order
pitch interval
- ordered
- unordered

pitch-class interval (pci)
- ordered
- unordered
segmentation
wedge

QUESTIONS FOR REVIEW

1. Why do we place sets in normal order? What is the process for doing so?
2. What musical factors do you focus on when choosing pitch or pitch-class sets for analysis?
3. What are the steps to construct ic vectors, and how can they be helpful in analysis?
4. What are the steps to transpose pcsets? pitch sets?
5. What are the steps to invert pcsets? pitch sets?

6. Describe how a clock face can be helpful for calculating (a) normal order, (b) transposition, and (c) inversion.

7. What are the steps to find the transpositional relationship between two pcsets? the inversional relationship?

Know It? Show It!

Focus by working through the tutorials.

Learn with InQuizitive.

Apply what you've learned to complete the workbook assignments.

37

Sets and Set Classes

Outline

Set classes and their prime forms
- Finding prime form
- Set-class labels

Characteristic trichords of familiar scales and modes
- Whole tone
- Pentatonic
- Hexatonic
- Octatonic
- Chromatic

Reading set-class tables
- Complementary sets
- Using ic vectors

Set classes and formal design

Overview

In this chapter, we group sets into set classes, and learn how to recognize some of the most distinctive set classes in twentieth-century compositions.

Repertoire

Béla Bartók

From *Mikrokosmos*: "Bulgarian Rhythm" (No. 115) and "Whole-Tone Scale" (No. 137)

Sonata for Two Pianos and Percussion

Claude Debussy, "La cathédral engloutie" ("The Sunken Cathedral"), from *Préludes*

Olivier Messiaen, "Liturgie de crystal" ("Liturgy of Crystal"), from *Quartet for the End of Time*

Anton Webern

Concerto, Op. 24

String Quartet, Op. 5, mvts. 3 and 4

Set Classes and Their Prime Forms

In Chapter 36, we learned to identify pcsets by writing their elements in normal order and how to compare sets when they were related by transposition or inversion. Repeating pcsets that share the same interval content or that are related by T_n or T_nI can lend coherence to nontonal works. And pcsets that differ in these respects provide contrast, just as motion to a new harmony or key provides contrast in tonal music.

If you prepared a thorough analysis of a piece like Bartók's "Bulgarian Rhythm," you would identify many different sets. To keep this number to a manageable size, however, you could consider transpositionally and inversionally related sets to be equivalent, serving a similar musical function. Sets grouped this way—into equivalence classes—are called set classes.

KEY CONCEPT A set class (SC) contains all possible distinct transpositions of a pcset, as well as all distinct transpositions of its inversion. Pcsets in the same set class share the same ic vector; their shared intervallic structure gives them a similar sound.

Listen once again to the beginning of Bartók's "Bulgarian Rhythm," while following Example 37.1. We know from Chapter 36 that pentachords A and B are related by inversion, which means they belong to the same set class.

EXAMPLE 37.1: Bartók, "Bulgarian Rhythm," mm. 1-4

Most pcsets belong to a set class with twenty-four members: the pcset's twelve transpositions and its inversion's twelve transpositions. Following are the members of the set class to which pentachord B—{8 9 t e 1} and its inversion {e 1 2 3 4}—belong.

transpositions: T_0 {0 1 2 3 5}, T_1 {1 2 3 4 6}, T_2 {2 3 4 5 7}, T_3 {3 4 5 6 8},
      T_4 {4 5 6 7 9}, T_5 {5 6 7 8 t}, T_6 {6 7 8 9 e}, T_7 {7 8 9 t 0}, T_8 {8 9 t e 1},
      T_9 {9 t e 0 2}, T_t {t e 0 1 3}, T_e {e 0 1 2 4}

transpositions of its inversion: T_0I {0 2 3 4 5}, T_1I {1 3 4 5 6}, T_2I {2 4 5 6 7}, T_3I {3 5 6 7 8}, T_4I {4 6 7 8 9}, T_5I {5 7 8 9 t}, T_6I {6 8 9 t e}, T_7I {7 9 t e 0}, T_8I {8 t e 0 1}, T_9I {9 e 0 1 2}, T_tI {t 0 1 2 3}, T_eI {e 1 2 3 4}

That this characteristic sound can be expressed in twenty-four different ways is a powerful idea. When we analyze music, it is helpful to collapse all twenty-four into a single label, the prime form. That way we can compare and contrast pcsets in a succinct way.

KEY CONCEPT   A prime form is a "token" that represents all the transpositions and inversions of a pcset that belong to a single set class.

- Prime forms always begin with a zero and are written with ascending pcs between square brackets [ ].

- Adjacent pcs of the prime form usually have smaller intervals to the left and larger ones to the right—for example, [0 1 2 5 6 9].

In music analysis, finding the prime form of pcsets allows us to compare two pcsets that may look different in the score (different contour, timbre, pitch classes, rhythm) and discover that they are actually members of the same class.

Finding Prime Form

There are a number of ways to arrive at the prime form of a pcset.

On a Clock Face   The now-familiar clock face can help you find prime form for pentachord A of Example 37.1.

1. Circle the pc numbers on a clockface (Figure 37.1), as we did in Chapter 36.

2. Choose the most compact arrangement, the normal order: {7 9 t e 0}.

3. If you find a "tie" between two possible normal orders (with equally small outer spans), keep both of them and follow the remaining steps.

4. Check the adjacent pcis to see whether the smaller intervals lie to the left; if not, invert. Draw an arrow from each pc to its inverse, and draw a box around the inverse {0 1 2 3 5}. (0 is its own inverse.)

5. Write in ascending order, then transpose to 0, if needed.

6. If you had a tie in step 3, choose the one with smallest intervals to the left. The prime form is [0 1 2 3 5].

FIGURE 37.1: Clock-face diagram (prime form)

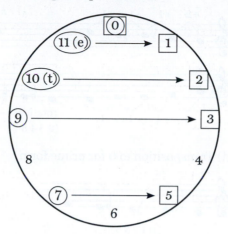

From Pitches on the Keyboard or Staff Another way to visualize this process is on a staff or an instrument.

1. Play or write the pitches of pentachord A from low to high (Example 37.2a).

2. Play each rotation (part b), then choose the normal order (smallest span).

3. Examine the adjacent intervals of the normal order (part c); this one has the largest interval near the bottom (whole step) and smaller intervals near the top (half steps); you need to invert it.

4. Choose any note on which to start your inversion (here, G4). Take the original pitch-interval sequence (+2 +1 +1 +1) and play it reversing the direction of each interval, (-2 -1 -1 -1).

5. Now find the normal order of the inverted set and transpose to C, or 0 (part c).

EXAMPLE 37.2: Bartók, "Bulgarian Rhythm," m. 1

(a) Ascending order 🎧

(b) Rotations

(c) Normal order with inversion around G4

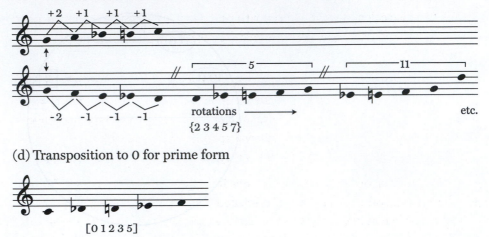

(d) Transposition to 0 for prime form

[0 1 2 3 5]

Let's look briefly at a pcset where there are two possible normal orders: {2 6 7 t}. Figure 37.2 shows the pcs circled on a clock face, where a gap of pci 4 appears in two places: between 2 and 6, and between t and 2. Retain both possible normal orders and complete the steps described above. Then transpose to 0 and choose the best prime form (smaller intervals to the left). The prime form is [0 1 4 8].

FIGURE 37.2: Clock-face diagram with two "tied" normal orders

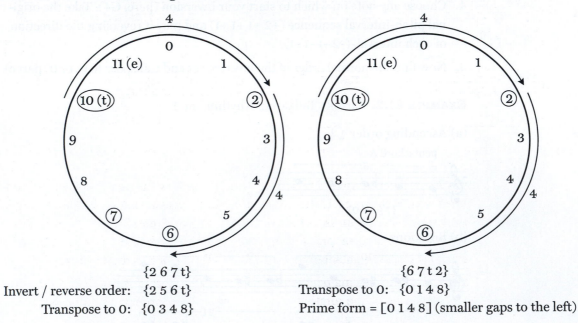

{2 6 7 t}	{6 7 t 2}
Invert / reverse order: {2 5 6 t}	Transpose to 0: {0 1 4 8}
Transpose to 0: {0 3 4 8}	Prime form = [0 1 4 8] (smaller gaps to the left)

Another Way

You can also calculate prime form with pcs in integer notation. Place the pc integers in ascending order, and calculate the pc interval between the first and last elements with subtraction mod12.

$\{9\ t\ e\ 0\ 7\}$ → $\{9\ t\ e\ 0\ 7\}$ interval spanned = t $(7 - 9) = (19 - 9) = t$
$\phantom{\{9\ t\ e\ 0\ 7\}}\quad\ \ \ \{t\ e\ 0\ 7\ 9\}$ interval spanned = e $(9 - t) = (21 - t) = e$
$\phantom{\{9\ t\ e\ 0\ 7\}}\quad\ \ \ \{e\ 0\ 7\ 9\ t\}$ interval spanned = e $(t - e) = (22 - e) = e$
$\phantom{\{9\ t\ e\ 0\ 7\}}\quad\ \ \ \{0\ 7\ 9\ t\ e\}$ interval spanned = e $(e - 0) = e$
$\phantom{\{9\ t\ e\ 0\ 7\}}\quad\ \ \ \{7\ 9\ t\ e\ 0\}$ interval spanned = 5 $(0 - 7) = (12 - 7) = 5$

The normal order is $\{7\ 9\ t\ e\ 0\}$, since it spans the smallest "outside" interval: pci 5. Because a larger interval is on the left, the set needs to be inverted. Replace each pc with its inverse: $\{7\ 9\ t\ e\ 0\}$ becomes $\{5\ 3\ 2\ 1\ 0\}$. You can use the rainbow method to reverse the order of the pcs at the same time, and you have the prime form: [0 1 2 3 5].

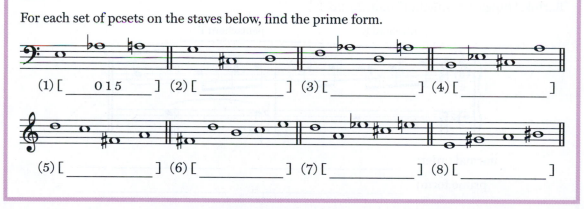

Try it #1

For each set of pcsets on the staves below, find the prime form.

(1) [0 1 5   ]   (2) [   ]   (3) [   ]   (4) [   ]

(5) [   ]   (6) [   ]   (7) [   ]   (8) [   ]

We return now to "Bulgarian Rhythm" to see how the pentachords are developed later in the piece. Listen to the **A′** section, measures 17 to the end. Example 37.3 shows the beginning of **A′** with pentachords C and D circled. Use integer notation to find their prime forms and determine whether they belong to the same set class as pentachords A and B, [0 1 2 3 5], or to a different one.

- Begin by placing pentachord C in normal order: $\{2\ 4\ 5\ 6\ 7\}$. If you imagine each of the rotations, you will see that this ordering spans the smallest outside interval.

- Since the larger interval is to the left and semitones are to the right, invert and reverse order: $\{5\ 6\ 7\ 8\ t\}$.

- Transpose to the 0 level to find the prime form: [0 1 2 3 5]. Pentachord C has the same prime form as A and B; the three pentachords are equivalent, and are members of the same set class.

Further, we know from Chapter 36 that pentachords C and D are inversionally related (C = T_tI D). Pentachord D thus belongs to the same set class as A, B, and C, helping to give Bartók's piece its consistent sound.

EXAMPLE 37.3: Bartók, "Bulgarian Rhythm," mm. 17-18 🎧

Try it #2

Find the normal order and prime form for the two pentachords in the example below. One of them is not equivalent to pentachords A-D. Which one?   pentachord _____

Bartók, "Bulgarian Rhythm," mm. 25-26 🎧

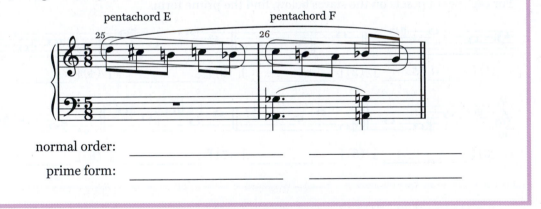

normal order: _____   _____

prime form: _____   _____

Finally, look at pentachord G of Example 37.4, where we need to apply the tie-breaker instructions to find the prime form.

- The pcs in ascending order are {1 4 6 9 t}.
- Looking for the rotation with the smallest span reveals a three-way tie: {9 t 1 4 6}, {1 4 6 9 t}, and {4 6 9 t 1}; all span pci 9. Retain all three.
- Pcset {9 t 1 4 6} transposed to 0 produces {0 1 4 7 9}.
- The other two choices need to be inverted: {1 4 6 9 t} becomes {2 3 6 8 e}, and {4 6 9 t 1} becomes {e 2 3 6 8}.
- Transpose each to 0: {0 1 4 6 9} and {0 3 4 7 9}.

- Of these three, {0 1 4 6 9} is the best choice as prime form because it has the smallest pci intervals to the left.

Example 37.4: Bartók, "Bulgarian Rhythm," m. 9

pentachord G

SUMMARY

To find a pcset's prime form:

1. Reorder the pcs so that they ascend numerically, and consider each rotation.

2. Look at the interval from first to last pc in each rotation, and choose the rotation with the smallest possible span. If you use a clock face, look for the shortest clockwise distance between first and last pc. This order is the normal order, written in curly braces.

3. If there are two possible normal orders, retain both for steps 4 and 5.

4. If the normal order has larger intervals toward the left and smaller toward the right, invert the set (replace each pc with its inverse) and look for the normal order of this inverted form (repeat steps 1 and 2).

5. When the normal order is found, transpose so that the first pc is 0. That is prime form, written between square brackets.

Set-Class Labels

Each set class can be identified with a label, just as "augmented triad," "Mm7," and "fully diminished seventh" identify three- and four-note sets in tonal music. We will use labels derived from music theorist Allen Forte's complete set-class list. Forte grouped together pcsets with the same number of elements (or cardinality) and then ordered them by ic vector. To each set class, he gave a hyphenated number (for example, 5-35). The number before the hyphen represents the cardinality of the pcset, and the number after represents the pcset's position on the list; for example, 5-35 is a pcset of five elements that appears thirty-fifth on the list. These numbers are sometimes called "Forte numbers." Forte's complete table, helpful for set-class analysis, is given in Appendix 6. When analyzing a nontonal work, first identify musical segments of interest, find the prime form, and then look up the set-class label. The labels will allow you to discuss sets without having to write out and compare all the pcs each time.

Characteristic Trichords of Familiar Scales and Modes

You will find it easier to analyze nontonal music as well as understand it aurally if you learn to recognize the trichord types. One effective way to do this is to associate trichords with the collections studied in Chapter 34: whole-tone, diatonic, pentatonic, hexatonic, octatonic, and chromatic. If you look at the set-class table in Appendix 6, you will see that there are only twelve three-element (trichord) set classes; try to learn the sound and scale membership for all of them. Many of these you already know—for example, triad types, [0 3 6], [0 4 7], and [0 4 8]. Spend some time at the piano playing through the excerpts below; identify as many trichords as you can. Sing them back after playing them, and find and play their inversions as well. When you can recognize the sound of the twelve trichord types, you will have a strong foundation upon which to build your appreciation of and skill in performing nontonal repertoire.

Whole Tone

Listen to Example 37.5, from Bartók's "Whole-Tone Scales." The circled sets belong to the set classes [0 2 4], [0 2 6], and [0 4 8]. These are the only trichords closely associated with the whole-tone collection. You can identify them by their whole steps, major thirds, or tritones, as their ic vectors show.

EXAMPLE 37.5: Bartók, "Whole-Tone Scales," mm. 1-3 🎧

prime form:	[0 2 6]	[0 4 8]	[0 2 4] (twice)
Forte name:	3-8	3-12	3-6
ic vector:	[010101]	[000300]	[020100]

Pentatonic

The most characteristic trichords of the pentatonic collection are [0 2 5] and [0 2 7], but pentatonic compositions also share [0 2 4] with the whole-tone and diatonic collections, and [0 3 7] with the diatonic collection. Example 37.6, from a Debussy piano prelude, includes all of these. Each pc in Debussy's melody is harmonized by a major or minor triad. The prime form for each triad in measure 73 is [0 3 7]; major and minor triads are equivalent by inversion, as we saw in Chapter 36.

EXAMPLE 37.6: Debussy, "La cathédral engloutie," mm. 72-75

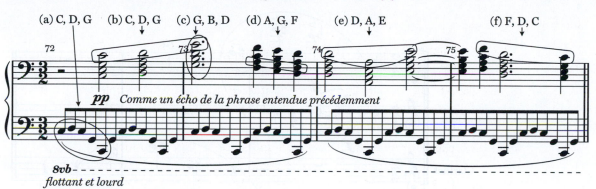

Try it #3

Provide the prime form for each trichord circled in Example 37.6. Then find the Forte number and ic vector in Appendix 6.

	Prime form	Forte number	ic vector
(a)	[0 2 7]	3-9	[010020]
(b)	_____	_____	_____
(c)	_____	_____	_____
(d)	_____	_____	_____
(e)	_____	_____	_____
(f)	_____	_____	_____

Hexatonic

The hexatonic collection—6-20 [0 1 4 5 8 9]—has as its trichordal subsets 3-3 [0 1 4], 3-4 [0 1 5], and 3-12 [0 4 8], the latter shared with the whole-tone scale. At the opening of Webern's Concerto (Example 37.7), there are two statements of the hexatonic collection: the first in the oboe and flute, and the second in the trumpet and clarinet. Every melodic trichord in this opening is a statement of 3-3 [0 1 4].

EXAMPLE 37.7: Webern, Concerto, Op. 24, mm. 1–3

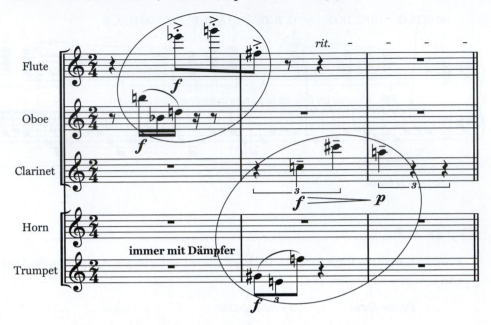

Try it #4

For each pair of trichords listed, provide the normal order, then give the T_n or T_nI relation between the two.

(a)   Oboe: { _____ }   Flute: { _____ } T_n or T_nI: _____

(b)   Trumpet: { _____ }   Clarinet: { _____ } T_n or T_nI: _____

Octatonic

To discover the characteristic trichords of the octatonic collection, look first at one form of the collection, {0 1 3 4 6 7 9 t }. The diminished triad [0 3 6] can be built on any element: {0 3 6}, {1 4 7}, {3 6 9}, and so on. Further, pcs 0, 3, 6, or 9 can support either a major or minor triad: {0 3 7} or {0 4 7}, {3 6 t} or {3 7 t}, {6 9 1} or {6 t 1}, and so on. These pcs can also support the "split-third" chord [0 3 4 7].

Just as characteristic of the octatonic collection are the subsets that begin with a semitone: [0 1 3], [0 1 4], and [0 1 6]. Example 37.8 shows two primary themes of Bartók's *Sonata for Two Pianos and Percussion*. The circled pitches (labeled x, y, and z) are examples of these trichords.

EXAMPLE 37.8: Bartók, *Sonata for Two Pianos and Percussion*

(a) Mm. 1-2 (piano 1)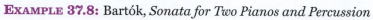

prime form: x: [0 1 4]   y: [0 1 6]   z: [0 1 4]
Forte number: 3-3   3-5   3-3

(b) Mm. 33-34 (piano 1)

Chromatic

The only trichord not yet discussed is the chromatic trichord [0 1 2]. We complete our study of trichords by looking at a passage from Webern's String Quartet (Example 37.9). This passage includes almost the entire chromatic collection and is saturated with SCs [0 1 2], [0 1 4], and [0 1 5].

EXAMPLE 37.9: Webern, String Quartet, mvt. 3, mm. 8-10

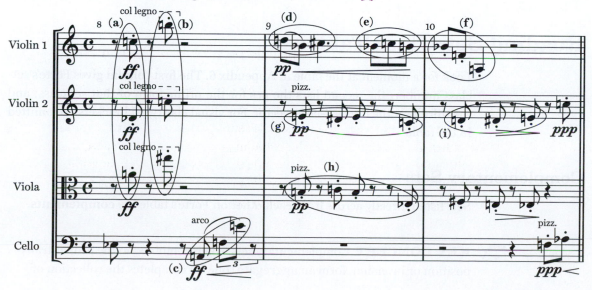

Try it #5

Provide the prime form and Forte number for each circled trichord in Example 37.9.

	Prime form	Forte number		Prime form	Forte number
(a)	[0 1 4]	3-3	(f)		
(b)			(g)		
(c)			(h)		
(d)			(i)		
(e)					

SUMMARY

There are only twelve distinct trichords. Learn them as characteristic subsets of familiar collections.

- Subsets of the whole-tone collection: [0 2 4], [0 2 6], [0 4 8].
- Subsets of the pentatonic and diatonic collections: [0 2 4], [0 2 5], [0 2 7], [0 3 7].
- Subsets of the hexatonic collection: [0 1 4], [0 1 5], [0 4 8].
- Subsets of the octatonic and diatonic collections: [0 3 6], [0 3 7].
- Subsets of the octatonic and chromatic collections: [0 1 3], [0 1 4], [0 1 6].
- Subsets of the chromatic collection: [0 1 2] and all other trichords.

Reading Set-Class Tables

Look for a moment at the table in Appendix 6. The first column gives Forte's set-class number; the second lists the pcs for the prime form of that set class; and the third lists the interval-class vector. For visual clarity, all brackets are omitted in the table.

Complementary Sets

Sets listed directly across from each other on Forte's table are **complements**.

 KEY CONCEPT Complementary sets, when combined in the proper transposition or inversion, form an **aggregate** (one set completes the collection of all twelve tones begun by the other). Complementary sets have parallel set-class numbers: 3-12 and 9-12 are complements, as are 4-28 and 8-28, 5-37 and 7-37, and so on.

As an example of complementation, consider SC 4-28 [0 3 6 9] and SC 8-28 [0 1 3 4 6 7 9 t]. These should be familiar to you as the fully diminished seventh chord and the octatonic scale. In their prime forms, the sets don't necessarily show their complementary relation, since {0 3 6 9} is actually a literal subset of {0 1 3 4 6 7 9 t}. But if you transpose 4-28 by T_2 to {2 5 8 e}, it is the **literal complement** of {0 1 3 4 6 7 9 t}; that is, the pcs {2 5 8 e} are "literally" missing from the larger set, and these two sets when combined include all twelve tones. When two set classes—such as [0 3 6 9] and [0 1 3 4 6 7 9 t]—are related by complementation in some transformation, though not necessarily the one you see in the score, they are called **abstract complements**.

For an example of abstract complementation in a musical context, look at Example 37.10. The circled tetrachord contains pcs {1 2 7 8}, a member of SC 4-9 [0 1 6 7]. The content of the entire example, chord plus melody, is {0 1 2 3 6 7 8 9}, SC 8-9. Since the 4-9 chord is embedded within 8-9, it can't be a literal complement; it is an abstract complement. (The pcs missing from 8-9— {4 5 t e}—also belong to 4-9, the literal complement.)

EXAMPLE 37.10: Webern, String Quartet, mvt. 4, mm. 12–13

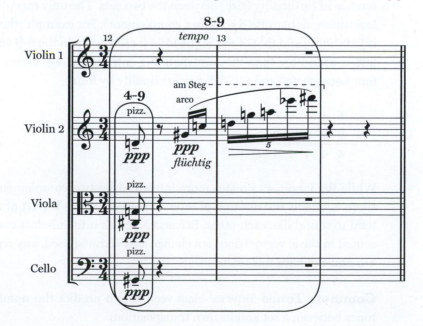

⌒ **KEY CONCEPT** When you analyze nontonal music, make note of repeated set classes, subset relationships, and complementary sets. These set relationships often correspond to a consistent sound within a section of music.

Using ic Vectors

Profile of ic Content To get a quick profile of the sound of a set class, examine its ic vector. For example, the ic vector of SC 6-37 [0 2 4 6 8 t], the whole-tone scale, is [060603]. This vector clearly gives the picture of a set class completely saturated with major seconds (6 in the ic 2 position), major thirds (6 in the ic 4 position), and tritones (3 in the ic 6 position). Similarly, the ic vector of SC 7-37 [0 1 3 5 6 8 t], the diatonic collection, is distinctive for the fact that no two entries in its vector are the same: [254371]. Another ic vector of interest is that for 4-15 [0 1 4 6] and 4-29 [0 1 3 7]: [111111]. These two tetrachords are often called the **"all-interval" tetrachords**, since their pcs span one each of every interval class. They also share a special relationship: although they have the same ic vector, they are not related by transposition or inversion; such set classes are said to be **Z-related** (Z comes from "zygotic," a biological term related to twins). Forte lists these as 4-Z15 and 4-Z29.

Complement Relation The ic vectors of complementary set classes are related in a particular way: the difference between entries is the same as the difference in cardinality (size) between the two sets. The only exception is in the last ic position, 6 (because 6 is its own complement). For example, the ic vector of 4-9 is [200022] and that of 8-9 is [644464]: each entry in the 8-9 vector, except the last, is four more than the corresponding entry in the 4-9 vector. (They differ by four because 4-9 and 8-9 differ in cardinality by four.)

$$
\begin{array}{r}
6\ 4\ 4\ 4\ 6\ 4 \\
-\ 2\ 0\ 0\ 0\ 2\ 2 \\
\hline
4\ 4\ 4\ 4\ 4\ (2)
\end{array}
$$

While the larger set creates more intervals, the two complementary set classes share a similar distribution of interval classes, which is part of the reason they tend to sound like each other. Because a pcset's interval-class content (as represented in the ic vector) does not change as it is transposed, any representatives of 4-9 and 8-9 have this relationship.

Common Tones Interval-class vectors can predict the number of common tones between a set and its own transposition.

KEY CONCEPT The number in each position of the ic vector tells how many common tones will be generated between a pcset and its transpositions. For example, 1 in the ic 3 position means that when the set is transposed by 3 (or 9), there will be one common tone. This property is sometimes called the **common-tone theorem**. The only exception is that the number in the ic 6 position must be doubled.

To see how the common-tone theorem works, consider the whole-tone scale and its ic vector. The whole-tone set class, 6-35, exists in only two distinct forms: {0 2 4 6 8 t} and {1 3 5 7 9 e}. In its ic vector, [060603], there are two entries of 6. These 6s indicate six common tones at these transposition levels. For example, when you transpose either of these pcsets by T_2 or T_t (both are ic 2), the transposition will yield six common tones with the original pcset. The same is true of T_4 and T_8, as well as T_6 (double the 3 in the ic vector to predict six common tones).

To sum up, transposing {0 2 4 6 8 t} by ic 2, 4, or 6 yields exactly the same pcset back again. On the other hand, transposing by ic 1, 3, or 5 produces no common tones; it produces the other whole-tone collection: {1 3 5 7 9 e}. The fact that 6-35 has only two distinct forms is also represented on the set-class listing in Appendix 6. While most set-classes contain twenty-four members (transpositions or inversions), those with fewer than that show the number in parentheses next to the Forte number. For example, the whole-tone hexachord is listed as 6-35(2)—the 2 indicates that there are only two forms of this set. SC 4-9 (Example 37.10) also has fewer than twenty-four and is listed as 4-9(6). Sets like this can be predicted by looking for common-tone properties in the ic vector. They also typically show symmetrical properties under inversion: the consecutive intervals of their prime forms will be identical whether you read them backward or forward. For example, the interval succession for 6-35 [0 2 4 6 8 t] is 2-2-2-2-2, and the succession for 4-9 [0 1 6 7] is 1-5-1.

Composer Olivier Messiaen was fascinated by sets like these; he called them "modes of limited transposition," and he identified seven. Three of them we already know: his mode 1 is SC 6-35 (the whole-tone collection); mode 2 is SC 8-28 (the octatonic collection); and mode 3 is SC 9-12 (the complement of the augmented triad). Example 37.11 gives a passage from his *Quartet for the End of Time*—featuring two modes of limited transposition in the piano part (and birdsong in the violin!).

EXAMPLE 37.11: Messiaen, "Liturgie de crystal," mm. 5-9

Try it #6

Identify the circled passages (a) and (b) as Messiaen's mode 1, 2, or 3.

	Mode	*Prime form*	*Forte number*
(a)	_____	_____	_____
(b)	_____	_____	_____

Set Classes and Formal Design

Composers may use different set classes to distinguish between contrasting sections; the first movement of Webern's String Quartet, an **A B A′** form, provides an example. The movement opens with two shimmering *am Steg* (on the bridge) tremolo chords played by the violins (set classes 4-8 [0 1 5 6] and 4-9 [0 1 6 7]), set off by a cello "foghorn" (Example 37.12). The two "shimmer" chords together combine to form SC 5-7 [0 1 2 6 7]. The pizzicato chord at the end of measure 2, with the same pitch content as the first shimmer chord, also belongs to SC 4-8. The second shimmer chord is arpeggiated into a melody in measure 3, which is passed in canonic fashion first to violin 2 (transposed down a perfect fifth), then to the cello (down three octaves) in measure 4. The cello then continues in measures 5-6 with a canonic imitation of the first violin. Listen to the passage to hear how counterpoint, texture, and repeated set classes 4-8 and 4-9 unite the section.

EXAMPLE 37.12: Webern, String Quartet, mvt. 4, mm. 1-6

The texture of the opening returns in the **A′** section, measures 11-13, as do many of the pcsets (see Example 37.13) and even a melody. The first violin's melody (mm. 4-5), pcs <0 5 1 0>, returns in 11-12, transposed up an octave in the viola and two octaves in violin 2. The circled texture in measures 11-12, pcs {0 1 2 5 6 7 8}, forms SC 7-7 [0 1 2 3 4 7 8 9], the abstract complement of the **A** section's combined shimmer chords SC 5-7. In measures 12-13, the pizzicato chord plus violin 2 melody articulate SC 8-9, the abstract complement of **A**'s first shimmer chord. The pizzicato chord in measure 12 also belongs to SC 4-9, as circled and labeled in the example.

These set classes—4-9 and 8-9, 5-7 and 7-7, and others of the opening and closing measures—are rich in tritones and semitones, creating a dissonant tapestry of sound typical of Webern's compositions. If you were to undertake a thorough analysis of these two passages, you would find that the pcsets marked in Examples 37.12 and 37.13 represent only a few of the sets shared by the **A** and **A′** sections.

EXAMPLE 37.13: Webern, String Quartet, mvt. 4, mm. 11-13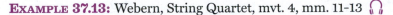

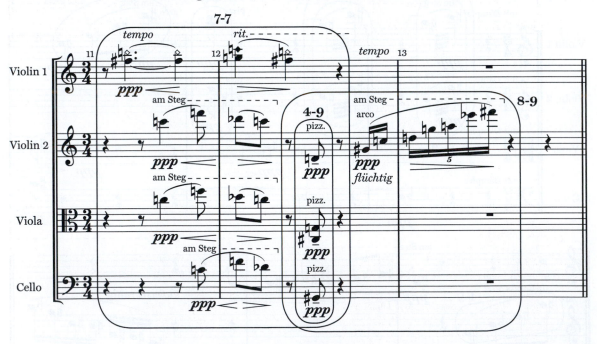

In contrast, the middle section, measures 7-10 (Example 37.14), features completely different sets. You should recognize the chord made by the viola pizzicato notes: D-B♭-G♭, an augmented triad (SC 3-12 [0 4 8]). When combined with the pc 4 in the cello, the resulting pcset {2 4 6 t} is the whole-tone subset 4-24 [0 2 4 8]. This whole-tone sound is disrupted by violin 2's pc e, which combines with the pizzicato notes to make {t e 2 6}: a statement of SC 4-19

[0 1 4 8], the augmented triad plus a semitone. The overall effect, represented by the collection of all the pcs in measures 7-10—{0 2 3 4 6 8 t e}, a member of SC 8-24—includes a strong whole-tone component, in contrast to the sets of the opening.

EXAMPLE 37.14: Webern, String Quartet, mvt. 4, mm. 7-14 🎧

In this movement, the formal divisions shown in the set analysis above are reinforced by the contrasting texture of the middle section, melody over ostinato accompaniment, and by the return of melodic and textural elements in measures 11-12. The movement is a ternary form: **A B A′**.

Did You Know?

You will find a complete list of Messiaen's modes of limited transposition in his book *The Technique of My Musical Language,* translated by John Satterfield (Paris: Leduc, 1956). Messiaen wrote the *Quartet for the End of Time* while incarcerated in a prisoner-of-war camp during World War II. He chose his text from the Revelation of St. John. Messiaen says this about the instrumental ensemble, all fellow prisoners:

> The unusual group for which I wrote this quartet—violin, clarinet, cello and piano—is due to the circumstances surrounding its conception.

I was a prisoner-of-war (1941), in Silesia, and among my fellow prisoners were a violinist . . . a clarinetist . . . and a cellist . . . myself being the pianist. . . . Why this choice of text? Perhaps because, in these hours of total privation, the basic forces which control life reasserted themselves. (From the liner notes to Angel/EMI recording S-37587.)

It is remarkable that an artwork of such power was composed in such dire circumstances—a testament to the human spirit.

TERMS YOU SHOULD KNOW

all-interval tetrachord	complement	mode of limited transposition
aggregate	• abstract complement	prime form
common-tone theorem	• literal complement	set class
	Forte number	Z-related sets

QUESTIONS FOR REVIEW

1. What properties do pcsets belonging to the same set class share?
2. What purpose does prime form serve in music analysis? Describe the process for finding prime form.
3. What is true of the ic vectors for sets related by transposition or inversion?
4. Which trichords are common subsets of the whole-tone scale? of the pentatonic scale? of the hexatonic scale? of the octatonic scale?
5. What characteristic of complementary sets is revealed by comparing their ic vectors?
6. In twentieth-century music for your own instrument, or a piece specified by your teacher, find a passage that seems to fall naturally into pc groupings of threes (in chords, motives, and so on). Analyze these trichords; find their prime forms. If applicable, show transposition or inversion levels of sets belonging to the same set class.

Know It? Show It!

Focus by working through the tutorials.

Learn with InQuizitive.

Apply what you've learned to complete the workbook assignments.

38

Ordered Segments and Serialism

Overview

This chapter explores how composers use ordered pitch and pitch-class segments in their works, and suggests strategies for listening to and composing twelve-tone and other serial music. We will see and hear how serial compositions differ in style by examining several contrasting works.

Repertoire

Alban Berg
    Lyric Suite, mvt. 1
    Violin Concerto
Pierre Boulez, *Structures Ia*
Luigi Dallapiccola, "Die Sonne kommt!" ("The Sun Comes Up!"), from *Goethe-lieder*
Arnold Schoenberg, *Klavierstück* (*Piano Piece*), Op. 33a
John Tavener, "The Lamb"
Anton Webern
    Concerto for Nine Instruments, Op. 24
    Symphonie, Op. 21, mvt. 2
    Variations for Piano, Op. 27, mvts. 2 and 3

Outline

Serial composition
- Ordered pitch segments
- Labeling pitch-class segments
- Operations on pitch classes

Twelve-tone rows
- Labeling rows
- Choosing row forms
- Hearing row relationships

Realizing twelve-tone rows
- The row matrix
- Hexachordal combinatoriality
- Finding combinatorial row pairs

Serialism and compositional style

Serialized durations

Serial Composition

Listen to the opening verse of John Tavener's 1982 anthem "The Lamb" without a score, and consider whether it is nontonal, centric, modal, or tonal. You might decide on more than one answer, as Tavener beautifully contrasts modal passages in E Aeolian (or natural minor) with centric ones that feature transformations of ordered pitch segments. Musicians have been experimenting with ordered pitch and rhythmic segments since medieval times; in the twentieth century, this method of composition reached its pinnacle.

> **KEY CONCEPT** Serial music is composed with ordered segments of musical elements—usually pitches or pitch classes, although elements such as durations, dynamics, and articulations may also be ordered.

Ordered Pitch Segments

Look at the first phrase of "The Lamb," given in Example 38.1. The tender opening melody sung by the sopranos sounds at first like G major. When the altos join them in measure 2, however, their melodic line creates dissonant intervals with the sopranos in unexpected ways. Sing each line, then examine the ordered sequence of pitch intervals in the soprano melody and compare it with that of the alto melody to discover their relationship.

EXAMPLE 38.1: Tavener, "The Lamb," mm. 1-2 🎧

The intervals in the soprano line appear in the same order in the alto—but with the direction of each interval reversed (+ becomes -). The two melodies are pitch **inversions** (**I**) of each other—that is, they share the same ordered sequence of pitch intervals, but with the direction reversed. Listen to the soprano and alto together in measure 2 to hear how the ordered intervals mirror each other.

KEY CONCEPT The distinction between sets and segments is an important one in nontonal and serial music analysis, indicated in analysis by the type of bracket.

For **sets** (*unordered* collections):

- Write the elements in curly braces: {0 5 6}. These are also used for sets in normal order.
- Write the prime form of sets and set classes in square brackets: [0 1 6].

For **segments** (*ordered* collections):

- Write the elements of segments in angle brackets: < 7 e 9 6 >.

The term **element** may refer to pitches, pitch classes, intervals, interval classes, durations, dynamics, or other musical features.

Following the introductory material of measures 1-2, we hear the second phrase in the soprano (Example 38.2). Because Tavener uses the melodic segment in measure 3 to generate much of the rest of the composition, we call it the **prime** (or **P**) form of the theme, and because its first note is pc 7, we call it P_7. If he transposed the melody to another pitch level elsewhere in the piece, it would still be a P segment, but would be named by its first pc (e.g., P_2 if it began on D). Likewise, any inversion that begins on G is I_7, and one that begins on D is I_2. Now compare the pitches of measures 3 and 4.

EXAMPLE 38.2: Tavener, "The Lamb," mm. 3-4

Soprano
Gave thee life, and bid thee feed   By the stream and o'er the mead;
pitch intervals: < +4   -2   -3   -3   +2   +3 >   < -3   -2   +3   +3   +2   -4 >

The pitches are identical in measure 4, except that they appear in reverse order. This relationship, called **retrograde** (**R**), is easiest to see and hear if you attend to the pcs (rather than the intervals). Because this retrograde form takes its identity from P_7 (played backward), we call it R_7. When you listen to a pitch segment in retrograde, you will hear its intervals reverse order and change direction (up or down) as well, as the labels below the staff show.

Now look at Example 38.3, the third phrase of this piece. Compare the pitches and intervals of P_7 (m. 5, soprano) with the other measures in both parts to determine their relationships.

EXAMPLE 38.3: Tavener, "The Lamb," mm. 5-6 🎧

Try it #1

Write the sequence of pitch intervals for each voice part in Example 38.3 in the blanks below (in angle brackets). For each measure and voice part indicated below, compare the interval pattern and pcs with the P form (m. 5, soprano). Then circle the appropriate word, if any, that applies to each pc sequence.

(a) m. 5 soprano   <+4 -2 -3 -3 +2 +3>   (prime)   inversion   retrograde

(b) m. 5 alto   prime   inversion   retrograde

(c) m. 6 soprano   prime   inversion   retrograde

(d) m. 6 alto   prime   inversion   retrograde

In Example 38.3, the sopranos sing P followed by R. The altos sing I, followed by a new transformation: the **retrograde inversion** (**RI**) of P. To spot the RI form, look for the I₇ in measure 5 (altos), and follow those pitches in reverse order in measure 6. All retrogrades of the inversion are named for the inversion's first pc; therefore this segment is RI_7.

SUMMARY

The first complete ordered segment in a piece is usually designated the prime (P), and later segments are compared with it, using one of four labels.

- P (prime): the pitch-interval sequence is identical to that of the prime segment.
- I (inversion): the direction of each pitch interval in the prime segment is inverted (Example 38.1).
- R (retrograde): the pcs of the prime segment are reversed in order, and the original pitch-interval sequence is inverted and reversed in order (Example 38.2).
- RI (retrograde inversion): the pcs of I are reversed in order, and the pitch-interval sequence of the prime segment is reversed in order (Example 38.3).

The transformations R, I, and RI are typically combined with transposition (T).

Labeling Pitch-Class Segments

As we have seen, labels for pitch-class (pc) segments have two parts: a letter (P, I, R, or RI) and a number. For P and I segments, the number is the first pc integer of that segment. For an R segment, the number comes from its associated P (that is, R_7 is the retrograde of P_7). RI forms likewise get their number from the associated I form.

SUMMARY

P_7: a segment P that begins with pc 7;

R_7: a retrograde of P_7 (this segment *ends* with pc 7);

I_7: an inversion of P that begins with pc 7;

RI_7: a retrograde of I_7 (this segment *ends* with pc 7).

Another Way

There are two main systems for labeling segments. The first system (P_7, R_7, and so on) you have just read about. But some analysts label the first appearance of the segment P_0, no matter which pc it begins with, to show that it is the first and "original" form, on which others are based. Each subsequent transposition is then calculated from this original. (That is, transposition up a whole step would be labeled P_2.) The two systems are akin to fixed *do* and movable *do*: the P_7 system is like fixed-*do*, the P_0 system like movable-*do*. Because the fixed-*do* system is most common today, we will follow it here, but you may encounter the other system in older books or articles on serial music.

Operations on Pitch Classes

To calculate the R, I, and RI forms for a given pc segment P, we will use many of the same operations on ordered segments that we did on sets in Chapters 36–37.

To transpose a segment, simply add the same integer to each element. For example, to transpose by a minor third, add 3 to each element. To invert a segment, take the pc complement of each pitch: 1 becomes e, 2 becomes t, 3 becomes 9, and so on (the complements add to 12). To write an R or RI form, run the P or I form backward.

Look again at Example 38.3, which demonstrates each of these operations.

- P_7 (m. 5, soprano) is $< 7 \, e \, 9 \, 6 \, 3 \, 5 \, 8 >$.
- The R_7 form (m. 6, soprano) is the same sequence in reverse order: $< 8 \, 5 \, 3 \, 6 \, 9 \, e \, 7 >$.

- To find the inversion of < 7 e 9 6 3 5 8 > (m. 5, alto), substitute for each pc its inverse: < 5 1 3 6 9 7 4 >. This yields I_5. To find I_7, transpose this segment by adding 2 to each element: < 7 3 5 8 e 9 6 >.
- To determine the RI_7 form, reverse the order of I_7: < 6 9 e 8 5 3 7 >.

KEY CONCEPT When working with row transformations, always invert *first* before transposing pcs or retrograding the order of pcs. Performing these operations in the opposite order will result in a different set of pcs.

Interestingly, Stravinsky was a self-taught serialist and did not follow all of the conventions for serial procedures established in the 1920s by Schoenberg and Webern. In the case of the combined retrograde and inversion operations, he retrograded first and then inverted. In analysis of his music, the correct label is actually IR: inversion of the retrograde.

SUMMARY

Following are the four classic operations for pitch classes in a prime segment (P).

Transposition (T): Add a constant integer (mod12) to each pc in P.

Retrograde (R): Reverse the pc order of P (so the pcs run backward).

Inversion (I): Replace each pc in P with its inverse (mod12), and then transpose as needed.

Retrograde inversion (RI): Reverse the pc order of I.

Try it #2

Write the notes for each P segment in the left-hand column on the staff (your choice of octave, contour, and rhythm). Then write the transformation requested in the right-hand column, using the Summary above as your guide, in both integer notation and on the staff.

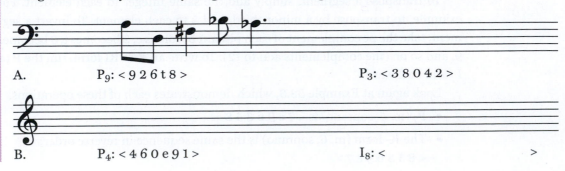

A. P_9: < 9 2 6 t 8 > P_3: < 3 8 0 4 2 >

B. P_4: < 4 6 0 e 9 1 > I_8: <   >

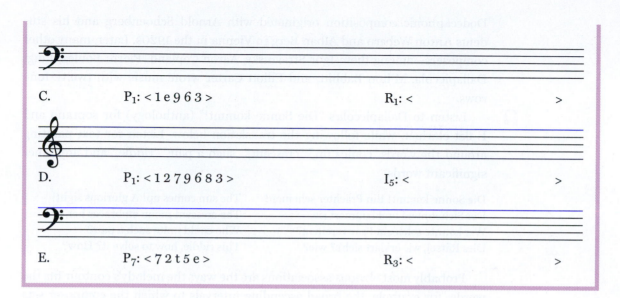

C. P_1: < 1 e 9 6 3 > R_1: <   >

D. P_1: < 1 2 7 9 6 8 3 > I_5: <   >

E. P_7: < 7 2 t 5 e > R_3: <   >

Another Way

You can use index numbers (see Chapter 36) as a shortcut for inverting a segment. Given a segment <7 e 9 6 3 5 8>, if you want to write its inversion beginning on a particular pc—let's say 7—you find the index number by adding 7 to the first pc of your segment (7 + 7 = 14 = 2): the index is 2.

$$
\begin{array}{r}
7\ e\ 9\ 6\ 3\ 5\ 8 \\
+\ 7 \\
\hline
2
\end{array}
$$

Now subtract all pcs of the original segment from the index number 2 to get the inverted segment:

$$
\begin{array}{r}
2\ 2\ 2\ 2\ 2\ 2\ 2 \\
-\ 7\ e\ 9\ 6\ 3\ 5\ 8 \\
\hline
<\ 7\ 3\ 5\ 8\ e\ 9\ 6\ > = \text{inversion.}
\end{array}
$$

Twelve-Tone Rows

Serial music composed with twelve-pc segments is called **twelve-tone**, or **dodecaphonic**, music (from the Greek for "twelve sounds").

KEY CONCEPT When an ordered segment consists of twelve distinct pcs, one from each pitch class, it is called a **twelve-tone row**. Twelve-tone compositions artfully combine the P form of the row (and its transpositions) with its R, I, and/or RI forms.

Dodecaphonic composition originated with Arnold Schoenberg and his students Anton Webern and Alban Berg in Vienna in the 1920s. Later, many other composers—among them Igor Stravinsky, Aaron Copland, Pierre Boulez, Luigi Dallapiccola, Milton Babbitt, and Elliott Carter wrote music with twelve-tone rows.

Listen to Dallapiccola's "Die Sonne kommt!" (anthology) for soprano and E-flat clarinet, while following the translation below. Listen for text painting around the words "comes up," "crescent," "such a pair," "riddle," and any other significant words.

Die Sonne kommt! Ein Prachter scheinen!	The sun comes up! A glorious sight!
Der Sichelmond umklammert sie.	The crescent moon embraces her.
Wer konnte solch ein Paar vereinen?	Who could unite such a pair?
Dies Rätsel, wie erklärt sich's? wie?	This riddle, how to solve it? How?

Probably most obvious associations are the ways the melody's contour fits the words: for example, the broad ascending intervals to which the composer sets "sun comes up" and the twisting of the musical line around "crescent." "Moon" is set to broad descending intervals, perhaps to contrast with the sun's ascent. "Such a pair" refers to the sun and moon, but Dallapiccola provides additional associations by scoring the piece for voice and clarinet duo, and by basing the primary pitch material on two transpositions of a twelve-tone row. We will return to the question of the riddle!

Analysis of a twelve-tone work often begins with determining the row; we number its elements in the score with **order numbers** 1 to 12. For retrograde rows, write the order numbers in reverse: 12 down to 1. As each row unfolds, label it using the system described above for ordered segments: P_5, RI_6, I_2, and so on. Analysis doesn't end with row labels, however—just as analysis of tonal music doesn't end with Roman numerals. Once you have identified the rows, consider the musical reasons that might motivate the composer's choice of particular row forms: How do the row choices interact with phrase and formal structure, or with the text of a song? Do particular row forms share common tones with others to create interesting relationships between contrapuntal lines? As you listen to more serial music, you will develop strategies for analysis beyond simple row labeling.

The vocal line in Example 38.4, from the opening of Dallapiccola's song, consists of two complete rows, with the second an inversion of the first. As is clear from the score, Dallapiccola divided the row into trichords by slurs, rhythm, rests, and register.

EXAMPLE 38.4: Dallapiccola, "Die Sonne kommt!" mm. 1-9 (voice)

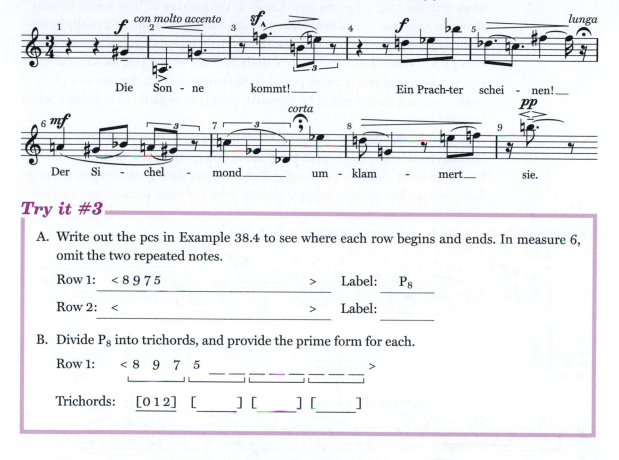

Try it #3

A. Write out the pcs in Example 38.4 to see where each row begins and ends. In measure 6, omit the two repeated notes.

Row 1: < 8 9 7 5   > Label: P_8

Row 2: <   > Label:

B. Divide P_8 into trichords, and provide the prime form for each.

Row 1: < 8   9   7   5   >

Trichords: [0 1 2]   [   ] [   ] [   ]

The first row in Example 38.4 (mm. 1-5) is the prime row. Label it P_8, since it begins with pc 8. The trichords are (in order) set classes 3-1 [0 1 2], 3-5 [0 1 6], 3-4 [0 1 5], and a repetition of 3-5 [0 1 6]; the two statements of 3-5 [0 1 6] provide some compositional opportunities that we will explore below. These trichords, as they appear in the P row, are {e 4 5} and {0 1 6}, and are related by T_5I. (If you have any difficulty understanding how the set-class labels for these trichords are determined, or the T_nI relation between them, review the discussion of set-class analysis in Chapter 37.) As we explore serial composition, we will continue to use angle brackets for ordered segments, curly braces for unordered sets and normal order, and square brackets for prime form.

Labeling Rows

A row is a precompositional idea—a sequence of pitch classes that composers then realize musically in various ways, just as Baroque composers could realize a figured bass in different ways. The repetitions of a row might involve an entirely different contour and sequence of pitches (the same pitch classes, but different octaves) and a different rhythm or tempo, or they might maximize common features with the original prime row. Listen to the passage of "Die Sonne kommt!" shown in Example 38.5 to hear Dallapiccola's strategy. You might initially be confused as you follow the row because Dallapiccola repeats pitches in measure 6: <9 8 t 9 8>. While a twelve-tone row itself does not repeat pcs, its musical realization may repeat one or more pcs when the composer sets the row in a piece of music, just as a motive might be repeated. Simply disregard the repetition when labeling rows.

Example 38.5 includes the entrance of the clarinet. Its melody should sound familiar, as it is an exact repetition of the opening vocal line (mm. 1-5). Label it P_8. An unusual aspect of this song is that Dallapiccola repeats not just the original row's pcs but its exact original pitches, with the same contour and rhythm.

EXAMPLE 38.5: Dallapiccola, "Die Sonne kommt!" mm. 6-12

Now compare the ordered pc intervals of the "Sichelmond" phrase with those of the original row. (Recall that pcis are measured from 0 to 11 and do not use plus or minus signs as pitch intervals do. Ordered pcis are calculated clockwise around the clock face, or subtracted (b - a) mod12.) Compare the two pci successions to see that the two rows are related by inversion. We can label the "Sichelmond" row I_9, because it begins with pc 9.

	"Die Sonne kommt! . . ."	"Der Sichelmond . . ."
pcs	<8 9 7 5 e 4 2 3 t 1 0 6>	<9 8 t 0 6 1 3 2 7 4 5 e>
ordered pcis	1 t t 6 5 t 1 7 3 e 6	e 2 2 6 7 2 e 5 9 1 6
	P_8	I → I_9

KEY CONCEPT When rows are related by inversion, each ordered pc interval in one row corresponds with its inverse in the other row.

As you probably noticed, in Example 38.5 the repeated B5 in measure 9 signals the beginning of a retrograde row—the same melody (pitch, contour, and rhythm) as I_9 in measures 6-8 but in reverse order, labeled RI_9. The rest of the song continues in the same vein, with exact repetitions of previous row forms and exact retrogrades, including contour and rhythm. When a segment of music is followed by a repetition entirely in retrograde (pitch, rhythm, and so on), as happens here, the two segments together are called a **palindrome**. Perhaps the palindromes represent the poem's "riddle." Dallapiccola builds an entire work out of simple repetition and transformation, in the same way that Renaissance and Baroque composers wrote "riddle" canons with melodies performed backward or upside-down.

KEY CONCEPT Sometimes composers make a row's construction, or relationships between row forms, clear by the musical context: by the rhythm, contour, register, or correspondence to motives or phrases. They may also obscure rows in various ways, such as setting them as chords where the ordering may be difficult to discern. (Look ahead at Example 38.7 for an example of a row presented chordally.)

Choosing Row Forms

The internal structure of a row has a great deal to do with larger decisions composers make about their pieces, just as a small-scale motive in a tonal work might foreshadow a change of key or large-scale tonal design. Consider, for example, the T_5I relationship between the two statements of SC 3-5 [0 1 6] in "Die Sonne kommt!" Because these two trichords are related by index number 5, any two rows whose T_nI numbers sum to 5 will reproduce the pcs of these two trichords as a unit within the row. (More advanced study of twelve-tone theory can explain why this is so.) For our purposes, we can simply observe that Dallapiccola has chosen row pairs—P_8 and I_9, plus their retrogrades—that sum to 5. You will find predictable pc duplications, called **invariant pcs** or **invariant sets**, between each pair of rows related by T_5I.

KEY CONCEPT Invariance means "kept the same," or "does not vary." Composers use pitch, pitch-class, or segment invariance to make connections between rows, sets, or segments. These invariant elements are often audible, and may contribute to a work's musical coherence.

To see invariance at work, look at the underlined trichords below, from the two rows in measures 8-12: P_8 (clarinet, beginning in m. 8) and RI_9 (voice, m. 9). These transposition levels, 8 and 9, sum to index number 5 (mod12). As you can see, trichords {e 4 5} and {0 1 6} reappear in each row, though their order varies. That the boxed pcs {8 9} and {2 3} appear consecutively in the two rows is also a predictable feature, since 8 + 9 sum to 5, and 2 + 3 sum to 5.

$$P_8: <\boxed{8\ 9}\ 7\ \underline{5\ e\ 4}\ \boxed{2\ 3}\ t\ \underline{1\ 0\ 6}>\qquad RI_9: <\underline{e\ 5\ 4}\ 7\ \boxed{2\ 3}\ \underline{1\ 6\ 0}\ t\ \boxed{8\ 9}>$$

$$T_5 1$$

Now observe how Dallapiccola features some of these pc recurrences in his musical setting (Example 38.6). The circles mark places where the composer has placed invariant pcs between rows in close proximity. His choice to realize many of them in the same pitch register makes audible the pc correspondences between rows, and the text painting of "such a pair" is played out by paired statements of {e 4 5}, {2 3}, and {0 1 6}.

EXAMPLE 38.6: Dallapiccola, "Die Sonne kommt!" mm. 6-12 (showing invariant pcs) 🎧

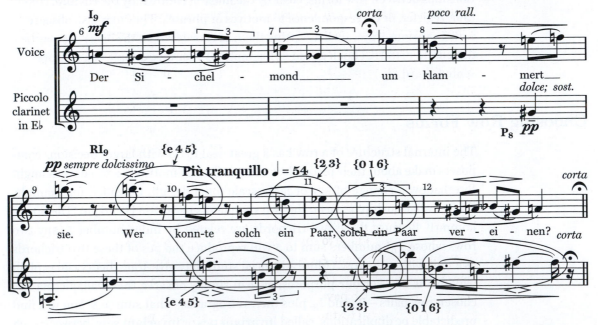

Hearing Row Relationships

You need no special abilities, other than patience and practice, to hear how rows are related. The first step is to analyze aurally the ordered pcis of a row. Write down this sequence as you hear it: often it will contain distinctive intervals or trichords at the beginning and end that will help you determine the row form. Since Dallapiccola's row begins with the [0 1 2] trichord, listen for opening chromaticism or leaps of major sevenths. It ends with a distinctive interval: a tritone. If you hear a row beginning with chromaticism, it must be a P or I form, but if you hear one beginning with a tritone, it must be an R or RI form.

If the beginning and end of the row are highly similar, then you will want to write down the entire sequence of intervals as you hear them. When you hear the next row, compare its pci sequence with the one you have written down. With time and practice, you can learn to do this, but don't forget to listen for other musical aspects: form, phrase, motivic repetition, and so on. The early twelve-tone composers saw their innovation as an outgrowth of motivic development and variation technique in Western music—not as a rejection of the earlier tradition but as a continuation and enrichment of that tradition.

Realizing Twelve-Tone Rows

Musical unity in a serial composition is created both by the row and by its realization through the compositional process. To learn how composers might create contrasting material from a single row, we turn now to a more extended work: Schoenberg's *Klavierstück*, Op. 33a. Schoenberg was convinced that a composer's craft included the ability to work with material from a row. "The time will come," he wrote, "when the ability to draw thematic material from a basic set of twelve tones will be an unconditional prerequisite for obtaining admission into the composition class of a conservatory" (*Style and Idea*, 1948).

Listen to the piece while following the score in your anthology. This piano work is sometimes described as a twelve-tone sonata form: listen for an expository first theme and lyrical second theme, then mark where those two themes return in the "recapitulation." Of course, we must expand our understanding of sonata form to hear the movement this way, since a tonal sonata's dramatic structure hinges on the tension between contrasting keys. Nevertheless, Schoenberg's composition does allude to sonata form. This type of borrowing is acknowledged by Schoenberg's student Anton Webern, who once claimed in a lecture (published after his death as *The Path to the New Music*, 1963), "We too are writing in classical forms, which haven't vanished."

From the chordal texture alone of the opening of the piece (Example 38.7a), it is not possible to determine the row's order; we need to look for a melodic statement, where the ordering is clearer. One possibility is to consult the return of this first theme in the "recapitulation" (part b). Here, the right hand brings back the chordal opening in measures 32-33, after the fermata, but now in arpeggiated form. Compare, for example, the first two chords of measure 1 with the right-hand arpeggiated chords of measure 32—the pcs are the same, and the arpeggios clarify the row's order. When you have determined the order of the row pcs in part (b), go back to label the order numbers in part (a).

EXAMPLE 38.7: Schoenberg, *Klavierstück*

(a) Mm. 1-2 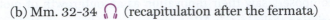 (exposition)

(b) Mm. 32-34 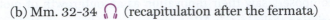 (recapitulation after the fermata)

Try it #4

Above the score in Example 38.7b, write the ordered pcs for the row, beginning in the right hand of measure 32, after the fermata.

A. Copy the pcs below, and write the corresponding order numbers beneath.

row pcs: < t 5 0 e   >

order numbers: 1 2 3 4

B. Write the order numbers for the three chords in measure 1 of Example 38.7a next to the notes, then copy them here, arranged from low to high.

1
2
3
Chord 1: __4__   Chord 2: _____   Chord 3: _____

⌒ **KEY CONCEPT** When the first row in a piece is presented chordally, look for a later appearance of the row as a melody to determine the pc order. Label individual row elements in the score with order numbers from 1 to 12 for P and I forms (and 12 to 1 for R and RI forms), to show their order clearly.

The distinctive set classes or intervals that lie at either end of this row (<t 5 0 e 9 6 1 3 7 8 2 4>) help make the row relationships audible. P and I forms begin with an ic 5, and the first trichord is the pentatonic subset 3-9 [0 2 7]. The R and RI forms begin with an ic 2, and the whole-tone subset 3-8 [0 2 6]. Listen for these different sounds to identify the row forms.

The Row Matrix

To label other row forms in this piece, take Schoenberg's row and build a **row matrix**—a 12 × 12 chart that displays all possible P, I, R, and RI forms of a row, and a convenient aid to analysis. Complete the matrix with either letter names or pc integers; we will use integers for now, to make calculating T and I forms easier.

⌒ **KEY CONCEPT** To build a row matrix:

1. Write the P form of the row across the top.

2. Write the I form—the inverse of each pc in the row—down the first column on the left.

3. Consider the pc at the beginning of each matrix row to be the first pc of each P form (transpose the original P form to begin on this pc).

4. Consider the pc at the top of each column to begin an I form.

If you begin your matrix by transposing the initial row to begin on 0, then the main diagonal from the upper left- to lower right-hand corner will contain all zeros. This is a helpful property, since you can judge from the diagonal of zeros whether you have calculated correctly. The diagonal directly below the main diagonal of zeros gives you the pc interval succession for the P rows, and the diagonal above the zeros gives you the pci succession for the I rows.

The matrix in the *Try it #5* below is only partially completed.

- Read P forms left to right; in this matrix, the first row is P_0, the second is P_5, the third is P_t, and so on.

- To find R forms, read the rows backward, right to left. The first row is R_0, the second is R_5, the third is R_t, and so on. (Remember, R forms are named by the first pc of their associated P form.)

- Read the I forms top to bottom as columns: the first column is I_0, the second is I_7, the third is I_2.

- Read the RI forms as columns bottom to top: the first column is RI_0, the second is RI_7, the third is RI_2. (Remember, RI forms are named by the first pc of their associated I form.)

Try it #5

Fill in the remaining positions in the matrix on your own. (You may find the task easier if you complete the matrix in this order: P_0, P_1, P_2, P_3, and so on. This way you only have to add 1 each time.) Making a matrix by hand is an important step in learning how rows are constructed and related, but a web search will find numerous websites for building matrices automatically.

↓ I

P →	I_0	I_7	I_2	I_1	I_e								← R
P_0	0	7	2	1	e	8	3	5	9	t	4	6	R_0
P_5	5	0	7	6	4	1	8	t	2	3	9	e	R_5
P_t	t	5	0	e	9	6	1	3	7	8	2	4	R_t
P_e	e	6		0			2						R_e
P_1	1	8			0		4						R_1
	4	e				0	7						
	9	4					0						
	7	2					t	0					
	3	t					6		0				
	2	9					5			0			
	8	3					e				0		
	6	1	8	7	5	2	9	e	3	4	t	0	
	RI_0	RI_7	RI_2	RI_1	RI_e								

↑ RI

When you have completed the matrix, refer to it as you label the remaining rows in Example 38.7a and b.

Try it #6

Fill in the requested row labels (the subscripts).

Example 38.7a:

m. 1: P _____t_____   m. 2: RI _____

Example 38.7b:

mm. 32-33, right hand: P _____   mm. 33-34, right hand: RI _____

left hand: I _____   left hand: R _____

Hexachordal Combinatoriality

Listen to the second theme of Schoenberg's piece, given in Example 38.8. This theme has a slower "harmonic rhythm"—that is, it takes longer for each row to be completed because of repeated notes. Label the row forms, one in the right hand and one in the left, from the matrix you completed. Interestingly, Schoenberg uses the same transpositions of the row as earlier in the piece, but to very different musical effect.

EXAMPLE 38.8: Schoenberg, *Klavierstück*, mm. 14-18

If you had not been tipped off to look for one row in each hand, you might have had difficulty identifying rows in this passage. This is because Schoenberg completes an **aggregate**—a collection of all twelve tones—in measures 14-16 (both hands together) before either row concludes. To understand this concept, we notate the passage in pc integers below. We divide the row in each hand into two hexachords, just as Schoenberg does (mm. 14-16, 16-18), by means of rests and changes in register. Remember that pitches can be repeated, but they will maintain row order.

		mm. 14-16	mm. 16-18
right hand:	P_t	<t 5 0 e 9 6	1 3 7 8 2 4>
left hand:	I_3	<3 8 1 2 4 7	0 t 6 5 e 9>
		aggregate	aggregate

As the diagram shows, the first hexachords of each row (each hand, mm. 14-16) together make an aggregate, as do the second hexachords of each row (mm. 16-18).

KEY CONCEPT **Hexachordal combinatoriality** occurs when two forms of the same row are paired so that one hexachord of the first row, combined with one hexachord of the second row, complete an aggregate. The rows' other hexachords, when combined, will likewise complete an aggregate. Such aggregates are sometimes called **secondary sets**.

Hexachordal combinatoriality may help create variety in the pcs and in the intervals between voices. It can also contribute to a faster harmonic rhythm—that is, the frequency with which one aggregate is completed and the next one begins. You can diagram the combinatorial relationship in one of two ways, where A represents the *unordered* pc content of one hexachord, and B the unordered content of the other. In the Schoenberg example, hexachord A is {5 6 9 t e 0} and hexachord B is {1 2 3 4 7 8}.

(a) Vertical aggregates

row:	A	B
transformation of row:	B	A
	aggregate	aggregate

(b) Linear aggregates

row: transformation of row:

A   B   A   B
aggregate

There are four types of combinatoriality: P-, I-, R-, and RI-combinatoriality. We have already seen an example of I-combinatoriality, where a row is paired with its inversion, in the Schoenberg example (P_t paired with I_3). In P-combinatoriality, a row is paired with another P form (a transposition of the original). In R- or RI-combinatoriality, a row is paired with a retrograde or retrograde-inversion form. A hexachord that can generate all four types of combinatoriality is called an **all-combinatorial hexachord**.

There are only six all-combinatorial hexachords. If you compose a row that begins with one of these hexachords, you are guaranteed that your row can be combined with some form of P, I, R, and RI to create hexachordally combinatorial music.

All-combinatorial hexachords		IC vectors
6-1	[0 1 2 3 4 5]	[5 4 3 2 1 0]
6-7	[0 1 2 6 7 8]	[4 2 0 2 4 3]
6-8	[0 2 3 4 5 7]	[3 4 3 2 3 0]
6-20	[0 1 4 5 8 9]	[3 0 3 6 3 0]
6-32	[0 2 4 5 7 9]	[1 4 3 2 5 0]
6-35	[0 2 4 6 8 t]	[0 6 0 6 0 3]

Finding Combinatorial Row Pairs

If you wanted to compose a twelve-tone work that featured combinatorial row pairs, you would need to know how to "find" pairs that work. The easiest way is by examining a row's matrix. As an example, let's take the row from the second movement of Webern's *Variations for Piano*. This row is constructed from an all-combinatorial hexachord (although, as we will see, the movement does not employ combinatoriality at all).

To find a combinatorial pair of rows, first divide the matrix into four quadrants, as shown below. This isolates the hexachords for comparison. If you wanted to find a P-combinatorial pair for P_5, whose first hexachord is <5 1 0 4 3 2>, you would circle this collection on the left side of the matrix and hunt for the same unordered collection, {0 1 2 3 4 5}, on the right side; the content of the A hexachord should appear in the second (B) hexachord of the new row. Once you have found it, you can see that P_5 and P_e are P-combinatorial.

	0	8	7	e	t	9	3	1	4	2	6	5
	4	0	e	3	2	1	7	5	8	6	t	9
P_5	(5	1	0	4	3	2)	8	6	9	7	e	t
	1	9	8	0	e	t	4	2	5	3	7	6
	2	t	9	1	0	e	5	3	6	4	8	7
	3	e	t	2	1	0	6	4	7	5	9	8
	9	5	4	8	7	6	0	t	1	e	3	2
P_e	e	7	6	t	9	8	(2	0	3	1	5	4)
	8	4	3	7	6	5	e	9	0	t	2	1
	t	6	5	9	8	7	1	e	2	0	4	3
	6	2	1	5	4	3	9	7	t	8	0	e
	7	3	2	6	5	4	t	8	e	9	1	0

P_5: <5 1 0 4 3 2   8 6 9 7 e t>

P_e: <e 7 6 t 9 8   2 0 3 1 5 4>

    aggregate   aggregate

Another way to find the same combinatorial pair, without a matrix, is to consider properties of invariance discussed earlier. In order for P-combinatoriality to work, we need to find out which transposition of hexachord A (set-class 6-1 [0 1 2 3 4 5]) produces zero common tones—thus generating the remainder of the row, or hexachord B. In other words, by what T_n level will hexachord A transform into hexachord B? Fortunately, the ic vector—[543210] (which may be found in Appendix 6)—provides just this information. The 0 in the ic 6 position of the vector tells us that transposition by T_6 will produce no common tones. In Chapter 37, we called this principle the common-tone theorem. This information produces precisely the row pairing we found by examining the matrix—the T_6 transposition of our P_5 row is P_e. The ic vectors for each of the all-combinatorial hexachords are shown in the listing above; each of them has a 0 in at least one position.

KEY CONCEPT To write a P-combinatorial row pairing, examine the ic vector for the first hexachord of the row. If there is a zero in any position of the vector, then a transposition of hexachord A by that interval will produce hexachord B. Pairing two rows by that same interval of transposition will result in P-combinatoriality.

Try it #7

Follow either procedure to find other P-combinatorial rows in the matrix above.

A. What row is P-combinatorial with P_9? _____

B. What row is P-combinatorial with P_7? _____

To find an I-combinatorial pair on the matrix, again begin by circling the first hexachord of the P form on the left side of the matrix. This time, hunt for the equivalent content of this unordered hexachord anywhere on the bottom half, as part of a vertical column. Look at columns rather than rows, because you are looking for I forms; and the bottom half because you want to find an I row whose second (B) hexachord is equivalent in content to hexachord A.

0	8	7	e	t	9	3	1	4	2	6	5
4	0	e	3	2	1	7	5	8	6	t	9
5	**1**	**0**	**4**	**3**	**2**	8	6	9	7	e	t
1	9	8	0	e	t	4	2	5	3	7	6
2	t	9	1	0	e	5	3	6	4	8	7
3	e	t	2	1	0	6	4	7	5	9	8
9	5	4	8	7	6	0	t	1	e	**3**	2
e	7	6	t	9	8	2	0	3	1	**5**	4
8	4	3	7	6	5	e	9	0	t	**2**	1
t	6	5	9	8	7	1	e	2	0	**4**	3
6	2	1	5	4	3	9	7	t	8	**0**	e
7	3	2	6	5	4	t	8	e	9	**1**	0

(P_5 labels the third row.)

Again, once you have found it, simply read the row forms from the matrix: P_5 and I_6 are I-combinatorial.

$$P_5: \quad <5\ 1\ 0\ 4\ 3\ 2 \quad 8\ 6\ 9\ 7\ e\ t>$$
$$I_6: \quad <6\ t\ e\ 7\ 8\ 9 \quad 3\ 5\ 2\ 4\ 0\ 1>$$

$\underbrace{\phantom{<6\ t\ e\ 7\ 8\ 9}}_{\text{aggregate}} \quad \underbrace{}_{\text{aggregate}}$

To find this I-combinatorial pairing without a matrix, look for the T_nI level of hexachord A that transforms it into hexachord B. There are several ways to do this. One way is to write the normal order of hexachord A, and below it write the normal order of hexachord B in *reverse*. When these integers are added, they should produce a consistent index number: their T_nI relationship. In this case, the hexachords are related by T_eI; therefore the I-combinatorial row that pairs with P_5 will also be related by T_eI. P_5 and I_6 are T_eI-related (you can see this by adding the subscripts $5 + 6$).

hexachord A: $\{0\ \ 1\ \ 2\ \ 3\ \ 4\ \ 5\}$
hexachord B: $+\{e\ \ t\ \ 9\ \ 8\ \ 7\ \ 6\}$
$\overline{\phantom{+\{e\ \ t\ \ 9\ \ 8\ \ 7\ \ 6\}}}$
          $e\ \ e\ \ e\ \ e\ \ e\ \ e$ The hexachords are related by T_eI.

Try it #8

Follow either procedure to find other I-combinatorial rows in the matrix above.

A. What row is I-combinatorial with P_9? _____

B. What row is I-combinatorial with P_7? _____

The R-combinatorial pair for this row is P_5 and R_5. Any row paired with its own retrograde will produce R-combinatoriality. Finally, to create an RI-combinatorial row, hexachord A must map onto itself under some T_nI. That operator can then be used to find a combinatorial row pair, or you can search for pairings on the row matrix.

R-combinatoriality:

P_5: ⟨5 1 0 4 3 2   8 6 9 7 e t⟩
R_5: ⟨t e 7 9 6 8   2 3 4 0 1 5⟩
        aggregate   aggregate

Combinatoriality is not limited to hexachord pairings: tetrachordal combinatoriality may be made from a combination of three related rows, and trichordal combinatoriality from four related rows, as shown below. In this example, taken from composer-theorist Robert Morris, the first trichords of each row when combined produce an aggregate (as shown by their vertical alignment), as do the second trichords, and so on.

P_0:   ⟨0 4 5   2 3 7   1 9 8   e t 6⟩
RI_7: ⟨1 9 8   e t 6   0 4 5   2 3 7⟩
I_7:   ⟨7 3 2   5 4 0   6 t e   8 9 1⟩
R_0: ⟨6 t e   8 9 1   7 3 2   5 4 0⟩
     aggregate aggregate aggregate aggregate

Serialism and Compositional Style

Together, the centric serialism of Tavener's "The Lamb," the riddle canons of the Dallapiccola song, and the sonata-like Schoenberg piano work demonstrate that not all serial music sounds alike. Indeed, there is a greater resemblance between Schoenberg's later twelve-tone works and his early, nonserial compositions than there is between his twelve-tone music and Webern's, or between Berg's and Webern's. Even the construction of these composers' rows—quite apart from their musical realization—has much to tell about their styles.

Look, for example, at two of Berg's rows and two of Webern's. The row for Berg's Violin Concerto (Example 38.9a) is shaped by many more consonant intervals than other rows, beginning with a series of ascending thirds (ics 3 and 4) and concluding with a rising whole-tone scale. These materials allow triadic harmonies in the midst of a serial work; and in a compositional tour de force, Berg sets the twelve-tone row against a quotation from a Bach chorale.

In part (b), from Berg's *Lyric Suite*, the row systematically states all twelve pcis, as marked. This principle of row construction—the **all-interval row**—was followed by other composers as well, Dallapiccola and Luigi Nono among them. An additional feature is that the intervals are arranged symmetrically around a central axis (ic 6), as marked by the arrows, so that each pc interval in the first half of the row is matched by its complement in the second half.

EXAMPLE 38.9: Rows of Alban Berg

(a) Violin Concerto, mm. 15-18 (solo violin, P₇)

row: < 7   t   2   6   9   0   4   8   e   1   3   5
interval classes: 3   4   4   3   3   4   4   3   2   2   2

(b) *Lyric Suite*, mvt. 1, mm. 2-4 (violin 1, P₅)

ordered pcis: e   8   9   t   7   ⑥   5   2   3   4   1   (all-interval row)
interval classes: 1   4   3   2   5   ⑥   5   2   3   4   1   (symmetrical ics)

Webern's rows demonstrate additional compositional principles: the first (Example 38.10a) is a **symmetrical row** (like Berg's, but without also being an all-interval row). Its symmetry can be seen in the palindromic arrangement of interval classes. Symmetrical rows can create a challenge for the analyst because two row labels are correct for every row. In the case of Webern's *Symphonie*, the row shown is P_t: <t 7 8 9 5 6 0 e 3 2 1 4>. Transposing this row by 6 semitones yields P₄ <4 1 2 3 e 0 6 5 9 8 7 t>—precisely the same pcs as P_t in reverse order (R_t). In analysis, either row label would be correct, but we prefer to assign P or I rather than retrograde labels, unless a composer has paired a row with its retrograde.

EXAMPLE 38.10: Rows of Anton Webern

(a) *Symphonie*, mvt. 2, mm. 12-17 (cello, P_t or R₄)

ordered pcis: 9   1   1   8   1   6   e   4   e   e   3
interval classes: 3   1   1   4   1   6   1   4   1   1   3

(b) *Concerto for Nine Instruments,* mm. 1–3

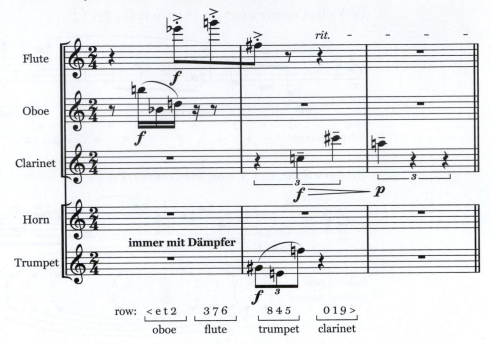

In a **derived row** (part b), the basic idea of the row—a pcset—is stated at the beginning, and the rest of the pcs of the row are derived from it (by T, I, R, or RI). As the example shows, Webern's concerto row is clearly divided into trichords by instrumentation: three notes in each instrument. You can see how the derived row works by listing each of the trichords in normal order and comparing them; all are SC 3-3 [0 1 4]. The arrows below show how the trichords are related.

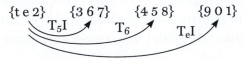

Webern's *Variations for Piano* demonstrates a few additional musical features that are typical of this composer's serial works. Webern is much less likely than Schoenberg or Berg to write long, lyrical melodies. Instead, he opts for short movements with a succession of brief melodies, creating a tapestry of sound. In the *Variations,* he uses the same row for all three movements. Example 38.11 gives the prime row, from the third movement—the movement he wrote first; this is the row for which we constructed the matrix earlier in the chapter.

EXAMPLE 38.11: Webern, *Variations for Piano*, mvt. 3, mm. 1-5

row: P₃ < 3 e t 2 1 0 6 4 7 5 9 8 >

Now listen to the second movement while following the score in your anthology. One thing that stands out on first hearing is that the movement sounds repetitive in ways that extend beyond the repeat signs of the binary form. Why, for instance, do we keep hearing the A4—a repeated pitch in the midst of so much other varied pitch activity? Other pitches stand out because of their extreme high register: the same high notes, G6 and E6, appear here and there.

The row for this movement begins with a retrograde form. Refer to the matrix (p. 811) to analyze the row forms in Example 38.12, and write the row labels in the blanks. Here are some hints to guide your analysis. First, there is one row in each hand; the order numbers of R₃ are provided for the right hand to get you started. Second, the row placement switches from one hand to the other midway through the phrase. Third, Webern employs a technique similar to phrase overlap, or elision—that is, the last pc in one row is the same as the first pc in the next. These shared pcs he states only once, so you'll need to "count" them twice. This technique is sometimes called **row elision** (or "row linkage").

EXAMPLE 38.12: Webern, *Variations for Piano*, mvt. 2, mm. 1-11

Think of the texture in this movement as a canon between hands. The rhythms, articulations, and dynamic levels are identical from the left hand (the **dux**, or leader) to the right (the **comes**, or follower). This relationship swaps within the row (in m. 5, the right hand becomes the leader), which helps identify the point at which the rows switch from one hand to the other. The dux/comes relationship continues to swap throughout the piece.

It is sometimes helpful to write out the row pairs in integer notation to consider relationships of interest, as you did for the combinatorial pairs. The rows in the first half of the movement are listed below (with the pcs that are elided in parentheses):

R_3: < 8 (9) 5 7 4 6 0 1 2 t e (3) > R_t: < (3) 4 0 2 e 1 7 8 (9) 5 6 t >
RI_3: < t (9) 1 e 2 0 6 5 4 8 7 (3) > RI_8: < (3) 2 6 4 7 5 e t (9) 1 0 8 >

Begin by exploring those repeated A4s, circled above. Webern specifically chose row forms where pc 9 appears in the same position (the same is true for pc 3, which makes the elisions possible). In his realization of the rows, the composer highlights this relationship by always writing pc 9 with the same register, rhythm, and dynamic level, to make the repetition stand out aurally. Every dyad (or pair of pcs) found "harmonically" between the rows is maintained as a dyad throughout the movement, and the pitches of these dyads are symmetrical around A4. Take, for instance, the dyad {8 t}, with which the first row pair begins. Search for any other pc 8 or t in the movement, and you will see that almost every 8 is paired with t. Now refer again to the score to see how Webern emphasizes this relationship: each pair is set in the same register, with the same rhythm and dynamic marking.

Another Way

You can predict which row forms will produce the repeated A4s by using index numbers. Any P and I form whose row labels add to six will produce the same relation.

R_3:   8 (9) 5 7 4 6 0 1 2 t e (3) P_5:   5 1 0 4 (3) 2 8 6 (9) 7 e t
RI_3: + t (9) 1 e 2 0 6 5 4 8 7 (3) I_1: + 1 5 6 2 (3) 4 t 0 (9) e 7 8
          ‾‾‾‾‾‾‾‾‾‾‾‾‾‾‾‾‾‾‾‾‾‾‾‾‾   ‾‾‾‾‾‾‾‾‾‾‾‾‾‾‾‾‾‾‾‾‾‾‾‾
          6 6 6 6 6 6 6 6 6 6 6 6   6 6 6 6 6 6 6 6 6 6 6 6

Another aspect of Webern's row realization may contribute to the repetitive sound of this movement: a technique called **registral invariance** (also sometimes called "frozen register" or "pitch fixation"). Over half of the pcs in the row appear in one and only one register. Example 38.13 gives these pitches in their frozen, or fixed, position.

EXAMPLE 38.13: Seven pitches from *Variations for Piano*, mvt. 2 🎧

To hear how registral invariance works, play these pitches on a piano (all together or as a rolled chord) while listening to the movement; they will stand out from the rest of the texture because of their repetition as pitches (rather than pitch classes). In *The Path to the New Music*, Webern hints that he composed rows according to certain guiding principles he was reluctant to share: "Now I'm asked, 'How did I arrive at this row?' Not arbitrarily, but according to certain secret laws." Perhaps he is referring to a system for predicting which row forms will produce the types of relationships discussed in this chapter. On the other hand, later in the same passage, Webern attributes his row composition to "inspiration."

Serialized Durations

One significant development in the 1950s and early 1960s was the extension of serial procedures to dimensions other than pitch—a procedure referred to as **total serialism**, or **integral serialism**. In a groundbreaking experimental piece for two pianos from the 1950s, *Structures Ia* (Example 38.14), Pierre Boulez serialized not only pitch classes, but also durations, articulation, and dynamic levels. Pitch-class rows were paired with duration rows, and each section of the work was assigned a dynamic level and articulation type from an ordered series of dynamics and articulations.

EXAMPLE 38.14: Boulez, *Structures Ia*

(a) Mm. 24–31 (piano 2) 🎧

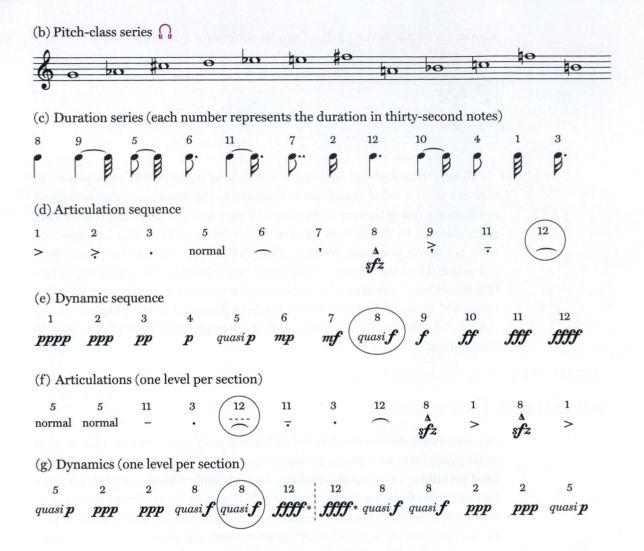

(b) Pitch-class series

(c) Duration series (each number represents the duration in thirty-second notes)

8   9   5   6   11   7   2   12   10   4   1   3

(d) Articulation sequence

1   2   3   5   6   7   8   9   11   12

(e) Dynamic sequence

1	2	3	4	5	6	7	8	9	10	11	12
pppp	*ppp*	*pp*	*p*	quasi *p*	*mp*	*mf*	quasi *f*	*f*	*ff*	*fff*	*ffff*

(f) Articulations (one level per section)

5	5	11	3	12	11	3	12	8	1	8	1
normal	normal	–	•			•		*sfz*	>	*sfz*	>

(g) Dynamics (one level per section)

5	2	2	8	8	12	12	8	8	2	2	5
quasi *p*	*ppp*	*ppp*	quasi *f*	quasi *f*	*ffff* *	*ffff* *	quasi *f*	quasi *f*	*ppp*	*ppp*	quasi *p*

In part (a), piano 2 plays the pitch-class and duration series shown in parts (b) and (c); the duration series is in retrograde form. To create serialized articulations and dynamics, the composer first created ordered sequences of these elements (for example, from very soft to very loud) and numbered each from 1 to 12. These are shown in parts (d) and (e); parts (f) and (g) give the serial ordering Boulez chose for the entire work (derived from the diagonals in his row matrices).

Now refer back to the piano score in part (a). This section is notated *legato* and *quasi forte*, corresponding to the fifth position in the articulation and dynamic series (circled in parts f and g). The articulation number 12 and dynamic number 8 refer to their place in the sequence of twelve possible articulations and dynamics. The next section of the work uses the sixth position (11 and 12) in these series. Though the structure of this work, on first listening, seems quite "random," it is actually just the opposite: every element is organized by the composer's pre-compositional choices.

Did You Know?

Like the musical palindromes that structure Dallapiccola's song, linguistic palindromes have charmed readers for many years. Some examples include "Doc, note; I diet on cod" and "Able was I, ere I saw Elba."

Webern was fascinated with what is called the Sator Square, made of the Latin words SATOR AREPO TENET OPERA ROTAS written in a square so that they may be read top-to-bottom, bottom-to-top, left-to-right, and right-to-left:

```
S A T O R
A R E P O
T E N E T
O P E R A
R O T A S
```

Webern cited this square as inspiration for his serial compositions. The earliest known copy, discovered in the early twentieth century, lay in the ruins of Pompeii, where it had been preserved in the volcanic ash of Mt. Vesuvius since 79 CE. The saying translates as "The farmer Arepo has work [with] wheels [i.e., a plow]."

TERMS YOU SHOULD KNOW

aggregate

all-combinatorial hexachord

comes

dodecaphonic

dux

invariance

- invariant pcs
- invariant sets

hexachordal combinatoriality

inversion (I)

integral serialism

order number

palindrome

prime (P)

retrograde (R)

retrograde inversion (RI)

registral invariance

row elision

secondary set

row

row matrix

total serialism

serial

twelve tone

QUESTIONS FOR REVIEW

1. What is serialism? What elements other than pitches can be ordered?

2. How does the pattern of pitch-class intervals change from P to I forms of a row? from P to R? from P to RI?

3. What are some characteristics to look for in studying the row for a serial piece?

4. The row numbers for R and RI forms come from which pc of the row, first or last?

5. If a row contains two equivalent sets related by T_nI, what happens when the entire row is transformed by that same T_nI?

6. How can properties of the row be brought out (or not) in its musical realization?

7. Are all serial works twelve tone? Explain, citing examples from this chapter.

8. Describe how to construct a row matrix. What goes along the top? down the side? What does the main diagonal reveal?

9. What is combinatoriality? What does it allow the composer to do in the music?

10. How is the term "harmonic rhythm" used in a twelve-tone context?

11. Is it always possible to tell by listening if a work is serial as opposed to freely nontonal?

12. In a work composed with integral (or total) serialism, what other musical elements may be serialized?

13. After consulting your teacher, find one twelve-tone work for your own instrument. Try to identify the row and at least one transformation. Does the composer align phrase structure with row forms?

14. What are some ways different composers use rows to make their compositions sound distinctive in style? (Hint: Compare the pieces by Webern, Schoenberg, Dallapiccola, and Tavener in this chapter.)

Know It? Show It!

Focus by working through the tutorials.

Learn with InQuizitive.

Apply what you've learned to complete the workbook assignments.

39

Rhythm, Meter, and Form after 1945

Overview

After 1945, composers began to explore new ways to conceptualize and notate rhythm, meter, and form. This chapter examines these new approaches.

Repertoire

Luciano Berio, *Sequenza III*, for voice

William Bolcom, *12 New Etudes for Piano*, mvt. 3

Earle Brown, *Folio and Four Systems*

John Cage, *4'33"*

Elliott Carter, String Quartet No. 2

John Corigliano, "Come now, my darling," from *The Ghosts of Versailles*

George Crumb, "¿Por qué nací entre espejos?" ("Why Was I Born Surrounded by Mirrors?"), from *Madrigals*, Book 4

Philip Glass, *Music in Fifths*

György Ligeti
Continuum
Hungarian Etudes, mvt. 3
Ten Pieces for Wind Quintet, mvt. 9
"Wenn aus der Ferne" ("If from the Distance"), from
    Three Fantasies on Texts by Friedrich Hölderlin

Kenneth Maue, *In the Woods*

Krzysztof Penderecki, *Threnody for the Victims of Hiroshima*

Steve Reich, *Piano Phase*

Terry Riley, *In C*

Karlheinz Stockhausen
Klavierstück XI
Zyklus

La Monte Young, *Composition 1960*, No. 5

Outline

New approaches to traditional form
- Sectional forms
- Canon and imitation

Variants on traditional rhythmic notation
- Ametric music
- New approaches to meter and polymeter
- Metric modulation

New developments in musical form and notation
- Time-line, graphic, and text notation
- Moment form and mobile form
- Indeterminacy and chance
- Minimalism and form as process

Analyzing form in recent music

New Approaches to Traditional Form

The three decades after World War II were marked by an intense exploration of compositional methods, including new approaches to rhythm, meter, durations, pitch, timbre, and their notation. The earlier trend of precisely notating every music element also continued into the postwar era, as we saw in Boulez's integral serial work *Stuctures Ia*. Innovations in instrumental techniques brought new timbres and types of articulations, leading to even more detailed performance instructions and score markings. These practices when taken to an extreme made the music difficult to perform, because of the need to pay attention to so many details. Some composers responded with innovative notation that made scores easier to read. Others added new levels of detail and complexity to the visual representation of the music. Even in traditionally notated scores, some composers added new rhythmic and metrical indications to represent new concepts of musical time.

Sectional Forms

Listen to the excerpt in your anthology from a piece by Krzysztof Penderecki. Originally called *Piece for 52 Strings*, it is best known as *Threnody for the Victims of Hiroshima* (1960), and its striking sound is different from anything we have studied thus far. Listen several times without the score. Think about where you hear formal divisions and how Penderecki creates subsections and closure at the end of the excerpt.

Now look at the score from the beginning to rehearsal number 10. Example 39.1 shows the opening. Although the markings are innovative, the formal design of the work draws on traditional elements studied in earlier chapters; the dotted vertical lines, for example, are like bar lines, with the number of seconds between them given at the bottom of the score.

EXAMPLE 39.1: Penderecki, *Threnody for the Victims of Hiroshima*, m. 1 🎧

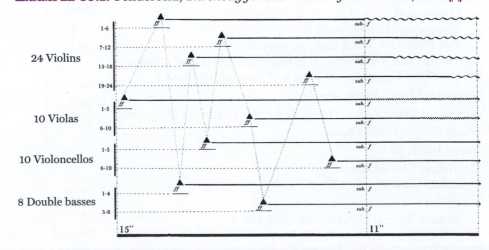

In Penderecki's notation (a key is provided on the score's first page), the triangles pointing up mean to play the highest note possible on the instrument, and the wavy lines indicate the presence and intensity of vibrato. The other symbols seen after rehearsal 6 indicate sound effects. After the imitative entrances at the beginning of the piece, the effect is of one large mass of sound, rather than of individual instruments. As you can hear, the sound quality up to rehearsal 10 changes smoothly, with one type of sound eliding to the next.

Now consider the next subsection, rehearsal numbers 10-17: the graphic notation here is intended to depict what the music sounds like, with the black pitch clusters expanding and then contracting. The outer boundaries of the clusters are notated exactly, but the players must listen carefully to fill in their portion of the space in between and to create the musical shape. In 15-16, the score specifies the pitches for each player within the cluster. Many listeners will hear each of these clusters as an individual phrase—with a starting point, midpoint, and close—even though each cluster is elided with the entry of the next. Together, the sonic similarity of the clusters and their elisions unify this subsection. Closure at the end (17) is achieved by the cadential *glissandi* in opposing directions.

The third subsection begins with individual, pointillistic entrances at rehearsal 18, the score indicating the exact pitches and order of entry for each instrument with an "arrowhead" notation. At the end (22), we hear elements that, in tonal music, would normally support a tonal cadence: a closing of range, a thinner texture, softer dynamics, arrival on a point of rest, and silence. When these elements are combined in contemporary pieces, they can create closure as definitive as any in tonal music, even without functional harmony. The entrance of contrasting music at 26 (not shown in the anthology) confirms the end of this first large section and the beginning of the second.

In another work from the same period (1961)—*Visage*, an electronic (tape) music composition by Luciano Berio—sectional divisions are marked by such elements as broken speech that becomes increasingly frantic and emotionally fraught, leading to the release of tension by the singer's recorded laugh, and a change in the emotional content of the following section.

The challenge in identifying formal divisions in nontonal music—especially works as innovative as these were at the time of their composition—is that there is no standard system of "markers" for closure, such as tonal cadences. The best approach for formal analysis is listening; become familiar with each piece, and then decide whether you can hear a musical gesture that suggests a phrase ending, cadence, or sectional division. If you can, take the next step: try to explain how and why the gesture conveys that musical function.

Canon and Imitation

Example 39.2a gives the entire ninth movement of Ligeti's *Ten Pieces for Wind Quintet* (1968). (In this score, the piccolo and clarinet are transposing instruments: the piccolo sounds one octave higher than notated, and the clarinet sounds a whole step lower.) All three instruments play the same melodic line, but with slightly different durations (the pitch sequence is shown in part b). The form of this piece is represented in the pitch-time graph in part (c). Interestingly, its beginning and end are similar to a description in one of the earliest written sources of information about counterpoint (from around 900), the *Musica enchiriadis*: it opens with a unison and ends with a gradual close to an octave.

EXAMPLE 39.2: Ligeti, *Ten Pieces for Wind Quintet*

(a) Ninth movement

(b) Pitch sequence

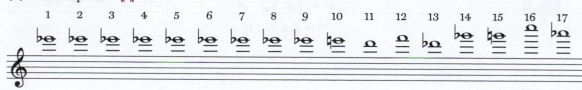

(c) Pitch/time graph

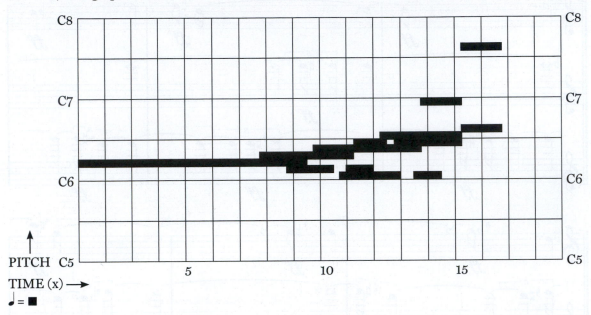

Ligeti employs other types of imitation in his compositions as well. Look at Example 39.3, from *Three Fantasies on Texts by Friedrich Hölderlin* (1982). This passage, consisting of the alto parts, shows a typical imitative entry at the unison. Sing the passage with your class. (The downward-pointing arrows on the B♭s mean to sing them a quarter tone flat.)

EXAMPLE 39.3: Ligeti, "Wenn aus der Ferne," mm. 19–23 (alto parts)

Translation: How flowed the lost hours, how calm was my soul.

For a final example of imitation, listen again to the beginning of Penderecki's *Threnody* while following the score, to see how the entrances of sound effects are organized. Example 39.4 shows the patterns for the four entrances in the cellos at rehearsal 6, labeled A, B, C, and D. Compare these entrances with those in the violas, violins, and basses (from there to rehearsal 10). Mark those entrances in your score with the same labels. Although this portion of the *Threnody* follows strict contrapuntal procedures (the individual parts enter in a kind of imitation), you probably did not hear it this way; instead, it sounds like a swirling ostinato of "insect" sounds. Yet the choice of imitative entries is significant to the sound of this passage: it allows Penderecki to balance the diverse string effects and thus achieve an even blending. The instructions to the performer—pizzicato (plucked), *arco* (bowed), and *battuto* (hitting the string with the wood of the bow)—also contribute to this aural effect.

EXAMPLE 39.4: Penderecki, *Threnody for the Victims of Hiroshima*, cello entrances at rehearsal number 6 🎧

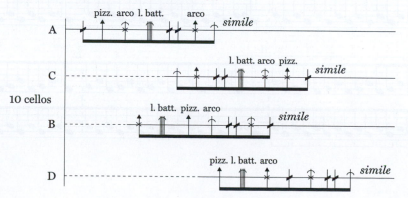

Variants on Traditional Rhythmic Notation

In compositions after 1945, you may also encounter new twists on traditional rhythmic notation—for example, meter signatures with a note rather than a lower number (such as $\frac{4}{\downarrow}$ instead of $\frac{12}{8}$). Other pieces may use simple and traditional notation, but create new effects nevertheless.

Ametric music

Look at the opening of Ligeti's *Continuum* (1967) in Example 39.5. Even though all durations are eighth notes, they combine to produce complex and detailed rhythmic interactions, which gradually change as the piece progresses. There are no traditional bar lines or notated meter, but Ligeti provides dotted lines as a visual reference.

EXAMPLE 39.5: Ligeti, *Continuum*, "measures" 1-22 (8-15 recorded) 🎧

Play through this passage slowly at the keyboard (Ligeti's tempo is "Extremely fast, so that individual tones can hardly be perceived, but rather merge into a continuum"), or listen to a complete recording online. You will hear that the work opens with a two-note minor-third pattern in both hands. In measure 10, the pattern changes in the right hand, enlarged to a three-note set spanning a perfect fourth; this three-note pattern heard against the two-note creates an unsettling rhythmic effect. The next change comes in measure 15: now each hand plays a three-note pattern, but the patterns are offset by one eighth note. Play the rest of the passage again, and listen for the remaining changes. Mark these in your score.

As the work proceeds, the length and starting point of patterns continue to change and occasionally become aligned again. In measures 21–22, for example, the patterns are realigned—now in five-note sets in contrary motion. Where patterns align like this, we hear clear accents, although none are notated in the score.

Another innovative approach to traditional notation is taken by George Crumb. While Example 39.6 (from 1969) is notated with a meter, this meter is very hard to perceive without following the score. The passage begins with sustained chords notated with unconventional fermatas—squared off, with a 7 above—indicating that the chord is to be held seven seconds. The changing meter is likewise notated unconventionally, beginning with 7 over a thirty-second note and changing to 7 over a sixty-fourth note (surely all these 7s must have a symbolic quality for Crumb). Perception of these meters is obscured by rests in all parts on nearly every downbeat. The "mirrors" of the song's title are reflected in the vocal part, where each measure is a rhythmic palindrome—the first two are pitch palindromes as well—further obscuring any sense of motion forward in time.

EXAMPLE 39.6: Crumb, "¿Por qué nací entre espejos?," first system

New Approaches to Meter and Polymeter

Even in music that is primarily notated in traditional meters, composers found ways to extend what is possible in metric music. Example 39.7, from William Bolcom's piano etudes (1977-86), shows two notational innovations—one of which is a new type of meter signature Bolcom calls a "relative-time" signature. Bar lines show a basic beat (or *tactus*), and the performer chooses where to place the notated pitches between these beats. The passage begins in $\frac{2}{8}$, with the relative-time signature (the oval) introduced in measure 63. Measure 67 shows pitches beamed together so that the beam grows from one to three, signaling to the performer to play these pitches increasingly rapidly.

EXAMPLE 39.7: Bolcom, *12 New Etudes for Piano*, mvt. 3, mm. 62-69

Some composers after 1945 took a new approach to polymeter (Chapter 35) as well; they created polymeter by assigning different tempi simultaneously to individual parts (with or without different meter signatures). In the third movement of Ligeti's *Hungarian Etudes* (1983), for example, all five choral parts are notated in $\frac{4}{4}$, but in five different tempi: ♩ = 90, 110, 140, 160, and 190. Example 39.8 shows the opening, with the entrances of the chorus 1 bass section at ♩ = 90 and the altos at ♩ = 160. Each part has its own tempo markings and measure numbers. Your class may want to discuss strategies a conductor might consider to keep the choir together!

EXAMPLE 39.8: Ligeti, *Hungarian Etudes*, mvt. 3, mm. 1–7

Translation:
Bass: Cheap apples! Here they are in a heap. Who buys them, eats them. Cheap apples!
Alto: The dog sled runs, it races truly, truly. I am the sled master.

Metric Modulation

Another type of metric music treats tempo in a different way, offering a means to "modulate" between tempi. For an example, listen to the duet "Come now, my darling," from John Corigliano's *The Ghosts of Versailles* (1980-87; anthology), sung by mezzo-soprano Cherubino and soprano Rosina—characters borrowed from Mozart's *The Marriage of Figaro*. (Corigliano's work features an "opera within an opera.") While this duet draws its inspiration from Mozart, its tonal and rhythmic compositional practices are decidedly of our own time. In the opening section, beginning at measure 19, we see and hear changing meters and find that Cherubino is characterized by primarily eighth notes in simple meters. Rosina (whom he is trying to seduce) sings of her fear and anger in contrasting broad quarter-note triplets. Once she gives in to the seduction (m. 50), however, the meter stabilizes in simple quadruple meter, and the two sing without rhythmic conflict.

Example 39.9 shows measures 60-66, near the close of the duet. Listen to the passage, focusing on the effect of the small rhythmic notations above the staff at the end of measures 60 and 61. The first notation, ♩ = ♪, changes nothing in the rhythm except for the beat unit; the duration that was once notated as a quarter is simply renotated as an eighth. The next notation, ♪ = ♪, however, indicates that the triplet subdivision should be reinterpreted as an eighth note, which speeds up the beat unit and tempo. (In mm. 60-62, try tapping the piano right-hand rhythm with your right hand and the beat unit with your left, to feel the tempo change.) This type of rhythmic and tempo change is called a metric modulation.

EXAMPLE 39.9: Corigliano, "Come now, my darling," mm. 60-66 🎧

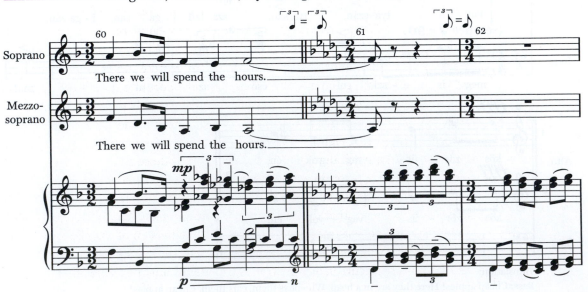

KEY CONCEPT In a **metric modulation**, a note value in one section of music is held constant but reinterpreted (like a "pivot duration") as a new rhythmic value in the next section, which results in a tempo change; for example, the duration of a triplet eighth note in one section is reinterpreted as a sixteenth note in the next.

Metric modulation is more accurately a tempo modulation—a means of smoothing what would otherwise be abrupt changes of tempo by introducing subdivisions or groups of beats in the first tempo that match durations in the new one. The new tempo is recognized in retrospect, much like a modulation by pivot chord.

The composer most often associated with metric modulation is Elliott Carter. Example 39.10, from his String Quartet No. 2 (1959), illustrates the technique in a characteristic way. The quartet begins with a tempo of ♩ = 105. In measure 9, performers need to think about the cello's sixteenth-note subdivisions of the beat as though they are grouped into threes, to make accurate dotted-eighth durations (violin 2) in measure 10. This dotted-eighth pulse is then renotated in the next section at a tempo of ♩ = 140. Between measures 9 and 10, the ♪ = ♪ indicates that the dotted eighths in measure 10 should be equal in duration to three sixteenths, with no change (yet) in the duration of those sixteenths. The dotted eighths become a pivot duration; since there are only three sixteenths per beat instead of four, the beat sounds faster. Then the notation between measures 10 and 11, ♪. = ♩, means that the duration formerly notated as a dotted eighth is now to be represented as a quarter note, restoring the division of each beat into four sixteenths. This makes the ♩ = 140 tempo in measure 11 faster by one-third than the ♩ = 105 in measure 9, but smooths the change from one to the other.

EXAMPLE 39.10: Carter, String Quartet No. 2, mm. 7–13

The pieces presented above represent only a small sampling of the variety of treatments of rhythm, meter, and duration in post-1945 avant-garde composition. Over this time period, a variety of technologies—from early reel-to-reel recording equipment to synthesizers, computers, MIDI sequencers, and other types of digital recording—have made it possible for composers to execute levels of rhythmic complexity and exact control over durations, articulations, and dynamics that would not be possible with human performers.

New Developments in Musical Form and Notation

Time-line, Graphic, and Text Notation

At the beginning of this chapter, we saw an example of a score written with unconventional notation. Example 39.11 provides another, a 1965 composition for solo voice by Luciano Berio; excellent recordings of this piece (some with the score shown) are available online. The text is from a poem by Markus Kutter; the poem itself is in a variable form, where nine short segments can be read in any order. Berio fragments the text into even smaller segments, some of which are single phonemes, indicated by a phonetic symbol.

EXAMPLE 39.11: Berio, *Sequenza III*, first 40 seconds 🎧

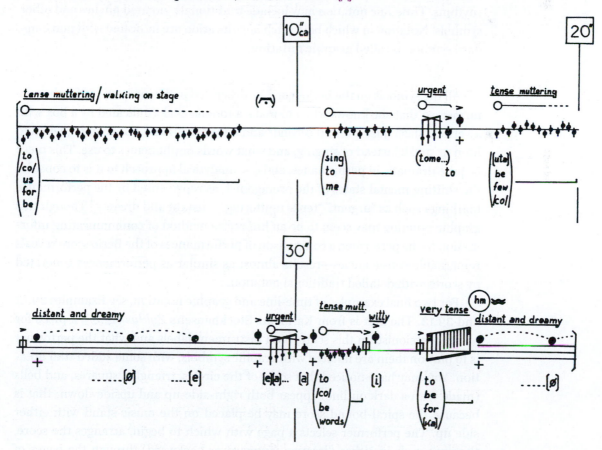

In this score, the relative placement of pitches is shown on a one-, three-, or five-line staff—with the five-line showing precise pitch indications, the three-line indicating intervals that are less precise, and the one-line showing only contour. The piece begins with the performer walking onstage, muttering the syllables in the large parentheses in any order (the black note heads with a small vertical slash indicate that they are to be spoken on different pitches). After a pause (making the first activity last about ten seconds), she repeats the words "sing to me" in any order, before proceeding to "to me to me to" in an ascending pitch contour.

The placement of the events on the time line—represented by numbers across the top of the score—tells the singer when to perform them, as do the notational symbols, some of which have stems and beams.

KEY CONCEPT In **time-line notation**, the passing of time is measured by the number of seconds elapsed between markers (10 seconds, 20 seconds, and so on), and the musical events take place between the markers, resulting in ametric rhythms. Time-line notation may include traditionally notated pitches and other symbols. Notation in which both pitch and duration are indicated with nonstandard symbols is called **graphic notation.**

All the symbols on the Berio score are described in the instructions for the performer, so that she knows when to make a tongue click (indicated by a box with a vertical slash, just after 20 seconds and between 30 and 40 seconds), when to hum or speak instead of singing, and what words or phonemes to use. This piece is quite dramatic in performance, and one analytical approach to it is to consider the shifting mental states of the protagonist, as represented by the performance markings such as "urgent," "tense muttering," "distant and dreamy." Though this graphic notation may seem to be an imprecise method of communicating information to the performer, a comparison of performances of the Berio score reveals remarkable consistencies—results almost as similar as performances generated by scores with detailed traditional notation.

For two final examples of time-line and graphic notation, see Examples 39.12 and 39.13. The first is from Karlheinz Stockhausen's *Zyklus* (1959), a piece for one percussionist. In this score, both instrument labels and what the performer is to play on them are notated with graphic symbols, with some added staff notation. You may have noticed that some of the circles, triangles, squares, and bells (made with a dark outline) appear both right-side-up and upside-down; that is because the spiral-bound score may be placed on the music stand with either side up. The performer selects a page with which to begin, arranges the score, then proceeds in either direction (forward or backward) through the pages of the score until he or she reaches the beginning point. Larger rectangular boxes enclose events that may be played in any order and at any point within the length of the rectangle; those in larger triangles may also be performed in any order, but one of the events must enter where each of the lines indicates.

EXAMPLE 39.12: Stockhausen, *Zyklus*, part of one page (unnumbered pages)

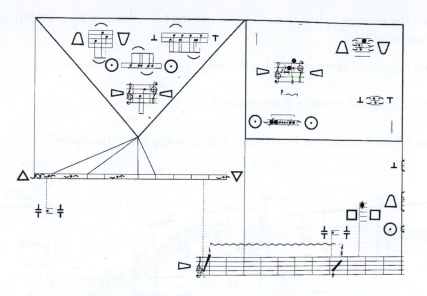

In other works with graphic notation, you may see pitches specified exactly, but without precise durations. For example, a group of pitches may be notated in a box, with instructions to play them in any order, as fast as possible, or with durations of the performer's choosing. Some composers may show note heads with horizontal lines extending from them to indicate that the pitch is held for a long time, without designating the precise duration. Other composers, such as Earle Brown, simply draw the lines representing the pitches, without any indication of clefs or specific placement on the instrument. In Example 39.13, from a 1954 work, the two long thin lines stretching across the top and bottom of the image represent the outer limits of the keyboard, and darker lines in between represent pitch and duration, with the thickness of the line reflecting dynamic levels or clusters. This score may also be played with either side up.

EXAMPLE 39.13: Brown, *Folio and Four Systems*, fourth system

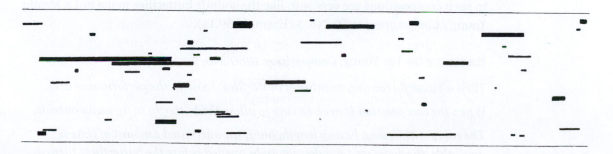

Try it #1

Examine the passage below from Bussotti's string trio *Phrase à Trois* (1960), and listen to a performance online.

(a) What aspects of this score are traditional in their notation and conception?

(b) What is nontraditional in this notation?

(c) What terms described in this chapter might be applied to this score?

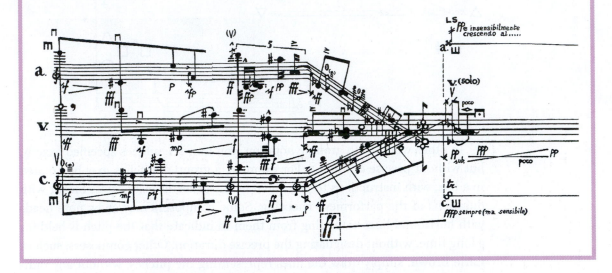

Finally, some pieces composed during the second half of the twentieth century are characterized by **text notation** (or "text scores"): instructions for performing the piece are written in prose or poetry, without any traditional notation at all. Some of these pieces explore the edges of musical performance—extremes of dynamics or instrument ranges, elements of noise, even dance or drama. Some indicate that a passage or a rhythmic pattern is to be played "as fast as possible" or a pitch is to be sustained "as long as possible." Sometimes the sounds produced in such compositions are very soft, like the sounds butterflies make in La Monte Young's *Composition 1960*, No. 5 (Example 39.14).

EXAMPLE 39.14: Young, *Composition 1960*, No. 5

Turn a butterfly (or any number of butterflies) loose in the performance area.

When the composition is over, be sure to allow the butterfly to fly away outside.

The composition may be any length, but if an unlimited amount of time is available, the doors and windows may be opened before the butterfly is turned loose and the composition may be considered finished when the butterfly flies away.

The entire score of John Cage's *4'33"* (1952) is given in Example 39.15. No sounds at all are notated for the performer; the durations for the three movements are intended to total four minutes and thirty-three seconds, but the performer's part is marked "Tacet" (do not play, or be silent). In concert, performers sometimes delineate movements by opening and closing a piano lid, lowering an instrument, or another visual clue. This work raised awareness of the role of silence in music, as well as appreciation for the role of environmental sounds as music.

EXAMPLE 39.15: Cage, *4'33"*

I

Tacet

II

Tacet

III

Tacet

SUMMARY

- Time-line notation: Time is measured by the number of seconds elapsed between markers (e.g., 10 seconds); musical events take place between the markers.

- Graphic notation: Both pitch and duration are indicated with nonstandard symbols, often of the composer's own invention.

- Text notation: Instructions for performing the piece are written in prose or poetry, without any traditional music notation.

Moment Form and Mobile Form

A related development in the second half of the twentieth century was the idea that formal sections of a piece did not have to connect in some logical way or in a predetermined order; compositions could feature abrupt changes from one style of music to another. Rather than hearing a piece as a structured and unified whole, listeners were to hear and enjoy whatever music was sounding at a particular time "in the moment"; hence the term **moment form**. This type of piece is said to have a **nonteleological form** (as opposed to the **teleological**, or goal-directed, structures of traditional tonal music).

A famous example of nonteleological form is Stockhausen's *Klavierstück XI* (1956), which consists of nineteen different independent musical fragments in (for the most part) traditional notation. Two of the fragments are shown in Example 39.16. Tempo, dynamics, and articulation for any given segment are specified at the end of the previous segment; for example, the end of the first segment (top line) specifies tempo 2, *forte*, and a sustained articulation, —. In performance, any one of the fragments may follow any other; the pianist chooses the order according to where his or her eye falls next on the score. (This is Stockhausen's instruction. However, many pianists select their order of segments initially at random, then practice the segments in that same order to prepare the performance. The piece is just too difficult to make formal decisions at sight!)

EXAMPLE 39.16: Stockhausen, *Klavierstück XI*, two segments

Pieces like *Klavierstück XI*, where segments, sections, or movements may be played in varying orders, have what is called a **mobile form**, after artist Alexander Calder's mobile sculptures, whose parts may move into different positions as a result of the wind or a mechanical action. Stockhausen's *Zyklus* and Brown's *Four Systems* display similar mobile aspects. In analyzing a piece with a mobile form, keep in mind the possible permutations of sections or segments. While the contents of segments may remain consistent from one performance to another, the overall organization of the piece will not.

SUMMARY

- Moment form is intended to be nonteleological, with each section to be appreciated in the moment—without expectation of, or desire for, formal repetition or goals.

- In works with mobile form, sections can be performed in varied orders, following instructions given by the composer or based on performer decisions.

Indeterminacy and Chance

Musical innovations after 1945 extended to the compositional process itself.

KEY CONCEPT **Indeterminate** pieces, composed primarily after 1950, incorporate some elements that either are not specified by the composer or are selected by chance.

Some chance procedures involve a mechanical action by the composer or performer (such as throwing dice or flipping coins to make musical decisions), while others are more serendipitous (turning on a radio and including whatever sounds it happens to be making at the time, whether tuned to a station or not). There are several terms associated with mechanical randomization: in music by American composers like John Cage, these are known as **chance operations**; for European composers like Karlheinz Stockhausen, they are known as **aleatoric procedures** (from the Latin word *alea*, which means "dice") and the music as aleatoric music. All these procedures belong to the more general principle of indeterminacy.

Indeterminacy is not really new in the twentieth century—in Mozart's time, musicians played dice games in which music was composed by a random selection of phrase beginnings and endings (indeterminacy of composition). Further, any realization of a figured bass required choices on the part of the performer that could result in different voicings of chords (indeterminacy of performance). Indeed, all music has an element of indeterminacy: performers must make many choices as they bring the notated music to life. You can think of indeterminacy on a continuum, with indeterminate compositions from the post–World War II era actually focusing on relinquishing control as an organizing feature.

Compositions in graphic scores, text notation, or mobile form often include a degree of indeterminacy in their performance. Some graphic scores, like Penderecki's *Threnody*, represent the tasks of the performer as accurately as (or even more accurately than) a traditionally notated piece; others leave much room for interpretation. Consider the piece *In the Woods* (1975), by Kenneth Maue, reproduced in Example 39.17.

EXAMPLE 39.17: Maue, *In the Woods*

Begin in the morning. Bring some lunch, four large discs of day-glo paper, some thumbtacks, and some tape. Choose a roughly rectangular or circular area of solid woods.

Enter the woods at different locations along the periphery. Start walking in any direction. Sometimes move toward specific locations; sometimes just wander here and there; sometimes follow streams or paths, sometimes bushwhack; sometimes just sit.

As you walk around, find places to tack or tape your day-glo discs, in such a way that they can be seen by other players as they walk by. And be on the lookout for other players' discs. When you come across one, take it down, carry it for a while, then put it in a new location for someone else to find.

In the middle of the day, find each other by making noises. Make noise by any available means. Make sounds and listen. Move toward sounds you hear. When everyone has gathered together, have lunch. Then set out again, each in a different direction. This time, when you find a disc, take it down and keep it. After the day seems to be ending, make your way to the periphery, and wait to be picked up by a car.

This piece, surprisingly enough, does have a consistent form that is comparable to traditional forms. There is a setting out (the first section), which lasts all morning; a span of time where performers are making noises to assemble (the middle section), which concludes with the eating of lunch together; and a return to the periphery (a final section), which takes all afternoon and is similar to the beginning section. The overall form is thus ternary: **A B A′** . *In the Woods* reminds us that each piece must be approached on its own terms. A score's appearance does not always indicate the presence or absence of form.

Surely by this point some of you are arguing, "This isn't music." Yet a definition of music contemporaneous with this piece is "Music is organized sound." There are indeed sounds in this piece, organized in such a way that any accurate performance should be recognizable as *In the Woods*. Musicians must choose for themselves how to define "music."

Minimalism and Form as Process

Beginning in the 1960s, some composers reacted to the extremes of integral serialism by composing pieces in a style known as **minimalism**, in which each piece was created from a "minimum" of musical materials. La Monte Young's *Composition 1960* (Example 39.14) is an example of an early minimalist piece. Other works feature the incessant repetition of pitches (usually from a diatonic collection) that change gradually over time. In these latter pieces—sometimes called "process pieces" and preferred in the 1960s by composers Terry Riley, Philip Glass, and Steve Reich—the gradual changes involve a process that, once started, must run to completion. For example, Riley's *In C* requires a group of players to move through a set of fifty-three melodic patterns, repeating each one for a while before proceeding to the next. (The first four patterns are shown in Example 39.18.) Each player chooses when to start a new pattern and how long to repeat the old one, but must stay with the group, so that all players move through the score within a few patterns of each other, creating a gradually changing musical kaleidoscope.

EXAMPLE 39.18: Riley, *In C*, first four patterns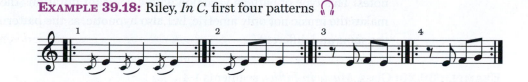

Several of Steve Reich's compositions from the 1960s draw on the idea of **phasing**: patterns moving in and out of alignment, creating additional sounds and patterns not present in the score. Reich discovered this effect by accident, when trying to get two reel-to-reel tape players to play copies of the same tape in synchronization (nearly impossible with the equipment he had). His composition *Piano Phase*, an excerpt of which is given in Example 39.19, begins with one pianist playing a repeated melodic pattern. A second pianist joins with the same pattern, in synchronization, then gradually accelerates until his or her part is one pitch off from the original aligned pairing. The process of pattern repetition, acceleration, and realignment one pitch off continues until the two parts are once more aligned.

Listen to the first section of *Piano Phase* (anthology). While listening, concentrate on the rhythmic and pitch patterns that emerge from the pairings of the two parts and the approach of the alignment at the end of the section. In a piece like this one, when the process is complete, the section (or whole composition) is also complete—the process defines the overall form.

EXAMPLE 39.19: Reich, *Piano Phase*, first three patterns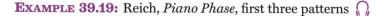

In *Music in Fifths* (Example 39.20), Philip Glass introduces a different pattern-manipulation technique. Pattern 2 repeats pattern 1 (thirteen eighth notes doubled at the fifth), but then varies the pattern in an additional eight eighth notes. This type of pattern variation with a constant duration (the eighth note) makes the music not only ametric, but also hypnotic, as the patterns sound both the same and different.

EXAMPLE 39.20: Glass, *Music in Fifths*, segments 1-4

Try it #2

Examine the passage in Example 39.20, and listen to a performance online.

A. How does pattern 3 relate to patterns 1 and 2?

B. How does pattern 4 relate to the preceding patterns?

Analyzing Form in Recent Music

Among the basic form-defining elements in the musics we have studied are repetition and contrast—involving key areas, motives, themes, or even types of musical activity (exposition, transition, or development). In more recent music, as we have seen, it is possible to create formal closure without functional tonality by incorporating other elements that help make a point of repose: a slowing of musical activity, a stop on a longer duration than normal, a rest that breaks the musical flow, a contrapuntal ending on a unison or octave or some other stable interval.

One of the challenges of analyzing form in recent music is that there is such a wide range of possibilities. If you examine the first movement of a Beethoven sonata, you have a good idea of what form to expect. On the other hand, music after 1945 tends to be less predictable. The starting point for any formal analysis is listening to the piece enough times that you can clearly hear it in your head—then attempting to explain what you hear. As you study and perform more repertoire from this era, you will become better able to predict which elements of style and form a composer will choose. While comparing form in nontonal pieces with tonal conventions is sometimes useful, be cautious in making these comparisons. Consider which elements of the piece are traditional in some way, but also the effect of nontraditional elements. Treat the examples in this chapter as an introduction, then move on to discover the formal processes in the contemporary pieces that you play or study.

When you perform contemporary music with traditional notation, you should execute the rhythms as precisely as possible. You may have to work carefully with a sequence of durations to get the timing exactly right, and also with the meter (if present) to get the metric accents correct. Familiarity and careful practice are key. For post-1945 pieces with unusual notation, composers often provide an explanation in either the individual parts or the score. As with any piece of music you are preparing for performance, it is essential to understand all the score notation to realize the piece correctly. These pieces can be very interesting to play—don't let unfamiliar notation keep you from learning a new work!

Did You Know?

The 1950s to mid-1970s were a time of great experimentation in music. In the years immediately following World War II, a new generation of European and American composers and performers—including Milton Babbitt, Luciano Berio, John Cage, György Ligeti, Olivier Messiaen, Luigi Nono, and Karlheinz Stockhausen—gathered in Germany at the Internationale Ferienkurse für Neue Musik, Darmstadt (Darmstadt International Summer Courses for New Music) to study new and early twentieth-century compositions (among them works of Webern and Schoenberg), and receive instruction in serialism and atonal composition. Though the instruction focused on the modernist styles prevalent in Europe before the war, composers from this group were also innovators in the development of electronic music, indeterminacy, and other postwar styles.

In the United States during the 1950s, New York City was one of the sites of musical innovation. During this time, John Cage taught at the New School for Social Research; among the students who audited his course was a young Yoko Ono—who later became a well-known public figure after marrying Beatle John Lennon. Ono had previously studied serial composition at Sarah Lawrence College, but found it limiting. Her compositions were influenced by Cage and by Eastern philosophies; among the text pieces included in her book *Grapefruit* is one that instructs the performer to play a note in the woods at dawn, accompanied by birdsong. Ono performed with both La Monte Young and John Cage, and is pictured on the cover of one of Cage's albums, lying across the strings of an open piano while the composer strikes the strings around her.

TERMS YOU SHOULD KNOW

aleatoric music
chance operations
graphic notation
indeterminacy
metric modulation

minimalism
mobile form
moment form
nonteleological form
phasing

pitch symmetry
teleological form
text notation
time-line notation

QUESTIONS FOR REVIEW

1. Name three innovations in rhythmic notation developed in music after 1945.
2. How does metric modulation work? With which composers is this technique associated?
3. How is closure achieved in pattern-repetition pieces?
4. Give two examples of indeterminacy in music composition and/or performance.
5. If a piece contains indeterminate elements, is its form also indeterminate? Explain.
6. In music for your own instrument, find one piece that incorporates indeterminacy, graphic notation, or text notation. (The date of composition can help you locate a piece of each type; ask your teacher for assistance, if needed.)

Know It? Show It!

Focus by working through the tutorials.

Learn with InQuizitive.

Apply what you've learned to complete the workbook assignments.

40

Recent Trends

Overview

This chapter considers some of the many compositional methods twenty-first century composers have at their disposal, from all historical eras.

Repertoire

Chen Yi, "Shan Ge," from *Three Bagatelles from China West*

John Corigliano, "Come now, my darling," from *The Ghosts of Versailles*

György Kurtág, from *Six Moments musicaux*, Op. 44: "Invocatio" ("Invocation") and ". . . rappel des oiseaux" ("Remembrance of Birds")

György Ligeti, "Désordre," from *Piano Etudes*, Book I

Arvo Pärt, *Magnificat*

Steve Reich
City Life
Proverb

Tōru Takemitsu, *Rain Tree Sketch*

Ellen Taaffe Zwilich, "Arlecchino," from *Commedia dell'Arte*

Outline

Contemporary composers and techniques of the past
- Materials from the pretonal era
- Materials from the Baroque, Classical, and Romantic periods
- Materials from the twentieth century

A look ahead

Contemporary Composers and Techniques of the Past

For most of the recorded history of Western music (or any music, for that matter), specific styles were associated with composers in their particular locations and time. These styles usually included (1) slightly older compositional methods practiced by traditionalists and the somewhat old-fashioned composers (these formed the bulk of what composers were taught); (2) the current style, practiced by those in vogue; and (3) the beginnings of a new style—whatever came next. For example, when J. S. Bach (1685-1750) was young, he was trained in the traditional styles of the late seventeenth century, including modal counterpoint and church music. As his career progressed, he incorporated newer ideas and developed his mature style, which included complex tonal counterpoint and pieces written in all twenty-four major and minor keys. Late in his life, his own compositions were considered old-fashioned by his sons and others writing in the new "galant" style.

From the early twentieth century through the 1970s, particular art-music styles came to be in vogue and others (such as functional tonality) were rejected, even though some composers still wrote in these older styles. The conflict of the **modernist** aesthetic—espoused by composers such as Schoenberg, Stravinsky, Bartók, and later Stockhausen and Babbitt—was to turn away from the past while at the same time venerating it. Modernist composers adopted the novel, scientific, mathematical, and revolutionary, yet wished to be considered the successors to the great musical masters of the past.

In the last decades of the twentieth century, this tendency changed. Both popular and art music began to draw more freely on earlier musical practices, creating a new style by combining materials from different times. This style is sometimes referred to as **postmodernism**, a term borrowed from literary and art criticism. As a result, the composer's materials today can include everything known from previous eras.

KEY CONCEPT Modernist compositions are unified in style and compositional methodology, while postmodern compositions may borrow from and combine multiple styles. Style juxtaposition, stylistic allusions, quotation, parody, and intertextuality (defined below) are associated with postmodern style.

Our fast-paced, information-age society is reflected in **style juxtaposition**: elements strongly associated with one style or musical culture appear side by side with another type of music without a transition between the two, or any attempt to reconcile the differences. Some pieces include literal **quotations** or **stylistic allusions** to works of other composers (both contemporaneous and from previous centuries) that are intended to be recognized by the listener; others employ

parody, where elements of previous styles are distorted or exaggerated for comic effect, again with the intent that listeners will make the connection and get the joke. Quotation, allusion, and parody are not new techniques, but recent compositions take them to extremes, juxtaposing radically different musical styles. These are all elements of **intertextuality**, the propensity of "texts" to communicate with and comment on each other: for newer texts to reference older ones, and for older texts to be reinterpreted in the presence of newer ones. The term "texts" here refers broadly to various types of artistic creations—not only prose and poetry, but also musical works, dance, visual art, plays, and movies or other video productions—any of which can be connected through intertextual relationships.

In the 1970s, composers also began to reemploy tonal materials: triads, melody and motivic development, regular beat and meter, consonant sonorities, and diatonic scales and collections. Of course, those materials were present through the entire century in a wide variety of popular and folk musics, and in works of some art-music composers, but they had been out of fashion in the mainstream modernist community. The resurgence of interest in older materials, though, did not mean a wholesale return to writing music that could be mistaken for that of an earlier century. Tavener's "The Lamb" (Chapter 38), for example, alternates serial passages with functional tonal sections.

Today's composers usually pick and choose among the older elements, making new music that features elements of the past—whether the recent past of the last few years, or the long past of the medieval or Renaissance eras. Their music is, for the most part, clearly "contemporary"—bearing the mark of the experimentation of the previous fifty years—even when it incorporates materials from earlier eras. In this chapter, we examine works inspired by compositional styles of the past. Consider it an introduction and a stimulus to further study. After all, the meaning and significance of many of the techniques considered here, especially those of the past quarter century, will not be fully understood until more time has passed and historical distance has clarified them.

Materials from the Pretonal Era

In the medieval and Renaissance eras, limited communications, a lack of printing facilities, and difficult travel conditions restricted musicians' knowledge of music to what was available in their native locales. Musicians today are not so restricted; in fact, by the end of the twentieth century, more was known about Western music written before 1650 than at any previous time, including the time when the music was originally composed. Partly as a result, the last century saw an upsurge of interest in historically accurate performance practice. This interest was backed by detailed research into traditions of composition and performance, the restoration of old instruments and the production of new "historical" instruments, as well as the publication of editions, translations, and treatises that describe "how it was done at the time." New recording technology has made it possible for pieces preserved in centuries-old manuscripts to be performed and distributed worldwide, and for today's listeners to appreciate their beauty. Who would have thought that one of the best-selling CDs of art music in the 1990s would be a recording of monks singing medieval chant? Yet that was the case.

One piece that draws on pretonal ideas is Steve Reich's *Proverb* (1995), a work for three sopranos, two tenors, two vibraphones, and two samplers or electronic organs, based on a text from the twentieth-century philosopher Ludwig Wittgenstein. The piece begins with a single soprano voice singing, "How small a thought it takes to fill a whole life . . . how small a thought" (Example 40.1). The soprano is soon joined by a second soprano, singing the same melody in canon. Perform the passage with your class or listen to a recording, and think of analytical questions you can ask and answer about this excerpt.

EXAMPLE 40.1: Reich, *Proverb*, mm. 1–22 (sopranos 1 and 2)

To analyze this passage, consider what we learned previously about older types of counterpoint, such as fugue and invention, combined with the effects of newer techniques like changing and asymmetrical meters.

Try it #1

Examine the passage from Reich's *Proverb* given in Example 40.1.

A. Into how many phrases and subphrases does the initial melody divide (mm. 1-11)? _____
   How do the subphrases relate to each other?

B. On the staff below, write out the pitch collection for measures 1-11 and determine its
   tonal/modal scale type and center.

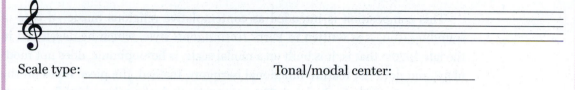

Scale type: _____   Tonal/modal center: _____

C. List the type of durations used. Why do you think Reich placed the bar lines where he did?
   How do the rhythms correspond to the phrases and subphrases?

   Duration values:

D. In the canonic passage (beginning in m. 12), what is the interval of time between entries?
   _____ On the example, write the harmonic intervals created by the counterpoint.

Although the haunting spirit of medieval plainchant continues to be present in Reich's counterpoint, the clashing half-step harmonic intervals produced by the time-delayed canonic voices and the changing asymmetric meters in which they are notated clearly mark this piece as a product of the twentieth century. The entire work combines contrapuntal techniques and an *a cappella* singing style that are almost a thousand years old with a text that is not much more than fifty years old, electronic organs (a familiar sound of the 1960s), and vibraphones (a percussion instrument invented in the early twentieth century).

A second piece that evokes the sounds of an earlier era is Arvo Pärt's *Magnificat* (1989). An excerpt is shown in Example 40.2; listen to or sing it with your class.

EXAMPLE 40.2: Pärt, *Magnificat*, mm. 5-12

Translation: And my spirit hath rejoiced in God my savior.

This composition is intended as contemplative religious music—a type of sounding icon. It is written in Pärt's *tintinnabuli* style, which he developed in the late 1970s: that is, it is built on a modal scale, is homophonic, does not modulate, and does not feature functional harmony. Instead, the piece relies on the resonance available in the triad. The primary melodic line (bass in this excerpt) is diatonic and generally moves by step, with occasional skips emphasizing accented words; the accompanying lines fill in the chord members of the primary triad of the work, F minor (F-A♭-C), or provide stepwise motion between members of the triad. The only dissonances are those occasionally created between a melody pitch and the triad, and they are not "resolved" in a traditional fashion, but dissipate as the melody moves to a chord tone.

Both pieces call for the "pure," vibrato-less singing style revived in the twentieth century for the performance of early music. In the *Magnificat*, singers are to listen carefully, blending to make pure triadic intervals—the resonant triads of the overtone series—rather than the slightly adjusted intervals of the equal-tempered chromatic scale. This blending gives Pärt's works their characteristic bell-like sound. Both the Reich and Pärt selections are "minimalist" in their use of a limited palette of compositional materials, but they are very different in sound from the pattern-repetition minimalist compositions examined in Chapter 39.

In addition to modal scales and counterpoint from the Renaissance, some recent composers have adopted the oldest types of contrapuntal cadences, such as contracting in to a unison or expanding out to an octave. Chant and monophonic techniques have been borrowed, as well as practices like **isorhythm** (a repeated series of durations combined with a repeated melodic idea; see, for example, Nono's *Il canto sospeso* or Messiaen's *Quartet for the End of Time*) and **quodlibet** (multiple texts, usually not all in the same language).

The idea of writing a piece without specifying the precise instrumentation (for example, Riley's *In C*, from Chapter 39) has also been adapted from earlier practice. Tunings other than equal temperament found their way into pieces from mid-century on, influenced by both non-Western and Western sources. Early works with alternative tunings, like those by American composers Harry Partch and Lou Harrison, were performed with handmade instruments or with altered fingerings or performance techniques on traditional instruments, but later composers used synthesizers and electronic means to create variant tunings. These composers also explored **microtonal tunings**, which include intervals smaller than a semitone, such as a quarter-tone or smaller.

SUMMARY

Compositional ideas from the medieval and Renaissance periods that are employed in some late twentieth- and early twenty-first century music include

- modal counterpoint and scales,
- imitation and canon,
- quodlibet (multiple texts),
- nonmetered rhythm, isorhythm, and
- non-equal-tempered tunings.

Materials from the Baroque, Classical, and Romantic Periods

Among the materials composers have borrowed from Baroque, Classical, and Romantic styles are traditional forms (binary, ternary, and sonata) and genres (concertos, sonatas, symphonies, and variation sets); traditional phrase structure and cadences; triads, seventh chords, and diatonic collections (often in a nonfunctional setting); tonal counterpoint, including fugue and canon; symmetrical meters and rhythms that reinforce them; motivic development and melodic embellishment; and functional tonal harmony and dissonance treatment. Elements of Romantic style—from lush orchestration to the use of recurring motives like Wagner's leitmotivs (to represent a person, action, idea, or place)—have appeared throughout the twentieth century in pieces that are not in a Romantic style overall.

Quotations from older pieces or stylistic allusions—newly composed music intended to capture the style of an older composer—while not a new idea, are prominent in some postmodern works. One example, as we have seen, is John Corigliano's opera *The Ghosts of Versailles*, which blends newly composed "faux Mozart" with characters and plot elements taken from operas by Mozart and Rossini (and references to quite a few other styles) into a work that clearly sounds like music of the late twentieth century. Listen to measures 1-72 of "Come now, my darling," while following the score in your anthology.

The setting is a flashback to Mozart's *The Marriage of Figaro*, where Cherubino, a young man of the Count's household (actually the singer is a mezzo-soprano, in a "pants" role), is seducing Rosina, the Count's wife. Two excerpts from this scene are given in Examples 40.3 and 40.4.

EXAMPLE 40.3: Corigliano, "Come now, my darling," mm. 10-13

Try it #2

A. How do the tonal harmonies in Example 40.3, including the key and mode, express Rosina's reluctance? Consider the key Cherubino is singing in at the beginning of the excerpt, and the key in which Rosina enters, then identify the harmonies.

B. What rhythmic and metrical aspects of Rosina's music indicate her internal conflict?

Example 40.4 exhibits many features that are associated with Mozart's music—the two-measure symmetrical subphrases, melodic style, chord choices, and keyboard right-hand figuration patterns. Indeed, the melody bears a striking resemblance to the beginning of Mozart's "Voi, che sapete," also sung by Cherubino (see anthology). Yet this duet could not be mistaken for one from Mozart's time. The changes of key and meter that come later in the passage are too extreme.

EXAMPLE 40.4: Corigliano, "Come now, my darling," mm. 38–41

The Ghosts of Versailles also includes "ghost music" reminiscent of Penderecki, an aria with Middle Eastern influences, and elements of musical stage productions from Rossini to Wagner to Broadway. In some ways, the scope and scale of this contemporary work resembles the grand operas of the Romantic period more than those of Mozart. Corigliano's opera is richly intertextual, and the listener's pleasure is enhanced if he or she recognizes these older styles.

The question of intertextuality is particularly interesting in the case of composer Ellen Taaffe Zwilich. In the 1970s and 1980s, at a time when most other composers were abandoning genre-based names for their works, Zwilich's traditional titles stood out (trumpet concerto, symphony, etc.). In contrast, many of her recent works for traditional ensembles have evocative names: *Rituals* (for five percussionists and orchestra, 2003), *Shadows* (Piano Concerto No. 3, 2011), *Voyage* (String Quartet No. 3, 2012), and *Peanuts® Gallery* (six pieces for pianist and orchestra based on the cartoons of Charles Schulz, 1999). Zwilich describes the earlier works as being "in conversation" with other concertos, symphonies, and string quartets that she knew well as an orchestral violinist. The inspiration for more recent works comes from extra-musical references—images, ideas, places, historical events, and characters. Unlike Corigliano's opera, Zwilich's works can be considered modernist, in that they are consistent in style and are nontonal. A limited number of motives introduced at the beginning of a movement establish the musical parameters within which the movement operates, an approach favored by Schoenberg and other early twentieth-century composers.

For an example of Zwilich's use of motives to create a character, consider "Arlecchino," from her 2012 *Commedia dell'Arte* (Example 40.5). Arlecchino, or Harlequin, is one of the comic servants (others include Pierrot, Pulcinella, Pagliacci, and Columbina) in the commedia's stock of characters. In an interview in advance of the premiere, Zwilich described Arlecchino as an acrobat who is "very active" and "all over the place"; one of his physical gestures consisted of "a kind of squat, then a jump up," which she represented musically through melodic and rhythmic motives (see the violin 1 and cello parts in mm. 5-7 and 9-10). Examine Example 40.5 with this character and motion in mind; pay attention also to the pitch materials, which seem to make tonal allusions but resist the establishment of a clear key or collection.

EXAMPLE 40.5: Zwilich, "Arlecchino," mm. 1-15

*all eighth notes in the string orchestra: short, but not staccato

This brief orchestral introduction consists of pitch class A sharply rearticulated in five octaves, alternating with slapstick (a percussion instrument made of thin slabs of wood that make a sharp "crack" when slapped together). Measures 5-11 introduce three intervallic motives associated with Arlecchino: (1) a minor-third alternation (A and C, doubled in octaves in the violins and cellos, mm. 5-7), implying $\hat{1}$ and $\hat{3}$ in A minor; (2) a tritone (A-E♭, $\hat{1}$ to ♭$\hat{5}$/♯$\hat{4}$, mm. 6 and 9-10); and (3) the motive of a half step and a whole step filling a minor third (WH or HW; E♭-D-C in mm. 6-7 and 10 and C-B-A in m. 9).

Pitch class A continues to be reinforced through measures 6-11, though the pitch-class collection of 9-10 hints at a possible octatonic reading (all pcs except the initial E are from OCT 23). The last orchestral stroke in measure 11 brings in five octaves of E—suggesting $\hat{5}$ in A major or minor, confirmed by the violin solo arpeggiating an A major triad (m. 13), then an A minor one (m. 14). The end of the violin melody encircles E6, embedding two HW motives (G-F♯-E and F♯-E-E♭).

Altogether, the three motives in measures 5-15 hint at A minor or an octatonic context but confirm neither of these, as both E♭ (octatonic) and E (diatonic) are emphasized.

This entire movement is built on the motives with which it began (though they travel through a variety of implied key areas); although there are no strongly contrasting sections, an extraordinary variety of scales and embellishments in the solo violin and the lively tempo maintain interest throughout. This is entirely in keeping with the commedia character Arlecchino, who makes up for a limited number of gestures with unpredictable changes of direction, acrobatic skill, and comic timing.

SUMMARY

Elements from the Baroque, Classical, and Romantic periods that may be found in recent music include

- traditional forms and genres,

- phrase structure and cadences,

- contrapuntal writing,

- symmetrical meters and the rhythmic patterns associated with them,

- motivic development and melodic embellishment,

- dissonance treatment derived from tonal styles.

Materials from the Twentieth Century

The composer's materials from the first half of the twentieth century include many of the techniques covered in Chapters 33-39: octatonic, pentatonic, whole-tone, and other nondiatonic scale materials; harmonies built on intervals other than thirds; pitch-class sets and serialism; and rhythmic innovations such as changing meters, asymmetrical meters, and ametric music. At the same time, they may also include the innovations of early jazz, the song forms of the Broadway musical, and elements of post-1950s popular music.

The second half of the century saw an increasing emphasis on timbre, rhythm, and electronic media—some pieces require a stage full of percussion instruments and others feature computer-manipulated sound, samplers, and video. Such timbres as environmental noises, speech, and electronically produced sounds were considered fair game, along with extended techniques on traditional instruments. World music influences have brought new ways of looking at time and rhythm, from the patterns of the Balinese gamelan to those of West African drumming. After their absence in avant-garde music for much of the century, a regular beat and traditional meter also found their way back into art music in the 1980s and

1990s, as we saw in Corigliano's *The Ghosts of Versailles*. In the last few decades, composers have combined these techniques in an astonishing variety of ways.

The *Six Moments musicaux* for string quartet by György Kurtág (2005) reflect the compositional diversity that can be explored in a single multi-movement work. Each movement is quite distinct from the others. The first includes a "hoquetus" (hocket) passage (Example 40.6) that is reminiscent of both Ligeti's *Ten Pieces for Wind Quintet* (Example 39.2) and Penderecki's *Threnody* (rehearsal number 18). (A hocket is the medieval practice of two alternating voices made to sound like a single line.) The entrances of the sustained tones—though marked ***ppp***—are accented, and in this way make a "hidden" melody, highlighted by the composer on the lowest staff.

EXAMPLE 40.6: Kurtág, "Invocatio," mm. 17-23

In Example 40.7, from the fifth movement, Kurtág creates the bird calls of the title by combining extended instrumental techniques with changing meter, a dance rhythm—described by the composer as "like a type of dance [habanera, etc.]"—and birdlike rhythms (m. 6, violin 2). The diamond-shaped open note heads are artificial harmonics: Roman numerals tell the performer where to touch the string so that the tone will sound up two octaves. Where a black note head is given below the diamond one (e.g., mm. 6-7, cello), the performer presses that note firmly down to shorten the string, then lightly touches the diamond note to produce a pitch two octaves above the black note. The little "o" symbols above a note head (m. 11, cello) indicate natural harmonics, which sound up one octave from the indicated note. Getting all of these harmonics to sound clearly with the given tempo of ♩ = 92 is quite a challenge! For the analyst (or performer), listening carefully (for the role of each instrument) and deciphering the visually complex score are first steps. The two violins, for example, are paired with similar gestures that begin with an ascending M6, while the viola and cello have more sustained tones, with syncopations of the Spanish habanera.

EXAMPLE 40.7: Kurtág, " . . . rappel des oiseaux . . . ," mm. 6-13

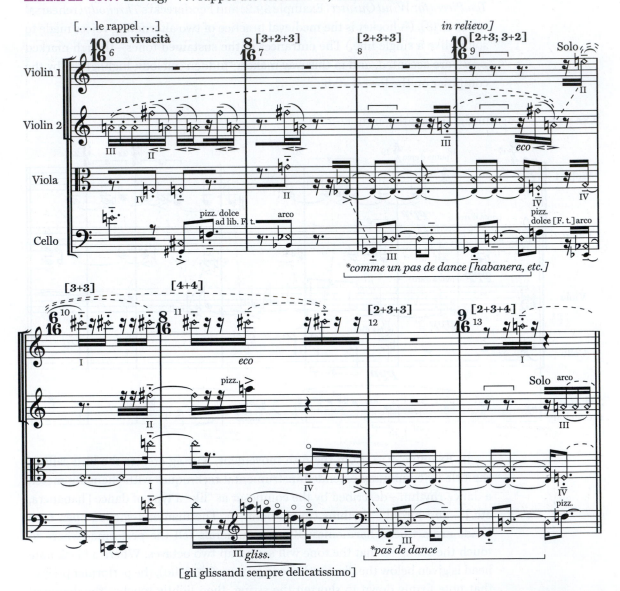

Ligeti's piano piece "Désordre" is an example of rhythmic eclecticism that includes non-Western influences (Example 40.8). At the time the piece was written (1985), Ligeti was very interested in the cross rhythms of African drumming, evidenced here by the shifting downbeats between hands after measure 4. His music also borrows rhythmic and metrical practices from Bartók (for example, the opening 3 + 5 grouping of eighth notes), and mimimalist pattern repetition from the 1960s.

EXAMPLE 40.8: Ligeti, "Désordre," mm. 1-9

Another composer combining Western compositional techniques with elements of non-Western styles is Chinese composer Chen Yi. Chen's works often incorporate traditional Chinese instruments like the pipa (a four-stringed fretted plucked lute), and many of her works for Western ensembles or instruments reference the melodies and accompaniments of Chinese folk songs.

In the excerpt from "Shan Ge" (2007; Example 40.9), the "long" measures for solo flute (mm. 6 and 10) evoke the pitch characteristics and performance style of the folk melody "Shan'ge Diao." The piano accompaniment was inspired by music for the *lusheng* (a type of mouth organ) ensembles of the Miao people, a minority group in Southwest China. (There are performances of both the folk song and *lusheng* ensembles available online, as well as performances of Chen Yi's arrangements of the piece in a different instrumentation so that you can compare the sound.)

EXAMPLE 40.9: Chen, "Shan Ge," mm. 6-13

Minimalism continues to serve as an active compositional resource in recent music, although in the hands of some composers it has became more "maximal," with larger ensembles contributing to a busier texture. Others have made minimalist music less obviously repetitive. A 1995 piece by Steve Reich, *City Life*, illustrates the first of these trends. In the first movement—scored for two flutes, two oboes, two clarinets, two pianos, two samplers (which play digitized snippets of recorded sounds), percussion, string quartet, and string bass—a recording of a New York street vender saying "Check it out" provides the primary rhythmic idea. Other movements bring in car horns, sirens, door slams, heartbeats, a pile driver, and speech samples from the New York City Fire Department's field communications on February 26, 1993, the day the basement of the World Trade Center was bombed—all treated as musical sounds and incorporated into the texture. Pattern repetition is a significant element in this piece, but the texture is much thicker, with a variety of layers combining to make a wall of sound. The excerpt in Example 40.10 includes some of the instrumental motives derived from the "Check it out" rhythm.

EXAMPLE 40.10: Reich, *City Life*, mvt. 1, mm. 30-35

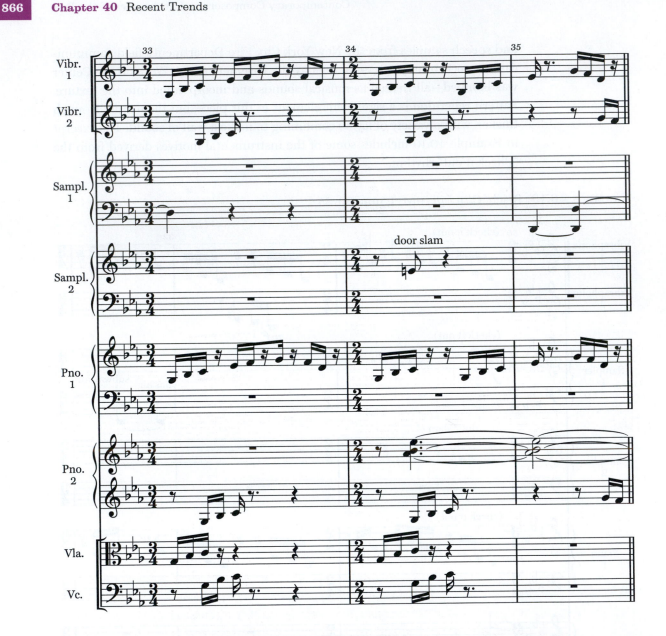

In many pieces written at the end of the century, the materials are so well integrated that their origin is not easy to determine. For example, Japanese composer Tōru Takemitsu, while primarily trained in Western compositional techniques, incorporates some elements of Japanese aesthetics. In Example 40.11, the Japanese concept of *ma* (space or gap) is illustrated in measure 6, where a pause is written in. For listeners, it is not obvious that there is a notated rest; rather, the little span of time allows them to absorb the musical thoughts that preceded the pause, to wonder what might follow, or simply to enjoy the brief absence of sound. Takemitsu's works are often evocative of Debussy, Ravel, and

Messiaen in their harmonies and rhythms, yet they bring to mind images of a Japanese garden—nature, balance, and calmness. Like many end-of-century works, his resist labeling; they do not belong to any one compositional practice.

EXAMPLE 40.11: Takemitsu, *Rain Tree Sketch*, mm. 1-6

A Look Ahead

Although it is impossible for us to know what changes in music lie ahead as the twenty-first century progresses, one thing that seems clear is that performers, composers, conductors, and music teachers will be expected to know more than ever about music of the past. All the styles of music discussed in this book are continuing to be studied and performed, a state of affairs that is unlikely to change. Musicians need to know the conventions of each period represented in their repertoire, and to apply these conventions in a stylistic and musical performance.

Your studies have just begun. The process of becoming a musician is a life's task, not something accomplished in a few semesters of a two-year theory curriulum, or even in an entire undergraduate course of study. What you should have acquired now, though, is a firm foundation for continuing your studies. Be curious, take more courses, and above all, perform and investigate music of many styles and periods. We are lucky to live, and to be able to make music, in the twenty-first century—everything is open to us. Enjoy and explore!

Did You Know?

Only since 1983 have any women won the prestigious Pulitzer Prize for Music, and the number of active female composers is a fraction of the number of male composers, as reflected in these chapters. Before the twentieth century, women who were composers mostly learned their craft growing up in a musical household, where siblings and/or parents were musicians. For example, Clara Schumann began learning piano and composition at an early age from her father, Friedrich Wieck, who also taught her future husband Robert Schumann; and Fanny Mendelssohn Hensel studied with the same musical tutors as her younger brother Felix. Even when educational opportunities were available, women were not expected to work as composers or performers, and most who succeeded against societal pressures were equipped with both self-determination and the strong support of a father or husband.

As educational opportunities expanded for women in the twentieth century, additional paths into composition and performance became available. It became possible for women to take composition lessons at women's colleges and universities in the early part of the century, and later they studied in the same classes as men. Though still outnumbered by men, there are more successful women composers today than ever before—including Ellen Taaffe Zwilich, the first woman to receive the Pulitzer Prize (1983). Other women whose work has been recognized by the Pulitzer board include winners Shulamit Ran (1991), Melinda Wagner (1999), Jennifer Higdon (2010), Caroline Shaw (2013), and Julia Wolfe (2015); and finalists Vivian Fine (1983), Joan Tower (1993), Chen Yi (2006), and Augusta Read Thomas (2007). Two more composers featured in this chapter, John Corigliano (2001) and Steve Reich (2009), have also won the award. Visit individual composers' websites to hear samples of their work.

TERMS YOU SHOULD KNOW

intertextuality	parody	quotation
isorhythm	postmodernism	style juxtaposition
microtonal tunings	quodlibet	stylistic allusion
modernism		

QUESTIONS FOR REVIEW

1. For each piece discussed in this chapter, make a list of elements in the music that are based on older styles, and a list of elements that indicate the piece is contemporary.
2. What aspects of counterpoint do you find in these compositions?
3. How would you determine if a piece that features triads has functional tonality?
4. What are some characteristics of rhythm and meter in the works discussed here?
5. What elements of minimalism are found in works in this chapter?
6. Find a piece of contemporary music for your own instrument that draws on stylistic elements of an earlier era. (Confer with your instrumental teacher for ideas.)

Know It? Show It!

Focus by working through the tutorials.

Learn with InQuizitive.

Apply what you've learned to complete the workbook assignments.

Try it Answers

Chapter 1

Try it #1

A. (1) F; (2) D; (3) E; (4) F; (5) A; (6) D; (7) G; (8) B; (9) B; (10) C; (11) G; (12) F; (13) C; (14) F; (15) D.

B. (1) G: B-D-F-A; (2) D: F-A-C-E; (3) A: C-E-G-B; (4) B: D-F-A-C; (5) C: E-G-B-D.

Try it #2 (1) F♯; (2) C; (3) B♭; (4) C♯; (5) C♭; (6) G♯; (7) F; (8) A♯; (9) E♭; (10) F♭; (11) G♭; (12) E♯.

Try it #3

A. (1) G♯ or A♭; (2) C or B♯; (3) F or E♯; (4) A; (5) D♯ or E♭; (6) E or F♭; (7) G; (8) G.

B. (1) W; (2) H; (3) W; (4) W; (5) H; (6) W; (7) N; (8) W.

Try it #4

A. (1) F♯; (2) D; (3) E♭; (4) B; (5) G♯; (6) A♭; (7) D; (8) C♯; (9) G; (10) D♯.

B.

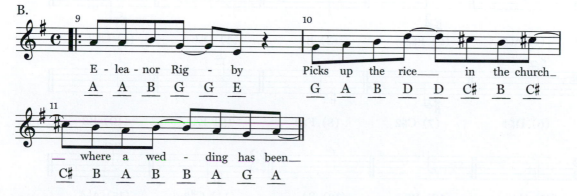

C. (1) H; (2) H; (3) W; (4) W; (5) H; (6) W; (7) N; (8) W; (9) W; (10) H; (11) W; (12) W; (13) H; (14) H.

Try it #5

A. (1) F♯; (2) G; (3) D♭; (4) B; (5) F♯; (6) A♭; (7) C; (8) G; (9) F; (10) E♯.

B.

A   E   F   A   B   F♯   G   B   C   G♯   A   C♯   D   A   B   D

C. (1) W; (2) H; (3) H; (4) W; (5) W; (6) H; (7) H; (8) H; (9) H; (10) H; (11) N; (12) W; (13) N; (14) W.

Try it #6

A. Clef: alto; (1) A; (2) F♯; (3) E; (4) E♭; (5) C; Clef: tenor; (6) B♭; (7) D; (8) F♯; (9) G; (10) C.

B.

E   A   B♮   G♯   E   F♯   G♯   A   G♯   F♯   E   E   F♯   G♮   F♯   E   D♯

C. (1) W; (2) H; (3) H; (4) W; (5) H; (6) W.

Try it #7

A. (1) G♯4; (2) B5; (3) A♭3; (4) E5; (5) D♭3; (6) F♯2; (7) E4; (8) B2.

   (1) D4; (2) C5; (3) F3; (4) G♭4; (5) E4; (6) C♯3; (7) B♭4; (8) B3.

B. (1) G3; (2) F3; (3) G1; (4) C2; (5) F1.

Try it #8

(1) A♭5   (2) F♯3   (3) B4   (4) D♭6   (5) G♯3

(6) D♯4   (7) C♯2   (8) F♯2   (9) E4   (10) B3

(11) G4   (12) B3   (13) B4   (14) C♯3   (15) A♭4

Chapter 2

Try it #1 (a) simple; (b) compound; (c) simple; (d) compound.

Try it #2 (a) duple or quadruple; (b) triple; (c) duple or quadruple; (d) triple.

Try it #7 (a) ♩. or ♩ 𝄾; (b) ♩ or ♩ 𝄾.

Try it #8

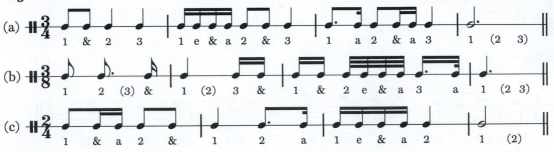

Chapter 3

Try it #1 Pitch-class collection: F G A B♭ C D E; collection is diatonic.

Try it #2

(a) F♭ E♭ D D♭ C C♭ B♭ A A♭

(b) G♭ F F♭ E♭ D D♭ C C♭ B♭

Try it #3

(a)

(c) "Are You Sleeping?": 1̂-2̂-3̂-1̂, 1̂-2̂-3̂-1̂, 3̂-4̂-5̂, 3̂-4̂-5̂, 5̂-6̂-5̂-4̂-3̂-1̂, 5̂-6̂-5̂-4̂-3̂-1̂, 1̂-5̲̂-1̂, 1̂-5̲̂-1̂.
do-re-mi-do, do-re-mi-do, mi-fa-sol, sol-la-sol-fa-mi-do, sol-la-sol-fa-mi-do, do-<u>sol</u>-do, do-<u>sol</u>-do.

"Happy Birthday": 5̲̂-5̲̂-6̂-5̲̂-1̂-7̲̂, 5̲̂-5̲̂-6̂-5̲̂-2̂-1̂, 5̲̂-5̲̂-5̂-3̂-1̂-7̲̂-6̂, 4̂-4̂-3̂-1̂-2̂-1̂. *<u>sol</u>-<u>sol</u>-la-<u>sol</u>-do-ti,*
<u>sol</u>-<u>sol</u>-la-<u>sol</u>-re-do, <u>sol</u>-<u>sol</u>-sol-mi-do-ti-la, fa-fa-mi-do-re-do.

Try it #4

(a) A major

(b) A♭ major

(c) G major

(d) B major

Try it #5

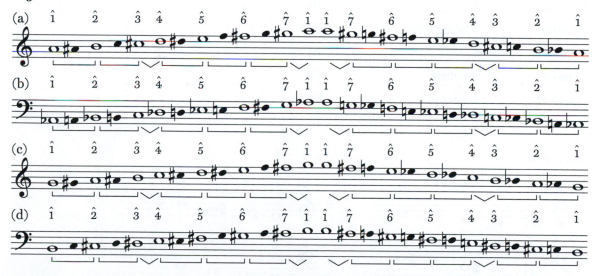

Try it #6

Try it #7

Try it #8
Key signature suggests what key?: A♭ major; First two scale degrees?: $\hat{5}$-$\hat{1}$ in A♭ major; Last scale degree?: $\hat{1}$; Key of piece: A♭ major.

Try it #9

SCALE	SCALE DEGREE	LETTER NAME
F major	$\hat{4}$	B♭
G major	leading tone	F♯
A♭ major	$\hat{5}$	E♭
E major	mediant	G♯
B major	supertonic	C♯
D♭ major	$\hat{6}$	B♭

Try it #10

Chapter 4

Try it #1

METER	METER TYPE	BEAT UNIT	BEATS PER MEASURE
$\frac{9}{8}$	compound triple	♩.	3
$\frac{2}{2}$	simple duple	♩	2
$\frac{12}{8}$	compound quadruple	♩.	4
$\frac{4}{8}$	simple quadruple	♪	4
$\frac{3}{2}$	simple triple	♩	3
$\frac{2}{4}$	simple duple	♩	2
$\frac{6}{8}$	compound duple	♩.	2

Try it #2

(a)

li 1 li 2 ta li 1 li 2 ta li 1 li 2 ta li 1 li 2

(b)

Ich wand-re durch die stil-le Nacht, da schleicht der Mond so Heim-lich sacht___
li 1 li 2 li 3 li 1 (2) 3 1 li 2 li 3 li 1 2 (3)

(c)

I don't___ like you,___ but I___ love you;
1 2 li 3 4 li (1) li 2 li 3 4

Seems that I'm al - ways___ think - ing of you.___
1 2 li 3 4 la (1) 2 li 3 4 la

Try it #3

A.

(2) li 1 la ta li 2 li ta 1 ta li 2 li ta 1 la li ta 2 ta li 1 (2)

B.

(1) 1 2 3 la ta li 1 ta li 2 ta la ta li ta 3 li ta 1 ta li 2 3

Chapter 5

Try it #1

KEY	RELATIVE MINOR	KEY	RELATIVE MINOR
E major	C♯ minor	A♭ major	F minor
D major	B minor	E♭ major	C minor
B major	G♯ minor	F major	D minor

Try it #2

KEY	RELATIVE MAJOR	KEY	RELATIVE MAJOR
A minor	C major	C♯ minor	E major
G♯ minor	B major	F minor	A♭ major
C minor	E♭ major	E minor	G major
D minor	F major	B♭ minor	D♭ major

Try it #3

G♯ minor   F♯ minor

G minor   B♭ minor

E♭ minor   B minor

Try it #4

	SIGNATURES		SIGNATURES
B major–B minor	5#–2#	F# major–F# minor	6#–3#
B♭ major–B♭ minor	2♭–5♭	A major–A minor	3#–0#
C major–C minor	0♭–3♭	C# major–C# minor	7#–4#

Try it #5

Try it #6 (a) B♭ major; (b) D minor; (c) G minor; (d) D♭ major; (e) E♭ major.

Try it #7 Natural signs are optional (only relevant if you are imagining a key signature).

(a) C harmonic minor

(b) B♭ melodic minor

(c) F melodic minor

(d) G# melodic minor

(e) B harmonic minor

(f) C# melodic minor

(g) F# harmonic minor

(h) E harmonic minor

Try it #8

(a) E major pentatonic

(b) E minor pentatonic

(c) B major pentatonic

(d) B minor pentatonic

(e) F# major pentatonic

(f) F# minor pentatonic

(g) B♭ major pentatonic

(h) B♭ minor pentatonic

Try it #9

(a) E Dorian

(b) B♭ Lydian

(c) B Aeolian

(d) A Mixolydian

(e) F♯ Phrygian

(f) E♭ Ionian

Chapter 6

Try it #1

(a)

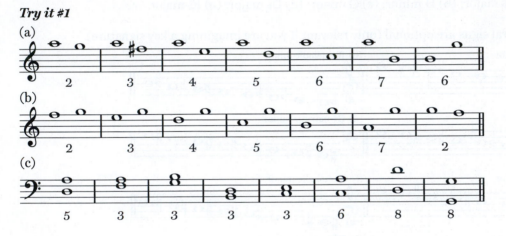

2   3   4   5   6   7   6

(b)

2   3   4   5   6   7   2

(c)

5   3   3   3   3   6   8   8

Try it #2

(1) 7; (2) 13 (6); (3) 8; (4) 13 (6); (5) 13 (6); (6) 12 (5); (7) 8; (8) 9 (2); (9) 10 (3); (10) 10 (3).

Try it #3

(a)

A♭ major

P5   M7   M2   P4   M6   PU   M3

G minor

m3   P4   m7   m6   M2   P5   PU

(b)

M6   P5   M7   PU   M3   P4   M2

Try it #4

(a)

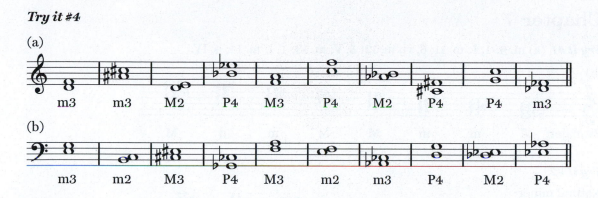

m3   m3   M2   P4   M3   P4   M2   P4   P4   m3

(b)

m3   m2   M3   P4   M3   m2   m3   P4   M2   P4

Try it #5

(a)

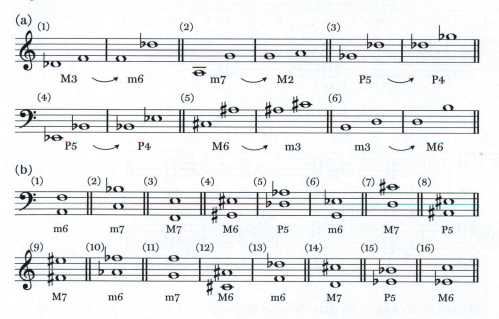

(1)   (2)   (3)

M3 ⌣ m6   m7 ⌣ M2   P5 ⌣ P4

(4)   (5)   (6)

P5 ⌣ P4   M6 ⌣ m3   m3 ⌣ M6

(b)

(1)   (2)   (3)   (4)   (5)   (6)   (7)   (8)

m6   m7   M7   M6   P5   m6   M7   P5

(9)   (10)   (11)   (12)   (13)   (14)   (15)   (16)

M7   m6   m7   M6   m6   M7   P5   M6

Try it #6

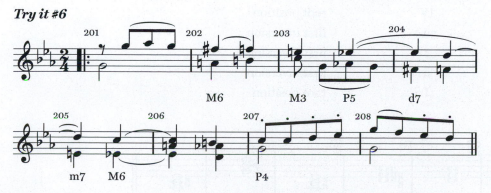

201   202   203   204

M6   M3   P5   d7

205   206   207   208

m7   M6   P4

Chapter 7

Try it #1 (a) m. 9: 1̂, I; m. 11: 6̂, vi; m. 12: 5̂, V; m. 13: 1̂, I; m. 14: 4̂, IV.

(b)

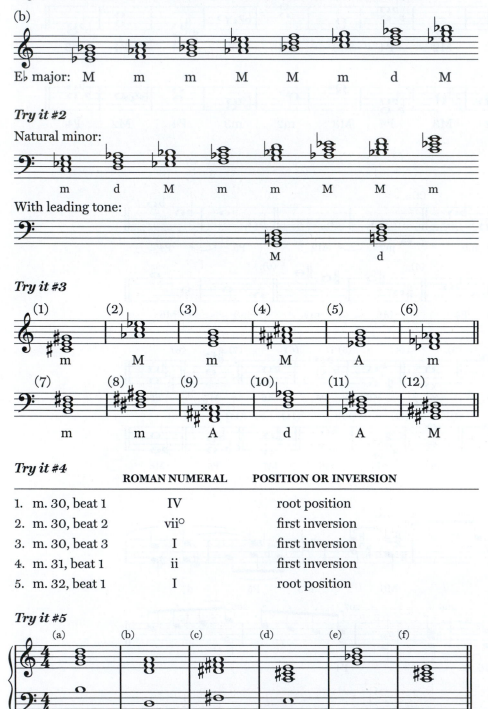

E♭ major: M   m   m   M   M   m   d   M

Try it #2

Natural minor:

     m   d   M   m   m   M   M   m

With leading tone:

                               M   d

Try it #3

(1)   (2)   (3)   (4)   (5)   (6)

 m   M   m   M   A   m

(7)   (8)   (9)   (10)   (11)   (12)

 m   m   A   d   A   M

Try it #4

	ROMAN NUMERAL	POSITION OR INVERSION
1. m. 30, beat 1	IV	root position
2. m. 30, beat 2	vii°	first inversion
3. m. 30, beat 3	I	first inversion
4. m. 31, beat 1	ii	first inversion
5. m. 32, beat 1	I	root position

Try it #5

  (a)   (b)   (c)   (d)   (e)   (f)

   6   (5/3)   6   #6/4   ♭   #

Try it #6

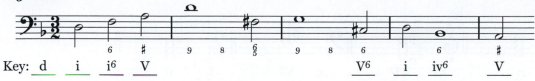

Key: d ___ i ___ i⁶ ___ V ___   V⁶ ___ i ___ iv⁶ ___ V

Chapter 8

Try it #1

A.

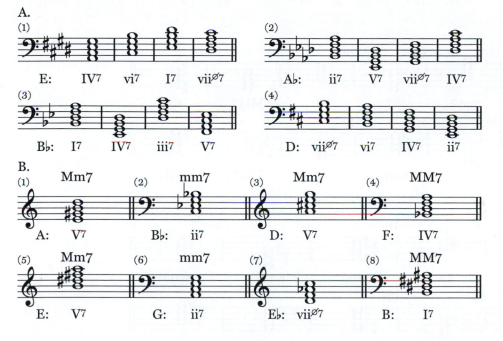

(1) E: IV⁷ vi⁷ I⁷ vii⁰⁷

(2) A♭: ii⁷ V⁷ vii⁰⁷ IV⁷

(3) B♭: I⁷ IV⁷ iii⁷ V⁷

(4) D: vii⁰⁷ vi⁷ IV⁷ ii⁷

B.

(1) Mm7 A: V⁷
(2) mm7 B♭: ii⁷
(3) Mm7 D: V⁷
(4) MM7 F: IV⁷
(5) Mm7 E: V⁷
(6) mm7 G: ii⁷
(7) Mm7 E♭: vii⁰⁷
(8) MM7 B: I⁷

Try it #2

A.

m.	QUALITY	BASS AND FIGURES
m. 2	mm7	seventh ($\frac{4}{2}$)
m. 3	Mm7	third ($\frac{6}{5}$)
m. 6	Mm7	seventh ($\frac{4}{2}$)

B.

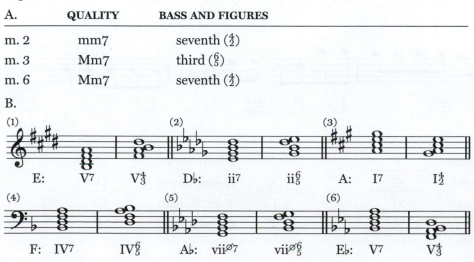

(1) E: V⁷ V$\frac{4}{3}$

(2) D♭: ii⁷ ii$\frac{6}{5}$

(3) A: I⁷ I$\frac{4}{2}$

(4) F: IV⁷ IV$\frac{6}{5}$

(5) A♭: vii⁰⁷ vii⁰$\frac{6}{5}$

(6) E♭: V⁷ V$\frac{4}{3}$

Try it #3

Try it #4

Try it #5

Try it #6

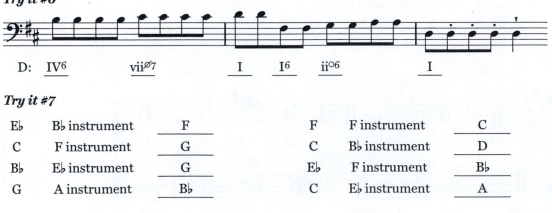

Try it #7

Eb	Bb instrument	F		F	F instrument	C
C	F instrument	G		C	Bb instrument	D
Bb	Eb instrument	G		Eb	F instrument	Bb
G	A instrument	Bb		C	Eb instrument	A

Chapter 9

Try it #1

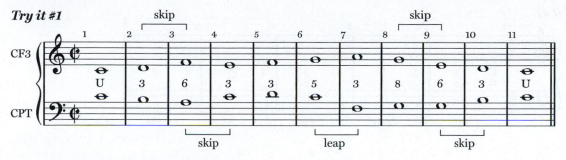

Upper part (cantus firmus): conjunct

Lower part (counterpoint): conjunct

Try it #2

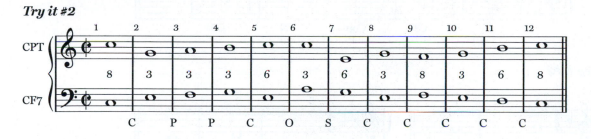

Try it #3

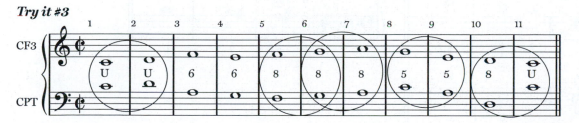

Try it #4

6	B♭	F	E	D	C	B♭	D	C♯ (LT)	B♭
5	A	E	D	C	B♭ (d5!)	A	C	B♭ (d5!)	A
3	F	C	B♭	A	G	F	A	G	F
8	D	A	G	F	E	D	F	E	D

Chapter 10

Try it #1

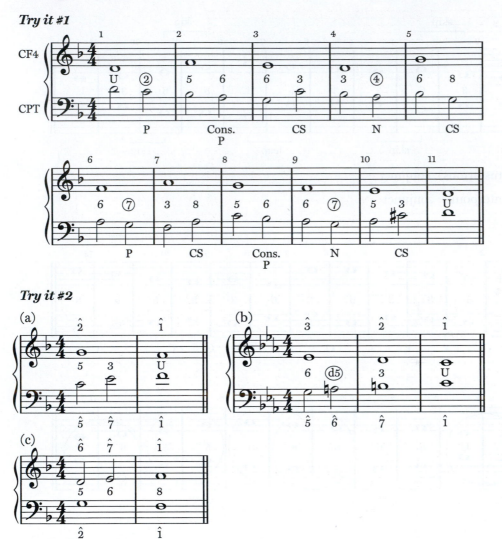

Try it #2

Try it #3

(a)

(b)

(c)

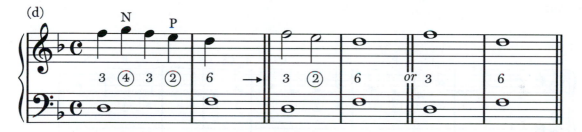

(d)

Try it #4

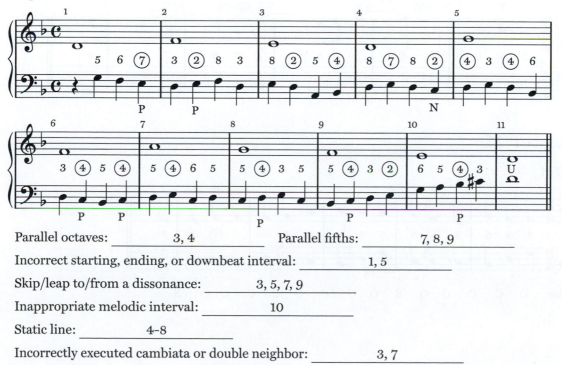

Parallel octaves: _____3, 4_____   Parallel fifths: _____7, 8, 9_____

Incorrect starting, ending, or downbeat interval: _____1, 5_____

Skip/leap to/from a dissonance: _____3, 5, 7, 9_____

Inappropriate melodic interval: _____10_____

Static line: _____4–8_____

Incorrectly executed cambiata or double neighbor: _____3, 7_____

Try it #5

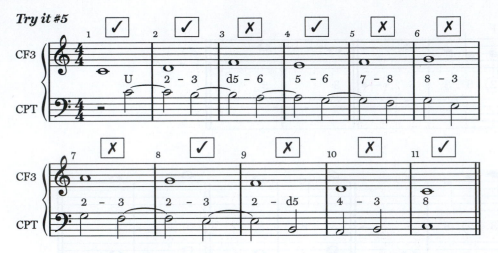

M. 3: incorrect use of d5. M. 5: improper suspension. M. 6: parallel octaves. M. 7: no preparation for the suspension. M. 9: 2 resolves improperly to d5. M. 10: 4-3 is an improper suspension in the lower voice.

Try it #6

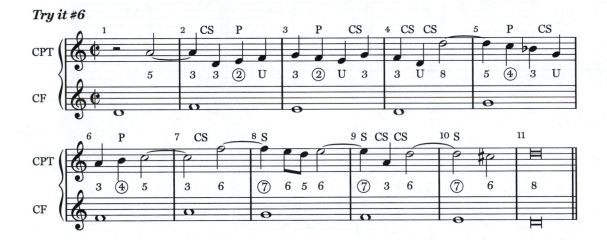

Chapter 11

Try it #1

Chapter 12

Try it #1 HC in m. 5, PAC in m. 10. The phrases are five measures long rather than four.

Try it #2

	(1)	(2)	(3)	(4)	(5)	(6)	(7)	(8)
Root:	A♭	F	G	C♯	F	F♯	G♭	F
Quality:	maj	maj	min	maj	min	min	maj	maj
Figure:	$^6_3$	$^6_3$	$^5_3$	$^5_3$	$^5_3$	$^6_3$	$^5_3$	$^5_3$
Voicing:	E	B	A	A	D	C	E	B

Try it #3

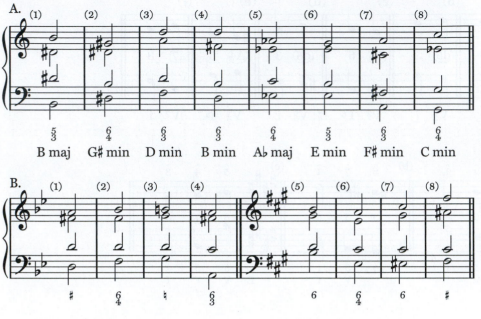

Chapter 13

Try it #1

Try it #2

With mistakes labeled:

With corrections:

Try it #3

Try it #4

Chapter 14

Try it #1

Try it #2

E: I⁵₃ ══ ⁶₄ ══ ⁵₃   g: i⁵₃ ══ ⁶₄ ══ ⁵₃   D: I⁵₃ ══ ⁶₄ ══ ⁵₃

Try it #3

F: I   V⁶₄   I⁶   c: i   V⁶₄   i⁶   D: I   V⁶₄   I⁶
          P   P   P

Try it #4

(a) 3̂ 2̂ 1̂   (b) 1̂ 2̂ 1̂   (c) 1̂ 7̂ 1̂   (d) 3̂ 4̂ 5̂   (e) 3̂ 4̂ 3̂

1̂ 2̂ 3̂   1̂ 7̂ 1̂   1̂ 4̂ 3̂   1̂ 2̂ 3̂   1̂ 7̂ 1̂

D: I V⁶₄ I⁶   A♭: I V⁶ I   g: i V⁴₂ i⁶   F: I V⁴₃ I⁶   b: i V⁶₅ i

Try it #5

e: i   iv⁶   V   i⁶   ii°⁶   V⁶₄ ══ ⁵₃
    T   (PD   D   T)   PD   D
    T ─────────────────────────── PD   D

Chapter 15

Try it #1

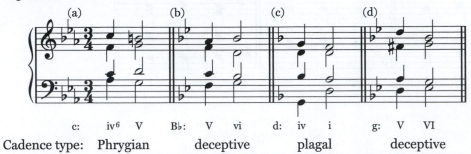

	(a)	(b)	(c)	(d)
	c: iv⁶ V	B♭: V vi	d: iv i	g: V VI
Cadence type:	Phrygian	deceptive	plagal	deceptive

Try it #2

	(a)	(b)	(c)	(d)
	F: I IV	e: i VI	a: VII III	B♭: IV ii
Root motion:	desc. 5th	desc. 3rd	desc. 5th	desc. 3rd

Try it #3

A.

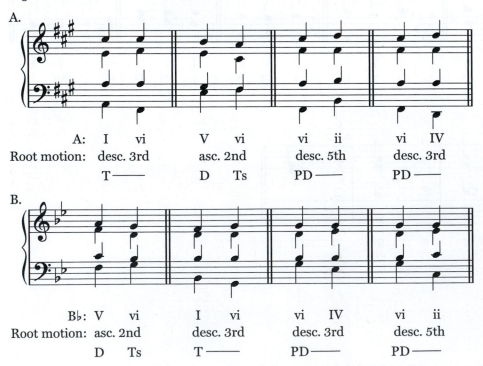

A: I vi	V vi	vi ii	vi IV
Root motion: desc. 3rd	asc. 2nd	desc. 5th	desc. 3rd
T ——	D Ts	PD ——	PD ——

B.

B♭: V vi	I vi	vi IV	vi ii
Root motion: asc. 2nd	desc. 3rd	desc. 3rd	desc. 5th
D Ts	T ——	PD ——	PD ——

Chapter 16

Try it #1

In m. 8, beat 2, the alto F♯ looks like a passing tone, but the ii-I progression is not idiomatic; instead, we analyze the chord on the second part of that beat as vii°⁶ to create an embedded PD-D-T. If you take both alto pitches in beat 2 as chord tones (F♯-A-C-E), you get a vii⌀⁶₅, but the chordal seventh does not resolve correctly.

Try it #2

The chord of resolution is in root position.

Try it #3

(a)   (b)   (c)   (d)

Try it #4

Chapter 17

Try it #1

g: vii°7   B: viiø7   D: viiø7   f♯: vii°7   e: vii°7

Try it #2

KEY	$\hat{7}$–$\hat{1}$	$\hat{4}$–$\hat{3}$ (or ♭$\hat{3}$)
F minor	E♮–F	B♭–A♭
C minor	B♮–C	F–E♭
A major	G♯–A	D–C♯
B minor	A♯–B	E–D
E minor	D♯–E	A–G
A♭ major	G–A♭	D♭–C

Try it #3

A.

g: vii°$^6_5$ i^6 A: viiø7 I   b: vii°7 i   e: viiø$^4_3$ i^6 G: viiø$^4_3$ I^6

B.

KEY	SOPRANO	BASS	HARMONIZATION 1	HARMONIZATION 2
major	$\hat{3}$–$\hat{2}$–$\hat{1}$	$\hat{1}$–$\hat{2}$–$\hat{3}$	I–V$^6_4$–I^6	I–vii°6–I^6
major	$\hat{1}$–$\hat{2}$–$\hat{1}$	$\hat{1}$–$\hat{7}$–$\hat{1}$	I–V^6–I^6	I–vii°7–I
minor	$\hat{1}$–$\hat{7}$–$\hat{1}$	$\hat{1}$–$\hat{4}$–♭$\hat{3}$	i–V$^4_2$–i^6	i–vii°$^4_3$–i^6
major	$\hat{3}$–$\hat{4}$–$\hat{5}$	$\hat{1}$–$\hat{2}$–$\hat{3}$	I–V$^4_3$–I^6	I–vii°6–I^6
minor	♭$\hat{3}$–$\hat{4}$–♭$\hat{3}$	$\hat{1}$–$\hat{7}$–$\hat{1}$	i–V$^6_5$–i	i–vii°7–i

Chapter 18

Try it #1

x:	inverted	measure:	2
y:	transposed	measure:	3

Try it #2

EXCERPT	MM. 1–4	MM. 5–8	PERIOD TYPE
(a) Hensel, "Neue Liebe, neues Leben"	**a** (HC)	**a′** (PAC)	parallel
(b) "Greensleeves"	**a** (HC)	**a′** (PAC)	parallel
(c) Mozart, Sonata, K. 284	**a** (HC)	**a** (PAC)	contrasting

The Mozart piece includes a modulating consequent. In addition, the second phrase begins the same as the first but only for three notes, before it continues with contrasting material.

Chapter 19

Try it #1

a = transposed down an octave plus a 6th
b = transposed down an octave plus a 4th
c = inverted and modified (the interval over the bar line is a 6th, not d7th)
d = inverted and modified
e = same as original but transposed up a P5

Try it #2

(1) The two passages use the same root progression.

(2) The LIP type is 10-10.

Try it #3 In m. 10 of the Kern song, the expected Gm7 (ii7) is replaced with G7 (a dominant seventh chord on G), and the expected C7 (the C dominant seventh that is V7 in F minor) in m. 11 is replaced with Cmaj7 (a major seventh chord on C). These replacements set up a cadence in m. 11 on the word "long." Incidentally, the G7 in m. 10 is a "secondary dominant" to C (marked V7/V) (to be discussed in Chapter 20).

Chapter 20

Try it #1

KEY	V CHORD	V7/V		KEY	V CHORD	V7/V
(a) B♭ major	F major	C-E♮-G-B♭		(f) D major	A major	E-G♯-B-D
(b) E minor	B minor	F♯-A♯-C♯-E		(g) E♭ major	B♭ major	F-A-C-E♭
(c) C minor	G minor	D-F♯-A-C		(h) B major	F♯ major	C♯-E♯-G♯-B
(d) A major	E major	B-D♯-F♯-A		(i) G minor	D minor	A-C♯-E♮-G
(e) A♭ major	E♭ major	B♭-D-F-A♭		(j) F minor	C♯ minor	G♯-B♯-D♯-F♯

Try it #2

KEY	V CHORD	VII°7/V		KEY	V CHORD	VII°7/V
(a) C minor	G minor	F♯-A♮-C-E♭		(f) F major	C major	B♮-D-F-A♭
(b) E♭ major	B♭ major	A♮-C-E♭-G♭		(g) B♭ major	F major	E-G-B♭-D♭
(c) F minor	C minor	B♮-D♮-F-A♭		(h) D♭ major	A♭ major	G♮-B♭-D♭-F♭
(d) A minor	E minor	D♯-F♯-A-C		(i) G minor	D minor	C♯-E♮-G-B♭
(e) E major	B major	A♯-C♯-E-G♮		(j) B major	F♯ major	E♯-G♯-B-D

Try it #3

A.

A: V/V   d: V6/V   G: V⁶₅/V   f: V⁴₂/V   B♭: vii°⁶/V   F: vii°⁶/V   g: vii°⁴₃/V

E♭: V6/V   b: V⁴₂/V   e: vii°⁶₅/V   c: vii°7/V   E: V⁴₃/V   D: vii°⁶/V   A♭: vii°⁴₂/V

B.

Bb: ii⁶₅   V⁶₅/V   V   d: iv   V⁶₅/V   V   G: V   vii°⁶/V   V⁶

Chapter 21

Try it #1 (2) V7/vi; (3) vii°7/iii; (4) vii°7/IV; (5) V7/IV; (6) vii°7/III.

Try it #2

F: vi⁶   V⁶₅/ii   ii   V7

The tendency tones in the V⁶₅/ii chord (m. 72, beat 2), F♯2 (LT) and C5 (7) do resolve correctly.

Try it #3

	KEY	ROMAN NUMERAL	TONICIZED CHORD	SECONDARY DOMINANT

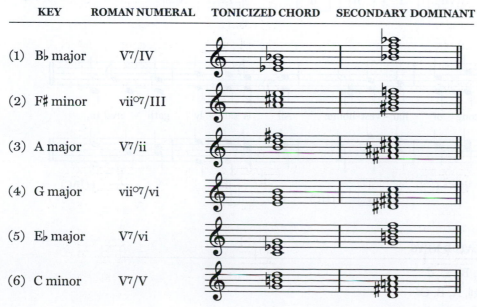

(1)	Bb major	V7/IV
(2)	F♯ minor	vii°7/III
(3)	A major	V7/ii
(4)	G major	vii°7/vi
(5)	Eb major	V7/vi
(6)	C minor	V7/V

Try it #4

A: ii⁶₅   V⁷/V   V   c: i   V⁴₂/iv   iv⁶   e: i   V⁶/III   III

Chapter 22

Try it #1

(a) *A♭ major*

Roman numerals:	I	ii	iii	IV	V	vi	vii°
Chords:	A♭	b♭	c	D♭	E♭	f	g°

(b) *E♭ major*

Chords:	A♭	B♭	c	d°	E♭	f	g
Roman numerals:	IV	V	vi	vii°	I	ii	iii

Try it #2

C♯ minor:	i	ii°	III	iv	v	V	VI	VII	vii°
Chords:	c♯	d♯°	E	f♯	g♯	G♯	A	B	b♯°
E major:	vi	vii°	I	ii	ii		IV	V	

Try it #3

Raise the song of har-vest-home: All is safe-ly gath-ered in,

F: I   V⁶   I   vi   ii⁶   ii   V   I (IAC)
              d: iv⁶   V(HC)   i   iv

Try it #4

A.	RELATED KEYS
F major	g, a, B♭, C, d
E major	f♯, g♯, A, B, C♯
A major	b, c♯, D, E, f♯
G major	a, b, C, D, e
B♭ major	c, d, E♭, F, g

B.   **CLOSELY RELATED KEYS**

E minor   G, a, b, C, D
G minor   B♭, c, d, E♭, F
C♯ minor   E, f♯, g♯, A, B
F minor   A♭, b♭, c, D♭, E♭
B minor   D, e, f♯, G, A

Try it #5

(a) *D major*

Roman numerals:	I	ii	iii	IV	V	vi	vii°
Chords:	D	e	f♯	G	A	b	c♯°

E minor

Chords:	D	e	f♯°	G	a	b	C
Roman numerals:	VII	i	ii°	III	iv	v	VI

(b) *D major*

Roman numerals:	I	ii	iii	IV	V	vi	vii°
Chords:	D	e	f♯	G	A	b	c♯°

F♯ minor

Chords:	D	E	f♯	g♯°	A	b	c♯
Roman numerals:	VI	VII	i	ii°	III	iv	v

(c) *D major*

Roman numerals:	I	ii	iii	IV	V	vi	vii°
Chords:	D	e	f♯	G	A	b	c♯°

G major

Chords:	D	e	f♯°	G	a	b	C
Roman numerals:	V	vi	vii°	I	ii	iii	IV

(d) *D major*

Roman numerals:	I	ii	iii	IV	V	vi	vii°
Chords:	D	e	f♯	G	A	b	c♯°

B minor

Chords:	D	e	F♯	G	A	b	c♯°
Roman numerals:	III	iv	V	VI	VII	i	ii°

Chapter 23

Try it #1 1. continuous; 2. sectional; 3. rounded; 4. simple; 5. simple binary; 6. rounded binary; 7. simple binary.

Try it #2 Example 23.5: sectional rounded; Example 23.6: continuous rounded; Example 23.7: sectional rounded.

Chapter 24

Try it #1 The answer is tonal: the P4 leap from C5 to G4 ($\hat{1}$ to $\hat{5}$) of the subject is transformed to a P5 leap, G5 to C5 ($\hat{5}$ to $\hat{1}$), in the answer; the interval following is also changed, so that $\flat\hat{6}$ of the subject is answered with $\flat\hat{3}$.

Try it #2

MEASURE	BEAT	VOICE PART	STARTING PITCH	COMPLETE OR INCOMPLETE ENTRY?
16	2	soprano	C5	complete
16	3	alto	G4	complete
17	1	tenor	A3	complete
17	3	bass	D3	complete; first note enlongated

Try it #3 There is an inverted answer entry in the alto on beat 3 of m. 47, which is missing the last note.

Chapter 25

Try it #1 Variation VIII is in C minor; Variation XII is in $\frac{3}{4}$.

Chapter 26

Try it #1

KEY	PARALLEL MINOR SIGNATURE	$\flat\hat{3}$	$\flat\hat{6}$	$\flat\hat{7}$
C major	3 flats	E♭	A♭	B♭
E major	1 sharp	G♮	C♮	D♮
B♭ major	5 flats	D♭	G♭	A♭
D major	1 flat	F♮	B♭	C♮
B major	2 sharps	D♮	G♮	A♮

Try it #2

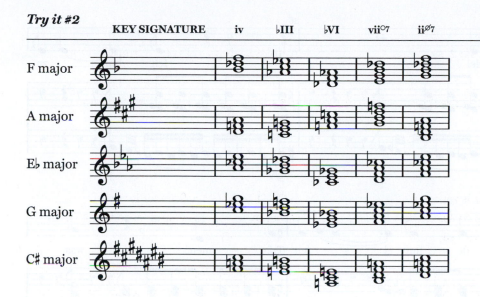

Try it #3

Chapter 27

Try it #1

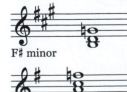

F♯ minor   G minor   A major

E minor   F major   B minor

Try it #2

m. 34		m. 35				m. 36			m. 37		m. 38		m. 39		m. 40	
ti	*fa*	*re*	*ti*	*sol*	*ti*	*ti*	*do*	*do*	*ra*	*mi*	*fa*	*me*	*ra*	*do*	*do*	*ti*
$\hat{7}$	$\hat{4}$	$\hat{2}$	$\hat{7}$	$\hat{5}$	$\hat{7}$	$\hat{7}$	$\hat{1}$	$\hat{1}$	$\flat\hat{2}$	$\hat{3}$	$\hat{4}$	$\flat\hat{3}$	$\flat\hat{2}$	$\hat{1}$	$\hat{1}$	$\hat{7}$

Try it #3

KEY	$\flat\hat{6}$	$\sharp\hat{4}$		KEY	$\flat\hat{6}$	$\sharp\hat{4}$
A minor	F	D$\sharp$		E major	C$\natural$	A$\sharp$
C$\sharp$ minor	A	F$\times$		B minor	G	E$\sharp$
F major	D$\flat$	B$\natural$		G$\sharp$ minor	E	C$\times$

Try it #4

g: Gr⁶   B: It⁶   C: Fr⁶

f: It⁶   f$\sharp$: Gr⁶   e: Fr⁶

Chapter 28

Try it #1 Introduction: mm. 1-8; **A**: 9-20; **B**: 21-61; **A′**: 62-79.

Try it #2

of heav-i-ness, He is full of heav-i-ness; Thy re-buke hath brok-en His heart;

g: V7   i   e: vii°7/V   V⁶₄ ——— ⁵₃

Try it #3

The rhyme scheme is ab ab ab ab. Each stanza is only two lines long, and each has the same rhyme scheme: ab. Rather than an objective-subjective contrast for the lines, this poem features a first-person speaker throughout. In line 1 of strophes 1-3, she begs her partner not to love her if it's for the wrong reason; in line 2, he is directed to love other things instead. In the final stanza, "nicht" (no) turns to "ja" (yes), if he loves for love. The musical setting might be strophic, given the parallel structure of text.

Try it #4

	Character(s)	Measures
Strophe 1:	narrator	mm. 16-32
Strophe 2:	father, son, father	mm. 37-40, 42-50, 52-54
Strophe 3:	elf king	mm. 58-72
Strophe 4:	son, father	mm. 73-79, 81-85
Strophe 5:	elf king	mm. 87-96
Strophe 6:	son, father	mm. 98-104, 106-112
Strophe 7:	elf king, son	mm. 117-123, 124-131
Strophe 8:	narrator	mm. 133-147

Chapter 29

Try it #1

Measures:	1-8a	8b-16a	16b-24a	24b-32a
Phrase letters:	a	a′	b	a
Period structures?	parallel period			

Try it #2

	Measure	Beat
Ninth chord:	16	(1) &
Added-sixth chord:	16	(2) &

Try it #3 M. 50, downbeat, is a Cm^{7-5}, $ii^{ø7}$ (a half-diminished seventh chord in an enharmonic respelling: C-E♭-G♭-B♭). M. 51, downbeat, is a C^{7-5}: C-E♮-G♭-B♭ (a dominant seventh chord with lowered fifth), $V^{7♭5}/V$.

Try it #4 There is no turnaround. The melody includes the blue notes E♭ and B♭.

Chapter 30

Try it #1

A.

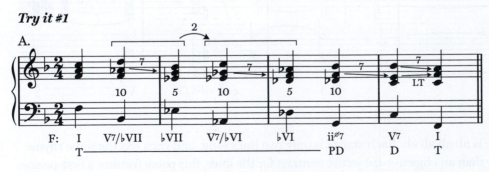

B.

F: I⁶   IV   V$^6_5$/iii   iii   V$^6_5$/ii   ii   V$^6_5$ I

or with additional accidentals   V/vi   V/V

       T   PD —————————————————————— D   T

Try it #2

A.

C: I —————— desc par $^6_3$ with 7–6 —————— I

B.

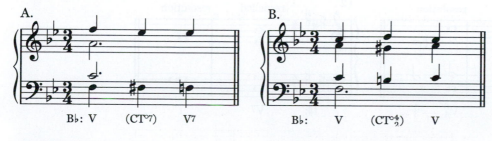

C: I⁶ —————— asc par $^6_3$ with 5–6 —————— I

Try it #3

A.   **B.**

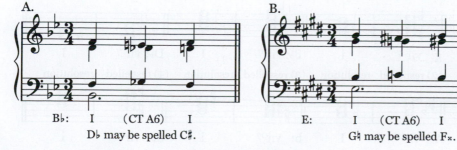

B♭: V   (CT°7)   V7   B♭: V   (CT°$^4_2$)   V

Try it #4

A.   **B.**

B♭: I   (CT A6)   I   E: I   (CT A6)   I

D♭ may be spelled C♯.   G♮ may be spelled F𝄪.

Try it #5

Chord	Root of chord	Relationship of root to tonic	Diatonic	Mixture chromatic mediants	Chromatic mediants
Mediant in E major	G♯ (♯$\hat{3}$)	M3 above	G♯–B–D♯ (iii)		G♯–B♯–D♯ (III)
	G (♭$\hat{3}$)	m3 above		G–B–D (♭III)	G–B♭–D (♭iii, rare)
Submediant in E major	C♯ ($\hat{6}$)	m3 below	C♯–E–G♯ (vi)		C♯–E♯–B♯ (VI)
	C (♭$\hat{6}$)	M3 below		C–E–G (♭VI)	C–E♭–G (♭vi, rare)

Chapter 31

Try it #1

Try it #3

e: i⁶   vii°⁷/G?   vii°⁷/G   V⁷/B♭?   d⁶ or vii°⁴₃/C   vii°⁴₂/A   V⁷/A   e⁷   vii°⁶₅/D

None of the chords resolve exactly as expected.

Chapter 32

Try it #1 The phrase of the second theme from mm. 23-26 is transposed down a perfect fifth in 90-93, while the following phrase, mm. 27-31, is transposed up a perfect fourth in 94-98, altering the registral relationship between the phrases. The same transposition pattern is followed for the two phrases of 45-51 (and 112-118).

Try it #2

Mm. 74-76, right hand, are similar to mm. 9-10.

Mm. 74-77, left hand, are drawn from mm. 35-38.

The right hand is reminiscent of the upper line in mm. 9-10, which are themselves an expansion of the melodic upper part in m. 4. Compare also m. 23, and the contour (although it is much slower-moving) of the second theme. The left hand is drawn from the chorale (second) theme.

Try it #3 Some of the elements include the main theme from measures 1-4 (see mm. 90-95 especially, though motives from the main theme persist through m. 111); the accompaniment pattern from 14-22 (in 96-103); the arpeggiation accompaniment from 23-28 (in 104-110); subsection 2b, with its syncopation and triplets, from 50-56a (in 112-141).

Try it #4

Chapter 33

Try it #1

A. five-part rondo

B.

Section:	A	B	A′	C	A″	Codetta
Measures:	1–16	17–24	25–32	33–48	49–64	65–74
Key:	G	D	G	g	G	G

Chapter 34

Try it #1

MODE	PC CENTER	
Mixolydian	F	
Dorian	C♯	
Lydian	B♭	
Aeolian	F♯	
Phrygian	G	
Locrian	E	
Ionian	A♭	
Lydian-Mixolydian	A	

Try it #2

(a) D♯ E F♯ G♯ A♮ C♯; pc center is D♯.

(b) B

(c) Aeolian; Locrian (♭$\hat{5}$)

(d) D♯

(e)
Instrument	Intervals featured	Pc list
flute	semitones	C♯ D D♯ E F (chromatic subset)
cello	P4 and P5	D G A (subset of the major pentachord)
piano RH	P5ths	D♯ F♯ A♯ C♯ (mm7 chord)
piano LH	M7 (also P5)	D F♯ G A (subset of the major pentachord)

Try it #3

SONORITY	INTEGER NOTATION	ASCENDING ORDER
Dominant seventh chord on A	9 1 4 7	{1 4 7 9}
Half-diminished seventh chord on D	2 5 8 0	{0 2 5 8}
Do-re-mi-fa-sol on E	4 6 8 9 e	{4 6 8 9 e}
Augmented triad on F♯	6 t 2	{2 6 t}
Diminished seventh chord on C♯	1 4 7 t	{1 4 7 t}
Major-major seventh chord on A♭	8 0 3 7	{0 3 7 8}
Dorian mode on D	2 4 5 7 9 e 0	{0 2 4 5 7 9 e}

Try it #4

SCALE TYPE	STARTING PC	LETTER NAMES	INTEGER NOTATION
octatonic 01	F♯	F♯ G A B♭ C D♭ E♭ E♮ (F♯)	6 7 9 t 0 1 3 4 (6)
whole tone	E♭	E♭ F G A B D♭ (E♭)	3 5 7 9 e 1 (3)
minor pentatonic	D	D F G A C (D)	2 5 7 9 0 (2)
octatonic 23	E♭	E♭ F F♯ G♯ A♮ B C D (E♭)	3 5 6 8 9 e 0 2 (3)
major pentatonic	B	B C♯ D♯ F♯ G♯ (B)	e 1 3 6 8 (e)
whole tone	B♭	B♭ C D E F♯ G♯ (B♭)	t 0 2 4 6 8 (t)

Try it #5

1. Diminished seventh on C: 0 3 6 9
   Diminished seventh on G: 7 t 1 4
   Combine to form which octatonic scale? 0 1 3 4 6 7 9 t

2. Augmented triad on C♯: 1 5 9
   Augmented triad on D: 2 6 t
   Combine to form which hexatonic scale? 1 2 5 6 9 t

3. Diminished seventh on D♭: 1 4 7 t
   Diminished seventh on E♭: 3 6 9 0
   Combine to form which octatonic scale? 0 1 3 4 6 7 9 t

The two octatonic scales are the same.

Chapter 35

Try it #1

Try it #2 (a) changing meter; (b) additive rhythm (or ametric); (c) polymeter.

Try it #3

SECTION	A	B	A′	B′	Coda
MEASURES	1-5	6-15	16-20	21-29	30-33
SCALE TYPE	OCT 23	OCT 12	OCT 12	OCT 23	Aeolian
FOCAL PCS	A/D♯	D/G♯	B♭/E	E♭/A	E♭

Chapter 36

Try it #1

A. {5 8 9 0}, {7 t e 2}, {1 4 5 8}, {4 7 8 e}

B. (1) {9 e 1 3}   (5) {9 1 4}

   (2) {e 2 6}   (6) {2 5 8 9}

   (3) {9 1 2 3 4}   (7) {6 9 0 2}

   (4) {9 e 1 3 4}   (8) {2 3 4 7 8}

Try it #2

TRICHORD	INTEGER NOTATION	TRANSPOSE BY	TRANSPOSED SET IN INTERGER NOTATION
{D F A}	{2 5 9}	minor third	{5 8 0}
{B C C♯}	{e 0 1}	minor second	{0 1 2}
{C♯ D F♯}	{1 2 6}	major second	{3 4 8}
{E F♯ A♯}	{4 6 t}	pci 5	{9 e 3}
{C E G♯}	{0 4 8}	pci 7	{7 e 3}
{G♭ A♭ B♭}	{6 8 t}	pci 4	{t 0 2}
{C D F}	{0 2 5}	pci 6	{6 8 t}

Try it #3

(a) (1) [001110]

    (2) [112101]

    (3) [032221]

    (4) [232341]

(b) {1 4 8}

(c) {0 1 3 5 7 8}

Try it #4

Ordered pitch intervals: -5 +3 +5 +1   Inverted: +5 -3 -5 -1

Bartók uses this inverted set in mm. 13-15.

Try it #5

{e 1 4}	{1 e 8}	{3 6 8 9}	{9 6 4 3}
{9 t 2 3}	{3 2 t 9}	{e 1 2 3 5}	{1 e t 9 7}
{e 2 5}	{1 t 7}	{6 9 0 1}	{6 3 0 e}

Try it #6

(a) {8 9 t e 1}

(b) {2 4 5 6 7}

(c) 3

(d) C = T_3I B.

$$
\begin{array}{r}
8\ 9\ t\ e\ 1 \\
+\ 7\ 6\ 5\ 4\ 3 \\
\hline
3\ 3\ 3\ 3\ 3
\end{array}
$$

Chapter 37

Try it #1

(1) [0 1 5]

(2) [0 1 6]

(3) [0 1 4 7]

(4) [0 2 4 6]

(5) [0 2 5 8]

(6) [0 1 3 5 7]

(7) [0 1 2 3 7]

(8) [0 1 4 8]

Try it #2

Normal order: {t e 0 1 2}   {7 9 t e 0}

Prime form: [0 1 2 3 4]   [0 1 2 3 5]

Try it #3

	Prime form	Forte number	ic vector
(a)	[0 2 7]	3-9	[010020]
(b)	[0 2 7]	3-9	[010020]
(c)	[0 3 7]	3-11	[001110]
(d)	[0 2 4]	3-6	[020100]
(e)	[0 2 7]	3-9	[010020]
(f)	[0 2 5]	3-7	[011010]

Try it #4

(a)   Oboe: {t e 2}   Flute: {3 6 7} T_n or T_nI: T_5I

(b) Trumpet: {4 5 8}   Clarinet: {9 0 1} T_n or T_nI: T_5I

Try it #5

	Prime form	Forte number			Prime form	Forte number
(a)	[0 1 4]	3-3		(f)	[0 1 5]	3-4
(b)	[0 1 4]	3-3		(g)	[0 1 4]	3-3
(c)	[0 1 5]	3-4		(h)	[0 1 4]	3-3
(d)	[0 1 4]	3-3		(i)	[0 1 2]	3-1
(e)	[0 1 2]	3-1				

Try it #6

	Mode	Prime form	Forte number
(a)	mode 3	[0 1 2 4 5 6 8 9 t]	9-12
(b)	mode 2	[0 1 3 4 6 7 9 t]	8-28

Chapter 38

Try it #1

(a) m. 5 soprano   <+4 -2 -3 -3 +2 +3>   prime

(b) m. 5 alto   <-4 +2 +3 +3 -2 -3>   inversion

(c) m. 6 soprano   <-3 -2 +3 +3 +2 -4>   retrograde

(d) m. 6 alto   <+3 +2 -3 -3 -2 +4>   (none of the above!)

Try it #2

A. P_9: < 9 2 6 t 8 > P_3: < 3 8 0 4 2 >

B. P_4: < 4 6 0 e 9 1 > I_8: < 8 6 0 1 3 e >

C. P_1: < 1 e 9 6 3 > R_1: < 3 6 9 e 1 >

D. P_1: < 1 2 7 9 6 8 3 > I_5: < 5 4 e 9 0 t 3 >

E. P_7: < 7 2 t 5 e > R_3: < 7 1 6 t 3 >

Pitches may be notated in any octave or enharmonic spelling.

Try it #3

A. Row 1: <8 9 7 5 e 4 2 3 t 1 0 6>   Label: P_8

Row 2: <9 8 t 0 6 1 3 2 7 4 5 e>   Label: I_9

B. Row 1:   < 8 9 7   5 e 4   2 3 t   1 0 6>

Trichords: [0 1 2]   [0 1 6]   [0 1 5]   [0 1 6]

Try it #4

(a) row pcs: < t 5 0 e 9 6 1 3 7 8 2 4 >

order numbers: 1 2 3 4 5 6 7 8 9 10 11 12

(b)

	1		6		9
	2		8		12
	3		7		11
Chord 1:	4	Chord 2:	5	Chord 3:	10

Try it #5

P →	I_0	I_7	I_2	I_1	I_e	I_8	I_3	I_5	I_9	I_t	I_4	I_6	← R
P_0	0	7	2	1	e	8	3	5	9	t	4	6	R_0
P_5	5	0	7	6	4	1	8	t	2	3	9	e	R_5
P_t	t	5	0	e	9	6	1	3	7	8	2	4	R_t
P_e	e	6	1	0	t	7	2	4	8	9	3	5	R_e
P_1	1	8	3	2	0	9	4	6	t	e	5	7	R_1
P_4	4	e	6	5	3	0	7	9	1	2	8	t	R_4
P_9	9	4	e	t	8	5	0	2	6	7	1	3	R_9
P_7	7	2	9	8	6	3	t	0	4	5	e	1	R_7
P_3	3	t	5	4	2	e	6	8	0	1	7	9	R_3
P_2	2	9	4	3	1	t	5	7	e	0	6	8	R_2
P_8	8	3	t	9	7	4	e	1	5	6	0	2	R_e
P_6	6	1	8	7	5	2	9	e	3	4	t	0	R_6
	RI_0	RI_7	RI_2	RI_1	RI_e	RI_e	RI_3	RI_5	RI_9	RI_t	RI_4	RI_6	

↓I (top), ↑RI (bottom)

Try it #6

Example 38.7a:

m. 1: P_t m. 2: RI_3

Example 38.7b:

mm. 32-33, right hand: P_t mm. 33-34, right hand: RI_3

left hand: I_3 left hand: R_t

Try it #7 A. P_3; B. P_1.

Try it #8 A. I_t; B. I_8.

Chapter 39

Try it #1

Some possible answers:

(a) Dynamic markings, notes on a five-line staff, articulation markings (bowings).

(b) Staff lines don't go straight across the page, no meter indication, some staves don't indicated a clef.

(c) Indeterminate, graphic score.

Try it #2

A. Pattern 3 is the same as pattern 1, but with an additional eighth on the descending scale at the end (doubled at the fifth); or it could be thought of as pattern 2, missing its middle portion.

B. Pattern 4 begins identically to pattern 1 and then adds an ascending/descending scale (like the end of patterns 2 and 3), repeated two times.

Chapter 40

Try it #1

A. There are three units—mm. 1-4, 5-8, and 9-11—separated by rests. The first two units seem to form a complete thought, as the text indicates; the third seems to be a shortened variant of the first (with A♯ and G omitted).

B. The scale (in descending order) includes D-C♯-B-A♯-G-F♯-E-D (intervals 1-2-1-3-1-2-2; the same collection as B harmonic minor). Like many early twentieth-century modal pieces, there is some ambiguity about the tonal or modal center. The A♯ seems to indicate B minor, but there is metrical and phrase placement emphasis on C♯ and F♯.

C. The durations are primarily quarters, dotted quarters, and those two tied. The downbeats after bar lines correspond to accented words. The sequence of durations in each subphrase is very similar to the others.

D. The entries are separated by five eighth notes. The intervals between voices are primarily major and minor seconds, with a few thirds and fourths.

Try it #2

A. The passage opens with Cherubino singing in G major. In m. 11, Rosina's entry (with a change of key signature to A major) disturbs an impending half cadence in G by introducing a B minor $\frac{6}{4}$ followed by a E dominant seventh chord, which progresses to an A major chord in 13—a harmonic destination quite distant from Cherubino's key. The chords in her section are also inverted, which weakens the harmonic strength of the progression.

B.   Rosina's accompaniment includes two-beat triplets, a striking contrast to Cherubino's even quarters and eighths.

Glossary

1:1 (one-to-one): See *first species*.

2:1 (two-to-one): See *second species*.

4:1 (four-to-one): See *third species*.

5-6 motion: Expansion of the opening tonic area with motion from a fifth to a sixth above the bass; an alternative analysis is I-vi⁶.

A

a a b a: See *quaternary song form*.

A B A: See *ternary form*.

abrupt modulation: See *direct modulation*.

abstract complement: Two sets are abstract complements if they can be combined in transposition or inversion to form a complete aggregate. Forte set labels show this relationship: the numbers before the hyphen sum to 12 and the numbers after the hyphen are the same (e.g., 4-z15 and 8-z15).

accent: Stress given to a note or other musical element that brings it to the listener's attention—may be created by playing louder or softer, using a different timbre or articulation, or slightly changing rhythmic durations.

accidental: A musical symbol (♯, ♭, ♮, ×, or ♭♭) that appears before a note to raise or lower its pitch.

added-sixth chord: A root-position triad that contains an extra pitch a major sixth above the bass note.

additive rhythm: An ametric rhythm created when a brief duration (often a sixteenth or smaller) is chosen as a basic element and then several are added together to form larger durations.

aeolian cadence: In popular music, the progression ♭VI-♭VII-I (in either a major or minor key), named for its association with folk-music progressions in the Aeolian mode.

Aeolian mode: An ordered collection with the pattern of whole and half steps corresponding to the white-key diatonic collection starting and ending on A; the same collection as the natural minor scale.

aggregate: A collection of all twelve pitch classes. The term generally refers to the combination of two or more twelve-tone rows to generate new twelve-note collections. Aggregates may also appear in non-twelve-tone music.

Alberti bass: A common Classical-era keyboard accompaniment formed by arpeggiating the pitches of each chord in a harmonic progression with a repeated contour of low-high-middle-high.

all-combinatorial hexachord: A hexachord capable of all four types of combinatoriality (P, I, R, and RI).

altered common-chord modulation: See *altered pivot-chord modulation*.

altered-fifth chord: A triad or seventh chord that has been colored and intensified by raising or lowering the fifth by a half step.

altered pivot-chord modulation: A modulation whose pivot chord is a chromatic chord (e.g., a mixture chord or secondary dominant) in one or both keys.

alto: The second-highest voice in four-part (SATB) writing, usually directly below the soprano.

alto clef: A C-clef positioned on a staff so that the middle line indicates middle C (C4).

ametric: Music for which no regular meter is perceived; may be notated in nontraditional ways.

anacrusis: Occurs when a melody starts just before the first downbeat in a meter; also called an upbeat, or pick-up.

anhemitonic pentatonic: A pentatonic scale with no half steps.

answer: The statement of a fugue subject, transposed up a fifth or down a fourth, that follows the statement of the subject in the exposition. See also *real answer* and *tonal answer*.

antecedent phrase: The first phrase of a period; ends with an inconclusive cadence (usually a half cadence).

anticipation: An unaccented embellishing tone resulting from the "early" arrival of a pitch. The embellishing tone is repeated as a consonance on the next beat.

applied chord: See *secondary dominant*.

appoggiatura: A dissonance that occurs on a strong beat and usually resolves down by step; sometimes refers to an accented dissonance approached by skip or leap, or an accented incomplete neighbor.

aria: A solo vocal movement within an opera, oratorio, or cantata.

arpeggiating $\frac{6}{4}$: A $\frac{6}{4}$ created when the bass line sounds each note of a triad in turn (root, third, fifth), or alternates between the root and the fifth.

arpeggio, arpeggiated: A chord played one pitch at a time.

articulation: Ways a note can be attacked and connected to other notes: played very short (*staccato*), held (*tenuto*), played suddenly and loudly (*sforzando*), highly connected (legato), or separated.

art song: A song, usually featuring a poetic text, written for performance outside the popular- and folk-music traditions.

ascending-second progression: Root motion by ascending seconds; frequently used to connect functional areas in the basic phrase.

asymmetrical meter: A compound meter with beat units of unequal duration, typically (though not always) created by five or seven beat divisions grouped into beat lengths such as 2 + 3 or 2 + 3 + 2.

asymmetrical period: A period containing two phrases of differing length.

atonal: See *nontonal*.

augmentation: The process of systematically lengthening the duration of pitches in a musical line, usually by a consistent proportion (e.g., doubling all note values).

augmented interval: An interval one half step larger than a major or perfect interval.

augmented-sixth chord: A chord featuring $\flat\hat{6}$ in the bass and $\sharp\hat{4}$ in an upper voice, creating an augmented sixth. Such chords usually resolve to V: $\flat\hat{6}$ and $\sharp\hat{4}$ resolve outward by half step to $\hat{5}$.

augmented triad: A triad with major thirds between the root and third and between the third and fifth, and an augmented fifth between the root and fifth.

B

B♭ instrument: An instrument whose sounding pitch is a whole step lower than the notated pitch.

balanced binary form: A continuous simple binary form in which material from the end of the first section returns at the end of the second section.

bar line: A vertical line that indicates the end of a measure.

Baroque era: The period in Western music dating roughly from 1600 until 1750. Some Baroque composers are Johann Sebastian Bach, George Frideric Handel, François Couperin, Antonio Vivaldi, and Henry Purcell. Genres associated with this era are the concerto grosso, oratorio, keyboard suite, and cantata.

basic phrase: A conclusive phrase that consists of an opening tonic area (T), an optional predominant area (PD), a dominant area (D), and tonic closure (T, a cadence on I). Written in contextual analysis as T-PD-D-T, beneath Roman numerals.

bass: The lowest voice in four-part (SATB) writing.

bass clef: Clef positioned on a staff to indicate F; its two dots surround the F3 line. (Also known as the F-clef.)

beat: The primary pulse in musical meter.

beat division: The secondary pulse in musical meter; the first level of faster-moving pulses beneath the primary beat.

bimodality: The simultaneous use of two modes in two different layers of music.

binary form: A composition organized into two sections. Usually each section is repeated.

bitonality: The simultaneous use of two keys in two different layers of music.

blue note: One of three pitches, derived from the blues scale, that can be altered in popular music for expressive effect: $\flat\hat{3}$, $\sharp\hat{4}$ (or $\flat\hat{5}$), and $\flat\hat{7}$.

blues scale: A collection of notes, $\hat{1}$, $\flat\hat{3}$, $\hat{4}$, $\sharp\hat{4}$ (or $\flat\hat{5}$), $\hat{5}$, and $\flat\hat{7}$, from which performers can choose when improvising a blues melody. Since it contains the minor modal scale degrees $\flat\hat{3}$ and $\flat\hat{7}$, the blues scale blurs the distinction between major and minor when it is used as the basis for improvisation against a major-key blues progression.

borrowed chord: See *mixture chord*.

bridge: (1) In a fugue exposition, music that harmonically prepares for a subject entry in the tonic after the conclusion of an answer. (2) In a quaternary song form, the contrasting **b** section. (3) In post-1950 popular music, a contrasting section that prepares for the return of the chorus.

build: In a popular song, an increase in intensity that anticipates the chorus.

C

C-clef: A movable clef that may be placed on a staff to identify any one of the five lines as middle C (C4).

C instrument: An instrument whose sounding pitch is the same as the notated pitch.

C score: A nontransposed score that shows all the parts in the concert key—i.e., all the pitches sound as notated, without transposition. Also known as concert-pitch score.

cadence: The end of a phrase, where harmonic, melodic, and rhythmic features articulate a complete musical thought.

cadential extension: An extension created by the repetition of the cadence with little new or elaborative melodic material.

cadential $^6_4$: A $^6_4$ chord that embellishes the V chord by displacing it with simultaneous 6-5 and 4-3 suspension-like motion above the sustained bass note $\hat{5}$. Usually occurs on a strong beat.

cadenza: A solo at the end of a concerto movement that features rapid passagework and other technical challenges. Can appear in any concerto movement, but is generally found in the first movement after a prominent cadential $^6_4$ harmony in the orchestra, before the beginning of the coda.

cambiata: Contrapuntal embellishment, involving an apparent skip from a dissonance, that combines passing and neighboring motion.

canon: A contrapuntal procedure where the second part can be derived from the first by following a set of instructions (e.g., transpose down a fifth and delay by a measure).

cantus firmus: The given melody against which a counterpoint is written.

cardinality: The number of elements in a collection.

center: A pitch or pitch class pervasively heard in a work or section of a work. A center does not imply a functional system of scale degrees (as would a tonic), but it can establish a sense of hierarchy.

centric: Music that focuses on a pitch or pitch-class center, but not in the sense of a conventional tonal hierarchy.

chaconne: A set of continuous variations in which the entire harmonic texture, not just the bass line, is repeated and varied. While the bass line may remain unchanged for several successive variations, it is usually altered as the chaconne progresses—through rhythmic variation, changes in inversion, or substitute harmonies.

chain of suspensions: A series of suspensions, often used in fourth-species counterpoint to set descending notes in the cantus firmus.

chance: A method of composition or performance that is determined by a random procedure, such as the toss of coins, dice, or the *I Ching*.

change of bass suspension: A type of suspension in which the bass changes when the suspension resolves; e.g., a 9-8 suspension that becomes a 9-6 because the bass skips up a third.

changes: A chord progression in a popular style; short for "chord changes."

changing meter: In contemporary pieces, meter that changes from measure to measure.

character variation: A variation intended to reproduce a particular musical style or evoke a certain genre.

chorale: A hymn set for four voices. The voices tend to move together, creating a chordal texture. Most often, the melody is given to the soprano.

chord: A group of pitches sounded together. In common-practice harmony, chords are generally built in thirds.

chord members: The pitches that make up a chord. In tonal music, each chord member is described by the interval it forms with the lowest (or bass) pitch of the chord.

chordal dissonance: A dissonant harmonic interval that originates as part of a seventh chord.

chordal skip: A melodic embellishment made by skipping from one chord member to another.

chromatic: Pitches from outside the diatonic collection. The chromatic collection consists of all twelve pitch classes.

chromatic half step: A semitone between two pitches with the same letter name (e.g., D and D♯).

chromatic inflection: A method of modulation effected by shifting one pitch of a chord by a half step.

chromatic mediant: A nondiatonic triad whose root is a major or minor third above or below $\hat{1}$. While chromatic mediants can appear as individual harmonies within a progression, they are most often employed as key areas.

chromatic neighbor tone: A nondiatonic half-step neighbor that embellishes a chord tone.

chromatic passing tone: A passing tone that divides a diatonic whole step into two half steps.

chromatic sequence: A diatonic sequence transformed by substituting chromatic harmonies for diatonic ones, or by chromatic embellishment.

chromatic submediant: A nondiatonic triad whose root is a major or minor third below $\hat{1}$. Also, the distantly related relationship of the key of that triad to the tonic key.

chromatic variation: A variation that contrasts with the original theme through increased chromaticism, embellishing the melodic line or elaborating the chord progressions.

chromatic voice exchange: The chromatic alteration of one of the pitches in a voice exchange (e.g., $\hat{2}$ and $\hat{4}$ in a ii(7) might exchange places to become $\sharp\hat{4}$ and $\hat{2}$ in a V7/V).

circle of fifths: A circular diagram showing the relationships between keys. The sharp keys appear around the right side of the circle, with each key a fifth higher moving clockwise. The flat keys appear around the left side, with each key a fifth lower moving counterclockwise.

Classical era: The period in Western music dating roughly from 1750 until 1830. Some Classical composers are Wolfgang Amadeus Mozart, Joseph Haydn, and Ludwig van Beethoven. Genres most associated with this era are the string quartet, the sonata, the symphony, and opera.

clef: A symbol that appears on the far left of every staff to designate which line or space represents which pitch (in which octave).

closely related key: Any key whose tonic is a diatonic triad (major or minor) in the original key. The key signatures of closely related keys differ at most by one accidental.

closing theme: A "third theme" that might be found near the end of a sonata-form exposition; part of the second theme group if it shares the same key.

coda: A section at the end of a piece, generally following a strong cadence in the tonic; extends the tonic area and brings the work to a close.

codetta: A "little coda" at the end of a section or piece.

coda/codetta theme: A distinctive, identifiable melody introduced in a coda or codetta.

collection: A group of unordered pitches or pitch classes that serve as a source of musical materials for a work or a section of a work; a large set.

comes: In a canon, the voice that follows.

common-chord modulation: See *pivot-chord modulation*.

common-dyad modulation: See *pivot-dyad modulation*.

common practice: The compositional and harmonic techniques of the Baroque, Classical, and Romantic eras.

common-tone augmented-sixth chord: A collection of neighbor or passing tones that makes an augmented-sixth chord; shares one pitch with the preceding or following chord.

common-tone diminished seventh chord: A collection of neighbor or passing tones that makes a diminished seventh chord; shares one pitch with the preceding or following chord.

common-tone modulation: See *pivot-tone modulation*.

common-tone theorem: The number in each position of a pcset's ic vector tells the number of common tones that will result when that particular interval class is used to transpose the pcset.

complement: See *literal complement* and *abstract complement*.

compound duple: Any meter with two beats in a measure, with each beat divided into three (e.g., $\frac{6}{8}$ or $\frac{6}{4}$).

compound interval: An interval larger than an octave.

compound melody: A melody created by the interaction of two or three voices, usually separated by register. Often features large leaps.

compound meter: Meter in which the beat divides into threes and subdivides into sixes. The top number of compound meter signatures is 6, 9, or 12 (e.g., $\frac{12}{8}$ or $\frac{6}{8}$).

compound quadruple: Any meter with four beats in a measure, with each beat divided into three (e.g., $\frac{12}{8}$ or $\frac{12}{4}$).

compound triple: Any meter with three beats in a measure, with each beat divided into three (e.g., $\frac{9}{8}$ or $\frac{9}{4}$).

concert pitch: The sounding pitch of an instrument. For transposing instruments, this differs from notated pitch.

concerto: A composition for a solo instrument and orchestra. Concertos often consist of three movements, arranged fast-slow-fast (following a formal pattern similar to the three-movement sonata).

conclusive cadence: A cadence that makes a phrase sound finished and complete. Generally the harmonic progression is V-I, with both soprano and bass ending on $\hat{1}$.

conjunct motion: Melodic motion by step.

consequent phrase: The second phrase of a period; ends with a conclusive cadence (usually a PAC).

consonance, imperfect: The intervals of a third and sixth.

consonance, perfect: The intervals of a unison, fourth, fifth, and octave. The harmonic interval of a fourth is treated as a dissonance in common-practice style.

consonant: A relative term based on acoustic properties of sound and on the norms of compositional practice. A consonant harmonic interval—unison, third, fifth, sixth, or octave—is considered pleasing to hear.

consonant skip: See *chordal skip*.

contextual analysis: A second level of harmonic analysis, showing how passing chords (and other voice-leading chords) function to expand the basic phrase model (T-PD-D-T).

continuo: An instrumental accompaniment that is read from only a given bass line (often with figures). The continuo typically consists of a low bass instrument (cello, bass viol, or bassoon) that plays a single-voice bass line, and an instrument capable of producing chordal harmonies (harpsichord, organ, guitar, or lute). The chordal instrument realizes the bass line harmonically—from figures if given, or following principles of harmonic progression and voice-leading.

continuous: Term referring to a section of a piece that has a tonally open ending and must therefore continue into the following section for tonal completion.

continuous binary: A binary form in which the first large section ends with a cadence that is not on the tonic. The piece must continue into the following section to conclude in the tonic.

continuous variation: A variation form characterized by a continuous flow of musical ideas—as opposed to strong, section-defining cadences—and *Fortspinnung* phrase structure. Continuous variations usually feature a short bass line or harmonic progression that remains constant.

contour motive: A motive that maintains its contour, or musical shape, but changes its intervals; its rhythm may or may not be altered.

contrapuntal: A composition based on the principles of counterpoint. See *counterpoint*.

contrapuntal chord: See *voice-leading chord*.

contrary fifths or octaves: Motion from one perfect interval to another of the same type, in which the voices move in opposite directions.

contrary motion: Contrapuntal motion in which two voices move in opposite directions.

contrasting period: A period in which the two phrases do not share the same initial melodic material.

counterpoint: A musical texture that sets two or more lines of music so that the independent lines together create acceptable harmony; or harmonies set one after another so that the individual voices make good, independent melodic lines.

couplet: Two paired lines of poetic text.

cross relation: The chromatic alteration of a pitch in one voice part, immediately after the diatonic version has sounded in another voice.

D

da capo aria: An A B A design where the final A section is not written out again; rather, performers are instructed to return to the beginning ("da capo") and repeat the first section until they come to a fermata or other indication marking the end.

deceptive cadence: The cadence V(7)-vi in major, or V(7)-VI in minor. Generally, any nontonic resolution from V at a cadence.

deceptive resolution: A midphrase resolution to the submediant from V.

descending-fifth progression: Root motion by descending fifths (or ascending fourths), creating a segment (or all) of the chain I-IV-vii°-iii-vi-ii-V-I in major, or i-iv-VII (or vii°)-III-VI-ii°-V-i in minor.

descending-third progression: Root motion by descending thirds, creating a segment (or all) of the chain I-vi-IV-ii-vii°-V-iii-I in major, or i-VI-iv-ii°-vii° (or VII)-V-III-i in minor.

design: The melodic or thematic aspects of musical form, as distinct from the harmonic structure.

development: The section of a sonata form devoted to the exploration and variation of motives and themes from the exposition. Generally features sequential and modulatory passages.

developmental coda: A coda having the character and structure of a sonata-form development; sometimes called a "second development."

diatonic: (1) The collection of seven pitch classes that, in some rotation, conforms to the pattern of the whole and half steps of the major scale. (2) Made up of pitches belonging to a given diatonic collection.

diatonic half step: A semitone between two pitches with different letter names (e.g., D and E♭).

diatonic sequence: A sequence made up of pitches belonging to the diatonic collection. When the sequence pattern is transposed, generic melodic intervals stay the same, but interval qualities change (e.g., major to minor, or perfect to diminished).

diminished interval: An interval one half step smaller than a minor or perfect interval.

diminished scale: Another name for *octatonic scale*, so called because of the two fully diminished seventh chords that are its subsets.

diminished seventh chord: See *fully diminished seventh chord.*

diminished triad: A triad with minor thirds between the root and third and between the third and fifth, and a diminished fifth between the root and the fifth.

diminution: (1) Unaccented notes added to a first-species framework in second- and third-species counterpoint; so called because they divide the whole-note durations of the first-species framework. (2) The process of systematically shortening the durations of pitches in a melodic line, usually by a consistent proportion (e.g., reducing all note values by half).

direct fifths or octaves: Similar motion into a perfect interval, permitted only in inner voices or if the soprano moves by step.

direct modulation: Modulation accomplished without the use of a pivot chord or pitch.

disjunct motion: Melodic motion by skip or leap.

displacement: (1) The rhythmic offsetting of a pitch so that it is "held over" like a suspension from one sonority to the next, or "arrives early" before the rest of a harmony. (2) The offsetting of a triadic pitch in a harmony by another pitch, as in a sus chord.

dissonant: A relative term based on acoustic properties of sound and on the norms of compositional practice. A dissonant harmonic interval—second, fourth (in common-practice harmony, as in a 4-3 suspension), tritone, or seventh—is considered unpleasant or jarring to hear.

dodecaphonic: See *twelve tone.*

dominant: (1) Scale degree $\hat{5}$. (2) The triad built on $\hat{5}$.

dominant area: The harmonic area in a basic phrase that precedes the final tonic, to create a conclusive cadence.

dominant expansion: See *expansion.*

dominant seventh chord: A seventh chord consisting of a major triad and a minor seventh. Occurs on $\hat{5}$ in a major key.

dominant substitute: The harmonies vii°, vii°⁷, or vii°7 (built on the leading tone), which may function as substitutes for the dominant. Because they lack $\hat{5}$, dominant substitutes have a weaker dominant function than V(7).

Dorian mode: An ordered collection with the pattern of whole and half steps corresponding to the white-key diatonic collection starting and ending on D; equivalent to a natural minor scale with $\hat{6}$ raised by a half step.

dot: Rhythmic notation that adds to a note half its own value (e.g., a dotted half equals a half note plus a quarter note).

double counterpoint: Two parts in invertible counterpoint.

double exposition: A feature of sonata form in some Classical-era concertos, where material in the exposition is heard twice: once played by the orchestra without modulation to the secondary key, and then by the soloist following the standard tonal scheme (and with the orchestra playing an accompanimental role).

double flat: An accidental (♭♭) that lowers a pitch two half steps (or one whole step) below its letter name.

double fugue: A fugue with two subjects.

double neighbor: The combination of successive upper and lower neighbors (in either order) around the same pitch.

double passing tones: Passing tones that occur simultaneously in two or more voices, usually creating parallel thirds or sixths.

double period: A group of four phrases in which a PAC appears only at the end of the fourth phrase, following three inconclusive cadences.

double sharp: An accidental (𝄪) that raises a pitch two half steps (or one whole step) above its letter name.

double suspension: Simultaneous suspensions in two voices combining 9-8 with either 4-3 or 7-6.

doubling: In four-part writing, a triad member represented in two different voices.

downbeat: Beat 1 of a metrical pattern.

drop: The return of the full texture in the chorus of a popular song.

duple meter: Meter in which beats group into units of two (e.g., $\frac{2}{4}$, $\frac{2}{2}$, or $\frac{6}{8}$).

duplet: In compound meters, a division of the beat into two, borrowed from simple meters, instead of the expected three parts.

dyad: A collection of two distinct pitches or pitch classes.

dynamic level: The degree of loudness or softness in playing. Common terms (from soft to loud) are *pianissimo, piano, mezzo piano, mezzo forte, forte,* and *fortissimo.*

E

E♭ instrument: An instrument whose sounding pitch

is a major sixth lower (or minor third higher) than the notated pitch.

échappée: A type of incomplete neighbor, approached by step and left by leap. Also called an escape tone.

eighth note: A stemmed black note head with one flag. In simple meters, two eighth notes divide a quarter-note beat; in compound meters, three eighth notes divide a dotted-quarter-note beat.

element: Most commonly, a pitch class in a set, segment, or collection. The elements of a set or segment may also be dynamic levels, durations, articulations, or other musical features.

elision: The simultaneous ending of one phrase and beginning of another, articulated by the same pitches.

embedded T-PD-D-T: A small-scale T-PD-D-T progression occurring within a larger basic phrase; used to embellish the opening tonic area.

enharmonic equivalence: The idea that two or more possible names for a single pitch (e.g., C♯, D♭, B𝄪) are musically and functionally the same.

enharmonic modulation: Modulation in which a chord resolves according to the function of its enharmonic equivalent. Chords that can be spelled (and therefore resolved) enharmonically include fully diminished sevenths, dominant sevenths, and German augmented sixths.

enharmonic pitches: Pitches with the same sound but different letter names, such as B♭ and A♯.

episode: (1) A contrasting section in a rondo; generally less tonally stable than the rondo's refrain. (2) A modulating passage in a fugue.

expansion: The extension of a T, D, or PD functional area in a phrase by means of contrapuntal motion and voice-leading chords.

exposition: (1) In sonata form, the first large section (often repeated), where the themes for the movement are "exposed" for the first time; features two primary key areas with a modulatory transition between them. (2) In a fugue or invention, the initial section where the subject is presented in each voice.

extension: (1) The lengthening of a motive, melody, or phrase. (2) A pitch added to a triad or seventh chord (e.g., an added sixth, ninth, or eleventh).

F

Fibonacci series: An infinite series in which each new member is the sum of the previous two (e.g., 0, 1, 1, 2, 3, 5, 8, 13, etc.). Associated with compositions by Bartók and others, and sometimes used in conjunction with time points.

fifth: (1) The distance spanned by five consecutive letter names. (2) The pitch in a triad that is five scale steps above the root.

fifth species: Counterpoint that combines the patterns of each of the other species. Sometimes known as free composition.

figural variation: A variation that features a specific embellishment pattern or figure throughout.

figuration prelude: A prelude featuring a rhythm based on a consistent arpeggiation scheme. The prelude could be notated as a series of chords, with each harmony unfolding according to the arpeggiation pattern.

figured bass: The combination of a bass line and Arabic numbers (figures), indicating chords without notating them fully; the numbers represent some of the intervals to be played above the bass line. Typically found in continuo parts.

first inversion: A triad or seventh chord voiced so that the chordal third is in the bass.

first species: Counterpoint written so that each note in one voice is paired with a single note in the other voice, using only consonant intervals. Also called note-to-note or 1:1 counterpoint.

first theme group: The opening section of a sonata form, featuring a tonic-key melody (or melodies) and accompaniment; may be preceded by an introduction.

five-part rondo: A rondo with the form **A B A C A** or **A B A B′ A**, plus optional coda.

flat: An accidental (♭) that lowers a pitch a half step.

focal pitch: A pitch or pitch class that is emphasized through repetition or other means, but does not establish a hierarchy with other pitches in the piece's collection.

Fonte: A type of progression, identified by Joseph Riepel, that could be used in the harmonic disturbance at the beginning of the second section of a binary form; literally, "fountain." Consists of a descending sequence, often with secondary dominants, such as V7/ii | ii | V7 | I.

Forte set label: A set-class-labeling system developed by Allen Forte, in which set classes are ordered by size (or cardinality) and then by ic vector. To each set class, Forte gave a hyphenated number (e.g., 5-35). The number before the hyphen represents the cardinality of the pcset, and the number after it represents the pcset's ordinal position on Forte's list; thus, 5-35 is a pcset of five elements that appears thirty-fifth on the list.

***Fortspinnung*:** A feature of Baroque-era works in which a melody is "spun out" in uninterrupted fashion. Continuous motion, uneven phrase lengths, melodic or harmonic sequences, changes of key, and elided phrases are all characteristics of *Fortspinnung* passages.

fourth species: Counterpoint in which one voice is rhythmically displaced by ties across the bar; characterized by its use of suspensions.

fragmentation: The isolation and/or development of a small but recognizable part of a motive.

French augmented-sixth chord (Fr⁶): An augmented-sixth chord with $\hat{1}$ and $\hat{2}$ in the upper voices. The distinctive sound of this chord is created by two dissonances above the bass: the augmented sixth and the augmented fourth.

fugue: An imitative contrapuntal composition, usually in three or four voices, that features repeated statements of a subject and its answer in various keys, with accompanying counterpoint and modulatory episodes in between.

full score: A score showing each instrumental part in the piece on a separate staff (or staves).

fully diminished seventh chord: A seventh chord consisting of a diminished triad and a diminished seventh. Because its thirds are all minor, it has no audible root. May be used as a means to modulate to distantly related keys.

fundamental bass: An analytical bass line consisting of the roots of a chord progression, as opposed to the sounding bass line.

G

German augmented-sixth chord (Gr⁶): An augmented-sixth chord with $\hat{1}$ and $\flat\hat{3}$ in the upper voices. This chord, characterized by its perfect fifth above the bass, is an enharmonic respelling of a dominant seventh chord.

golden section (or mean): A proportion associated with balance in architecture, painting, and music; about 62 percent (.618) of the total length of a piece. In music analysis, works by Debussy and Bartók (among others) reflect this proportion in their formal divisions or moments of climax. The golden mean is related to the Fibonacci series: if you divide two adjacent numbers in the series, they approximate the golden mean.

grand staff: Two staves, one in the treble clef and one in the bass clef, connected by a curly brace; typically found in piano music.

graphic notation: Nonstandard symbols used to indicate pitch, duration, articulation, etc., in some nontonal scores.

groove: The underlying rhythmic "feel" of a performance, created by a recurring pattern of pitch and rhythm performed by the rhythm section—drums, electric bass or double bass, guitar, and keyboards.

ground bass: A set of continuous variations built on a repeating bass line.

H

half cadence (HC): An inconclusive cadence on the dominant.

half-diminished seventh chord: A seventh chord consisting of a diminished triad and a minor seventh.

half note: A stemmed white note head; its duration is equivalent to two quarter notes.

half step: The musical space between a pitch and the next-closest pitch on the keyboard.

harmonic ambiguity: Characteristic of highly chromatic passages in late-Romantic music. The musical coherence comes not through "strength of progression" (strong root-movement-based chord progressions) but rather through "strength of line": smooth linear connections between chords.

harmonic disturbance: A term for the beginning of the second large section in a binary form, so called for its unstable sequential harmonies.

harmonic interval: The span between two pitches played simultaneously.

harmonic minor: See *minor scale*.

harmonic rhythm: The rate at which harmonies change in a piece (e.g., one chord per measure or one chord per beat).

harmonic sequence: A succession of harmonies based on a root progression; includes a harmonic pattern that is successively transposed and a repeated intervallic pattern between the bass and upper voice.

harmonically closed: Term referring to a melody or formal section that ends with a conclusive cadence on the tonic.

harmonically open: A harmonic feature of a phrase or section of a piece in which the end is inconclusive, or in a different key from the beginning.

harmony: (1) A chord. (2) A progression of chords,

usually implying common-practice principles of voice-leading.

head: In jazz, a clearly recognizable melody and harmonic progression that is the basis for improvisation over the course of the piece.

hemiola: A temporary duple rhythmic grouping in the context of an underlying triple meter (e.g., two measures of $\frac{3}{4}$ meter heard as three measures of $\frac{2}{4}$); or a temporary two-part division of the beat in the context of an underlying three-part division (e.g., a measure of $\frac{6}{4}$ heard as a measure of $\frac{3}{2}$).

hexachord: A collection of six distinct pitches or pitch classes.

hexachordal combinatoriality: A compositional technique in which two forms of the same row are paired so that the rows' initial hexachords, when combined, complete an aggregate. Similarly, the rows' second hexachords, when combined, complete an aggregate. There are four kinds of hexachordal combinatoriality: P, I, R, and RI.

hidden fifths or octaves: See *direct fifths* or *octaves*.

hook: In popular songs, a musical setting of a few words or a phrase, usually including the title, that is the most "catchy" or memorable part of the song.

hypermeter: A high-level metric grouping that interprets groups of measures as though they were groups of beats within a single measure.

I

I-combinatoriality: Pairing a row and its inversion form(s) to make aggregates.

imitation: The contrapuntal "echoing" of a voice in another part.

imperfect authentic cadence (IAC): An authentic cadence weakened by (1) placing the I or V harmony in inversion (contrapuntal IAC), or (2) ending with the soprano on a scale degree other than $\hat{1}$ (strong IAC).

imperfect consonance: The intervals of a third and sixth.

incomplete neighbor: A neighbor tone without either (1) the initial stepwise motion from the main pitch to the neighbor, or (2) the returning stepwise motion of the neighbor to the main pitch.

inconclusive cadence: A cadence that makes a phrase sound less complete than a PAC. Generally, either the soprano or the bass ends on a scale degree other than $\hat{1}$.

indeterminate: Some musical element or event in a score that is left to chance (either in performance or during composition).

index number: The value that measures the "distance" between two inversionally related pcsets. If pcsets A and B are inversionally related by the index number n, then A = T_nI B, and B = T_nI A. When paired correctly, every pc in one set added to the corresponding pc in the other set will sum uniformly to the index number.

instrumental break: An instrumental section in the middle of a popular song.

instrumental chorus: Chorus of a popular song performed with instrumental solos rather than vocals.

integer notation: The system of labeling pcs by number instead of letter name: C = 0, C♯ or D♭ = 1, D = 2, D♯ or E♭ = 3, and so on. The letter t may substitute for 10 (B♭ or A♯) and e for 11 (B).

interlude: A passage that serves as a transition between or a change of pace from other sections.

internal expansion: The lengthening of a phrase between its beginning and end. Results from immediate repetitions of material, an elongation of one or more harmonies, or the addition of new material within the phrase.

interval: The musical space between two pitches or pitch classes.

interval class (ic): All pitch intervals that can be made from one pair of pitch classes belong to the same interval class (e.g., M3, m6, and M10). Also called unordered pitch-class interval.

interval-class vector (ic vector): A concise summary of all interval classes within a given pcset; written as six numbers within square brackets, without commas. For example, the ic vector for the trichord {0 4 6}, [010101], shows that it contains one whole step, one major third, and one tritone.

intro: Music, usually instrumental, that introduces a popular song.

invariance: The retention of pitch classes between a pcset or row and its transposition or inversion.

invention: A contrapuntal composition, usually in two voices, that features repeated statements of a subject, imitated at the octave, with accompanying counterpoint and modulatory episodes in between.

inverse: Given a pc or pc interval, the inverse is the corresponding pc or pc interval such that the two sum to 0 (mod12). For example, the inverse of pc 5 is pc 7.

inversion (chordal): A voicing in which a chord member other than the root is the lowest-sounding pitch.

inversion (motivic): A melodic or motivic transformation in which successive generic intervals reverse direction (e.g., an ascending third becomes a descending third).

inversion (pitch): A melodic or motivic transformation in which successive ordered pitch intervals reverse direction (e.g., a +2 becomes a -2).

inversion (pitch class): A transformation in which each pc in a pcset is replaced by its inverse (e.g., the inversion of {0 1 6 7} is {0 e 6 5}). To find the transposed inversion of a pcset, always invert first, then transpose.

inversion (row): The form of a twelve-tone row in which each pc is replaced by its inverse; abbreviated I_n, where n is the pc integer of the row's first element.

inversionally related intervals (tonal): Two intervals that, when combined, span an octave (e.g., E3-G♯3, a major third; plus G♯3-E4, a minor sixth). When inverted, major intervals become minor (and vice versa), diminished become augmented (and vice versa), and perfect stay perfect. The interval numbers of inversionally related intervals sum to 9 (third and sixth, second and seventh, etc.).

invertible counterpoint: Counterpoint that is structured intervallically so that the two lines can exchange register.

Ionian mode: An ordered collection with the pattern of whole and half steps corresponding to the white-key diatonic collection starting and ending on C; the same collection as the major scale.

isochronous: Term characterizing beats that are spaced evenly. Isochronous beats are found in simple and compound meters.

isorhythm: A repeating series of durations (which may be associated with repeating pitch materials); used in various style periods, but most prominently in the Middle Ages and twentieth century.

Italian augmented-sixth chord (It⁶): An augmented-sixth chord with (doubled) $\hat{1}$ in the upper voices.

K

key: (1) The key of a tonal piece takes its name from the first scale degree of the major or minor tonality in which that piece is written; this pitch class is the primary scale degree around which all other pitches in the piece relate hierarchically. (2) A lever on an instrument that can be depressed with a finger (like a piano key).

key signature: A sign that appears at the beginning of each line of a musical score, after the clef, showing which pitches are to be sharped or flatted consistently; helps determine the key.

L

lament bass: Chromatic bass line descending from $\hat{1}$ to $\hat{5}$; so called because of its association in early opera with sadness and death.

large ternary: A formal scheme created by joining smaller, composite forms into an **A B A** form (e.g., minuet and trio, or scherzo and trio). The **A** and **B** sections themselves may have their own form (such as rounded binary).

lead-in: A musical passage that connects the end of one melodic phrase with the beginning of the next.

leading tone: $\hat{7}$ of the major scale and harmonic or ascending-melodic minor scale; a half step below the tonic.

leading-tone chord: Harmonies built on the leading tone: vii°, viiø7, or vii°7.

lead-sheet notation: A type of notation, commonly used in popular music, where roots are indicated by capital letters and qualities by added abbreviations or symbols (e.g., Fm indicates an F minor triad).

leap: A melodic interval larger than a third (larger than a skip).

ledger line: Extra lines drawn through stems and/or note heads to designate a pitch above or below a staff.

libretto: The text of an opera.

Lied: German art song of the Romantic era (plural is Lieder).

linear chord: See *voice-leading chord*.

linear-intervallic pattern (LIP): The intervallic framework between outer voices. LIPs underlie all harmonic sequences, although sometimes they are hidden behind complicated surface elaborations.

link: (1) In a fugue exposition, a rhythmic or metrical adjustment of a few beats to allow the subject to enter on the appropriate part of the measure. (2) In popular styles, a short instrumental passage, used to connect sections. (3) A lead-in.

literal complement: The pcset that, when combined with a given pcset, produces the complete aggregate.

Locrian mode: An ordered collection with the pattern of whole and half steps corresponding to the white-key diatonic collection starting and ending on B; equivalent to a natural minor scale with $\hat{2}$ and $\hat{5}$ lowered by half steps.

loop: In a popular song, three or more chords repeated in the same sequence and harmonic rhythm.

Lydian mode: An ordered collection with the pattern of whole and half steps corresponding to the white-key diatonic collection starting and ending on F; equivalent to a major scale with $\hat{4}$ raised by a half step.

Lydian-Mixolydian mode: A mixed mode created by combining the lower tetrachord of the Lydian mode with the upper tetrachord of the Mixolydian (e.g., C D E F♯ G A B♭ C); equivalent to a major scale with $\hat{4}$ raised by a half step and $\hat{7}$ lowered by a half step.

M

major interval: The quality of the intervals second, third, sixth, and seventh above $\hat{1}$ in the major scale.

major-minor seventh chord: See *dominant seventh chord*.

major-minor tetrachord: See *split-third chord*.

major pentatonic: A five-note subset of the diatonic collection that features major-key $\hat{1}$, $\hat{2}$, $\hat{3}$, $\hat{5}$, and $\hat{6}$.

major scale: An ordered collection of pitches arranged according to the pattern of whole and half steps W-W-H-W-W-W-H.

major seventh chord: A seventh chord consisting of a major triad and a major seventh.

major triad: A triad with a major third between the root and third, a minor third between the third and fifth, and a perfect fifth between the root and the fifth. Corresponds to $\hat{1}$, $\hat{3}$, and $\hat{5}$ of a major scale.

measure: A unit of music grouped by beats; generally, a measure begins and ends with notated bar lines.

medial caesura: An abrupt silence marking the end of the transition in the exposition of a sonata-form movement before the second-theme group.

mediant: (1) Scale degree $\hat{3}$. (2) The triad built on $\hat{3}$.

medieval era: The period in Western music dating roughly from 800 to 1430. Some medieval composers are Hildegard of Bingen, Pérotin, and Guillaume de Machaut. Genres associated with this era are Gregorian chants, motets, chansons, and organum.

melisma: A vocal passage that sets one syllable of text to many notes.

melodic interval: The span between two notes played one after another.

melodic minor: See *minor scale*.

melodic sequence: A motive repeated several times in successive transpositions (often up or down by step).

mélodie: Romantic-era art song in the French tradition.

meter: A hierarchical arrangement of beats and their divisions that repeat from measure to measure and are perceived as relatively strong and weak. The first beat of each measure is perceived as strongest.

meter signature: A sign that appears at the beginning of a piece, after the clef and key signature: the upper number indicates meter type and the lower number indicates which note gets the beat; also called a time signature.

metric modulation: A means of smoothing what would otherwise be abrupt changes of tempo by introducing subdivisions or groups of beats in the first tempo that match durations in the new tempo. The new tempo is recognized in retrospect, much like a modulation by pivot chord.

metric reinterpretation: A disruption in the established hypermetric pattern at the cadence. This can occur when a measure simultaneously functions as strong and weak in the case of a phrase elision.

metrical accent: The pattern of strong and weak beats based on the "weight" of the downbeat and the "lift" of the upbeat.

Middle Ages: See *medieval era*.

middle C: C4, the C located at the center of the piano keyboard.

minimalism: A style in which music is composed through the repetition and gradual change of "minimal" musical elements.

minor interval: The quality of the intervals third, sixth, and seventh from $\hat{1}$ in the minor scale. A minor second (diatonic half step) is formed between $\hat{7}$ and $\hat{1}$ in a major, harmonic minor, or ascending melodic minor scale.

minor pentatonic: A five-note subset of the diatonic collection: minor-key $\hat{1}$, ♭$\hat{3}$, $\hat{4}$, $\hat{5}$, and ♭$\hat{7}$.

minor scale: The natural minor scale is an ordered collection of pitches arranged according to the pattern of whole and half steps W-H-W-W-H-W-W. The harmonic minor scale raises ♭$\hat{7}$ to $\hat{7}$ (the leading tone). The melodic minor raises ♭$\hat{6}$ and ♭$\hat{7}$ ascending, but takes the natural minor form descending.

minor seventh chord: A seventh chord consisting of a minor triad and a minor seventh.

minor triad: A triad with a minor third between the root and third, a major third between the third and fifth, and a perfect fifth between the root and the fifth. Corresponds to $\hat{1}$, $\flat\hat{3}$, and $\hat{5}$ of a minor scale.

minuet and trio: The most common type of composite ternary form, generally written in triple meter. Typically the third (dance-like) movement of a Classical-era sonata, string quartet, or symphony.

Mixolydian mode: An ordered collection with the pattern of whole and half steps corresponding to the white-key diatonic collection starting and ending on G; equivalent to a major scale with $\hat{7}$ lowered by one half step.

mixture (or modal mixture): (1) Shifting temporarily from a major key to the parallel minor (or vice versa) in a musical passage. (2) "Mixing" the parallel major and minor modes, most often in major keys, where the modal scale degrees, $\flat\hat{3}$, $\flat\hat{6}$, and $\flat\hat{7}$ are borrowed from the parallel minor.

mixture chord: A chord whose spelling and chord quality are derived from the parallel mode. Most often, chords from the parallel minor mode appear in a major key. Also called borrowed chords.

mobile form: Form consisting of segments, sections, or movements that may be played in varying orders. While the contents of segments may remain consistent from one performance to another, the overall form of the piece will not.

mod12 arithmetic: Arithmetic that keeps integers in the range 0 to 11. To convert a number greater than 11, divide by 12 and take the remainder. Used to label pcs in integer notation and perform operations such as transposition or inversion.

modal scale degrees: The scale degrees that differ between major and natural minor scales: $\hat{3}$, $\hat{6}$, and $\hat{7}$.

mode: (1) Rotations of the major (or natural minor) scale (e.g., the Dorian mode is a rotation of the C major scale beginning and ending on D). (2) Term used to distinguish between major and minor keys (e.g., a piece in "the minor mode").

mode of limited transposition: Composer Olivier Messiaen's term for pc collections that can be transposed by only a few intervals; other transpositions replicate the original collection (the whole-tone and octatonic collections are examples).

modified strophic: A variation of strophic form. Rather than repeating the melody exactly, the music is slightly altered from verse to verse.

modulating period: A period whose consequent phrase modulates, leading to an authentic cadence in a different key from the antecedent phrase.

modulation: A change of key, usually confirmed by a (perfect) authentic cadence.

moment form: The concept that sections of a piece do not have to connect in some logical way or in a predetermined order, but can change abruptly from one style of music to another.

Monte: A type of progression, identified by Joseph Riepel, that could be used in the harmonic disturbance at the beginning of the second section of a binary form; literally, "mountain." Consists of an ascending sequence, usually with secondary dominants, such as V7/IV | IV | V7/V | V.

motet: A polyphonic choral work.

motive: The smallest recognizable musical idea. Motives may be characterized by their pitches, contour, and/or rhythm, but rarely contain a cadence. Generally they are repeated (exactly or varied).

musical form: The overall organization of a composition into sections, defined by harmonic structure—change of key, mode, pcset, collection, or row form—as well as by changes in (or a return to) a theme, texture, instrumentation, rhythm, or other feature.

musical topic: In Classical and Romantic instrumental music, design elements that evoke a location, activity, emotion, or musical style. Examples include minuet, brilliant style, singing style, and *Sturm und Drang* (storm and stress).

N

natural minor: See *minor scale*.

natural sign: An accidental (♮) that cancels a sharp or flat.

Neapolitan: The major triad built on ♭II; typically occurs in first inversion (Neapolitan sixth), with $\hat{4}$ in the bass and $\flat\hat{2}$ and $\flat\hat{6}$ in the upper voices.

neighbor tone: An embellishment that decorates a melody pitch by moving to a pitch a step above or below it, then returning to the original pitch; approached and left by step in opposite directions.

neighboring $\substack{4 \\ 2}$: A $\substack{4 \\ 2}$ chord arising from neighbor tones in all three of the upper parts (e.g., in the tonic expansion I-ii$\substack{4 \\ 2}$-I).

neighboring $\substack{6 \\ 4}$: A $\substack{6 \\ 4}$ chord, usually unaccented, that shares a bass note with the harmony it embellishes, while two upper voices move in stepwise upper-neighbor motion. Also called a pedal $\substack{6 \\ 4}$.

ninth chord: A triad or seventh chord with a ninth added above the bass.

nonad: A collection of nine distinct pitches or pitch classes.

non-isochronous: Term characterizing beats that are unevenly spaced. Non-isochronous beats are found in asymmetrical meters, such as $\frac{5}{8}$ and $\frac{7}{8}$, where beats last for either a quarter-note or dotted-quarter duration.

nonmetric: See *ametric*.

nonteleological form: Form, such as moment form and mobile form, in which the music lacks a sense of a goal or direction.

nontonal: Music that freely employs all twelve pitch classes. The pervasive chromaticism and absence of whole- and half-step scale patterns make a true "tonic" pitch class impossible to discern in nontonal music.

normal order: The order of consecutive pcs in a pcset that (1) spans the smallest interval and (2) places the smallest intervals toward the left.

notated meter: The way in which rhythms are notated in a score. In common-practice music, notated meter and perceived meter are usually the same; in music of the twentieth century and later, they may not be.

note-to-note: See *first species*.

O

oblique motion: Contrapuntal motion in which one part repeats the same pitch while the other moves by leap, skip, or step.

octad: A collection of eight distinct pitches or pitch classes.

octatonic scale: A scale composed of eight distinct pcs in alternating whole and half steps.

octave: The distance of eight musical steps.

octave equivalence: The concept that two pitches an octave apart are functionally equivalent.

offbeat: A weak beat or weak portion of a beat.

omnibus: A special chromaticized voice exchange, usually prolonging the dominant. The exchanged pitches form the interval of a tritone, which enables the voice exchange to continue chromatically until the exchanged voices arrive where they began (but up or down an octave). All the resulting chromatic simultaneities are *voice-leading chords*.

open score: A score with a staff for every part, unlike a piano score; for example, an SATB choral score on four staves.

orchestration: Setting or composing for a large ensemble.

ostinato: A repeated rhythmic and/or pitch pattern.

outro: Music, often instrumental, that brings a popular song to its close.

overlap: A means of phrase connection in which one or more voices begin a new phrase while one or more voices simultaneously finish the previous phrase.

overlapping voices: A voice-leading error in which one voice moves into the register of an adjacent voice on an adjacent beat.

P

P-combinatoriality: Pairing a row and its transposed form(s) to make aggregates.

palindrome: A segment (of pitches, pcs, intervals, and/or rhythms) that reads the same backward and forward.

parallel fifths or octaves: Contrapuntal and voice-leading error that results from approaching a perfect fifth in parallel motion from another perfect fifth, or perfect octave from another perfect octave.

parallel keys: Keys in different modes that share the same letter name and tonic, such as F major and F minor.

parallel major: The major key that shares the same tonic as a given minor key. The parallel major raises the third, sixth, and seventh scale degrees of the minor key.

parallel minor: The minor key that shares the same tonic as a given major key. The parallel minor lowers the third, sixth, and seventh scale degrees of the major key.

parallel motion: Contrapuntal motion in which both parts move in the same direction by the same interval.

parallel period: A period in which the two phrases share the same beginning melodic material.

parody: The compositional borrowing or reshaping of another composer's materials, emphasizing particular features.

passacaglia: Continuous variations with a repeated bass line (or ground bass).

passing chord: A voice-leading "chord" arising from passing motion.

passing $\frac{6}{4}$: A $\frac{6}{4}$ chord created by passing motion in the bass (e.g., in the progression I–I$\frac{6}{4}$–IV^6).

passing $^6_4$: A voice-leading $^6_4$ chord, usually connecting root-position and first-inversion chords of the same harmony and harmonizing a bass-line passing tone.

passing tone: A melodic embellishment that fills in the space between chord members by stepwise motion; approached and left by step in the same direction.

pc: Abbreviation of *pitch class*.

pcset: Abbreviation of *pitch-class set*.

pedal $^6_4$: See *neighboring $^6_4$*.

pedal point: A note held for several measures while harmonies change above it. Chords above a pedal point do not participate in the harmonic framework.

pentachord: A collection of five distinct pitches or pitch classes.

pentatonic scale: A scale with five pcs. In Western music, the pentatonic scale is a subset of the diatonic collection. The two most common are the minor pentatonic ($\hat{1}$, $\flat\hat{3}$, $\hat{4}$, $\hat{5}$, $\flat\hat{7}$) and the major pentatonic ($\hat{1}$, $\hat{2}$, $\hat{3}$, $\hat{5}$, $\hat{6}$).

perfect authentic cadence (PAC): A strong conclusive cadence in which a root-position V(7) progresses to a root-position I, and the soprano moves from $\hat{2}$ or $\hat{7}$ to $\hat{1}$.

perfect consonance: The intervals of a unison, fourth, fifth, and octave. The harmonic interval of a fourth is treated as a dissonance in common-practice style.

period: A musical unit consisting (usually) of two phrases. Generally, the first phrase ends with a weak cadence (typically a HC), answered by a more conclusive cadence (usually a PAC) at the end of the second.

phasing: The compositional technique of moving musical patterns in and out of alignment, creating additional sounds and patterns that are not present in the original materials.

phrase: A basic unit of musical thought, similar to a sentence in language, with a beginning, a middle, and an end. In tonal music, a phrase must end with a cadence; in nontonal music, other musical features provide closure.

phrase group: Three or more phrases with tonal and/or thematic design elements that group them together.

phrase modulation: See *direct modulation*.

phrase rhythm: The interaction of hypermeter and phrase structure.

phrase structure: The melodic and harmonic characteristics of a phrase or group of phrases, identified by cadence type, harmonic motion, number of measures, and melodic or motivic repetition or contrast.

Phrygian cadence: The half cadence iv⁶-V in minor, so called because of the half-step descent in the bass.

Phrygian mode: An ordered collection with the pattern of whole and half steps corresponding to the white-key diatonic collection starting and ending on E; equivalent to a natural minor scale with $\hat{2}$ lowered by a half step.

Phrygian II: See *Neapolitan*.

Picardy third: In a minor key, the raised third of a tonic chord (making the harmony major), typically at an authentic cadence at the end of a piece.

pitch: A tone sounding in a particular octave.

pitch class (pc): A class that assumes octave and enharmonic equivalence. Notes an octave (or several octaves) apart share the same name (e.g., F3, F5, and F2 all belong to pc F).

pitch-class interval (pci): The interval spanned by two pcs. Ordered pitch-class intervals measure the distance from pc a to b by subtracting (b - a) mod 12; the distance can range from 0 to 11. Unordered pitch-class intervals measure the shortest distance between two pcs, either from the first to the second or vice versa; the distance ranges from 0 to 6. See *interval class*.

pitch interval: The musical space between two pitches, described either with tonal labels (e.g., minor second, augmented sixth, perfect fifth) or by the number of half steps from one pitch to the other. Unordered pitch intervals measure distance; ordered pitch intervals measure distance and direction (shown with a + or -).

pitch symmetry: The spacing of pitches at equal distances above and below a central pitch.

pitch-time graph: A graph that plots pitch (the vertical axis) against time (the horizontal axis).

pivot area: In a pivot-chord modulation, a series of harmonies that function diatonically in both the old and new key.

pivot chord: In a pivot-chord modulation, a harmony that functions diatonically in both the old and new key.

pivot-chord modulation: Modulation from one key to another by means of a harmony (the pivot chord) that functions diatonically in both keys.

pivot-dyad modulation: Modulation in which two pitches of a chord function as a "pivot." Other pitches of this modulating chord may shift up or down a half step, making a chromatic connection.

pivot-tone modulation: Modulation in which only a single pitch of a chord or melodic line functions as a "pivot." Other pitches of this modulating chord may shift up or down a half step, making a chromatic connection.

plagal cadence: The cadence IV-I (iv-i in minor), sometimes called the Amen cadence.

planing: Twentieth-century technique of connecting chords via parallel motion.

polymeter: Music with two or more different simultaneous metric streams.

polymodality: Music with several modes sounding in different layers of music simultaneously.

polyphonic variation: A variation with independent voices; may include imitative entries.

polytonality: Music with several keys sounding in different layers of music simultaneously.

Ponte: A type of progression, identified by Joseph Riepel, that could be used in the harmonic disturbance at the beginning of the second section of a binary form; literally, "bridge." Consists of a dominant prolongation, such as V | V | V$^{8-7}$ | I.

postchorus: In a popular song, a short passage of music following the chorus that prepares for the return of the verse.

postmodernism: Combining materials originating from different times and styles. The term is borrowed from literary and art criticism.

post-tonal music: Music composed after 1900 that is not restricted to compositional principles of the common-practice era.

power chords: Chords featuring only the root and fifth (missing the third), played by electric guitars and typically moving in parallel motion.

prechorus: In popular styles, a short passage of music with text that comes between the verse and the chorus.

predominant: (1) The triad or seventh chord built on $\hat{2}$, $\hat{4}$, or $\hat{6}$. (2) A category of harmonic function that includes chords that precede the dominant, typically ii and IV (ii$^{\varnothing}$ and iv in minor keys), but also the Neapolitan sixth and augmented-sixth chords.

predominant area: A harmonic area in a basic phrase that often precedes the dominant area (T-PD-D-T).

primary theme (**group**): See *theme (group)*.

prime (**row**): Row in a twelve-tone composition considered a starting point, usually the first appearance of the row; labeled P$_n$, where n is the first pc of the row.

prime form: The representative pcset for a set class, beginning with 0 and enclosed in square brackets; the set's normal order (or the normal order of its inversion) transposed to begin with 0.

prolong: To expand the function of a harmony by means of contrapuntal motion and contrapuntal or linear chords.

pset: Abbreviation of "pitch set."

Q

quadruple meter: Meter in which beats group into units of four (e.g., $\frac{4}{8}$ or $\frac{12}{8}$).

quadruplet: In compound meter, a subdivision group in four parts borrowed from simple meter.

quarter note: A stemmed black note head, equivalent in duration to two eighth notes.

quaternary song form: A song form consisting of four (usually eight-bar) phrases. The first two phrases begin the same (they may be identical or may differ at the cadence). They are followed by a contrasting section (bridge) and then a return to the opening material, making the overall form **a a b a**. Also known as thirty-two-bar song form.

quodlibet: A medley, or amalgamated borrowing, of songs; may feature multiple texts, sometimes in different languages.

R

R-combinatoriality: Hexachordal combinatoriality achieved by pairing a row and its appropriate retrograde form(s) to make aggregates.

raised submediant: Raised $\hat{6}$ in melodic minor.

real answer: Exact transposition of a fugue subject up a fifth (or down a fourth); the answer directly follows the subject, with accompanying counterpoint, in a fugue exposition.

realization: (1) A full musical texture created from a figured (or unfigured) bass. (2) In pieces composed with pcsets or rows, pitch classes in a specific register and rhythm. (3) Performance of a work from a text or graphic score.

rearticulated suspension: A suspension in which the suspended voice sounds again (instead of being held over) at the moment of dissonance.

recapitulation: The final section of a sonata form (or penultimate section, if the movement ends with a coda), in which the music from the exposition is heard again, this time with the theme groups usually in the tonic key.

recitative: A short vocal movement, usually paired with an aria, written in a style intended to simulate speech.

reduction: (1) A score transcribed so that it can be performed by fewer instrumental forces (usually by piano). (2) The underlying harmonic framework and linear counterpoint of a passage of music, revealed after embellishing tones or harmonies have been eliminated.

refrain: (1) The section of a song that recurs with the same music and text. (2) In popular-music verse-refrain form, the second portion of the song, after the verse; generally in **a a b a**, or quaternary, song form. (3) In rondo form (usually **A B A C A** or **A B A C A B (D) A**), the refrain is the **A** section, which returns with opening thematic material in the tonic key. Another word for *ritornello*.

register: The particular octave in which a pitch sounds.

registral invariance: A compositional technique in which certain pcs are realized as pitches only in one specific register. Also known as frozen register and pitch fixation.

relative keys: Major and minor keys that share the same key signature (e.g., C major and A minor).

relative major: The major key that shares the same key signature as a given minor key. The relative major is made from the same pitch-class collection as its relative minor, but begins on ♭$\hat{3}$ of the minor key.

relative minor: The minor key that shares the same key signature as a given major key. The relative minor is made from the same pitch-class collection as its relative major, but begins on $\hat{6}$ of the major key.

Renaissance era: The period in Western music dating roughly from 1430 until 1600. Some Renaissance composers are Josquin des Prez, Palestrina, Guillaume Dufay, and Carlo Gesualdo. Genres most associated with the era are the mass, madrigal, masque, and instrumental dances.

resolution: The way a harmony or scale step progresses to the next harmony or pitch. The term usually refers to the manner in which a dissonant interval moves to a consonant one.

rest: A duration of silence.

retardation: A rhythmic embellishment where a consonance is held over to the next beat, creating a dissonance with the new harmony. The dissonance is resolved upward by step, creating another consonant interval.

retransition: A musical passage that harmonically prepares for the return of previously heard material. In sonata form, it appears at the end of the development section and prolongs the dominant harmony in preparation for the tonic return of the recapitulation's first theme group. In rondo form, a retransition may appear before any recurrence of the refrain (**A** section).

retrograde: The form of a twelve-tone row in which the pcs are in the reverse order of the prime. Abbreviated R_n, where n refers to the last pc of the row, i.e., the first pc of the original, prime row.

retrograde inversion: The form of a twelve-tone row in which the pcs are in the reverse order of the inversion. Abbreviated RI_n, where n refers to the last pc of the row, i.e., the first pc of the inverted row.

retrogression: Progressions that reverse typical common-practice harmonic norms; common in other musical idioms (e.g., V–IV in blues and rock music).

rhyme scheme: The pattern of rhyming in a poetic verse or stanza, generally designated with lowercase letters. Repeated letters indicate lines that end with rhyming words.

rhythm: The patterns made by the durations of pitch and silence (notes and rests) in a piece.

rhythmic acceleration: The gradual move from long note values to shorter note values in a passage of music; also called a rhythmic *crescendo*.

rhythmic motive: A motive that maintains its rhythm but changes its contour and interval structure.

RI-combinatoriality: Hexachordal combinatoriality achieved by pairing a row and its appropriate retrograde-inversional form(s) to create aggregates.

riff: A repeated instrumental motive.

ritornello: An instrumental section of a piece that returns. Another word for *refrain*.

Romantic era: The period in Western music dating roughly from 1830 until 1910. Some Romantic composers are Robert Schumann, Frédéric Chopin, Giuseppe Verdi, and Richard Wagner. Genres most associated with this era are the art song, program symphony, character piece, tone poem, and grand opera.

rondo: A musical form characterized by a repeated section (refrain, or ritornello) alternating with sections that contrast in key, mode, texture, harmonic complexity, thematic content, and/or style (usually **A B A C A** or **A B A C A B (D) A**). The contrasting sections are called episodes.

root: The lowest pitch of a triad or seventh chord when the chord is spelled in thirds.

root position: A chord voiced so that the root is in the bass.

rounded binary: A binary form in which melodic or motivic features in the initial phrase return at the end of the piece, "rounding out" the formal plan.

row: A specific ordering of all twelve pitch classes.

row elision: One way of connecting rows in a twelve-tone piece: the same pc or pcs are shared at the end of one row and the beginning of the next.

row matrix: A twelve-by-twelve array that displays all possible P, I, R, and RI forms of a row.

S

SATB: An abbreviation for the four main voice ranges: soprano, alto, tenor, and bass. Also indicates a particular musical style or texture: chorale style.

scale: A collection of pitch classes arranged in a particular order of whole and half steps.

scale degree: A name for each pitch class of the scale, showing its relationship to the tonic pitch (for which the key is named). Scale-degree names may be numbers ($\hat{1}$, $\hat{2}$, $\hat{3}$), words (tonic, supertonic, mediant), or solfège syllables (*do*, *re*, *mi*).

scale step: Same as scale degree.

scherzo and trio: A composite ternary form in a fast tempo, usually in triple meter. Typically the third movement of a Romantic-era sonata, quartet, or symphony.

second inversion: A triad or seventh chord voiced so that the chordal fifth is in the bass.

second species: Counterpoint written so that one voice has two notes for every single note in the other voice. Permits consonances and passing tones, according to specific rules of voice-leading; some authors also allow neighbor tones. Another name for *2:1 counterpoint*.

second theme group: The second large part of a sonata exposition, in a secondary key area (usually V, or III in minor keys). When this material returns in the recapitulation, it is usually transposed to the tonic key.

secondary dominant: A dominant-function harmony (V or vii°, with or without the chordal seventh) "applied" to a chord other than tonic (may also refer only to a secondary V chord). A secondary dominant typically includes chromatic alterations (relative to the tonic key). Also called an applied dominant, or applied chord.

secondary leading-tone chord: A leading-tone chord that functions as an applied, or secondary, dominant; usually a fully diminished seventh chord.

secondary set: An aggregate formed by combining segments belonging to more than one row form.

section: A large division within a composition, usually set off by a cadence (or other elements denoting closure). May be delineated by repeat signs or a double bar.

sectional: A harmonic feature of tonal forms, in which a section is tonally closed (with an authentic cadence in the tonic key); the section could stand on its own.

sectional binary: A binary form in which the first section ends with a cadence on the tonic. The section is tonally complete and could stand on its own.

sectional variation: A variation form in which each variation is clearly distinguished from the next by a strong conclusive cadence (and often by double bars). Each variation could be played as a complete stand-alone section.

segment: An ordered sequence of pitches or pcs.

sentence: A phrase design with a 1 + 1 + 2 (or 2 + 2 + 4) motivic structure. Typically shaped by an opening idea that is repeated, then a continuation that works out the idea further and brings the phrase to a cadence.

sequence: A musical pattern that is restated successively at different pitch levels. See *harmonic sequence* and *melodic sequence*.

sequence pattern: A short (one- or two-measure) melodic or harmonic idea, transposed up or down to form a sequence.

serial music: Music composed with (ordered) pitch-class segments and ordered transformations of these segments; may also feature ordered durations, dynamics, and articulations.

set: A group of unordered pitches or pitch classes. See *collection*.

set class: The collection of pcsets that contains all possible distinct transpositions of the pcset, as well as all distinct transpositions of its inversion. Pcsets in the same set class also share the same ic vector.

seven-part rondo: A rondo whose form is **A B A C A B (D) A**, plus optional coda.

seventh chord: A chord that can be arranged as a root-position triad with another third stacked on top. This third forms a seventh with the root. There are five types of seventh chords in common-practice tonal music: major seventh, minor seventh, major-minor seventh (dominant seventh), half-diminished seventh, and fully diminished seventh.

sharp: An accidental (♯) that raises a pitch a half step.

short score: A score that shows several parts combined on each staff.

shuttle: The alternation of two chords in a popular song.

similar motion: Contrapuntal, or voice-leading, motion in which both parts move in the same direction, but not by the same generic interval.

simple binary: A binary form that generally has an ‖: A :‖‖: B :‖ or ‖: A :‖‖: A′ :‖ design.

simple duple: Any meter with two beats in a measure, with each beat divided into two (e.g., $\frac{2}{4}$).

simple meter: Meter in which the beat divides into twos and subdivides into fours. The top number of the meter signature will be 2, 3, or 4 (e.g., $\frac{4}{8}$ or $\frac{3}{2}$).

simple quadruple: Any meter with four beats in a measure, with each beat divided into two (e.g., $\frac{4}{4}$).

simple ternary: A ternary form that is relatively brief (as opposed to composite ternary), with three distinct sections, usually in the form **A B A**. The **B** section generally expresses both a contrasting key and contrasting thematic material.

simple triple: Any meter with three beats in a measure, with each beat divided into two (e.g., $\frac{3}{4}$ or $\frac{3}{2}$).

sixteenth note: A stemmed black note head with two flags. In duple beat divisions, two sixteenths divide an eighth-note beat; in triple beat divisions, three sixteenths divide a dotted-eighth-note beat.

skip: A melodic interval of a third or fourth.

slur: An arc that connects two or more different pitches. Slurs affect articulation but not duration.

solfège, fixed-*do*: A singing system in which a particular syllable is associated with a particular pitch class; e.g., *do* is always C, *re* is always D, etc., no matter what the key.

solfège, movable-*do*: A singing system in which a particular syllable is associated with a particular scale step; e.g., *do* is always $\hat{1}$, *re* is always $\hat{2}$, etc., no matter what the key.

sonata: A multimovement composition for piano or a solo-line instrument (usually with keyboard accompaniment), typically in three or four movements. The first movement is almost always in sonata form.

sonata form: A formal plan with a three-part design (exposition, development, recapitulation) and a two-part harmonic structure (the most common is ‖: I-V :‖‖: → I :‖ for major keys, with motion to III instead of V in minor keys). Sonata form can be thought of as an expanded continuous rounded binary form.

sonatina: A "little sonata." The first movement of a sonatina is usually a reduced sonata form, with compact first and second themes and a very short development section or no development at all.

song cycle: A group of songs, generally performed as a unit, either set to a single poet's cycle of poetry or set to poems that have been grouped by the composer into a cycle.

soprano: The highest voice in four-part (SATB) writing.

sounding pitch: The pitch that is heard when a performer plays a note on an instrument. For transposing instruments, this differs from notated pitch. Also called concert pitch.

spacing: The arrangement of adjacent parts in four-part writing, in which vocal range and the intervals between voices are considered.

species: A particular type of counterpoint, used as a tool for teaching composition. The various species (types) of counterpoint differ by the embellishments permitted and the rhythmic relationship between the voices. See *first species* (1:1), *second species* (2:1), *third species* (4:1), *fourth species*, and *fifth species*.

split-third chord: A four-note "triad" with both a major and a minor third above the root.

staff: The five parallel lines on which music is written.

step: The melodic interval of a half or whole step.

step progression: A technique for writing compound melody, in which nonadjacent pitches are connected by an overall stepwise motion.

strain: In marches, the sections corresponding to the **A** and **B** portions of binary (or ternary) forms.

stratification: The layering of distinct musical materials.

strophe: A stanza, or verse, in a song.

strophic: A song form in which more than one strophe (verse) of text is sung to the same music.

style juxtaposition: A method of composing in which elements strongly associated with one musical style are placed side-by-side with another style without a transition between the two.

stylistic allusion: A musical passage that either literally quotes another composition, or is written in imitation of a previous style, intended to be recognized by the listener as belonging to another time or piece.

subdivision: The third level of pulse in musical meter, after beat and division.

subdominant: (1) Scale degree $\hat{4}$. (2) The triad built on $\hat{4}$.

submediant: (1) Scale degree $\hat{6}$. (2) The triad built on $\hat{6}$.

subordinate theme (group): Another name for *second theme (group)*.

subphrase: A melodic and harmonic unit smaller than a phrase. Subphrases complete only a portion of the basic phrase progression and do not conclude with a cadence.

subset: A subgroup of a given set.

substitute chord: A harmony that can stand for another. The most common are vi for I, ii for IV, and vii° for V.

subtonic: (1) Scale degree ♭$\hat{7}$ of the natural minor scale, so called because it is a whole step below tonic. (2) The triad built on ♭$\hat{7}$ of natural minor.

supertonic: (1) Scale degree $\hat{2}$. (2) The triad built on $\hat{2}$.

sus chord: In popular music, a chord with a fourth above the bass instead of a third. The fourth does not necessarily resolve, as in a typical 4-3 suspension.

suspension: A rhythmic embellishment where a consonance is held over to the next beat, creating a dissonance with the new harmony. The dissonance is resolved downward by step, creating another consonant interval. Suspensions are designated by intervals above the bass; the most common are 7-6, 4-3, and 9-8.

suspension chain: A combined succession of suspensions, sometimes of a single type (e.g., 4-3, 4-3) or alternations of two kinds (e.g., 7-6, 4-3, 7-6, 4-3); the resolution of each suspension prepares the next.

symmetrical meter: A meter with equally spaced primary beats within each measure, each beat having the same number of divisions.

symmetrical phrase: A phrase with an even number of measures.

symmetrical set: A set whose pcs can be ordered so that the intervals between adjacent elements are the same when read left to right or right to left. The whole-tone scale, octatonic scale, and chromatic collection are all symmetrical sets.

symmetry: Having the same pattern from start to middle as end to middle.

syncopation: Off-beat rhythmic accents created by dots, ties, rests, dynamic markings, or accent marks.

T

teleological form: Form that gives the listener a sense that the music moves toward a goal; usually associated with common-practice forms.

tempo: How fast or slow music is played. Examples of tempo markings include *adagio* (slow), *andante* (medium speed), and *allegro* (fast).

temporary tonic: The chord to which a secondary dominant or secondary leading-tone harmony is applied; also known as a "tonicized harmony."

tendency tone: A chord member or scale degree whose dissonant relation to the surrounding tones requires a particular resolution in common-practice style (i.e., chordal sevenths resolve down, and leading tones resolve up).

tenor: The second-lowest voice in four-part (SATB) writing. Usually directly above the bass.

tenor clef: A C-clef positioned on a staff so that the fourth line from the bottom indicates middle C (C4); typically read by bassoons, cellos, and tenor trombones in their higher registers.

ternary form: A composition divided into three sections. The outer sections usually consist of the same musical material, while the inner section features contrasting musical qualities (including key), creating an overall **A B A** form. In some song forms, the contrasting section may occur last (**A A B**).

tessitura: The vocal or instrumental range most used by a singer or instrumentalist.

tetrachord: (1) A collection of four distinct pitches or pitch classes. (2) A segment of four consecutive members of a scale.

text notation: A musical score with instructions written in prose or poetry, without any traditional musical notation.

textural variation: A variation written in a texture that contrasts with that of surrounding variations or the original theme. Two possibilities are (1) the simplifying variation, which features only a few voices, resulting in a thin texture; and (2) the contrapuntal variation, which features imitative entries of the voices.

theme and variations: A variation set based on a given theme, in which each variation differs in melody, rhythm, key, mode, length, texture, timbre, character, style, or motive. Theme and variation sets after the Baroque era are usually sectional variations, in which each variation could be considered a brief, stand-alone piece. See also *continuous variation*.

third inversion: A seventh chord voiced so that the chordal seventh is in the bass.

third species: Counterpoint written so that one voice has four notes for every single note in the other voice; allows consonances, passing tones, and neighboring tones, according to strict rules of voice-leading. Another name for *4:1 counterpoint*.

thirty-second note: A stemmed black note head with three flags; equal in duration to two sixty-fourth notes.

thirty-two-bar song form: *Quaternary song form*, with each phrase eight measures long; common formal design for show tunes and songs that have become jazz standards.

through composed: A composition organized so that each section (e.g., each verse in a song) consists of different music, with little or no previous material recurring as the work progresses.

tie: A small arc connecting the note heads of two (or more) identical pitches, adding the durations of the notes together.

timbral variation: A variation that exploits instrumentation and/or sound color different from previous variations.

time-line notation: Music written so that the passing of time is measured out in the number of seconds elapsed between markers.

time points: Locations in a score indicating a musical event; determined by a duration series, a numerical pattern, chance, or a series of proportions.

time signature: Another term for *meter signature*.

tonal answer: The modified transposition of a fugue subject up a fifth or down a fourth.

tonal music: Music based on the following organizational conventions: (1) melodies built from major and minor scales using scale-degree function, in relation to a tonic (e.g., $\hat{7}$ resolving to $\hat{1}$); (2) harmonies that relate to each other in functional progressions leading toward a tonic harmony; (3) identifiable embellishing tones (dissonant suspensions, neighbors, passing tones) that resolve (or imply a resolution).

tonal plan: The progression of keys in a composition.

tonic: (1) Scale degree $\hat{1}$. (2) The triad built on $\hat{1}$.

tonic area: Usually the opening and closing area in a basic phrase (T-PD-D-T).

tonic closure: A conclusive ending that confirms the key of a musical passage, usually accomplished by means of an authentic cadence.

tonic expansion: An extension of tonic function effected by means of contrapuntal motion and voice-leading chords.

tonic substitute: A chord other than tonic (most often the submediant) that fulfills tonic function in the basic phrase model.

tonicization: The result when a chord becomes a temporary tonic by means of a secondary, or applied, dominant. The key of the passage does not really change, and the temporary tonic soon returns to its normal functional role in the primary key.

tonicized half cadence (THC): a half cadence preceded by a secondary dominant (or diminished seventh chord).

total serialism: The extension of serial procedures to musical elements other than pitch. Also called integral serialism.

transferred resolution: The movement of a tendency tone from one voice part to another prior to resolution.

transition: A musical passage that modulates from one key and establishes another, often by means of sequential treatment. In sonata form, the transition links the first and second theme groups.

transpose: (1) To notate a score for transposing instruments so that pitches will sound correctly in the concert key. (2) To rewrite a section of music at a different pitch level. (3) To add or subtract a constant to pitches or pitch classes in integer notation.

transposed score: A score that shows the pitches as notated in the performers' parts (which may be transposed for certain instruments), rather than the sounding pitches.

transposing instrument: An instrument (e.g., clarinet, saxophone, or horn) whose notated pitches are not the same as the pitches that sound when played.

transposition (row): The form of a twelve-tone row derived by transposing the prime. Abbreviated P_n, where n is the pc integer of the row's first element.

transpositional equivalence: The relationship between two sets such that each one can be transposed to make the other.

treble clef: On a staff, the treble clef (also known as G-clef) denotes the line for G4, by means of the end of its curving line; typically read by flutes, clarinets, oboes, horns, sopranos, altos, and piano right hand.

triad: A chord made from two stacked thirds.

triad quality: The description of a triad according to the quality of its stacked thirds and fifth: major, minor, diminished, or augmented.

trichord: A collection of three distinct pitches or pitch classes.

triple meter: Meter in which beats group into units of three (e.g., $\frac{3}{2}$ or $\frac{9}{8}$).

triplet: In simple meters, a division group borrowed from compound meters.

tritone: An interval made up of three whole tones or six semitones: an augmented fourth or diminished fifth. By some definitions, only an augmented fourth is a tritone, since in this spelling the interval spans three whole steps.

tritone axis: Music (in nontonal pieces) that moves from a first pitch center to a second pitch center a tritone away, and then returns; analogous to the tonic-dominant axis in tonal music.

tritone substitution: A dominant-seventh-quality chord that replaces a V7 chord a tritone away. The substitution results in a Neapolitan (♭II) with a minor seventh, to make a dominant seventh quality.

twelve-bar blues: Standardized blues format of three subphrases, each four measures long. The harmonic plan is usually ‖ I | I | I | I | IV | IV | I | I | V | IV | I | I ‖, where any triad may add a minor seventh.

twelve-tone: Music with a specific ordering of all twelve pitch classes, called a row. The row is musically realized by means of transformations (transposition, inversion, retrograde, or retrograde inversion) throughout a composition.

U

unequal fifths: Similar motion from a d5 to P5 or P5 to d5; d5 to P5 is prohibited in strict counterpoint, but allowable in some situations in four-part writing if not placed in the outer voices.

unison: The interval size 1, or the distance from a pitch to itself; interval 0 if measured in semitones. Sometimes abbreviated U.

upbeat: Occurs when a melody starts just before the first strong beat in a meter; named for the upward lift of the conductor's hand. Another word for *anacrusis*.

V

verse: (1) The section of a song that returns with the same music but different text. (2) In early twentieth-century popular song forms, the first section of verse-refrain form; the verse is usually not repeated, and it may be tonally less stable than the refrain.

verse-refrain form: A typical form of early twentieth-century popular songs and show tunes: an introductory verse, possibly modulatory, precedes a chorus that is often in quaternary song form (**a a b a**).

vocal range: The range of pitches (high and low) that may be sung comfortably by singers of a particular voice type (e.g., alto or tenor).

voice crossing: In four-part writing, one voice written higher than the part above it or lower than the part below it; considered poor voice-leading in common-practice SATB style.

voice exchange: The expansion of a functional area in which two voices exchange chord members (e.g., $\hat{1}$ moves to $\hat{3}$ in the bass, and $\hat{3}$ moves to $\hat{1}$ in the soprano). This skip is often filled in with a passing tone or passing chord.

voice-leading: The combination of melodic lines to create harmonies according to principles of common-practice harmony and counterpoint.

voice-leading chord: A "chord" created by combining embellishing tones in the expansion of a structural harmony. In analysis, label the individual embellishments rather than the chord, or label the chord as "voice-leading" (VL) or as a passing or neighboring chord.

W

whole note: A stemless open note head; equal in duration to two half notes.

whole step: The combination of two adjacent half steps.

whole-tone scale: An ordered collection of pcs arranged so that each scale step lies a whole step away from the next. A whole-tone scale consists of six elements and exists in two distinct forms: pcs {0 2 4 6 8 t} and {1 3 5 7 9 e}.

APPENDIX 3

The Overtone Series

Every musical pitch played by an instrument, or sung by a voice, is a complex tone, consisting of a fundamental (lowest) pitch plus a series of overtones that sound faintly above it. Example A3.1 shows an overtone series above C2. Overtones (also called partials) are naturally occurring phenomena, created by the vibrations of strings, vocal chords, or columns of air. Partials are often numbered: the fundamental is the first partial, the octave above is the second partial, and so on. The partials shown with black note heads sound out of tune compared to a piano.

EXAMPLE A3.1: Overtone series with C2 Fundamental

The characteristic timbre—or color—of an instrument is created by the different strengths (or amplitudes) of overtones, resulting from the shape of the instrument's resonating space. For example, a flute has a strong fundamental, a somewhat weaker second partial, and very weak higher partials. An oboe has more sound from higher overtones than from lower overtones.

The interval between the first and second partials (the octave from C to C) may be represented by the ratio 2:1 (relating the frequencies of the two pitches). Throughout the series, each ratio between partial numbers represents the interval between the pitches, such as 3:2 (C–G, perfect fifth), 4:3 (G–C, perfect fourth), 5:4 (C–E, major third), and so on. The intervals with smaller numbers tend to correspond with acoustic consonances, and higher numbers (e.g., 16:15, minor second) with dissonances. These ratios also represent the divisions of a string (e.g., on violin, guitar, or cello) where a performer would place his or her fingers to create these intervals, as Figure A3.1 shows. If you play an open string, then divide it in half and play the string again, the second pitch is an octave above the first. For brass players, the overtones are open notes (played without depressing any valves or moving the slide on a trombone); changing the air pressure and speed moves the sound between pitches in the overtone series.

FIGURE A3.1: Divisions of a string to produce P8, P5, and P4

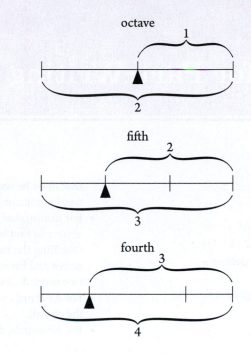

Guidelines for Part-Writing

Contents

I. Vocal Ranges
II. Doubling Guidelines
III. Spacing Guidelines
IV. General Voice-Leading Guidelines
V. Realizing Figured Bass
VI. Voice-Leading Considerations for Specific Harmonies

I. Vocal Ranges

Typical ranges for common-practice SATB writing:

- Soprano: C4 to G5
- Alto: G3 to D5
- Tenor: C3 to G4
- Bass: E2 to D4

II. Doubling Guidelines

- If the triad is in *root position* (and major or minor quality), double the root. Sometimes you double the third or fifth, but these doublings are much less common.
- If the triad is in *first inversion*, double any chord member that is not a tendency tone or other altered tone. Doubling the soprano is a common strategy (for major or minor triads only).
- If the triad is in *second inversion*, double the fifth (the bass).
- Never double a tendency tone. This guideline applies most frequently to the leading tone ($\hat{7}$) and to the seventh of the dominant seventh chord ($\hat{4}$), but includes any tone that must be resolved, such as a chromatic passing tone or altered tone.
- For *diminished triads* (which typically appear in first inversion), double the third. Doubling the root emphasizes the dissonance and causes voice-leading problems. Occasionally, the fifth may be doubled.
- For *N6 chords*, double the bass (the third of the chord).
- For *It6 chords*, double $\hat{1}$.

III. Spacing Guidelines

When writing SATB parts, check to see that

- the interval between soprano and alto, and the interval between alto and tenor, is an octave or less;
- the interval between the tenor and bass line usually remains within a tenth;
- no alto pitch is higher than soprano or lower than tenor;
- no tenor pitch is higher than alto or lower than bass.

IV. General Voice-Leading Guidelines

A. Work to achieve smooth voice-leading:

- Resolve tendency tones correctly, and never double them.
- Move each voice to the closest possible member of the following chord (without creating parallel perfect intervals or errors in doubling or spacing).
- Avoid skipping down to a chordal seventh.

- If two chords share a common tone, keep the common tone in the same voice.

B. Aim for independence of the four voices based on principles of good counterpoint:

- Keep each voice within its own characteristic range.
- Write the soprano-bass counterpoint first before filling in the inner voices.
- Avoid moving all four voices in the same direction.
- Avoid placing a pitch in one voice part so that it crosses above or below the pitch sung by an adjacent voice part—either within a single chord (voice crossing) or between two consecutive chords (overlapping).
- Avoid prolonged parallel or similar motion; balance with contrary and oblique motion.

C. Make each voice a "singable" melody:

- Write primarily stepwise motion or chordal skips, with few large leaps (except bass leaps between chord members).
- Avoid melodic motion by augmented or diminished intervals (e.g., the augmented second between scale degrees $\flat\hat{6}$ and $\hat{7}$ in harmonic minor).
- Use passing or neighboring tones to create a smooth line or add melodic interest.

D. Pay careful attention to voice-leading to and from perfect intervals:

- Choose contrary or oblique motion when you approach and leave any perfect interval (unison, octave, fifth), since parallel perfect intervals are prohibited in this style.
- Do not use
  (1) direct octaves or fifths (similar motion into a perfect interval in the soprano-bass pair)—these are permitted only in inner voices or if the soprano moves by step;
  (2) contrary octaves or fifths (contrary motion from one perfect interval to another of the same size);
  (3) unequal fifths (motion from a diminished fifth to a perfect fifth, especially in the soprano-bass pair), since they interfere with proper resolution of the tendency tones ($\hat{7}$ resolving up to $\hat{1}$ and $\hat{4}$ resolving down to $\hat{3}$); motion from a perfect fifth to a diminished fifth is acceptable.

E. Keep in mind typical voice-leading based on root progressions:

- Roots a fifth apart: hold the common tone in the same voice, and move all the other parts to the closest possible chord member.
- Roots a third apart: hold the common tones, and move the other part to the closest possible chord member.
- Roots a second apart: move the upper parts in contrary motion to the bass line.

F. Remember to write musically:

- When a harmony is repeated, create some variety by changing the soprano pitch, the inversion, and/or the spacing of the chord.
- Where possible, avoid static or repetitive melodic lines.

V. Realizing Figured Bass

- Sing the given line(s) to help orient yourself tonally.
- Place pitches above the bass in an appropriate octave according to the generic intervals written in the figured bass.
- Use pitches diatonic in the key, unless indicated otherwise by the bass or figures.
- An accidental next to a number means to raise or lower the pitch associated with that number by one half step.
- An accidental by itself means to raise or lower the third *above the bass* (not necessarily the third of the chord).
- A slash through a number means to raise the pitch associated with that number.
- Accidentals in the figure apply only to that single chord.
- A figured bass does not list all intervals above the bass; some, like octaves and thirds, may be implied by the figures.
- Follow all doubling and voice-leading guidelines when voicing or connecting chords.
- A dash between two numbers means that those intervals belong in the same voice-leading strand (like a suspension: 4-3).
- Melodic embellishing tones (other than suspensions) are not shown in the figures because they are not a part of the main harmonic framework.

VI. Voice-Leading Considerations for Specific Harmonies

A. When resolving V7 to I (or i):

- Two tendency tones resolve at once.
- The chordal seventh moves down ($\hat{4}$ moves to $\hat{3}$), and
- the leading tone resolves up by half step ($\hat{7}$ resolves to $\hat{1}$).
- When both chords are in root position, either the V7 or I will be incomplete (lacking the fifth) to avoid parallels.
- At a cadence, $\hat{7}$ in an inner voice may leap to $\hat{5}$ to complete the tonic triad.
- The same rules apply when resolving secondary dominant chords, except that scale-degree numbers refer to the "temporary" tonic.

B. When resolving the leading-tone triad or seventh chord:

- If the tritone is spelled as a diminished fifth ($\hat{7}$ below $\hat{4}$), it normally resolves inward to a third: $\hat{1}$-$\hat{3}$.
- If the tritone is spelled as an augmented fourth ($\hat{4}$ below $\hat{7}$), it may follow the voice-leading of the tendency tones and resolve outward to a sixth, or it may move in similar motion to a perfect fourth ($\hat{5}$-$\hat{1}$).
- When the tritone is spelled as a diminished fifth, resolve $\hat{4}$ up to $\hat{5}$ in only one context: when the soprano-bass counterpoint moves upward in parallel tenths ($\hat{2}$ to $\hat{3}$ in the bass, $\hat{4}$ to $\hat{5}$ in the soprano). The strength of the parallel motion in this contrapuntal pattern overrides the voice-leading tendency of $\hat{4}$ to resolve down.
- Resolve the tendency tones of viiø7 and viio7 like V7: resolve $\hat{7}$ up to $\hat{1}$, resolve $\hat{4}$ down to $\hat{3}$, and resolve the chordal seventh down ($\hat{6}$ to $\hat{5}$).
- The same rules apply when resolving secondary leading-tone chords, except that scale-degree numbers refer to the "temporary" tonic.

C. When writing a cadential $^6_4$:

Always double the bass.

- Hold the common tones between the chord of approach and the $^6_4$, and move other voices the shortest distance.

- Write the cadential $^6_4$ on a strong beat in the measure; it displaces the V or V7 to a weaker beat.
- Resolve the "suspended" tones of the $^6_4$ downward: the sixth above the bass moves to a fifth, and the fourth above the bass moves to a third.
- If there is a seventh in the dominant harmony that follows the cadential $^6_4$, the doubled bass note (an octave above the bass) usually moves to the seventh of the dominant seventh chord.

D. When writing other types of $^6_4$s:

- Each second-inversion triad will be one of the following types: cadential $^6_4$, passing $^6_4$, neighboring (or pedal) $^6_4$, or arpeggiating $^6_4$.
- Always double the bass (fifth) of the chord.
- In all $^6_4$s except arpeggiating (which are consonant), all voices should approach and leave chord members by step (forming neighbor or passing tones) or by common tone.
- Arpeggiating $^6_4$s may include skips within members of the chord that is arpeggiated, but must resolve correctly to the next harmony.

E. When writing N6 chords:

- Use the Neapolitan harmony most often in minor keys. Build it on $\flat\hat{2}$ with a major quality, and (usually) in first inversion ($\flat$II6). In major keys, be sure to include $\flat\hat{6}$ (from mixture) to ensure the chord's major quality.
- Precede the Neapolitan with any harmony that would normally precede a predominant-function harmony: e.g., I, VI, iv6, a string of parallel $^6_3$ chords.
- Double $\hat{4}$ (the bass note, when the harmony appears in its characteristic first inversion). If $\flat\hat{2}$ is doubled, it may move to $\natural\hat{2}$ in an inner voice only—never in the soprano.
- Place the N6 in a predominant role and resolve it to V, with both its tendency tones moving down: ($\flat$)$\hat{6}$ to $\hat{5}$, and $\flat\hat{2}$ (usually through the passing-tone $\hat{1}$) to $\hat{7}$. Note: Don't resolve $\flat\hat{2}$ to $\natural\hat{2}$ (unless it has been doubled in an inner voice), since this voice-leading conflicts with the tendency of $\flat\hat{2}$ to move downward.
- If you harmonize the passing-tone $\hat{1}$ when resolving the N6, choose viio7/V or V$^{6-5}_{4-3}$.

- Typically, $\flat\hat{2}$ or $\hat{4}$ appears in the highest voice. Don't place $(\flat)\hat{6}$ in the highest voice if the N^6 moves through a tonic chord before progressing to V, because the resolution of $(\flat)\hat{6}$-$\hat{5}$ above $\flat\hat{2}$-$\hat{1}$ invariably leads to parallel fifths in the voice-leading.

F. When writing augmented-sixth chords:

- Place $\hat{5}$ of the V chord (the chord of resolution) in the bass and an upper voice (the soprano is a characteristic but not required voicing), leaving an empty space before it for the augmented sixth.
- In the empty space, write in the two tendency tones leading by half step to $\hat{5}$: $(\flat)\hat{6}$-$\hat{5}$ in the bass, and $(\sharp)\hat{4}$-$\hat{5}$ in the upper voice. In major keys, don't forget to add the correct accidental to lower $\hat{6}$.

- Add $\hat{1}$ in one of the inner voices.
- Add a fourth note, following these guidelines.
  (1) Italian 6 (It^6): double $\hat{1}$;
  (2) French 6 (Fr^6): add $\hat{2}$ (an augmented fourth above the bass note);
  (3) German 6 (Gr^6): add $\hat{3}$ from the minor mode (a perfect fifth above the bass note—in major keys, you will need to add an accidental).
- Resolve the tendency tones by half step to $\hat{5}$, and move the remaining tones to the closest possible chord tone in the dominant harmony.
- Resolve an It^6 or a Fr^6 directly to V; Gr^6 chords often resolve to V$^{6-5}_{4-3}$ to avoid parallel fifths.

Ranges of Orchestral Instruments

INSTRUMENT	WRITTEN RANGE	SOUNDING RANGE
Strings		
Violin		as written
Viola		as written
Cello		as written
Bass		octave lower
Harp		as written
Guitar		octave lower
Banjo		as written, but tenor banjo sounds an octave lower

SOURCE: Samuel Adler, *The Study of Orchestration*, 4th ed. (New York: Norton, 2016)

INSTRUMENT	WRITTEN RANGE	SOUNDING RANGE

Woodwinds

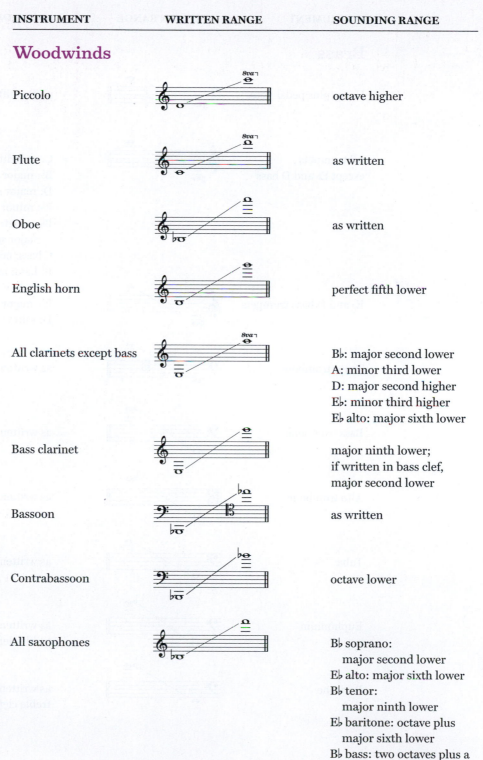

Piccolo	octave higher
Flute	as written
Oboe	as written
English horn	perfect fifth lower
All clarinets except bass	Bb: major second lower
	A: minor third lower
	D: major second higher
	Eb: minor third higher
	Eb alto: major sixth lower
Bass clarinet	major ninth lower;
	if written in bass clef,
	major second lower
Bassoon	as written
Contrabassoon	octave lower
All saxophones	Bb soprano:
	major second lower
	Eb alto: major sixth lower
	Bb tenor:
	major ninth lower
	Eb baritone: octave plus
	major sixth lower
	Bb bass: two octaves plus a
	major second lower

INSTRUMENT	WRITTEN RANGE	SOUNDING RANGE

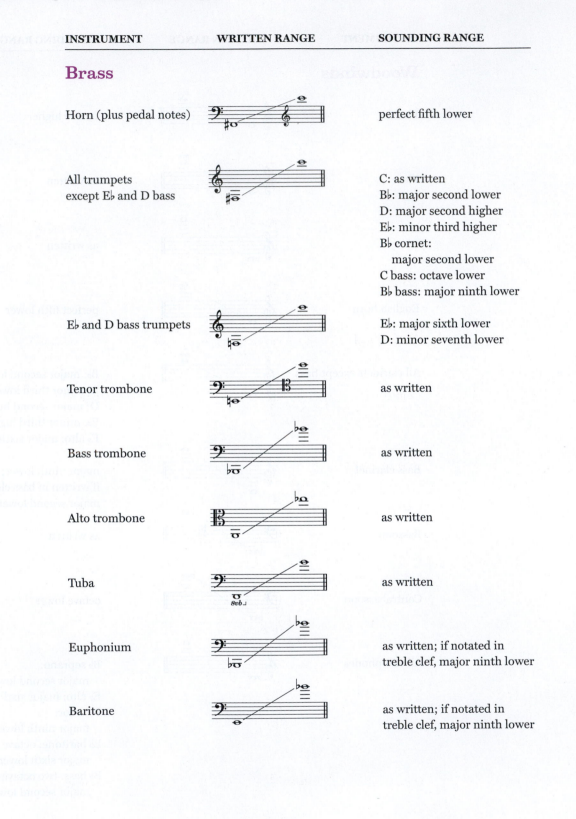

Brass

Horn (plus pedal notes) — perfect fifth lower

All trumpets except E♭ and D bass
- C: as written
- B♭: major second lower
- D: major second higher
- E♭: minor third higher
- B♭ cornet: major second lower
- C bass: octave lower
- B♭ bass: major ninth lower

E♭ and D bass trumpets
- E♭: major sixth lower
- D: minor seventh lower

Tenor trombone — as written

Bass trombone — as written

Alto trombone — as written

Tuba — as written

Euphonium — as written; if notated in treble clef, major ninth lower

Baritone — as written; if notated in treble clef, major ninth lower

INSTRUMENT	WRITTEN RANGE	SOUNDING RANGE

Percussion

Timpani — as written

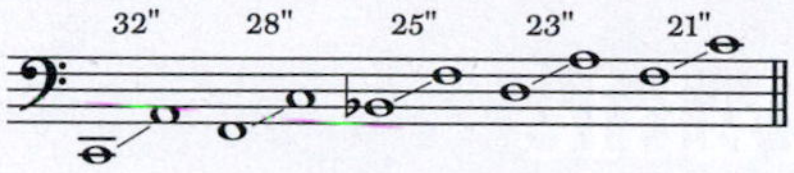

Xylophone — octave higher

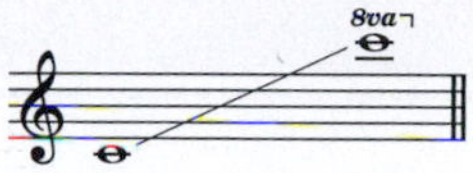

Marimba — as written

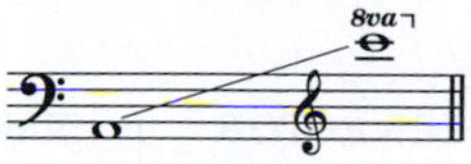

Vibraphone — as written

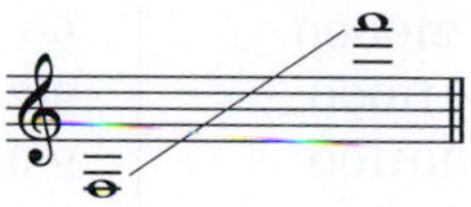

Glockenspiel — two octaves higher

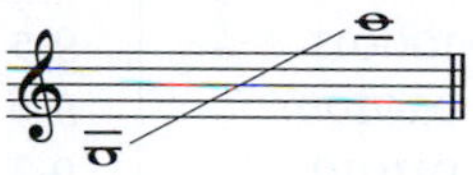

Chimes — as written

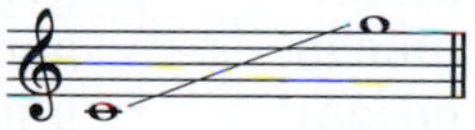

Keyboard

Piano — as written

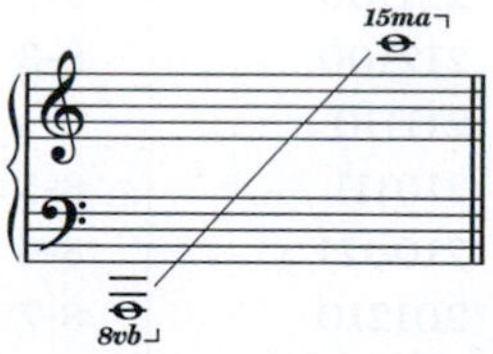

Celesta — octave higher

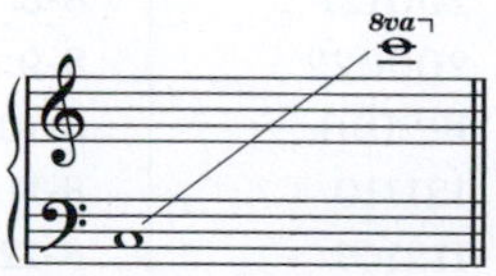

Harpsichord — as written

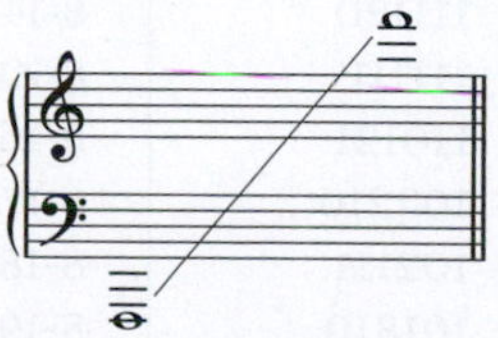

Organ — as written

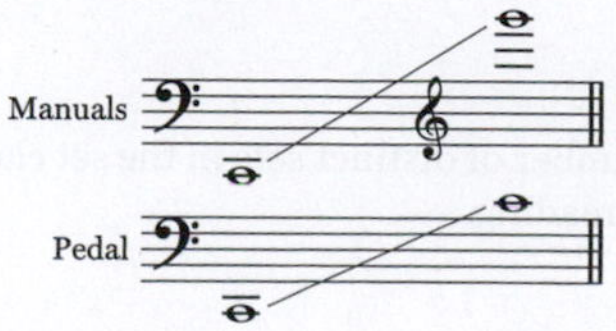

Set-Class Table

NAME	PCS	IC VECTOR	NAME	PCS	IC VECTOR
3-1(12)	0,1,2	210000	9-1	0,1,2,3,4,5,6,7,8	876663
3-2	0,1,3	111000	9-2	0,1,2,3,4,5,6,7,9	777663
3-3	0,1,4	101100	9-3	0,1,2,3,4,5,6,8,9	767763
3-4	0,1,5	100110	9-4	0,1,2,3,4,5,7,8,9	766773
3-5	0,1,6	100011	9-5	0,1,2,3,4,6,7,8,9	766674
3-6(12)	0,2,4	020100	9-6	0,1,2,3,4,5,6,8,t	686763
3-7	0,2,5	011010	9-7	0,1,2,3,4,5,7,8,t	677673
3-8	0,2,6	010101	9-8	0,1,2,3,4,6,7,8,t	676764
3-9(12)	0,2,7	010020	9-9	0,1,2,3,5,6,7,8,t	676683
3-10(12)	0,3,6	002001	9-10	0,1,2,3,4,6,7,9,t	668664
3-11	0,3,7	001110	9-11	0,1,2,3,5,6,7,9,t	667773
3-12(4)	0,4,8	000300	9-12	0,1,2,4,5,6,8,9,t	666963
4-1(12)	0,1,2,3	321000	8-1	0,1,2,3,4,5,6,7	765442
4-2	0,1,2,4	221100	8-2	0,1,2,3,4,5,6,8	665542
4-3(12)	0,1,3,4	212100	8-3	0,1,2,3,4,5,6,9	656542
4-4	0,1,2,5	211110	8-4	0,1,2,3,4,5,7,8	655552
4-5	0,1,2,6	210111	8-5	0,1,2,3,4,6,7,8	654553
4-6(12)	0,1,2,7	210021	8-6	0,1,2,3,5,6,7,8	654463
4-7(12)	0,1,4,5	201210	8-7	0,1,2,3,4,5,8,9	645652
4-8(12)	0,1,5,6	200121	8-8	0,1,2,3,4,7,8,9	644563
4-9(6)	0,1,6,7	200022	8-9	0,1,2,3,6,7,8,9	644464
4-10(12)	0,2,3,5	122010	8-10	0,2,3,4,5,6,7,9	566452
4-11	0,1,3,5	121110	8-11	0,1,2,3,4,5,7,9	565552
4-12	0,2,3,6	112101	8-12	0,1,3,4,5,6,7,9	556543
4-13	0,1,3,6	112011	8-13	0,1,2,3,4,6,7,9	556453
4-14	0,2,3,7	111120	8-14	0,1,2,4,5,6,7,9	555562
4-Z15	0,1,4,6	111111	8-Z15	0,1,2,3,4,6,8,9	555553
4-16	0,1,5,7	110121	8-16	0,1,2,3,5,7,8,9	554563
4-17(12)	0,3,4,7	102210	8-17	0,1,3,4,5,6,8,9	546652
4-18	0,1,4,7	102111	8-18	0,1,2,3,5,6,8,9	546553
4-19	0,1,4,8	101310	8-19	0,1,2,4,5,6,8,9	545752

Note: Numbers in parentheses show the number of distinct sets in the set class if other than 48.
All brackets are eliminated here for ease of reading.

NAME	PCS	IC VECTOR	NAME	PCS	IC VECTOR
4-20(12)	0,1,5,8	101220	8-20	0,1,2,4,5,7,8,9	545662
4-21(12)	0,2,4,6	030201	8-21	0,1,2,3,4,6,8,t	474643
4-22	0,2,4,7	021120	8-22	0,1,2,3,5,6,8,t	465562
4-23(12)	0,2,5,7	021030	8-23	0,1,2,3,5,7,8,t	465472
4-24(12)	0,2,4,8	020301	8-24	0,1,2,4,5,6,8,t	464743
4-25(6)	0,2,6,8	020202	8-25	0,1,2,4,6,7,8,t	464644
4-26(12)	0,3,5,8	012120	8-26	0,1,2,4,5,7,9,t	456562
4-27	0,2,5,8	012111	8-27	0,1,2,4,5,7,8,t	456553
4-28(3)	0,3,6,9	004002	8-28	0,1,3,4,6,7,9,t	448444
4-Z29	0,1,3,7	111111	8-Z29	0,1,2,3,5,6,7,9	555553
5-1(12)	0,1,2,3,4	432100	7-1	0,1,2,3,4,5,6	654321
5-2	0,1,2,3,5	332110	7-2	0,1,2,3,4,5,7	554331
5-3	0,1,2,4,5	322210	7-3	0,1,2,3,4,5,8	544431
5-4	0,1,2,3,6	322111	7-4	0,1,2,3,4,6,7	544332
5-5	0,1,2,3,7	321121	7-5	0,1,2,3,5,6,7	543342
5-6	0,1,2,5,6	311221	7-6	0,1,2,3,4,7,8	533442
5-7	0,1,2,6,7	310132	7-7	0,1,2,3,6,7,8	532353
5-8(12)	0,2,3,4,6	232201	7-8	0,2,3,4,5,6,8	454422
5-9	0,1,2,4,6	231211	7-9	0,1,2,3,4,6,8	453432
5-10	0,1,3,4,6	223111	7-10	0,1,2,3,4,6,9	445332
5-11	0,2,3,4,7	222220	7-11	0,1,3,4,5,6,8	444441
5-Z12(12)	0,1,3,5,6	222121	7-Z12	0,1,2,3,4,7,9	444342
5-13	0,1,2,4,8	221311	7-13	0,1,2,4,5,6,8	443532
5-14	0,1,2,5,7	221131	7-14	0,1,2,3,5,7,8	443352
5-15(12)	0,1,2,6,8	220222	7-15	0,1,2,4,6,7,8	442443
5-16	0,1,3,4,7	213211	7-16	0,1,2,3,5,6,9	435432
5-Z17(12)	0,1,3,4,8	212320	7-Z17	0,1,2,4,5,6,9	434541
5-Z18	0,1,4,5,7	212221	7-Z18	0,1,2,3,5,8,9	434442
5-19	0,1,3,6,7	212122	7-19	0,1,2,3,6,7,9	434343
5-20	0,1,3,7,8	211231	7-20	0,1,2,4,7,8,9	433452
5-21	0,1,4,5,8	202420	7-21	0,1,2,4,5,8,9	424641
5-22(12)	0,1,4,7,8	202321	7-22	0,1,2,5,6,8,9	424542
5-23	0,2,3,5,7	132130	7-23	0,2,3,4,5,7,9	354351
5-24	0,1,3,5,7	131221	7-24	0,1,2,3,5,7,9	353442
5-25	0,2,3,5,8	123121	7-25	0,2,3,4,6,7,9	345342
5-26	0,2,4,5,8	122311	7-26	0,1,3,4,5,7,9	344532
5-27	0,1,3,5,8	122230	7-27	0,1,2,4,5,7,9	344451
5-28	0,2,3,6,8	122212	7-28	0,1,3,5,6,7,9	344433
5-29	0,1,3,6,8	122131	7-29	0,1,2,4,6,7,9	344352
5-30	0,1,4,6,8	121321	7-30	0,1,2,4,6,8,9	343542
5-31	0,1,3,6,9	114112	7-31	0,1,3,4,6,7,9	336333
5-32	0,1,4,6,9	113221	7-32	0,1,3,4,6,8,9	335442
5-33(12)	0,2,4,6,8	040402	7-33	0,1,2,4,6,8,t	262623
5-34(12)	0,2,4,6,9	032221	7-34	0,1,3,4,6,8,t	254442
5-35(12)	0,2,4,7,9	032140	7-35	0,1,3,5,6,8,t	254361

NAME	PCS	IC VECTOR	NAME	PCS	IC VECTOR
5-Z36	0,1,2,4,7	222121	7-Z36	0,1,2,3,5,6,8	444342
5-Z37(12)	0,3,4,5,8	212320	7-Z37	0,1,3,4,5,7,8	434541
5-Z38	0,1,2,5,8	212221	7-Z38	0,1,2,4,5,7,8	434442
6-1(12)	0,1,2,3,4,5	543210			
6-2	0,1,2,3,4,6	443211			
6-Z3	0,1,2,3,5,6	433221	6-Z36	0,1,2,3,4,7	*
6-Z4(12)	0,1,2,4,5,6	432321	6-Z37(12)	0,1,2,3,4,8	
6-5	0,1,2,3,6,7	422232			
6-Z6(12)	0,1,2,5,6,7	421242	6-Z38(12)	0,1,2,3,7,8	
6-7(6)	0,1,2,6,7,8	420243			
6-8(12)	0,2,3,4,5,7	343230			
6-9	0,1,2,3,5,7	342231			
6-Z10	0,1,3,4,5,7	333321	6-Z39	0,2,3,4,5,8	
6-Z11	0,1,2,4,5,7	333231	6-Z40	0,1,2,3,5,8	
6-Z12	0,1,2,4,6,7	332232	6-Z41	0,1,2,3,6,8	
6-Z13(12)	0,1,3,4,6,7	324222	6-Z42(12)	0,1,2,3,6,9	
6-14	0,1,3,4,5,8	323430			
6-15	0,1,2,4,5,8	323421			
6-16	0,1,4,5,6,8	322431			
6-Z17	0,1,2,4,7,8	322332	6-Z43	0,1,2,5,6,8	
6-18	0,1,2,5,7,8	322242			
6-Z19	0,1,3,4,7,8	313431	6-Z44	0,1,2,5,6,9	
6-20(4)	0,1,4,5,8,9	303630			
6-21	0,2,3,4,6,8	242412			
6-22	0,1,2,4,6,8	241422			
6-Z23(12)	0,2,3,5,6,8	234222	6-Z45(12)	0,2,3,4,6,9	
6-Z24	0,1,3,4,6,8	233331	6-Z46	0,1,2,4,6,9	
6-Z25	0,1,3,5,6,8	233241	6-Z47	0,1,2,4,7,9	
6-Z26(12)	0,1,3,5,7,8	232341	6-Z48(12)	0,1,2,5,7,9	
6-27	0,1,3,4,6,9	225222			
6-Z28(12)	0,1,3,5,6,9	224322	6-Z49(12)	0,1,3,4,7,9	
6-Z29(12)	0,1,3,6,8,9	224232	6-Z50(12)	0,1,4,6,7,9	
6-30(12)	0,1,3,6,7,9	224223			
6-31	0,1,3,5,8,9	223431			
6-32(12)	0,2,4,5,7,9	143250			
6-33	0,2,3,5,7,9	143241			
6-34	0,1,3,5,7,9	142422			
6-35(2)	0,2,4,6,8,t	060603			

*Z-related hexachords share the same ic vector; use vector in the third column.

SOURCE: Allen Forte, *The Structure of Atonal Music* (New Haven: Yale University Press, 1973) (adapted)

Credits

Audacity® software is copyright © 1999-2018 Audacity Team. The name Audacity® is a registered trademark of Dominic Mazzoni.

Béla Bartók, "44 Duos." © Copyright 1933 by Universal Edition A.G., Wien/UE 10452 A/B. Copyright renewed 1960 by Boosey & Hawkes, Inc., New York. All rights in the USA owned and controlled by Boosey & Hawkes, Inc., New York.

Béla Bartók, "Mikrokosmos, Sz.107." © Copyright 1940 by Hawkes & Son (London) Ltd. Reprinted by permission of Boosey & Hawkes, Inc.

Luciano Berio, "Sequenza III, for voice." © Copyright 1965 by Universal Edition (London) Ltd., London, © assigned to Universal Edition A.G., Wien/UE 18101. Reprinted with permission.

William Bolcom, "Twelve New Etudes for Piano." Copyright © 1988 by Edward B. Marks Music Company. This arrangement © 2015 by Edward B. Marks Music Company. International copyright secured. All rights reserved. Used by permission. Reprinted by permission of Hal Leonard Corporation.

Earle Brown, "Folio and Four Systems." Copyright © 1961 (Renewed) by Associated Music Publishers, Inc. (BMI). International copyright secured. All rights Reserved. Used by permission.

Sylvano Bussotti, "Phase à Trois." © Renewed 1994 by Casa Ricordi Srl - Milano. Reproduced by permission of Hal Leonard MGB Srl - Milano.

John Cage, "4'38"." Copyright © 1960 by Henmar Press Inc. All rights reserved. Used by permission.

John Corigliano, "Come Now, My Darling." Words by William Hoffman. Music by John Corigliano. Copyright © 1991 by G. Schirmer, Inc. (ASCAP). International copyright secured. All rights reserved. Used by permission.

George Crumb, "Madrigals Book IV." © 1971 C. F. Peters Corp. All rights reserved. Used by permission.

Luigi Dallapiccola, "Goethe-Lieder." Copyright © 1953 by Edizioni Suvini Zerboni. Copyright © renewed. All rights reserved. Used by permission of European American Music Distributors Company, sole U.S. and Canadian agent for Edizioni Suvini Zerboni.

George and Ira Gershwin, "I Got Rhythm." Music and lyrics by George Gershwin and Ira Gershwin. © 1930 (Renewed) WB Music Corp. and Ira Gershwin Music. All rights administered by WB Music Corp. All rights reserved. Reprinted with permission.

Gerry Goffin and Michael Masser, "Saving All My Love For You." Words by Gerry Goffin. Music by Michael Masser. © 1978, 1985 Screen Gems-EMI Music Inc., Lauren-Wesley Music Inc., and Universal Music Corp. This arrangement © 2015 Screen Gems-EMI Music Inc., Lauren-Wesley Music Inc., and Universal Music Corp. All rights for Lauren-Wesley Music Inc. Controlled and administered by Screen Gems-EMI Music Inc. All rights reserved. International copyright secured. Used by permission. Reprinted by permission of Hal Leonard Corporation.

Berry Gordy, Hal Davis, Willie Hutch, and Bob West, "I'll Be There." Words and music by Berry Gordy, Hal Davis, Willie Hutch, and Bob West. © 1970, 1975 (Renewed 1998, 2003) Jobete Music Co., Inc. This arrangement © 2015 Jobete Music Co., Inc. All rights controlled and administered by EMI April Music Inc. All rights reserved. International copyright secured. Used by permission. Reprinted by permission of Hal Leonard Corporation.

Oscar Hammerstein II and Jerome Kern, "All the Things You Are," from *Very Warm for May*. Lyrics by Oscar Hammerstein II. Music by Jerome Kern. Copyright © 1939 Universal - Polygram International Publishing, Inc. Copyright renewed. This arrangement © 2015 Universal - Polygram International Publishing, Inc. All rights reserved. Used by permission. Reprinted by permission of Hal Leonard Corporation.

Oscar Hammerstein II and Jerome Kern, "Can't Help Lovin' Dat Man," from *Show Boat*. Lyrics by Oscar Hammerstein II. Music by Jerome Kern. Copyright © 1927 Universal - Polygram International Publishing, Inc. Copyright renewed. This arrangement © 2015 Universal - Polygram International Publishing, Inc. All rights reserved. Used by permission. Reprinted by permission of Hal Leonard Corporation.

Otto Harbach and Jerome Kern, "Smoke Gets In Your Eyes," from *Roberta*. Words by Otto Harbach. Music by Jerome Kern. Copyright © 1933 Universal - Polygram International Publishing, Inc. Copyright renewed. This arrangement © 2015 Universal - Polygram International Publishing, Inc. All rights reserved. Used by permission. Reprinted by permission of Hal Leonard Corporation.

Neal Hefti, "Splanky." © 1958 (Renewed) WB Music Corp. All rights reserved. Reprinted with permission.

Fanny Mendelssohn Hensel, "Neue Liebe, neues Leben." Edited by Eva Rieger and Kaete Walter. © 1985 Schott Music, Mainz, Germany. All rights reserved. Used by permission of European American Music Distributors LLC, sole U.S. and Canadian agent for Schott Music, Mainz, Germany.

Peter Jackson Jr. and Gerald Jackson, "Turn the Beat Around." Words and music by Peter Jackson Jr. and Gerald Jackson. © 1975 (Renewed) Unichappell Music, Inc. All rights reserved. Reprinted with permission.

Dennis Lambert and Brian Potter, "One Tin Soldier," from *Billy Jack*. Words and music by Dennis Lambert and Brian Potter. Copyright © 1969, 1974 Songs of Universal, Inc. Copyright renewed. This arrangement © 2015 Songs of Universal, Inc. All rights reserved. Used by permission. Reprinted by permission of Hal Leonard Corporation.

John Lennon and Paul McCartney, "Eleanor Rigby." Words and music by John Lennon and Paul McCartney. Copyright © 1966 Sony/ATV Music Publishing LLC. Copyright renewed. This arrangement © 2015 Sony/ATV Music Publishing LLC. All rights administered by Sony/ATV Music Publishing LLC, 424 Church Street, Suite 1200, Nashville, TN 37219. International copyright secured. All rights reserved. Reprinted by permission of Hal Leonard Corporation.

John Lennon and Paul McCartney, "Nowhere Man." Words and music by John Lennon and Paul McCartney. Copyright © 1965 Sony/ATV Music Publishing LLC. Copyright renewed. This arrangement copyright © 1965 Sony/ATV Music Publishing LLC. All rights administered by Sony/ATV Music Publishing LLC, 424 Church Street, Suite 1200, Nashville, TN 37219. International copyright secured. All rights reserved. Reprinted by permission of Hal Leonard Corporation.

Gyorgy Ligeti, "Continuum." © 1970 by Schott Music, Mainz, Germany. © Renewed. All rights reserved. Used by permission of European American Music Distributors LLC, sole U.S. and Canadian agent for Schott Music, Mainz, Germany.

Gyorgy Ligeti, "Desorde," from *Piano Etudes, Book I*. Published by Schott Music, Mainz, Germany. Used by permission of European American Music Distributors LLC, sole U.S. and Canadian agent for Schott Music, Mainz, Germany.

Gyorgy Ligeti, "Ten Pieces for Wind Quintet." © 1969 by Schott Music, Mainz, Germany. © Renewed. All rights reserved. Used by permission of European American Music Distributors LLC, sole U.S. and Canadian agent for Schott Music, Mainz, Germany.

Andrew Lloyd Webber, "Memory," from *Cats*. Music by Andrew Lloyd Webber. Text by Trevor Nunn after T.S. Eliot. Music copyright © 1981 Andrew Lloyd Webber licensed to The Really Useful Group Ltd. Text copyright © 1981 Trevor Nunn and Set Copyrights Ltd. This arrangement © 2015 Andrew Lloyd Webber licensed to The Really Useful Group Ltd. All rights in the text controlled by Faber and Faber Ltd. and administered for the United States and Canada by R&H Music Co., a division of Rodgers & Hammerstein: an Imagem Company. International copyright secured. All rights reserved. Reprinted by permission of Hal Leonard Corporation.

Kenneth Maue, "In the Woods," from *Water in the Lake: Real Events for Imagination*. Copyright 1979, Harper & Row. Reprinted by permission.

Don McLean, "Vincent (Starry Starry Night)." Words and music by Don McLean. Copyright © 1971, 1972 Benny Bird Co., Inc. Copyright renewed. This arrangement © 2015 Benny Bird Co., Inc. All rights controlled and administered by Songs of Universal, Inc. All rights reserved. Used by permission. Reprinted by permission of Hal Leonard Corporation.

Alan Menken and Tim Rice, "A Whole New World," from Walt Disney's *Aladdin*. Music by Alan Menken. Lyrics by Tim Rice. © 1992 Wonderland Music Company, Inc., and Walt Disney Music Company. This arrangement © 2015 Wonderland Music Company, Inc., and Walt Disney Music Company. All rights reserved. Used by permission. Reprinted by permission of Hal Leonard Corporation.

Freddie Mercury, "Bohemian Rhapsody." Words and music by Freddie Mercury. Copyright © 1975 Queen Music Ltd. Copyright renewed. This arrangement © 2015 Queen Music Ltd. All rights administered by Sony/ATV Music Publishing LLC, 424 Church Street, Suite 1200, Nashville, TN 37219. International copyright secured. All rights reserved. Reprinted by permission of Hal Leonard Corporation.

James Myers and Max Freedman, "Rock Around The Clock." Words and music by Max C. Freedman and Jimmy DeKnight. Copyright © 1953 Myers Music Inc., Kassner Associated Publishers Ltd., and Capano Music. Copyright renewed. This arrangement © 2015 Myers Music Inc., Kassner Associated Publishers Ltd., and Capano Music. All rights on behalf of Myers Music Inc. and Kassner Associated Publishers Ltd. administered by Sony/ATV Music Publishing LLC, 424 Church Street, Suite 1200, Nashville, TN 37219. International copyright secured. All rights reserved. Reprinted by permission of Hal Leonard Corporation.

Dolly Parton, "I Will Always Love You." Words and music by Dolly Parton. Copyright © 1973 (Renewed 2001) Velvet Apple Music. This arrangement © 2015 Velvet Apple Music. All rights reserved. Used by permission. Reprinted by permission of Hal Leonard Corporation.

Elvis Presley and Vera Matson, "Love Me Tender," from *Love Me Tender*. Words and music by Elvis Presley and Vera Matson. Copyright

© 1956; Renewed 1984 Elvis Presley Music (BMI.) This arrangement © 2015 Elvis Presley Music (BMI). All rights in the U.S. administered by Imagem Sounds. International copyright secured. All rights reserved. Reprinted by permission of Hal Leonard Corporation.

Henry Purcell, "When I am laid in earth," from *Dido and Aeneas*. Edited and arranged by Edward J. Dent. © Oxford University Press, 1925. Extract reproduced by permission.

Steve Reich, "Piano Phase." © Copyright 1980 in the USA by Hendon Music, Inc., a Boosey & Hawkes Company. Reprinted by permission of Boosey & Hawkes, Inc. © Copyright 1980 by Universal Edition (London) Ltd., London/UE 16156. World, except for the USA.

Steve Reich, "Proverb." © Copyright 1997 by Hendon Music, Inc., a Boosey and Hawkes Company. Reprinted by permission of Boosey & Hawkes, Inc.

William "Smokey" Robinson, "You've Really Got A Hold On Me." Words and music by William "Smokey" Robinson. © 1962, 1963 (Renewed 1990, 1991) Jobete Music Co., Inc. This arrangement © 2015 Jobete Music Co., Inc. All rights controlled and administered by EMI April Music Inc. All rights reserved. International copyright secured. Used by permission. Reprinted by permission of Hal Leonard Corporation.

William "Smokey" Robinson and Ronald White, "My Girl." Words and music by William "Smokey" Robinson and Ronald White. © 1964, 1972, 1973, 1977 (Renewed 1992, 2000, 2001, 2005) Jobete Music Co., Inc. This arrangement © 2015 Jobete Music Co., Inc. All rights controlled and administered by EMI April Music Inc. All rights reserved. International copyright secured. Used by permission. Reprinted by permission of Hal Leonard Corporation.

Lalo Schifrin, "Mission: Impossible Theme," from the Paramount Television Series *Mission Impossible*. Copyright © 1965 Sony/ATV Music Publishing LLC. Copyright renewed. This arrangement © 2015 Sony/ATV Music Publishing LLC. All rights administered by Sony/ATV Music Publishing LLC, 424 Church Street, Suite 1200, Nashville, TN 37219. International copyright secured. All rights reserved. Reprinted by permission of Hal Leonard Corporation.

Arnold Schoenberg, "Klavierstuck, Op. 33a." Used by permission of Belmont Publishers, Los Angeles.

Karlheinz Stockhausen, "Klavierstück 11, für Klavier, Nr. 7." © Copyright 1957 by Universal Edition (London) Ltd., London/UE 12654. Reprinted with permission.

U2 and Bono, "Miracle Drug." Music by U2. Lyrics by Bono. Copyright © 2004 Universal Music Publishing International B.V. This arrangement © 2015 Universal Music Publishing International B.V. All rights in the U.S. and Canada controlled and administered by Universal - Polygram International Publishing, Inc. All rights reserved. Used by permission. Reprinted by permission of Hal Leonard Corporation.

Anton Webern, "5 Sätze für Streichquartett, Op. 5." © Copyright 1922, 1949 by Universal Edition A.G., Wien/PH358. Reprinted with permission.

Anton Webern, "Variationen für Klavier, Op. 27." © Copyright 1937, 1979 by Universal Edition A.G., Wien/UE 10881/UE16845. Reprinted with permission.

Meredith Willson, "Till There Was You," from Meredith Willson's *The Music Man*. © 1950, 1957 (Renewed) Frank Music Corp. and Meredith Willson Music. This arrangement © 2015 Frank Music Corp. and Meredith Willson Music. All rights reserved. Reprinted by permission of Hal Leonard Corporation.

La Monte Young, "Composition 1960, No. 5, June 1960." Reproduced with permission from An Anthology (1963). Copyright © La Monte Young 1963, 1970.

Ellen Taaffe Zwilich, *Commedia dell'Arte*, movement I, "Arlecchino." Copyright © 2012 by Theodore Presser Company. Used with permission.

Index of Music Examples

"Agincourt Song," 69-70
Anonymous, Minuet in D Minor, from the *Anna Magdalena Bach Notebook*, 29, 42, 474-75
"Ash Grove, The," 114, 594-95

Bach, Johann Sebastian
  "Ach Gott, vom Himmel sieh' darein," 231-32, 267, 268
  "Aus meines Herzens Grunde," 269-71, 322-25, 348
  Cantata No. 140, "Wachet auf," mvts. 4 and 7, 347-48, 358
  Cello Suite No. 2 in D Minor, Prelude, 491-92, 493
  "Christ ist erstanden," 330
  "Er kommt," 464-65
  "Ermuntre dich, mein schwacher Geist," 414
  "Es ist gewisslich an der Zeit," 429
  "Ein feste Burg ist unser Gott," 223-24, 346-47
  Fugue in C Major, from *The Well-Tempered Clavier*, Book I, 495-96, 498, 506
  Fugue in C Minor, from *The Well-Tempered Clavier*, Book I, 491, 499-502
  Fugue in D♯ Minor, from *The Well-Tempered Clavier*, Book I, 494-95, 496-98, 507-9
  "Heut' ist, o Mensch," 329
  Invention in C Minor, 510
  Invention in D Minor, 61, 94-95, 121-22, 299-300, 340, 386-90, 494, 495, 498
  "Jesu, der du meine Seele," 339
  "Liebster Jesu," 329
  "O Haupt voll Blut und Wunden," 138, 328, 349, 461-62
  Passacaglia in C Minor, 517
  Prelude in C Major, BWV 924, 404
  Prelude in C Major, from *The Well-Tempered Clavier*, Book I, 147, 151, 157, 339-40, 356-57, 358, 435-36
  "Schafe können sicher weiden," 29, 570-72
  St. Anne Fugue (in E♭ Major), 75, 81, 328-29, 331, 503-6
  Violin Partita No. 2 in D Minor, Chaconne, 92-93, 309, 315, 515-16, 518
  "Wachet auf," 224, 225, 231, 238, 298, 410, 415
Bartók, Béla
  Bagatelle, Op. 6, No. 2, 742-44
  "Bulgarian Rhythm," from *Mikrokosmos* (No. 115), 731-32, 745-46, 753-54, 757, 763-64, 766-67, 773-79
  "Five-Tone Scale," from *Mikrokosmos* (No. 78), 721-23
  "In Lydian Mode," from *Mikrokosmos* (No. 37), 103
  "Six Dances in Bulgarian Rhythm," from *Mikrokosmos* (No. 148), 732-33
  Sonata for Two Pianos and Percussion, 782-83
  "Song of the Harvest," 709-12, 725-26, 736, 740-42
  "Syncopation," from *Mikrokosmos* (No. 133), 733
  "Whole-Tone Scale," from *Mikrokosmos* (No. 137), 780
Basie, Count, "Splanky," 602-3, 604
Beethoven, Ludwig van
  Piano Sonata in C Major, Op. 53 (*Waldstein*), mvt. 1, 644-45, 655-56, 674-83
  Piano Sonata in C Minor, Op. 13 (*Pathétique*)
    Mvt. 1, 651-52
    Mvt. 2, 432-33, 642-43, 645-46, 652-53, 693-97
    Mvt. 3, 370, 527
  Piano Sonata in C♯ Minor, Op. 27 (*Moonlight*), mvt. 1, 549-50
  Piano Sonata in D Minor, Op. 31, No. 2 (*Tempest*), mvt. 3, 230-31
  Sonatina in F Major, Op. Posth., mvt. 2, 234, 366-67, 370-71
  Variations on "God Save the King," 526-27
Berg, Alban
  Lyric Suite, mvt. 1, 814-15
  "Sahst du nach dem Gewitterregen," from *Altenberg-Lieder*, Op. 4, No. 2, 750-53, 755-56, 768-69
  Violin Concerto, 814-15
Berio, Luciano, *Sequenza III*, 837-38
Bettis, John (with Lind), "Crazy for You," 341
Bolcom, William, *12 New Etudes for Piano*, mvt. 3, 832
Bono and U2, "Miracle Drug," 29
Boulez, Pierre, *Structures Ia*, 819-20, 824

Brahms, Johannes
    Intermezzo in A Major, Op. 118, No. 2, 636-37
    "Die Mainacht," 80-81, 350
    Variations on a Theme by Haydn, 288, 334, 379-80
Brown, Earle, *Folio and Four Systems*, 839, 842
Bussotti, Sylvano, *Phrase à Trois*, 840

Cage, John, *4′33″*, 841
Carter, Elliott, String Quartet No. 2, 835-36
"Chartres" (harmonization by Charles Wood), 220
Chen Yi, "Shan Ge," from *Three Bagatelles from China West*, 863-64
Chopin, Frédéric
    Mazurka in F Minor, Op. 68, No. 4, 23
    Nocturne in E♭ Major, Op. 9, No. 2, 80, 82
    Prelude in C Minor, Op. 28, No. 20, 559, 656-57
    Prelude in E Minor, Op. 28, No. 4, 657-58
Clementi, Muzio, Sonatina in C Major, Op. 36, No. 1, mvt. 1, 229-30, 363-65, 371, 378-79, 463-64, 684-85
"Clementine," 248
Corelli, Arcangelo
    Sonata in D Minor, Op. 4, No. 8, Preludio, 96, 139-40, 266, 305, 458-59, 664
    Trio Sonata in A Minor, Op. 4, No. 5, Allemanda, 88-89, 394, 454-55, 477-79, 664
Corigliano, John, "Come now, my darling," from *The Ghosts of Versailles*, 834-35, 855-57, 861
Crumb, George, "¿Por qué nací entre espejos?", from *Madrigals*, Book 4, 831-32

Dallapiccola, Luigi, "Die Sonne kommt!" from *Goethe-lieder*, 800-804, 814
Davis, Hall (with Gordy, Hutch, and West), "I'll Be There," 143

Debussy, Claude
    "La cathédral engloutie," 780-81
    "Fantoches," from *Fêtes Galantes*, 718
    "Mandoline," 719
    "Voiles," from *Preludes*, Book I, 723-24
"Down in the Valley," 69
Dozier, Lamont (with Holland and Holland Jr.), "Baby Love," 606, 608

Fauré, Gabriel, "Après un rêve," 589-90, 632
Foster, Stephen, "Oh! Susanna," 368-69
Freedman, Max (with Myers), "Rock Around the Clock," 605, 607, 608
Fux, Johann Joseph, cantus firmi, 167, 182, 185, 195, 203

Gershwin, George (with Ira Gershwin), "I Got Rhythm," from *Girl Crazy*, 596-601, 604
Glass, Philip, *Music in Fifths*, 845-46
Goffin, Gerry (with Masser), "Saving All My Love for You," 155
Gordy, Barry (with Davis, Hutch, and West), "I'll Be There," 143
Gottwald, Lukasz, Max Martin, Bonnie McKee, Katy Perry, and Henry Walter, "Roar," 610–11, 615
"Greensleeves," 68, 71, 74, 102-3

Hammerstein, Oscar, II (with Kern)
    "All the Things You Are," from *Very Warm for May*, 396-97
    "Can't Help Lovin' Dat Man," from *Showboat*, 558-59
Handel, George Frideric
    Chaconne in G Major, 30, 110, 130-31, 137-38, 139, 329, 392-93, 404, 608, 623-24, 639
    "Hallelujah!" from *Messiah*, 301-3
    "Rejoice greatly," from *Messiah*, 22, 33, 34-35, 395

"Thy rebuke hath broken His heart," from *Messiah*, 575-77
Harbach, Otto (with Kern), "Smoke Gets in Your Eyes," from *Roberta*, 628, 643-44
Haydn, Joseph
    Concerto in D Major for Horn and Orchestra, mvt. 1, 159, 687-88
    Piano Sonata No. 9 in F Major, Scherzo, 229-30, 261
    String Quartet in D Minor, Op. 76, No. 2, mvt. 3, 487
Hensel, Fanny Mendelssohn
    "Nachtwanderer," 71, 564-65
    "Neue Liebe, neues Leben," 38-39, 399, 406, 621-22
Heyman, Edward (with Young), "When I Fall in Love," 156
Holland, Brian (with Dozier and Holland Jr.), "Baby Love," 606, 608
Holst, Gustav, Second Suite for Military Band, mvt. 4 ("Fantasia on the 'Dargason'"), 80, 525, 739
"Home on the Range," 73
Hutch, Willie (with Gordy, Davis, and West), "I'll Be There," 143

Ives, Charles, "The Cage," 739

Jacquet de la Guerre, Elisabeth-Claude, Gigue, from Suite No. 3 in A Minor, 74
Jeppesen, Knud, cantus firmi, 168, 178-79, 197
Joplin, Scott
    "Pine Apple Rag," 22, 36, 417
    "Solace," 13-14, 17-18, 36-37, 434-35

Kern, Jerome
    "All the Things You Are," from *Very Warm for May* (with Hammerstein), 396-97
    "Can't Help Lovin' Dat Man," from *Showboat* (with Hammerstein), 560-61
    "Smoke Gets in Your Eyes," from *Roberta* (with Harbach), 628, 643-44
King, Carole, "You've Got a Friend," 608-9

Kirnberger, Johann Philipp, cantus firmi, 184, 185, 187, 188, 191, 199, 200

Kurtág, György
"Invocatio," from *Six Moments musicaux*, Op. 44, 861
". . . rappel des oiseaux," from *Six Moments musicaux*, Op. 44, 861-62

Lambert, Dennis (with Potter), "One Tin Soldier," from *Billy Jack*, 400
Leiber, Jerry (with Stoller), "Hound Dog," 604-5
Lennon, John (with McCarthy)
"Eleanor Rigby," from *Revolver*, 107, 613
"Nowhere Man," from *Rubber Soul*, 303-4
Ligeti, György
Continuum, 830-31
"Désordre," from *Piano Etudes*, Book I, 862-63
Hungarian Etudes, mvt. 3, 833
Ten Pieces for Wind Quintet, mvt. 9, 825-28, 861
"Wenn aus der Ferne," from *Three Fantasies on Texts by Friedrich Hölderlin*, 828-29
Lind, Jon (with Bettis), "Crazy for You," 341
Lloyd Webber, Andrew, "Memory," 462-63
Love, Mike (with Wilson), "Help Me, Rhonda," 606-7

Masser, Michael (with Goffin), "Saving All My Love for You," 155
Matson, Vera (with Presley), "Love Me Tender," 412
Maue, Kenneth, *In the Woods*, 843-44
McCarthy, Paul (with Lennon)
"Eleanor Rigby," from *Revolver*, 107, 613
"Nowhere Man," from *Rubber Soul*, 303-4
McLean, Don, "Vincent," 310-11
Menken, Alan (with Rice), "A Whole New World," *Aladdin*, 436-37

Mercury, Freddie
"Bohemian Rhapsody," 342
"Crazy Little Thing Called Love," 614
"Merrily We Roll Along," 247, 248-51
Messiaen, Olivier
"Danse de la fureur," from *Quartet for the End of Time*, 738
"Liturgie de crystal," from *Quartet for the End of Time*, 787-88
Mozart, Wolfgang Amadeus
"Alleluia," 50
Dies irae, from *Requiem*, 402-3, 553-56
Kyrie, from *Requiem*, 511
Lacrymosa, from *Requiem*, 69-70
Minuet in F Major, K. 2, 331
Piano Sonata in B♭ Major, K. 333, mvt. 1, 290, 381
Piano Sonata in C Major, K. 545
Mvt. 1, 3, 4, 46-47, 50, 158, 247, 255, 280, 375, 380-81, 383, 415
Mvt. 2, 293, 376-77, 382
Piano Sonata in D Major, K. 284
Mvt. 1, 543-44
Mvt. 3, 276, 292, 307, 318-19, 336, 443, 449-50, 471-73, 552-53, 558-59, 639
Piano Sonata in G Major, K. 283, mvt. 1, 40, 367-68, 665-73
"Quanto duolmi, Susanna," from *The Marriage of Figaro*, 574-75
Rondo in E♭ Major for Horn and Orchestra, K. 371, 423-24
Sonata for Violin and Piano, K. 296, mvt. 2, 279-80
Sonata for Violin and Piano in C Major, K. 6, mvt. 3, 479
String Quartet in C Major, K. 170, mvt. 2, 481-82
String Quartet in D Minor, K. 421
Mvt. 1, 647
Mvt. 3, 560, 619-20
Variations on "Ah, vous dirai-je Maman," 126, 332-33, 334, 336, 337, 433, 441-42, 480-81, 520-25

Variations on "Unser dummer Pöbel meint," 483
"Voi, che sapete," from *The Marriage of Figaro*, 157-58, 264, 373-74, 531, 572-74, 856
"My Country, 'Tis of Thee," 60, 210, 218, 235-36, 240, 246, 277, 282-83, 291, 298-99
Myers, James (with Freedman), "Rock Around the Clock," 605, 607, 608

Newton, John, "Amazing Grace," 27, 28, 63

"Old Hundredth" (harmonization by Bourgeois), 211, 216, 218, 301
"Old Joe Clark," 103

Pachelbel, Johann, Canon in D, 398-99, 517
Pärt, Arvo, *Magnificat*, 853-54
Parton, Dolly, "I Will Always Love You," 54-55
Penderecki, Krzysztof, *Threnody for the Victims of Hiroshima*, 824-25, 829, 843, 861
Perry, Katy (with Gottwald, Martin, McKee, and Walter), "Roar," 610-11, 615
Peter, Paul and Mary, "Puff the Magic Dragon," 315
Phillips, Joel, "Blues for Norton," 304
Potter, Brian (with Lambert), "One Tin Soldier," from *Billy Jack*, 400
Presley, Elvis (with Matson), "Love Me Tender," 412
Purcell, Henry
"Music for a While," 330, 338, 515-16, 518-19
"When I am laid in earth" ("Dido's Lament"), from *Dido and Aeneas*, 46-47, 317-18, 517, 534, 639

Ravel, Maurice
"Aoua!" from *Chansons madécasses*, 715-16
Pavane pour une infant défunte, 717

Reich, Steve
   City Life, 864-66
   Piano Phase, 845
   Proverb, 852-53
Rice, Tim (with Menken), "A
      Whole New World," from
      Aladdin, 435-36
Riley, Terry, *In C*, 844-45, 854
Robinson, Vicki Sue, "Turn the
      Beat Around," 614
Robinson, William "Smokey"
   "My Girl" (with White), 143
   "You've Really Got a Hold on
      Me," 71, 77
"Rosa Mystica" (harmonization by
      Praetorius), 216, 225

"St. George's Windsor" ("Come, Ye
      Thankful People, Come"),
      133, 292, 347
   harmonization by Elvey, 210,
      213, 216, 218
Schenker, Heinrich, cantus firmi,
      171, 173, 174, 178
Schoenberg, Arnold, *Klavierstück*,
      Op. 33a, 805-11, 814
Schubert, Franz
   "Am Meer," from
      Schwanengesang, 630
   "Der Doppelgänger," from
      Schwanengesang, 566
   "Du bist die Ruh," 539-40
   "Erlkönig," 556-57, 585-88
   "Im Dorfe," from *Winterreise*,
      541-42
   "Der Lindenbaum," from
      Winterreise, 77-79, 86-88
   Moment musical in A♭ Major,
      Op. 94, No. 6, 544-45
   "Morgengruss," from *Die schöne
      Müllerin*, 281, 579-80
   "Nur wer die Sehnsucht kennt
      (Lied der Mignon)," 466-68
   Waltz in A♭ Major, Op. 9, No. 2,
      653-54
   Waltz in B Minor, Op. 18, No. 6,
      86, 362
   "Der Wegweiser," from
      Winterreise, 626-27, 639

Schumann, Clara Wieck
   Drei Romanzen, Op. 21, No. 1,
      452-54, 699-704
   "Liebst du um Schönheit," 581
Schumann, Robert
   "Ich grolle nicht," from
      Dichterliebe, 401, 442-43,
      532, 628
   "Im wunderschönen Monat
      Mai," from *Dichterliebe*,
      577-79, 581-84
   "Trällerliedchen," 64-65, 484-85
   "Volksliedchen," 484-85
"Simple Gifts," 61
Sousa, John Philip, "The Stars and
      Stripes Forever," 23, 41,
      47-48, 124, 125-26, 283,
      428, 434, 487-88, 561
Stockhausen, Karlheinz
   Klavierstück XI, 841-42
   Zyklus, 838-39, 842
Stoller, Mike (with Leiber),
      "Hound Dog," 604-5
Stravinsky, Igor
   "Bransle Gay," from *Agon*, 734
   "Chez Petrouchka," from *Trois
      mouvements de
      "Petrouchka,"* 715
   "Danse Russe," from *Trois
      mouvements de
      "Petrouchka,"* 712-13
   "Lento," from *For the Five
      Fingers*, 718
   Les noces, Tableau II, 735
   *Trois mouvements de
      "Petrouchka,"* mvt. 2, 739

Takemitsu, Toru, *Rain Tree Sketch*,
      866-67
Tavener, John, "The Lamb,"
      794-96, 814, 851
Tiësto, "Red Lights," 611-12
"Twinkle, Twinkle, Little Star," 49

U2 and Bono, "Miracle Drug," 29
"Ubi caritas et amor" (Gregorian
      chant), 8

Varèse, Edgard, *Density 21.5*,
      736-37
Victoria, Tomás Luis de, "O
      magnum mysterium," 29,
      204-5
Vivaldi, Antonio, "Domine Fili
      unigenite," from *Gloria*,
      37-38

Wagner, Richard, Prelude to
      Tristan und Isolde, 658-59
"Wayfaring Stranger," 101, 287,
      316-17
Webern, Anton
   Concerto for Nine Instruments,
      Op. 24, 781-82, 816
   "Dies ist en Lied für dich allein,"
      745
   String Quartet, Op. 5
      Mvt. 3, 709-12, 783
      Mvt. 4, 785, 789-91
   Symphonie, Op. 21, mvt. 2, 113,
      815
   Variations for Piano, Op. 27
      Mvt. 2, 733, 811-14
      Mvt. 3, 816-19
West, Bob (with Gordy, Davis, and
      Hutch), "I'll Be There," 143
White, Ronald (with Robinson),
      "My Girl," 143
Willson, Meredith, "Till There
      Was You," 40
Wilson, Brian (with Love), "Help
      Me, Rhonda," 606-7
Wolf, Hugo, "In dem Schatten
      meiner Locken," from
      Spanisches Liederbuch,
      633-34

Young, La Monte, *Composition
      1960*, No. 5, 840, 843
Young, Victor (with Heyman),
      "When I Fall in Love," 156

Zwilich, Ellen Taaffe, "Arlecchino,"
      from *Commedia dell'Arte*,
      858-60

Index of Terms and Concepts

abrupt modulations. *See* modulation(s): direct
accented neighbor tone, 324-25. *See also* neighbor tone(s)
accented passing tone, 224, 324-25. *See also* passing tone(s)
accent marks, syncopation and, 76
accidental(s). *See also* double flat(s); double sharp(s); flat(s); natural(s); sharp(s)
    defined, 6
    in figured-bass notation, 141, 267
    in harmonic minor scale, 95
    key signatures and, 54-56, 125-26
    in major scales, 51
    in minor scales, 87, 95, 97, 242
    placement of, 10
    types of, 6, 8
accompaniment styles, 249-50
    in Lieder, 582
adagio, 24
added-sixth chord, 597
additive rhythm, 738-39
aeolian cadence. *See* cadence(s)
Aeolian mode, 104-6, 106, 714
Aerosmith, 400
    "Cryin'," 407
African drumming, 862
Afro-Cuban music, *clave* patterns, 35, 36
aggregate, 720, 784-85, 809
A instruments, 161. *See also* transposing instruments
Alberti, Domenico, 162
Alberti bass, 158, 162, 247, 250, 292, 359, 665
aleatoric music. *See* chance operations

alla breve, 28, 41
all-combinatorial hexachord, 810-11
allegretto, 24
allegro, 24
all-interval row, 814-15
all-interval tetrachords, 786
altered fifth chords, 600-601
alternative tunings, 854-55
alto clef, 12
alto vocal range, 237
"Amen" cadence. *See* cadence(s): plagal
ametric music, 736-37, 830-32, 860
anacrusis, 28, 38-40, 219-20
andante, 24
andantino, 24
answer (in fugue), 495-98, 502
    real, 495-97, 502
    tonal, 495-97, 502
antecedent phrase, 369. *See also* phrase
anticipations, 338
apparent chords. *See* voice-leading chords
applied chord(s), 410-11. *See also* secondary dominants; secondary leading-tone chords
applied dominants. *See* secondary dominants
appoggiatura, 333-34, 343
arco, 829
aria(s)
    da capo, 486, 570-72, 590
    defined, 570
    ternary, 572-74
Arne, Thomas, 251
arpeggiated triad, 130, 286
arpeggiating $^6_4$, 282-83

arpeggiation(s), 162
    of accompaniment, 247, 249-51
    defined, 157-58
    of tonic, 230-31
    arranging, 160
ars permutoria, 488
articulation, 34-35
    serialized, 820
art songs, 577-90
    Lieder, 577-88
    mélodie, 589-90
asymmetrical meters, 731-33, 853, 860
atonal music, 847. *See also* nontonal music, serial composition
    defined, 711
augmentation, 508
augmented fifths, 121-23
augmented fourths, 121-23, 170
augmented intervals, 121-23. *See also specific intervals*
    dissonance of, 124
augmented seconds, 93, 121-23, 538
    intonation of, 556
augmented-sixth chords, 558-67. *See also* French augmented-sixth chord; German augmented-sixth chord; Italian augmented-sixth chord
    approaches to, 563-64
    aural identification and performance, 564
    chromatic inflection in, 644-45
    common-tone, 630-31
    defined, 558
    enharmonic modulation with, 646-50
    less common spellings and voicings, 564-66

augmented-sixth chords
    (*continued*)
  secondary, 566
  voice-leading, spelling, and
      resolution of, 561-63
augmented sixths, 121-23
augmented triad, 131, 134, 135-37.
    See also triad(s)
  limited transposition of, 787
  raised chordal fifth and, 632
  Roman numerals for, 131-32,
      134
  whole-tone scale and, 724
authentic cadence. *See* cadence(s)

Babbitt, Milton, 800, 847, 850
Bach, Johann Sebastian, 107, 850
  cantatas of, 591
  Clavierübung III, 512
  Goldberg Variations, 512
  "O Haupt voll Blut und
      Wunden," 546
  St. Anne fugue, 512
bar(s). *See* measure(s)
baritone clef, 12
bar line(s), 23, 31
Baroque era
  binary forms in, 476, 477
  counterpoint education in, 166
  da capo arias in, 570, 590
  deceptive cadences in, 299
  double-dotted rhythm in, 37
  figured bass in, 139-42, 266-72
  Fortspinnung in, 491-92, 493,
      515
  harmonic thinking in, 273
  hemiola in, 37
  hypermeter in, 380
  leading-tone triads and seventh
      chords in, 359
  melody in, 491-93
  modes in, 103, 107
  musical elements used in recent
      music, 855-60
  Phrygian cadence in, 304-5
  plagal cadence in, 301-3
  recitatives in, 575-77
  retardations, 331
  sonatas in, 664
  style in, 19
  suspensions in, 327-30
  ternary form in, 485-86
  text painting in, 546
  variations in, 515-19

Bartók, Béla, 850, 863
  Mikrokosmos, 770
  *Music for Strings, Percussion,
      and Celesta*, 744, 745
  *Sonata for Two Pianos and
      Percussion*, 744
basic phrase (T-D-T; T-PD-D-T),
    229-35, 251, 294. *See also*
    phrase(s)
  cadential area and cadence
      types, 232-35
  chord choices from, 265
  defined, 230
  embedded PD–D–T, 292-93,
      346-47, 348
  establishing tonic area, 230-32
  expanding with ⁶₄ chords,
      276-87
  expanding with voice-leading
      chords, 345-59
  mixture chords in, 535-36
  secondary dominants to V in,
      416-17
  secondary-function chords
      within, 428-31, 432-35
  T-D-T model, 230-34
  T-PD-D-T model, 261-65
  T-PD-D-T model expansions,
      275-94
bass (in triads), 138
bass clarinet, transposition for,
    159
bass clef, 11, 13
bass lines, 95-96
  Alberti bass, 158
  arpeggiated, 158
  in chorale melodies, 269-70
  in chorale-style counterpoint,
      208-27
  in continuous variations, 516-17
  descending chromatic, 621-24
  for descending-fifth sequences,
      392-93, 620
  in hymns, 216
  lament bass, 317-18, 517, 534,
      639
  for Pachelbel sequences,
      398-401
bass vocal range, 237
battuto, 829
Beach Boys, the, "Help Me,
    Rhonda," 606-7, 608
beam(s), 25-26
  notation of, 30-32, 72-73

beat(s)
  defined, 22
  divisions and subdivisions of,
      28-30, 70-73
  grouping of, 23, 30-31
  notation of, 27-30, 70-76
  syncopation within, 76-77
  units other than quarter note,
      40-42
beat division, 22, 68, 71
Beatles, the, "Eleanor Rigby," 607
beat units, 26-28
  compound meter, 72-73, 74-76
Beck, Jeff, 616
Beethoven, Ludwig van
  setting of "God Save the King,"
      251
  Waldstein Sonata, 690
Bell, Freddie, and the Bellboys,
    616
Berg, Alban, serial compositions,
    800
Berio, Luciano, 847
  Visage, 825
Berry, Chuck, "Rock and Roll
    Music," 606
B-flat instruments, 160. *See also*
    transposing instruments
bimodality, 715, 742
binary forms, 471-83
  balanced, 479, 480
  composite, 487-88
  continuous, 472, 474-75, 480
  defined, 471
  harmonic disturbance in, 473,
      475, 477, 480
  phrase design in, 471-75
  in recent music, 855
  rounded, 472-73, 480, 486, 488,
      520, 685-86
  distinguished from ternary, 485
  sectional, 472, 480
  sections in, 475-76
  simple, 475, 480
  simple continuous, 474-75, 479
  simple with balanced sections,
      479
  tonal structures, 476-80
  tonicization and modulation in,
      449
  writing, 480-83
bitonality, 715
black keys, 5-6
blue notes, 603

blues
    plagal cadence in, 303-4
    twelve-bar, 602-5, 613
blues scale, 602-4
borrowed chords. *See* mixture
        chords
Bourgeois, Louis, 227
Brahms, Johannes, 701
bravura style, 527. *See also* musical
        topics
breaking species, 199-200, 202
breve(s), 26, 33, 179
bridge, 595
    in fugue, 497
    in popular songs, 601
    in post-1950 popular songs,
        608-9, 610-11
Brown, Dan, *The Da Vinci Code*,
        747
build, 610
Bussine, Romain, 589

cadence(s)
    aeolian, 614
    authentic, 232-33
    in minor keys, 242
    in basic phrase, 232-35
    conclusive, 215-18, 229-30
    deceptive, 298-300, 502
    defined, 210
    eighteenth-century style, 211,
        215-18
    evaded, 435-36, 661
    exposition closed with, 664
    in *Fortspinnung* passages, 492
    half (HC), 233-34, 298, 369,
        372-73, 376
    in minor keys, 242
    harmonic rhythm at, 248
    imperfect authentic (IAC), 232-
        33, 298, 369, 372-73, 376
    contrapuntal IAC, 233
    strong IAC, 233
    inconclusive, 215-18, 229-30
    less conclusive, 215-18
    in nontonal music, 711
    perfect authentic (PAC),
        232-33, 255, 298
    in periods, 369, 372-73, 376
    Phrygian, 304-5, 317-18, 458,
        478, 563, 581
    plagal and extension, 301-4
    in post-1905 popular songs, 613
    retardations at, 331

species, 211
    tonicized half (THC), 414-15
cadential $^6_4$, 276-79, 286
    approach and resolution,
        276-77, 278
    function of, 276-77
    mixture chords and, 540-42
    Neapolitan sixth chord and,
        551-52
    prolongation with neighbor and
        passing tones, 542
    writing, 277-78
cadential extensions, 382
cadenza, 688
Cage, John, 843, 847
Calder, Alexander, 842
Callcott, Jolin, *A Musical
        Grammar*, 567
cambiata, 191-92, 196
canon(s), 509-10, 740, 745-46,
        818, 825-29, 853, 855
cantatas, 591
cantus firmus
    defined, 166
    in first-species counterpoint,
        167-75
    in hymns and patriotic songs,
        209, 220-23
    in second-species counterpoint,
        182-88
cardinality, 720
Carter, Elliott, 800
C-clefs, 12-13, 205
center, 711
centricity, 750
centric music, 711
chaconne(s), 516
    formal organization, 517-19
chains of suspensions. *See*
        suspension chains
chance operations, 843-44
changes, 604
changing meter, 734-36, 832, 860,
        861-63
character variations. *See*
        variation(s)
Charakter, 528
"Chartres," 227
Chen Yi, 868
Chinese music, 863-64
chorale style
    in Bach cantatas, 591
    bass and melody lines, 214-20,
        269-70

chordal dissonance, 212-14
closing patterns, 216-18, 221
completing inner voices, 270-71
contrapuntal motion, 210
first-species style compared
        with, 209
harmonizing melodies, 268-72
melodic embellishment in,
        223-27
notation of, 235-41
note-to-note counterpoint in,
        208-23
opening patterns, 219-20, 221
passing and neighbor tones in,
        323-25
suspensions in, 225-26
writing counterpoint with given
        line, 220-23
choral tenor clef, 13
chord(s)
    arpeggiated, 157-58
    defined, 130
chordal dissonance, 212-14. *See
        also* dissonance
chordal seventh
    approach and resolution, 162,
        213-14, 255-57, 263, 271,
        309, 394, 620
    in Baroque era, 273
    in twentieth-century music, 717
chordal skip(s). *See* consonant
        skips
chord substitutes, theory of, 319
chord symbols, 598
chorus (in popular song), 606, 610
chromatic (defined), 47
chromatic collection, 46-47
chromatic embellishment(s),
        332-33
    common-tone diminished
        seventh and augmented
        chords, 627-31
    descending chromatic bass
        lines, 621-24
    of diatonic sequences, 619-21
    mixture chords and, 540
    Neapolitan sixth chord and,
        551-52
    in popular music, 342
    stepwise voice-leading and,
        622-24
    in variation movements, 523-24
    voice exchanges, 563-64, 625-27
chromatic half step(s), 53

chromatic harmony and voice-leading, 618-39
chromaticized descending-fifth sequences, 619-21
descending chromatic bass lines, 621-24
elaboration of diatonic frameworks, 619-32
mediant relations, 633-37
raised chordal fifth, 632
chromatic inflection, modulation by, 644-45, 646
chromatic mediant relations, 633-38
chromatic modulation, 641-62
by common dyad and chromatic inflection, 644-45
employing common tones, 642-53
enharmonic through augmented-sixth chords, 646-50
linear, 656-61
with sequences, 653-56
through mixture, 645-46
chromatic scale, 47-48
spelling pitches within, 52-54
chromatic sequences
descending-fifth, 443-44, 601, 619-21, 622, 680-81
with all root-position seventh chords, 444
modulation by, 654-55
diatonic sequences transformed into, 620
interval sizes and qualities in, 388
modulation with, 653-56
patterns, 619-21
secondary dominants in, 443-44, 681
sequential transposition, 655-56
chromatic submediant, 633-37
chromatic trichord, 783
chromatic variations. See variation(s)
chromatic voice exchange, 416-17, 420, 563-64
wedge progressions and, 625-27
chromatic wedge progressions, 625-27, 639
church modes, 104, 107
C instruments, 159
circle of fifths, 56-57, 91
finding key signatures with, 91

Clapton, Eric, 616
clarinet, transpositions for, 159, 160
Classical era. See also eighteenth century
augmented-sixth chords in, 560
basic phrase in, 228-52
binary forms in, 477, 488
figured bass in, 266-72
hypermeter in, 377, 380
indeterminacy during, 843
leading-tone triads and seventh chords in, 359
musical elements used in recent music, 855-60
musical topics in, 526-27
recitatives in, 574-75
retardations, 331
seventh chords in, 162
sonata form in, 664-73, 689
style in, 19
ternary arias in, 572-74
ternary form in, 485-86
variations in, 515, 520
clave patterns, 35, 36
clefs, 9-13
alto, 12
baritone, 12
bass, 11, 13
C, 12-13, 205
choral tenor clef, 13
mezzo-soprano, 12
in SATB style, 236
soprano, 12
tenor, 12, 13
treble, 9-10, 13
"Clementine," 369
closely related keys
defined, 456
finding, 456-57
modulation to, 448-68
close position, 237
closing theme (CT), 668-69
coda, 382-83, 521, 608, 682-83
developmental, 682
in rondo, 697
codetta, 293, 383, 682
collection, 46-47, 710
form and, 740
col legno, 709
comes, 818
commedia dell'arte, 728, 858
common chords. See pivot chords
common-dyad modulation, 642, 644-45

common-practice style. See also Baroque era; Classical era; eighteenth century
eras, 19
rhythm and meter in, 25
common time, 28
common-tone chromatic modulation, 642-53
common-tone diminished seventh chord, 627-30
common-tone German augmented sixth chord, 630-31
common-tone theorem, 786-87, 812
complement
abstract, 785
literal, 722, 785
complementary intervals, 757
complementary sets, 784-86
composite ternary forms. See ternary forms
compound interval(s). See interval(s)
compound melody, 492-93
compound meter(s). See meter(s), compound
concerto form, 686-88, 855
concert pitch, 160
concert-pitch instruments, 159
conclusive cadence. See under cadence(s)
conducting patterns, 23-24, 43, 68
conjunct motion, 167. See also motion types
consequent phrase, 369. See also phrase(s)
consonance
imperfect, 124
of intervals, 124-27, 171-75
perfect, 124
tying, 199-200
consonant skips
in chorale textures, 223-24
defined, 184
as embellishing tones, 336-38
in second-species counterpoint, 184, 187-89
in third-species counterpoint, 191-94, 195-96
contemporary musical styles, 19. See also twentieth-century music
contextual analysis, 230

continuous binary form. *See* binary forms

continuous variations. *See* variation(s)

contour motive. *See* motive(s)

contrabassoon, transposition for, 159

contrary fifths
avoiding, 243
dominant seventh chord and, 257-58

contrary motion
in counterpoint, 170-71, 172, 173-74, 210, 243, 262, 264
root movement by second and, 313

contrary octaves, avoiding, 243

contrasting period. *See* period(s)

contrasting verse-chorus, 606-7

Corigliano, John, 868

counterpoint
augmentation, 508
canon, 509-10
chorale style
melodic embellishment, 223-26
note-to-note, 208-23
consonant harmonic intervals in, 171-75
defined, 166
diminution, 508
double, 499
early, 179
free, 204-5, 497, 498
inversion, 507-8
invertible, 178-79, 499-500
note-to-note (chorale style), 208-26
note-to-note (first species; 1:1), 165-80
eighteenth-century style compared with, 209
species
first (1:1), 165-80
second (2:1), 181-90
third (4:1), 191-97
fourth, 197-202
fifth, 203-4
stretto technique, 506-7
triple, 499-500
types of motion in, 170-71

countersubject, 498

counting in thirds, 3-4

couplets, 578, 584, 589

Coven, "One Tin Soldier," 407

cover versions, 616

crescendo, 18

Croce, Jim, "Bad, Bad Leroy Brown," 614

crossed voices, 176

cross relations, 168-69, 419-20, 537

C score, 159

cut time. *See alla breve*

da capo aria. *See* aria(s)

da capo indication, 570, 579

dal segno, 570

Dal segno al Fine, 486

da Ponte, Lorenzo, 574

Darmstadt Ferienkurse für Neue Musik, 847

Debussy, Claude, 589, 866
"Fantoches," 728
golden section used by, 747

deceptive cadence. *See* cadence(s)

deceptive resolution, 291, 298-300, 441-43

decrescendo, 18

Deep Purple, "Smoke on the Water," 606

dependent transitions, 666, 675-76

derived row, 816

design (of a piece), 473

developing variation, 701

development, 689
in sonatas, 669, 671-72, 679-81, 684
in sonatinas, 684

diatonic collection, 46-47
modes, 102-7, 711, 713-19
in nonfunctional setting, 855

diatonic half step(s), 53

diatonic scale, 47

diatonic sequences, 385-407
ascending-fifth, 404-5, 406-7
ascending parallel 6/3 chords, 405-7
with 5-6 motion, 405-7
descending-fifth, 389-97, 406-7, 492, 622
with all root-position triads, 390, 391-93
with alternating root-position and first-position triads or sevenths, 390, 391-93
bass lines for, 392-93

characteristics, 390
in popular music, 396-97
with seventh chords, 390, 394-96
writing, 393
descending parallel 6/3 chords, 402-4, 406-7
with 7-6 motion, 403-4, 406-7
interval sizes and qualities in, 387-88
Pachelbel, 398-401, 407
transforming into chromatic sequences, 620

diminished fifths, 121-23, 170
intonation of, 556

diminished fourths, 121-23

diminished intervals, 121-23. *See also specific intervals*
dissonance of, 124

diminished minor seventh chord. *See* half-diminished seventh chord

diminished scale. *See* octatonic scale(s)

diminished seconds, 121-23

diminished seventh chord, 152-53, 154
common-tone, 627-30
enharmonic modulation with, 650-53
as mixture chord, 537
octatonic collection and, 726
secondary, 420-22, 430-44, 551-52

diminished sevenths (interval), 121-23

diminished sixths (interval), 121-23

diminished third chord, 574

diminished thirds (interval), 121-23, 551, 564

diminished triad(s), 131-33, 135-37. *See also* triad(s)
doubling in, 240
in first inversion, 261
Roman numerals for, 131-32, 134

diminuendo, 18

diminution(s), 182, 508

direct modulations. *See* modulation(s)

direct octaves and fifths. *See* hidden octaves and fifths

disjunct motion, 167. *See also motion types*

dissonance
  chordal, 212-14
  of embellishing tones, 322
  of intervals, 124-27, 172
dodecaphonic music. *See* twelve-
    tone rows
dominant (scale degree), 62
dominant area in phrase, 231-32
dominant chord, minor, 316-18
dominant expansion
  with cadential $^6_4$ chord, 276-79
  with secondary-function chords,
    423-25
dominant harmony
  cadential $^6_4$ and, 276-77
  in minor keys, 453
  Neapolitan sixth chord and, 552
  prolonging tonic with, 288-89
  resolving leading tone, 242
dominant key, minor, modulation
    to, 458-59
dominant key, modulation to,
    451-52, 476-77
dominant seventh chord (V7),
    148-50, 153-54
  approaching perfect intervals,
    257-60
  chromatically inflected, 644-45,
    646
  in descending-fifth sequences,
    620
  German sixth chord and,
    646-49
  incomplete, 346-47
  inversions of, 213
  in perfect authentic cadence,
    255
  prolongation of, 260
  resolutions of, 212-14, 255-57
  as secondary dominant, 411-20,
    427-44
  as source of chordal disso-
    nances, 212, 231-32
  writing, 255-60
dominant substitutes, 314-15
  leading-tone chords as, 346-55,
    359
Dorian mode, 102-3, 104-6, 107,
    713, 714
dot(s), 33-34
dotted-eighth note(s), 34
dotted-half note(s), 74-76
dotted-quarter note(s), 34, 68,
    70-71

double counterpoint. *See*
    counterpoint
double-dotted rhythms, 33, 34, 37
double exposition, 686
double flat(s), 8. *See also*
    accidentals
double neighbor. *See* neighbor
    tones
double period. *See* period(s)
double sharp(s), 8, 95. *See also*
    accidentals
double suspension. *See*
    suspension(s)
doubling
  augmented-sixth chords and,
    562-63
  cadential $^6_4$ chord and, 278
  deceptive cadence and, 300
  dominant seventh chord and,
    255-56
  for mixture chords, 535
  Neapolitan sixth chord and,
    552-54
  in SATB settings, 239-40, 256
  in twentieth-century music,
    717-18
downbeat, 23, 182
drop (in popular song), 610-11
Duparc, Henri, 589
duple meter, 23-24
  compound duple, 68-70, 74-76
duplets, 79-80
durations, serialized, 819-20
dux, 818
dyad(s), 720, 818
Dylan, Bob, "Blowin' in the Wind,"
    606
dynamic markings, 17-18
  metrical accent, 82-83
  serialized, 820

early music style periods, 18
E-flat instruments, 161. *See also*
    transposing instruments
eighteenth century. *See also*
    Baroque era; chorale style;
    Classical era
  contrapuntal style in, 166,
    209-27
  cross relations in, 420
eighth note(s), 26, 77-79
  notation of, 31, 77
eighth rest, 26
electronic music, 847

elements, 720, 795
elevenths, 112-13
Elvey, George J., 227
embedded PD-D-T, 292-93,
    346-47, 348
embellishing chords. *See*
    voice-leading chords
embellishing diminished seventh
    chord. *See* common-tone
    diminished seventh chord
embellishment(s). *See* chromatic
    embellishment(s); melodic
    embellishment(s); rhyth-
    mic embellishment(s)
English horn, transposition for, 160
enharmonic equivalents, 6, 8,
    123-24, 709-10
  within scales, 53
enharmonic modulation, 646-53
  with augmented-sixth chords,
    646-50
  with diminished seventh
    chords, 650-53
enharmonic reinterpretation,
    648-50
episodes
  in fugue, 500-502
  in rondo, 693, 694-95
escape tone (*échappée*), 333-34,
    343
euphonium, transposition for, 159
evaded cadence. *See* cadence(s)
exposition, 688-89
  double, 686
  in invention and fugue, 493-500
  in sonatas, 664-69, 674-79
extended techniques, 860, 861-62
extensions, 597

Fauré, Gabriel, 589
fauxbourdon, 402
fermata, 231, 299, 570
Fibonacci series, 746-47
fifth (in triads), 131, 138
  doubling of, 240
fifths, 111-12. *See also* diminished
    fifths; perfect fifths
  in first-species counterpoint,
    176-78
fifth species, 203-4
figural variations. *See* variation(s)
figured bass, 139-42
  realizing, 266-72
  for seventh chords, 150-51

Fine, 570

Fine, Vivian, 868

F instruments, 161. *See also* transposing instruments

first inversion (of seventh chords), 150-51

first inversion (of triads), 137-39, 157-58

  doubling in, 240

  figured bass for, 140-41

first species (1:1), 166-80. *See also* counterpoint

  connecting harmonic intervals in, 169-75

  connecting melodic intervals in, 167-69

  defined, 166

  eighteenth-century counterpoint compared with, 209

  writing note-to-note counterpoint in strict style, 175-79

first theme group (FTG), 665, 686

flag(s), 25-26

  notation of, 30-32

flat(s), 5-6. *See also* accidental(s)

  order in key signatures, 58

focal pitches/pcs, 712

folk music

  modes in, 103

  pentatonic collections in, 63

Fonte, 482-83

form, musical. *See also specific types*

  after common-practice era, 740-46

  analysis of in recent music, 846-47

  binary, 471-83

    composite, 487-88

  concerto, 686-88

  defined, 471

  mobile, 842

  moment, 841-42

  post-1945 approaches to, 824-29, 837-46, 855

  as process, 844-46

  register and, 742-44

  rondo, 693-98

  sectional, 824-25

  set classes and, 789-91

  sonata, 664-90

  strophic, 577-84

  substitutes for tonal function, 744-45

ternary, 699-705, 791, 843

  composite, 486-87

  simple, 484-86

through-composed, 585-88

variation, 514-24

vocal, 569-91

forte, 18. *See also* dynamic markings

Forte, Allen, 779

  Tonal Harmony in Concept and Practice, 426

Forte numbers, 779, 784

Fortspinnung, 491-92, 493, 515

fourths, 111-12. *See also* augmented fourths; perfect fourths

fourth species, 197-202. *See also* counterpoint

  breaking species and tying consonances, 199-200

  rhythmic character of, 199

  rhythmic displacement in, 197-201

  suspension chains, 200-201

  writing, 201-2

fragmentation. *See* motive(s)

free counterpoint. *See* counterpoint

French augmented-sixth chord, 559, 560. *See also* augmented-sixth chords

  approaches to, 563-64

  aural identification and performance, 564

  voice-leading, spelling, and resolution of, 562-63

French horn, transpositions for, 159, 160

fretboard diagram, 143

fugue(s)

  answer, 495-98

  contrapuntal techniques in, 506-10

  defined, 494

  double, 503-6

  episodes, 500-502

  exposition, 493-500

  invention compared with, 502

  later expositions (middle and final entries), 500-502

  in recent music, 855

  stretto technique, 506-7

  subject in, 493-95

  triple, 503-6

vocal, 510-11

fully diminished seventh chord. *See* diminished seventh chord

fundamental bass, 144, 359

Fux, Johann Joseph, 167

  Gradus ad Parnassum, 203-4, 205

German augmented-sixth chord, 559, 560. *See also* augmented-sixth chords

  approaches to, 563-64

  aural identification and performance, 564

  voice-leading, spelling, and resolution of, 562-63

German diminished-third chord, 564-65

Glass, Philip, 844

"God Save the Queen," 251

Goethe, Johann Wolfgang von, 585

golden section (or mean), 746-47

Gordon, Edwin, 31, 72

Gounod, Charles, 589

grand staff, 13-14

graphic notation, 737, 825, 837-39, 843

grave, 24

Green Day, 400

  "Basket Case," 407

groove, 607-8

ground bass, 516, 518-19. *See also* variations

Guido of Arezzo, 65

  Guidonian hand, 65

guitar, transposition for, 159

guitar chord symbols, 155

guitar tablature, 155, 156

half cadence. *See* cadence(s)

half-diminished seventh chord, 149-50, 153-54. *See also* leading-tone seventh chord

half note(s), 26

  notation of, 31

half rest, 26, 32-33

half step(s), 6-7, 110, 115

  intervals counted with, 121

  in major scale, 48-49

Handel, George Frideric, 107

  Messiah, 591

  use of sevenths, 125

harmonic disturbance
  in binary form, 473, 475, 477, 480
  Fonte in, 482–83
  Monte in, 481
  Ponte in, 480
harmonic intervals. *See* interval(s)
harmonic loops, 615
harmonic minor scale, 93–95,
  97–99
harmonic minor tetrachord, 93–94
harmonic rhythm, 247
harmonic sequences, 387, 388. *See
  also* chromatic sequences;
  diatonic sequences
  based on root progressions,
  306–14
Harnish, Otto Siegfried, 144
Harrison, Lou, 854
Haydn, Franz Joseph, 107
  setting of "God Save the King,"
  251
head, 605
Heine, Heinrich, 577, 581
  Lyrisches Intermezzo, 444
hemiola, 37–38, 81
Hendrix, Jimi, 616
Hensel, Fanny Mendelssohn, 868
heptachord(s), 720
heptad(s), 720
hexachord(s), 720
hexachordal combinatoriality,
  809–14
  combinatorial row pairs, 811–14
hexatonic scale(s), 726–27
hexatonic trichord, 781–82
hidden octaves and fifths, 172–73
  avoiding in second-species
  counterpoint, 189
  dominant seventh chord and,
  257–58
  in SATB style, 243–44
Higdon, Jennifer, 868
hip-hop, 608
hocket, 861
"Home on the Range," 369
homophonic texture, 246
homorhythmic texture, 210
hook, 596, 606
Howat, Roy, *Debussy in
  Proportion*, 747
hymns. *See also* chorale style
  bass lines, 216
  melodic cadential patterns,
  216–17

melodies of, 227
note-to-note counterpoint in,
  209
hypermeter, 43, 376–77, 380, 697

ic vector. *See* interval-class vector
"I Got Rhythm" tetrachord, 722
imitation, 740, 745–46, 825–29
imperfect authentic cadence. *See*
  cadence(s)
imperfect consonances, 124, 171,
  173–75
  in SATB style, 242
incomplete neighbors. *See*
  neighbor tones
inconclusive cadence. *See under*
  cadence(s)
independent transitions, 666
indeterminacy, 843–44, 847. *See
  also* chance operations
index numbers, 767–68, 799
instrumental break, 608
instrumental interlude, 608
integer notation, 720, 724, 777
integral serialism, 819
intentional harmonic ambiguity,
  658–59
intertextuality, 851, 855–60
interval(s), 6–7, 109–28
  analyzing, 125–26
  compound, 112–14
    analytical reduction of,
    169–70
    figured bass and, 139
  consonance and dissonance of,
    124–27, 182–83
  defined, 110
  enharmonically equivalent,
    123–24
  harmonic, 111–12, 168, 169–75
  inverting, 116–17
  labeling in counterpoint, 167,
    170
  large, 119–21
  melodic, 111–12, 167–69
  naming, 114
  pitch combinations, 110–14
  qualities of, 114–21
  simple, 113
  size of, 110–11
  small, 117–19
  spelling, 117–24
  in two-voice composition,
    165–206

interval class, 759–62
interval-class vector (ic vector),
  759–62, 769, 786–88
intro (in popular song), 607, 610
invariance, 803–4
invariant pcs, 803
invariant sets, 803
invention(s), 494–502
  canon in, 509–10
  defined, 494
  exposition, 493–500
  fugue compared with, 502
inverses, 757
inversion (in counterpoint), 507–8
inversion (of pitch sets and
  pitch-class sets) (I),
  762–70, 794, 796
  identifying, 766–70
inversion (of triads), 137–39, 144
  figured bass for, 140–41
inversion (of seventh chords),
  figured bass for, 150–51
inversionally related intervals, 117,
  119–21
invertible counterpoint. *See*
  counterpoint
Ionian mode, 104–6, 714
  spelling, 105–6
irregular resolution, 441–43
isochronous beats, 731
isorhythm, 854
Italian augmented-sixth chord,
  558, 560. *See also* augmented-sixth chords
  approaches to, 563–64
  aural identification and
  performance, 564
  voice-leading, spelling, and
  resolution of, 562–63

Japanese aesthetics, 866–67
jazz
  modes in, 103, 106–7, 713
  pentatonic collections in, 63
  recent, 860
  triads and seventh chords in,
    155–57, 162
  tritone substitution in, 602
  use of sevenths, 125
Joplin, Scott, 19

key(s)
  identification of, 57–58, 59–61,
    95–96

major, 47-52
  seventh chords in, 148-50
  triads in, 131-33
  minor, 85-100
    seventh chords in, 152-53
    triads in, 152-53
  parallel, 86-88
  relative, 88-92
keyboard, writing for, 245-47
keyboard spacing, 237
key signature(s)
  accidentals and, 54-56, 87
  circle of fifths and, 56-57
  key identification from, 57-58
  major, 55-56
  minor scales and, 97
  pitch intervals and, 125-26
  purpose of, 55
  triad spelling and, 136-37
  writing, 58-59
King, Carole, "You've Got a
    Friend," 608
King, Martin Luther Jr., 251
Kirnberger, Johann Philipp, 83
Kutter, Markus, 837

lament bass progression, 317-18,
    517, 534, 639
large ternary form, 699-705
larghetto, 24
largo, 24
Lavigne, Avril, 400
  "Sk8er Boi," 407
lead-in, 380-81
leading tone (scale degree), 62
  approach and resolution,
      213-14, 242, 255-57, 271,
      620
  avoiding doubling for, 240,
      255-56
  in minor, 100
leading-tone seventh chord, fully
    diminished (vii°7)
  contexts for, 346-50
  inversions of, 354-55
  as mixture chord, 537
  in popular music, 599
  resolution of, 350, 352-55
  secondary, 420-22, 430-44,
    551-52
  writing, 352-53
leading-tone seventh chord,
    half-diminished (viiø7), 149
  contexts for, 346-50

inversions of, 354-55
in popular music, 599
resolution of, 350, 352-55
secondary, 420-22, 430-44
leading-tone triad, first inversion
  contexts for, 346-50
  prolonging tonic with, 346-47
  resolution of, 350-52
  secondary, 420-22
leading-tone triad, root position,
    307
lead-sheet notation, 142-43, 155-56
leap(s), 167-68, 171, 173, 176, 184.
    See also consonant skips
  in second-species counterpoint,
    187-89
learned style, 527. *See also* musical
    topics
ledger lines, 9, 13-16
legato, 34
Leiber, Jerry, 616
leitmotivs, 383, 855
Lendvai, Erno, 744-45
Lennon, John, 616
Leonardo da Vinci, 747
Leoncavallo, Ruggiero, *I Pagliacci*,
    728
letter names of pitches, 3-4, 9, 47,
    51
level of transposition, 386
Lewis, Jerry Lee, 616
Lied(er), 577-88
  analysis and interpretation,
    583-84
  strophic, 577-84
  text and song structure, 577-84
  text painting in, 581-83
Ligeti, György, 847
linear chords. *See* voice-leading
    chords
linear chromaticism, 656-61
  intentional harmonic ambiguity
    and, 658-59
  voice-leading chords and,
    656-58
linear intervallic pattern (LIP),
    387, 388, 391-92, 402, 405
link
  in fugue, 497
  in popular styles, 608
Lippius, Johannes, 144
Little Richard, "Tutti Frutti," 606
Locrian mode, 107, 713, 714
loop (in popular song), 614-15

lower neighbors, 184, 192, 335-36.
    See also neighbor tone(s)
Lully, Jean-Baptiste, 43
Luther, Martin, 267
Lutosławski, Witold, golden
    section used by, 747
Lydian-Mixolydian mode, 713, 714
Lydian mode, 104-6, 714
  spelling, 105-6

Madonna, 341
major intervals, 115-21
  as inversion of minor intervals,
    116-17
major keys, 47-63
  closely related, 456
  mixture chords in, 532-33
  predominant chords in, 261
  seventh chords in, 148-50
  triads in, 131-33
major-major seventh chord
    (MM7). *See* major seventh
    chord (MM7)
major-minor seventh chord
    (Mm7). *See* dominant
    seventh chord (V7)
major-minor tetrachord, 718
major pentachord, 64-65, 86-87,
    105
major pentatonic scale, 63-64, 65,
    721-22
major scale(s), 47-52
major seconds, 114, 117-19
major seventh chord (MM7),
    148-50, 153-54
  in popular music, 597, 599
major sevenths (interval), 115-17,
    119-21
major sixths (interval), 115-17,
    119-21
  in contrapuntal settings, 173-75
major tetrachord, 51, 94
major thirds (interval), 114,
    115-19, 117-19
  in contrapuntal settings, 173-75
major triads, 131-33, 135-37. *See*
    also triad(s)
  Roman numerals for, 131-32,
    134
march(es)
  alla breve in, 41
  form of, 487-88
Massenet, Jules, 589
Mattheson, Johann, 43

measure(s), 23
  incomplete, 38–39
medial caesura (MC), 666
mediant (scale degree), 62
mediant key, modulation to, 459–61
mediant triads, 314–16
  flatted, 635
  in minor keys, 316–18
melodic embellishment(s), 321–43. *See also specific types*
  in chorale textures, 223–27
  figured bass and, 266
  function of, 322
  in harmonic framework, 322–25
  identifying, 322–23
  labeling, 343
  mixture chords and, 540
  in popular music, 341–42
  in second-species counterpoint, 182–85
  of suspensions, 329–30
  in third-species counterpoint, 191–94
melodic-harmonic divorce, 615
melodic intervals. *See* interval(s)
melodic minor scale, 94, 97–99
melodic minor tetrachord, 94
melodic motion, 167–69
  in first-species counterpoint, 175–79
melodic sequences, 387, 388
mélodie, 589–90
melody
  Baroque, 491–93
  chorale-style harmonization, 214–20, 269–70
  compound, 492–93
  harmonization of modulating, 466–68
melody-and-accompaniment texture
  creating an accompaniment, 248–51
  features of, 246
  melody harmonization, 247–48
  voice distribution, 247
  writing for keyboard, 245–47
Messiaen, Olivier, 847, 867
  Quartet for the End of Time, 791, 854
  The Technique of My Musical Language, 791

meter(s)
  ametric music, 736–37, 830–32, 860
  asymmetrical, 731–33, 853, 860
  changing, 734–36, 832, 860, 861–63
  compound, 67–84
    compound duple, 68–70, 74–76
    compound quadruple, 68–70, 79–80
    compound triple, 68–70
    conducting patterns for, 68
    defined, 22–23, 68
    performance implications of, 82–83
    rhythmic notation in, 70–76
    simple mixed with, 77–81, 83
  defined, 22
  notation of, 830–36
  perceived and notated, 733–34
  "relative-time" signature, 832–33
  simple, 21–44
    compound mixed with, 77–81, 83
    defined, 22–23
    rhythmic notation in, 28–40
    rhythmic values in, 25–26
    signatures for, 26–27
    simple duple, 23
    simple quadruple, 23
    simple triple, 23
  symmetrical, 731, 860–61
  in twentieth-century music, 731–39
meter signature(s)
  changing, 731–36, 830
  compound, 67–76
  interpreting, 68–70
  simple, 26–28
metric accent, 23, 24, 35–36, 82–83
  in second-species counterpoint, 182
metric hierarchy, 42–43
metric symbols, 82–83
metric modulation, 834–36
metric organization, 22–25
metric reinterpretation, 379
mezzo forte, 18. *See also* dynamic markings
mezzo piano, 18. *See also* dynamic markings

mezzo-soprano clef, 12
microtonal tunings, 855
Middle Ages
  characterization of perfect intervals in, 127
  counterpoint in, 179
  musical materials used in recent music, 851–55
  as style era, 18
  tritone in, 124
middle C, 5
middle entries, 500–502
minimalism, 844–46, 854, 863, 864–66
minor dominant. *See* dominant chord, minor
minor intervals, 115–21
  as inversion of major intervals, 116–17
minor keys, 85–100
  closely related, 456
  mixture chords in, 533–34
  predominant chords in, 261
  seventh chords in, 152–53
  triads in, 133–35
minor-minor seventh chord (mm7). *See* minor seventh chord (mm7)
minor pentachord, 87, 92–93, 94–95, 98, 105
minor pentatonic scale, 101–2, 721–22
minor scale(s)
  Dorian mode and, 107
  forms of, 93–95
  hearing, 96–97
  writing, 97–99
minor seconds, 114, 117–19
minor seventh chord (mm7), 148–50, 153–54
  in popular music, 597, 599
minor sevenths (interval), 115–17, 119–21
minor sixths (interval), 115–17, 119–21
  in contrapuntal settings, 173–75
minor thirds (interval), 114, 115–19
  in contrapuntal settings, 173–75
minor triads, 131–33, 135–37. *See also* triad(s)
  Roman numerals for, 131–32, 134
minuet(s), 41
minuet and trio, 486–87

Mixolydian mode, 103, 104-6, 714
  spelling, 105-6
mixture chords, 530-46
  augmented-sixth chords and, 563-64
  cadential $^6_4$ chord and, 540-42
  chromatic mediants and submediants, 633-37
  chromatic predominant, 548-68
  in deceptive cadences, 537
  defined, 532
  embellishing tones and, 540
  expanding the basic phrase with, 535-36
  in instrumental music, 543-44
  intonation and, 542-43
  in minor keys, 533-34
  modulation and, 544-45
  modulation through, 645-46
  in popular songs, 598-99
  spelling and function of, 534-38
  tonicizing, 538-40
mobile form, 842
mod12 arithmetic, 756-59, 777
modal mixture. See mixture chords
modal scale degrees, 100, 102-3, 115, 533
moderato, 24
modernism, 19, 850
modes
  defined, 102
  diatonic, 102-7
  of limited transposition, 787-88
  parallel identification of, 105-6
  relative identification of, 104, 105-6
  spelling, 105-6
  in twentieth-century music, 713-19, 740-42
modified strophic form, 584
modulation(s)
  altered common-chord, 645-46
  altered pivot-chord, 645-46
  in binary forms, 476-80
  chromatic, 641-62
  to closely related keys, 448-68
  common pivot-chord, 449-61
  defined, 414
  direct, 461-64, 633, 642
  harmonizing modulating melodies, 466-68
  locating, 464
  from major key to dominant, 451-52, 476-77

from major key to supertonic, mediant, subdominant, or submediant, 459-61
from minor key to minor dominant, 458-59, 476-77
from minor key to relative major, 452-55, 476-77
mixture chords and, 544-45
in musical contexts, 464-68
by secondary dominants, 463-64
tonicization compared with, 414, 450-51
moment form, 841-42
Monte, 481
Morris, Robert, 814
motion types
  conjunct, 167
  disjunct, 167
  oblique, 170-71, 210, 243
  parallel, 170-71, 210
  similar, 170-71, 210
motive(s)
  analysis of, 363-65
  arpeggiated, 364-65
  contour, 363
  defined, 363
  extending, 364
  fragmenting, 364
  identifying, 363-64
  inverting, 364-65
  labeling, 363
  leitmotivs, 383, 855
  in phrases, 362-68
  rhythmic, 363
  sentences and, 366-68
  transposing, 364-65
  truncating, 364
motivic parallelism, 588
movable-do solfège, 49
Mozart, Leopold, 83
Mozart, Wolfgang Amadeus, Piano Sonata in C Major, K. 545, 162
multibar rests, 33
Musica enchiriadis, 179, 826
musical alphabet, 3-4
musical forms. See also specific types
  defined, 471
musical topic, 526-27
"My Country, 'Tis of Thee," 251

natural(s), 6
natural harmonics, 861-62

natural minor scale, 93-94, 97-99, 101
natural minor tetrachord, 94, 614
Neapolitan sixth chord, 549-57
  defined, 550
  intonation and performance, 556
  spelling and voicing, 550-51
  text painting and, 627
  tonicization of, 556-57, 588
  voice-leading and resolution, 551-55
neighboring $^4_2$ chords, 356-58
neighboring $^6_4$ chords, 279-82, 286
neighbor tones
  accented, 324-25
  cadential $^6_4$ prolonged with, 542
  in chorale textures, 223-24, 231, 323-25
  chromatic, 332-33
  defined, 184
  double (changing tones), 192, 196, 335-36, 343
  incomplete, 333-34, 343
  in popular music, 341-42
  in second-species counterpoint, 184-85, 187-89
  text painting with, 586
  in third-species counterpoint, 191-94, 195-96
Newman, Paul, 19
ninth chords, 397, 597
ninths (interval), 112-13
  in twentieth-century music, 717
nonachord(s), 720
nonad(s), 720
non-isochronous beats, 731
nonmetric pieces, 25
Nono, Luigi, 814, 847
  Il canto sospeso, 854
nonteleological form, 841
nontonal music, 711-19. See also atonal music; serial composition
  defined, 711
normal order, 751-52, 773, 775-77
notation
  ametric music, 830-32
  anacrusis, 38-40
  clefs, 9-13, 236
  dots and ties, 33-35
  figured bass, 140-41
  of four-part harmony, 235-41
  grand staff, 13-14

notation (*continued*)
  graphic, 737, 825, 837-39, 843
  guidelines for, 30-31, 73
  guitar chord symbols, 155
  guitar tablature, 155, 156
  innovative practices, 824,
    830-36
  integer, 720, 724, 777
  lead-sheet, 142-43, 155-56
  ledger lines, 13-16
  meter signatures, 26-28, 67-76,
    731-36
  metric modulation, 834-36
  of pitch, 3-4
  of rests, 32-33, 73
  of rhythm, 25-26, 28-40, 70-76,
    830-36
  staff, 8, 236
  of stems, 30-32, 236
  text, 840-41
  ties, 76-77
  time-line, 837-38
note head, 10
note-to-note counterpoint (1:1).
    See counterpoint

objective-subjective stance, 578-79
oblique motion, 170-71, 210, 243
octachord(s), 720
octad(s), 720
octatonic scale(s), 725-26, 740-42,
    744-45, 860
octatonic trichord, 782-83
octave(s), 111, 127
  as consonant interval, 124
  in contrapuntal settings, 172-73
  defined, 4
  in first-species counterpoint,
    176-78
  perfect, 115
  symmetrical divisions of, 634
  transposition by, 13
octave doubling, 125
octave equivalence, 4, 114, 709-10
offbeat, 27, 28, 182
"Old Hundredth," 227
omnibus progression. *See* chro-
    matic wedge progression
Ono, Yoko, 847
open position, 237
opera buffa, 728
oratorios, 591
orchestration, 160
order numbers, 800

ostinato(s), 712, 713, 724
ottava sign, 15
outro (in popular song), 608
overlapping voices, 176, 238-39,
    259

Pachelbel sequences, 398-401, 407
palindrome(s), 738-39, 803, 821,
    832
parallel $\frac{6}{3}$ chords, 318-19
  ascending, 405-7
  descending, 402-4
parallel fifths
  avoiding, 172-73, 189-90, 196,
    242, 256, 271
  in descending-fifth sequences,
    394
  with Neapolitan chord, 550
  in root motion by second,
    262-63, 290, 313
  with secondary dominant
    chords, 418
  in tonic to mediant root
    motion, 315
  in third-species counterpoint,
    193-94
  in twentieth-century music, 715,
    717
parallel keys, 86-88, 532
parallel motion, 170-71, 210
  root movement by second and,
    313
  in twentieth-century music,
    717-18, 724
parallel octaves
  avoiding, 172-73, 189-90, 242,
    255, 271
  in descending-fifth sequences,
    394
  with Neapolitan chord, 550
  in root motion by seconds,
    262-63, 313
  with secondary dominant
    chords, 418
  in tonic to mediant root
    motion, 315
  in third-species counterpoint,
    193-94
parallel period. *See* period(s)
parallel thirds in SATB style, 243
parallel unisons, avoiding, 172-73
Paravonian, Rob, 407
parlando style, 574
parody (in music), 851

Partch, Harry, 854
passacaglia(s), 516
  formal organization, 517-19
passing $\frac{6}{4}$ chords, 283-85, 286
passing tone(s)
  accented, 224, 324-25
  between chord tones, 336-38
  cadential $\frac{6}{4}$ prolonged with, 542
  in chorale textures, 223-24, 231,
    323-25
  chromatic, 332-33
  defined, 183
  in popular music, 341-42
  in second-species counterpoint,
    183-84, 187-89
  in third-species counterpoint,
    191-94, 195-96
  unaccented, 224, 324-25
pcsets. *See* pitch-class sets; pitch
    sets
pedal $\frac{4}{2}$ chords, 356-58
pedal $\frac{6}{4}$, 279-82, 286. *See also*
    neighboring $\frac{6}{4}$
pedal points, 339-40, 342, 502,
    723
pentachord(s), 720, 777-78
pentatonic collection, 63-64,
    101-2
  major, 63-64
pentatonic scales, 63-64, 65,
    101-2, 602-4, 721-23, 860
  major, 63-64, 65, 721-72
  minor, 101-2, 721-22
pentatonic trichord, 780-81
perfect authentic cadence. *See*
    cadence(s)
perfect consonances, 124
  approaching, 174, 242-43
  in contrapuntal settings, 171-73
  in SATB style, 242-44
perfect fifths, 115, 119-21
  as consonant intervals, 124
  in contrapuntal settings, 172-73
perfect fourths, 115-19
  as consonant interval, 172
  in contrapuntal settings, 172-73
  as dissonant interval, 124, 172
perfect intervals, 115-21, 127,
    257-60. *See also* octave(s);
    perfect fifths; perfect
    fourths
performance implications
  of ametric music, 736-37
  of asymmetrical meters, 732-33

of augmented-sixth chords, 564
of chromatic passages, 627, 660
of harmonic analysis, 538-40
of indeterminacy and chance,
    843-44
in Lieder, 583-84
metrical accent and, 82-83
metrical hierarchy and, 42-43
mixture chords and intonation,
    542-43
mixture chords in instrumental
    music, 543-44
of Neapolitan sixth chord, 556
of scales, 64-66
of secondary-function chords,
    434-35
of sonata-form movements,
    688-89
tempo indications and, 24
textual analysis and, 590
of time-line notation, 837-38
of variations, 528
period(s), 368-75
    asymmetrical, 371
    contrasting, 370-73, 372
    double, 374-75
    modulating, 371, 372, 700
    parallel, 369-73, 376, 379, 700
    symmetrical, 371
    three-phrase, 373-74
Perry, Katy, "Roar," 610, 615
"Petrouchka chord," 715
Pet Shop Boys, "Go West," 407
phasing, 845
phrase(s)
    antecedent-consequent, 369
    basic, in SATB style, 228-52
        establishing tonic area,
        230-32
    defined, 210, 229, 362
    design in binary form, 471-75
    diagrams, 369
    elision (overlap) of, 378-79
    expansion of, 379-83
    Fortspinnung passages, 491-92,
        493, 515
    linking, 378-79
    motive and, 362-68
    in nontonal music, 711
    period and, 368-75
    structure, 361-84, 604-5
phrase group, 376-77
phrase modulations. See modula-
    tion(s): direct

phrase rhythm, 376-83
    cadential extensions, 382
    coda, 382-83
    defined, 377
    expansion and, 379-83
    in Fortspinnung passages,
        491-92
    hypermeter, 376-77, 380
    lead-in, 380-81
Phrygian cadence. See cadence(s)
Phrygian II chord. See Neapolitan
    sixth chord
Phrygian mode, 103, 104-6, 714
piano, 18
piano accompaniment
    in Lieder, 582
    textures, 249-50
piano keyboard, 5-6, 14
Picardy third, 534
piccolo, transposition for, 159
pick-up. See anacrusis; upbeat
pitch(es), 2-20
    defined, 4
    enharmonic equivalents, 6, 8
    letter names of, 3-4
    notation of, 3-4, 8-17
    on piano keyboard, 5-6
    spelling within scales, 50-52
pitch class, 4
pitch-class collections, 45-66. See
        also key(s); scale(s)
    form and, 740
    in recent music, 860
    relative keys and, 88
    sets, 720
    in music after 1900, 709-12, 713
pitch-class intervals, 753-62, 777
    ordered, 754-55, 757, 758
    unordered, 754-55, 759-60
pitch-class segments
    labeling, 797
    operations on, 797-99
    ordered, 794-96
    pitch-class sets distinguished
        from, 795
pitch-class sets (pcsets), 720
    analyzing, 750-70
    elements of, 751-53
    inversion of, 764-66
    octave displacement, 769
    ordered and unordered, 753-55,
        794-96
    transposition and mod12
        arithmetic, 755-59, 777

pitch intervals, 753-62. See also
        interval(s)
    ordered, 754-55
    unordered, 754-55
pitch sets (psets), 750
    analyzing, 750-70
    inversion of, 763-74
pitch symmetry, 743-44
pitch-time graph, 743
pivot chords, 449-61
    defined, 450
    finding, 464
    from major key to mediant,
        459-61
    from major key to subdominant,
        459-61
    from major key to submediant,
        459-61
    from major key to supertonic,
        459-61
    from minor key to minor
        dominant, 458-59
    from minor key to relative
        major, 452-55
    modulation vs. tonicization by,
        450-51
    from tonic to dominant in
        major, 451-52
    writing a modulation, 461
pivot-dyad modulation. See
        common-dyad modulation
pivot-tone modulation. See
        common-tone chromatic
        modulation
pizzicato, 709, 829
plagal cadence. See cadence(s)
planing, 717-18
point of imitation, 204, 205, 495,
        502
polymeter, 734-36, 832-33
polymodality, 715, 742
polyphonic variation. See
        variations
polyrhythm, 80-81
polytonality, 715
Ponte, 480
popular music, 593-616. See also
        popular songs
    augmented-sixth chords in, 560
    descending-fifth sequences in,
        396-97
    direct modulations in, 462-63
    embellishing tones in, 341-42
    modes in, 103, 106-7

popular music (*continued*)
  pentatonic collections in, 63
  quaternary and verse-refrain
      forms, 594-96
  triads and seventh chords in,
      155-57, 162
  twelve-bar blues, 602-5
  use of sevenths, 125
popular songs, 594-602, 860
  harmonic practices, 596-99
  post-1950, 606-16
  quaternary form, 594-95
  suspensions and rhythmic
      displacement in, 600
  verse-refrain form, 596
postchorus, 609, 610
postmodernism, 850
post-tonal music. *See* nontonal
  music
power chords, 613
prechorus, 609, 610
predominant-function chords,
      261-64. *See also* subdomi-
      nant chords; supertonic
      chords
  chromatic, 548-68
  in major keys, 261
  in minor keys, 261
  seventh chords, 264
  voice-leading to dominant,
      262-63
preparation
  of chordal seventh, 263, 264
  of dissonance, 183, 212
  of suspension, 197, 226
Presley, Elvis
  "Heartbreak Hotel," 606
  "Hound Dog," 605, 616
prestissimo, 24
presto, 24
primary theme (PT), 665
prime form (P), 773-79, 795, 796
program music, 582-83
Pythagoras, 127

quadruple meter, 23-24
  compound, 68-70, 79-80
quadruplets, 79-80
quartal harmonies, 719
quarter note(s), 26, 77-78
quarter rest, 26
quaternary song form, 594-95
quintal harmonies, 719
quintuplets, 80

quodlibet, 854
quotation (in music), 850-51,
      855-57

rags, 19
  form of, 487-88
raised chordal fifth, 632
raised submediant (scale degree),
      100
Raison, André, 516-17
Rameau, Jean-Philippe, 144, 319,
      359
Ran, Shulamit, 868
range, in SATB style, 237
rap, 608
Ravel, Maurice, 589, 866
R&B, 616
realization, figured bass, 266-72
rearticulated suspension, 225
recapitulation, 689
  in sonatas, 669-71, 681-82
  in sonatinas, 685
recitatives, 574-77
recitativo accompagnato, 574
recitativo secco, 574
Redford, Robert, 19
"Red River Valley," 369
refrain, 596, 607, 698
  in rondo, 693-94
  in verse-refrain form, 596
registers
  form and, 742-44
  naming, 13
registral invariance, 818-19
Reich, Steve, 844, 868
relative keys, 88-92
relative major, 89-91
  modulation to, 452-55
relative minor, 88-92
"relative-time" signature, 832-33
Renaissance era
  characterization of perfect
      intervals in, 127
  consonance and dissonance in,
      124
  counterpoint in, 179
  fauxbourdon in, 402
  harmonic thinking in, 273
  modes in, 103, 107
  musical materials used in recent
      music, 851-55
  style in, 18
  text painting in, 546
repeat signs, 471, 475-76

resolution (of dissonance), 183
  in dominant seventh chords,
      212-14
  in dominant triads, 242
resolution (of suspension), 197, 226
rest(s), 25, 26, 32-33
  notation of, 73
retardations, 331
retransition
  in rondo, 695-97
  in sonatas, 672-73, 680
  in sonatinas, 684
retrograde (R), 795, 796
retrograde inversion (RI), 796
rhyme schemes, 577-78, 581
rhythm
  additive, 738-39
  defined, 25
  isorhythm, 854
  notation of, 28-40, 830-36
  syncopated, 35-37, 76-77
  in twentieth-century music,
      731-39
  values in simple meter, 25-26
rhythm clefs, 32
rhythmic acceleration, 518, 528
rhythmic counting, 23, 31, 68, 78,
      80
rhythmic *crescendo*, 518
rhythmic displacement
  in fourth-species counterpoint,
      197-201
  in popular songs, 600
rhythmic embellishment(s). *See
      also* suspension(s)
  anticipations, 338
  retardations, 331
rhythmic motive. *See* motive(s)
Riemann, Hugo, 319, 426
Riepel, Joseph, 468, 480
riff, 607
ritornello, 570, 693, 698
rock
  modes in, 103
  pentatonic collections in, 63
  plagal cadence in, 303
  triads and seventh chords in,
      155-57
Rolling Stones, the, 616
romanesca, 517
Roman numerals
  for 5-6 motion, 405-7
  for altered chords, 532-33, 545,
      635

for altered fifth harmonies, 601
for applied dominants, 411
for ascending sequences, 407
for augmented triads, 131-32, 134
for cadential $\begin{smallmatrix}6\\4\end{smallmatrix}$, 277-78
figured bass combined with, 142
levels of, 230
for parallel $\begin{smallmatrix}6\\3\end{smallmatrix}$ chords, 319
for pedal points, 340
for seventh chords, 150-51
for triads, 131-32
for voice-leading seventh chords, 357-59
Romantic era
augmented-sixth chords in, 560
binary forms in, 477
chromatic mediants in, 633-34
chromatic voice exchanges in, 625-27
common-tone chromatic modulation in, 642-45
harmonic ambiguity in, 658-59
hypermeter in, 380
instrumental program music in, 582-83
Lieder in, 577-88
mélodie in, 589-90
musical materials used in recent music, 855-60
musical topics in, 526-27
rhythmic notation in, 81
seventh chords in, 162
sonata form in, 674-83, 689
style in, 19
ternary form in, 485-86
rondo
coda in, 697
five-part, 693-98
refrains and episodes in, 693-95, 698
seven-part, 698-99
sonata-rondo, 698-99
transitions and retransitions in, 695-97, 698
root (in triads), 131
doubling of, 138, 240
identifying, 139
root position
of seventh chords, 150-51
of triads, 131, 137-39, 157-58
root progressions
ascending-second, 306
ascending-third, 309

descending-fifth, 306-9, 316-17, 319, 620, 622
descending-third, 262, 306, 309-11
with mediant triads, 314-16
Rameau's theory of, 319
by second, 312-14
rounded binary form. *See* binary forms
row elision, 817
row matrix, 807-9
rows, twelve-tone, 799-814
choosing forms, 803-4
compositional style and, 814-19
derived, 816
form and, 740
hearing relationships, 804-5
labeling, 801-3
realizing twelve-tone, 805-14
symmetrical, 815
rubato, 83
Rückert, Friedrich, 584

"St. George's Windsor," 227
SATB style. *See also* chorale style
basic phrase in, 228-52
connecting dominant and tonic areas, 242-45
doubling in, 239-40
harmonizing chorale melodies, 268-72
hidden octaves and fifths in, 243-44
independent melodic lines in, 238-39
notation of, 235-41
perfect consonances in, 242-44
predominant to dominant in, 262-63
range in, 237
spacing in, 237-38
voice-leading guidelines, 272
Satie, Erik, 747
saxophone, transpositions for, 159, 160
scale(s), 47-54. *See also* scale degrees
analysis and formal design, 740-42
chromatic, 47-48, 52-54
defined, 47
diatonic, 47
hexatonic, 726-27
major, 47-52

minor, 93-95, 96-99
modal, 104-6
octatonic, 725-26, 740-42, 860
pentatonic, 602-4, 721-23, 860
major, 63-64, 65, 721-22
minor, 101-2, 721-22
spelling pitches within, 50-52
spelling pitch intervals with, 117-19
whole-tone, 723-24, 860
scale degrees, 49-50
for augmented-sixth chords, 558-59
in first-species counterpoint, 176-78
identifying keys from, 95-96
interval qualities and, 115-21
in major, 49, 132, 148-50
in mediant triads, 314
in minor, 93-94, 100, 134
modal, 100, 102-3
names of, 62-63
in Neapolitan sixth chord, 549-50
in Phrygian cadence, 304
relative keys and, 90-91
in secondary dominant, 409, 412
seventh chords and, 148-54
triads and, 131-43
scale-degree triads, 132
scherzo and trio, 486-87
Schoenberg, Arnold, 850
Pierrot lunaire, 728
serial compositions, 798, 800
Schubert, Franz, "Der Wegweiser," 639
Schumann, Clara Wieck, 705, 868
"Liebst du um Schönheit," 584
Schumann, Robert, 705, 868
"Ich grolle nicht," 444
score(s), 3
reading pitches from, 8-16
writing pitches on, 16-17
secondary dominants, 409-26, 638
augmented-sixth chords and, 563-64
with basic phrase, 428-31
in chromatic sequences, 443-44, 681
defined, 410
identifying, 429-31

secondary dominants (*continued*)
  intensifying the dominant, 410-11
  modulation by, 463-64
  musical contexts, 432-37
  with raised fifth, 632
  resolving, 440-43
  seventh chords, 411-12
  spelling, 430-31, 438-39
  systems for analyzing, 426
  text painting with, 436-37, 444
  to V, 411-20
    in basic phrase, 416-17
    cross relations and, 419-20
    spelling, 411-13
    tonicization and modulation, 414-15
    writing and resolving, 418-19
secondary leading-tone chords
  chromatically inflected, 644-45
  identifying, 429-31
  musical contexts, 432-37
  resolving, 440-43
  spelling, 430-31, 438-39
  text painting with, 436-37, 444
  to V, 420-22
    in dominant expansions, 423-25
secondary sets, 810
second inversion (of seventh chords), 150-51
second inversion (of triads), 137-39
  doubling in, 240
  figured bass for, 140-41
seconds, 111-12, 114. *See also* augmented seconds; major seconds; minor seconds
  as dissonant intervals, 124
second species (2:1), 181-90. *See also* counterpoint
  defined, 182
  harmonic considerations, 189-90
  melodic considerations, 187-89
  melodic embellishment, 182-85
  metric accent in, 182
  middle section, 187-89
  opening and closing patterns, 186-87
  writing, 186-90
second theme group (STG), 666-68, 686
sectional binary form. *See* binary forms

sectional variations. *See* variations
sections, 475-76
segmentation, 753
semitone(s). *See* half step(s)
sentence(s), 366-68, 372
septuplets, 80
sequence(s), 386. *See also* chromatic sequences; diatonic sequences; harmonic sequences; melodic sequences
serial composition, 794-99, 847, 860. *See also* twelve-tone rows
  compositional style and, 814-19
  labeling segments, 797
  operations on pitch classes, 797-99
  ordered pitch segments, 794-96
  total serialism, 819-20
  with twelve-tone rows, 799-814
set classes, 772-91
  defined, 773
  formal design and, 789-91
  labeling segments, 779, 797
  prime forms, 773-79
  tables, 784-88
sets
  analysis with, 749-70
  complementary, 784-86
  defined, 720
  form and, 740
  pitch and pitch-class intervals, 753-62
    inversion of, 762-70
  relationships between, 752-53
  trichord types, 780-84
set theory, 719-21. *See also* set classes; sets
seventh chords, 146-64, 638. *See also specific chords*
  in descending-fifth root progressions, 308-9
  in major keys, 148-50
  in minor keys, 152-53
  musical style and, 162
  in musical textures, 157-62
  in popular styles, 155-57, 597, 599
  predominant, 264
  Roman numerals and figures for, 150-51
  spelling, 153-54, 155
  in transposing scores, 159-61
  types of, 147-48

uncommon, 156
sevenths (interval), 111-12. *See also* diminished sevenths; major sevenths; minor sevenths
  as dissonant intervals, 124
sextuplets, 80
sharp(s), 5-6. *See also* accidental(s)
  order in key signatures, 57-58
Shaw, Caroline, 868
shuttle, 614
sight-reading skills
  beat-unit patterns and, 30, 40
  key signatures and, 91
  pitch spellings and, 53
  reading compound meters, 72
  for rhythm, 30
  spelling triads, 135-37
similar motion, 170-71, 210
simple binary form. *See* binary forms
simple meter(s). *See* meter(s), simple
simple ternary form. *See* ternary forms
simple verse form, 606, 607
simplifying variation. *See* variations
sinfonias, 494, 502
sixteenth note(s), 26, 78
  notation of, 31, 77
sixteenth rest, 26
sixths (interval), 111-12. *See also* augmented sixths; major sixths; minor sixths
  as consonant intervals, 124
  in first-species counterpoint, 176-78
sixty-fourth note(s), 26
skip(s), 167, 171, 173, 176. *See also* consonant skip(s)
  tonic expansion with bass-line, 289
slash notation, 143
slur(s), 34-35
Smith, Samuel Francis, 251
solfège syllables, 49, 65
solo break, 608
sonata(s), 664, 855. *See also* sonata form
sonata (or sonata-allegro) form, 664-90
  Classical, 664-73, 689
  coda in, 682
  concerto and, 686-88

defined, 664
development in, 669, 671–72, 679–81, 689
exposition in, 664–69, 674–79, 688–89
key areas in, 674–79
recapitulation in, 669–71, 681–82, 689
in recent music, 855
retransition in, 672–73, 680
in Romantic era, 674–83, 689
tonicization and modulation in, 449
twelve-tone rows and, 805
sonata-rondo, 698–99
sonatina, 684–86
song cycle, 583
song forms
    modified strophic, 584
    quaternary and verse-refrain, 594–96
    strophic, 577–84
    ternary (three-part), 570–77
    through-composed, 585–88
soprano clef, 12
soprano vocal range, 237
sounding pitch. *See* concert pitch
spacing
    keyboard, 237
    in SATB settings, 237–38
species counterpoint. *See* counterpoint
split-third chord, 718
staff, 8
    keyboard notation on, 245–47
    in SATB style, 236
stem(s), 16–17, 25–26
    notation of, 30–32, 236
    in SATB style, 236
step, stepwise motion, 167, 171, 173, 176
step progressions, 492–93
Stevens, Halsey, *The Life and Music of Béla Bartók*, 770
Sting, The (film), 19
Stockhausen, Karlheinz, 843, 847, 850
Stoller, Mike, 616
strains, 487–88
Strassburg, Gottfried von, 661
stratification, 715, 742
Stravinsky, Igor, 850
    Petrouchka, 728
    serial compositions, 798, 800

stretto, 506–7
string bass, transposition for, 159
strophes, 577, 589
strophic form, 577–84
    defined, 579
structure (in music), 476–80
Sturm und Drang, 526–27
style juxtaposition, 850–51
style periods, 18–19
stylistic allusions, 850–51, 855–60
subdominant (scale degree), 62
subdominant chords, prolonging tonic with, 279–82, 287–88
subdominant key, modulation to, 459–61
subject (in fugue), 493–95
    alteration of, 507–9
submediant (scale degree), 62
submediant chords
    flatted, 537–38, 635
    prolonging tonic with, 290–92
submediant key, modulation to, 459–61
subphrase, 367
subsets, 720
subtonic (scale degree), 100
suffix. *See* cadential extension
supertonic (scale degree), 62
supertonic key, modulation to, 459–61
supertonic seventh chord, 356–57
supertonic triad in first inversion, 261
Supremes, the, "Baby Love," 606, 608
sus chords, 600
suspension(s)
    2–3 type, 198, 201–2, 205, 327
    4–3 type, 198, 202, 326–27, 328–29, 330, 600
    7–6 type, 198, 201–2, 203, 326–27, 328–29, 403–4, 581, 586, 622–24
    9–8 type, 198, 202, 323, 326–27, 328–29
    with change of bass, 327–28
    in chorale textures, 225–26
    consonant, 200, 202
    defined, 197
    double, 328–29
    embellishing, 329–30
    expressive interpretation of, 343
    figured bass and, 266

in four parts, 326–27
in fourth-species counterpoint, 197–201
lower-voice, 198
in popular music, 341–42
in popular songs, 600
rearticulated, 225
upper-voice, 198
suspension chains, 329
    defined, 200
    in fourth-species counterpoint, 200–201
symmetrical divisions of the octave, 634
symmetrical form, 740
symmetrical meter, 731
symmetrical row, 815
symmetrical scale(s)
    defined, 724
    hexatonic, 726–27
    octatonic, 725–26
    whole-tone, 724
syncopation(s), 35–37, 76–77

tablature. *See* notation
Tagg, Phillip, 614
"tape" loops, 615
Taylor, James, 608, 616
teleological form, 841
Telesco, Paula, 639
tempo
    defined, 24–25
    indications, 24
    metric modulation, 834–36
temporary tonic. *See* tonicization
tendency tones, 62, 65. *See also* chordal seventh; leading tone
    in augmented-sixth chords, 549, 560
    in dominant seventh chord, 213–14, 231–32, 260
    doubling avoided for, 240, 255–56
    in first-inversion leading-tone triad, 351
tenor clef, 12, 13
tenor vocal range, 237
tenths, 112–13
ternary forms
    comparison of, 705
    composite, 486–87, 705
    defined, 484
    full sectional, 485

ternary forms (*continued*)
  large, 699-705
  in nontonal music, 791, 843
  in recent music, 855
  rounded binary distinguished
    from, 485
  sectional closure possibilities in,
    486
  simple, 484-86, 705
  vocal, 570-77
tetrachord(s), 720, 722
  major, 51
  minor, 92-94, 614
text notation, 840-41
text painting
  in arias, 574
  defined, 582
  with diminished third chord,
    565
  in instrumental program music,
    582-83
  in Lieder, 581-83, 586-87
  mixture chords and, 538, 546
  with Neapolitan sixth chord,
    552, 557
  secondary-function chords and,
    436-37, 444
  in twelve-tone music, 800
text setting
  harmonic color and, 531-32
  in Lieder, 577-84
  in twelve-tone music, 800
textual analysis, 577-79, 589-90
textural variations. *See* variations
texture(s). *See also* counterpoint
  contrapuntal, 246
  defined, 246
  homophonic, 246
  melody-and-accompaniment,
    246-51
thematic design, 473
theme, 130
theme and variations, 520-25. *See
  also* variations
third (in triads), 131, 138
  doubling of, 240
thirds, 111-12, 114. *See also* major
    thirds; minor thirds
  as consonant intervals, 124
  in first-species counterpoint,
    176-78
third species (4:1), 191-97. *See also*
    counterpoint
  melodic embellishment, 191-94

middle section, 194
opening and closing patterns,
    194
thirty-second note(s), 26
thirty-two-bar song form. *See*
    quaternary song form
Thomas, Augusta Read, 868
Thornton, Willie Mae "Big Mama,"
    "Hound Dog," 604-5, 616
through-composed form, 585-88
tie(s), 34-35
  syncopation and, 76-77
Tiësto, "Red Lights," 611-12
timbral variations. *See* variations
time-line notation, 837-38
time signature. *See* meter
    signature
Tin Pan Alley, 596
tintinnabuli style, 854
tonic (scale degree), 49, 62
tonic area in phrase, 230-31
tonic expansions
  with 5-6 motion, 290-91
  with $^6_4$ chords, 279-86
  with bass-line skips, 289
  with dominant $^6_4$, dominant $^4_3$,
    and first-inversion leading
    tone triad, 351-52
  dominant in, 288-89
  embedding PD-D-T progres-
    sion, 292-93, 346-47, 348
  extending final area, 293-94
  I-vi motion, 291-92
  with mixture chords, 537
  subdominant in, 279-82,
    287-88
tonicization, 414-15
  defined, 414
  of dominant, 409-26
  of mixture chords, 538-40
  modulation compared with,
    414, 450-51
  of Neapolitan sixth chord,
    556-57, 588
  within a phrase, 432-35
  sequential transposition and,
    655-56
  in sonata development sections,
    681
  spanning more than two chords,
    429
topic theory. *See* musical topics
total serialism, 819
Tower, Joan, 868

T-PD-D-T phrase. *See* basic phrase
transferred resolution, 260
transitions (TR)
  in rondo, 695-97
  in sonata form, 666, 675-76
transposing instruments, 159-61.
    *See also specific
    instruments*
transposing scores, triads and
    seventh chords in, 159-61
transposition
  identifying, 766-70
  of modes, 106-7
  modes of limited, 787-88
  octave, 13
  pcset, 755-59
  R, I, and RI combined with,
    796-98
  sequential, 655-56
treble clef, 9-10, 13
triad(s), 129-45, 638. *See also
    specific chords*
  analyzing, 138-39
  components of, 131
  defined, 130
  doubling guidelines, 240
  figured bass for, 140-41
  inversion of, 137-39, 144
  in musical contexts, 147-48
  in musical textures, 157-62
  in popular styles, 155-57
  qualities in major keys, 131-33
  qualities in minor keys, 133-35
  Roman numerals for, 131-32
  spelling, 131, 135-37
  in tonal music, 131-43
  in transposing scores, 159-61
trichord(s), 720
  chromatic, 783
  hexatonic, 781-82
  octatonic, 782-83
  pentatonic, 780-81
  whole-tone, 780
triple counterpoint. *See*
    counterpoint
triple meter, 23-24
  compound, 68-70
triplets, 77-79, 80
tritone, 123
  dissonance of, 124
  in dominant seventh, 212
  in leading-tone triad, 350
  Locrian mode and, 713
tritone axis, 744-45

tritone substitution, 602

truncation. *See* motive(s)

tunings
  alternative, 854-55
  microtonal, 855
  nontempered, 546

tuplets, 79-81

turnaround (in jazz), 604

twelfths, 112-13

twelve-bar blues, 602-5, 613
  harmonic progressions and phrase structure, 604-5
  scales in, 602-4

twelve-tone rows, 799-814
  choosing row forms, 803-4
  defined, 799
  labeling rows, 801-3
  realizing, 805-14

twentieth-century music. *See also* jazz; popular music; rock; serial composition
  compound intervals in, 113
  consonance and dissonance in, 125
  listening to, 709
  materials in recent music, 860-67
  modal practice in, 106-7
  modernism, 19, 850
  modes, scales, and sets, 708-28
  new technologies, 836, 860
  recent trends, 849-68
  rhythm, meter, and form after 1900, 730-47
  rhythm, meter, and form after 1945, 823-48
  serial composition, 793-822
  set analysis, 749-91
  styles, 19
  techniques of the past in, 850-67

twenty-first century music, 19, 849-68

U2, "City of Blinding Lights," 609

unaccented neighbor tone, 324-25. *See also* neighbor tone(s)

unaccented passing tone, 224, 324-25. *See also* passing tone(s)

unequal fifths, dominant seventh chord and, 257-58

unison, 110-11, 115, 121, 124
  notating in SATB style, 236

upbeat(s), 23, 28, 38-40, 182. *See also* anacrusis

upper neighbors, 184, 192, 335-36. *See also* neighbor tone(s)

variable meter. *See* changing meter

variations, 130, 514-29
  character, 527
  chromatic, 523-24
  continuous, 515-19, 528
  developing, 701
  figural, 522-23
  musical topics in, 526-27
  paired, 517
  polyphonic or contrapuntal, 525
  procedures, 521
  in recent music, 855
  rhythmic acceleration in, 518, 528
  sectional, 486, 515, 520-25, 528
  simplifying, 524
  textural, 524-25
  timbral, 525

verse, 596, 606, 610

verse-chorus form, 606-7

verse-refrain form, 596

Village People, "Go West," 407

vivace, 24

vocal forms, 569-91
  modified strophic, 584
  strophic, 577-84
  three-part, 570-77
  through-composed, 585-88

vocal ranges, 237

voice crossings, 238-39, 259

voice exchanges, 174, 284, 346, 416-17, 420
  chromatic, 563-64, 625-27

voice-leading
  in augmented-sixth chords, 561-63, 566
  for cadential $^6_4$ chord, 276-77
  in chorale melodies, 268-72
  in chorale-style counterpoint, 220-22
  chromatic, 600-601
  for deceptive cadences, 300
  defined, 166
  descending-fifth root progressions, 308
  for descending-fifth sequences, 391-92, 393, 394-95, 619-21
  for dominant seventh chords, 255-60
  in fifth-species and free counterpoint, 203-5
  in first-species counterpoint, 166-75
  in fourth-species counterpoint, 201-2
  for I-iii-IV, 315
  I-vi motion, 291
  for mixture chords, 535, 537-38
  for Neapolitan sixth chord, 551-55
  for passing $^6_4$, 357
  in post-1950 popular songs, 613
  from predominant to dominant, 262-63
  secondary dominants, 419-20, 440-43
  in dominant expansions, 423-25
  in second-species counterpoint, 187-90
  in third-species counterpoint, 191-94
  in twentieth-century music, 717-19, 724

voice-leading chords, 345-59
  chromaticism and, 656-58
  leading-tone triads and seventh chords, 345-55
  pedal or neighboring $^6_4$ chords, 356-58

Wagner, Melinda, 868

Wagner, Richard, 383, 661

Waldstein, Ferdinand Ernst Gabriel von, 690

waveform, 611

Webern, Anton
  The Path to the New Music, 805, 819
  serial compositions, 800
  use of sevenths, 125

wedge melody, 768-69

West, Kanye, "Stronger," 317

white keys, 5

White Stripes, the, "Dead Leaves and the Dirty Ground," 317

whole note(s), 26

whole rest, 26, 32-33

whole step(s), 6-7, 110, 115
  in major scale, 48-49

whole-tone scale(s), 723-24, 860
  ic vector, 787

whole-tone trichord, 780
Wieck, Friedrich, 705, 868
Wolfe, Julia, 868
women composers, 868

Wood, Charles, 227
world music, 860, 862, 863-64,
    866-67
    pentatonic collections in, 63

xylophone, transposition for, 159

Z-related sets, 786
Zwilich, Ellen Taaffe, 857, 868